REFERENCE SERIES

Air Force Combat Wings

Lineage and Honors Histories

1947–1977

Charles A. Ravenstein
United States Air Force Historical Research Center

OFFICE OF AIR FORCE HISTORY
UNITED STATES AIR FORCE
WASHINGTON, D.C., 1984

Library of Congress Cataloging in Publication Data

Ravenstein, Charles A.
Air Force Combat Wings; Lineage and Honors Histories, 1947–1977.

Includes index.
1. United States. Air Force—History. 2. Aeronautics, Military—United States—History. I. Title.
UG633.R36 1984 358.4'00973 83-24954
ISBN 0-912799-12-9

For sale by the Superintendent of Documents, U.S. Government Printing Office,
Washington, D.C. 20402

United States Air Force Historical Advisory Committee

(As of June 1, 1984)

Lt. Gen. Charles G. Cleveland, USAF
Commander, Air University

Mr. DeWitt S. Copp
The National Volunteer Agency

Dr. Philip A. Crowl
Annapolis, Maryland

Dr. Warren W. Hassler, Jr.
Pennsylvania State University

Brig. Gen. Harris B. Hull, USAF, Retired
National Aeronautics and Space Administration

Dr. Alfred F. Hurley
Brig. Gen., USAF, Retired
North Texas State University

Gen. Bryce Poe II, USAF, Retired
Alexandria, Virginia

Lt. Gen. Winfield W. Scott, Jr.
Superintendent, USAF Academy

Dr. David A. Shannon (*Chairman*)
University of Virginia

Mr. Eugene R. Sullivan
The General Counsel, USAF

The Author

CHARLES A. RAVENSTEIN is a historian with the Research Division, USAF Historical Research Center, Maxwell Air Force Base, Alabama, where for the past seventeen years he has specialized in organizational lineage and honors. He holds a BS in history (1970) and an MS in education (1973) from Troy State University, and is also a graduate of the USAF Ground Photography School (1949) and the USAF Recruiter's School (1959). Before joining the Historical Research Center, he served twenty years in the Air Force as an enlisted historian, retiring as a senior master sergeant. Mr. Ravenstein has written or collaborated on the following Air Force histories: Charles W. Dickens, *Air Weather Service and Meteorological Satellites, 1950–1960,* (Weather Service Historical Study No. 5, 1973); with Maurer Maurer, *Constraints on Army Air Forces Operations* (Historical Research Division, Aerospace Studies Institute, Air University, June 1969); *U.S. Air Force Victory Credits, Southeast Asia, A Preliminary List* (Historical Research Division, Air University, and Office of Air Force History, HQ USAF, October 1971); with Maurer Maurer, "Peaceful Employment of U.S. Airpower," a chapter in *A Quarter Century of Air Power* (John H. Scrivner, Jr., ed.) Air Force Reserve Officers Training Corps, Air University, 1973); *U.S. Air Force Combat Victory Credits, Southeast Asia* (Albert F. Simpson Historical Research Center, Air University, HQ USAF, 1974); "Combat Narratives: 1965–1968," "Combat Narratives: 1972–1973," and "Glossary of Terms and Abbreviations" in *Aces and Aerial Victories, The United States Air Force in Southeast Asia, 1965–1973* (Albert F. Simpson Historical Research Center, Air University, and the Office of Air Force History, HQ USAF, 1976); *A Guide to Air Force Lineage and Honors,* 2d ed., revised (Research Division, USAF Historical Research Center, 1984).

Foreword

The United States Air Force Historical Research Center and its predecessor organizations have over the years received thousands of requests for brief histories of Air Force organizations. Wing commanders ask for historical data that can be used to introduce the unit to new personnel, build morale, and improve *esprit de corps*. Headquarters USAF and the major commands require historical information to plan organizational changes. Officers throughout the Air Force need historical material for public affairs purposes. Former members of the Army Air Forces and the Air Force are interested in the heritage and history of the organizations in which they served. Government agencies and private individuals, for a variety of reasons, also want to know about Air Force establishments and units and their histories.

Because of the interest in these lineage and honors histories, the USAF Historical Division in the late 1950s compiled a reference volume of Air Force combat organizations—groups, wings, divisions, commands, and air forces. Published in 1961, this volume focused exclusively on organizations active during World War II.* Historians traced each organization from its origin to 1 January 1956. A companion volume followed, containing the histories of combat squadrons active between 7 December 1941 and 2 September 1945.† These squadron histories were carried through 5 March 1963 (the fiftieth anniversary of the 1st Aero Squadron, the first Army unit to be equipped with aircraft for tactical operations). This present volume, the third in the series, is devoted to the Air Force-controlled (AFCON) combat wings of the post-World War II United States Air Force. All of these wings feature numerical designations up to three digits (1 through 706); only five possess history and honors from World War II.** Each wing's history is traced from its origin through September 1977, when the Air Force celebrated its thirtieth anniversary as a separate service.

---

*Maurer Maurer (ed.), *Air Force Combat Units of World War II* (Washington: USGPO, 1983; New York: Franklin Watts, Inc., 1963; New York: Arno Press, 1979; Washington: Zenger, 1981).

†Maurer Maurer (ed.), *Combat Squadrons of the Air Force, World War II* (Washington: USGPO, 1982).

**These wings are therefore not involved in the temporary bestowal of history and honors described in the introduction to this volume. They are: 1st Special Operations Wing, which began its existence as the 1st Air Commando Group; 24th Composite Wing, which had the same designation during World War II; 26th Tactical Reconnaissance Wing, which dates from 1942 thanks to consolidation in 1965 with the wartime 5th Reconnaissance Group; 54th Tactical Fighter Wing, established in February 1943 as the 54th Troop Carrier Wing; and 301st Tactical Fighter Wing, which began its life in October 1944 as the 301st Fighter Wing.

Readers should study carefully the explanatory notes (pages ix to xiii) after looking up the unit or units of interest. Each wing entry contains a great deal of information. The way in which units, names, and dates are listed—particularly the punctuation—has specific meaning.

RICHARD H. KOHN
CHIEF, OFFICE OF AIR FORCE HISTORY

Preface

Permanent organizations of the Air Force, whether active or inactive, are Air Force-controlled (AFCON) organizations with a continuing lineage and history. Although some AFCON organizations are named, most are numbered and contain from one to three digits in the numerical part of their designation. (Examples: 1st Tactical Fighter Wing; 28th Bombardment Wing, Heavy; 374th Tactical Airlift Wing.) AFCON organizations, when activated a second or subsequent time, regain their previous lineage, history, honors, and emblem. Temporary organizations, on the other hand, are major command-controlled (MAJCON) organizations without a continuing lineage or history. MAJCON organizations always have four digits in the numerical portion of their designation. (Example: 6510th Test Wing.) Because MAJCON organizations are by nature temporary—designed originally to let major commands meet the exigencies of fast changing circumstances—once inactivated their lineage and history is permanently retired.

This volume deals with one category and echelon of AFCON organization—the "combat" (category) "wing" (echelon). A *combat* wing is one that has, or previously has had, a specific functional designation and mission in combat: bombardment, fighter, strategic and tactical reconnaissance (all types), airlift, air refueling, or missile.* Besides the combat aspects of their flying or fighting mission, combat wings are often charged with operating a base. Whether combat or support in category, all wings occupy an intermediate echelon in the Air Force organizational hierarchy, above groups and squadrons, but below divisions and air forces. Although there are no "typical" combat wings, most usually have two or more assigned combat squadrons in the same functional areas as the wing, or in a closely related functional area. For instance, a tactical fighter wing generally has two or more tactical fighter squadrons, and may also have a tactical fighter training squadron. A bombardment wing will generally have a bombardment squadron and an air refueling squadron. Combat wings often have a variety of support organizations that are permanently aligned with the parent wing through similarity in numerical designation. Combat wings further possess, as a general rule, a significant self-supporting capability in the areas of materiel, maintenance, and munitions. The strength of the United States Air Force is often calculated by the number of active combat wings it controls.

---

*Some functional designations disguise the combat function under such terms as "Air Commando," or "Special Operations," or "Composite," but the unit is nonetheless involved in one or more of these basic combat missions.

A few wings other than combat wings appear in this volume. The 1st and 377th Air Base Wings, although support establishments, are included because they have in their history controlled combat components. The 46th Aerospace Defense Wing (a "disguised" air base wing) appears because it possesses the temporarily bestowed history and honors of a World War II combat group and may at some future date be employed as a combat wing. Many Air National Guard (ANG) combat wings (designated in the 101–300 block of numbers) have served one or more brief tours of active service with the Air Force, but these wings are controlled in peacetime by the individual states of the United States and do not normally fall into either the AFCON or MAJCON category. For this reason, because the ANG in recent years abandoned strict adherence to the Air Force lineage system, and because histories of these units are sometimes unavailable or records for peacetime periods are lost, the Air Force can no longer determine with certainty the lineage, history, and honors of ANG combat wings. They are therefore excluded. Finally, 66 of the 281 AFCON wings that have existed either as active or inactive establishments since World War II are, or were, either support organizations or did not have a combat flying mission; for these reasons they have been by category also excluded.* Some of these organizations operated under combat conditions, while others have or had flying support functions. Because these wings were organized either to support combat flying operations, or because they had no specific flying mission, they do not fall into the category of "combat flying" wings and therefore do not appear in the volume.

Every AFCON wing appearing in this work is identified by the designation it possessed on 30 September 1977. For each of these wings I have provided information about the lineage, assignments, tactical components, stations, commanders, aircraft and missiles, operations, service and campaign streamers, decorations, and emblem. An explanation of these elements and their treatment is contained in the explanatory notes. In preparing any reference work, one has finally to draw a line between what can and cannot be reasonably included. Thus, some important elements, such as the wing support components and the full designation of tactical components, have been purposefully, if reluctantly, excluded.

Most of the sources used to prepare this volume are located in the document collection of the United States Air Force Historical Research Center at Maxwell AFB, Alabama. Perhaps most important among these sources are histories that Air Force organizations at all echelons have prepared periodically and sent to the

---

*They are: 1st Medical Service Wing; 1st through 7th, plus the 43d and 59th, Weather Wings; 9th Weather Reconnaissance Wing; 13th 24th, 25th, 29th, 30th, 39th, 59th, 73d, 75th, 77th, 80th, 85th, and 88th Air Depot Wings; 39th and 40th Aerospace Rescue and Recovery Wings; 41st Aerospace Rescue and Weather Reconnaissance Wing; 73d Aerospace Surveillance Wing; 82d Combat Security Police Wing; 501st and 601st Tactical Control Wings; 507th and 602d Tactical Air Control Wings; 544th Strategic Intelligence Wing; 554th Operations Support Wing; 603d Air Base Wing; 901st–907th, 910th–918th, 920th–926th, and 928th–930th Reserve Training Wings; and 941st–944th Reserve Air Depot Training Wings.

Historical Research Center under the auspices of the Air Force history program. Wing histories and their supporting documents served as the primary sources, of course; but histories of wing components, or of divisions and numbered air forces that controlled the wings, were frequently consulted. These related histories often furnished crucial information during those periods when a wing history was poorly prepared, or not prepared at all. The organization record cards of each USAF unit and establishment, maintained by Headquarters USAF until early 1978 and thereafter by the Historical Research Center, provided an important source of information. Most of the material on wing emblems was obtained at the Air Force Manpower and Personnel Center, Randolph AFB, Texas, although many emblems also came from the Defense Audio Visual Agency's Still Photo Depository at Arlington, Virginia. The periodic *Directory of United States Air Force Organizations,* published by Headquarters USAF from September 1947 through November 1973, provided valuable information about active wings, their assignments, and stations.* Finally, primary source documents in the Historical Research Center collection, including command station lists, G–series special orders, operations plans and reports, organizational directories, Department of the Air Force Manpower and Organization numbered letters, and similar records, were indispensable.

Unfortunately, even among this plenitude of sources, it sometimes proved impossible to ascertain specific facts. The full names of wing commanders and the exact dates they assumed command, for example, were often not to be found. To determine a particular fact from fragmentary and sometimes conflicting evidence, some choices necessarily represent my best judgment.

I prepared this volume between 1969 and 1982, usually in addition to other duties, as time permitted. Other Air Force historians also contributed significantly to the research and writing of this book: Harry R. Fletcher, Gerard E. Hasselwander, Donald D. Little, and Lieutenant Colonel Forrest B. Dowdy (an Air Force Reservist who performed his training at the Historical Research Center). Guidance for this work was provided by Maurer Maurer, James N. Eastman, Jr., Lloyd H. Cornett, Jr., and R. Cargill Hall. Pauline Tubbs, Dorothy M. McCluskie, and Peggy C. Brown ably assisted in the editing and typing. I wish to extend special thanks to personnel in the Recognition Branch, Air Force Manpower and Personnel Center, and to personnel of the Defense Audio Visual Agency, who went out of their way to furnish illustrations for the wing emblems.

CHARLES A. RAVENSTEIN — March 1984
USAF Historical Research Center

*The Historical Research Center has recently resumed preparation of this inventory semiannually, under the title *List of Active United States Air Force Organizations*.

Explanatory Notes (How to Use this Book)

The following notes explain how the information in this book is arranged, and the terms and format used in Air Force lineage and honors histories.

Heading. The heading comprises the numerical and functional designation of the wing as of 30 September 1977. Each combat wing appears in numerical order, and, when required, in alphabetical order under the number. (Three wings carry the number "1," two are numbered "301," and two are numbered "322.")

Lineage. (See Appendix I.) The official USAF statement of lineage, or "genealogy," forms the foundation of the wing's history and governs the wing's inheritance of emblem and honors. The Air Force lineage system, described in Air Force Pamphlet 210–2, applies to Reserve organizations and the regular Air Force. (As noted earlier, the Air Force can no longer determine with certainty the lineage, history, and honors of ANG combat wings, and thus the Guard wings are not included in this volume.)

One peculiarity will be noticed in the lineage of some wings that appear in this book. In August 1947, the Air Force began a service test of what was called the "wing-base" plan. This test, conducted with 29 combat wings, proved the wing-base plan to the satisfaction of the Air Force. In 1948 the service discontinued all of the temporary service-test units and establishments and replaced them with new, permanent units and establishments with the same numerical and generally the same functional designations. Beginning in July 1948, the new wings replaced the discontinued wings; in most instances the permanent wings activated on the same day the temporary wings discontinued, but in a few cases the permanent wings activated a day or two before the discontinuance of the temporary wings. On the surface, these overlapping lineages appear erroneous; nevertheless, they conform to the orders of the time. Because the personnel, assignments, components, stations, facilities, equipment, and missions of the service-test wings passed completely to the new, permanent wings that replaced them, the Air Force has unofficially considered both variants of the wings to be the same organization. But without an official consolidation directive, they remain separate establishments. In this book, the temporary and permanent wings are treated as single establishments.* The overlapping of dates in the lineage statement therefore carries over to other sections including assignments, components, stations, and commanders.

Assignments. Each of the wing's immediate higher "parent" organizations is listed chronologically. A single date indicates the date of assignment; where a double date appears, the second date indicates termination of assignment. A semicolon is used to show a change of assignment while the wing remained active; a period indicates the wing was disbanded, discontinued, or inactivated. If the wing was attached for operational control to another organization, the attachment appears in parentheses, with brackets used to set off parenthetical elements within parentheses. Each attachment contains double dates.

Components. Tactical components assigned, or attached for operational control, to the wing are listed in hierarchical and numerical order. Each list shows only those components at the first subordinate echelon; the lists do not show subordinate squadrons of an assigned or attached group because these squadrons were not directly assigned to the wing. Of the tactical components, only the numerical designation appears if the functional designations (e.g., fighter, bombardment) were identical for both the component and wing. If the numerical designation of a component changed during its period(s) of assignment or attachment, the later designation is shown parenthetically. Example: 705th (later, 962d). Support-type components (medical units, an air base or combat support group, maintenance squadrons, and other support squadrons and flights) are excluded.

A semicolon separating dates indicates a break in assignment or attachment. A comma indicates a change with no break in wing control. A squadron attached for a time and then assigned (with no break in wing control), for example, would be shown: attached 1 Jan–29 Jul 1952, assigned 30 Jul 1952–12 Jul 1957. Interrupted, attached service in a series would read: attached 12 Jul–10 Aug 1956, 17 Nov 1956–3 Jan 1957, 10 Jul–19 Aug 1957, and so forth, with commas separating the series entries. This same procedure is used to show detached status of wing components, when such detached periods are frequent.

Periods of detached service, when components are detached from wing control for duty with another organization, appear in parentheses. Likewise, components not operational for specific periods are shown in parentheses. In some cases the exact dates for detached service, or dates for those periods when a component was not operational, could not be determined with certainty. A *circa* (c.) date is used in these instances.

---

*A more detailed explanation of the pivotal wing-base service test appears in the introduction to this book.

Stations. Permanent locations of the wing headquarters are listed chronologically. The name of each base is the one in use at the time the wing arrived, with any changes appearing in parentheses. Some foreign nations that hosted wings are identified by their "popular" name, rather than their official name. Thus, the Republic of Korea appears as South Korea, the Republic of Vietnam as South Vietnam, and the Republic of China as either Formosa or Taiwan, depending upon the period. Wings located in the Federal Republic of Germany, or in occupied Germany prior to 1 September 1949, are listed as being in West Germany. A single date indicates the arrival of the wing at a base. Semicolons separate the station-and-date entries while the wing remained active, but changed stations. If a wing moved from one theater of operations to another, a double date is provided for the station being vacated. A double date is also provided whenever a wing arrived at a base and was subsequently disbanded, discontinued, or inactivated. A period at the end of a second date indicates disbandment, discontinuance, or inactivation.

Commanders. Wing commanders are listed chronologically, along with the highest rank attained during the command tenure. Commanders are shown for all periods when the wing was active. Between 1959 and 1968 the Air Force required two organizational actions (activate and organize) to place personnel in a wing headquarters (and in other units). During the time a wing was activated but not yet organized, the entry shows "None (not manned)," together with double dates, followed by a semicolon and the actual list of commanders. Whenever active wings were not manned at other times, the "None (not manned)" statement and double dates also appear. If for some reason a wing commander was at first temporarily and then permanently appointed, the commander's name may be followed by one date and a parenthetical "temporary," followed by a second date and a parenthetical "permanent."

Lists of commanders are as accurate as the sources permitted. Some wings kept excellent historical records; others kept poor records, or none at all. Commander lists, therefore, sometimes contain "unknown" as an entry, and in many of the commander lists, *circa* (c.), or some other indicator such as "by" this date, are to be found. A second date followed by a semicolon indicates a gap in the commander list. A second date followed by a period indicates the wing headquarters inactivated.

Aircraft/Missiles. The aircraft, aircraft and missiles, or missiles used by wing components assigned and attached for operational control appear in this section. In the missile category, only strategic or tactical surface-to-surface missiles are included. (Air-to-air, air-to-ground, or surface-to-air missiles are considered ordnance and are not included.) The section title accounts for the type(s) of weapon systems. Aircraft are listed by series and number (e.g., F–86 or EC–135), but not by model (e.g., B–52H or KC–135A). Missiles are listed by their popular names (e.g., Atlas, Titan I, Minuteman III). The years during which the wing possessed the weapon systems are also listed (e.g., RF–101, 1959–1965). Because many wings often possessed different weapon systems simultaneously, these different systems, with the dates of possession, are separated by semicolons. The final entry is followed by a period. A wing may also have had the same weapon systems at different times. Example (for a wing activated in 1950, inactivated in 1961, activated again in 1963, and inactivated in 1967): Aircraft. B–47, 1950–1955; KC–97, 1953–1955; B–52, 1956–1961; KC–135, 1955–1961. B–52, 1963–1967; KC–135, 1963–1967; EC–135, 1966–1967.

A wing often lost possession on a temporary basis of one or more of its weapon systems. This occurred, for example, when its tactical components were detached with all of the aircraft for duty elsewhere. Such temporary absences of a weapon system are shown by a comma. Example: B–52, 1957–1960, 1960–1962, 1963–1965; KC–135, 1956–1958, 1958–1960, 1960–1961, 1961–1965. In other words, for a time in 1960 and in 1962–1963, the wing had no B–52 aircraft for its own use, all being under the control of another organization. Likewise, for short periods in 1958, 1960, and in 1961, the wing did not control KC–135 aircraft.

Operations. Information in this section, though abbreviated, includes all combat and other significant operations, often with a discussion of the particular aspects of combat. Oversea deployments of the wing are mentioned, together with changes in wing status and its mission. Speed or distance records are frequently cited. For reasons of security classification, numerous significant wing operations during the decade 1967–1977 are excluded, or mentioned only briefly.

Readers who wish to know more about a wing's operations can visit the Historical Research Center to conduct research, or purchase through the mail microfilm copies of the unclassified wing histories.

Service Streamers. (See Appendix II.) Service streamers represent noncombat service in the various theaters of military operations. Those service streamers earned by a wing are listed here. (If a wing participated in combat operations in a theater, it earned a campaign streamer instead of a service streamer.)

Campaign Streamers. (See Appendix II.) The Historical Research Center evaluates and verifies unit combat credits. Verified combat credit entitles a unit to the appropriate campaign streamers representing the named campaigns in which a wing participated. Research often shows that a wing is entitled to campaign credits never awarded on orders, or has received improper campaign credit awarded in error. This official list of campaign streamers is based upon each wing's verified combat record.

Decorations. (See Appendix III.) Decorations include citations and awards recognizing distinguished or meritorious acts by the wing. In this list, the type of decoration is cited together with specific dates, if dates appeared in the award document. Erroneous dates were revised and corrected dates shown within brackets. For example, the dates stated in an order may cover a time before a wing was active or after it became inactive; indeed, an order may cite a date before the wing even became engaged in the activity for which it received an award. Air Force Pamphlet 900–2, produced by the Air Force Manpower and Personnel Center, contains the official listing of unit decorations, including wing decorations. The decorations listed in this volume generally agree with those appearing in the pamphlet, but some revisions have been made based on research into actual wing operations.

Emblem. For those wings holding an official emblem approved by Headquarters USAF (and most do possess emblems), the wording of the "blazon" is provided in its official heraldic language. Many wings have had two or more emblems in the 30 years covered by this book; the emblem in use on 30 September 1977 is the one included here. Headquarters USAF authorized a temporary history bestowal in 1954 that allowed combat wings to use, under certain circumstances, the history, honors, and emblem of the older combat group of the same number. Thus, many postwar combat wings use the same emblem that their like-numbered combat groups used in World War II.*

If the emblem included a crest, the crest is described. Any official motto is cited, and translated to English if necessary. Finally, the date Headquarters USAF approved the emblem is cited within parentheses. If a motto was approved separately, the date of approval is also shown.

---

*cf., Maurer Maurer (ed.), *Air Force Combat Units of World War II* (Washington: USGPO, 1983; New York: Franklin Watts, Inc., 1963; New York: Arno Press, 1979; Washington: Zenger, 1981).

Contents

Page

Page

Page

Page

Appendices

Indexes

Introduction

Organizations known as "wings" have been used by the Air Force for many years. Indeed, in July 1918 the American Expeditionary Forces of the United States Army organized its first aircraft establishment higher than a group: the 1st Pursuit Wing. Although this wing did not survive demobilization after World War I, new wings were created in the 1920s and 1930s. During World War II numerous wings existed; some provided training in the United States, others controlled combat groups and support organizations overseas. Rapid demobilization after September 1945 meant that a new Air Force had to be built with the remnants of the wartime Army Air Forces.

The service test of a wing-base plan in 1947–1948 prompted an important change in the field structure and organization of the Air Force. Old-style World War II wings supervised a mixture of combat groups and support organizations. None of the subordinate organizations were permanently affiliated with the wings, or possessed similar numerical designations or standard functions. The wings organized for the service test featured standard functions. Each wing had a combat group, a maintenance and supply group, an airdrome group (to operate base facilities and services), and a station medical group, all with identical numerical designations. The 1947–1948 wing-base service test rendered more nearly uniform the functions of the wing elements, and permanently aligned, or affiliated, support units with the parent wings through similarity in numerical designations.

All of the Air Force wings involved in the postwar service test, whether manned by Table of Distribution (T/D) or Table of Organization (T/O) manning authority, were Air Force-controlled (AFCON) establishments.* The Air Force reserved the numbers 1 through 999 for these permanent organizations. In addition to the permanent AFCON wings that replaced the service-test organizations in 1948, USAF provided for temporary organizations to be controlled by major commands. The commands wanted a flexible organization at the lower echelons to permit the rapid adjustments in manning that short-term requirements often dictated. Because the manning of permanent T/O organizations was judged to be too rigid, in 1948 the Air Force created a new type of temporary organization, to be manned under T/D authorization.

---

*The term "AFCON" applies to all those units under the direct control of Headquarters USAF for organizational actions. The term applies retroactively to the service-test wings.

For a time, the Air Force differentiated between its temporary and permanent organizations by calling the temporary ones "designated" or "T/D," while the permanent organizations were referred to as "constituted" or "T/O." The temporary major command-controlled organizations would eventually become identified as "MAJCON," with the permanent ones known as "AFCON." The new MAJCON organizations* would not have a continuous lineage or history. The commands would designate (i.e., give a number and functional designation), organize (later, activate), redesignate, and discontinue (later, inactivate) them as needed, using the four-digit numbers allotted to each command by Headquarters USAF.† When a temporary establishment or unit was discontinued (later, inactivated), its life ended, never to be revived. The number of this establishment or unit could then be reused to designate another, entirely new, temporary establishment or unit. Although the original intent was to provide major command flexibility in establishing and terminating short-lived, temporary organizations, some MAJCON organizations have now existed as long as their AFCON counterparts—well over 30 years.

Generally, postwar AFCON combat wings have had a double mission: train for and conduct combat operations (through the combat group and that group's combat squadrons), and operate a permanent installation (through assigned support components). AFCON organizations have two privileges not shared by MAJCON organizations. One of these is reincarnation with full lineage, history, and honors through reconstitution of units or reestablishment of establishments. AFCON organizations can also be consolidated with one or more separate AFCON organizations that existed at different times to form a single entity, with the lineage, history, and honors of all retained.

In 1952 many of the World War II combat group headquarters began to be phased out as more wings assumed direct control of the combat squadrons, particularly those assigned to the Strategic Air Command (SAC) and Air Defense Command (ADC). At this time, Air Force strength began to be calculated in wings instead of groups, and the service possessed 95 wings. By the end of Korean hostilities on 27 July 1953 the number of combat wings had increased to 106, in part achieved by ordering Reserve and Air National Guard organizations to active service. Although these additions to the regular Air Force served only a specified number of months, many of them were replaced at the termination of their active duty by newly-established wings of the regular Air Force. The elimination of combat groups and retention of wings soon raised a question about honors. The groups—all veterans of World War II combat operations—held collectively many

*The term "MAJCON" applies to all those units under the direct control of major commands for organizational actions. Although the term did not exist in 1948, it applies retroactively to the temporary organizations of that period.

†The Air Force assigned blocks from the numbers 1000 through 9999 to the major commands for their use.

honors, while the postwar wings possessed few if any honors. Could not the World War II history and honors be assigned to the wings?

Both SAC and ADC wanted to retain the honors of these groups. In 1954 the two commands asked Headquarters USAF to assign these honors to the like-numbered postwar combat wings, thereby perpetuating the history and honors of the World War II groups. After study, Headquarters USAF decided to bestow the history and honors of combat groups on like-numbered combat wings. For example, the 9th Bombardment Wing, established after World War II, received by temporary bestowal the history of the 9th Bombardment Group, together with the campaign credits and decorations that had been earned by the group during World War II. In "bestowing" group history and honors on wings, USAF directives did not specify any conditions or limitations except to advise, in letters authorizing such bestowals, that these bestowals were temporary. In 1963 interested USAF agencies developed rules governing temporary bestowal (see Appendix V), but the act of assigning combat group history and honors to combat wings remains today probably the most misunderstood aspect of USAF lineage and honors.*

Although most of the wings included in this volume are authorized temporary use of the history, honors, and emblem of their aligned or affiliated combat group (the combat group having the same number in its designation as the wing), the group's lineage and honors are not included here. Maurer's *Air Force Combat Units of World War II* provides these details for the groups, at least through World War II and up to January 1956. In a few instances, however, we have used the emblem authorized the combat group if the combat wing possessed no later emblem of its own.

---

*On 31 March 1982 the Department of the Air Force acted to eliminate some of the confusion in the temporarily bestowed histories, issuing MPM letter 422q that consolidated the 11th Strategic Group and the 11th Air Refueling Wing; the 307th Bombardment Wing, Very Heavy, the 307th Strategic Wing, and the 307th Air Refueling Group, Heavy; and the 340th Bombardment Wing, Heavy, and the 340th Air Refueling Group, Heavy. In each case, the group and wing(s) became a single organization. Two years later on 31 January 1984, Department of the Air Force letter 539q consolidated more World War II combat groups with their like-numbered postwar combat wings bearing the following numerical designations: 15th, 25th, 29th, 32d, 34th, 35th, 39th, 40th, 42d, 46th, 70th, 72d, 75th, 80th, 95th, 96th, 99th, 100th, 310th, 320th, 321st, 328th, 341st, 345th, 351st, 355th, 379th, 380th, 381st, 384th, 385th, 389th, 390th, 392d, 397th, 401st, 407th, 410th, 413th, 416th, 432d, 449th, 451st, 455th, 460th, 462d, 478th, 484th, 494th, 497th, 499th, 500th, 506th, and 508th. Where a group or wing was active, the designation of the active establishment was retained. These consolidations virtually end USAF-bestowed history and honors, for few wings now remain that qualify for that program.

Air Force Combat Wings

THE COMBAT WINGS

1st AIR BASE WING

Lineage. Established as 1st Composite Wing on 9 May 1969. Activated on 1 Jul 1969. Redesignated 1st Air Base Wing on 1 Jul 1976. Inactivated on 30 Sep 1977.

Assignments. Headquarters Command, USAF, 1 Jul 1969; 76th Airlift Division, 1 Jul 1976–30 Sep 1977.

Components. *Squadrons.* 1st Air Transport: 1 Jul 1969–30 Jun 1971. 1st Airborne Command and Control: 1 Jul 1969–1 Nov 1975. 1st Flying Training: 1 Jul 1969–30 Jun 1971. 1st Helicopter: 1 Jul 1969–1 Jul 1976. 1st Composite: 1 Jul 1971–30 Jun 1975. 2d Composite: 1 Jul 1971–30 Jun 1975.

Stations. Andrews AFB, Md, 1 Jul 1969–30 Sep 1977.

Commanders. Brig Gen Richard A. Knobloch, 1 Jul 1969; Col Benjamin M. Matlick, Jr., 1 Feb 1970; Brig Gen Carlton L. Lee, 1 Mar 1970; Brig Gen Clarence J. Douglas, Jr., 25 Aug 1972; Brig Gen William E. Brown, Jr., 31 Jan 1975; Col Leonard R. Peterson, 17 Jun–30 Sep 1977.

Aircraft. C–47, 1969–1972; C–54, 1969–1970; C–118, 1969–1975; C–131, 1969–1975; CH–21, 1969–1971; EC–135, 1969–1975; T–29, 1969–1973; T–33, 1969–1973; T–39, 1969–1975; TH–1, 1969–1971; UH–1, 1969–1976; CH–3, 1970–1976; VC–131, 1971–1975; KC–135, 1973–1975; E–4, 1974–1975.

Operations. Replaced 1001st Composite Wing, absorbing its personnel and resources, on 1 Jul 1969. Provided airborne and ground alert operations required for the support of a National Emergency Airborne Command Post (NEACP). Exercised command jurisdiction over Andrews AFB, Md, and over assigned elements. Supported tenant organizations at Andrews AFB. Provided flight management of mission support operations, including high priority airlift. Supported proficiency flying training of assigned and attached personnel, and for personnel of HQ USAF, HQ AFSC, and other organizations within the greater Washington, D.C., area. Furnished base support and services for transient aircraft, both domestic and foreign. Engaged in emergency airlift and search and rescue missions. Two composite squadrons inactivated on 30 Jun 1975, and the 1st AC&CS transferred on 1 Nov 1975, leaving only the CH–3s and UH–1s operated by the 1st Helicopter Squadron.

The latter transferred on 1 Jul 1976. From then until inactivation on 30 Sep 1977 the wing operated, administered, and maintained Andrews AFB, providing logistical support for tenants. Replaced by 76th Air Base Group on 1 Oct 1977.

Service Streamers. None.

Campaign Streamers. None.

Decorations. Air Force Outstanding Unit Award: 1 Jul 1976–30 Jun 1977.

Emblem. On a shield per bend gules and azure, a conventional air base runway, throughout argent. *Crest:* On a wreath of the unit's colors (argent and azure), a quill or and a wrench gules in saltire, interlaced with a cogwell azure. (Approved on 22 Apr 1955 for 1401st Air Base [later, 1001st Composite] Wing; used 1 Jul 1969–30 Sep 1977 by 1st Composite [later, 1st Air Base] Wing.)

1st SPECIAL OPERATIONS WING

Lineage. Established as 1st Air Commando Group on 9 Aug 1944, replacing the 1st Air Commando Group (a miscellaneous unit) that was constituted on 25 Mar 1944, activated on 29 Mar 1944, and consolidated on 9 Aug 1944 with the headquarters unit of the new establishment. Inactivated on 3 Nov 1945. Disestablished on 8 Oct 1948. Reestablished on 18 Apr 1962. Activated, and organized, on 27 Apr 1962. Redesignated: 1st Air Commando Wing on 1 Jun 1963; 1st Special Operations Wing on 8 Jul 1968; 834th Tactical Composite Wing on 1 Jul 1974; 1st Special Operations Wing on 1 Jul 1975.

Assignments. Army Air Forces India-Burma Sector, 29 Mar 1944 (original unit assigned to 9 Aug 1944, establishment assigned thereafter); Tenth Air Force, 10 Jul 1945; Army Service Forces, 6 Oct–3 Nov 1945. USAF Special Air Warfare Center (later, USAF Special Operations Force), 27 Apr 1962; Tactical Air Command, 1 Jul 1974; Ninth Air Force, 1 Jul 1976–.

Components. *Groups*. 549th Tactical Air Support Training: 15 Dec 1975–1 Jan 1977. 930th Tactical Airlift (later, 930th Air Commando; 930th Special Operations): 1 Jun 1968–18 Jun 1969 (not operational, Dec 1968–18 Jun 1969). *Squadrons*. 5th Fighter, Commando (later, 605th Air Commando, Composite): 1 Sep 1944–3 Nov 1945; 15 Nov 1963–1 Jul 1964 (detached 15 Nov 1963–1 Jul 1964). 6th Fighter, Commando (later, 6th Air Commando, Fighter; 6th Special Operations Training): 30 Sep 1944–3 Nov 1945; 27 Apr 1962–29 Feb 1968; 31 Jul 1973–1 Jan 1974. 8th: 1 Mar 1974– (not operational, 1 Mar–31 May 1974). 16th: 12 Dec 1975–. 18th: 25 Jan–15 Jul 1969. 20th: 1 Jan 1976–. 71st Tactical Airlift (later, 71st Air Commando; 71st Special Operations): 1 Jun–16 Dec 1968. 164th Liaison: 1 Sep 1944–3 Nov 1945. 165th Liaison: 1 Sep 1944–3 Nov 1945. 166th

Liaison: 1 Sep 1944–3 Nov 1945. 310th Attack: 15 May–15 Jul 1969. 311th Attack: 15 May–15 Jul 1969. 317th Air Commando, Troop Carrier (later, 317th Air Commando, Utility; 317th Special Operations): 1 Jul 1964–15 Jul 1969 (not operational, 1 Jan–30 Jun 1966); 15 Apr 1970–30 Apr 1974. 318th: 15 Nov 1971–1 Jun 1974. 319th Troop Carrier, Commando (later, 319th Air Commando, Troop Carrier; 319th Air Commando, Tactical Airlift; 319th Special Operations): 1 Sep 1944–2 Sep 1945; 27 Apr 1962–15 Jul 1969; 30 Jul 1969–15 Jan 1972. 360th Tactical Electronic Warfare: 1–31 Jul 1973. 415th Special Operations Training: 19 Jul 1971–30 Jun 1975. 424th Special Operations (later, 424th Tactical Air Support) Training: 1 Jul 1970–1 Jan 1972. 547th Special Operations (later, 547th Tactical Air Support) Training: 15 Oct 1969–30 Apr 1975. 549th Tactical Air Support Training: 15 Oct 1969–15 Dec 1975. 602d Fighter, Commando: 1 May 1963–1 Oct 1964. 603d Fighter, Commando (later, 603d Air Commando; 603d Air Commando, Strike/Reconnaissance; 603d Special Operations; 603d Special Operations Training): 1 Jul 1963–15 May 1971; 1 Jul 1973–1 Jul 1974. 604th Fighter, Commando: 1 Jul 1963–8 Nov 1964. 775th Troop Carrier, Assault: 15 Apr–1 Jul 1964. 4406th Combat Crew Training: 1 Oct 1968–15 Jul 1969. 4407th Combat Crew Training: 15 Jul 1969–30 Apr 1973. 4408th Combat Crew Training: 15 Jul–22 Sep 1969. 4409th Combat Crew Training: 15 Jul–15 Oct 1969. 4410th Combat Crew Training: 27 Apr 1962–1 Dec 1965; 15 Jul–15 Oct 1969. 4412th Combat Crew Training: 25 Oct 1967–15 Jul 1969. 4413th Combat Crew Training: 1 Mar 1968–15 Jul 1969. 4473d Combat Crew Training: 8 Aug 1969–1 Jul 1970. 4532d Combat Crew Training: 25 Oct 1967–15 Jul 1969. *Flight.* 7th Special Operations: 1 Jul 1969–31 May 1972.

Stations. Hailakandi, India, 29 Mar 1944 (original unit); Asansol, India, 20 May 1944–6 Oct 1945 (original unit to 9 Aug 1944, establishment thereafter); Camp Kilmer, NJ, 1–3 Nov 1945. Eglin Air Force Auxiliary Field No. 9 (Hurlburt Field), Fla, 27 Apr 1962; England AFB, La, 15 Jan 1966; Eglin Air Force Auxiliary Field No. 9 (Hurlburt Field, Fla, 15 Jul 1969–.

Commanders. Col Philip G. Cochran, 29 Mar 1944 (original unit); Col Clinton B. Gaty, 20 May 1944 (original unit to 9 Aug 1944; establishment thereafter); Col Robert W. Hall, c. 7 Apr 1945–unkn. Lt Col Miles M. Doyle, 27 Apr 1962; Col Chester A. Jack, 29 Apr 1962; Col Gerald R. Dix, 19 Mar 1963; Col Harry C. Aderholt, 28 Mar 1964; Col Gordon F. Bradburn, 10 Jul 1964; Col Hugh G. Fly, Jr., 1 Dec 1965; Col Alpheus W. Blizzard, Jr., 3 Apr 1967; Col Albert S. Pouloit, 9 Sep 1967; Col Leonard Volet, 14 Feb 1969; Col Robert W. Gates, 15 Jul 1969; Col Michael C. Horgan, 31 Oct 1970; Col James H. Montrose, 1 Apr 1973; Brig Gen William J. Holton, 11 Jan 1974; Col Edward Levell, Jr., 1 Jul 1976; Col Richard H. Dunwoody, 29 Jul 1977–.

Aircraft. B–25, 1944; P–47, 1944–1945; P–51, 1944, 1945; UC–64, 1944–1945; L–1, 1944; L–5, 1944–1945; C–47, 1944–1945; YR–4, 1944–1945; CG–4 (glider), 1944–1945; TG–5 (glider), 1944–1945. C–46, 1962–1964; C/TC/VC–47, 1962–1970, 1973–1975; B/RB–26, 1962–1966; T/AT–28, 1962–1973; L–28 (later, U–10),

1962–1973; C/UC–123, 1963–1973; A–1, 1963–1966, 1969–1972; YAT–28, 1964–1965; YAT–37, 1964; O–1, 1964–1967, 1969–1971; AC–47, 1965, 1967–1969; U–3, 1966–1967; U–6, 1966–1967; UH–1, 1966, 1969–1974, 1976–; A/RA–26, 1966–1969; A–37, 1967–1969, 1969–1971, 1973–1974; EC/HC–47, 1967–1969, 1973; AC–123, 1967; C/MC–130, 1968–; AC–130, 1968, 1971–; EC–130, 1969; C/AC–119, 1968–1969, 1971–1972; O–2, 1969–1976; OV–10, 1969–1976; YQU–22 (drone), 1969–1970; QU–22 (drone), 1970–1971; CH–3, 1973–1974, 1976–. In addition to the primary aircraft listed above, also flew T–29, 1969–1973; VT–29, 1969–1975; T–33, 1969–1975; T–39, 1969–1975; C/VC–47, 1969–1970; C–130, 1969; C–131, 1970–1973; and VC–131, 1973–1975.

Operations. Replaced the 5318th Provisional Air Unit in India in Mar 1944. As a miscellaneous unit, the group was comprised until Sep 1944 of operational sections (rather than units): bomber; fighter; light-plane (and helicopter); transport; glider; and light-cargo. The group provided fighter cover, bomb striking power, and air transport services for Wingate's Raiders, fighting behind enemy lines in Burma. Operations included airdrop and landing of troops, food, and equipment; evacuation of casualties; and attacks against enemy airfields and lines of communication. Converted from P–51 to P–47 fighters and eliminated its B–25 bomber section in May 1944. In Sep 1944, after the original unit was consolidated with the headquarters component of the new establishment (also called 1st Air Commando Group), the sections were replaced by a troop carrier, two fighter, and three liaison squadrons. The group continued performing supply, evacuation, and liaison services for allied forces in Burma until the end of the war, including the movement of Chinese troops from Burma to China in Dec 1944. It also attacked bridges, railroads, airfields, barges, oil wells, and troop positions in Burma and escorted bombers to Burmese targets, including Rangoon. Switched back to P–51s in May 1945. Left Burma in Oct and inactivated in NJ in Nov 1945.

Replaced the 4400th Combat Crew Training Group in Apr 1962 and assumed air commando operations and training responsibility. Also assumed a detachment in South Vietnam from the prior group and continued training USAF and South Vietnamese Air Force aircrews in the United States and South Vietnam throughout the Southeast Asian conflict. The group (later, wing) maintained a quick reaction force and conducted specialized operations in unconventional warfare, counterinsurgency, psychological activities, and civic actions at trouble spots around the world by deploying mobile training teams, detachments, and components as required. Although Southeast Asia received the bulk of the unit's attention until 1973, air commando (later, special operations) personnel were active in Panama, Central and South America, Europe, Africa, and the Middle East at various times. Trained personnel of friendly states, sometimes in the United States and sometimes by deployed teams. States receiving training included Iran, Greece, Saudi Arabia, Mali, El Salvador, the Dominican Republic, Costa Rica, Guatemala, the Republic of Vietnam, Thailand, Ethiopia, Venezuela, Ecuador, Nicaragua, Bolivia, and the Republic of the Congo.

The group (wing) also worked closely with U.S. Army Special Forces, developed combat tactics for numerous types of aircraft, and conducted combat crew training for USAF and foreign aircrews. It participated in a number of tactical exercises, both at home and abroad, and occasionally participated in mercy missions and humanitarian operations. One such operation involved eradication of screwworm flies in Puerto Rico and the Virgin Islands, requiring numerous missions in the early 1970s.

Between 11 Jan and 30 Jun 1974, the USAF Special Operations Force and 1st Special Operations Wing merged their operations, and on 1 Jul 1974, the wing—temporarily known as 834th Tactical Composite Wing—assumed responsibility for operating the USAF Special Operations School and the USAF Air Ground Operations School, the former training selected American and allied personnel in special operations, and the latter training personnel in concepts, doctrine, tactics, and procedures of joint and combined operations.

Service Streamers. None.

Campaign Streamers. India-Burma; Central Burma.

Decorations. Distinguished Unit Citation (Burma and India): [Mar]–20 May 1944. Air Force Outstanding Unit Awards: Jul 1963–Jun 1965; 1 Jul 1969–15 Apr 1971; 1 Jan 1976–31 Mar 1977.

Emblem. Per fess azure and play of 13 gules and argent, in pale a sword point to base light blue, winged fesswise in chief of the like, the blade surmounted in base by a lamp or enflamed of the third and fourth, all within a diminished bordure of the fifth. *Motto:* ANY TIME, ANY PLACE. (Approved on 6 Jun 1963.)

1st TACTICAL FIGHTER WING

Lineage. Established as 1st Fighter Wing on 28 Jul 1947. Organized on 15 Aug 1947. Discontinued on 24 Aug 1948. Activated on 22 Aug 1948. Redesignated 1st Fighter-Interceptor Wing on 16 Apr 1950. Inactivated on 6 Feb 1952. Redesignated 1st Fighter Wing (Air Defense) on 14 Sep 1956. Activated on 18 Oct 1956. Redesignated 1st Tactical Fighter Wing on 1 Oct 1970.

Assignments. Twelfth Air Force, 15 Aug 1947–24 Aug 1948. Twelfth Air Force, 22 Aug 1948; Fourth Air Force, 20 Dec 1948; Fifteenth Air Force, 1 May 1949 (attached to 22d Bombardment Wing, 1 Jul 1949–1 Apr 1950); Fourth Air Force, 1 Jul 1950 (attached to Western Air Defense Force, 1–31 Jul 1950); Western Air Defense Force, 1 Aug 1950–6 Feb 1952 (attached to Southern California Air Defense Sector [Provisional], 19 Jul–19 Sep 1950; 27th

Air Division [Defense], 20 Sep 1950–c. 6 Feb 1952). 30th Air Division (Defense [later, SAGE]), 18 Oct 1956; Detroit Air Defense Sector, 1 Apr 1959; 34th Air Division, 1 Apr 1966; 23d Air Division, 1 Dec 1969; 26th Air Division, 31 Dec 1969; 836th Air Division, 1 Oct 1970; Ninth Air Force, 30 Jun 1971–.

Components. *Wings.* 22d Bombardment Wing, Medium: attached 10 May–30 Jun 1949. 67th Reconnaissance (later, 67th Tactical Reconnaissance) Wing: attached 25 Nov 1947–24 Aug 1948 and 22 Aug 1948–28 Mar 1949. *Groups.* 1st: 15 Aug 1947–24 Aug 1948; 22 Aug 1948–6 Feb 1952 (detached 15 Aug 1950–3 Jun 1951); 18 Oct 1956–1 Feb 1961. 67th Reconnaissance: 15 Aug–25 Nov 1947. *Squadrons.* 6th Airborne Command and Control: 19 Aug 1976–. 7th Liaison: 1 Sep 1947–24 Aug 1948; 22 Aug 1948–28 Mar 1949. 27th: 1 Jul 1971–. 45th: 1 Oct 1970–1 Jul 1971. 46th: 1 Oct 1970–1 Jul 1971. 47th: 1 Oct 1970–1 Jul 1971. 71st: 1 Feb 1961–16 Jan 1967; 1 Jul 1971–. 84th: 31 Dec 1969–1 Oct 1970. 94th: attached 15 Aug 1950–3 Jun 1951; assigned 1 Feb 1961–1 Dec 1969 (detached 24 May–3 Nov 1969); assigned 1 Jul 1971–. 188th: attached 15 Jun 1951–6 Feb 1952. 4424th Combat Crew Training: 1 Oct 1970–30 Jun 1972. 4501st Tactical Fighter Replacement: 1 Oct 1971–30 Jun 1975.

Stations. March Field (later, AFB), Calif, 15 Aug 1947–24 Aug 1948. March AFB, Calif, 22 Aug 1948; George AFB, Calif, 18 Jul 1950; Norton AFB, Calif, 1 Dec 1951–6 Feb 1952. Selfridge AFB, Mich, 18 Oct 1956; Hamilton AFB, Calif, 31 Dec 1969; MacDill AFB, Fla, 1 Oct 1970; Langley AFB, Va, 30 Jun 1975–.

Commanders. Col Carl J. Crane, 15 Aug 1947; Col Elvin F. Maughn, 19 Jan 1948; Col Clifford H. Rees, 17 May–24 Aug 1948. Col Clifford H. Rees, 22 Aug 1948; Col Joseph H. Davidson, 13 Jan 1949; Col George McCoy, Jr., 14 Jun 1949; Col William L. Lee, 19 Aug 1949; Col Wiley D. Ganey, 4 Jan 1950; Col George McCoy, Jr., 17 Feb 1950; Brig Gen Donald R. Hutchinson, c. 17 Oct 1950; Col Dolf E. Muehleisen, 14 Dec 1950; Col Robert F. Worley, c. Jun 1951–6 Feb 1952. Col Glenn E. Duncan, 18 Oct 1956; Col Charles D. Sonnkalb, c. Aug 1959; Col George J. La Breche, c. Dec 1960; Col Ralph G. Taylor, Jr., 15 Jun 1962; Col Wallace B. Frank, 11 Sep 1963; Col Converse B. Kelly, 16 Sep 1963; Col Kenneth E. Rosebush, Aug 1966; Col Taras T. Popovich, 29 Apr 1968; Col Morris B. Pitts, c. 31 Oct 1969–c. 31 Dec 1969; unkn, c. 31 Dec 1969–unkn; Col Mervin M. Taylor, Jan 1970; Col Travis R. McNeil, 1 Oct 1970; Col Robert F. Titus, 1 Mar 1971; Col Howard W. Leaf, 6 May 1971; Col Walter D. Druen, Jr., 1 Nov 1971; Col Sydney L. Davis, 18 Apr 1972; Col Gerald J. Carey, Jr., 25 Jun 1973; Col Ernest A. Bedke, (by 30 Jun) 1975; Lt Col George H. Miller, 1 Jul 1975; Brig Gen Larry D. Welch, 1 Aug 1975; Col John T. Chain, Jr., 1 Aug 1977–.

Aircraft. P (later, F)–80, 1947–1948; RF–80, 1947–1948; FA (later, RB)–26, 1947–1948; L–13, 1947–1948. F–80, 1948–1949; RF–80, 1948–1949; RB–26, 1948–1949; B–26, 1948–1949; L–13, 1948–1949; L–4, 1948–1949; L–5, 1948–1949; F–86, 1949–1952; B–29, 1949; F–51, 1951–1952. F–86,

1956–1960; F/TF–102, 1958–1960; F–106, 1960–1969, 1969–1970; F–4, 1970–1975; B–57, 1970–1972; T–38, 1975–; F–15, 1975–; EC–135, 1975–.

Operations. Trained in fighter and reconnaissance operations and supported strategic bombardment training, 1947–1948 and 1948–1950. Was integrated experimentally with a reconnaissance wing, 1947–1948 and 1948–1949, and with a bombardment wing, 1949–1950, sharing commanders in common during much of this time. Supported Operation Haylift, a humanitarian effort to deliver feed to snowbound cattle in the western United States, 1949. Provided air defense in southern Calif from mid-1950 until inactivated in 1952. Provided air defense in the upper Midwest area, 1956 through 1969, then moved to central Calif, still in an air defense role. Had no tactical units under its control, May–Nov 1969. Moved to Fla in Oct 1970, where its mission changed to tactical fighter, assuming operational commitments of the 15th TFW. Assumed an F–4 transitional and replacement pilot training role in 1971, some of its aircrews and equipment being deployed from time to time in a variety of tactical exercises. Moved to Langley AFB, Va, in 1975 and converted to F–15s, participated in the F–15 weapons system evaluation program in 1976 and in deployments to Europe in 1977.

Service Streamers. None.

Campaign Streamers. None.

Decorations. Air Force Outstanding Unit Award: 1 Jul 1975–31 Oct 1976.

Emblem. Vert, five bendlets enhanced sable fimbriated or, as many crosses patee in bend debased three and two of the second fimbriated argent. *Crest:* Upon a wreath of the colors (or and vert) upon a hurte wavy an arrow palewise reversed between two wings displayed conjoined in lure or. *Motto:* AUT VINCERE AUT MORI—Conquer or die. (Approved for 1st Group on 10 Feb 1924 and for 1st Wing on 22 May 1957.)

2d BOMBARDMENT WING, HEAVY

Lineage. Established as 2d Bombardment Wing, Very Heavy, on 15 Oct 1947. Organized on 5 Nov 1947. Discontinued on 12 Jul 1948. Redesignated 2d Bombardment Wing, Medium, and activated on 12 Jul 1948. Redesignated 2d Bombardment Wing, Heavy, on 1 Apr 1963.

Assignments. Eighth Air Force, 5 Nov 1947–12 Jul 1948 (attached to 43d Bombardment Wing, Very Heavy, 17 Nov 1947–12 Jul 1948). Eighth Air Force, 12 Jul 1948 (attached to 43d Bombardment Wing, Medium, 12 Jul–31 Dec 1948); Second Air Force, 1 Apr 1950 (attached to 7th Air Division, 4 May–31 Aug 1951); 38th Air Division, 10 Oct 1951 (attached to 7th Air Division, 10 Sep–4 Dec 1952; 5th Air

Division, 4 Aug–20 Sep 1954 and 6 Jul–26 Aug 1956); 6th Air Division, 1 Nov 1959; 823d Air Division, 1 Apr 1961; 4th Air Division, 1 Apr 1963; 19th Air Division, 1 Sep 1964; 42d Air Division, 1 Jul 1965; 19th Air Division, 2 Jul 1969–.

Components. *Group.* 2d: 5 Nov 1947–12 Jul 1948 (detached 17 Nov 1947–12 Jul 1948); 12 Jul 1948–16 Jun 1952 (detached 12 Jul–31 Dec 1948 and 18 Feb–16 May 1950; not operational, 10 Feb 1951–16 Jun 1952). *Squadrons.* 2d Air Refueling: attached 10 Feb 1951–15 Jun 1952, assigned 16 Jun 1952–1 Apr 1963. 20th: attached 10 Feb 1951–15 Jun 1952, assigned 16 Jun 1952–25 Jun 1965 (not operational, c. 12 Feb–c. 5 May 1965). 49th: attached 10 Feb 1951–15 Jun 1952, assigned 16 Jun 1952–1 Apr 1963. 62d: 25 Jun 1965– (not operational, c. 31 May 1972–c. 26 Oct 1973). 71st Air Refueling: 15 Apr 1968–. 98th: attached 10 Feb 1951–15 Jun 1952, assigned 16 Jun 1952–1 Apr 1963. 308th Air Refueling: 1 Jul 1959–1 Mar 1960. 429th: 1 Oct 1958–1 Jan 1962 (not operational, 6 Nov 1961–1 Jan 1962). 596th: 15 Apr 1968– (not operational, c. 31 May 1972–c. 26 Oct 1973). 913th Air Refueling: 1 Apr 1963–.

Stations. Davis-Monthan Field (later, AFB), Ariz, 5 Nov 1947–12 Jul 1948. Davis-Monthan AFB, Ariz, 12 Jul 1948; Chatham AFB, Ga, 1 Apr 1949; Hunter Field (later, AFB), Ga, 22 Sep 1950; Barksdale AFB, La, 1 Apr 1963–.

Commanders. None (not manned), 5 Nov 1947–12 Jul 1948. None (not manned), 12 Jul–31 Dec 1948; Col William E. Eubank, Jr., 1 Jan 1949; Brig Gen Frederic E. Glantzberg, 4 Apr 1949; Brig Gen John M. Reynolds, c. 31 Jan 1952; Col Rollin M. Winingham, 12 Aug 1953; Col Osce V. Jones, 5 Oct 1953; Col Austin J. Russell, 26 Oct 1953; Col Arthur J. Walker, 14 Jul 1955; Col Robert M. Tuttle, 10 Sep 1956; Col Seth J. McKee, 15 Dec 1956; Col Robert C. Whipple, 26 Aug 1958; Brig Gen William B. Kieffer, 1 Jun 1959; Col Brooks A. Lawhon, 13 Jun 1960; Col John W. Kline, 19 Jun 1961; Col Harrison R. Christy, Jr., 7 Mar 1963; Col Frank B. Elliott, 1 Apr 1963; Col Louis M. Sowers, 15 May 1964; Col Melvin R. Schultz, 16 May 1966; Col Arthur W. Holderness, Jr., 17 Dec 1966; Col Edmund A. Rafalko, 13 Oct 1967; Brig Gen Edward O. Martin, 11 Nov 1968; Col Samuel E. Dyke, 5 May 1970; Col Harold R. Jewell, 16 Jun 1972; Col Stanley C. Beck, 2 Apr 1973; Col Jerome R. Barnes, Jr., 10 Jun 1974; Col Kelly H. Burke, 1 Jul 1974; Col Jerome E. Wechter, 2 Jun 1975; Col Jerome R. Barnes, Jr., 1 Jun 1976; Col George A. Dugard, 2 Feb 1977; Col Jerome R. Barnes, Jr., c. 20 Mar 1977; Col George R. Dugard, 18 Apr 1977; Col Jerome R. Barnes, Jr., 8 May 1977; Col Kenneth M. Patterson, 27 May 1977–.

Aircraft. B–29, 1949–1950; B–50, 1949–1953; KB–29, 1950–1953; KC–97, 1953–1963; B–47, 1954–1963; B–52, 1963–1965, 1965–1977, 1977–; KC–135, 1963–; EC–135, 1966–1970.

Operations. Wing headquarters not operational, 5 Nov 1947–12 Jul 1948 and 12 Jul–31 Dec 1948. Tactical group attached to 43d Bombardment Wing during these periods (except for a short period it spent in England, in 1948). Entire wing moved from Ariz to Ga on 1 Jan 1949 and manned from resources of other organizations. Converted from B–29 to B–50 bombers in 1949–1950 and trained in global bombardment operations from Jan 1949. Added air refueling to mission in Dec 1950. Deployed at RAF Mildenhall, England, May–Aug 1951, RAF Upper Heyford, England, Sep–Dec 1952, and Sidi Slimane AB, French Morocco, Aug–Sep 1954 and Jul–Aug 1956. Converted to B–47 jet bombers in 1954. Service tested a "super wing" concept with 70 B–47s, Jul 1959–Apr 1961. Moved to Barksdale AFB, La, on 1 Apr 1963, replacing 4238th Strategic Wing and absorbing that wing's B–52 and KC–135 resources. Supported Second Air Force's post attack command and control system, Apr 1963–Mar 1970. Conducted bombardment training and air refueling operations, Apr 1963 to date except for periods when all aircraft and crews were on loan to SAC organizations involved in combat operations in Southeast Asia. Began supporting SAC operations in Southeast Asia with aircraft and personnel in 1965, and increasingly supported these operations in 1966 and 1967. On 15 Apr 1968, gained a second B–52 and a second KC–135 squadron, again becoming a SAC "super" wing. From late May 1972 until 26 Oct 1973, all wing B–52 resources loaned to SAC organizations in the Far East and Southeast Asia; from May 1972 to early Nov 1972, all but four of the wing's KC–135s and a few aircrews loaned to other SAC units. After the return of combat resources, the wing continued supporting SAC operations in Southeast Asia into 1975, on a reduced scale.

Service Streamers. None.

Campaign Streamers. None.

Decorations. Air Force Outstanding Unit Award: 1 Nov 1956–1 Apr 1957.

Emblem. Or, in fess four aerial bombs dropping bend sinisterwise azure, on an Air Force shield, paly of five, vert and sable, a fleur-de-lis argent. *Motto:* LIBERTATEM DEFENDIMUS—Liberty we defend. (Approved on 25 Apr 1966.)

3d TACTICAL FIGHTER WING

Lineage. Established as 3d Bombardment Wing, Light, on 10 Aug 1948. Activated on 18 Aug 1948. Redesignated: 3d Bombardment Wing, Tactical, on 1 Oct 1955; 3d Tactical Fighter Wing on 8 Jan 1964.

Assignments. 314th Air Division, 18 Aug 1948; Fifth Air Force, 1 Mar 1950; 41st Air Division, 1 Mar 1955; Fifth Air Force, 1 Feb 1957; 41st Air Division, 10 Nov 1958; Twelfth Air Force, 8 Jan 1964 (attached to 4481st Air Division, Provisional, 8 Jan–30 Jun 1964); 834th Air Division, 1 Jul 1964; 2d Air Division, 8 Nov 1965; Seventh Air Force, 1 Apr 1966; Fifth Air Force, 15 Mar 1971; 314th Air Division, 15 Mar 1971; Thirteenth Air Force, 16 Sep 1974–.

Components. *Group.* 3d: 18 Aug 1948–25 Oct 1957 (detached 20 Jul–30 Nov 1950; not operational, 13 Aug

1956–25 Oct 1957). *Squadrons*. 1st Air Commando: attached 21 Nov 1965–8 Mar 1966. 1st Test: 16 Sep 1974–. 3d: 15 Dec 1975– (detached 15–16 Dec 1975). 7th Airborne Command and Control: 31 Mar–14 Aug 1975 (detached). 8th Bombardment (later, 8th Attack): attached 13 Aug 1956–24 Oct 1957, assigned 25 Oct 1957–8 Jan 1964 (detached 1 Sep 1963–8 Jan 1964); assigned 15 Nov 1969–30 Sep 1970. 8th Tactical Reconnaissance: attached 18 Apr 1949–1 Apr 1950. 10th Fighter: 8 Apr 1966–17 Apr 1967. 13th Bombardment: attached 13 Aug 1956–24 Oct 1957, assigned 25 Oct 1957–8 Jan 1964 (detached 1 Sep 1963–8 Jan 1964). 20th Operations: 16 Sep 1974–31 Mar 1975. 25th: 18–19 Dec 1975. 26th Tactical Fighter (later, 26th Tactical Fighter Training; 26th Tactical Fighter Training Aggressor): 16 Sep 1974– (not operational, 16 Sep 1974–30 Aug 1975). 35th: 15 Mar 1971–16 Sep 1974 (detached 1 Apr–12 Oct 1972). 36th: 15 May 1971–16 Sep 1974. 40th Fighter-Interceptor: attached 1 Dec 1961–31 May 1962. 44th: attached 3 Apr–2 Jun 1972 and 28 Jul–8 Sep 1972. 67th: attached 2 Jun–28 Jul 1972 and 8 Sep–16 Oct 1972. 68th: 16 Sep 1974–30 Sep 1975 (not operational). 80th: 15 Mar 1971–16 Sep 1974. 90th Bombardment (later, 90th Tactical Fighter; 90th Attack; 90th Tactical Fighter): attached 13 Aug 1956–24 Oct 1957, assigned 25 Oct 1957–8 Jan 1964 (detached 1 Sep 1963–8 Jan 1964); assigned 9 Jun 1964–19 Nov 1965 (detached 3 Feb–10 May 1965 and 3 Aug–19 Nov 1965); assigned 3 Feb 1966–31 Oct 1970; assigned 16 Sep 1974–. 307th: attached 21 Nov–6 Dec 1965. 308th: 2 Dec 1965–25 Dec 1966 (detached 15 Nov–25 Dec 1966). 310th Attack: 15–30 Nov 1969. 311th Attack: 15 Nov–15 Dec 1969. 416th: 16 Jun 1964–8 Nov 1965 (detached 14 Mar–21 Jul 1965); 16 Nov 1965–15 Apr 1967 (detached 16 Nov 1965–15 Jun 1966). 421st Air Refueling: attached 21 Nov 1960–1 Jun 1962. 429th: attached c. 21 Nov–14 Dec 1965. 510th: 16 Mar 1964–15 Nov 1969 (detached 5 May–c. 20 Aug 1965). 531st: 16 Jun 1964–19 Nov 1965 (detached 2 Nov 1964–18 Mar 1965); 7 Dec 1965–31 Jul 1970. 602d Fighter: attached 21 Nov 1965–8 Mar 1966. 604th Air Commando (later, 604th Special Operations): attached 15 Nov 1967–1 Mar 1970, assigned 1 Mar–30 Sep 1970. 731st: attached 1 Dec 1950–25 Jun 1951. 6091st Reconnaissance: attached 21 Nov 1960–c. 5 Jun 1962.

Stations. Yokota AB, Japan, 18 Aug 1948; Johnson AB, Japan, 1 Apr 1950; Yokota AB, Japan, 14 Aug 1950; Iwakuni AB, Japan, 1 Dec 1950; Kunsan AB, South Korea, 22 Aug 1951; Johnson AB, Japan, 1 Oct 1954; Yokota AB, Japan, 18 Nov 1960–8 Jan 1964; England AFB, La, 8 Jan 1964; Bien Hoa AB, South Vietnam, 8 Nov 1965; Kunsan AB, South Korea, 15 Mar 1971; Clark AB, Philippines, 16 Sep 1974–.

Commanders. Col James R. Gunn, Jr., 18 Aug 1948; Col Gerry L. Mason, 16 Jun 1949; Lt Col Wilmer A. Hardesty, 17 Jun 1949; Col Robert W. Witty, 24 Jun 1949; Col Lawrence C. Coddington, 1 Apr 1950; Col Thomas B. Hall, c. Jun 1950; Col Strother B. Hardwick, Jr., c. Jul 1950; Col Virgil L. Zoller, 14 Aug 1950; Col Donald L. Clark, 23 Aug 1950; Col Virgil L. Zoller, 1 Dec 1950; Col Nils O. Ohman, 24 Jul 1951; Col Marshall R. Gray, 4 Mar 1952; Col Eugene B. LeBailly, 14

Aug 1952; Col Roger E. Phelan, 12 Aug 1953; Col William H. Matthews, 2 Feb 1954; Col Edwin A. Doss, 22 Feb 1954; Col William B. Reed, 2 Apr 1954; Col Homer C. Munsan, 1 Aug 1954; Col Howard F. Bronson, Jr., 6 Aug 1954; Col Cecil P. Lessig, 10 Sep 1954; Col Anthony V. Grossetta, 1 Mar 1955; Col Edward R. Casey, 3 May 1955; Col Rufus H. Holloway, 9 Jun 1955; Col George Y. Jumper, 16 Aug 1955; Col Clarence L. Elder, 10 Jun 1958; Col James B. Tipton, 10 Jul 1958; Col Robert J. Ahern, 22 Jun 1959; Col Leo Hawel, Jr., 22 Jun 1961; Col Carl R. Norton, 28 Jun 1962; Col Francis E. Timlin, 1 Aug 1962; Col Charles S. Overstreet, Jr., 3 Sep 1963–8 Jan 1964 (additional duty); unkn, 9 Jan–18 Feb 1964; Col Philip Brooks, 19 Feb 1964; Col Waring W. Wilson, 28 May 1965; Col Robert A. Ackerly, 19 Jul 1965; Col Richard C. Catledge, 1 Nov 1966; Col George W. McLaughlin, 30 Sep 1967; Col Homer K. Hansen, 5 May 1968; Col Howard M. Lane, 1 Apr 1969; Col William E. Charlson, 11 Apr–31 Oct 1970; none (not manned), 1 Nov 1970–14 Mar 1971; Col Abner M. Aust, Jr., 15 Mar 1971; Col Charles A. Watry, 17 Nov 1971; Col Paul A. Kauttu, 5 Oct 1972; Col Harry W. Schurr, 19 Nov 1973; Col George L. Schulstad, 16 Sep 1974; Col Lacy W. Breckenridge, 14 Mar 1975; Col Alfred M. Miller, Jr., 25 Mar 1975; Col James R. Brown, 13 Oct 1976–.

Aircraft. B–26, 1948–1950, 1950–1956; F–15, 1949; RF–80, 1949–1950; C–47, 1951; B–57, 1956–1963; RB–50, 1960–1961; KB–50, 1960–1962; C–130, 1961–1962; F–102, 1961–1962; F–100, 1964–1970; F–5, 1965–1967; A–1, 1965–1966; U–10, 1965–1966; C/AC/HC–47, 1965–1966; A–37, 1967–1970; F–4, 1971–1974, 1974–; T–33, 1974; C–9, 1974–1975; CH–3, 1974–1975; T–38, 1976–.

Operations. Trained as a bombardment and reconnaissance wing prior to Korean war. Combat in Korea, 1–19 Jul 1950. Tactical units operated under wing control from Iwakuni AB, Japan, 1–19 Jul 1950. On 20 Jul 1950 the tactical group and its squadrons served under operational control of another organization. The wing assumed a supporting role, initially from Johnson AB, Japan, but later from Yokota AB, Japan. Wing returned to Iwakuni AB on 1 Dec 1950, regaining control of its tactical units, performing combat in Korea. Moved to South Korea in Aug 1951. After Korean war, wing participated successively in bombardment, air defense, reconnaissance, and air refueling training (its headquarters being non-operational 1 Sep 1963 to 8 Jan 1964).

Moved to the United States without personnel or equipment in Jan 1964, then trained and rotated its squadrons in detached status to Southeast Asia for combat duty. Moved to South Vietnam in Nov 1965 and took an active combat role until 31 Oct 1970. During this time, wing also participated in combat evaluation of F–5 and F–37 aircraft. Unmanned and unequipped on 31 Oct 1970, the wing remained active in a "paper" status until it moved without personnel or equipment to South Korea on 15 Mar 1971. Manned and equipped in South Korea with F–4 aircraft, and underwent numerous organizational changes. In Sep 1974, moved without personnel or equipment to Clark AB,

Philippines, replacing 405th Fighter Wing. Participated in frequent operational exercises and evaluations. Between 5 Apr and 31 May 1975, wing used its facilities as a staging area for Operations Baby Lift (evacuation of Vietnamese orphans from South Vietnam to the United States) and New Life (evacuation of Vietnamese adults to the United States for resettlement). T–38 fighter training operations began in Jan 1976.

Service Streamers. None.

Campaign Streamers. UN Defensive; CCF Intervention; First UN Counteroffensive; CCF Spring Offensive; UN Summer–Fall Offensive; Second Korean Winter; Korea Summer–Fall, 1952; Third Korean Winter; Korea Summer–Fall, 1953; Vietnam Defense; Vietnam Air; Vietnam Air Offensive; Vietnam Air Offensive, Phase II; Vietnam Air Offensive, Phase III; Vietnam Air/Ground; Vietnam Air Offensive, Phase IV; TET 69/Counteroffensive; Vietnam Summer–Fall, 1969; Vietnam Winter–Spring, 1970; Sanctuary Counteroffensive; Southwest Monsoon.

Decorations. Presidential Unit Citations (Vietnam): 8 Jun 1966–16 Apr 1967; 6 Mar 1968–31 Jul 1969. Air Force Outstanding Unit Awards with Combat "V" Device: 31 Jan–5 Mar 1968; 1 Aug 1969–20 Jan 1970; 21 Jan–31 Oct 1970. Air Force Outstanding Unit Awards: 1 Jun 1958–30 Jun 1960; 1 Jul 1960–31 Mar 1962; 1 May 1964–16 Jul 1965; 1 Jul 1972–31 Dec 1973. Republic of Korea Presidential Unit Citation: 27 Jun–31 Jul 1950. Republic of Vietnam Gallantry Crosses with Palm: 25 Nov 1965–19 May 1969; 1 Apr 1966–[31 Oct 1970]; 1 May–30 Sep 1970.

Emblem. Party per bend vert and sable in chief a cactus (prickly pear) or, a bend azure fimbriated of the third, all within a bordure argent charged with 19 crosses patee of the second. (Approved for 3d Group on 17 Jan 1922 and for 3d Wing on 22 Dec 1952.)

4th TACTICAL FIGHTER WING

Lineage. Established as 4th Fighter Wing on 28 Jul 1947. Organized on 15 Aug 1947. Discontinued on 1 Aug 1948. Activated on 1 Aug 1948. Redesignated: 4th Fighter-Interceptor Wing on 20 Jan 1950; 4th Fighter-Bomber Wing on 8 Mar 1955; 4th Fighter-Day Wing on 25 Apr 1956; 4th Tactical Fighter Wing on 1 Jul 1958.

Assignments. Strategic Air Command, 15 Aug 1947–1 Aug 1948. Strategic Air Command, 1 Aug 1948; Fourteenth Air Force, 1 Dec 1948 (attached to First Air Force, 15 Jan–22 Feb 1949); Ninth Air Force, 23 Feb 1949 (attached to Eastern Air Defense Force, 10 Nov 1949–; further attached to 26th Air Division [Defense], 20 Feb 1950–); First Air Force, 1 Aug 1950 (remained attached to Eastern Air Defense Force and further attached to 26th Air Division [Defense]); Eastern Air Defense Force, 1 Sep 1950 (remained attached to 26th Air Division [Defense] to c. 19 Nov 1950; attached to Fifth Air Force, 28 Nov 1950–7 Mar 1955; further attached to 314th Air Division, 22 Dec 1950–7 May 1951; further attached to 39th Air Division, 1–7 Mar 1955); 39th Air Division, 8 Mar 1955; Ninth Air Force, 8 Dec 1957; Twelfth Air Force, 1 Jul 1960; Ninth Air Force, 1 Jan 1962 (attached to 2d Air Division [Provisional], 21 Oct–c. 29 Nov 1962); 833d Air Division, 1 Oct 1964 (attached to Fifth Air Force ADVON, 29 Jan–c. 29 Jul 1968); Ninth Air Force, 24 Dec 1969–.

Components. *Wing*. 354th Tactical Fighter: attached 5–24 Jul 1968. *Groups*. 4th: 15 Aug 1947–1 Aug 1948; 1 Aug 1948–8 Dec 1957 (not operational, 17 Oct–8 Dec 1957). 363d Tactical Reconnaissance: attached 26 Apr 1949–c. 1 Aug 1950. *Squadrons*. 7th: attached 21 Mar–1 Jul 1957. 333d: 8 Dec 1957–4 Dec 1965 (detached 10 Mar 1964–c. 15 Mar 1965). 334th: 8 Dec 1957– (detached 1 Apr–13 Aug 1963, 15 Feb–29 May 1965, 28 Aug 1965–5 Feb 1966, 13 Dec 1969–c. 31 May 1970). 335th: 8 Dec 1957– (detached 1 May 1960–22 Nov 1961, 16 Nov 1964–21 Feb 1965, 3 Jul–15 Dec 1965, 4 Dec 1969–c. 25 May 1970). 336th: 8 Dec 1957– (detached 12 Aug 1963–7 Jan 1964, 25 May–30 Aug 1965; not operational, 1 Apr 1966–8 Feb 1967). 339th: attached 18 Nov 1954–15 Sep 1957. 476th: 25 Sep 1968–18 Mar 1969 (not operational). 558th: attached 4 Feb–10 Mar 1968 and 26 Mar–22 Jul 1968.

Stations. Andrews Field (later, AFB), Md, 15 Aug 1947–1 Aug 1948. Andrews AFB, Md, 1 Aug 1948; Langley AFB, Va, 26 Apr 1949; New Castle County Aprt, Del, 8 Sep–19 Nov 1950; Johnson AB, Japan, 28 Nov 1950; Suwon AB, South Korea, 7 May 1951; Kimpo AB, South Korea, 23 Aug 1951; Chitose AB, Japan, 1 Oct 1954–8 Dec 1957; Seymour Johnson AFB, NC, 8 Dec 1957–.

Commanders. Brig Gen Yantis H. Taylor, 15 Aug 1947–1 Aug 1948. Brig Gen Yantis H. Taylor, 1 Aug 1948; Col Arthur C. Agan, Jr., 17 Feb 1949; Col Robert W. C. Wimsatt, 26 Apr 1949; Col Henry B. Fisher, 14 Jun 1949; Col Albert L. Evans, Jr., 13 Aug 1949; Col Bela A. Harcos, 22 Aug 1949; Brig Gen George F. Smith, 3 Oct 1949; Col Herman A. Schmid, May 1951; Col Harrison R. Thyng, 1 Nov 1951; Col Charles E. King, 2 Oct 1952; Col James K. Johnson, 11 Nov 1952; Col Donald P. Hall, 9 Aug 1953; Col Neil A. Newman, 30 Jun 1954; Col Alvin E. Hebert, 10 Aug 1954; Col Grover C. Brown, 1 May 1955; Col Robert P. Montgomery, 17 Aug 1956; Col Earle R. Myers, 6 Jun 1957; Col James M. Smelley, 2 Jul 1957; Col Robert C. Richardson III, 8 Dec 1957; Col Timothy F. O'Keefe, 5 Jan 1958; Brig Gen Joseph H. Moore, 28 Feb 1959; Col Albert L. Evans, Jr., 18 Oct 1961; Brig Gen Gordon M. Graham, 15 Jul 1962; Col John R. Murphy, 16 Oct 1963; Col William E. Bryan, Jr., 4 Jan 1965; Col Homer C. Boles, 27 Jan 1966; Col William R. Eichelberger, 30 May 1966; Col Robert V. Spencer, 1 Jul 1966; Col William R. Eichelberger, 28 Jan 1967; Col Paul C. Watson, 17 Feb 1967; Col Everett N. Farrell, 6 Jan 1968; Col Jack W. Hayes, Jr., 26 Jan 1968; Col Charles E. Yeager, 23 Mar 1968; Col Marion L. Boswell, 30 May 1969; Col Walter P. Paluch, Jr.,

16 May 1970; Col James R. Hildreth, 19 Feb 1971; Col John E. Ralph, 21 Apr 1972; Col Len C. Russell, 21 May 1973; Col James N. Portis, 11 Feb 1974; Col Robert D. Russ, 7 Aug 1975; Col Robert S. Beale, 6 Jun 1976–.

Aircraft. P (later, F)–80, 1947–1948. F–80, 1948–1949, 1954; RB–26, 1949–1950; B–45, 1949–1950; FP–80, 1949–1950; RF–80, 1949–1950; F–86, 1949–1957, 1957–1958; F–100, 1957–1960; F–105, 1958–1966; F–4, 1967–.

Operations. Performed tactical operations as part of air defense in the United States, 1947–1948. Flew air defense with own components, and reconnaissance and bombardment with attached 363d Tactical Reconnaissance Group (which itself had two fighter-bomber squadrons attached), 1948–1950. Moved to Japan in Nov 1950. The tactical group moved to South Korea for combat in Dec 1950, but the wing remained in Japan, performing air defense operations. Moved to South Korea in May 1951 and conducted combat operations, 7 May 1951–27 Jul 1953. Provided air defense and reconnaissance in Korea, Japan, Formosa, and the Philippines, 1953–1957. Returned to the United States in Dec 1957. Worldwide tactical operations and training, Dec 1957–. Participated in tactical evaluation of the F–105 aircraft, May 1958–Oct 1961. Deployed in Fla during the Cuban missile crisis, 21 Oct–29 Nov 1962. Operated an F–105 replacement training function, Mar–Nov 1966. Deployed at Kunsan AB, South Korea, following the *Pueblo* crisis, Jan–Jul 1968. Rotated tactical squadrons to Ubon RTAFB, Thailand, as augmentees of the 8th TFW for combat operations, Apr 1972 until the end of the Southeast Asian conflict.

Service Streamers. None.

Campaign Streamers. CCF Spring Offensive; UN Summer–Fall Offensive; Second Korean Winter; Korea Summer–Fall, 1952; Third Korean Winter; Korea Summer–Fall, 1953.

Decorations. Air Force Outstanding Unit Awards: 1 Jul 196730 Jun 1968; 16 Sep 1973–15 Apr 1974; 2 Feb 1976–18 Apr 1977. Republic of Korea Presidential Unit Citations: 1 Nov 1951–30 Sep 1952; 1 Oct 1952–31 Mar 1953.

Emblem. Azure on a bend or, a spear garnished with three eagle feathers and shaft flammant to base all proper. *Crest:* On a wreath of the colors (or and azure) a lion's face or. *Motto:* FOURTH BUT FIRST. (Approved for 4th Group on 26 Sep 1949 and for 4th Wing on 7 Oct 1952.)

5th BOMBARDMENT WING, HEAVY

Lineage. Established as 5th Strategic Reconnaissance Wing on 1 Jul 1949. Activated on 16 Jul 1949. Redesignated: 5th Strategic Reconnaissance Wing,

Heavy, on 14 Nov 1950; 5th Bombardment Wing, Heavy, on 1 Oct 1955.

Assignments. 311th Air Division, 16 Jul 1949; Second Air Force, 1 Nov 1949 (attached to 9th Strategic Reconnaissance Wing, 12 Nov 1949–); Fifteenth Air Force, 1 Apr 1950 (remained attached to 9th Bombardment Wing, Heavy [later, 9th Bombardment Wing, Medium] to 10 Feb 1951); 14th Air (later, 14th Strategic Aerospace) Division, 10 Feb 1951 (attached to 3d Air Division, 14 Jan–12 Apr 1955); 810th Strategic Aerospace Division, 25 Jul 1968; 47th Air Division, 30 Jun 1971; Fifteenth Air Force, 30 Nov 1972 (attached to Air Division Provisional, 810th, 30 Nov 1972–14 Jan 1973); 47th Air Division, 15 Jan 1973; 57th Air Division, 22 Jan 1975–.

Components. *Group.* 5th: 16 Jul 1949–16 Jun 1952 (detached 12 Nov 1949–10 Feb 1951; not operational, 10 Feb 1951–16 Jun 1952). *Squadrons.* 23d: attached 10 Feb 1951–15 Jun 1952, assigned 16 Jun 1952–. 31st: attached 10 Feb 1951–15 Jun 1952, assigned 16 Jun 1952–1 Oct 1959, attached 2 Oct 1959–18 Jan 1960. 72d: attached 10 Feb 1951–15 Jun 1952, assigned 16 Jun 1952–1 Jul 1958. 129th: attached 14 Oct 1952–1 Jan 1953. 347th: attached 1 Jan–12 Sep 1953 (not operational, 20 Aug–12 Sep 1953). 906th Air Refueling: 25 Jul 1968–. 916th Air Refueling: 1 Sep 1959–25 Jul 1968.

Stations. Mountain Home AFB, Idaho, 16 Jul 1949; Fairfield-Suisun (later, Travis) AFB, Calif, 12 Nov 1949; Minot AFB, ND, 25 Jul 1968–.

Commanders. Col Waldine W. Messmore, 16 Jul 1949; Col Horace M. Wade, 12 Nov 1949; Col John H. Davis, 26 Nov 1949; Brig Gen Robert F. Travis, 1 Feb 1950; Col Carlos J. Cochrane, 6 Aug 1950; Col Joe W. Kelly, 10 Aug 1950; Col Walter E. Arnold, 10 Feb 1951; Col Willis E. Beightol, 27 Sep 1953; Brig Gen Edwin B. Broadhurst, 1 Oct 1953; Col Albert F. Fahy, Jr., 14 Jan 1955; Col Edwin G. Simenson, 9 Mar 1955; Col Albert F. Fahy, Jr., 3 Mar 1956; Col Lucion N. Powell, 23 Mar 1956; Col Charles J. Beck, 17 Apr 1960; Col Martin E. Plocher, 2 Jun 1962; Col William R. Smith, 4 Jun 1962; Col Robert E. Blauw, 21 Apr 1964; Col Rodger L. Howard, 7 Jul 1964; Col Richard M. Hoban, 27 Jun 1966; Col Robert E. Blauw, 10 Jun 1967; Col George E. Burch, 2 Jul 1968; Col William W. Culbertson, 25 Jul 1968; Col Bob M. Garner, 18 Jul 1970; Col William G. MacLaren, Jr., 10 May 1972; Col William A. Eveland, 24 Jul 1974; Col Kenneth L. Peek, Jr., 28 Jul 1975; Col James D. Gormley, 31 Jan 1977–.

Aircraft. B–29, 1949; RB–29, 1949, 1951; RB–36, 1951–1958; B–36, 1955–1958; B–52, 1959–1968, 1968–; KC–135, 1959–1968, 1968–; EC–135, 1968–1969.

Operations. Performed long-range strategic reconnaissance, Jul 1949–Oct 1955, with some limited reconnaissance to Sep 1958. Fully integrated with 9th Strategic Reconnaissance (later, 9th Bombardment) Wing, 12 Nov 1949–10 Feb 1951; maintained a manned headquarters, but had no operational control over assigned units, and from 1 Feb 1950 to 10 Feb 1951 shared a commander in common with the 9th Wing. Began maintaining proficiency in strategic bombardment in Jul 1953, but was not redesignated as a bombardment wing until Oct 1955. Added air refueling to other missions in Dec 1959. Phased down at Travis AFB, Calif, in 1968 and moved without personnel or equipment to Minot AFB, ND, absorbing resources of the 450th Bombardment Wing, Heavy. Continued global strategic bombardment training and air refueling operations, including loan of KC–135 aircraft and crews and B–52 crews to SAC organizations involved in combat operations in Southeast Asia, 1968–1975. Supported the post attack command and control system (PACCS), Jul 1968–Dec 1969.

Service Streamers. None.

Campaign Streamers. None.

Decorations. None.

Emblem. Party per pale nebuly vert and sable a death's head argent, winged or. *Crest:* On a wreath of the colors (argent and vert), a bull's head caboshed azure and armed or. *Motto:* KIAI O KA LEWA—Guardians of the upper regions. (Approved for 5th Group on 21 Jun 1924 and for 5th Wing on 12 Aug 1954.)

6th STRATEGIC WING

Lineage. Established as 6th Bombardment Wing, Medium, on 20 Dec 1950. Activated on 2 Jan 1951. Redesignated: 6th Bombardment Wing, Heavy, on 16 Jun 1952; 6th Strategic Aerospace Wing on 1 May 1962; 6th Strategic Wing on 25 Mar 1967.

Assignments. Eighth Air Force, 2 Jan 1951; 47th Air (later, 47th Strategic Aerospace) Division, 10 Feb 1951 (attached to 3d Air Division, 31 Oct 1955–26 Jan 1956); 22d Strategic Aerospace Division, 1 Jul 1963; 12th Strategic Aerospace Division, 1 Jul 1965; 18th Strategic Aerospace Division, 25 Mar 1967; 12th Strategic Aerospace Division, 2 Jul 1968; 14th Strategic Aerospace Division, 30 Jun 1971; 47th Air Division, 1 Oct 1976–.

Components. *Group.* 6th: 2 Jan 1951–16 Jun 1952 (not operational). *Squadrons.* 6th Air Refueling: 3 Jan 1958–25 Jan 1967. 24th: attached 2 Jan 1951–15 Jun 1952, assigned 16 Jun 1952–25 Jan 1967. 24th Strategic Reconnaissance: 25 Mar 1967–. 39th: attached 2 Jan 1951–15 Jun 1952, assigned 16 Jun 1952–15 Sep 1963. 40th: attached 2 Jan 1951–15 Jun 1952, assigned 16 Jun 1952–25 Jan 1967. 307th Air Refueling: attached c. 1 Aug 1951–16 Jun 1952. 310th Air Refueling: 25 Jun 1965–25 Jan 1967. 579th Strategic Missile: 1 Sep 1961–25 Mar 1965. 4129th Combat Crew Training: 1 Aug 1959–15 Sep 1963.

Stations. Walker AFB, NM, 2 Jan 1951; Eielson AFB, Alaska, 25 Mar 1967–.

Commanders. Col Thomas S. Jeffrey, Jr., 2 Jan 1951; Col William K. Martin, 15 Jan 1951; Col Glen W. Martin, 20 May 1955; Col Everett W. Best, 21 Sep 1956; Col Daniel V. Mac Donald, 3 Jun 1957; Lt Col Lewis R. Riley, 15 Aug 1957; Col Edwin C. Evans, 16 Sep

1957; Col Everett W. Best, 23 Sep 1957; Col Donald E. Hillman, 23 Feb 1960; Col Ernest C. Eddy, 18 Jul 1962; Col Floyd H. Haywood, Jr., 15 Jul 1963; Col Richard M. Hoban, 15 Apr 1965; Col Lester F. Miller, 15 Jun 1965; Col George P. Cole, 9 Jul 1966; Col Rowland H. Worrell, Jr., 2 Sep 1966; Col Martin E. Plocher, 25 Mar 1967; Col Ray M. Watkins, 11 Jul 1967; Col Leslie W. Brockwell, 4 Jun 1969; Col Melford W. Lewis, 23 Jun 1970; Col Doyle F. Reynolds, 5 Jun 1972; Col Joe L. Church, 6 Dec 1973; Col William J. Campbell, 11 Jul 1974; Col Donald M. Griffin, 7 Oct 1975; Col Jimmy S. Lassetter, 28 May 1976–.

Aircraft and Missiles. B–29, 1951–1952; KB–29, 1951–1952; B–36, 1952–1957; B–52, 1957–1967; Atlas, 1962–1965; KC–135, 1958–1967, 1967–(attached); RC–135, 1967–.

Operations. Conducted strategic bombardment training from activation in 1951 until 1 Sep 1959, with air refueling as additional mission in 1951–1952, and again from Apr 1958. Deployed at Andersen AFB, Guam, Oct 1955–Jan 1956. Two bombardment squadrons (24th and 30th) joined the 4129th CCTS in Sep 1959, training B–52 and KC–135 crews, while the 40th Bombardment Squadron continued flying operational missions until 10 Jun 1960. From 10 Jun 1960 to 1 Dec 1961 the wing flew but a few operational missions in a non-combat ready status. A missile squadron joined the wing's resources in Sep 1961. The 40th Squadron returned to operational status on 1 Dec 1961 and on 5 Sep 1963 the other two bomb squadrons also regained tactical status. The 39th discontinued a few days later, but the 24th and 40th Squadrons continued global bombardment training through Dec 1966, when they phased down for inactivation. The missile squadron phased out its Atlas operations in Feb 1965 and inactivated a month later. On 25 Mar 1967 the wing moved without personnel or equipment to Eielson AFB, Alaska, where it replaced the 4157th Strategic Wing and assumed resources and missions of that wing. In Alaska, the wing flew RC–135 strategic reconnaissance missions with an assigned squadron, and KC–135 air refueling missions with aircraft deployed to Eielson from other SAC wings. From Apr 1968 to Jul 1972 the wing periodically served as the airborne monitor of the Alaskan ballistic missile early warning station. The wing maintained a detachment at Shemya AFS, in the Aleutians, and operated from that base except for the periods Feb–May 1975 and Jun–Sep 1976, when the base closed for the repair of earthquake damage.

Service Streamers. None.

Campaign Streamers. None.

Decorations. Air Force Outstanding Unit Awards: 1 May 1960–31 May 1962; 1 Jul 1971–30 Jun 1973; 1 Jul 1973–30 Jun 1975.

Emblem. Per fess debased or and azure issuant against the rays of the setting sun, a full rigged ship (black hull and white sails) in the Gaillard Cut (light and dark green), in chief a biplane (black) diving bend sinisterwise all proper. *Crest:* On a wreath of the colors (or and azure) a pirate's head and shoulders tattooed on the chest with skull and bones proper, garbed and coifed or and sable. *Motto:* PARATI DEFENDERE—Ready to defend. (Approved on 22 Jan 1924 for 6th Group [Composite]; used since 1951 by 6th Wing.)

7th BOMBARDMENT WING, HEAVY

Lineage. Established as 7th Bombardment Wing, Very Heavy, on 3 Nov 1947. Organized on 17 Nov 1947. Discontinued on 1 Aug 1948. Redesignated 7th Bombardment Wing, Heavy, and activated on 1 Aug 1948.

Assignments. Eighth Air Force, 17 Nov 1947–1 Aug 1948. Eighth Air Force, 1 Aug 1948; 19th Air Division, 16 Feb 1951– (attached to 5th Air Division, 10 Jul–13 Sep 1955).

Components. *Groups*. 7th: 17 Nov 1947–1 Aug 1948; 1 Aug 1948–16 Jun 1952 (not operational, 16 Feb 1951–16 Jun 1952). 11th: attached 1 Dec 1948–16 Feb 1951. *Squadrons*. 7th Air Refueling: 1 Apr 1958–15 Apr 1960; 1 Mar 1964– (not operational, c. 6 May–c. 1 Dec 1965 and c. 10 Sep 1969–c. 31 Mar 1970). 9th: attached 16 Feb 1951–15 Jun 1952, assigned 16 Jun 1952–25 Jun 1968 (not operational, c. 6 May–1 Dec 1965); assigned 31 Dec 1971–. 20th: 25 Jun 1965– (not operational, c. 1 Aug–1 Dec 1965 and c. 1 Sep 1969–c. 28 Mar 1970). 98th: attached 1–10 Dec 1957. 436th: attached 16 Feb 1951–15 Jun 1952, assigned 16 Jun 1952–1 Aug 1958 (not operational, c. 1 Apr–1 Aug 1958). 492d: attached 16 Feb 1951–15 Jun 1952, assigned 16 Jun 1952–15 Jun 1959. 919th Air Refueling: 15 Apr–15 Jul 1960. 920th Air Refueling: 15 Apr–15 Jul 1960. 4018th Combat Crew Training: 1 Apr 1974–.

Stations. Fort Worth AAFld (later, Griffiss AFB; Carswell AFB), Texas, 17 Nov 1947–1 Aug 1948. Carswell AFB, Texas, 1 Aug 1948–.

Commanders. Col Alan D. Clark, 17 Nov 1947–1 Aug 1948. Col Alan D. Clark, 1 Aug 1948; Col William P. Fisher, 11 May 1949; Brig Gen Clarence S. Irvine, 3 Jan 1950; Col John A. Roberts, 16 Feb 1951; Col George T. Chadwell, 29 Oct 1951; Col John A. Roberts, 14 Apr 1952; Col George T. Chadwell, 2 Jan 1953; Col Clarence A. Neely, 1 May 1954; Col Raymond S. Sleeper, 1 Jul 1955; Col Frederick D. Berry, Jr., 3 Jul 1957; Col John A. Roberts, 16 Jul 1957; Col James Y. Parker, 5 Jan 1959; Col George J. Eade, 6 Jul 1961; Col Don W. Bailey, 17 Jul 1963; Col Vincent M. Crane, c. 28 Apr 1965; Col Don W. Bailey, c. 12 Jun 1965; unkn (wing headquarters depleted), c. 1 Aug–c. 30 Nov 1965; Col Don W. Bailey, c. 1 Dec 1965; Col Benjamin B. Shields, 1 Aug 1966; Col Ralph T. Holland, 12 Aug 1966; Col Carlton L. Lee, 23 Jun 1967; Col Winston E. Moore, 28 Jul 1968; Col Samuel E. Dyke, 30 Apr 1969; Col Edward R. Van Sandt, 11 Sep 1969; Lt Col Paul A. Warner, 16 Sep 1969; Col Samuel E. Dyke, c. 31 Mar 1970; Col Donald D. Adams, 27 Apr 1970; Col Robert L. Holladay, Jr., 2 Jun 1971; Col Walter C. Schrupp, 26 May 1972; Col John D. Beeson, 31 May 1973; Col Walter C. Schrupp, 1 Nov 1973; Col David

E. Blais, 9 Aug 1974; Col Edward L. Todd, 31 Jan 1977–.

Aircraft. B–29, 1947–1948; B–36, 1948. B–29, 1948; B–36, 1948–1958; XC–99, 1949; RB–36, 1950; B–52, 1957, 1958–1965, 1965–1969, 1970–; KC–135, 1958–1960, 1964–1965, 1965–1969, 1970–.

Operations. Trained with B–29s in global bombardment operations, Nov 1947–Jul 1948 and Aug–Dec 1948. Began converting to B–36 bombers in Jun 1948. Controlled two B–36 groups, Dec 1948–Feb 1951, and three B–36 squadrons, Feb 1951–May 1958. Flight tested XC–99 in Jun 1949 and evaluated RB–36 in 1950. Deployed at Nouasseur AB, French Morocco, 10 Jul–13 Sep 1955. Had an attached B–52 squadron, 1–10 Dec 1957, and converted to B–52 bombers and KC–135 tankers, May–Jun 1958. Trained in global strategic bombardment and air refueling operations. Beginning 13 Apr 1965 the wing deployed its forces to the Pacific area to support SAC combat operations in Southeast Asia. All wing bombers and tankers, along with aircrews and some support personnel, deployed in Apr–May 1965. In the United States, the wing gained the assets of a second B–52 squadron from another wing in Jun 1965, giving it a bomber capability again. From Jun 1965 until Jun 1968 the wing operated with two B–52 squadrons. All B–52 resources deployed to the Pacific area by 1 Aug 1965, along with most of the wing's remaining support personnel, leaving the 7th Wing as a small non-flying cadre to operate Carswell AFB, Texas. Wing headquarters remained non-operational to c. 1 Dec 1965, when B–52/KC–135 resources began returning. The wing continued to support SAC operations in Southeast Asia through the remainder of the conflict and into 1975, but on a reduced scale except for the period c. 1 Sep 1969–c. 28 Mar 1970, when most wing resources were required overseas and only a small cadre remained at home. The wing again became a two B–52 squadron wing on 31 Dec 1971. In addition to its other activities the wing conducted B–52D consolidated training for SAC, 1 May 1972–c. 15 Dec 1972 and 5 Jan–15 Dec 1973. By mid–1973 most wing KC–135 resources had redeployed, and most B–52 resources returned by Jan 1974. The wing resumed nuclear alert status on 3 Jan 1974. From 4 Dec 1973 to May 1975 the wing conducted B–52D replacement training, and from Jan 1974 also conducted B–52D combat crew training, i.e., providing B–52 flight training to novice crews. Beginning in Jun 1974 the wing also conducted B–52 and KC–135 Central Flight Instructors' courses.

Service Streamers. None.

Campaign Streamers. None.

Decorations. Air Force Outstanding Unit Award with Combat "V" Device: 1 Sep 1969–28 Mar 1970. Air Force Outstanding Unit Awards: 18 Jun–1 Dec 1965; 1 Jul 1976–30 Jun 1977. Republic of Vietnam Gallantry Cross with Palm: 1 Sep 1969–28 Mar 1970.

Emblem. On a shield or, an eagle preying sable, markings argent, feet and beak or, grasping with its talons a bomb proper, in base an escutcheon, charged with the arms of the 7th Bombardment Group; azure, on a bend or three crosses pattee sable. *Motto:* MORS AB ALTO—Death from above. (Approved on 12 Sep 1952.)

8th TACTICAL FIGHTER WING

Lineage. Established as 8th Fighter Wing on 10 Aug 1948. Activated on 18 Aug 1948. Redesignated: 8th Fighter-Bomber Wing on 20 Jan 1950; 8th Tactical Fighter Wing on 1 Jul 1958.

Assignments. 315th Air Division, 18 Aug 1948; Fifth Air Force, 1 Mar 1950; 43d Air Division, 1 Mar 1955; Fifth Air Force, 1 Feb 1957; 41st Air Division, 10 Nov 1958; Fifth Air Force, 1 Jun 1962; Pacific Air Forces, 18 Jun 1964; Tactical Air Command, 8 Jul 1964; 831st Air Division, 10 Jul 1964; Thirteenth Air Force, 8 Dec 1965 (attached to 2d Air Division, 8 Dec 1965–31 Mar 1966; Seventh Air Force, 1 Apr 1966–15 Sep 1974); 314th Air Division, 16 Sep 1974–.

Components. *Wings*. 51st Fighter-Interceptor: attached 25 Sep–12 Oct 1950. 452d Bombardment: attached 15–30 Nov 1950. *Groups*. 8th: 18 Aug 1948–1 Oct 1957 (detached 14 Aug–30 Nov 1950; not operational, 1 Feb–1 Oct 1957). 49th: attached c. 9 Jul–30 Sep 1950. *Squadrons*. 4th: attached 26 Jun–13 Jul 1950. 9th: attached c. 27 Jun–c. 9 Jul 1950. 13th Bombardment: attached 1–30 Oct 1970, assigned 31 Oct 1970–24 Dec 1972 (not operational, 12 Apr–24 Dec 1972). 16th Special Operations: 30 Oct 1968–8 Dec 1975 (detached 19 Jul 1974–8 Dec 1975). 25th: 28 May 1968–5 Jul 1974. 35th: attached 1 Feb–30 Sep 1957, assigned 1 Oct 1957–18 Jun 1964 (detached 13 May–18 Jun 1964); assigned 16 Sep 1974–. 36th: attached 1 Feb–30 Sep 1957, assigned 1 Oct 1957–18 Jun 1964 (detached 13 May–18 Jun 1964); assigned 16–30 Sep 1974 (not operational). 58th: attached Jun–11 Sep 1973. 68th: attached 1 Mar–1 Dec 1950, 20 Oct 1954–1 Mar 1955, and 1 Dec 1961–15 Jun 1964; assigned 25 Jul 1964–6 Dec 1965 (detached 24 Aug–6 Dec 1965). 77th Squadron, Royal Australian Air Force: attached 2 Jul–10 Oct 1950 and 25 Jun–22 Aug 1951. 80th: attached 11 Aug–1 Oct 1950 and 1 Feb–30 Sep 1957, assigned 1 Oct 1957–18 Jun 1964 (detached 13 May–18 Jun 1964); assigned 16 Sep 1974–. 308th: attached Dec 1972–Jun 1973. 319th Fighter-Interceptor: attached 20 Feb–17 Aug 1954. 334th: attached 11 Apr–8 Jul 1972 and 25 Sep 1972–Mar 1973. 335th: attached 8 Jul–Dec 1972. 336th: attached 12 Apr–25 Sep 1972 and Mar–7 Sep 1973. 339th Fighter Squadron, All Weather: attached 26 Jun–5 Jul 1950. 431st: 25 Jul 1964–6 Dec 1965 (detached 26 Aug–6 Dec 1965). 433d: 25 Jul 1964–23 Jul 1974. 435th: attached 5 Jun–23 Jul 1966, assigned 24 Jul 1966–8 Aug 1974. 497th: 25 Jul 1964–6 Dec 1965; 8 Dec 1965–16 Sep 1974. 555th: attached c. 25 Feb–24 Mar 1966, assigned 25 Mar 1966–1 Jun 1968.

Stations. Ashiya Afld, Japan, 18 Aug 1948; Itazuke Afld, Japan, 25 Mar 1949; Pyongyang, North Korea, 1 Dec 1950; Seoul AB, South Korea, 9 Dec 1950; Itazuke AB, Japan, 10 Dec 1950;

Kimpo AB, South Korea, 25 Jun 1951; Suwon AB, South Korea, 23 Aug 1951; Itazuke AB, Japan, 20 Oct 1954–10 Jul 1964 (deployed at Kunsan AB, South Korea, 14–22 Oct 1955); George AFB, Calif, 10 Jul 1964–c. 6 Dec 1965; Ubon Afld, Thailand, 8 Dec 1965–16 Sep 1974; Kunsan AB, South Korea, 16 Sep 1974–.

Commanders. Col Charles T. Olmsted, 18 Aug 1948; Col Daniel A. Cooper, 22 Jan 1949; Col John M. Price, 1 Mar 1949; Col Charles W. Stark, 9 Dec 1950; Col James B. Tipton, 3 Apr 1951; Col Raymond K. Gallagher, 20 Feb 1952; Col James J. Stone, Jr., 24 Jan 1953; Col William E. Elder, 29 May 1953; Col Ernest H. Beverly, 11 Sep 1953; Col John B. Murphy, 11 Jul 1954; Col William W. Momyer, 4 Aug 1954; Col Orville H. Rehmann, 26 Feb 1955; Col Robert P. Montgomery, 8 Jun 1957; Col Raymond K. Gallagher, 8 Jul 1959; Col Chesley G. Peterson, 20 Jul 1959; Col William A. Daniel, 23 May 1960; Col John R. Roche, 16 May 1962; Col William E. Buck, Jr., 29 Jun 1962; Col Jack G. Milne, 12–18 Jun 1964; none (not manned), 19 Jun–24 Jul 1964; Col John L. Gregory, Jr., 25 Jul 1964; Col Joseph G. Wilson, 8 Dec 1965; Col Robin Olds, 30 Sep 1966; Col Robert V. Spencer, 23 Sep 1967; Col Charles C. Pattillo, 5 Jul 1968; Col Donald N. Stanfield, 8 May 1969; Col David J. Schmerbeck, 6 May 1970; Col Lloyd R. Leavitt, Jr., 2 Oct 1970; Col Larry M. Killpack, 4 Oct 1970; Col James A. Young, 20 May 1971; Col Carl S. Miller, 28 Feb 1972; Col Francis A. Humphreys, Jr., 25 Nov 1972; Col Tom M. Arnold, Jr., 25 Jan 1974; Col Harry W. Schurr, 16 Sep 1974; Col Alfred M. Miller, Jr., 22 Nov 1974; Col Charles R. Hamm, 12 Mar 1975; Col Reginald R. Davis, 12 Mar 1976; Col Thomas S. Swalm, 7 Mar 1977–.

Aircraft. Primarily F–51, 1948–1950, 1950; F–80, 1949–1950, 1950–1953; F–82, 1950; F–86, 1953–1957; F–100, 1956–1963; F–102, 1961–1964; F–105, 1963–1964; F–4, 1964–1974, 1974–; F–104, 1966–1967; AC–130, 1968–1974; AC–123, 1969–1970; and B–57, 1970–1972; but also included Meteor–8, 1951; F–94, 1954; and F–84, 1956.

Operations. Air defense in Japan, Aug 1948–Jun 1950. Combat operations in Korea, Jun 1950–Jul 1953, at times operating from bases in North and South Korea and at other times from bases in Japan. Air defense in South Korea, Jul 1953–Oct 1954. Air defense in Japan, and maintenance of a quick reaction strike force, Oct 1954–May 1964. Tactical squadrons detached on 13 May 1964, and on 18 Jun 1964 all wing components except wing headquarters inactivated. The wing moved without personnel or equipment to Calif, absorbing resources of the 32d TFW. For the next year the wing trained with F–4 aircraft and participated in numerous exercises, operational readiness inspections, and the like. Moved to Thailand in Dec 1965 and commenced combat operations. Operations included bombardment, ground support, air defense, interdiction, and armed reconnaissance. Numerous enemy aircraft fell prey to wing components and wing became known as the "MiG Killer." In the latter stages of the Southeast Asian conflict the wing's mission shifted away from combat air patrol as new types of aircraft became part of the wing's force, and in this stage of the war the wing gained fame as the "Bridge Busters." During its final years of combat the wing used B–57s for night attacks, AC–130 gunships for ground support and armed reconnaissance, and F–4s for fast-forward air control, interdiction, escort, armed reconnaissance, and other special missions. After North Vietnam invaded the Republic of Vietnam in Mar 1972 the 8th Wing was augmented by additional F–4 units from the United States. To make room for these forces the B–57 squadron became non-operational and moved to the Philippines. The wing continued combat in Vietnam until mid-Jan 1973, in Laos until 22 Feb 1973, and in Cambodia until 15 Aug 1973. F–4 augmentation forces were released in Sep 1973. In mid-1974 action began to phase down Ubon Afld, Thailand, and the wing began to lose personnel, aircraft, and units. The last scheduled F–4 training flight occurred on 16 Jul 1974, and on 16 Sep the wing and most of its components moved without personnel or equipment to Kunsan AB, South Korea, where the wing absorbed resources of the 3d TFW that had moved without personnel or equipment to the Philippines. At Kunsan, the wing became responsible for air defense of South Korea and other operational commitments. In Apr 1975 the wing gained an air base squadron at Kwang Ju, often used during numerous tactical exercises. Following the killing of two U.S. Army officers by North Koreans on 18 Aug 1976, the 8th TFW went on increased alert and was quickly augmented by F–4s from the 12th and 67th Squadrons at Kadena AB, Okinawa. The alert status relaxed on 8 Sep 1976 and the augmentation forces were released.

Service Streamers. None.

Campaign Streamers. UN Defensive; UN Offensive; CCF Intervention; First UN Counteroffensive; CCF Spring Offensive; UN Summer–Fall Offensive; Second Korean Winter; Korea Summer–Fall, 1952; Third Korean Winter; Korea Summer–Fall, 1953; Vietnam Defense; Vietnam Air; Vietnam Air Offensive; Vietnam Air Offensive, Phase II; Vietnam Air Offensive; Phase III; Vietnam Air/Ground; Vietnam Air Offensive, Phase IV; TET 69/Counteroffensive; Vietnam Summer–Fall, 1969; Vietnam Winter–Spring, 1970; Sanctuary Counteroffensive; Southwest Monsoon; Commando Hunt V; Commando Hunt VI; Commando Hunt VII; Vietnam Ceasefire.

Decorations. Presidential Unit Citations (Vietnam): 16 Dec 1966–2 Jan 1967; 1 Mar 1967–31 Mar 1968; 1 Jan–1 Apr 1971. Air Force Outstanding Unit Awards with Combat "V" Device: 16 Dec 1965–15 Dec 1966; 1 Apr–30 Sep 1968; 1 Jan–31 Dec 1970; 1 Oct 1971–31 Mar 1972; 1 Apr–22 Oct 1972; 18 Dec 1972–15 Aug 1973. Air Force Outstanding Unit Award: 12 May 1963–21 Mar 1964. Republic of Korea Presidential Unit Citations: 27 Jun 1950–31 Jan 1951; 1 Feb 1951–31 Mar 1953. Republic of Vietnam Gallantry Cross with Palm: 1 Apr 1966–28 Jan 1973.

Emblem. Azure, a chevron nebule or. *Crest:* On a wreath of the colors (or and azure) three fleur-de-lis or, in front of a propeller fesswise azure. *Motto:* ATTAQUEZ ET CONQUEREZ—Attack and conquer. (Approved for 8th Group on 6 Sep 1934 and for 8th Wing on 3 Jul 1952.)

9th STRATEGIC RECONNAISSANCE WING

Lineage. Established as 9th Strategic Reconnaissance Wing on 25 Apr 1949. Activated on 1 May 1949. Redesignated: 9th Bombardment Wing, Heavy, on 1 Apr 1950; 9th Bombardment Wing, Medium, on 2 Oct 1950; 9th Strategic Aerospace Wing on 1 Apr 1962; 9th Strategic Reconnaissance Wing on 25 Jun 1966.

Assignments. 311th Air Division, 1 May 1949; Second Air Force, 1 Nov 1949; Fifteenth Air Force, 1 Apr 1950; 14th Air Division, 10 Feb 1951; Fifteenth Air Force, 1 May 1953 (attached to 7th Air Division, 23 May–11 Jul 1955; 3d Air Division, 3–22 Oct 1955 and 1 Oct 1957–c. 10 Jan 1958); 813th Air (later, 813th Strategic Aerospace) Division, 15 Jul 1959; 14th Strategic Aerospace (later, 14th Air) Division, 25 Jun 1966–.

Components. *Wing*. 5th Strategic Reconnaissance: attached 12 Nov 1949–10 Feb 1951. *Groups*. 5th Strategic Reconnaissance: attached 9 Nov 1949–10 Feb 1951. 9th: 1 May 1949–16 Jun 1952 (not operational, 10 Feb 1951–16 Jun 1952). *Squadrons*. 1st: attached 10 Feb 1951–15 Jun 1952, assigned 16 Jun 1952–. 5th: attached 10 Feb 1951–15 Jun 1952, assigned 16 Jun 1952–25 Jun 1966. 9th Air Refueling: 16 Jun 1952–15 Dec 1965 (detached 16 Jun 1952–30 Apr 1953). 38th Reconnaissance: attached 26 May–1 Jun 1949. 97th Air Refueling: 15 Jul 1961–1 Jul 1962 (detached). 99th: attached 10 Feb 1951–15 Jun 1952, assigned 16 Jun 1952–1 Apr 1971; assigned 30 Jun 1976–. 569th Strategic Missile: 1 Jun 1961–25 Jun 1965. 658th: 1 Oct 1958–1 Jan 1962 (not operational, 1 Oct 1961–1 Jan 1962). 4364th Support (later, 4364th Post Attack Command and Control): 20 Jul 1962–25 Mar 1965 (not operational, 20 Jul–c. 1 Dec 1962).

Stations. Fairfield-Suisun (later, Travis) AFB, Calif, 1 May 1949; Mountain Home AFB, Idaho, 1 May 1953; Beale AFB, Calif, 25 Jun 1966–.

Commanders. Col Raymond L. Winn, 1 May 1949; Brig Gen Robert F. Travis, 16 Jun 1949; Col Carlos J. Cochrane, 6 Aug 1950; Col Joe W. Kelly, 10 Aug 1950; Col Clifford J. Heflin, 10 Feb 1951; Brig Gen William C. Kingsbury, 5 Jan 1953; Col Robert V. De Shazo, 27 Jul 1957; Col Rufus H. Holloway, 15 Jul 1959; Col Walter Y. Lucas, 7 Jun 1960; Col William L. Gray, 5 Jul 1962; Col William R. Smith, 2 Apr 1964; Col Walter Y. Lucas, 10 Jun 1965; Maj Adelbert J. Lemke, c. May 1966; Col Douglas T. Nelson, 25 Jun 1966; Col William R. Hayes, 14 Dec 1966; Col Charles F. Minter, Sr., 27 Jun 1969; Col Harold E. Confer, 1 Jul 1970; Col Jerome F. O'Malley, 31 May 1972; Col Patrick J. Halloran, 10 May 1973; Col John H.

Storrie, 30 Jun 1975; Col Lyman M. Kidder, 30 Sep 1977–.

Aircraft and Missiles. B/RB–17, 1949–1950; B–29, 1949–1954; RB–29, 1949–1951; RB–36; 1949–1950, 1951; KB–29, 1953; B–47, 1954–1966; KC–97, 1954–1965; Titan, 1962–1965; EB–47, 1962–1965; SR–71, 1977–; U–2, 1976–.

Operations. Conducted strategic reconnaissance with assigned components, May 1949–Mar 1950, and with components of 5th Strategic Reconnaissance Wing, Nov 1949–Feb 1951. Conducted strategic bombardment training, Feb 1951–Dec 1965. Performed air refueling, May–Jul 1953 and Sep 1954–Dec 1965. Conducted SAC airborne communications relay missions, Dec 1962–Mar 1965. Deployed at Fairford RAF Station, England, May–Jul 1955, at Kadena AB, Okinawa, 3–22 Oct 1955, at Eielson AFB, Alaska, 18–22 Jan 1956, and at Andersen AFB, Guam, Oct 1957–Jan 1958. Controlled a Titan missile complex, Jun 1961–Jun 1965. Phased down operations at Mountain Home AFB, Idaho, Jan–Jun 1966, then moved to Beale AFB, Calif. Performed strategic reconnaissance, Jun 1966–.

Service Streamers. None.

Campaign Streamers. None.

Decorations. Presidential Unit Citation: 31 Mar–31 Dec 1968. Air Force Outstanding Unit Award with Combat "V" Device: 1 Jul 1972–30 Jun 1973. Air Force Outstanding Unit Awards: 1 Jan 1957–31 Jan 1958; 1 Jul 1967–30 Jun 1968; 1 Jul 1970–30 Jun 1971; 1 Jul 1971–30 Jun 1972; 1 Jul 1973–30 Jun 1975; 1 Jul 1975–30 Jun 1977.

Emblem. Per pale vert and sable a pallet wavy argent fimbriated or, over all on a fess or four crosses patee of the second (sable). *Crest:* On a wreath of the colors (argent and vert) a rattlesnake entwined about a prickly pear cactus all proper. *Motto:* SEMPER PARATUS—Always ready. (Approved for 9th Group on 20 Mar 1924 and for 9th Wing on 1 Jul 1952.)

10th TACTICAL RECONNAISSANCE WING

Lineage. Established as 10th Reconnaissance Wing on 14 Nov 1947. Organized on 3 Dec 1947. Discontinued on 27 Aug 1948. Redesignated 10th Tactical Reconnaissance Wing, and activated on 25 Aug 1948. Inactivated on 1 Apr 1949. Activated on 10 Jul 1952.

Assignments. Ninth Air Force, 3 Dec 1947–27 Aug 1948. Ninth Air Force, 25 Aug 1948; Fourteenth Air Force, 1 Feb–1 Apr 1949. Twelfth Air Force, 10 Jul 1952; United States Air Forces in Europe, 1 Jan 1958; Third Air Force, 25 Aug 1959; Seventeenth Air Force, 1 Jul 1961; Third Air Force, 1 Sep 1963–.

Components. *Group.* 10th: 3 Dec 1947–27 Aug 1948; 25 Aug 1948–1 Apr 1949; 10 Jul 1952–8 Dec 1957. *Squad-*

rons. 1st: 8 Dec 1957–. 19th: attached 8 Jan–7 Mar 1958, assigned 8 Mar 1958–1 Jul 1965. 30th: attached 8 Jan–7 Mar 1958, assigned 8 Mar 1958–1 Apr 1976. 32d: 8 Dec 1957–8 Mar 1958 (detached 8 Jan–8 Mar 1958); 15 Aug 1966–1 Jan 1976 (not operational, 15 Aug–31 Oct 1966). 38th: 8 Dec 1957–8 Mar 1958 (detached 8 Jan–8 Mar 1958). 42d: 8 Dec 1957–1 Jul 1965. 45th: attached 13 Jun–6 Jul 1973. 62d: attached 7–24 Mar 1976. 527th Tactical Fighter Training Aggressor: 1 Apr 1976–.

Stations. Pope Field (later, AFB), NC, 3 Dec 1947–27 Aug 1948. Pope AFB, NC, 25 Aug 1948–1 Apr 1949. Toul-Rosieres AB, France, 10 Jul 1952; Spangdahlem AB, West Germany, 9 May 1953; RAF Alconbury, England, 25 Aug 1959–.

Commanders. Col Louis M. Merrick, 3 Dec 1947–27 Aug 1948. Col Louis M. Merrick, 25 Aug 1948–1 Apr 1949. Col Dixon M. Allison, 10 Jul 1952; Col Brian O'Neill, 1 Oct 1952; Col Franklin S. Allen, Jr., 30 Jun 1955; Col Kenneth R. Powell, 22 Jul 1955; Col James D. Kemp, 3 Jul 1959; Col Victor N. Cabas, 21 Jun 1962; Col Arthur Small, 8 Jul 1963; Col DeWitt S. Spain, 25 Mar 1964; Col James A. Shannon, 22 Jun 1966; Col Theodore S. Coberly, 15 May 1967; Brig Gen Winston P. Anderson, 17 Jul 1968; Col Ralph F. Findlay, 29 Jun 1970; Col Lovic P. Hodnette, Jr., 9 Jul 1971; Col Daniel J. Nelson, 5 Jun 1972; Col LaVerne H. Griffin, 6 Mar 1973; Col Paul H. Hodges, 22 Feb 1974; Col Buford D. Lary, 17 Mar 1977–.

Aircraft. P (later, F)–51/F–6, 1947–1948; RF–51, 1947–1948. RF–51, 1948–1949. RF–80, 1952–1956; RB–26, 1952–1957; RB–57, 1954–1957; RF–84, 1955–1958; T/WT–33, 1955–1957; RB–66, 1956–1965; WB–66, 1957–1960; B–66, 1960–1965; RF–4, 1965–; F–5, 1976–.

Operations. Performed tactical reconnaissance, 1947–1948, and 1948–1949. Replaced 117th Tactical Reconnaissance Wing at Toul-Rosieres AB, France, in Jul 1952. Provided weather reconnaissance, 1952–c. 1960, and tactical reconnaissance (day and night, multi-sensor), 1952–. Replaced 7560th Air Base Group at RAF Alconbury, England, in Aug 1959, and became responsible for operation and maintenance of that installation. Operated from RAF Wethersfield, England, 3 Jul–31 Oct 1972. Took part in frequent tactical exercises of USAFE and NATO. Dropped two (of three) reconnaissance squadrons in 1976 and gained the 527th Tactical Fighter Training Aggressor Squadron. This unit, equipped with F–5Es in May 1976, began providing "dissimilar" air combat training for USAFE fighter and reconnaissance wings in Sep 1976.

Service Streamers. None.

Campaign Streamers. None.

Decorations. Air Force Outstanding Unit Awards: 31 Dec 1959–1 Jan 1962; 15 Jul 1968–15 Jul 1969; 1 Jun 1972–1 Jun 1973.

Emblem. Azure a sphere or, latitude and longitude lines sable, in chief the head and arms of the Greek mythical god Argus, head facing base, arms fesswise both hands toward dexter of the second, outlined of the field. *Motto:* ARGUS—Ceaseless watch. (Approved for 10th Group on 29 Dec 1942 and for 10th Wing on 28 Jun 1954.)

11th AIR REFUELING WING

Lineage. Established as 11th Bombardment Wing, Heavy, on 18 Nov 1948. Activated on 16 Feb 1951. Redesignated: 11th Strategic Aerospace Wing on 1 Apr 1962; 11th Air Refueling Wing on 2 Jul 1968. Inactivated on 25 Mar 1969.

Assignments. 19th Air Division, 16 Feb 1951 (attached to 5th Air Division, 4 May–2 Jul 1955); Second Air Force, 13 Dec 1957; 816th Air (later, 816th Strategic Aerospace) Division, 1 Jul 1958; 819th Strategic Aerospace Division, 1 Jul 1965; 19th Air Division, 2 Jul 1966–25 Mar 1969.

Components. *Group.* 11th: 16 Feb 1951–16 Jun 1952 (not operational). *Squadrons.* 11th Air Refueling: 25 Jun 1965–25 Mar 1969. 26th: attached 16 Feb 1951–15 Jun 1952, assigned 16 Jun 1952–2 Jul 1968. 42d: attached 16 Feb 1951–15 Jun 1952, assigned 16 Jun 1952–1 Jun 1960. 96th Air Refueling: 3 Dec 1957–1 Oct 1960; 15 Dec 1960–25 Jun 1965. 98th: attached 16 Feb 1951–15 Jun 1952, assigned 16 Jun 1952–10 Dec 1957. 577th Strategic Missile: 1 Jun 1961–25 Mar 1965. 918th Air Refueling: 1 Oct–15 Dec 1960. 921st Air Refueling: 1 Oct–15 Dec 1960.

Stations. Carswell AFB, Texas, 16 Feb 1951; Altus AFB, Okla, 13 Dec 1957–25 Mar 1969.

Commanders. Brig Gen Thomas P. Gerrity, 16 Feb 1951; Col Louis W. Rohr, 15 Nov 1952; Col William T. Seawell, 2 Mar 1953; Col Howard W. Moore, 7 Aug 1954; Col John S. Samuel, 16 Jul 1957; Col Frederick R. Ramputi, 5 Sep 1958; Col Bernard J. Finan, Jr., 15 Jul 1961; Col Kenneth S. Steele, 1 Aug 1961; Brig Gen William B. Kyes, 4 Mar 1963; Col Merrill N. Moore, Jan 1965; Col Earl S. Kimbell, c. Jul 1965; Col Harold A. Radetsky, 2 Aug 1965; Col Earl S. Kimbell, 5 Jul 1966; Col Raymond J. Bryan, 8 Jul 1966; Col Raymond R. Deitch, 11 Jul 1966; Col Joseph J. Young, 29 Jun 1967–25 Mar 1969.

Aircraft and Missiles. B–36, 1951–1957; KC–97, 1957–1958; B–52, 1958–1968; KC–135, 1958–1969; Atlas, 1961–1965.

Operations. Strategic bombardment training, 1951–1968, aerial refueling, 1957–1969, and Atlas missile operations, 1961–1965, to meet SAC's global commitments. Deployed at Nouasseur AB, French Morocco, 4 May–2 Jul 1955.

Service Streamers. None.

Campaign Streamers. None.

Decorations. Air Force Outstanding Unit Awards: 6 Aug 1954–15 Jul 1957; 27 Oct 1958–16 Sep 1960.

Emblem. Azure, on a bend or, three grey geese volant proper. *Crest:* On a wreath or and azure a grey goose proper with wings displayed and inverted. *Motto:* PROGRESSIO SINE TIMORE AUT PRAEJUDICIO—Progress without fear or prejudice. (Approved for

11th Group on 11 Jun 1941 and for 11th Wing on 3 Aug 1956.)

12th FLYING TRAINING WING

Lineage. Established as 12th Fighter-Escort Wing on 27 Oct 1950. Activated on 1 Nov 1950. Redesignated: 12th Strategic Fighter Wing on 20 Jan 1953; 12th Fighter-Day Wing on 1 Jul 1957. Inactivated on 8 Jan 1958. Redesignated 12th Tactical Fighter Wing, and activated, on 17 Apr 1962. Organized on 25 Apr 1962. Inactivated on 17 Nov 1971. Redesignated 12th Flying Training Wing on 22 Mar 1972. Activated on 1 May 1972.

Assignments. Second Air Force, 1 Nov 1950; Eighth Air Force, 5 Dec 1950; 42d Air Division, 9 Apr 1951–8 Jan 1958 (attached 7th Air Division, 20 Jul–30 Nov 1951; 39th Air Division [Defense], 18 May–10 Aug 1953 and 10 May–7 Aug 1954). Tactical Air Command, 17 Apr 1962; Ninth Air Force, 25 Apr 1962; 836th Air Division, 1 Jul 1962; 2d Air Division, 8 Nov 1965; Seventh Air Force, 1 Apr 1966–17 Nov 1971. Air Training Command, 1 May 1972–.

Components. *Group.* 12th: 1 Nov 1950–16 Jun 1952 (not operational, 10 Feb 1951–16 Jun 1952). *Squadrons.* 27th Air Refueling: attached 1 Apr–1 Sep 1955. 43d: attached 8 Nov 1965–c. 4 Jan 1966. 45th: attached 8 May–1 Jul 1962. 389th: 31 Mar 1970–15 Oct 1971. 391st: attached 26 Jan–22 Jun 1966, assigned 23 Jun 1966–22 Jul 1968. 480th: 31 Mar 1970–17 Nov 1971. 506th Air Refueling: attached 8 Aug 1955–1 Jul 1957. 555th: 8 Jan 1964–25 Mar 1966 (detached 8 Dec 1964–18 Mar 1965, 6 Nov 1965–25 Mar 1966). 557th: 25 Apr 1962–8 Nov 1965, 1 Dec 1965–31 Mar 1970 (not operational, 10–31 Mar 1970). 558th: 25 Apr 1962–31 Mar 1970 (detached 9 Mar–16 Jun 1965, 3 Feb–22 Jul 1968; not operational, 10–31 Mar 1970). 559th: attached 10 Feb 1951–15 Jun 1952, assigned 16 Jun 1952–8 Jan 1958; assigned 25 Apr 1962–8 Nov 1965 (detached 9 Jun–7 Sep 1965); assigned 27 Dec 1965–31 Mar 1970 (not operational, 23–31 Mar 1970); assigned 1 May 1972–. 560th: attached 10 Feb 1951–15 Jun 1952, assigned 16 Jun 1952–8 Jan 1958; assigned 1 May 1972–. 561st: attached 10 Feb 1951–1 Apr 1952; assigned 16 Jun 1952–8 Jan 1958 (detached 16 Jun–16 Dec 1952).

Stations. Turner AFB, Ga, 1 Nov 1950; Bergstrom AFB, Texas, 5 Dec 1950–8 Jan 1958. MacDill AFB, Fla, 25 Apr 1962–31 Oct 1965; Cam Ranh Bay AB, South Vietnam, 8 Nov 1965; Phu Cat AB, South Vietnam, 31 Mar 1970–17 Nov 1971. Randolph AFB, Texas, 1 May 1972–.

Commanders. Capt James M. Ross, 1 Nov 1950; Col Cy Wilson, 20 Nov 1950; Col Charles A. Gayle, 1 Apr 1952; Col Richard O. Hunziker, 4 Aug 1952; Col Howard G. Cook, 23 Apr

1954; Col Robert W. Stephens, 20 Jul 1956; Col William D. Dunham, 10 Aug 1956–8 Jan 1958. None (not manned), 17 Apr–3 May 1962; unkn, 4–13 May 1962; Col Harold M. McClelland, 14 May 1962; Col Raymond A. Bradley, 17 Jul 1965; Col Levi R. Chase, 8 Oct 1965; Col Jones E. Bolt, 18 Oct 1966; Col Joel D. Thorvaldson, Mar 1967; Col Woodard E. Davis, Jr., 9 Apr 1967; Col Floyd White, 5 Apr 1968; Col Ramon R. Melton, 7 Apr 1969; Col Harry B. Trimble, 31 Mar 1970; Col Larry M. Killpack, 13 Apr 1970; Col Ralph S. Parr, 4 Oct 1970; Col Richard H. Schoeneman, 19 Feb 1971; Col Albert L. Melton, 4 Oct–17 Nov 1971. Col Hoyt S. Vandenberg, Jr., 1 May 1972; Brig Gen Malcolm E. Ryan, 14 Aug 1972; Col John P. Rollston, 1 Nov 1973; Col Kenneth R. Fleenor, 30 Jun 1975–.

Aircraft. F–84, 1950–1957; KB–29, 1955–1957. F–84, 1962–1964; F–4, 1964–1970, 1970–1971. TH–1, 1972–; T–29, 1972–1974; T–37, 1972–; T–38, 1972–; T–39, 1972–; T–41, 1972–1973.

Operations. Provided fighter escort, air defense, and exercised SAC bomber forces, 1950–1957. Deployed at Manston RAF Station, England, 20 Jul–30 Nov 1951, and at Misawa AB, Japan, 15 May–10 Aug 1953 and 10 May–11 Aug 1954. Provided air refueling support, 1955–1957. From mid-1957 until inactivation in 1958, and from Apr 1962 until deployed to Southeast Asia, maintained preparedness for world-wide tactical operations. Engaged in aerial combat in Southeast Asia, 19 Nov 1965–21 Oct 1971. Provided close air support, interdiction, rescue combat patrol, MiG patrol, and other activities. Replaced, and absorbed resources of, the 3510th Flying Training Wing at Randolph AFB, Texas, in May 1972. Became responsible for operation and maintenance of Randolph AFB, pilot instructor training, and operation of the USAF Instrument Flight Center, itself including the USAF Instrument Pilot Instructor School plus Flight Standards and Research and Development Divisions. The Center was responsible not only for instructor pilot training but also for development, testing, and evaluation of flight instruments and flight instrument systems. From 2 May 1973 to 12 Nov 1976, the wing also provided T–37, T–38, and T–39 pilot requalification training for over 150 USAF ex-prisoners of war.

Service Streamers. None.

Campaign Streamers. Vietnam Defense; Vietnam Air; Vietnam Air Offensive; Vietnam Air Offensive, Phase II; Vietnam Air Offensive, Phase III; Vietnam Air/Ground; Vietnam Air Offensive, Phase IV; TET 69/Counteroffensive; Vietnam Summer–Fall, 1969; Vietnam Winter–Spring, 1970; Sanctuary Counteroffensive; Southwest Monsoon; Commando Hunt V; Commando Hunt VI; Commando Hunt VII.

Decorations. Presidential Unit Citation (Southeast Asia): 8 Feb–8 Apr 1971. Air Force Outstanding Unit Awards with Combat "V" Device: 15 Oct 1965–30 May 1966; 1 Jun 1966–31 May 1967; 1 Jun 1967–31 May 1968; 1 Jun 1968–31 May 1969; 1 Jun 1969–31 Mar 1970; 1 Apr 1970–21 Oct 1971. Air Force Outstanding Unit Awards: 1 May 1972–28 Feb 1973; 1 Jan–31 Dec 1975. Republic of Vietnam Gallantry Crosses with Palm: 15 Oct 1965–10 Nov 1971; 1 Apr 1966–17 Nov 1971.

Emblem. Azure, a sword point to base or, hilt flamant proper; a bordure gyronny of twelve of the second and first, fimbriated of the second. *Motto:* SPIRITUS OMNIA VINCET—The spirit conquers all. (Approved for 12th Group on 3 Feb 1942 and, slightly modified, for 12th Wing on 15 Mar 1963.)

14th FLYING TRAINING WING

Lineage. Established as 14th Fighter Wing on 29 Jul 1947. Organized on 15 Aug 1947. Discontinued on 26 Jul 1948. Activated on 26 Jul 1948. Inactivated on 2 Oct 1949. Redesignated 14th Air Commando Wing, and activated, on 28 Feb 1966. Organized on 8 Mar 1966. Redesignated 14th Special Operations Wing on 1 Aug 1968. Inactivated on 30 Sep 1971. Redesignated 14th Flying Training Wing on 22 Mar 1972. Activated on 1 Jun 1972.

Assignments. First Air Force, 15 Aug 1947–26 Jul 1948. First Air Force, 26 Jul 1948–2 Oct 1949. Pacific Air Forces, 28 Feb 1966; 2d Air Division, 8 Mar 1966; Seventh Air Force, 1 Apr 1966–30 Sep 1971. Air Training Command, 1 Jun 1972–.

Components. *Group.* 14th: 15 Aug 1947–26 Jul 1948; 26 Jul 1948–2 Oct 1949. *Squadrons.* 1st: 8 Mar 1966–20 Dec 1967. 3d: 1 May 1968–15 Sep 1969. 4th: 8 Mar 1966–15 Dec 1969. 5th: 8 Mar 1966–15 Oct 1969. 6th: 29 Feb–15 Jul 1968. 9th: 25 Jan 1967–30 Sep 1971 (not operational, 25 Jan–28 Feb 1967). 14th: 25 Oct 1967–1 May 1968 (not operational, 25 Oct 1967–14 Jan 1968). 15th: 15 Mar 1968–31 Oct 1970. 17th: 1 Jun 1969–30 Sep 1971. 18th: 1 Oct 1969–25 Aug 1971. 20th: 8 Mar 1966–1 Sep 1971. 37th: 1 Jun 1972–. 50th: 1 Jun 1972–. 71st: 20 Dec 1968–10 Jun 1969. 90th: 31 Oct 1970–1 Sep 1971. 602d: 8 Mar 1966–8 Apr 1967. 604th: 15 Nov 1967–1 Mar 1970 (detached).

Stations. Dow Field (later, AFB), Maine, 15 Aug 1947–26 Jul 1948. Dow AFB, Maine, 26 Jul 1948–2 Oct 1949. Nha Trang AB, South Vietnam, 8 Mar 1966; Phan Rang AB, South Vietnam, 15 Oct 1969–30 Sep 1971. Columbus AFB, Miss, 1 Jun 1972–.

Commanders. Col Loring F. Stetson, Jr., 1947; Col George A. McHenry, c. 7 Jan–26 Jul 1948. Col George A. McHenry, 26 Jul 1948; Col Arvid E. Olson, Jr., c. 30 Sep–2 Oct 1949. None (not manned), 28 Feb–7 Mar 1966; Col Robert J. Jones, 8 Mar 1966; Col Gordon F. Bradburn, 17 Apr 1966; Col Forrest L. Rauscher, 10 Apr 1967; Col John M. Patton, 21 Nov 1967; Col Conrad S. Allman, 3 Jun 1968; Col William K. Bush, 5 Mar 1969; Col Clyde S. Cherry, 2 Sep 1969; Col William H. Fairbrother, 3 Apr 1970; Col Alfred F. Eaton, 13 Sep 1970; Col Mark W. Magnan, 14 Mar 1971; Col Malcolm L. Nurnburg, 13–30 Sep 1971. Col William A. Boutwell, 1 Jun 1972; Col Robert B. Tanguy, 9 Jun 1972; Col

James S. Creedon, c. 18 Jul 1973; Col Horace W. Miller, 8 Mar 1976–.

Aircraft. P (later, F)–47, 1947–1948; P–84, 1947–1948. F–47, 1948–1949; F–84, 1948–1949. A–1, 1966–1967, 1968; AC–47, 1966–1969; C–47, 1966–1971; HC–47, 1966–1969; U–10, 1966–1969; CH–3, 1966–1969; O–2, 1967–1971; UH–1, 1967–1971; C–130, 1968–1971; C–123, 1968–1971; AC–130, 1968; AC–119, 1968–1971. T–41, 1972–1973; T–37, 1972–; T–38, 1972–.

Operations. Provided air defense for the northeastern United States, 1947–1948, and 1948–1949. Performed combat operations in Southeast Asia, Mar 1966–Sep 1971, operating from numerous locations in South Vietnam and Thailand. Operations included close and direct air support, interdiction, combat airlift, aerial resupply, visual and photographic reconnaissance, unconventional warfare, counterinsurgency operations, psychological warfare (including leaflet dropping and aerial broadcasting), forward air control operations and FAC escort, search and rescue, escort for convoy and defoliation operations, flare drops, civic actions, and humanitarian actions. The wing also operated Nha Trang AB, South Vietnam, Mar 1966–Oct 1969, and provided maintenance support to a number of tenants. Trained South Vietnamese Air Force (VNAF) personnel in AC–119 operations and maintenance, Feb–Aug 1971, and transferred some of its AC–119s to the VNAF, Aug–Sep 1971 as part of a phase-down for inactivation. Replaced, and absorbed resources of, the 3650th Pilot Training Wing in Jun 1972 at Columbus AFB, Miss, and assumed an undergraduate pilot training program, plus base operation and maintenance.

Service Streamers. None.

Campaign Streamers. Vietnam Air; Vietnam Air Offensive; Vietnam Air Offensive, Phase II; Vietnam Air Offensive, Phase III; Vietnam Air/Ground; Vietnam Air Offensive, Phase IV; TET 69/Counteroffensive; Vietnam Summer–Fall, 1969; Vietnam Winter–Spring, 1970; Sanctuary Counteroffensive; Southwest Monsoon; Commando Hunt V; Commando Hunt VI.

Decorations. Presidential Unit Citations (Southeast Asia): 8 Mar 1966–7 Mar 1967; 21 Jun 1968–30 Jun 1969. Air Force Outstanding Unit Awards with Combat "V" Device: 16 Jun 1967–20 Jun 1968; 1 Jul 1970–30 Jun 1971. Meritorious Unit Commendation: 1 Jan–31 Dec 1968. Air Force Outstanding Unit Award: 1 Jan–31 Dec 1974. Republic of Vietnam Gallantry Crosses with Palm: 1 Apr 1966–30 Sep 1971; 1 Jan–30 Aug 1968.

Emblem. Azure, in chief an escutcheon per bend argent and sable over two laurel branches in saltire or, above in bend two flight symbols ascending, one argent surmounting one gules, encircled by five mullets, one in sinister chief and four in dexter base; all within a diminished bordure or. *Motto:* DAY AND NIGHT—PEACE AND WAR. (Approved on 19 Jun 1967.)

15th AIR BASE WING

Lineage. Established as 15th Tactical Fighter Wing, and activated, on 17 Apr 1962. Organized on 1 Jul 1962. Inactivated on 1 Oct 1970. Redesignated 15th Air Base Wing on 20 Oct 1971. Activated on 1 Nov 1971.

Assignments. Tactical Air Command, 17 Apr 1962; 836th Air Division, 1 Jul 1962–1 Oct 1970. Pacific Air Forces, 1 Nov 1971–.

Components. *Squadrons.* 9th Airborne Command and Control: 1 Nov 1971–. 13th Bombardment Squadron, Tactical: 8 Feb 1969–1 Oct 1970 (detached 15 Sep–1 Oct 1970). 22d Tactical Air Support: 1 Nov 1971–. 43d: 8 Jan 1964–15 Jul 1970 (detached 17 Aug 1965–c. 4 Jan 1966). 45th: 1 Jul 1962–1 Oct 1970 (detached 4 Apr–10 Aug 1965). 46th: 1 Jul 1962–1 Oct 1970 (detached 11 May–22 Aug 1965 and 1–10 Nov 1965). 47th: 1 Jul 1962–1 Oct 1970 (detached 22 Jul–27 Nov 1965). 421st: 25 Apr–1 Jul 1967. 4424th Combat Crew Training: 15 Oct 1968–1 Oct 1970.

Stations. MacDill AFB, Fla, 1 Jul 1962–1 Oct 1970. Hickam AFB, Hawaii, 1 Nov 1971–.

Commanders. None (not manned), 17 Apr–30 Jun 1962; Col George L. Jones, 1 Jul 1962; Col Francis J. Vetort, 8 Jun 1964; Col Levi R. Chase, 6 Jul 1964; Col Raymond A. Bradley, 4 Oct 1965; Col Woodrow W. Ramsey, 6 Oct 1965; Col Donald N. Stanfield, 12 Jun 1966; Col Charles J. Bowers, 29 Jul 1966; Col James D. Catington, 15 Aug 1966; Col Roy D. Carlson, 21 Jun 1967; Col Clifford H. Meier, 20 May 1968; Col Travis R. McNeil, 1 Feb–1 Oct 1970. Col Ernest W. Pate, 1 Nov 1971; Col Howard R. Inks, 3 Jun 1972; Col Wilmot E. Y. Paxton, 23 Aug 1972; Col Richard L. Thompson, 1 May 1976; Col Howard F. O'Neal, 17 May 1976–.

Aircraft. F–84, 1962–1964; T–33, 1962–1970; F–4, 1964–1970; B–57, 1968–1970. EC–135, 1971–; O–2, 1972–; T–33, 1972–1977.

Operations. Conducted tactical fighter combat crew training, 1962–1963, participated in a variety of exercises, operations and readiness tests of Tactical Air Command, 1963–1965. Trained pilots and provided logistical support for the 12th Tactical Fighter Wing. Reorganized as a mission–capable unit at the time of the Cuban missile crisis of 1962, returning afterwards to a training mission. Deployed the 43d, 45th, 46th, and 47th Squadrons to Southeast Asia in 1965. Functioned as a replacement training unit for F–4 aircrews from 1965–1970. In 1968 the 15th Wing also began B–57 light bomber aircrew training. Deployed 16 F–4s at Seymour Johnson AFB, NC, during the *Pueblo* crisis in 1968. Inactivated in 1970. Activated as an air base wing on 1 Nov 1971 at Hickam AFB, Hawaii. Controlled Hickam, Wheeler, Dillingham, and Johnston Island AF Bases, Bellows AFS, Kilauea Military Camp, and several smaller subsidiary bases. Wing supported about 100 tenant units. Commanded, operated, maintained, and provided internal security for all AF installations and assigned units in the Hawaiian Islands, Wake Island, and other island groups in the Central and South Pacific Ocean. Provided base support for Pacific Air Forces (PACAF) and tenant organizations. Its 15th Operations Squadron provided special air transport in VC–118s for CINCPAC, CINCPACAF, Commander in Chief, USARPAC, and for the Commander, Hawaiian Air National Guard, and provided full flight and operational services for visitors and special groups. The 9th Airborne Command and Control Squadron, assigned to the 15th Wing, provided airborne command and control support for the Commander in Chief Pacific, Nov 1971–.

Service Streamers. None.

Campaign Streamers. None.

Decorations. Air Force Outstanding Unit Awards: 1 Jan 1965–1 Jun 1966; 1 Jan–31 Dec 1969; 4 Apr–3 Sep 1975.

Emblem. Or, on a bend azure, two terrestrial lightning flashes issuant from base of the first, over all a gunsight counter-changed. *Motto:* PROSEQUOR ALIS—I pursue with wings. (Approved for 15th Group on 5 Oct 1942 and for 15th Wing on 15 Mar 1963.)

17th BOMBARDMENT WING, HEAVY

Lineage. Established as 17th Bombardment Wing, Light, on 8 May 1952. Activated on 10 May 1952. Redesignated 17th Bombardment Wing, Tactical, on 1 Oct 1955. Inactivated on 25 Jun 1958. Redesignated 17th Bombardment Wing, Heavy, and activated, on 15 Nov 1962. Organized on 1 Feb 1963. Inactivated on 30 Sep 1976.

Assignments. Fifth Air Force, 10 May 1952; Ninth Air Force, 1 Apr 1955–25 Jun 1958 (attached to Nineteenth Air Force, 15 Dec 1956–15 Dec 1957). Strategic Air Command, 15 Nov 1962; 40th Air Division, 1 Feb 1963; 6th Air Division, 1 Jul 1963; 57th Air Division, 1 Jul 1965; 817th Air Division, 2 Jul 1968; 45th Air Division, 2 Jul 1969; 40th Air Division, 1 Jul 1971; 42d Air Division, 1 Jul 1973; 14th Air Division, 30 Sep 1975–30 Sep 1976.

Components. *Group.* 17th: 10 May 1952–25 Jun 1958 (not operational, 8 Jun 1957–25 Jun 1958). *Squadrons.* 9th Air Refueling: 30 Sep 1975–30 Sep 1976. 34th: attached 8 Jun 1957–25 Jun 1958 (not operational, 17 Jan–25 Jun 1958); assigned 1 Feb 1963–30 Sep 1976 (not operational, 8 Jul–29 Sep 1975 and 14 Jul–30 Sep 1976). 37th: attached 8 Jun 1957–25 Jun 1958 (not operational, 10 May–25 Jun 1958). 95th: attached 8 Jun 1957–25 Jun 1958 (not operational, 20–25 Jun 1958). 903d Air Refueling: 30 Sep 1975–30 Sep 1976. 922d Air Refueling: 1 Feb 1963–30 Sep 1975 (not operational, 8 Jul–30 Sep 1975).

Stations. Pusan-East AB, South Korea, 10 May 1952; Miho AB, Japan, 10 Oct 1954–20 Mar 1955; Eglin Air Force Auxiliary Field No. 9 (Hurlburt Field), Fla, 1 Apr 1955–25 Jun 1958. Wright-Patterson AFB, Ohio, 1 Feb

1963; Beale AFB, Calif, 30 Sep 1975–30 Sep 1976.

Commanders. Col Albert W. Fletcher, 10 May 1952; Col Glen C. Nye, 3 Jun 1952; Col William C. Lindley, Jr., 7 Oct 1952; Col Clinton C. Wasem, 10 Oct 1952; Col Murdoch W. Campbell, c. Aug 1953; Col Daniel F. Tatum, c. Sep 1953; Col George D. Hughes, 8 Jul 1954; Col Walter H. Williamson, 4 Aug 1954; Col George D. Hughes, 4 Sep 1954; Col Howard F. Bronson, Jr., 10 Sep 1954; Col Carroll H. Bolender, 9 May 1956; Col Reginald J. Clizbe, 25 Jun 1956; Col Kenneth C. Dempster, 31 Mar–25 Jun 1958. None (not manned), 15 Nov 1962–31 Jan 1963; Col George H. Fulcher, 1 Feb 1963; Col Mason A. Dula, 1 Jun 1965; Col Clifford W. Hargrove, 1 Jan 1967; Col Raymond P. Lowman, 17 Jul 1967; Col James B. Vogler, Jr., 20 Nov 1968; Col Alfred R. Grimm, 12 Jan 1970; Brig Gen Ray B. Sitton, 26 Jun 1970; Col Thomas F. Rew, 24 May 1971; Col John D. Mash, 8 Jun 1972; Col Thomas P. Conlin, 12 Jun 1972; Col Andrew Pringle, Jr., 12 Feb 1973; Col Henry W. Boardman, 3 Jun 1974; Col George R. Savage, 8 Jul 1975; Lt Col Ovidio Pugnale, 4 Aug 1975; Col Philip A. Brennan, 30 Sep 1975; Col John J. Tobin, 6 Apr–30 Sep 1976.

Aircraft. B–26, 1952–1956; B–57, 1955–1956; B–66, 1956–1958. B–52, 1963–1975, 1975–1976; KC–135, 1963–1975, 1975–1976.

Operations. Replaced 452d Bombardment Wing, Light, in South Korea in May 1952. Conducted combat operations in Korea, 10 May 1952–27 Jul 1953. Operations included light bombardment, interdiction, and armed reconnaissance. Afterwards, maintained operational proficiency for light bombardment in Japan until moved to the United States, then trained to maintain tactical proficiency under TAC until inactivation. Replaced 4043d Strategic Wing in Feb 1963 and trained to maintain proficiency in strategic bombardment and aerial refueling on a global basis. Furnished B–52 aircrews and KC–135 aircraft and crews to SAC units involved in combat operations in Southeast Asia, 1965–1975. Taken off alert at Wright-Patterson AFB, Ohio, on 30 Jun 1975 and phased down, transferring aircraft by 7 Jul. Moved without personnel or equipment to Beale AFB, Calif, and absorbed resources of the 456th Bombardment Wing, including B–52G and KC–135Q aircraft. Continued global strategic bombardment alert to 30 Jun 1976 and used tanker aircraft primarily to refuel SR–71s of the 9th Strategic Reconnaissance Wing. Inactivated on 30 Sep 1976 and replaced by 100th Air Refueling Wing.

Service Streamers. None.

Campaign Streamers. Korea Summer–Fall, 1952; Third Korean Winter; Korea Summer–Fall, 1953.

Decorations. Air Force Outstanding Unit Awards: 1 Jul 1963–31 Mar 1964; 1 Jul 1971–30 Jun 1973. Republic of Korea Presidential Unit Citation: 24 May 1952–31 Mar 1953.

Emblem. Or, seven crosses pattee in pale sable. *Crest:* On a wreath of the colors (or and sable) a griffin rampant of the first, beaked, forelegged and winged of the second, and langued gules. *Motto:* TOUJOURS AU DANGER—Ever into danger. (Approved for 17th Group on 2 Nov 1937 and for 17th Wing on 27 May 1952.)

18th TACTICAL FIGHTER WING

Lineage. Established as 18th Fighter Wing on 10 Aug 1948. Activated on 14 Aug 1948. Redesignated 18th Fighter-Bomber Wing on 20 Jan 1950; 18th Tactical Fighter Wing on 1 Jul 1958.

Assignments. Thirteenth Air Force, 14 Aug 1948; Far East Air Forces, 1 Dec 1948; Thirteenth Air Force, 16 May 1949 (attached to Fifth Air Force, 1 Dec 1950–31 Oct 1954; Twentieth Air Force, 1 Nov 1954; 6332d Air Base Wing, 1–9 Nov 1954; Twentieth Air Force, 10 Nov 1954–31 Jan 1955; Air Task Group Fifth, Provisional, 1–15 Feb 1955; Twentieth Air Force, 16–28 Feb 1955; 314th Air Division, 1 Mar 1955–31 Jan 1957; Fifth Air Force, 1 Feb–30 Sep 1957); Fifth Air Force, 1 Oct 1957; 313th Air Division, 10 Nov 1958– (attached to Fifth Air Force ADVON, 28 Jan–13 Jun 1968).

Components. *Groups*. 5th Reconnaissance: attached 1 Dec 1948–16 May 1949. 18th: 14 Aug 1948–1 Oct 1957 (detached 16 May–16 Dec 1949, 28 Jul–1 Dec 1950, 1–8 Nov 1954, and c. 3 Sep–c. 30 Sep 1955; not operational, 1 Feb–1 Oct 1957). 35th Fighter-Interceptor: attached 7–24 May 1951. *Squadrons*. (Note: Because of the extreme number of deployments by the 15th, 44th, and 67th Squadrons in the 1960s and 1970s, detached periods are not shown for these squadrons.) 1st Special Operations: 15 Dec 1972–. 12th: attached 15 Mar–15 Aug 1957; assigned 25 Mar 1958– (detached 1 Feb–15 Mar 1965, 15 Jun–25 Aug 1965, 23–28 Jan 1968). 13th: 15 May 1966–15 Nov 1967 (detached). 15th Tactical Reconnaissance: attached 15 Mar 1960–19 Apr 1970, assigned 20 Apr 1970–. 19th Tactical Electronic Warfare: 31 Dec 1968–30 Oct 1970 (detached 31 Dec 1968–10 May 1969). 21st Troop Carrier: attached 17 Feb–28 Jun 1950. 25th Liaison: attached 1 Dec 1948–25 Mar 1949. 25th: 19 Dec 1975–. 39th Fighter-Interceptor: attached 7 May 1951–1 Jun 1952. 44th: attached 28 Jul–30 Nov 1950; attached 1 Feb–30 Sep 1957, assigned 1 Oct 1957–25 Apr 1967; assigned 15 Mar 1971– (not operational, 15 Mar–14 May 1971). 67th: attached 1 Feb–30 Sep 1957, assigned 1 Oct 1957–15 Dec 1967 (not operational, 1–15 Dec 1967); assigned 15 Mar 1971–. 90th Special Operations: 15 Apr–15 Dec 1972. 306th: attached 24 Apr–19 Jul 1962. 307th: attached Dec 1962–Mar 1963. 308th: attached Mar–Jul 1963. 309th: attached c. 20 Jul–Dec 1962. 336th Fighter-Day: attached 7 Aug 1956–1 Feb 1957. 6200th Troop Carrier: attached c. 1 Dec 1948–16 May 1949. Flying Training Squadron, Provisional: attached 15 Oct 1957–25 Mar 1958. *Flight*. 6204th Photo-Mapping: attached 17 Dec 1949–1 Dec 1950.

Stations. Clark AFB, Philippine Islands, 14 Aug 1948; Pusan AB, South Korea, 1 Dec 1950; Pyongyang East, North Korea, 1 Dec 1950; Suwon AB, South Korea, 4 Dec 1950; Chinhae,

South Korea, 10 Dec 1950; Osan-ni, South Korea, 26 Dec 1952; Kadena AB, Okinawa (later, Japan), 1 Nov 1954–.

Commanders. Brig Gen Robert C. Oliver, 14 Aug 1948; Col Herbert K. Baisley, c. 25 Oct 1948; Brig Gen Jarred V. Crabb, 1 Dec 1948 (additional duty after 16 May 1949); Maj Gen Harold M. Turner, Jun 1949 (additional duty); Col Clinton W. Davies, 17 Dec 1949; Col Curtis R. Low, 1 Dec 1950; Brig Gen Turner C. Rogers, 1 Feb 1951; Col Ernest G. Ford, 2 Feb 1952; Col William H. Clark, 7 Mar 1952; Col Frank S. Perego, 1 Jan 1953; Col John C. Edwards, 15 Jun 1953; Col Maurice L. Martin, 5 Jul 1953; Col Avelin P. Tacon, Jr., 31 Jul 1953; Col William D. Gilchrist, 17 Jul 1954; Col Cecil P. Lessig, 26 Jul 1954; Col Nathan J. Adams, 1–8 Nov 1954 (additional duty); Col John B. Murphy, 9 Nov 1954; Col Homer C. Rankin, 4 Feb 1955; Col Glendon P. Overing, 5 Apr 1955; Col Robert C. Orth, 3 May 1956; Col William S. Chairsell, 5 Jul 1958; Col Gust Askounis, 15 Aug 1958; Col Francis R. Royal, 23 Aug 1958; Col James A. Wilson, 14 Jul 1960; Col Francis S. Gabreski, 2 Aug 1960; Col George B. Simler, 19 Jun 1962; Col Jones E. Bolt, 16 May 1964; Col Robert L. Cardenas, 19 Jul 1964; Col Neil J. Graham, 28 Jun 1966; Col Clarence E. Anderson, Jr., 17 Jun 1967; Col Monroe S. Sams, 22 Dec 1967; Col Philip V. Howell, Jr., 24 Jun 1970; Brig Gen Robert F. Titus, 19 May 1971; Col Harold K. Wimberley, 29 May 1973; Col Charles H. Hausenfleck, 1 Jun 1974; Brig Gen Clyde F. McClain, 1 Dec 1974 (additional duty); Maj Gen Lynwood E. Clark, 14 Jul 1975 (additional duty); Brig Gen Walter H. Baxter III, 9 Jun 1976– (additional duty).

Aircraft. P (later, F)–47, 1948; F–51, 1948–1950, 1950–1953; RB–17, 1948–1949; F–2, 1948–1949; L–5, 1948–1949; C–47, 1948–1949; VB–17, 1948–1949; C–46, 1949; RB–17, 1949–1950; RC–45, 1949–1950; F–80, 1949–1950; F–86, 1953–1955, 1955, 1955–1957; T–33, 1954; F–100, 1957–1963; F–105, 1962–1965, 1965–1968, 1968–1972; RF–101, 1960–1967; RF–4, 1967–; F–4, 1971–; C–130, 1972–; T–39, 1975–1976; CT–39, 1977–; MC–130, 1977–.

Operations. Maintained proficiency in tactical aircraft; from 1 Dec 1948 to 16 May 1949 was the major Far East Air Forces organization in the Philippines. Aerial mapping, 1948–1950. Wing headquarters unmanned, 16 May–17 Dec 1949. Combat operations in Korea, 1 Dec 1950 through remainder of war. Moved to Okinawa on 1 Nov 1954, supporting tactical operations there and in Korea, Japan, Formosa (now Taiwan), and the Philippines. Deployed at Yonton Auxiliary AB, Okinawa, 10 Nov–11 Dec 1954. Deployed at Chia-Yi, Formosa, 1–16 Feb 1955. Aerial reconnaissance added to the wing's mission in 1960. Supported combat operations in Southeast Asia from 1961 with deployed reconnaissance forces, and from 1964 with deployed tactical fighter forces until the end of that conflict. Deployed at Osan AB, South Korea, following the *Pueblo* crisis (28 Jan–c. 13 Jun 1968). Continued to maintain assigned aircraft, crews, and supporting personnel in a high state of readiness for tactical air requirements of 313th Air Division, Fifth Air Force, and the Pacific Air Forces.

Service Streamers. None.

Campaign Streamers. CCF Intervention; First UN Counteroffensive; CCF Spring Offensive; UN Summer–Fall Offensive; Second Korean Winter; Korea Summer–Fall, 1952; Third Korean Winter; Korea Summer–Fall, 1953.

Decorations. Air Force Outstanding Unit Awards: 1 Dec 1959–30 Nov 1960; 1 Sep 1962–31 Aug 1963; 1 Aug 1964–5 Jun 1965; 6 Jun 1965–31 Dec 1966. Republic of Korea Presidential Unit Citations: 1 Dec 1950–31 Jan 1951; 1 Feb 1951–31 Mar 1953. Republic of Vietnam Gallantry Cross with Palm: 1 Apr 1966–28 Jan 1973.

Emblem. Or, a fighting cock with wings displayed sable, wattled and combed gules. *Crest:* On a wreath or and sable two wings conjoined and displayed tenne. *Motto:* UNGUIBUS ET ROSTRA—With talons and beak. (Approved for 18th Group on 21 Feb 1931 and for 18th Wing on 17 Apr 1953.)

19th BOMBARDMENT WING, HEAVY

Lineage. Established as 19th Bombardment Wing, Medium, on 10 Aug 1948. Activated on 17 Aug 1948. Redesignated 19th Bombardment Wing, Heavy, on 1 Jul 1961.

Assignments. Twentieth Air Force, 17 Aug 1948; Far East Air Forces, 16 May 1949; Twentieth Air Force, 17 Oct 1949 (attached to Far East Air Forces Bomber Command, Provisional, 1 Jun 1953–c. 28 May 1954); Second Air Force, 11 Jun 1954 (attached to Air Division Provisional, 813th, 11 Jun–14 Jul 1954); 813th Air Division, 15 Jul 1954 (attached to 5th Air Division, 7 Jan–11 Apr 1956); 823d Air Division, 1 Jun 1956 (attached to 5th Air Division, 8 May–7 Jul 1957); 57th Air Division, 25 Jul 1968; 823d Air Division, 2 Jul 1969; 42d Air Division, 30 Jun 1971–.

Components. *Group.* 19th: 17 Aug 1948–1 Jun 1953 (detached 28 Jun 1950–1 Jun 1953). *Squadrons.* 19th Air Refueling: 1 Feb 1956–1 Apr 1960 (detached 1 Feb–1 Jun 1956). 28th: 1 Jun 1953– (not operational, Jul 1972–Oct 1973). 30th: 1 Jun 1953–1 Jan 1962. 93d: 1 Jun 1953–1 Aug 1961. 100th Air Refueling: attached 2 Feb 1955–16 Aug 1956. 303d Air Refueling: 1 Nov 1959–1 Apr 1961. 407th Air Refueling: 1 Apr 1962–2 Jul 1968. 525th: 9 Jan–15 Mar 1961. 526th: 9 Jan–1 Jun 1961. 659th: 1 Nov 1958–1 Jul 1961. 912th Air Refueling: 25 Jul 1968– (not operational, Jul 1972–Mar 1973).

Stations. North Guam (later, Andersen) AFB, Guam, 17 Aug 1948; Kadena AB, Okinawa, 1 Jun 1953–28 May 1954; Pinecastle AFB, Fla, 11 Jun 1954; Homestead AFB, Fla, 1 Jun 1956; Robins AFB, Ga, 25 Jul 1968–.

Commanders. Lt Col Clarence G. Poff, 17 Aug 1948; Col Robert V. DeShazo, 24 Sep 1948; Maj Gen Alvan C. Kincaid, 16 May 1949; Brig Gen Alfred

R. Maxwell, 1 Jun 1949; Col Frederick E. Calhoun, 26 Nov 1949; Brig Gen Adlai H. Gilkeson, 29 Nov 1949; Brig Gen Robert W. C. Wamsatt, 27 May 1951; Col Harvey C. Dorney, 1 Jun 1953; Col Lloyd H. Dalton, Jr., 31 Aug 1953; Col John W. Livingston, 24 Apr 1954; Col Virgil M. Cloyd, Jr., 26 Jul 1954; Col John W. Livingstone, 9 Feb 1958; Col James H. Thompson, 14 Apr 1958; Col Roland W. Bergamyer, 1 Aug 1960; Col Richard R. Stewart, 5 Jul 1961; Col Mason A. Dula, 24 Oct 1963; Col Edward D. Edwards, 14 Dec 1963; Col Gordon F. Goyt, 4 Jun 1966; Col Clifford W. Hargrove, 1 Aug 1967; Col James S. Howard, 1 Jul 1968; Col Wesley L. Pendergraft, 25 Jul 1968; Col Gerhard R. Abendhoff, 1 Apr 1969; Col William R. Thorstenson, 13 Feb 1970; Col Dudley G. Kavanaugh, 3 Sep 1971; Col Stanley C. Beck, 9 Aug 1972; Col Nathaniel A. Gallagher, 1 Dec 1972; Col John F. Wylam, 9 Apr 1973; Col William E. Masterson, 9 Jul 1973; Col Nathaniel A. Gallagher, 29 Oct 1973; Col Frank H. McArdle, 15 Feb 1974; Col Edwin L. Smith, 11 Jul 1975; Col Charles W. Reeves, Jr., 28 Jun 1977–.

Aircraft. B–29, 1948–1950, 1953–1954; B–47, 1954–1961; KC–97, 1955–1961; B–52, 1962–1968, 1968–1972, 1973–; KC–135, 1962–1968, 1968–1972, 1973–.

Operations. Formed in Aug 1948 from resources of the former North Guam Air Force Base Command (Provisional). Operated North Guam (later, Andersen) AFB, Guam, and maintained proficiency in B–29s. When HQ Twentieth Air Force moved from Guam to Okinawa in May 1949, the former staff of that organization joined the HQ 19th Bombardment Wing. At the same time the wing assumed responsibility for administering two active and one semi-active bases plus an assortment of communications, weather, radar, rescue, and other facilities and units including the Marianas Air Materiel Area, a wing-size unit. Many of the units and facilities inactivated within a few months, and when the 19th Wing became subordinate to Twentieth Air Force again in Oct 1949, most of the remaining attached units in the Marianas and Bonin Islands transferred to other organizations. From 17 Oct 1949 to 28 Jun 1950 the wing continued B–29 training, operation of Andersen AFB, and some rescue and reconnaissance missions. When the Korean war broke out, the 19th Bombardment Group was immediately detached from wing control and operated from Kadena AB, Okinawa. The wing, meanwhile, remained at Andersen AFB in an administrative and logistical capacity, operating ammunition dumps and providing maintenance to transient aircraft. On 1 Jun 1953 the wing headquarters moved without personnel or equipment to Kadena and absorbed personnel and equipment of the inactivated 19th Bombardment Group. Through 27 Jul 1953 the wing flew 281 B–29 combat sorties (23 missions) in Korea. After hostilities concluded, the wing continued B–29 training, using SAC procedures and techniques. The wing moved to Fla in May–Jun 1954, turning in its B–29s at Davis-Monthan AFB, Ariz, en route to its new base. Began receiving B–47s later in 1954, and gained a KC–97 air refueling unit early in 1955. The entire wing deployed at Sidi Slimane AB, French Morocco, Jan–Apr 1956, and at Ben Guerir AB, Morocco, May–Jul 1957. From Jul 1957 to Apr 1961 the wing maintained a portion of its tactical resources on overseas alert. The wing operated Homestead AFB, Fla, 9 Jan 1961–2 Jul 1968. Converted to B–52 and KC–135 aircraft in 1961–1962. Won the Fairchild Trophy in the SAC bombing and navigation competition of 1966. The wing moved without personnel or equipment to Robins AFB, Ga, on 25 Jul 1968 and absorbed resources of the former 465th Bombardment Wing. Furnished B–52/KC–135 aircraft and crews to other SAC organizations involved in combat operations in Southeast Asia, and in Jul 1972 the wing no longer was capable of operations because all aircraft and most crews as well as support personnel were loaned to other SAC organizations. Late in 1972 the wing headquarters reduced to a small housekeeping unit because of personnel deployments. Some KC–135 aircraft and crews began returning to wing control in late Mar 1973, but B–52s and their crews did not return to wing control until 28 Oct 1973. Normal operations resumed in Nov 1973.

Service Streamers. None.

Campaign Streamers. Korea Summer–Fall, 1953.

Decorations. Air Force Outstanding Unit Awards: 1 Jul 1964–30 Jun 1965; 1 Jul 1967–30 Jun 1968. Republic of Korea Presidential Unit Citation: [1 Jun 1953]–27 Jul 1953.

Emblem. Azure, within the square of the constellation of Pegasus, a winged sword, point to base, all or. *Crest:* On a wreath of the colors (or and azure) an osprey guardant, rising, wings elevated and addorsed proper. *Motto:* IN ALIS VINCIMUS—On wings we conquer. (Approved for 19th Group on 19 Oct 1936 and for 19th Wing on 9 May 1952.)

20th TACTICAL FIGHTER WING

Lineage. Established as 20th Fighter Wing on 28 Jul 1947. Organized on 15 Aug 1947. Discontinued on 26 Aug 1948. Activated on 24 Aug 1948. Redesignated: 20th Fighter-Bomber Wing on 20 Jan 1950; 20th Tactical Fighter Wing on 8 Jul 1958.

Assignments. Ninth Air Force, 15 Aug 1947–26 Aug 1948. Ninth Air Force, 24 Aug 1948; Fourteenth Air Force, 1 Feb 1949; Tactical Air Command, 1 Aug 1950; Ninth Air Force, 22 Jan 1951 (attached to Tactical Air Division, Provisional, 25 Apr–10 Oct 1951; Tactical Air Command, 6–30 Nov 1951); Tactical Air Command, 1 Dec 1951 (attached to 49th Air Division, Operational, 12 Feb 1952–); United States Air Forces in Europe, 31 May 1952 (remained attached to 49th Air Division, Operational); Third Air Force, 5 Jun 1962 (remained attached to 49th Air Division, Operational [later, 49th Air Division (Operational)], to 1 Jul 1956); Seventeenth Air Force, 1 Jul 1961; Third Air Force, 1 Sep 1963–.

Components. *Group.* 20th: 15 Aug 1947–26 Aug 1948; 24 Aug 1948–8 Feb 1955 (detached 26 Jul–c. 17 Dec 1950 and 25 Apr–10 Oct 1951; not operational, 15 Nov 1952–8 Feb 1955). *Squadrons.* 55th: attached 15 Nov 1952–7 Feb 1955, assigned 8 Feb 1955–. 77th: attached 15 Nov 1952–7 Feb 1955, assigned 8 Feb 1955–. 79th: attached 15 Nov 19527 Feb 1955, assigned 8 Feb 1955–.

Stations. Shaw Field (later, AFB), SC, 15 Aug 1947–26 Aug 1948. Shaw AFB, SC, 24 Aug 1948; Langley AFB, Va, 9 Nov 1951–22 May 1952; Wethersfield RAF Station (later, RAF Wethersfield), England, 31 May 1952; RAF Upper Heyford, England, 1 Apr 1970–.

Commanders. Col Phineas K. Morrill, Jr., 15 Aug 1947–26 Aug 1948. Col Phineas K. Morrill, Jr., 24 Aug 1948; none (not manned), 25 Apr–10 Oct 1951; Col Reginald F. C. Vance, c. 11 Oct 1951; Col John A. Dunning, 22 Oct 1951; Col Arthur G. Salisbury, 6 Jun 1955; Col Raymond F. Toliver, 4 Apr 1957; Col Jay T. Robbins, 21 Jun 1959; Col Wendell J. Kelly, 26 Jun 1961; Col Royal N. Baker, 9 Jul 1961; Brig Gen John W. Baer, 10 Jun 1963; Col Ernest T. Cragg, 26 Jun 1965; Col Paul C. Watson, 10 Jul 1966; Brig Gen Edmund B. Edwards, 12 Aug 1966; Col Joseph A. Hagemann, 11 Jul 1968; Col Grant R. Smith, 1 Apr 1970; Brig Gen Richard M. Baughn, 15 Jun 1971; Brig Gen William C. Norris, 2 Feb 1973; Col James H. Ahmann, 12 Nov 1973; Col Kenneth D. Burns, 17 Aug 1974; Col Robert D. Anderson, 23 Jun 1975; Col Gerald D. Larson, 9 Jun 1977–.

Aircraft. P (later, F)–51, 1947–1948; P (later, F)–84, 1948. F–84, 1948–1950, 1950–1951, 1951–1957; F–100, 1957–1971; F–111, 1970–.

Operations. Trained to maintain proficiency as a tactical fighter unit, 1947–1948, and 1948–1950. The tactical group participated in firepower demonstrations, field exercises, and special operations. Trained Turkish officers in P–51s, Feb–Apr 1948. Tactical group detached, supporting SAC's 3d Air Division at RAF Manston, England, Dec 1950–Apr 1951. Wing headquarters not operational, 25 Apr–10 Oct 1951; all personnel detached for duty with Tactical Air Division, Provisional, which assumed operational control over all wing elements. Moved to England in May 1952 with a mission of maintaining proficiency for tactical operations with conventional and nuclear weapons in support of NATO operations in the European area. Replaced the 66th Tactical Reconnaissance Wing at RAF Upper Heyford, England, on 1 Apr 1970. Transferred last F–100 in Feb 1971 and received first F–111 in Sep 1970 as part of general aircraft conversion. Trained to conduct conventional or nuclear tactical air operations, primarily through firepower demonstrations and tactical exercises. Operated from RAF Greenham Common, England, 29 Apr–17 Aug 1976.

Service Streamers. None.

Campaign Streamers. None.

Decorations. Air Force Outstanding Unit Awards: 1 Jul 1956–30 Sep 1957; 1 May 1963–31 Dec 1964; 1 Jan 1965–31 Mar 1966; 1 Jul 1968–31 Mar 1970; 1 Sep 1970–30 Jun 1972; 31 Mar 1973–30 Jun 1974.

Emblem. Per fess azure and gules, a fess nebule or. *Crest:* On a wreath of the colors (or and azure) a sun in spendor proper, radiating from the center thereof thirteen darts gules. *Motto:* VICTORY BY VALOR. (Approved on 18 Dec 1934 for 20th Group and on 31 Oct 1951 for 20th Wing.)

21st COMPOSITE WING

Lineage. Established as 21st Fighter-Bomber Wing on 15 Nov 1952. Activated on 1 Jan 1953. Inactivated on 8 Feb 1958. Redesignated 21st Tactical Fighter Wing on 19 May 1958. Activated on 1 Jul 1958. Discontinued, and inactivated, on 18 Jun 1960. Redesignated 21st Composite Wing, and activated, on 6 May 1966. Organized on 8 Jul 1966.

Assignments. Ninth Air Force, 1 Jan 1953; Twelfth Air Force, 12 Dec 1954; United States Air Forces in Europe, 1 Jan–8 Feb 1958. Fifth Air Force, 1 Jul 1958; 39th Air Division, 10 Nov 1958–18 Jun 1960. Alaskan Air Command, 6 May 1966–.

Components. *Group.* 21st Fighter-Bomber: 1 Jan 1953–8 Feb 1958 (not operational, 15 Apr 1957–8 Feb 1958). *Squadrons.* 17th Troop Carrier (later, 17th Tactical Airlift): 8 Jul 1966–31 Mar 1975. 43d: 15 Jul 1970–. 72d: attached 15 Apr 1957–8 Feb 1958 (not operational, 15 Dec 1957–8 Feb 1958). 317th Fighter-Interceptor: 8 Jul 1966–31 Dec 1969. 416th: attached 15 Apr 1957–8 Feb 1958 (not operational, 10 Jan–8 Feb 1958); assigned 1 Jul 1958–18 Jun 1960. 531st: attached 15 Apr 1957–8 Feb 1958 (not operational, 15 Dec 1957–8 Feb 1958); assigned 1 Jul 1958–18 Jun 1960. 5040th Helicopter: 15 Jul 1969–30 Sep 1975. 5041st Tactical Operations: 1 Oct 1971–.

Stations. George AFB, Calif, 1 Jan 1953–28 Nov 1954; Chambley AB, France, 12 Dec 1954–8 Feb 1958. Misawa AB, Japan, 1 Jul 1958–18 Jun 1960. Elmendorf AFB, Alaska, 8 Jul 1966–.

Commanders. Col James B. Buck, 1 Jan 1953; Col Robert R. Rowland, 27 Apr 1953; Col Robert N. Baker, 29 Jun 1956–8 Feb 1958. Col Frank J. Collins, 1 Jul 1958; Col William W. Ingenhutt, 21 Aug 1958; Col Dean Davenport, 28 Sep 1959–18 Jun 1960. None (not manned), 6 May–7 Jul 1966; Col Donald H. Lynch, 8 Jul 1966; Col Charles W. Johnson, Jr., Jun 1968; Col Kennieth D. Dunaway, 23 Sep 1969; Col John A. Nelson, 15 Jan 1970; Col Kennieth D. Dunaway, 1 Sep 1970; Col James R. Larkins, 23 Jul 1971; Col James R. Brickel, 9 Aug 1971; Col David T. Stockman, 12 Jul 1972; Col Charles F. Loyd, 4 Jun 1973; Col Frederick C. Eaton, 1 Jul 1974; Col Edward L. Trixier, 1 Jul 1975; Col John T. Wotring, 29 Apr 1977–.

Aircraft. F–51, 1953; F–86, 1953–1958. F–84, 1958–1959; F–100, 1958–1960. F/TF–102, 1966–1969; C–130, 1966–1975; C–124, 1969–1971, 1971–1974; H–21, 1969–1970; F–4, 1970–; HH–3, 1970–1975; B–57, 1971–1975; C–118, 1971–1975; T–33,

1971–; T–39, 1971–1977; VC–118, 1972–1975; EC–118, 1973–1975; CH–3, 1974–1975; EB–57, 1974–1976; C–12, 1977–.

Operations. Maintained tactical proficiency and provided air defense augmentation in the United States, Jan 1953–Nov 1954. Became part of the NATO defense forces in Europe, performing special weapons tactical air operations, Dec 1954–Jan 1958. Participated in numerous actual and simulated tactical air operations and provided air defense augmentation in Japan and Korea, Jul 1958–Jun 1960. Assumed air defense responsibility for Alaska and contiguous areas in support of the Commander in Chief, North American Air Defense and Aerospace Defense Commands through the Alaskan NORAD Region and ADCOM Region. Provided support for the Alaskan Air Command, the Military Airlift Command, 1931st Communications Group, and tenant organizations. Provided support for Army and Air Force special operations in arctic and polar areas and participated in numerous search and rescue operations, Jul 1966–.

Service Streamers. None.

Campaign Streamers. None.

Decorations. Air Force Outstanding Unit Awards: 8 Jul 1966–1 May 1967; 2 May 1967–1 Jan 1968; 2 Jan–31 Dec 1968; 1 Jan–31 Dec 1969; 1 Jan–31 Dec 1970; 1 Jan–31 Dec 1971; 1 Jan–31 Dec 1972; 1 Jan–31 Dec 1974; 1 Jan–31 Dec 1975.

Emblem. On a shield azure, a broad sword argent, shaded silver, hilt and pommel or, shaded yellow, outlined of the field, between four red lightning streaks proper, two and two, bendwise. *Motto:* FORTITUDO ET PREPARATIO—Strength and preparedness. (Approved on 23 Jul 1957.)

22d BOMBARDMENT WING, HEAVY

Lineage. Established as 22d Bombardment Wing, Medium, on 28 Jul 1948. Activated on 1 Aug 1948. Redesignated 22d Bombardment Wing, Heavy, on 15 Mar 1963.

Assignments. Fifteenth Air Force, 1 Aug 1948 (attached to 301st Bombardment Wing, Medium, 1 Aug 1948–9 May 1949; 1st Fighter Wing, 10 May–30 Jun 1949); 12th Air Division, 10 Feb 1951 (attached to 7th Air Division, 5 Sep–4 Dec 1951 and 7 Dec 1953–5 Mar 1954; 3d Air Division, 1 Apr–5 Jul 1957); 47th Air (later, 47th Strategic Aerospace; 47th Air) Division, 1 Jan 1962; 14th Strategic Aerospace Division, 31 Mar 1970; 47th Air Division, 30 Jun 1971; 12th Strategic Missile (later, 12th Air) Division, 1 Aug 1972–.

Components. *Wings.* 1st Fighter: attached 1 Jul 1949–1 Apr 1950. 330th Bombardment: attached 27 Jun 1949–30 Apr 1951. *Group.* 22d: 1 Aug 1948–16 Jun 1952 (detached 1 Aug

1948–30 Jun 1949, 14 Nov 1949–20 Feb 1950, 4 Jul–c. 31 Oct 1950; not operational, 10 Feb 1951–16 Jun 1952). *Squadrons*. 2d: attached 10 Feb 1951–15 Jun 1952, assigned 16 Jun 1952–15 Mar 1963; assigned 15 Sep 1963– (not operational, 10 Mar–c. 1 Oct 1967 and 10 Apr 1972–4 Dec 1973). 19th: attached 10 Feb 1951–15 Jun 1952, assigned 16 Jun 1952–15 Mar 1963. 22d Air Refueling: attached 10 Feb 1951–15 Jun 1952 (not operational, 10 Feb 1951–31 May 1952), assigned 16 Jun 1952–15 Jun 1960; assigned 1 Jul 1963– (not operational, 10 Mar–c. 1 Oct 1967 and 10 Apr 1972–Sep 1972). 33d: attached 10 Feb 1951–15 Jun 1952, assigned 16 Jun 1952–15 Mar 1963. 320th Air Refueling: 16 Jun 1960–15 Sep 1962. 352d: attached 20 Sep–c. Nov 1951. 408th: 1 Jan 1959–1 Jan 1962 (not operational, 21 Oct 1961–1 Jan 1962). 486th: 2 Oct 1966–1 Jul 1971 (not operational, 10 Mar–c. 1 Oct 1967). 909th Air Refueling: 25 Jun 1966–1 Jul 1971 (not operational, 10 Mar–c. 1 Oct 1967).

Stations. Smoky Hill AFB, Kans, 1 Aug 1948; March AFB, Calif, 10 May 1949–.

Commanders. Col Leslie G. Mulzer, 1 Aug 1948; Col Joe W. Kelly, 3 Jan 1949; Col Joseph H. Davidson, 10 May 1949; Col George McCoy, Jr., 14 Jun 1949; Col William L. Lee, 19 Aug 1949; Col Wiley D. Ganey, 4 Jan 1950; Col Howell M. Estes, Jr., 5 Jul 1950; Col Wiley D. Ganey, 10 Nov 1950; Col James V. Edmundsen, 10 Feb 1951; Col John B. Henry, Jr., 14 Mar 1952; Col Ernest C. Eddy, c. 17 Dec 1952; Col Selmon W. Wells, 8 Jan 1953; Col John B. Henry, Jr., c. 16 Mar 1953; Col William F. Coleman, 9 Jul 1954; Col Lloyd H. Dalton, Jr., (by 20) Oct 1954; Col Pinkham Smith, 11 Feb 1956; Col Leon Stann, 20 Aug 1957; Col Edward W. Scott, Jr., 30 Aug 1957; Col William F. Savois, 29 Apr 1960; Col George Pfeiffer, Jr., Nov 1961; Col John F. Harvey, 15 Jun 1965; Col Mitchell A. Cobeaga, 3 Jan 1967; Col Robert L. Bennett, c. 10 Mar 1967; Col Edward G. Butler, c. May 1967; Col Mitchell A. Cobeaga, c. 1 Oct 1967; Col Lester E. Gunter, 31 Jul 1968; Col Lawrence W. Steinkraus, 28 Apr 1969; Col Glenn R. Sullivan, 16 Jan 1970; Col Michael Perrone, 31 May 1972; Lt Col Samuel Tyson, 13 Jun 1972; Col Donald A. Jensen, 3 Jul 1972; Col Michael Perrone, 16 Dec 1972; Col Jerome F. O'Malley, 1 Jun 1973; Col Ernest J. Stirman, 25 Sep 1973; Col Guy D. Perham, 1 Apr 1974; Col Harry L. Brown, 28 Feb 1975; Col Stanford E. Brown, 4 Aug 1975; Col Lawrence E. Pennington, 12 Jan 1977–.

Aircraft. B–29, 1949, 1950, 1950–1953; F–86, 1949–1950; KC–97, 1952–1962; B–47, 1953–1963; B–52, 1963–1966, 1966–1967, 1967–1972, 1973–; EC–135, 1963–1970; KC–135, 1963–1967, 1967–1972, 1972–.

Operations. From 1 Aug 1948 to 9 May 1949, while based at Smoky Hill AFB, Kans, shared a commander in common with the 301st Bombardment Wing. The 22d Wing's headquarters was at the time non-operational and its components detached. From 10 May 1949 to 16 Feb 1950, after moving to March AFB, Calif, shared a commander in common with the 1st Fighter Wing. Until 30 Jun 1949 the 22d Wing was non–operational, attached to the 1st Wing, but on 1 Jul 1949 the 22d was made operational and assumed host status, with the 1st Wing attached to it for control until 1 Apr 1950. The 22d Bombardment Group was detached from 14 Nov 1949 to 20 Feb 1950, during which time the wing controlled only the attached fighters of the 1st Wing. The bomb group was detached again for combat in Korea, 4 Jul–c. 31 Oct 1950, and during this period the wing controlled no aircraft. When operational, the wing trained to maintain proficiency in global strategic bombardment, adding air refueling to its mission in 1952. The wing deployed at Mildenhall RAF Station, England, Sep–Dec 1951, and at Upper Heyford RAF Station, England, Dec 1953–Mar 1954. From Apr to Jul 1957 it deployed at Andersen AFB, Guam. The wing was not tactically operational, 11 Mar–15 Sep 1963, while converting to B–52 bombers and KC–135 tankers. Supported Fifteenth Air Force's post attack command and control system with EC–135s, Sep 1964–Mar 1970. The 22d was a "super" wing, 1966–1971, with two bombardment and two tanker squadrons. From 10 Mar to c. 1 Oct 1967 the wing was reduced to a small "rear echelon" non-tactical organization with all tactical resources and most support resources loaned to SAC organizations involved in combat operations in Southeast Asia. The wing continued to support SAC operations in the Far East and Southeast Asia through 1975, and from 10 Apr 1972 to 29 Oct 1973 again had all of its bomber resources loaned to other organizations for combat and contingency operations. KC–135 resources were also on loan from 10 Apr to Sep 1972; afterwards a few tankers returned to wing control. The wing resumed bomber alert in Dec 1973.

Service Streamers. None.

Campaign Streamers. None.

Decorations. Air Force Outstanding Unit Awards: 1 Apr–1 Oct 1967 and 1 Feb–1 Mar 1968; 25 Mar–1 May 1968; 1 Jul 1969–30 Jun 1970; 1 Sep 1970–30 Jun 1972.

Emblem. Azure, a cougar's left gamb erased palewise, claws to base or armed gules. *Motto:* DUCEMUS—We lead. (Approved for 22d Group on 19 Jun 1941 and for 22d Wing on 28 Jun 1951.)

23d TACTICAL FIGHTER WING

Lineage. Established as 23d Fighter Wing on 10 Aug 1948. Activated on 16 Aug 1948. Inactivated on 24 Sep 1949. Redesignated 23d Fighter-Interceptor Wing on 19 Dec 1950. Activated on 12 Jan 1951. Inactivated on 6 Feb 1952. Redesignated 23d Tactical Fighter Wing, and activated, on 28 Jan 1964. Organized on 8 Feb 1964.

Assignments. Twentieth Air Force, 16 Aug 1948; Caribbean Air Command, 25 Apr–24 Sep 1949. Eastern Air Defense Force, 12 Jan 1951–6 Feb 1952. Tactical Air Command, 28 Jan 1964; Twelfth Air Force, 8 Feb 1964; 835th Air Division, 1 Jul 1964; Twelfth Air

Force, 30 Jun 1971; Ninth Air Force, 1 Jul 1972–.

Components. *Group.* 23d: 16 Aug 1948–24 Sep 1949; 12 Jan 1951–6 Feb 1952. *Squadrons.* 6th Special Operations Training: 1 Jan–15 Sep 1974. 74th: 1 Jul 1972– (detached 2 Jul–28 Dec 1973). 75th: 1 Jul 1972–. 76th: 1 Oct 1972–. 132d: attached 21 Jul 1951–6 Feb 1952. 134th: attached 1 Apr 1951–6 Feb 1952. 333d: 15 Oct 1970–22 Mar 1971 (not operational). 357th: 15–22 Mar 1971 (not operational). 419th Tactical Fighter Training: 15 Oct 1969–1 Oct 1971 (not operational, 8 May–1 Oct 1971). 421st: 8 Dec 1957–16 Apr 1959 (not operational). 560th: 8 Feb 1964–25 Sep 1968 (not operational, 19 Jun–25 Sep 1968). 561st: 8 Feb 1964–1 Jul 1972 (detached 6 Mar–10 Jul 1965 and 9 Apr–30 Jun 1972). 562d: 8 Feb 1964–1 Jul 1972 (detached 13 Aug–6 Dec 1965). 563d: 8 Feb 1964–1 Jul 1972 (detached 8 Apr–15 Aug 1965; not operational, 15 Aug–2 Nov 1966). 4519th Combat Crew Training: 1 Aug 1967–16 Oct 1969 (not operational, 1 Aug 1967–21 Jan 1968).

Stations. Northwest Guam AFB, Guam, 16 Aug 1948–3 Apr 1949; Howard AFB, CZ, 25 Apr–24 Sep 1949. Presque Isle AFB, Maine, 12 Jan 1951–6 Feb 1952. McConnell AFB, Kans, 8 Feb 1964; England AFB, La, 1 Jul 1972–.

Commanders. Col Romulus W. Puryear, 16 Aug 1948; Col John T. Shields, 22 Sep 1948; Col Angier H. Foster, 25 Apr 1949; Col Louis R. Hughes, Jr., c. 28 Apr–24 Sep 1949. Col Charles H. MacDonald, 12 Jan 1951–6 Feb 1952. None (not manned), 28 Jan–7 Feb 1964; Col Olin E. Gilbert, 8 Feb 1964; Col Edmund B. Edwards, 17 Aug 1964; Col Deward E. Bower, 12 Jul 1965; Col Max T. Beall, 9 Oct 1967; Col James V. Hartinger, 28 Aug 1968; Col Walter D. Dreun, Jr., 15 Jun 1970; Col Garry A. Willard, Jr., 21 Oct 1971; Col Harry W. Schurr, 28 Apr 1972; Col Louis W. Weber, 1 Jul 1972; Col Waymond C. Nutt, 20 Nov 1973; Col Charles W. McClarren, 28 Jun 1975; Col Bernard J. Bogoslofski, 12 Dec 1975; Col Paul L. Wieland, 1 Jan 1977–.

Aircraft. F–47, 1948–1949; RF–80, 1949. F–86, 1951–1952; F–51, 1951–1952; F–80, 1951–1952. F–105, 1964–1972; AT–33, 1966–1969; T–39, 1966–1972; A–7, 1972–; A–37, 1974.

Operations. Air defense of Guam, 1948–1949, and of the Canal Zone, 1949. Air defense of the northeastern United States, 1951–1952. Conducted basic training for about 500 Air Force recruits, 1951. Replaced 388th Tactical Fighter Wing in Feb 1964. Maintained proficiency in tactical fighter operations, frequently deploying whole units or segments thereof to support contingency and combat operations in overseas areas, 1964–1965. Conducted F–105 replacement training, Jan 1966–Nov 1970, and training for ANG units, Nov 1970–Apr 1971. Maintained proficiency in tactical fighter operations, 1970–1972. Replaced 4403d Tactical Fighter Wing at England AFB, La, in Jul 1972 and switched to A–7 aircraft operations. Also controlled an A–37B special operations training squadron in 1974.

Service Streamers. None.

Campaign Streamers. None.

Decorations. Air Force Outstanding Unit Award: 1 Jun 1970–15 Jun 1971.

Emblem. On a shield azure over a bolt of lightning, in pale, or, a flying tiger proper, tongue red, winged argent; all outlines black; a diminutive bordure silver-grey. *Motto:* FLYING TIGERS: GENTLE PAWS–SHARP CLAWS. (Emblem approved for 23d Fighter Group on 24 Jan 1957 and used by 23d TFW since Jan 1964. Motto approved on 9 May 1979.)

24th COMPOSITE WING

Lineage. Established as 24th Composite Wing (Special) on 19 Nov 1942. Activated on 25 Dec 1942. Disestablished on 15 Jun 1944. Reestablished as 24th Composite Wing on 5 Aug 1946. Activated on 25 Aug 1946. Inactivated on 28 Jul 1948. Activated on 30 Oct 1967. Organized on 8 Nov 1967. Redesignated: 24th Air Commando Wing on 15 Mar 1968; 24th Special Operations Wing on 15 Jul 1968; 24th Special Operations Group on 30 Jun 1972; 24th Composite Group on 15 Nov 1973; 24th Composite Wing on 1 Jan 1976.

Assignments. Iceland Base Command, U.S. Army Forces, Iceland, 25 Dec 1942–15 Jun 1944. Caribbean Air Command, 25 Aug 1946–28 Jul 1948. United States Air Forces Southern Command, 30 Oct 1967; United States Air Force Southern Air Division, 1 Jan 1976–.

Components. *Groups.* 130th Special Operations: attached 30 Jan–27 Feb 1971; attached 5–14 Feb 1973. 134th Anti-Aircraft Artillery: attached 1 Nov 1943–15 Jun 1944. 143d Air Commando: attached 8 Feb–9 Mar 1969. 342d Composite: 25 Dec 1942–18 Mar 1944. *Squadrons.* 24th Air Transport: 15 Mar 1968–30 Jun 1971 (not operational, 15 Apr–30 Jun 1971). 24th: 18 Mar 1969–1 Jul 1975; 1 Jan 1976–. 33d Fighter: 18 Mar–15 Jun 1944. 91st Reconnaissance: 12 Jan–26 Jul 1948. 330th Transport: 25 Aug–15 Oct 1946. 605th: 8 Nov 1967–30 Apr 1972. *Detachments.* Det A, Fighter Command (IBC, U.S. Army Forces, Iceland): attached 12 Feb–15 Jun 1944. Det, 314th Troop Carrier Group: attached 1 Oct 1946–26 Jul 1948. TAC C–130 Rotational Element (various detachments): attached 8 Nov 1967–30 Sep 1977. TAC A–7D Rotational Element (various detachments): attached 13 Nov 1972–.

Stations. Camp Olympia, Reykjavik, Iceland, 25 Dec 1942; Camp Tripoli, Reykjavik, Iceland, 13 Mar–15 Jun 1944. Borinquen Field (later, Borinquen AAFld; Borinquen Field; Ramey AFB), PR, 25 Aug 1946–28 Jul 1948. Albrook AFB, CZ, 8 Nov 1967; Howard AFB, CZ (later, Panama), 3 Jan 1968–.

Commanders. Brig Gen George P. Tourtellot, 25 Dec 1942; Brig Gen Early E. W. Duncan, 5–15 Jun 1944. Col George H. Steel, 25 Aug 1946; Brig Gen John A. Samford, c. 6 Mar 1947–28 Jul 1948. None (not manned), 30 Oct–7 Nov 1967; Col Richard Jones, 8 Nov 1967; Col James G. Silliman, 13

Dec 1967; Col Joseph A. Stuart, Jr., 14 Jun 1968; Col Leslie E. Gaskins, 1 Jun 1971; Col Robert S. Beale, 30 Mar 1974; Col William E. Roth, 15 Aug 1975; Col Paul M. Davis, 1 Jan 1976; Col Alton J. Thogersen, 16 Jan 1976–.

Aircraft. P–38, 1942–1944; P–39, 1942–1943; P–40, 1943–1944; P–47, 1944. B–17, 1946–1947; B–17/F–9, 1948; C–47, 1946–1948; C–54, 1947–1948; F–2, 1948. A–26, 1967–1968; C–46, 1967–1968; C–47, 1967–1970; VC–47, 1967–c. 1970; C–54, 1967–c. 1972; C–118, 1967–1971; VC–118, 1967–unkn; C–130, 1967–; C–131, 1967–1968; CH–3, 1967–1970; HH–19, 1967–1969; T–28, 1967–1970; VT–29, 1967–1970; U–10, 1967–1971; UH–1, 1967–; A–37, 1969–1972; HU–16, 1969; C–123, 1970–1973; UC–123, 1970–1975; VC–123, 1970–1973; C–119, 1971, 1973; O–2, 1971–; A–7, 1972–.

Operations. Served in the defense of Iceland, Dec 1942–Jun 1944. From Aug 1946 until replaced by the Antilles Air Division in Jul 1948, supervised large numbers of major and minor bases and Air Force units in the Caribbean area from Puerto Rico to British Guiana. Organized once more in Nov 1967 in the Canal Zone, replacing the 5700th Air Base Wing. The wing assumed operation and maintenance responsibilities for Howard and Albrook Air Force Bases and a special operations mission which included air transport, paramilitary operations, exercise participation, civic actions in Central and South America, search and rescue missions, humanitarian operations, mercy missions, aeromedical evacuation, and support of Army Special Forces, U.S. military assistance units, and training of Latin American air forces. From activation in 1967 until mid-1972, the 24th Wing operated the USAF Tropic Survival School at Albrook. It controlled rotational C–130 detachments from TAC, Nov 1967–Sep 1977, rotational A–7D detachments from TAC, Nov 1972– , and rotational UC–123 detachments from the Air Force Reserve, Apr 1973–Dec 1975.

Service Streamers. None.

Campaign Streamers. Air Combat, EAME Theater.

Decorations. Air Force Outstanding Unit Awards: 2 Jun–3 Jul 1970; 16 Mar 1971–15 Mar 1973.

Emblem. Azure, above an arched olive branch to dexter and an arched lightning flash to sinister conjoined in base, a pellet fimbriated argent and charged with a torch enflamed and a sword in saltire of the like, all within a diminished bordure of the last. *Motto:* LOS PROFESIONALES—The professionals. (Approved in 1968.)

25th TACTICAL RECONNAISSANCE WING

Lineage. Established as 25th Tactical Reconnaissance Wing, and activated, on 24 Sep 1965. Organized on 1 Oct 1965. Discontinued, and inactivated, on 15 Oct 1966.

Assignments. United States Air Forces in Europe, 24 Sep 1965; Seventeenth Air Force, 1 Oct 1965–15 Oct 1966.

Components. *Squadrons.* 19th: 1 Oct 1965–1 Sep 1966. 42d: 1 Oct 1965–22 Aug 1966.

Stations. Chambly AB, France, 1 Oct 1965–15 Oct 1966.

Commanders. None (not manned), 24–30 Sep 1965; Col Jack N. Fancher, 1 Oct 1965; Col Clayton L. Peterson, 6 Oct 1965; Col Jack N. Fancher, 1 Jul–15 Oct 1966.

Aircraft. EB/RB–66, 1965–1966.

Operations. Maintained proficiency in night and day photographic and day visual reconnaissance and electronic warfare techniques. Furnished aircraft and aircrews for reconnaissance in Southeast Asia.

Service Streamers. None.

Campaign Streamers. None.

Decorations. None.

Emblem. Azure, issuing out of sinister side and arm embowed grasping a trident bend sinisterwise prongs to base or, on and over the junction of the shaft and prongs a compass rose of the first on a background of the second. *Motto:* GUARD WITH POWER. (Approved for 25th Group on 3 Oct 1940; used by 25th Wing since Oct 1965.)

26th TACTICAL RECONNAISSANCE WING

Lineage. Established as 5th Photographic Group on 14 Jul 1942. Activated on 23 Jul 1942. Redesignated: 5th Photographic Reconnaissance and Mapping Group on 15 May 1943; 5th Photographic Reconnaissance Group on 11 Aug 1943; 5th Photographic Group, Reconnaissance, on 13 Nov 1943; 5th Reconnaissance Group on 4 May 1945. Inactivated on 28 Oct 1945. Disestablished on 6 Mar 1947. Reestablished, and consolidated on 19 Apr 1965 with 26th Strategic Reconnaissance Wing, Medium, which was established on 9 May 1952, activated on 28 May 1952, and inactivated on 1 Jul 1958. Redesignated 26th Tactical Reconnaissance Wing, and activated, on 19 Apr 1965. Organized on 1 Jul 1965.

Assignments. Second Air Force, 23 Jul 1942; Third Air Force, 8 Mar 1943; Twelfth Air Force, 4 Sep 1943 (attached to Northwest African Photographic Reconnaissance Wing, 4 Sep–21 Nov 1943); 90th Photographic Wing, Reconnaissance, 22 Nov 1943; Fifteenth Air Force, 1 Oct 1944; Army Service Forces, New York Port of Embarkation, c. 26–28 Oct 1945. 801st Air Division, 28 May 1952–1 Jul 1958 (attached to 7th Air Division, 13 Sep–29 Oct 1954). United States Air Forces in Europe, 19

Apr 1965; Third Air Force, 1 Jul 1965; Seventeenth Air Force, 1 Sep 1965–.

Components. *Squadrons*. 3d: 28 May 1952–1 Jul 1958 (not operational, 28 May 1952–1 Mar 1953 and 15 Apr–1 Jul 1958). 4th: 28 May 1952–1 Jul 1958 (not operational, 28 May 1952–2 Sep 1953 and 15 Apr–1 Jul 1958). 7th Special Operations: 17 Mar 1972–31 Jan 1973. 7th Tactical Fighter: attached 24 Aug–1 Oct 1971. 8th Tactical Fighter: attached 15 Sep–8 Oct 1970 and 24 Aug–1 Oct 1971. 10th: 28 May 1952–1 Jul 1958 (not operational, 28 May 1952–c. 1 Oct 1953 and 15 Aprl Jul 1958). 12th Photographic (later, 12th Photographic Reconnaissance): attached 27 Oct–21 Nov 1943. 15th Photographic (later, 15th Combat Mapping; 15th Photographic Reconnaissance): attached 21 Nov 1943–20 Jan 1944, assigned 21 Jan 1944–28 Oct 1945. 19th: 1 Jul–1 Oct 1965. 21st: 2 Sep 1942–28 Apr 1943 (not operational, 2 Sep 1942–c. 12 Jan 1943). 22d: 2 Sep 1942–7 Jul 1943 (not operational, 2 Sep 1942–c. 12 Jan 1943; detached 18 May–7 Jul 1943). 22d (no relation to previous squadron): 1 Dec 1965–20 Sep 1966; attached 9–26 Oct 1968. 23d: 2 Sep 1942–15 Nov 1944 (not operational, 2 Sep 1942–c. 12 Jan 1943; detached c. 15 Jul–8 Sep 1943, 9 Feb–9 Mar 1944, 23 Aug–15 Nov 1944). 24th Photographic Mapping (later, 24th Photographic; 24th Combat Mapping): 2 Sep 1942–9 Oct 1943 (not operational, 2 Sep 1942–c. 12 Jan 1943; detached c. 8 Aug–9 Oct 1943). 26th Air Refueling: 28 May 1952–1 Apr 1955 (detached 28 May 1952–31 May 1953). 32d Photographic (later, 32d Tactical) Reconnaissance: attached 30 Apr–14 Nov 1944, assigned 15 Nov 1944–28 Oct 1945; assigned 1 Oct 1965–15 Aug 1966. 37th: 15 Nov 1944–28 Oct 1945. 38th: 1 Jan 1966–. 321st Air Refueling: 16 Aug 1956–15 Apr 1958. 526th Fighter-Interceptor (later, 526th Tactical Fighter): 1 Nov 1968–31 Jan 1973. 4713th Defense Systems Evaluation: attached 20 Oct–4 Nov 1966, 21 May–30 Jun 1967, 21 Sep–6 Oct 1967. *Flight*. Flight, 5th Combat Mapping Squadron: attached 10 Mar–5 May 1944. *Detachment*. Det, 4713th Defense Systems Evaluation Squadron: attached 16 Jan 1968–28 Sep 1969.

Stations. AAB, Colorado Springs (later, Peterson AAFld), Colo, 23 Jul 1942; Camp Kilmer, NJ, 11–19 Aug 1943; Bizerte, Tunisia, 4 Sep 1943; La Marsa, Tunisia, 8 Sep 1943; San Severo, Italy, 6 Dec 1943; Bari, Italy, 11 Oct 1944–c. 8 Oct 1945; Camp Kilmer, NJ, 26–28 Oct 1945. Lockbourne AFB, Ohio, 28 May 1952–1 Jul 1958. Toul-Rosieres AB, France, 1 Jul 1965; Ramstein AB, West Germany, 5 Oct 1966; Zweibrucken AB, West Germany, 31 Jan 1973–.

Commanders. 2d Lt Frederick A. Williams, 23 Jul 1942; Maj J. D. Russell, c. Sep 1942; Maj James F. Stechell, 12 Jan 1943; Lt Col Waymond A. Davis, 27 Feb 1943; Capt Paul M. Thorngren, 1 Apr 1943; Maj John S. Adams, 17 Apr 1943; Lt Col Waymond A. Davis, 8 May 1943; Maj Leon W. Gray, 23 Oct 1943; Maj Lloyd R. Nuttall, 4 Feb 1944; Col Wilbur H. Stratton, 21 Sep 1944; Lt Col Bernard S. Hendler, 9 Aug 1945–unkn. None (not manned), 28 May 1952–9 Jan 1953; Col Henry R. Sullivan, Jr., 10 Jan 1953; Col George W. Humbrecht, 10 Feb 1953; Brig Gen Henry R. Sullivan, Jr., 27 Apr 1953; Col Lawson C. Horner, Jr., 22 Jul 1955; Col William J. Meng, 16 Aug

1955; Col Robert F. Layton, 4 Jun 1957; Col William H. Reddell, 10 Jun 1957; Maj Lester Meltzer, 15 Apr 1958–unkn. None (not manned), 19 Apr–30 Jun 1965; Col Robert L. Boardman, 1 Jul 1965; Col Harvey P. Hall, c. Jun 1966; Col Glyn W. Ramsey, 21 Jun 1966; Col William R. MacDonald, 5 Oct 1966; Col William T. Douthwaite, Jr., 23 Jun 1967; Col Bryce Poe II, 1 Jul 1969; Col Howard M. Lane, 23 Jun 1970; Brig Gen William F. Georgi, 1 Mar 1971; Col James E. McInerney, Jr., 31 Jan 1973; Col Lloyd C. Ulrich, 2 Jul 1973; Brig Gen George M. Browning, Jr., 6 May 1974; Col Robert C. Karns, 4 Jun 1976–.

Aircraft. Primarily P–38/F–4 and P–38/F–5, 1943–1945; but also included B–17, 1943–1944; B–24/F–7, 1943; B–25, 1943–1944; A–20, 1944; F–8, 1944. YRB–47, 1953–1955; B–47, 1953–1954; KC–97, 1953–1955, 1956–1958; RB–47, 1954–1958. RB–66, 1965; RF–4, 1965–; F–4, 1966–1973; RF–101, 1966; EB–57, 1966, 1967, 1968–1969; F/TF–102, 1968–1970; C–130, 1972–1973; C–47, 1972–1973; UH–1, 1972–1973.

Operations. Not operational from activation to Jan 1943. Tactical components assigned in Sep 1942, but unit remained unmanned until 12 Jan 1943. Trained in photographic reconnaissance and mapping, Jan–Aug 1943. Arrived in Tunisia Sep 1943, thereafter performed combat reconnaissance in the MTO and ETO until 4 May 1945. Received DUC for action on 6 Sep 1944 when the group secured photographic intelligence of German installations in the Balkans, enabling fighter units to destroy many enemy transport and fighter planes. Returned to United States and inactivated in Oct 1945. Activated in May 1952, but unmanned until Jan 1953. Maintained proficiency in strategic reconnaissance, Jan 1953–Apr 1958, and in aerial refueling, May 1952–Apr 1955 and Aug 1956–Apr 1958. Not operational 15 Apr–1 Jul 1958. Maintained proficiency in tactical reconnaissance, both visual and photographic, day and night from Jul 1965, adding regional air defense capabilities in Nov 1968, electronic countermeasures training and requirements in Oct 1966, and special operations in Mar 1972.

Service Streamers. American Theater.

Campaign Streamers. Air Combat, EAME Theater; Air Offensive, Europe; Naples-Foggia; Rome-Arno; Normandy; Northern France; Southern France; North Apennines; Rhineland; Central Europe; Po Valley.

Decorations. Distinguished Unit Citation (Balkans): 6 Sep 1944. Air Force Outstanding Unit Awards: 21 Mar–9 May 1956; 5 Oct 1966–23 Jun 1967; 1 Mar 1971–30 Jun 1972; 1 Jul 1973–31 May 1975.

Emblem. Per fess nebuly abased azure and vert, overall on a saltire argent change to light green on the vert part of the shield, two lightning flashes throughout tenne behind an eye vert, vitreous body argent, pupil and outlines sable. Motto: SABER ES PODER—Knowledge is power. (Approved on 4 Sep 1953.)

27th TACTICAL FIGHTER WING

Lineage. Established as 27th Fighter Wing on 28 Jul 1947. Organized on 15 Aug 1947. Discontinued on 1 Aug

1948. Activated on 1 Aug 1948. Redesignated: 27th Fighter-Escort Wing on 1 Feb 1950; 27th Strategic Fighter Wing on 20 Jan 1953; 27th Fighter-Bomber Wing on 1 Jul 1957; 27th Tactical Fighter Wing on 1 Jul 1958.

Assignments. Eighth Air Force, 15 Aug 1947–1 Aug 1948. Eighth Air Force, 1 Aug 1948 (attached to Far East Air Forces, 19 Nov–29 Nov 1950; Fifth Air Force, 30 Nov 1950–15 Jul 1951); 42d Air Division, 6 Aug 1951 (attached to Far East Air Forces, 6–13 Oct 1952; 39th Air Division [Defense], 13 Oct 1952–c. 13 Feb 1953; 7th Air Division, 7 May–17 Aug 1955); Twelfth Air Force, 8 Jan 1958 (attached to 834th Air Division, 15 Jul 1958–18 Feb 1959); 832d Air Division, 18 Feb 1959 (attached to 3d Air Division [Provisional], 21 Oct–1 Dec 1962); Twelfth Air Force, 1 Jul 1975–.

Components. *Wing.* 136th Fighter-Bomber: attached 20 May–30 Jun 1951. *Group.* 27th: 15 Aug 1947–1 Aug 1948; 1 Aug 1948–16 Jun 1952 (not operational, 6 Aug 1951–16 Jun 1952). *Squadrons.* 27th Air Refueling: 25 Oct 1953–1 Jul 1957 (detached 7 May–17 Aug 1955). 307th Air Refueling: attached 6 Jun–25 Oct 1953. 429th: attached 15 May 1967–15 May 1968 (not operational, 15 May–c. 30 Jun 1967). 465th Tactical Fighter Training: 1 Dec 1972–1 Aug 1973. 481st: 25 Sep 1957–31 Aug 1973 (not operational, 25 Sep–c. 17 Dec 1957 and c. 28 Jan–17 Feb 1959; detached 1–25 Jun 1959, 9 Jun–11 Oct 1961, 24 Apr–20 May 1963, 19 Nov 1963–1 Feb 1964, 9–c. 20 Apr 1964, 2 Sep–4 Dec 1964, and 15 Jun–30 Nov 1965; not operational, 5 Sep 1968–30 Jun 1969 and 31 Jul 1971–12 Nov 1972); 15 Jan 1976–. 522d: attached 6 Aug 1951–15 Jun 1952, assigned 16 Jun 1952– (detached 6 Sep–18 Dec 1958; not operational, c. 28 Jan–17 Feb 1959; detached 18 Oct 1959–22 Feb 1960, 13 Feb–c. 7 Mar 1961, 5 Feb–15 Jun 1962, 12 Dec 1962–c. 15 Feb 1963, 16 Mar–6 May 1964, 8 Aug–15 Nov 1964, 15 Aug–25 Nov 1965; not operational, 19 Jun–c. Sep 1969 and 31 Mar–c. 15 Sep 1971). 523d: attached 6 Aug 1951–15 Jun 1952, assigned 16 Jun 1952–20 Nov 1965 (not operational, c. 28 Jan–17 Feb 1959; detached c. 24 Feb–17 Jun 1960, c. 5 Sep–20 Nov 1961, c. 12 Oct 1962–c. 15 Jan 1963, c. 17 Sep–20 Nov 1963, 12 Jun–4 Sep 1964, and 22 Mar–30 Jun 1965); 31 Aug 1973–. 524th: attached 6 Aug 1951–15 Jun 1952, assigned 16 Jun 1952– (not operational, c. 28 Jan–17 Feb 1959; detached 17 Jun–8 Jul 1959, 10 Feb–16 Jun 1961, 30 Oct–14 Nov 1961, 9 Jun–c. 27 Jun 1963, 21 Jan–19 Mar 1964, and 1 Dec 1964–28 Mar 1965; not operational, 7 Mar–c. Jul 1969). 4427th Tactical Fighter Replacement: 1 Oct 1971–15 Jan 1976. 4429th Combat Crew Training: 20 Dec 1968–1 Dec 1972. *Detachment.* Det 1, HQ 27th TFW: 15 Jul 1963–4 May 1964.

Stations. Kearney AAFld (later, AFB), Nebr, 15 Aug 1947–1 Aug 1948. Kearney AFB, Nebr, 1 Aug 1948; Bergstrom AFB, Texas, 16 Mar 1949; Cannon AFB, NM, 18 Feb 1959–.

Commanders. Col Gwen G. Atkinson, 15 Aug 1947; Col Ashley B. Packard, 7 Jan–1 Aug 1948. Col Ashley B. Packard, 1 Aug 1948; Col Raymond F. Rudell, 1 May 1951; Col Donald J. M. Blakeslee, 6 Jul 1952; Col Richard N. Ellis, 2 Aug 1954; Col Charles M. Walton, Jr., Jul 1957; Brig Gen Ivan W. McElroy, 8 Jan 1958; Col John L. Gregory, Jr., 15 Jul 1958–c. 28 Jan 1959; unkn, c. 28 Jan–17 Feb 1959; Col Gilbert L. Meyers, 18 Feb 1959; Col Arlie J. Blood, 10 May 1959; Col Gilbert L. Meyers, 4 Aug 1959; Col Thomas A. Robertson, 22 Aug 1959; Col Arvis L. Hilpert, 12 Oct 1959; Col Jack C. Berger, 17 Jul 1961; Col Charles E. Simpson, 15 Jul 1963; Col Dale S. Sweat, 15 Aug 1963; Col Robert A. Tyler, 31 Dec 1965; Col Herndon F. Williams, 25 May 1967; Col Homer K. Hansen, 24 Jul 1967; Col William L. Ford, 1 Apr 1968; Col Jimmy J. Jumper, 16 Apr 1968; Col Frank C. Buzze, 15 Jul 1968; Col Charles E. Francis, 12 May 1970; Col Richard E. Little, 28 Jan 1972; Col John H. Bennett, 25 May 1973; Col Cecil D. Crabb, 18 Jul 1975; Col Thomas J. Hickey, 6 Aug 1976–.

Aircraft. P (later, F)–51, 1947–1948; F–82, 1948. F–51, 1948–1949; F–82, 1948–1950; F–84, 1950–1951, 1951–1958; KB–29, 1953–1955, 1955–1957; F–101, 1957–1958; F–100, 1959–1972; T/AT–33, 1968–1973; F–111, 1969–1970, 1970–.

Operations. Fighter escort operations to meet SAC commitments, 1947–1948 and 1948–1950. Won the Mackay Trophy for successful deployment of 90 F–84Es from Bergstrom AFB, Texas, to Furstenfeldbruck AB, West Germany, in Sep 1950, via Labrador, Greenland, Iceland, and England. This was the first long-range mass flight of jet aircraft in aviation history. Deployed at Yokota AB, Japan, 19–30 Nov 1950, then split into two echelons. The advance echelon deployed at Taegu AB, South Korea, 1 Dec 1950–30 Jan 1951, while the rear echelon deployed at Itazuke AB, Japan, 9 Dec 1950–31 Jan 1951. Flew combat in Korea, 6 Dec 1950–30 Jun 1951. The two echelons of the wing combined at Itazuke on 1 Feb 1951, continuing combat from that base. Returned to the United States in Jul 1951, but deployed at Misawa AB, Japan, 6 Oct 1952–13 Feb 1953, to provide air defense. Had air refueling as an additional mission, Jun 1953–May 1955 and Aug 1955–Jun 1957. Wing pilot Capt Forrest W. Wilson, in an F–84G, won the Allison Trophy jet aircraft race of the National Aircraft Show at Dayton, Ohio, on 6 Sep 1953, flying the 110.3-mile course at an average speed of 537.802 mph in 12:17.2 minutes. Deployed at Sturgate RAF Station, England, 7 May–17 Aug 1955. Converted to F–101s in 1957 after joining Tactical Air Command. Maj Adrian E. Drew, wing F–101 project officer, broke the world speed record on 12 Dec 1957 when he flew an F–101A over a Mojave Desert course at 1,212.8 mph in one direction and 1,207.5 mph in the opposite direction. Converted to F–100s in late 1958 and early 1959. Deployed at England AFB, La, 29 Mar–5 May 1961, and at MacDill AFB, Fla, 21 Oct–1 Dec 1962, the latter deployment during the Cuban missile crisis. Conducted F–100 pilot and mechanic replacement training, Jan 1966–Jun 1969. Deployed at Holloman AFB, NM, 13 Apr–12 May 1966. Conducted T/AT–33 forward air controller/air liaison officer training, Dec 1968–Jul 1973, phasing out F–100s in mid–1972, and phasing in F–111s beginning Oct 1969. Continued F–111 operations to 4 Aug 1970, and resumed F–111 operations again on 28 Oct 1970. Began conducting F–111 aircrew replacement training in Oct 1971.

Service Streamers. None.

Campaign Streamers. CCF Intervention; First UN Counteroffensive; CCF Spring Offensive.

Decorations. Republic of Korea Presidential Unit Citation: 9 Nov 1950–31 May 1951.

Emblem. Per bend azure and or, in sinister chief a right clenched fist couped at the wrist in dexter base a magnolia blossom leaved all argent, fimbriated sable. *Motto:* INTELLIGENT STRENGTH. (Approved for 27th Group on 12 Sep 1940 and for 27th Wing on 11 Jul 1952.)

28th BOMBARDMENT WING, HEAVY

Lineage. Established as 28th Bombardment Wing, Very Heavy, on 28 Jul 1947. Organized on 15 Aug 1947. Discontinued on 12 Jul 1948. Redesignated 28th Bombardment Wing, Medium, and activated on 12 Jul 1948. Redesignated: 28th Bombardment Wing, Heavy, on 16 May 1949; 28th Strategic Reconnaissance Wing on 1 Apr 1950; 28th Strategic Reconnaissance Wing, Heavy, on 16 Jul 1950; 28th Bombardment Wing, Heavy, on 1 Oct 1955.

Assignments. Fifteenth Air Force, 15 Aug 1947–12 Jul 1948. Fifteenth Air Force, 12 Jul 1948; Eighth Air Force, 1 Apr 1950; Fifteenth Air Force, 1 Apr 1955 (attached to 3d Air Division, 14 Apr–24 Jul 1955); 821st Air (later, 821st Strategic Aerospace) Division, 1 Jan 1959; 47th Air Division, 30 Jun 1971; 4th Strategic Missile (later, 4th Air) Division, 15 Jan 1973–.

Components. *Group.* 28th: 15 Aug 1947–12 Jul 1948; 12 Jul 1948–16 Jun 1952 (detached 19 Jul–18 Oct 1948; not operational, 10 Feb 1951–16 Jun 1952). *Squadrons.* 4th Airborne Command and Control: 1 Apr 1970–. 28th Air Refueling: 1 Oct 1960– (detached c. 9 Mar–c. 21 Sep 1966, c. 15 Jan–c. 19 Jul 1968, c. 19 Aug 1969–c. 23 Mar 1970). 37th: 1 Jul 1977–. 77th: attached 10 Feb 1951–15 Jun 1952, assigned 16 Jun 1952– (detached c. 9 Mar–c. 21 Sep 1966, c. 15 Jan–c. 19 Jul 1968, c. 19 Aug 1969–c. 23 Mar 1970). 97th Air Refueling: 1 Jul 1962–15 Mar 1964. 717th: attached 10 Feb 1951–15 Jun 1952, assigned 16 Jun 1952–1 Feb 1960. 718th: attached 10 Feb 1951–15 Jun 1952, assigned 16 Jun 1952–20 Feb 1960. 850th Strategic Missile: 1 Dec 1960–1 Jan 1962. 928th Air Refueling: 1 Feb 1959–1 Oct 1960.

Stations. Rapid City AAFld (later, AFB), SD, 15 Aug 1947–12 Jul 1948. Rapid City (later, Ellsworth) AFB, SD, 12 Jul 1948–.

Commanders. Col Thomas J. Gent, Jr., 15 Aug 1947; Col Raymond L. Curtice, 17 Sep 1947; Lt Col Everett W. Holstrom, 28 Sep 1947; Col Raymond L. Curtice, 9 Oct 1947; Col Thomas J. Gent, Jr., 15 Oct 1947; Col William W. Jones, c. 10–12 Jul 1948. Col William W. Jones, 12 Jul 1948; Col Albert T. Wilson, Jr., 19 Aug 1948; Brig Gen Richard E. Ellsworth, 15 Nov 1950; Col Howard W. Moore, 18 Mar 1953; Col Ariel W. Nielsen, 30 Apr 1953; Col Neil D. Van Sickle, 15 Jun 1955; Col Loran D. Briggs, 20 Apr 1957; Col Francis W. Nye, 6 Jul 1959; Col Allen B. Rowlett, Jun 1962; Col Leo C. Lewis, c. 1 Jul 1962; Col Albert H. Schneider, 10 Jul 1965; Col Edgar S. Harris, Jr., 27 Dec 1966; Col Albert H. Schneider, 4 May 1967; Col Edgar S. Harris, Jr., 2 Jun 1967; Col James Wagner, 24 Jul 1968; Col Richard L. Lawson, 1 Feb 1970; Col Junior B. Reed, 18 Jun 1971; Col Harold B. Coffee, 30 May 1973; Col James E. Light, Jr., 8 Apr 1974; Col Harold J. M. Williams, 21 Apr 1976; Col Clinton H. Winne, Jr., 11 May 1976–.

Aircraft. B–29, 1947–1948. B–29, 1948–1950; B–36, 1949–1950; RB–29, 1950; RB–36, 1950–1957; B–52, 1957–1966, 1966–1968, 1968–1969, 1970–; KC–135, 1959–1966, 1966–1968, 1968–1969, 1970–; KC–97, 1962–1964; EC–135, 1965–.

Operations. Maintained proficiency in heavy bombardment, 1947–1948. Maintained proficiency in global bombardment, deploying tactical components or segments thereof as needed, 1948–1950. Performed global strategic reconnaissance, 1950–1955, with bombardment as a secondary mission, 1954–1955. Trained primarily as a bombardment wing from 1955, but retained a reconnaissance capability to Sep 1956. Deployed at Andersen AFB, Guam, Apr–Jul 1955. Added aerial refueling to mission in 1959, and began operating post-attack command and control system for Fifteenth Air Force in Jan 1965, maintaining this capability through a rear echelon during the absences of the remainder of the wing. Controlled a non-equipped Titan missile squadron, Dec 1960–Dec 1961. Except for a small rear echelon left at Ellsworth AFB, SD, the wing's headquarters staff, tactical aircraft and crews, and most support personnel were integrated into SAC's Arc Light force for combat in Southeast Asia, c. 9 Mar–c. 21 Sep 1966, c. 15 Jan–c. 19 Jul 1968, and c. 9 Sep 1969–c. 18 Mar 1970. From Apr 1972 to Oct 1973 the wing also had most of its tactical aircraft and crews on loan to SAC organizations involved in combat operations, and the wing continued supporting Pacific forces with planes and crews into 1975. Converted from B–52G to B–52H models in 1977.

Service Streamers. None.

Campaign Streamers. None.

Decorations. Air Force Outstanding Unit Awards: 1 Sep 1957–30 Jun 1958; 1 Jan–31 Dec 1966; 1 Jan–1 Mar 1968; 2 Mar–1 Jul 1968; 9 Jun–10 Jul 1972.

Emblem. Per pale nebuly or and azure. *Crest:* On a wreath of the colors or and azure, a fleur-de-lis vert, shaded sable, the outer leaves terminated the form of wings or. *Motto:* GUARDIAN OF THE NORTH. (Approved for 28th

Group on 14 Nov 1941 and for 28th Wing on 11 Jun 1952.)

29th FLYING TRAINING WING

Lineage. Established as 29th Flying Training Wing on 22 Mar 1972. Activated on 1 Jul 1972. Inactivated on 30 Sep 1977.

Assignments. Air Training Command, 1 Jul 1972–30 Sep 1977.

Components. *Squadrons.* 43d: 1 Jul 1972–30 Sep 1977 (not operational, 12 Aug–30 Sep 1977). 52d: 1 Jul 1972–30 Sep 1977 (not operational, 12 Aug–30 Sep 1977).

Stations. Craig AFB, Ala, 1 Jul 1972–30 Sep 1977.

Commanders. Col Sam P. McClurkin, 1 Jul 1972; Col Robert B.Tanguy, 28 Jul 1973; Col Leroy W. Svendsen, Jr., 14 Feb 1974; Col Thomas H. Kirk, Jr., 14 Apr 1975; Col Charles E. Bishop, 12 Jan 1976; Col William M. Pugh, 12 May– c. 30 Sep 1977.

Aircraft. T–37, 1972–1977; T–38, 1972–1977; T–41, 1972–1973.

Operations. Replaced, and absorbed resources of, the 3615th Flying Training Wing on 1 Jul 1972. Provided undergraduate pilot training and operated Craig AFB, Ala, facilities. Last class graduated in mid-Aug 1977.

Service Streamers. None.

Campaign Streamers. None.

Decorations. Air Force Outstanding Unit Award: 1 Jan–31 Dec 1973.

Emblem. Azure, a lightning flash or surmounted by a Pegasus argent, saltirewise between in dexter chief a mullet of five points of the like and in base two mullets of five points fesswise of the second, all within a diminished bordure of the last. (Approved on 12 Mar 1973.)

31st TACTICAL FIGHTER WING

Lineage. Established as 31st Fighter Wing on 6 Nov 1947. Organized on 20 Nov 1947. Discontinued on 25 Aug 1948. Activated on 23 Aug 1948. Redesignated: 31st Fighter-Bomber Wing on 20 Jan 1950; 31st Fighter-Escort Wing on 16 Jul 1950; 31st Strategic Fighter Wing on 20 Jan 1953; 31st Fighter-Bomber Wing on 1 Apr 1957; 31st Tactical Fighter Wing on 1 Jul 1958.

Assignments. Ninth Air Force, 20 Nov 1947–25 Aug 1948. Ninth Air Force, 23 Aug 1948; Fourteenth Air

Force, 1 Feb 1949; Second Air Force, 1 Jul 1950; 40th Air Division, 14 Mar 1951 (attached to 39th Air Division [Defense], 10 Jul–11 Oct 1952 and 10 Nov 1953–12 Feb 1954); Ninth Air Force, 1 Apr 1957; 831st Air Division, 15 Mar 1959; Ninth Air Force, 1 Jun 1962 (attached to Air Force Atlantic Command, 24 Oct–9 Nov 1962; 1st Air Division Provisional, 10 Nov–c. 30 Nov 1962); 836th Air Division, 1 Oct 1964; 834th Air Division, 1 Jan 1965; 836th Air Division, 1 Aug 1966 (attached to Seventh Air Force, 16–24 Dec 1966); Seventh Air Force, 25 Dec 1966; 836th Air Division, 15 Oct 1970; Ninth Air Force, 30 Jun 1971–.

Components. *Group.* 31st: 20 Nov 1947–25 Aug 1948; 23 Aug 1948–16 Jun 1952 (detached 15 Dec 1950–10 Feb 1951; not operational, 10 Feb 1951–16 Jun 1952). *Squadrons.* 68th: 15–30 Oct 1970. 136th: 14 Jun 1968–25 May 1969. 188th: 7 Jun 1968–18 May 1969. 306th: 25 Sep 1957–28 Sep 1970 (not operational, c. Nov 1958–14 Mar 1959; detached 8 Apr–16 Jul 1960, 15 Feb–1 Mar 1961, 20 Aug–1 Sep 1961, 24 Apr–19 Jul 1962, 27 Jun–30 Sep 1963, 1 May–8 Aug 1964, 7 Jul 1965–27 Jan 1966; not operational, 8–28 Sep 1970); 30 Oct 1970–15 Jul 1971. 307th: attached 27 Jul 1951–15 Jun 1952, assigned 16 Jun 1952–27 Apr 1966 (detached 7 Nov–7 Dec 1956, 25 Feb–17 Aug 1958; not operational, c. Nov 1958–14 Mar 1959; detached 15 Mar–19 Jul 1959, 8 Nov 1960–9 Mar 1961, 11–24 Sep 1961, 18–28 Feb 1962, 17 Dec 1962–16 Mar 1963, 27 Dec 1963–5 Mar 1964, 6–21 Jun 1964, 23 Nov 1964–14 Mar 1965, 24 Jun–7 Dec 1965); 15 Jul 1971– (detached 29 Jul–28 Oct 1972). 308th: attached 27 Jul 1951–15 Jun 1952, assigned 16 Jun 1952–2 Dec 1965 (detached 5 Dec 1956–7 Jan 1957, 15 Aug 1958–19 Jan 1959; not operational, Mar–14 Mar 1959; detached 11 Jul–c. Dec 1959, 7 Mar–c. 19 Jul 1961, 13 Mar–3 Jul 1963, 9 Feb–5 May 1964, 9 Mar–8 Jul 1965); attached 16–24 Dec 1966, assigned 25 Dec 1966–5 Oct 1970 (not operational, 10 Sep–5 Oct 1970); assigned 30 Oct 1970– (detached 28 Apr–29 Jul 1972, 11 Dec 1972–11 Jun 1973). 309th: attached 27 Jul 1951–15 Jun 1952, assigned 16 Jun 1952–5 Oct 1970 (detached 5 Jan–9 Feb 1957; not operational, Feb–14 Mar 1959; detached 5 Jul–15 Nov 1960, 7 Oct–26 Nov 1961, 15 Jul–23 Dec 1962, 26 Sep–31 Dec 1963, 5 Aug–27 Nov 1964, 18 Jan–24 Apr 1966; not operational, 10 Sep–5 Oct 1970); assigned 30 Oct 1970–. 355th: 15 May 1969–30 Sep 1970 (not operational, 20–30 Sep 1970). 416th: 28 May 1969–28 Sep 1970 (not operational, 5–28 Sep 1970). 431st Air Refueling: attached 1 Apr–24 Nov 1957, assigned 25 Nov 1957–1 Jul 1958. 436th: 15–30 Oct 1970. 478th: 15–30 Oct 1970. 508th Air Refueling: attached 10 Feb–1 Jun 1954; assigned 11 May 1956–1 Apr 1957. 560th: 15–31 Oct 1970. 4431st Tactical Fighter Replacement: 1 Oct 1971–1 May 1973 (not operational).

Stations. Turner Field (later, AFB), Ga, 20 Nov 1947–25 Aug 1948. Turner AFB, Ga, 23 Aug 1948; George AFB, Calif, 15 Mar 1959; Homestead AFB, Fla, 31 May 1962–6 Dec 1966; Tuy Hoa AB, South Vietnam, 16 Dec 1966–15 Oct 1970; Homestead AFB, Fla, 15 Oct 1970–.

Commanders. Col William L. Lee, 20 Nov 1947; Col Eugene H. Snavely, 16–25 Aug 1948. Col Eugene H.

Snavely, 23 Aug 1948; Col Alvan C. Gillem II, c. 26 Dec 1950; Col Eugene H. Snavely, 10 Mar 1951; Col Carl W. Stapleton, 14 Mar 1951; Lt Col Charles W. Lenfrost, 9 Apr 1951; Col David C. Schilling, 1 May 1951; Lt Col Charles W. Lenfrost, c. 27 May 1951; Lt Col William D. Dunham, 22 Jun 1951; Lt Col Gerald W. Johnson, 1 Jul 1951; Col David C. Schilling, 20 Jul 1951; Col Robert P. Montgomery, 16 May 1955; Col Gordon M. Graham, 15 Jul 1955; Col Hubert Zemke, 1 Aug 1955; Col Gordon M. Graham, 13 Oct 1955; Lt Col Harold L. Williams, Feb 1959–unkn; Col Robert W. Stephens, 15 Mar 1959; Col Herbert E. Ross, 26 Aug 1959; Col William D. Ritchie, 5 Oct 1959; Col Jack R. Brown, 2 Oct 1961; Col Frank J. Collins, 14 Oct 1961; Col William E. Bethea, 9 Mar 1964; Col Franklin A. Nichols, 16 Mar 1964; Col Ernest T. Burnett, 30 May 1965; Col James Jabara, 17 Jun 1965; Col Raymond C. Lee, Jr., 17 Nov 1966; Col Warren R. Lewis, 28 Nov 1966; Col William J. Evans, 7 Dec 1967; Col Abner M. Aust, Jr., 3 May 1968; Col Cuthbert A. Pattillo, 8 Feb 1969; Col William B. Yancey, Jr., 8 Aug 1969; Col Gilbert D. Hereth, 15 Jun 1970; Brig Gen Wiltz P. Segura, 15 Oct 1970; Col David E. Rippetoe, Jr., 28 May 1971; Col Alonzo J. Walter, Jr., 16 Jun 1972; Col Dudley J. Foster, 1 Mar 1974; Col Walter J. Bacon II, 7 Mar 1975; Col Samuel R. Johnson, 14 Jun 1976–.

Aircraft. P (later, F)–51, 1947–1948. F–51, 1948–1949; F–84, 1948–1950, 1951–1957; KB–29, 1954, 1956–1957; F–100, 1957–1959, 1959–1970; KB–50, 1957–1958; F–4, 1970–.

Operations. Trained to maintain tactical proficiency, 1947–1948, and 1948–1950. From Dec 1950 through Jul 1951, all tactical components and most support components detached from the wing and deployed in England. Trained to maintain tactical proficiency, Jul 1951–1959, twice deploying as a wing to provide air defense in Japan, Jul–Oct 1952 and Nov 1953–Feb 1954. Made first jet fighter crossing of the Pacific Ocean to reach Japan in Jul 1952, and earned an outstanding unit award for this feat. Rotated tactical components to Alaska, 1956–1957, and to Europe, 1958–1959. Became completely non-operational by early Mar 1959, and moved to Calif in mid-month, absorbing personnel and equipment of inactivated units. From then until Dec 1966, maintained tactical proficiency by participating in exercises, firepower demonstrations, and rotating tactical components on a global scale. Deployed in Fla during the Cuban missile crisis of 1962. Moved to Southeast Asia in Dec 1966, and performed in combat, 16 Dec 1966–9 Sep 1970. Moved to the United States without personnel or equipment on 15 Oct 1970 and absorbed new personnel and equipment. Maintained tactical proficiency from that date, operated F–4 replacement training from 1 Jul 1971, and rotated components to Southeast Asia, Apr 1972–Jun 1973. Assumed responsibility for providing air defense in southern Fla on 1 Apr 1976.

Service Streamers. None.

Campaign Streamers. Vietnam Air Offensive; Vietnam Air Offensive, Phase II; Vietnam Air Offensive, Phase III; Vietnam Air/Ground; Vietnam Air Offensive, Phase IV; TET 69/Counteroffensive; Vietnam Summer–Fall, 1969; Vietnam Winter–Spring, 1970;

Sanctuary Counteroffensive; Southwest Monsoon.

Decorations. Presidential Unit Citation (Vietnam): 1 May–31 Dec 1968. Air Force Outstanding Unit Award with Combat "V" Device: 17 Dec 1966–30 Apr 1968. Air Force Outstanding Unit Awards: 4–16 Jul 1952; 1 Mar–30 Nov 1962; 1 Jun–16 Dec 1966. Republic of Vietnam Gallantry Crosses with Palm: 17 Dec 1966–31 Oct 1970; 1 Jan 1968–19 May 1969.

Emblem. Per bend nebule or and azure, in chief a wyvern, sans legs, wings endorsed of the second. *Motto:* RETURN WITH HONOR. (Approved for 31st Group on 28 Jun 1941 and for 31st Wing on 13 Dec 1951.)

32d TACTICAL FIGHTER WING

Lineage. Established as 32d Composite Wing on 10 Aug 1948. Activated on 24 Aug 1948. Inactivated on 1 Apr 1949. Redesignated 32d Fighter-Bomber Wing on 23 Mar 1953. Redesignated 33d Fighter Wing (Air Defense), and activated, on 28 Dec 1960. Organized on 1 Feb 1961. Discontinued, and inactivated, on 1 Jul 1962. Organized on 1 Apr 1964 prior to redesignation and activation as 32d Tactical Fighter Wing on 6 Apr 1964. Discontinued, and inactivated, on 25 Jul 1964.

Assignments. 1st Air Division, 24 Aug 1948; Thirteenth Air Force, 1 Dec 1948–1 Apr 1949. Air Defense Command, 28 Dec 1960; Minot Air Defense Sector, 1 Feb 1961–1 Jul 1962. 831st Air Division, 1 Apr–25 Jul 1964.

Components. *Wing.* 71st Tactical Reconnaissance: attached 24 Aug–25 Oct 1948 (not operational). *Squadrons.* 5th Fighter-Interceptor: 1 Feb 1961–1 Jul 1962. 23d Reconnaissance: attached 24 Aug 1948–16 Mar 1949. 31st Reconnaissance: 16 Mar–1 Apr 1949. 68th Fighter-Interceptor: 16 Jun–25 Jul 1964. 431st Fighter-Interceptor: 18 May–25 Jul 1964. 497th Fighter-Interceptor: 18 Jun–25 Jul 1964. 782d: 1 Apr–25 Jul 1964. 783d: 1 Apr–25 Jul 1964. 784th: 1 Apr–25 Jul 1964. 785th: 1 Apr–25 Jul 1964.

Stations. Kadena AB, Okinawa, 24 Aug 1948–1 Apr 1949. Minot AFB, ND, 1 Feb 1961–1 Jul 1962. George AFB, Calif, 1 Apr–25 Jul 1964.

Commanders. Col Edwin M. Day, 24 Aug 1948; Col Walter E. Arnold, 22 Jan 1949; Col Charles P. Prime, 1 Feb 1949; Col Walter E. Arnold, 21 Mar–1 Apr 1949. None (not manned), 28 Dec 1960–31 Jan 1961; Col Richard F. Weltzin, 1 Feb 1961–1 Jul 1962. Col John L. Gregory, Jr., 1 Apr–25 Jul 1964.

Aircraft. B/FB–17, 1948; C–46, 1948; B/RB–29, 1948–1949. F–106, 1961–1962. F–4, 1964.

Operations. Replaced 71st Tactical Reconnaissance Wing at Kadena, Okinawa, in Aug 1948. Provided photographic reconnaissance and search and rescue support, 1948–1949.

Provided air defense for a segment of the north-central United States, 1961–1962. Was being organized when replaced by 8th Tactical Fighter Wing in 1964.

Service Streamers. None.

Campaign Streamers. None.

Decorations. None.

Emblem. Argent, a flight symbol bendwise azure bearing a stylized aircraft or, in sinister chief a globe per pale sable and of the third, grid lines counterchanged, in dexter base a lion rampant of the fourth, all within a diminished bordure of the third fimbriated gules. (Approved for 32d Group on 8 Aug 1960; used by 32d Wing, 1961–1962 and 1964.)

33d TACTICAL FIGHTER WING

Lineage. Established as 33d Fighter Wing on 15 Oct 1947. Organized on 5 Nov 1947. Discontinued on 1 Aug 1948. Activated on 1 Aug 1948. Redesignated 33d Fighter-Interceptor Wing on 20 Jan 1950. Inactivated on 6 Feb 1952. Redesignated 33d Fighter Wing (Air Defense) on 14 Sep 1956. Activated on 18 Oct 1956. Inactivated on 18 Aug 1957. Redesignated 33d Tactical Fighter Wing, and activated, on 9 Feb 1965. Organized on 1 Apr 1965.

Assignments. Eighth Air Force, 5 Nov 1947–1 Aug 1948 (attached to 509th Bombardment Wing, Very Heavy, 17 Nov 1947–1 Aug 1948). Eighth Air Force, 1 Aug 1948 (attached to 509th Bombardment Wing, Medium, 1 Aug–15 Nov 1948); First Air Force, 1 Dec 1948 (attached to Eastern Air Defense Force, 10 Nov 1949–31 Aug 1950, and further attached to 32d Air Division [Defense], 20 Feb 1950–); Eastern Air Defense Force, 1 Sep 1950–6 Feb 1952 (remained attached to 32d Air Division [Defense] to 1 Feb 1952). 26th Air Division (Defense), 18 Oct 1956 (attached to 4622d Air Defense Wing [SAGE], 18 Oct 1956–7 Jan 1957); Boston Air Defense Sector, 8 Jan–18 Aug 1957. Tactical Air Command, 9 Feb 1965; 836th Air Division, 1 Apr 1965; Ninth Air Force, 30 Jun 1971–.

Components. *Wing*. 50th Fighter (later, 50th Fighter-Interceptor): attached 1 Jun 1949–2 Jun 1951. *Group*. 33d: 5 Nov 1947–1 Aug 1948 (detached); 1 Aug 1948–6 Feb 1952 (detached 1 Aug–15 Nov 1948); 18 Oct 1956–18 Aug 1957 (detached 1 Jul–18 Aug 1957). *Squadrons*. 4th: 20 Jun 1965–12 Apr 1969. 16th: 20 Jun 1965–1 Nov 1970 (detached 27 Aug–13 Sep 1966, 13–31 Oct 1967, 26 May–9 Sep 1970). 25th: 20 Jun 1965–28 May 1968. 40th: 20 Jun 1965–15 Oct 1970 (not operational, c. 10 May 1969–15 Oct 1970). 58th: 1 Sep 1970– (not operational, 1 Sep–31 Oct 1970; detached 29 Apr–14 Oct 1972, 8 Jun–14 Sep 1973, 8–22 Aug 1975, 31 Jan–14 Feb 1977). 59th: 1 Sep 1970– (not operational, 1 Sep 1970–30 Jun 1973; detached 24–29

Mar 1974). 60th: 1 Sep 1971– (not operational). 133d: attached 21 Jul 1951–6 Feb 1952. 786th: 1 Apr–20 Jun 1965. 787th: 1 Apr–20 Jun 1965. 788th: 1 Apr–20 Jun 1965. 789th: 1 Apr–20 Jun 1965. 4533d Tactical Training Squadron (Test): 7 Dec 1967–12 Apr 1971.

Stations. Roswell AAFld (later, Walker AFB), NM, 5 Nov 1947–1 Aug 1948. Walker AFB, NM, 1 Aug 1948; Otis AFB, Mass, 16 Nov 1948–6 Feb 1952. Otis AFB, Mass, 18 Oct 1956–18 Aug 1957. Eglin AFB, Fla, 1 Apr 1965–.

Commanders. Lt Col Joseph C. Smith, 5 Nov 1947 (additional duty); Col Gwen G. Atkinson, Jan–1 Aug 1948 (additional duty). Col Gwen G. Atkinson, 1 Aug 1948 (additional duty to 16 Nov 1948); Col Arthur C. Agan, Jr., 23 May 1949; Col Harrison R. Thyng, Apr 1951; Col Leon W. Gray, Oct 1951–6 Feb 1952. Col Hilmer C. Nelson, 18 Oct 1956; Col Delbert H. Hahn, (by May)–c. 30 Jun 1957; none (not manned), 1 Jul–18 Aug 1957. None (not manned), 9 Feb–31 Mar 1965; Col David C. Jones, 1 Apr 1965; Col George I. Ruddell, 1 Oct 1965; Col Robert W. Maloy, 26 Aug 1966; Col Abner M. Aust, Jr., 12 May 1967; Col Franklin L. Fisher, 15 Jun 1967; Col Richard C. Henry, 30 Sep 1970; Col William E. Skinner, 24 Mar 1972; Col Gordon B. Mickelson, 10 May 1973; Col Donald C. Hanto, 15 Feb 1975; Col David L. Nichols, 29 Apr 1977–.

Aircraft. F–51, 1948–1950; F–84, 1948–1950; F–86, 1950–1952; F–94, 1951–1952; F–47, 1951–1952. F–89, 1956–1957; F–94, 1956–1957. F–4, 1965–.

Operations. Wing headquarters not operational and all components detached, Nov 1947–1 Aug 1948 and 1 Aug–15 Nov 1948. The 509th Bombardment Wing at Walker AFB, NM, controlled the wing's tactical units. Headquarters of the 33d Fighter Wing became operational upon movement to Otis AFB, Mass, in mid-Nov 1948. The wing trained to maintain tactical proficiency and participated in exercises and aerial demonstrations Nov 1948–Nov 1949. Assumed an air defense mission in Dec 1949 and provided air defense in the northeastern United States until inactivated in Feb 1952. Again provided air defense in the northeastern United States, Oct 1956–Jun 1957. Non-operational, 1 Jul–18 Aug 1957. In Apr 1965 the wing activated at Eglin AFB, Fla, and embarked on a program of tactical training operations to maintain proficiency. Operated a test support division, Jul 1965–Dec 1967, and a special test squadron, Dec 1967–Apr 1971, in support of tests for weapon systems, aircraft armament and munitions, and tactical procedures of the Tactical Air Warfare Center. The wing also provided F–4 replacement training, 15 Dec 1966–28 Feb 1967. Through deployment of combat-ready tactical components, with personnel and equipment transferred to PACAF units upon arrival, the wing provided fresh aircraft and aircrews for the forces in Southeast Asia and in Korea. Entire resources of squadrons were released as follows: 40th TFS, May 1967, Nov 1968, and May 1969; 4th TFS, Jul 1967; and 16th TFS, Oct 1967 and Apr 1969. In all cases except for the 40th, in May 1969, the squadrons were immediately remanned and reequipped. The wing also transferred two of its combat-ready squadrons to PACAF, the 25th TFS in

May 1968 and the 4th TFS in Apr 1969. The wing's last combat-ready squadron, the 58th TFS, deployed to Southeast Asia for combat operations from Apr to Oct 1972 and again from Jun to Sep 1973. The wing supported the 4485th Test Squadron of the Tactical Air Warfare Center, Jan–Dec 1973, 16–18 Jun 1974, 7–11 Oct 1974, 15–18 Oct 1974, 13–17 Jan 1975, 7–11 Apr 1975, and 8 May–1 Jul 1977, in weapon systems evaluation program tests. Aircrews ferried F–4Es to Israel in Oct 1973. Effective 1 Jan 1976, the wing began augmenting air defenses in the Gulf Coast area. By mid-1977 the wing prepared for conversion to F–15 aircraft in late 1978.

Service Streamers. None.

Campaign Streamers. None.

Decorations. Air Force Outstanding Unit Awards: 1 Jan 1967–30 Jun 1968; 1 Jul 1968–30 Jun 1969.

Emblem. Azure, on a pale nebuly or, a sword point to chief inpale of the field, flammant gules, all within a bordure of the second. *Motto:* FIRE FROM THE CLOUDS. (Approved for 33d Group on 21 Feb 1942 and for 33d Wing on 5 Oct 1965.)

35th TACTICAL FIGHTER WING

Lineage. Established as 35th Fighter Wing on 10 Aug 1948. Activated on 18 Aug 1948. Redesignated 35th Fighter-Interceptor Wing on 20 Jan 1950. Inactivated on 1 Oct 1957. Redesignated 35th Tactical Fighter Wing, and activated, on 14 Mar 1966. Organized on 8 Apr 1966. Inactivated on 31 Jul 1971. Activated on 1 Oct 1971.

Assignments. 314th Air Division, 18 Aug 1948; Fifth Air Force, 1 Mar 1950; 314th Air Division, 25 May 1951; Japan Air Defense Force, 1 Mar 1952; Fifth Air Force, 1 Sep 1954; 41st Air Division, 1 Mar 1955–1 Oct 1957 (attached to 6102d Air Base Wing, 1 Jul–1 Oct 1957). Pacific Air Forces, 14 Mar 1966; Seventh Air Force, 8 Apr 1966–31 Jul 1971. Twelfth Air Force, 1 Oct 1971–.

Components. *Group.* 35th: 18 Aug 1948–1 Oct 1957 (detached c. 9 Jul–1 Dec 1950 and 7–24 May 1951; not operational, 15 Jan–14 Jul 1954; detached 14 Aug–30 Sep 1954; not operational, 8 Oct 1956–1 Oct 1957). *Squadrons.* Royal Australian Air Force, No. 2: attached c. 19 Apr 1967–4 Jun 1971. 8th Tactical Reconnaissance: attached 1 Apr–14 Aug 1950. 8th Bombardment, Tactical (later, 8th Special Operations): attached 8–18 Apr 1966, 15 Jun–15 Aug 1966, 12 Oct–12 Dec 1966, 11 Feb–12 Apr 1967, 7 Jun–2 Aug 1967, 26 Sep–21 Nov 1967; assigned 15 Jan 1968–15 Nov 1969; assigned 30 Sep 1970–31 Jul 1971 (detached c. 16–31 Jul 1971). 13th Bombardment, Tactical: attached 17 Apr–17 Jun 1966, 14 Aug–13 Oct 1966, 12 Dec 1966–11 Feb 1967, 11 Apr–8 Jun 1967, 1 Aug–26 Sep 1967, 21 Nov 1967–15 Jan 1968. 20th Tactical Fighter Training: 1 Dec 1972–. 21st Tactical Fighter Training: 1 Dec 1972–. 39th Fighter-Interceptor (later, 39th

Tactical Fighter Training): attached 8 Oct 1956–1 Jul 1957; assigned 1 Jul 1977–. 40th: attached 15 Jan–14 Jul 1954 and 8 Oct 1956–1 Jul 1957; assigned 1 Jun 1972– (not operational, 1 Jun 1972–). 41st: attached 9 Jul–1 Dec 1950 and 15 Jan–14 Jul 1954. 77th Royal Australian Air Force: attached 1 Dec 1950–6 Apr 1951. 120th: 30 Apr 1968–18 Apr 1969. 319th: attached 17 Aug–1 Oct 1954. 339th: attached 1 Jul 1949–1 Dec 1950 and 25 May 1951–20 Jul 1954. 352d: 10 Oct 1966–31 Jul 1971. 390th: 8 Apr–10 Oct 1966. 431st Tactical Fighter Training: 15 Jan 1976–. 434th Tactical Fighter (later, 434th Tactical Fighter Training): 1 Oct 1971–1 Jan 1977 (detached 12 Aug–6 Oct 1972; not operational, 11 Jan 1976–1 Jan 1977). 480th: attached 8 Apr–22 Jun 1966, assigned 23 Jun–10 Oct 1966. 561st: attached 1–14 Jul 1973, assigned 15 Jul 1973–. 562d: 31 Oct 1974– (detached 12–30 Aug 1977). 563d Tactical Fighter Training (later, 563d Tactical Fighter): 31 Jul 1975– (not operational, 1 Jul 1977–). 612th: 15 Mar–31 Jul 1971. 614th: 10 Oct 1966–31 Jul 1971. 615th: 10 Oct 1966–31 Jul 1971. 4435th Combat Crew Training: 1 Oct 1971–1 Dec 1972. 4435th Tactical Fighter Replacement: 1 Oct 1971–15 Jan 1976. 4452d Combat Crew Training: 1 Oct 1971–1 Dec 1972. *Detachment.* Det 1, 612th Tactical Fighter Squadron: attached 10 Oct 1966–8 Jan 1967 and 14 Apr 1969–15 Mar 1971.

Stations. Johnson AB, Japan, 18 Aug 1948; Yokota AB, Japan, 1 Apr 1950; Johnson AB, Japan, 14 Aug 1950; Yonpo, North Korea, 1 Dec 1950; Pusan AB, South Korea, c. 7 Dec 1950; Johnson AB, Japan, 25 May 1951; Yokota AB, Japan, 1 Oct 1954–1 Oct 1957. Da Nang AB, South Vietnam, 8 Apr 1966; Phan Rang AB, South Vietnam, 10 Oct 1966–31 Jul 1971. George AFB, Calif, 1 Oct 1971–.

Commanders. Col Edgar M. Scattergood, Jr., 18 Aug 1948; Col Ray W. Clifton, 7 Sep 1948; Col William O. Moore, 3 Feb 1949; Col Lawrence C. Coddington, 22 Aug 1949; Col Robert W. Witty, 1 Apr 1950; Col Virgil L. Zoller, 10 May 1950; Col Thomas B. Hall, 14 Aug 1950; Col Frederic C. Gray, 1 Dec 1950; Col Brooks A. Lawhon, 18 Feb 1951; Col Strother B. Hardwick, Jr., 25 May 1951; Col William A. Schulgen, 28 May 1951; Col Jack S. Jenkins, 19 Jan 1952; Col Thomas J. Barrett, 7 Jun 1952; Col Richard S. Morrison, 19 Jun 1954; Col Fred D. Stevers, 1 Oct 1954; Col Eugene B. Fletcher, 31 Jul 1955; Col James E. Johnston, 15–30 Jun 1957; unkn, 1 Jul–1 Oct 1957. None (not manned), 14 Mar–7 Apr 1966; Col Franklin H. Scott, 8 Apr 1966; Col Allan P. Rankin, 10 May 1966; Col George S. Weart, 10 Oct 1966; Col James A. Wilson, 1 Mar 1967; Col Herndon F. Williams, 1 Feb 1968; Col Frank L. Gailer, Jr., 23 Sep 1968; Brig Gen Walter Galligan, 9 Aug 1969; Col Walter C. Turnier, 10 Jun 1970; Col Cregg P. Nolan, Jr., 1 Jan–c. 31 Jul 1971. Col Fred A. Treyz, 1 Oct 1971; Col William J. Holton, 20 Jul 1972; Col Charles R. Beaver, 24 Aug 1973; Col Richard A. Haggren, 11 Jul 1975; Brig Gen Robert W. Clement, 2 Feb 1976; Brig Gen Cecil D. Crabb, 9 Aug 1976–.

Aircraft. Principally F–51, 1948–1950, 1950–1951, 1951–1953; F–61, 1949–1950; F–80, 1949–1950, 1951–1954; F–82, 1949–1950; F–94, 1951–1954; F–86, 1952–1953,

1953–1957; but also included F–86, 1951; RF–80, 1950, 1951–1952, 1953–1954; RF–51, 1952–1953; RC–45, 1952–1954; and RT–7, 1952–1953. Principally F–4, 1966; F–100, 1966–1971; and B–57, 1966–1969; but also included F–102, 1966; MK–20 (Canberra), 1967–1971; and A–37, 1970–1971. F–4, 1971–; F–105, 1973–.

Operations. Flew air defense missions in Japan, Aug 1948–Nov 1950. In Jul 1950 the wing's tactical group and two squadrons deployed to Korea for combat, but the wing (with one assigned and one attached squadron) continued flying air defense missions in Japan, as well as photographic reconnaissance of the Japanese coasts. Wing headquarters moved without personnel or equipment to South Korea on 1 Dec 1950, assuming resources of the 6150th Tactical Support Wing. Flew combat missions in Korea until 25 May 1951, then returned to Japan and resumed an air defense mission with some reconnaissance work. The tactical group was non–operational, 15 Jan–14 Jul 1954; during this time the wing directly controlled the 40th, 41st and 339th Squadrons. The group returned to operational status on 15 Jul 1954, and from 14 Aug to 30 Sep 1954 was detached from the wing. From 8 Oct 1956 the tactical group was again non-operational, and wing headquarters controlled the tactical squadrons until 1 Jul 1957, when it also became non-operational. From 1 Jul until inactivated on 1 Oct 1957, the wing was a "paper" unit, its units controlled by 41st Air Division. Organized again in Apr 1966 at Da Nang AB, South Vietnam, replacing the 7252d Tactical Fighter Wing. Controlled two F–4C squadrons, two rotational B–57 squadrons, and F–102 flights of the 64th Fighter-Interceptor Squadron, to conduct combat operations in Southeast Asia. On 1 Oct 1966 the 35th and 366th Wings moved in name only, the 35th Wing replacing the 366th Wing at Phan Rang AB, South Vietnam, and becoming an F–100 organization. The two B–57 squadrons also shifted bases, following the 35th Wing to Phan Rang. Also attached to the wing at Phan Rang was RAAF Squadron No. 2, equipped with MK–20 Canberra bombers. Another attached component, actually a *de facto* squadron, was the F–100 equipped Detachment 1, 612th TFS. On 15 Mar 1971, the 612th moved from Japan to Phan Rang in name only, replacing the detachment. Gained an A–37B squadron (8th SOS) in Sep 1970. Began phasing down for inactivation in Apr 1971, standing down from operations on 26 Jun 1971. Remaining resources passed to the 315th Tactical Airlift Wing on 31 Jul 1971 when the 35th Wing inactivated. A few months later the 35th Wing activated at George AFB, Calif, replacing the 479th Tactical Fighter Wing. Participated in tactical exercises, tests, and operations. Provided F–4 aircrew and maintenance personnel replacement training. Gained F–105 units beginning Jul 1973, in addition to F–4 units, and assumed a "Wild Weasel" (radar detection and suppression) mission with these aircraft. Began "Wild Weasel" aircrew training in F–105 and F–4 aircraft in late 1975.

Service Streamers. None.

Campaign Streamers. CCF Intervention; First UN Counteroffensive; CCF Spring Offensive; Vietnam Air; Vietnam Air Offensive; Vietnam Air Offensive, Phase II; Vietnam Air Offensive, Phase III; Vietnam Air/ Ground; Vietnam Air Offensive, Phase IV; TET 69/ Counteroffensive; Vietnam Summer–Fall, 1969; Vietnam Winter–Spring, 1970; Sanctuary Counteroffensive; Southwest Monsoon; Commando Hunt V; Commando Hunt VI.

Decorations. Presidential Unit Citation (Vietnam): 10 Oct 1966–10 Apr 1967. Air Force Outstanding Unit Awards with Combat "V" Device: 8 Apr–9 Oct 1966; 2 Apr–2 Sep 1967; 3 Sep 1967–2 May 1968; 1 Oct 1968–13 Apr 1969; 14 Apr 1969–13 Apr 1970; 1 Dec 1970–25 Jun 1971. Air Force Outstanding Unit Award: 2 Feb 1976–31 Mar 1977. Republic of Korea Presidential Unit Citation: 7 Sep 1950–7 Feb 1951. Republic of Vietnam Gallantry Crosses with Palm: 1 Apr 1966–31 Jul 1971; 1 Sep 1968–9 Oct 1970; 24 Feb–30 Mar 1971.

Emblem. Azure, a dexter cubit arm or grasping a dagger point to base gules. *Motto:* ATTACK TO DEFEND. (Approved on 24 Mar 1941 for 35th Group, and on 16 Dec 1953 for 35th Wing.)

36th TACTICAL FIGHTER WING

Lineage. Established as 36th Fighter Wing on 17 Jun 1948. Activated on 2 Jul 1948. Redesignated: 36th Fighter-Bomber Wing on 20 Jan 1950; 36th Fighter-Day Wing on 9 Aug 1954; 36th Tactical Fighter Wing on 8 Jul 1958.

Assignments: Caribbean Air Command, 2 Jul 1948 (attached to 6th Fighter Wing, 2–28 Jul 1948); United States Air Forces in Europe, 13 Aug 1948 (attached to 2d Air Division, 6–17 Sep 1949); 2d Air Division, 10 Oct 1949; Twelfth Air Force, 7 May 1951 (attached to Flight A, HQ Twelfth Air Force [Advanced Echelon], 7–20 May 1951; Twelfth Air Force [Advanced Echelon], 21 May 1951–26 Apr 1953); United States Air Forces in Europe, 1 Jan 1958 (attached to United States Air Forces in Europe [Advanced Echelon], 1 Jan 1958–14 Nov 1959); Seventeeth Air Force, 15 Nov 1959–.

Components. *Wings.* 121st Tactical Fighter: attached 12–27 May 1977. 7149th Tactical Fighter: attached 15 Apr–15 Sep 1969. *Group.* 36th: 2 Jul 1948–8 Dec 1957 (not operational, 1 Oct 1956–8 Dec 1957). *Squadrons.* 1st Pilotless Bomber (later, 1st Tactical Missile): attached 14 Mar 1955–15 Apr 1956. 7th: attached 2 Mar–4 Apr 1973; attached 3 Apr–3 May 1974; attached 4 Oct–6 Nov 1975. 9th: attached 12 Sep–6 Oct 1970; attached 4 Feb–15 Mar 1973; attached 6 Sep–7 Oct 1975. 18th Tactical Reconnaissance: attached 12–28 Apr 1977. 22d: attached 1 Oct 1956–7 Dec 1957, assigned 8 Dec 1957– (not operational, 25 Oct 1976–30 Jun 1977). 23d: attached 1 Oct 1956–7 Dec 1957, assigned 8 Dec 1957–31 Dec 1971. 32d: attached 1 Oct 1956–7 Dec 1957, assigned 8 Dec 1957–8 Apr 1960. 39th Tactical Electronic Warfare: 1 Apr

1969–31 Dec 1971. 45th Tactical Reconnaissance: attached 13 Aug 1948–25 Mar 1949. 53d: attached 1 Oct 1956–7 Dec 1957, assigned 8 Dec 1957– (not operational, 1 Feb–Jul 1977). 71st Tactical Missile: 1 Oct 1965–30 Apr 1969. 461st: attached 1 Oct 1956–7 Dec 1957, assigned 8 Dec 1957–1 Aug 1959. 525th: 1 Nov 1968– (not operational, 9 Mar–26 Apr 1977).

Stations. Howard AFB, CZ, 2–25 Jul 1948; Furstenfeldbruck (later, Furstenfeldbruck AB), West Germany, 13 Aug 1948; Bitburg AB, West Germany, 13 Dec 1952–.

Commanders: Col Henry R. Spicer, 2 Jul 1948 (additional duty); Col Malcolm N. Stewart, 13 Aug 1948; Col John C. Crosthwaite, 16 Sep 1948; Col Hubert Zemke, 2 Nov 1949; Col Thomas K. Hampton, 10 Nov 1949; Col Richard A. Legg, 3 Dec 1949; Col Robert L. Scott, Jr., 1 Mar 1951; Col Thomas B. Whitehouse, 30 May 1953; Col William H. Dick, 5 Jun 1954; Col Roy R. Brischetto, 17 Aug 1954; Col William H. Dick, 11 Jan 1955; Col John A. Brooks III, 7 Feb 1955; Brig Gen Walter B. Putnam, 21 Jul 1956; Col James D. Berry, 10 Jun 1960; Brig Gen Robert L. Delashaw, 18 Jul 1960; Col John H. Buckner, c. 11 Jun 1963; Brig Gen Gordon F. Blood, 11 Jul 1963; Col James F. Hackler, Jr., 22 Aug 1964; Col Benjamin B. Cassiday, Jr., 6 Aug 1966; Col Charles C. Pattillo, 12 May 1967; Col Joseph C. Secino, 26 Mar 1968; Col Richard G. Cross, Jr., 15 May 1968; Col Forrest L. Rauscher, 15 Jun 1969; Brig Gen Edwin W. Robertson II, 19 Nov 1969; Col Billy F. Rogers, 8 Oct 1971; Brig Gen Don H. Payne, 25 May 1972; Brig Gen Frederick C. Kyler, 31 Jul 1974–.

Aircraft and Missiles. Primarily flew F–80, 1948–1950; F–84, 1950–1953; F–86, 1953–1956; F–100, 1956–1961; F–105, 1961–1966; F–4, 1966–1977; F–102, 1968–1969; EB–66, 1969–1971; and F–15, 1977–; but also flew, in fewer numbers, B–17, 1948; B/RB–26, 1948–1949; Matador, 1955–1956, Mace, 1965–1969; RF–4, 1977; and A–7, 1977.

Operations. Wing headquarters activated in the Canal Zone, but was not manned because of pending movement to Europe. Tactically operational from mid–Aug 1948, introduced the first allied jet fighters in Europe. During the next three decades, introduced other new jet aircraft in Europe, including the F–84 in 1950, the F–86 in 1953, the F–100 in 1956, the F–105 in 1961, the F–4 in 1966, and the F–15 in 1977. Tactical operations included air defense, tactical exercises and manuvers, photographic reconnaissance (1948–1949), tactical missile operations (1955–1956 and 1965–1969), and tactical electronic warfare operations (1969–1971). Formed the Skyblazers aerial demonstration team in May 1949 and controlled it until Aug 1952, and again from Oct 1956 to Jan 1962. In addition to its primary installation (Bitburg AB, West Germany), the wing controlled Oberpfaffenhofen AB, West Germany, Dec 1949–Feb 1950, and Spangdahlem AB, West Germany, Sep 1969–Dec 1971.

Service Streamers. None.

Campaign Streamers. None.

Decorations. Air Force Outstanding Unit Awards: [1] May 1956–[1] May 1958; 1 Jan–31 Dec 1968; 1 Dec 1973–30 Apr 1975; 1 Jul 1975–30 Jun 1977.

Emblem. Or, an arrowhead point upward gules, in a chief, azure, a demiwing argent. *Motto:* PREPARED TO PREVAIL. (Emblem approved on 19 Jun 1940 for 36th Group and on 17 Jul 1952 for 36th Wing; motto approved 14 Aug 1979.)

37th TACTICAL FIGHTER WING

Lineage. Established as 37th Fighter-Bomber Wing on 3 Mar 1953. Activated on 8 Apr 1953. Inactivated on 25 Jun 1953. Redesignated 37th Tactical Fighter Wing, and activated, on 26 Oct 1966. Organized on 1 Mar 1967. Inactivated on 31 Mar 1970.

Assignments. Ninth Air Force, 8 Apr–25 Jun 1953. Pacific Air Forces, 26 Oct 1966; Seventh Air Force, 1 Mar 1967–31 Mar 1970.

Components. *Group.* 37th: 8 Apr–25 Jun 1953. *Squadrons.* 174th: 14 May 1968–11 May 1969. 355th: attached 3 Feb–4 Jul 1968, assigned 5 Jul 1968–15 May 1969. 389th: 15 Jun 1969–31 Mar 1970 (detached 15–24 Jun 1969). 416th: 15 Apr 1967–27 May 1969. 480th: 15 Apr 1969–31 Mar 1970. *Detachment.* Det 1, 612th Tactical Fighter Squadron: attached 8 Jun 1967–13 Apr 1969.

Stations. Clovis AFB, NM, 8 Apr–25 Jun 1953. Phu Cat AB, South Vietnam, 1 Mar 1967–31 Mar 1970.

Commanders. Lt Col George W. Bacon, 8 Apr 1953; Col Wallace E. Hopkins, 27 Apr 1953; Col Stephen B. Mack, 4 May–25 Jun 1953. None (not manned), 26 Oct 1966–28 Feb 1967; unkn, 1 Mar–5 May 1967; Col Raymond C. Lee, Jr., 6 May 1967; Col Edwin A. Schneider, 15 May 1967; Col Leroy J. Manor, 15 May 1968; Col Harry B. Trimble, 1 May 1969–31 Mar 1970.

Aircraft. F–100, 1967–1969; F–4, 1969–1970.

Operations. Not tactically operational, 1953. The 37th Combat Support Group was already operational at Phu Cat AB, South Vietnam, when the wing activated in 1967. Personnel for the wing headquarters and tactical components were in transit from the United States and elsewhere, and tactical operations did not commence until mid-April. Combat in Southeast Asia, 15 Apr 1967–31 Mar 1970. Flew interdiction, bombardment, escort, and close air support missions. From Jun 1967 to May 1969, also used F–100F two-place aircraft for visual and weather reconnaissance and forward air control operations.

Service Streamers. None.

Campaign Streamers. Vietnam Air Offensive; Vietnam Air Offensive, Phase II; Vietnam Air Offensive, Phase III; Vietnam Air/Ground; Vietnam Air Offensive, Phase IV; TET 69/Counteroffensive; Vietnam Summer–Fall, 1969; Vietnam Winter–Spring, 1970.

Decorations. Presidential Unit Citation (Vietnam): 1 Jul–31 Dec 1968. Air Force Outstanding Unit Awards with Combat "V" Device: 1 Apr 1967–30 Jun

1968; 1 Apr 1969–31 Mar 1970. Republic of Vietnam Gallantry Cross with Palm: 1 Mar 1967–30 Mar 1970.

Emblem. Azure, a saltire or. *Crest:* On a wreath of the colors, or and azure, a griffin sejant azure armed and winged or. *Motto:* DEFENDERS OF THE CROSSROADS. (Approved for 37th Group on 23 Jun 1941 and for 37th Wing on 4 Aug 1953.)

38th FLYING TRAINING WING

Lineage. Established as 38th Bombardment Wing, Light, on 10 Aug 1948. Activated on 18 Aug 1948. Inactivated on 1 Apr 1949. Activated on 1 Jan 1953. Redesignated: 38th Bombardment Wing, Tactical, on 1 Oct 1955; 38th Tactical Missile Wing on 18 Jun 1958. Discontinued, and inactivated, on 25 Sep 1966. Redesignated 38th Flying Training Wing on 22 Mar 1972. Activated on 1 Aug 1972. Inactivated on 30 Sep 1973. Activated on 1 Dec 1973. Inactivated on 1 Dec 1975.

Assignments. 315th Air Division, 18 Aug 1948–1 Apr 1949. Twelfth Air Force, 1 Jan 1953; United States Air Forces in Europe, 1 Jan 1958; Seventeenth Air Force, 15 Nov 1959–25 Sep 1966. Air Training Command, 1 Aug 1972–30 Sep 1973. Air Training Command, 1 Dec 1973–1 Dec 1975.

Components. *Groups.* 38th: 18 Aug 1948–1 Apr 1949; 1 Jan 1953–8 Dec 1957. 585th: 18 Jun 1958–25 Sep 1962. 586th: 18 Jun 1958–25 Sep 1962. 587th: 18 Jun 1958–25 Sep 1962. *Squadrons.* 70th: 1 Aug 1972–30 Sep 1973; 1 Dec 1973–1 Dec 1975. 71st: 8 Dec 1957–18 Jun 1958; 25 Sep 1962–1 Oct 1965; 1 Aug 1972–30 Sep 1973; 1 Dec 1973–1 Dec 1975. 89th: 25 Sep 1962–25 Sep 1966. 405th: 8 Dec 1957–18 Jun 1958; 25 Sep 1962–25 Sep 1966. 822d: 8 Dec 1957–18 Jun 1958; 25 Sep 1962–25 Sep 1966. 823d: 25 Sep 1962–25 Sep 1966. 887th: 25 Sep 1962–25 Sep 1966.

Stations. Itami Afld, Japan, 18 Aug 1948–1 Apr 1949. Laon AB, France, 1 Jan 1953; Hahn AB, West Germany, 18 Jun 1958; Sembach AB, West Germany, 20 Aug 1959–25 Sep 1966. Laredo AFB, Texas, 1 Aug 1972–30 Sep 1973. Moody AFB, Ga, 1 Dec 1973–1 Dec 1975.

Commanders. Col Preston P. Pender, 18 Aug 1948; Col Robert W. Witty, 16 Nov 1948–1 Apr 1949. Col William L. Kennedy, 1 Jan 1953; Col Albert W. Satterwhite, 4 Jul 1954; Col Wilbur W. Aring, 17 Jul 1954; Col John N. Ewbank, Jr., 20 Jul 1957; Col Theodore H. Runyon, 18 Jun 1958; Col Arthur T. Frontczak, 15 Jul 1958; Col Harry J. Sands, Jr., 21 Jul 1958; Col Arthur T. Frontczak, 16 Jun 1961; Col Rollo C. Lawrence, 6 Jun 1962; Col Linus F. Upson, Jr., 4 Aug 1963; Col Otto R. Haney, 10 Aug 1963; Col Britt S. May, 18 Jun 1965; Col Bertram A. Kibler, 5 Jul–25 Sep 1966. Col LeRoy W. Svendsen, Jr., 1 Aug 1972; Col Robert W. Bazley, 8 Nov 1972–30 Sep 1973.

Col Philip C. Gast, 1 Dec 1973; Col George T. Kertesz, 11 Apr 1975; Col Frank D. Hardee, 12 Sep–1 Dec 1975.

Aircraft and Missiles. A (later, B)–26, 1948–1949. B–26, 1953–1956; B–57, 1955–1958; Matador, 1958–1962; Mace, 1960–1966. T–37, 1972–1973; T–38, 1972–1973. T–37, 1973–1975; T–38, 1973–1975.

Operations. Assisted in the air defense of Japan and participated in tactical exercises, Aug 1948–Mar 1949. Participated in tactical operations, tests, and exercises of U.S. Air Forces in Europe with B–26 and B–57 aircraft, 1953–1958. In Jun 1958, replaced 701st Tactical Missile Wing at Hahn AB, West Germany, and became involved in tactical missile operations and training with TM–61 Matador and later with TM–76 (later, MGM–13) Mace tactical missiles. Inactivated in Sep 1966. Replaced, and absorbed resources of, the 3640th Pilot Training Wing at Laredo AFB, Texas, on 1 Aug 1972 and performed pilot training to 28 Aug 1973. Replaced, and absorbed resources of, the 3550th Pilot Training Wing at Moody AFB, Ga, on 1 Dec 1973. Performed pilot training until 21 Nov 1975. Inactivated on 1 Dec 1975 and replaced by 347th Tactical Fighter Wing.

Service Streamers. None.

Campaign Streamers. None.

Decorations. Air Force Outstanding Unit Awards: 1 Apr 1956–1 Mar 1958; 1 Apr 1959–30 Jan 1961; 1 Jun 1964–1 Jun 1966.

Emblem. Quarterly or and azure, in the first quarter on a shield dark blue, a winged sword point downward argent, the hilt and pommel charged with a torteau, a pomeis and a bezant, a fleur-de-lis fretting the blade of the first between two cloud formations of the fourth issuing from dexter and sinister base; in the second quarter a griffin segreant of the first; in the third quarter a wreath of olive branches surmounted by a torch of the last; in the fourth quarter an arrow fesswise below a winged crown jewelled with a mullet all of the third. *Motto:* VALOR WITH PROGRESS. (Approved on 11 Dec 1958.)

39th BOMBARDMENT WING, HEAVY

Lineage. Established as 39th Bombardment Wing, Heavy, and activated, on 15 Nov 1962. Organized on 1 Feb 1963. Discontinued, and inactivated, on 25 Jun 1965.

Assignments. Strategic Air Command, 15 Nov 1962; 822d Air Division, 1 Feb 1963–25 Jun 1965.

Components. *Squadron.* 62d: 1 Feb 1963–25 Jun 1965.

Stations. Eglin AFB, Fla, 1 Feb 1963–25 Jun 1965.

Commanders. None (not manned), 15 Nov 1962–31 Jan 1963; Col Earl L. Johnson, 1 Feb 1963; Col Fred W. Miller, 26 Jul 1963–25 Jun 1965.

Aircraft. B–52, 1963–1965.

Operations. Bombardment training operations to meet SAC's global commitments, 1963–1965.

Service Streamers. None.

Campaign Streamers. None.

Decorations. None.

Emblem. Or, a globe argent rimmed and grid lined sable, in sinister flaunch a lightning bolt arched point to chief gules, and fracted and rolled back per bend azure, a globe of the second, grid lined of the third between two olive branches arched of the first, the rolled back edge of the fourth, all within a diminished bordure of the second. (Approved on 6 Jan 1954.)

40th STRATEGIC AEROSPACE WING

Lineage. Established as 40th Bombardment Wing, Medium, on 9 May 1952. Activated on 28 May 1952. Redesignated 40th Strategic Aerospace Wing on 1 Feb 1964. Discontinued, and inactivated, on 1 Sep 1964.

Assignments. 802d Air Division, 28 May 1952 (attached to 310th Bombardment Wing, Medium, 6 Feb–1 May 1953; 7th Air Division, 9 Jun–9 Sep 1955 and c. 1 Jul–c. 1 Oct 1957); 21st Air Division, 20 Jun 1960–1 Sep 1964.

Components. *Squadrons.* 25th: 28 May 1952–1 Sep 1964 (not operational, 28 May 1952–c. 3 Apr 1953 and 15 Aug–1 Sep 1964). 40th Air Refueling: 8 Jul 1952–1 Jun 1960 (not operational, 8 Jul–7 Sep 1952; detached 8 Sep 1952–30 Apr 1953, 1–10 Mar 1954, 4 May–27 Jun 1954, 25 Jun–5 Sep 1956, c. 1 Jul–c. 1 Oct 1957, c. 1 Oct 1958–10 Jan 1959). 44th: 28 May 1952–1 Sep 1964 (not operational, 28 May 1952–31 May 1953 and 15 Aug–1 Sep 1964). 45th: 28 May 1952–1 Sep 1964 (not operational, 28 May 1952–30 Sep 1953 and 15 Aug–1 Sep 1964). 90th Air Refueling: 20 Jun 1960–15 Nov 1962. 548th Strategic Missile: 1 Jan–1 Sep 1964 (detached 1 Aug–1 Sep 1964). 660th: 1 Feb 1959–1 Jan 1962.

Stations. Smoky Hill (later, Schilling) AFB, Kans, 28 May 1952; Forbes AFB, Kans, 20 Jun 1960–1 Sep 1964.

Commanders. None (not manned), 28 May 1952–5 Feb 1953; Col Stanley J. Donovan, 6 Feb 1953; Col David A. Burchinal, 2 May 1953; Col Robert J. Nolan, 26 Oct 1953; Col Berton H. Burns, 11 Jun 1954; Col Charles L. Wimberly, 15 Jul 1954; Col Robert J. Nolan, 27 Jul 1954; Col Berton H. Burns, 16 Sep 1954; Col Andrew S. Low, Jr., 1 Jun 1957; Col George Y. Jumper, 4 Jul 1958; Col Woodward B. Carpenter, 7 Jul 1959; Col Norman J. McGowan, 20 Jun 1960; Col Joel A. Carroll, Jr., 8 Jul 1961–10 Aug 1964; unkn (possibly Col Joe B. Disana), 11 Aug–1 Sep 1964.

Aircraft and Missiles. B–29, 1953–1954; KC–97, 1953–1960,

1960–1962; B–47, 1954–1964; Atlas E, 1964.

Operations. Although activated in May 1952, the 40th Wing was not manned until early Feb 1953, when it gained personnel and equipment from a provisional squadron originally established at Davis-Monthan AFB, Ariz, as a holding unit for people and equipment surplus to another SAC wing. Received control and guidance from the 310th Bombardment Wing at Smoky Hill AFB, Kans, to 1 May 1953. By Oct 1953, all tactical squadrons were minimally operational. Converted from B–29s to B–47s in 1954 and became combat ready in Apr 1955. Deployed at Lakenheath RAF Station, England, 9 Jun–9 Sep 1955. Performed bombardment training and air refueling operations to meet SAC's global commitments, 1955–1964. Deployed at Greenham Common RAF Station, England, Jul–Oct 1957. Gained an Atlas missile squadron in Jan 1964. Began phasing down for inactivation shortly thereafter and was non–operational, c. 15 Aug–1 Sep 1964.

Service Streamers. None.

Campaign Streamers. None.

Decorations. None.

Emblem. A shield divided in an angular manner with the apex of angle toward the upper left, yellow and light green, and with a base of blue; on the green area a black silhouette of a modernistic aircraft with trail above a wavy circular symbol in gray, light gray and white with a yellow center bearing a red and black atom symbol; on and over the base a yellow wreath outlined in black. (Approved on 6 Jan 1954.)

42d BOMBARDMENT WING, HEAVY

Lineage. Established as 42d Bombardment Wing, Heavy, on 19 Feb 1953. Activated on 25 Feb 1953.

Assignments. Eighth Air Force, 25 Feb 1953; 45th Air Division, 8 Oct 1954 (attached to 7th Air Division, 18 Oct–18 Nov 1955); Eighth Air Force, 18 Jan 1958; 45th Air Division, 1 Dec 1958–.

Components. *Squadrons.* 42d Air Refueling: 18 Jan 1955–. 69th: 25 Feb 1953– (not operational, 25 Feb–c. 31 Mar 1953). 70th: 25 Feb 1953–25 Jun 1966 (not operational, 25 Feb–21 May 1953 and c. Jun–2 Nov 1959). 75th: 25 Feb 1953–15 Oct 1959 (not operational, 25 Feb–c. 31 Jul 1953 and c. Jun–15 Oct 1959). 407th Air Refueling: 2 Jul 1968–.

Stations. Limestone (later, Loring) AFB, Maine, 25 Feb 1953–.

Commanders. None (not manned), 25 Feb 1953; Col Frederick B. Ramputi, 26 Feb 1953; Col Bertram C. Harrison, 4 Apr 1953; Col William B. Campbell, 28 Feb 1954; Brig Gen Bertram C. Harrison, (by 16) Mar 1954; Col Jerome Tartar, 8 Oct 1954; Col Don W. Bailey, 4 May 1956; Col Woodrow P. Swancutt, 14 May 1956; Col Donald E. Hillman, 1 Jun 1956; Brig Gen William K. Martin, 18 Jan 1958; Col Don W. Bailey, 11 Jun 1958; Col Selmon W. Wells, 23 Jun 1958; Col John W. Gaff, Jr., 24 Nov 1958; Col Walter V. Gresham, Jr., 25 May 1960; Col William H. Reddell, 31 May 1960; Col Robert J. Nolan, 25 Jul 1963; Col Clifton Pyle, 10 Jul 1964; Col William M. Shy, 11 Jul 1966; Col Eugene L. Hudson, 13 Jul 1968; Col James E. Maxwell, 17 Apr 1970; Col John R. Kelly, Jr., 12 Jan 1971; Col Robert J. Bogan, 13 Feb 1972; Col James H. McGrath, 23 Mar 1972; Col Ruger W. Winchester, 9 Jun 1972; Col James H. McGrath, 8 Dec 1972; Col Grady L. Friday, Jr., 13 Oct 1973; Col Robert E. Chapman, 12 Sep 1974; Col Larry S. DeVall, 15 Nov 1975–.

Aircraft. B–36, 1953–1956; KC–97, 1955–1957; B–52, 1956–; KC–135, 1957–.

Operations. When formed "from scratch" in early 1953, the wing had few resources and used personnel loaned on temporary duty from Carswell AFB, Texas, some of whom formed a cadre to train new personnel. Of three bombardment squadrons, only the 69th could be manned. Operational training began in Apr for this unit. The 70th Bombardment Squadron began manning in May and commenced flying in Jul. In Aug 1953, the 75th Bombardment Squadron became operational. A portion of the wing deployed at Upper Heyford and Burtonwood, England, 15–23 Sep 1954, and the entire wing deployed at Upper Heyford, 18 Oct–18 Nov 1955. Gained an air refueling squadron in 1955 and lost one bombardment squadron in 1959, just before deploying entire air echelon to Ramey AFB, PR, for 3 months. Converted from B–36 to B–52 bombers in 1956. Lost another bombardment squadron in 1966, and gained a second air refueling squadron in 1968. Supported SAC's bombardment and air refueling operations in Southeast Asia from the mid-1960s to mid-1975 furnishing aircraft and aircrews, and at times, support personnel to other units.

Service Streamers. None.

Campaign Streamers. None.

Decorations. None.

Emblem. Azure, on a bend engrailed or, four annulets gules, between two aerial bombs palewise of the second, all within a diminutive bordure of the last. *Motto:* AETHERA NOBIS—The skies for us. (Approved for 42d Group on 11 Mar 1942 and for 42d Wing on 16 Apr 1954.)

43d STRATEGIC WING

Lineage. Established as 43d Bombardment Wing, Very Heavy, on 3 Nov 1947. Organized on 17 Nov 1947. Discontinued on 1 Aug 1948. Redesignated 43d Bombardment Wing, Medium, and activated on 1 Aug 1948. Inactivated on 31 Jan 1970. Redesignated 43d Strategic

Wing on 4 Feb 1970. Activated on 1 Apr 1970.

Assignments. Eighth Air Force, 17 Nov 1947–1 Aug 1948. Eighth Air Force, 1 Aug 1948; Fifteenth Air Force, 1 Apr 1950; 36th Air Division, 4 Sep 1951 (attached to 7th Air Division, c. 10 Mar–5 Jun 1953 and 5 Sep–10 Dec 1954; 3d Air Division, 1 Jul–1 Oct 1957); 19th Air Division, 15 Mar 1960 (attached to 825th Strategic Aerospace Division, 19–31 Aug 1964); 825th Strategic Aerospace Division, 1 Sep 1964; 42d Air Division, 1–31 Jan 1970. Eighth Air Force, 1 Apr 1970 (attached to Air Division Provisional, 57th, 1 Jun 1972–14 Nov 1973); 3d Air Division, 1 Jan 1975–.

Components. *Wing*. 2d Bombardment: attached 17 Nov 1947–1 Aug 1948 (not operational) and 1 Aug–31 Dec 1948 (not operational). *Groups*. 2d: attached 17 Nov 1947–1 Aug 1948, 1–10 Aug 1948, and 9 Nov–31 Dec 1948. 43d: 17 Nov 1947–1 Aug 1948; 1 Aug 1948–16 Jun 1952 (detached 16 Aug–16 Nov 1949; not operational, 10 Feb 1951–16 Jun 1952). 459th: attached 27 Jun 1949–16 Jun 1951. *Squadrons*. 2d Air Refueling: attached c. 30 Apr 1949–16 Sep 1950 (not operational, 30 Apr–30 Jun 1949; further attached to 43d Bombardment Group, 1 Jul 1949–16 Sep 1950). 9th Air Refueling: attached 1 Aug 1951–15 Jan 1952 and 6 Oct–14 Nov 1952. 43d Air Refueling: attached 10 Feb 1951–15 Jun 1952, assigned 16 Jun 1952–15 Mar 1960 (detached 18 Oct–28 Dec 1955). 60th: 1 Jul 1971– (not operational, 1 Jul 1971–c. Feb 1972). 63d: attached 10 Feb 1951–15 Jun 1952, assigned 16 Jun 1952–31 Jan 1970. Bombardment Squadron Provisional, 63d: attached 15 Jun 1972–30 Jun 1975 (not operational, c. Nov 1973–30 Jun 1975). 64th: attached 10 Feb 1951–15 Jun 1952, assigned 16 Jun 1952–31 Jan 1970 (not operational, 15 Mar–Aug 1960). 65th: attached 10 Feb 1951–15 Jun 1952, assigned 16 Jun 1952–31 Jan 1970 (not operational, 15 Mar–Aug 1960). 70th Air Refueling: attached 19–31 Aug 1964, assigned 1 Sep 1964–1 Jan 1970. 307th Air Refueling: attached 16 Sep 1950–1 Aug 1951 (further attached to 43d Bombardment Group, 16 Sep 1950–9 Feb 1951). 403d: 1 Dec 1958–15 Mar 1960; 15 May 1960–1 Jan 1961 (not operational). 4182d: 1 Apr 1970–1 Jan 1971 (not operational).

Stations. Davis–Monthan Field (later, AFB), Ariz, 17 Nov 1947–1 Aug 1948. Davis-Monthan AFB, Ariz, 1 Aug 1948; Carswell AFB, Texas, 15 Mar 1960; Little Rock AFB, Ark, 1 Sep 1964–31 Jan 1970. Andersen AFB, Guam, 1 Apr 1970–.

Commanders. Col James C. Selser, Jr., 17 Nov 1947–1 Aug 1948. Col James C. Selser, Jr., 1 Aug 1948; Col Lawrence M. Thomas, 15 Aug 1949; Col James C. Selser, Jr., 15 Sep 1949; Col William P. Fisher, 7 Jan 1950; Col Lawrence M. Thomas, 29 Aug 1950; Col William P. Fisher, c. 28 Sep 1950; Col John S. Hardy, 4 Sep 1951; Col Delmore P. Wood, Oct 1951; Col John K. Hester, (by 16) Oct 1951; Col Delmore P. Wood, (by 9) Nov 1951; Col John S. Hardy, (by 15) Nov 1951; Col Nils O. Ohman, 6 Sep 1952; Col Joseph D. White, 30 Aug 1953; Col Sam J. Byerley, Oct 1953; Brig Gen Nils O. Ohman, 30 Oct 1953; Col Jean B. Miller, Jr., 6 Nov 1953; Col David A. Burchinal, 4 Jan 1954; Col Jack J. Catton, 26 Jul 1955; Col Louis M. Sowers, (by

30) Apr 1956; Col Jack J. Catton, c. 2 Jun 1956; Col Louis M. Sowers, 8 Jun 1956; Col Roger M. Crow, 6 Jul 1956; Col Herbert I. Shingler, Jr., 1 Jul 1958; Col Thomas G. Netcher, 2 Apr 1959; Col Jean B. Miller, Jr., 13 Apr 1959; Col Reuben A. Baxter, 27 Feb 1960; Col James K. Johnson, 15 Mar 1960; Brig Gen Everett W. Holstrom, 19 Jun 1961; Col Howard J. Fry, 19 Aug 1964; Col Frank L. Voightmann, 1 Jul 1966; Col Hugh B. Robertson, Jr., 24 Jul 1967; Col Sherwin G. Desens, 12 Jul 1968; Col Roy L. Harris, Jr., 8–31 Jan 1970. Col Lawrence E. Stephens, 1 Apr 1970; Col Glen R. Dunlap, 1 Jul 1970; Col William P. Armstrong, 28 Apr 1972; Col James H. McGrath, 15 Jun 1972; Col James R. McCarthy, 1 Dec 1972; Col Morris E. Shiver, 25 May 1973; Col Lawton W. Magee, 25 Aug 1973; Col James R. McCarthy, 9 Nov 1973; Col Andrew Pringle, Jr., 15 Jun 1974; Col Donald C. Bass, 14 Jun 1975; Col David L. Patton, 27 Mar 1976; Col William F. Moses, Jr., 27 Jun 1977–.

Aircraft. B–29, 1947–1948; B–50, 1948. B–29, 1948–1950; B–50, 1948–1954; KB–29, 1949–1953; KC–97, 1953–1955, 1955–1960; B–47, 1954–1960; YRB–58, 1960; B/TB–58, 1960–1970; TF–102, 1960–1962; KC–135, 1964–1970. Primarily B–52, 1970–; and KC–135, 1970–1972, 1973–; but also flew (on logistical support missions) C–97, 1970–1972; and C–118, 1973–1974.

Operations. Strategic bombardment training, 1947–1948 and 1948–1960, and air refueling, 1949–1960, to meet SAC's global commitments. Wing personnel established flight records, flying two B–29s around the world in 1948 in 15 days, flying the B–50 *Lucky Lady II* nonstop around the world in 94 hours and 40 seconds in 1949, and setting a jet endurance record in 1954 by keeping a B–47 airborne for 47:35 hours. Converted to B–58 aircraft in 1960. From Mar 1960 to Jul 1961 flew YRB–58, TB–58, B–58, and TF–102 aircraft during Category II and III evaluations of the new supersonic bomber, while at the same time operating a combat crew training school to train SAC aircrews in the B–58 weapons system. Continued B–58 evaluations to Jul 1962, and from then until late 1969 served as one of two SAC B–58 wings with a strategic bombardment mission. Also controlled an air refueling squadron from Aug 1964 until inactivated in 1970. During the 1960s the wing continued to establish flight records. On 12 Jan 1961, wing personnel flew a B–58 over a 2,000 kilometer course at an average speed of 1,061.68 mph, and over a 1,000 kilometer course at an average speed of 1,200.194 mph. Two days later, another wing B–58 averaged 1,284.73 mph over a 1,000 kilometer course. In May 1961, a wing B–58 flew a closed course of 669.438 miles at 1,302.048 mph. That same month, another wing B–58 flew from New York City to Paris, France, in 3 hours, 14 minutes, and 44:53 seconds, establishing a new transatlantic speed record of 1,089.36 mph. During a race in 1962, a wing B–58 flew from Los Angeles to New York City at an average speed of 1,214.65 mph, from New York City to Los Angeles at an average speed of 1,081.8 mph, and from Los Angeles to New York City and back in 4 hours, 41 minutes, and 14.91 seconds. The 43d inactivated in Jan 1970, but activated again in Apr 1970, replacing the 3960th Strategic Wing at Andersen AFB, Guam. On 1 Jul 1970, the 43d also assumed tasks formerly handled by the Bombardment Wing Provisional, 4133d, assuming a combat role at this time. Employed attached aircraft and aircrews of other SAC units to participate in SAC's "Arc Light" combat mission in Southeast Asia from 1 Jul to mid-Aug 1970, and again from Feb 1972 to Aug 1973. Following the end of combat operations, provided routine training and ground alert with B–52 and KC–135 aircraft, the latter provided by other SAC units on loan. During 1975, provided logistical and medical support to thousands of Vietnam refugees evacuated from their homeland and located temporarily at Guam awaiting resettlement.

Service Streamers. None.

Campaign Streamers. Southwest Monsoon; Commando Hunt VII; Vietnam Ceasefire.

Decorations. Air Force Outstanding Unit Awards with Combat "V" Device: 1 Apr 1972–28 Jan 1973; 29 Jan–15 Nov 1973. Air Force Outstanding Unit Awards: 1 Aug 1960–1 Aug 1962; 1 May 1975–30 Apr 1977. Republic of Vietnam Gallantry Cross with Palm: 1 Apr 1970–28 Jan 1973.

Emblem. Per fess nebuly or and azure, a drop bomb counterchanged. *Motto:* WILLING, ABLE, READY. (Approved for 43d Group on 31 Jan 1942 and for 43d Wing on 14 May 1968.)

44th STRATEGIC MISSILE WING (ICBM–MINUTEMAN)

Lineage. Established as 44th Bombardment Wing, Medium, on 20 Dec 1950. Activated on 2 Jan 1951. Discontinued on 15 Jun 1960. Redesignated 44th Strategic Missile Wing (ICBM–Minuteman) on 24 Nov 1961. Organized on 1 Jan 1962.

Assignments. Fifteenth Air Force, 2 Jan 1951; 12th Air Division, 10 Feb 1951; 21st Air Division, 4 Aug 1951; 806th Air Division, 16 Jun 1952–15 Jun 1960 (attached to 5th Air Division, 19 Jan–22 Feb 1953 and 19 Apr–17 Jun 1954); Department of the Air Force, 15 Jun 1960–23 Nov 1961; Strategic Air Command, 24 Nov 1961; 821st Air (later, 821st Strategic Aerospace) Division, 1 Jan 1962; 4th Strategic Missile (later, 4th Air) Division, 30 Jun 1971–.

Components. *Group.* 44th: 2 Jan 1951–16 Jun 1952 (not operational, 10 Feb 1951–16 Jun 1952). *Squadrons.* 44th Air Refueling: 20 Apr 1953–1 Jun 1960 (not operational, 20 Apr– c. 15 May 1953; detached 27 Jun–11 Oct 1957). 66th: attached 10 Feb 1951–15 Jun 1952 (not operational, 10 Feb–c. 5 Mar 1951), assigned 16 Jun 1952–15 Jun 1960; assigned 1 Jul 1962– (not operational, 1 Jul 1962–c. Feb 1963). 67th: attached 10 Feb 1951–15 Jun 1952 (not operational, 10–22 Feb 1951), assigned 16 Jun 1952–15 Jun 1960; assigned 1

Aug 1962– (not operational, 1 Aug 1962–c. Feb 1963). 68th: attached 10 Feb 1951–15 Jun 1952 (not operational, 10 Feb–c. 27 Mar 1951), assigned 16 Jun 1952–15 Jun 1960; assigned 1 Sep 1962– (not operational, 1 Sep 1962–c. Feb 1963). 506th: 1 Dec 1958–15 Jun 1960. 850th: 1 Jan 1962–25 Mar 1965 (not operational, 15 Feb–25 Mar 1965).

Stations. March AFB, Calif, 2 Jan 1951; Lake Charles (later, Chennault) AFB, La, 1 Aug 1951–15 Jun 1960. Ellsworth AFB, SD, 1 Jan 1962–.

Commanders. Col Howell M. Estes, Jr., 2 Jan 1951; Col Carlos J. Cochrane, 7 Mar 1951; Col Herbert O. Wangeman, 1 Apr 1953; Col Frank W. Ellis, 2 May 1953; Col Joel A. Carroll, Jr., 14 May 1953; Col Frank W. Ellis, 3 Aug 1953; Col Jacob J. Brogger, 1 Feb 1956; Col Robert M. Tuttle, 27 Jul 1957; Col Louis W. Rohr, 25 Jul 1958–15 Jun 1960; none (not manned), 16 Jun 1960–31 Dec 1961; Col Virgil M. Cloyd, Jr., 1 Jan 1962; Col Wilson E. Burrill, 15 Jul 1965; Col Ernest B. Wilson, 1 Feb 1967; Col Charles J. Adams, 15 Aug 1969; Col Ralph H. Dowell, Jr., 31 Jan 1970; Col Thaddeus P. J. Gicewicz, 12 Feb 1971; Col Miles C. Wiley, Jr., 2 Jul 1971; Col George F. Bennett, 9 Jun 1972; Brig Gen Kermit C. Kaericher, 27 Jun 1973; Col William H. Bush, 24 Oct 1973; Col Judson C. Faurer, 20 Jun 1975; Col Ralph E. Spraker, 9 Jun 1977–.

Aircraft and Missiles. TB–29, 1951; B–29, 1951–1953; B–47, 1953–1960; KC–97, 1953–1957, 1957–1960. Titan I, 1962–1965; Minuteman I, 1963–1973; Minuteman II, 1972–.

Operations. Activated in training status when Korean war was 6 months old. Depended on 22d Bombardment Wing for initial cadre and help in becoming organized. Commenced operational training in Mar 1951. From 1 Oct 1951 to 29 Aug 1952, served as operational training unit for B–29 aircrews and maintenance personnel for Far East Air Forces. From 10 Oct 1951 to 15 May 1952, trained all elements of the 68th Strategic Reconnaissance Wing. Became a first-line strategic bombardment wing in Aug 1952 and gained an air refueling mission in 1953. Deployed at Sidi Slimane AB, French Morocco, 19 Jan–22 Feb 1953 and 19 Apr–17 Jun 1954. Discontinued in 1960. Organized in 1962 as a strategic missile wing, initially with a single Titan missile squadron, but later with three Minuteman missile squadrons.

Service Streamers. None.

Campaign Streamers. None.

Decorations. Air Force Outstanding Unit Awards: 1 Jul 1969–30 Jun 1970; 9 Jun–10 Jul 1972; 1 Jul 1974–30 Jun 1976.

Emblem. Azure, a missile palewise nose to base or, the warhead encircled by three electronic orbits argent, between eight mullets palewise, four in dexter flank and four in sinister flank of the last, all within a diminished bordure of the second. *Motto:* AGGRESSOR BEWARE. (Approved on 18 Jul 1962.)

46th AEROSPACE DEFENSE WING

Lineage. Established as 46th Aerospace Defense Wing on 10 Feb 1975. Activated on 15 Mar 1975.

Assignments. Aerospace Defense Command, 15 Mar 1975–.

Components. *Squadron.* 46th Flying Training: 15 Mar 1975–.

Stations. Peterson Field (later, AFB), Colo, 15 Mar 1975–.

Commanders. Col Donald J. Parsons, 15 Mar 1975; Col Edward L. Ellis, 12 Aug 1976; Col Alfred H. Uhalt, Jr., 2 Mar 1977–.

Aircraft. C–118, 1975; C–131, 1975; T–29, 1975; T–33, 1975–; T–37, 1975–; T–39, 1975; U–4, 1975–.

Operations. Replaced 4600th Air Base Wing in Mar 1975, taking over the mission of administering facilities of North American Air Defense Command (NORAD), Aerospace Defense Command (ADC), and Army Air Defense Command (ARADCOM) located on Ent AFB, Peterson Field (later, AFB), and Cheyenne Mountain Complex, all located in Colo, plus various other nearby off-base facilities. Although the provision of administrative and logistical support was the wing's primary mission, its flying training squadron served NORAD and ADC mission requirements and provided flying training for cadets of the USAF Academy.

Service Streamers. None.

Campaign Streamers. None.

Decorations. Air Force Outstanding Unit Award: 1 Jul 1975–30 Jun 1977.

Emblem. Azure, a foot embattled arraswise golden brown detailed or, issuant therefrom bendwise arched the jet trails of three stylized rockets of the third detailed dark blue and argent between, fesswise, issuant from sinister to dexter honor point a stylized aircraft with contrail of the last detailed of the fourth, and a similar charge from sinister nombril to dexter nombril flank, in sinister chief a mullet of the fifth shaded of the fourth, all within a diminished bordure of the third. *Motto:* SUPPORT. (Approved for 4600th ABW on 13 Jul 1961; used by 46th ADW since 15 Mar 1975 without official approval.)

47th FLYING TRAINING WING

Lineage. Established as 47th Bombardment Wing, Light, on 28 Jul 1947. Organized on 15 Aug 1947. Discontinued on 24 Aug 1948. Activated on 22 Aug 1948. Inactivated on 2 Oct 1949. Activated on 12 Mar 1951. Redesignated 47th Bombardment Wing, Tactical, on 1 Oct 1955. Discontinued, and inactivated, on 22 Jun 1962. Redesignated 47th Flying Training Wing on 22 Mar 1972. Activated on 1 Sep 1972.

Assignments. Twelfth Air Force, 15 Aug 1947–24 Aug 1948. Twelfth Air Force, 22 Aug 1948–2 Oct 1949. Tactical Air Command, 12 Mar 1951 (attached to 49th Air Division, Operational, 12 Feb 1952–); Third Air Force, 5 Jun 1952 (remained attached to 49th Air Division, Operational, to 1 Jul 1956); Seventeenth Air Force, 1 Jul 1961–22 Jun 1962. Air Training Command, 1 Sep 1972–.

Components. *Wing*. 392d: attached 27 Jun–2 Oct 1949. *Groups*. 47th: 15 Aug 1947–24 Aug 1948; 22 Aug 1948–2 Oct 1949; 12 Mar 1951–8 Feb 1955 (not operational, 17 Nov 1952–8 Feb 1955). 4400th Combat Crew Training: attached 12 Mar 1951–12 Feb 1952. *Squadrons*. 19th Tactical Reconnaissance: attached 7 May 1954–1 Dec 1956. 84th: attached 17 Nov 1952–7 Feb 1955, assigned 8 Feb 1955–22 Jun 1962. 85th: attached 17 Nov 1952–7 Feb 1955, assigned 8 Feb 1955–22 Jun 1962; assigned 1 Sep 1972–. 86th: attached 23 Mar 1954–7 Feb 1955, assigned 8 Feb 1955–22 Jun 1962; assigned 1 Sep 1972–. 422d: attached 20 Dec 1953–23 Mar 1954. 420th Air Refueling: attached 15 Mar 1960–7 Nov 1961, assigned 8 Nov 1961–22 Jun 1962.

Stations. Biggs Field (later, AFB), Texas, 15 Aug 1947–24 Aug 1948. Biggs AFB, Texas, 22 Aug 1948; Barksdale AFB, La, 19 Nov 1948–2 Oct 1949. Langley AFB, Va, 12 Mar 1951–21 May 1952; Sculthorpe RAF Station (later, RAF Sculthorpe), England, 1 Jun 1952–22 Jun 1962. Laughlin AFB, Texas, 1 Sep 1972–.

Commanders. Col William M. Prince, 15 Aug 1947; Col Newton Longfellow, Sep 1947–24 Aug 1948. Col Newton Longfellow, 22 Aug 1948; Col Willis F. Chapman, 19 Nov 1948–2 Oct 1949. Col Willis F. Chapman, 12 Mar 1951; Col Charles D. Jones, 1 Aug 1951; Col David M. Jones, 12 Feb 1952; Col John G. Glover, 16 Jun 1955; Brig Gen Joseph R. Holzapple, 30 Jun 1955; Col John G. Glover, Oct 1956; Col Reginald J. Clizbe, 29 Jun 1958; Col Kenneth C. Dempster, 19 Jun 1959; Col George H. Kneen, Jr., 1 Dec 1961–22 Jun 1962. Col Charles E. Woods, 1 Sep 1972; Col Harry Falls, Jr., 8 Jun 1973; Col Lawrence D. Garrison, 8 Jul 1975; Col Ralf M. Miller, 16 Aug 1977–.

Aircraft. A (later, B)–26, 1947–1948. B–26, 1948–1949; B–45, 1949. B–45, 1951–1958; B–26, 1951–1952; RB–45, 1954–1956; B–66, 1958–1962; KB–50, 1960–1962. T–41, 1972–1973; T–37, 1972–; T–38, 1972–.

Operations. Trained in night tactical operations, conducted firepower demonstrations, and participated in tactical exercises, 1947–1948 and 1948–1949. Trained in light bombardment operations, becoming proficient with nuclear weapons, 1951–1952. Provided combat crew training in B–26 aircraft and operated USAF Air Crew School (Light Bombardment and Tactical Reconnaissance, Night Photographic), May 1951–Feb 1952. Moved to England in mid-1952, and, for the next decade, performed tactical training operations, including participation in exercises and firepower demonstrations in support of NATO. Converted from B–45 to B–66 aircraft in 1958. Also performed air refueling with KB–50s, 1960–1962. Replaced, and absorbed resources of, the

3646th Pilot Training Wing at Laughlin AFB, Texas, on 1 Sep 1972 and conducted undergraduate pilot training for USAF, Air Force Reserve, and friendly foreign nation air forces.

Service Streamers. None.

Campaign Streamers. None.

Decorations. Air Force Outstanding Unit Awards: 1 Jul 1958–30 Jun 1960; 1 Jan–31 Dec 1973; 1 Jan 1976–28 Feb 1977.

Emblem. Per bend azure and light blue, a lightning bolt bendwise throughout argent between in sinister chief a stylized wing or and in dexter base on olive branch vert, within a diminished bordure of the fourth. (Approved on 2 Jan 1973.)

48th TACTICAL FIGHTER WING

Lineage. Established as 48th Fighter-Bomber Wing on 25 Jun 1952. Activated on 10 Jul 1952. Redesignated 48th Tactical Fighter Wing on 8 Jul 1958.

Assignments. Twelfth Air Force, 10 Jul 1952; United States Air Forces in Europe, 1 Jan 1958; Third Air Force, 1 Oct 1959; United States Air Forces in Europe, 12 Oct 1959; Seventeenth Air Force, 15 Nov 1959; Third Air Force, 15 Jan 1960; Seventeenth Air Force, 1 Jul 1961; Third Air Force, 1 Sep 1963–.

Components. *Group.* 48th: 10 Jul 1952–8 Dec 1957 (not operational, 15 Mar–8 Dec 1957). *Squadrons.* 492d: attached 15 Mar–7 Dec 1957, assigned 8 Dec 1957– (not operational, 1 Oct 1971–31 Jan 1972 and 22 Apr–c. 1 Jul 1977). 493d: attached 15 Mar–7 Dec 1957, assigned 8 Dec 1957– (not operational, 1 Dec 1971–c. Apr 1972 and 22 Apr–28 Jun 1977). 494th: attached 15 Mar–7 Dec 1957, assigned 8 Dec 1957– (not operational, 1 Feb 1972–c. 25 Jul 1974 and 22 Apr–31 May 1977). 495th: 1 Apr 1977– (not operational, 1 Apr–c. 29 Jul 1977). 509th: attached 5 Oct 1957–15 Jan 1958.

Stations. Chaumont AB, France, 10 Jun 1952; RAF Lakenheath, England, 15 Jan 1960–.

Commanders. Col Joseph H. Moore, 10 Jul 1952; Col Chesley G. Peterson, 27 May 1953; Col William L. Leverette, 1 Jun 1955; Brig Gen Albert P. Clark, Jr., 1 Aug 1955; Col Stanton T. Smith, Jr., Dec 1956; Col Edward F. Roddy, 24 Jun 1959; Col Victor E. Warford, 4 Aug 1959; Col Emmett S. Davis, 1 May 1961; Col Robert L. Petit, 6 Jun 1962; Col Allen P. Rankin, 1 Jun 1964; Col Ross L. Blachly, 3 Aug 1964; Col Edward B. Burdett, 14 Jul 1965; Col Cullen A. Brannon, Jr., 7 Jun 1967; Col Henry W. Brown, 2 Jun 1969; Col Frank L. Gailer, Jr., 19 Sep 1969; Col William T. Whisner, 1 Feb 1970; Col Don D. Pittman, 29 Mar 1971; Col John R. Paulk, 21 May 1973; Col Richard H. Head, 18 Apr 1974; Col Robert E. Messerli, 17 Jun 1975–.

Aircraft. F–84, 1952–1954; F–86, 1953–1956; F–100, 1956–1972; F–4, 1972–1977; F–111, 1977–.

Operations. Served as one of USAFE's fighter-bomber (later, tactical fighter) wings with a commitment to NATO. Operated a special aerobatic team, the "Sky Blazers," c. Jun–Nov 1953 and Jul 1954–Oct 1956. Equipped with very few aircraft, Feb 1972–Jul 1974. Converted to F–111F aircraft in 1977.

Service Streamers. None.

Campaign Streamers. None.

Decorations. Air Force Outstanding Unit Awards: 1 Jul 1961–29 Feb 1964; 1 Jul 1966–30 Jun 1968.

Emblem. Azure, an orle of mullets 13 visible argent, and issuant from sinister base throughout the head and arm of the Statue of Liberty vert, all within a diminished bordure of the second charged with a bordure gules. *Motto:* STATUE DE LA LIBERTE—The Statue of Liberty. (Approved on 5 Jul 1962.)

49th TACTICAL FIGHTER WING

Lineage. Established as 49th Fighter Wing on 10 Aug 1948. Activated on 18 Aug 1948. Redesignated: 49th Fighter-Bomber Wing on 1 Feb 1950; 49th Tactical Fighter Wing on 8 Jul 1958.

Assignments. 314th Air Division, 18 Aug 1948; Fifth Air Force, 1 Mar 1950 (attached to 58th Fighter-Bomber Wing, 16–31 Mar 1953); Japan Air Defense Force, 1 Apr 1953 (attached to Fifth Air Force, 1 Apr–7 Nov 1953; 39th Air Division [Defense], 7 Nov 1953–); Fifth Air Force, 1 Sep 1954 (remained attached to 39th Air Division [Defense] to 1 Mar 1955); 39th Air Division (Defense) (later, 39th Air Division), 1 Mar 1955; Fifth Air Force, 15 Apr–10 Dec 1957; United States Air Forces in Europe, 10 Dec 1957; Seventeenth Air Force, 15 Nov 1969; 832d Air Division, 1 Jul 1968 (attached to Seventeenth Air Force, 15 Jan–4 Apr 1969); 835th Air Division, 1 Feb 1970 (attached to Seventeenth Air Force, 14 Sep–7 Oct 1970); Twelfth Air Force, 30 Jun 1971 (attached to Thirteenth Air Force, 5 May–2 Oct 1972); Tactical Training, Holloman, 1 Aug 1977–.

Components. *Groups*. 49th: 18 Aug 1948–10 Dec 1957 (detached 9 Jul–30 Nov 1950, 16–31 Mar 1953, 2 Nov 1953–15 Apr 1957; not operational, 15 Apr–10 Dec 1957). 543d Tactical Support: attached 1 Dec 1950–26 Jan 1951. *Battalions*. 76th Anti-Aircraft Artillery Automatic Weapons: attached 5–c. 25 Jan 1951. 753d Anti-Aircraft Artillery Gun: attached c. Sep–c. Nov 1950. 865th Anti-Aircraft Artillery Automatic Weapons: attached c. Sep–c. 30 Nov 1950. *Squadrons*. 4th Fighter-Interceptor: attached 10 Aug 1954–15 Apr 1957. 7th: attached 9 Jul–17 Aug 1950 and 7 Aug 1956–15 Apr 1957; assigned 10 Dec 1957– (detached 10 Sep–6 Oct 1971, 2 Mar–4 Apr 1973, 2 Apr–3 May 1974, 4 Oct–6 Nov 1975, 23 Aug–25 Sep 1976). 8th: attached 15 Apr–15 Oct 1957; assigned 10 Dec 1957– (detached

c. 12 Sep–c. 11 Oct 1970, 10 Sep–6 Oct 1971, 3 Mar–5 Apr 1973, 5 Sep–6 Oct 1975, 21 Sep–20 Oct 1976, 22 Aug–22 Sep 1977). 9th: attached 17 Aug– c. 6 Sep 1950 and 15 Apr–9 Dec 1957, assigned 10 Dec 1957– (detached c. 12 Sep–c. 11 Oct 1970, 9 Sep–7 Oct 1971, 4 Feb–15 Mar 1973, 6 Sep–7 Oct 1975, 22 Sep–21 Oct 1977, 10 Sep–10 Oct 1977). 39th Fighter-Interceptor: attached 14–20 Jul 1954. 45th Tactical Reconnaissance: attached 27 Dec 1950–24 Feb 1951. 334th Fighter-Interceptor: attached 24 Feb–1 Mar 1951. 336th Fighter-Interceptor (later, 336th Fighter-Bomber; 336th Fighter-Day): attached 18 Nov 1954–6 Aug 1956. 339th Fighter-Interceptor: attached 20 Jul–18 Nov 1954. 356th: attached 12 Oct–9 Nov 1959. 417th: 15 Nov 1970–30 Apr 1977 (detached 9 Sep–2 Oct 1971, 3 Feb–14 Mar 1973, 5 Mar–5 Apr 1974, 3 Oct–5 Nov 1975, 24 Aug–26 Sep 1976; not operational, 1–30 Apr 1977). 421st Air Refueling: 15 Feb 1954–1 Oct 1957 (detached). 434th: attached 12 Aug–6 Oct 1972. 465th Tactical Fighter Training: 1 Aug 1973–1 Jan 1977. 4449th: 12 Jul–10 Oct 1972. *Batteries*. Battery A, 76th AAA Automatic Weapons Battalion: attached 1–25 Jan 1951. Battery A, 933d AAA Automatic Weapons Battalion: attached 18 Dec 1950–5 Jan 1951. *Flights*. Unnumbered (of 41st Fighter-Interceptor Squadron): attached 6 Sep–30 Nov 1950. Unnumbered (of 339th Fighter-All Weather Squadron): attached c. Oct–c. 30 Nov 1950. 6113th Air Weather: 18 Aug 1948–26 Jan 1949, attached 27 Jan–10 Apr 1949.

Stations. Misawa AB, Japan, 18 Aug 1948; Taegu AB, South Korea, 1 Dec 1950; Tsuki AB, Japan, 26 Jan 1951; Taegu AB, South Korea, 24 Feb 1951; Kunsan AB, South Korea, 1 Apr 1953; Misawa AB, Japan, 7 Nov 1953–10 Dec 1957; Etain/Rouvres (later, Etain) AB, France, 10 Dec 1957 (operated from Chalons–Vatry AB, France, 1 Sep–30 Nov 1958); Spangdahlem AB, West Germany, 25 Aug 1959–30 Jun 1968; Holloman AFB, NM, 1 Jul 1968–.

Commanders. Col Brooks A. Lawhon, 18 Aug 1948; Col Jack S. Jenkins, 22 Apr 1950; Col Aaron W. Tyer, 1 Dec 1950; Col Kenneth W. Northamer, 20 Apr 1951; Col Aaron W. Tyer, 27 May 1951; Col Joe L. Mason, 1 Sep 1951; Col David T. McKnight, 1 Feb 1952; Col Robert J. Rogers, c. 19 Aug 1952–15 Mar 1953; none (not manned), 16–31 Mar 1953; Col William W. Ingenhutt, 1 Apr 1953; Col Edwin A. Doss, 24 Apr 1953; Col George W. Pardy, 18 Nov 1953; Col John P. Randolph, 24 May 1954; Col Thomas C. Conroy, (by 31) May 1956; Col Elbert Helton, 14 Aug 1956; Col Joseph A. Barrett, Jr., 21 Oct 1957; Capt Paul E. Moore, 1 Nov 1957; Col Joseph L. Dickman, 10 Dec 1957; Col Wilbur J. Grumbles, 7 Jul 1958; Col Thomas D. DeJarnette, 15 Jun 1962; Col William P. McBride, 26 Feb 1963; Col William S. Chairsell, 17 Aug 1964; Col John C. Giraudo, 21 Jun 1966; Col Alphonse J. Coleman, 19 May 1967; Col Francis E. Binnell, 20 Mar 1968; Col Ramon R. Melton, 15 Jul 1968; Col Joseph C. Secino, 8 Mar 1969; Col Harry H. Moreland, 22 Aug 1969; Brig Gen Jack Bellamy, 24 Apr 1970; Col Wayne E. Whitlatch, 24 May 1972; Col George G. Hupp, 8 May 1973; Col William L. Kirk, 3 Jun 1974; Col Eleas Casillas, 5 Jan 1976–.

Aircraft. Primarily P (later, F)–51, 1948–1950; F–80, 1948–1951; F–84,

1951–1953, 1953, 1957; F–86, 1951, 1954–1957; F–100, 1957–1962; F–105, 1961–1967; F–4, 1967–1971, 1971–; T–38, 1973–1976; and F–15, 1977–; but also flew F–61, 1948–1949; F–82, 1950; RF–80, 1950–1951; F/RF–51, 1950–1951; and RB–26, 1950–1951.

Operations. Trained to maintain tactical proficiency while participating in the military occupation and air defense of Japan, 1948–Jun 1950. Remained in Japan until 1 Dec 1950, although components detached for combat operations. The wing's tactical mission was greatly reduced, but did include F–80 pilot training from late Jun to 1 Dec 1950. From 6 Sep to 1 Dec 1950 the wing had no tactical units except a detachment of the 41st Fighter-Interceptor Squadron, which provided strip alert and F–80 pilot training. On 1 Dec the wing moved without personnel or equipment to Taegu AB, South Korea, absorbing resources of another wing, and commenced combat operations. The wing was attached to 68th Fighter-Bomber Wing at Taegu, 16–31 Mar 1953, and on 1 Apr moved without personnel or equipment to Kunsan AB, South Korea, where it absorbed resources of the 474th Fighter-Bomber Wing and continued combat operations to 27 Jul 1953. Moved without tactical components to Misawa AB, Japan, on 7 Nov 1953 and absorbed resources of the 6016th Air Base Wing. Served as an administrative and support wing without tactical operations until Jul 1954, and then assumed an air defense mission with attached squadrons. On 15 Apr 1957 the detached 49th Fighter-Bomber Group became a paper unit and the wing assumed the fighter-bomber mission the group had been performing, continuing it to 15 Sep 1957, when the wing stood down and prepared to move to France. Replaced the 388th Fighter-Bomber Wing in France in Dec 1957. Participated in tactical exercises and operations in Europe, in support of NATO, Dec 1957–Jun 1968, initially with F–100s, later with F–105s and then F–4s. Replaced by 7149th Tactical Fighter Wing at Spangdahlem AB, West Germany, on 1 Jul 1968, and reformed at Holloman AFB, NM, largely with recent returnees from Southeast Asia. Served as USAF's first "dual-based," NATO-committed wing, subject to immediate return to Europe if and when needed. The entire wing deployed back to Spangdahlem AB 15 Jan–4 Apr 1969 and 14 Sep–7 Oct 1970, receiving the Mackay Trophy for the 1969 deployment. At Holloman AFB, the wing continued participation in tactical exercises and firepower demonstrations to maintain combat readiness. It assumed base host responsibility on 1 Jan 1971. In the autumn of 1971 the wing's four tactical squadrons deployed in Europe. On 4 May 1972 after North Vietnam invaded South Vietnam, the entire wing, except for a rear echelon to run Holloman, deployed at Takhli RTAFB, Thailand. Conducted combat operations in Southeast Asia, 11 May–27 Sep 1972. Returned to Holloman AFB in early Oct 1972, and continued rotating tactical components to Europe to support NATO through Sep 1977. Also provided USAF fighter lead-in training in T–38s, Feb 1974–Dec 1976. Became part of a new organization—Tactical Training, Holloman—on 1 Aug 1977 and lost responsibility for operating Holloman AFB. Began preparing for conversion to

F–15s in 1977 and received the first of the new planes on 8 Sep (officially accepted on 15 Oct) 1977.

Service Streamers. None.

Campaign Streamers. CCF Intervention; First UN Counteroffensive; CCF Spring Offensive; UN Summer–Fall Offensive; Second Korean Winter; Korea Summer–Fall, 1952; Third Korean Winter; Korea Summer–Fall, 1953; Vietnam Ceasefire.

Decorations. Air Force Outstanding Unit Award with Combat "V" Device: 5 May–6 Oct 1972. Air Force Outstanding Unit Awards: 1 Mar 1964–28 Feb 1966; 1 Mar 1966–30 Jun 1967; 1 Jan 1971–15 Apr 1972. Republic of Korea Presidential Unit Citations: 27 Jun 1950–7 Feb 1951; 8 Feb 1951–31 Mar 1953.

Emblem. A gyronny of three, gules, or and azure, a bolt of lightning, bend sinisterwise argent, in chief, a knight's helmet, winged of the last, in dexter chief, five stars (Southern Cross) argent, two on gules, and three on azure, in sinister base a covered wagon, trees and road scene, all proper. *Motto:* TUTOR ET ULTOR—I protect and avenge. (Approved for the 49th Group on 29 Dec 1951 and for the 49th Wing on 2 Jul 1959.)

50th TACTICAL FIGHTER WING

Lineage. Established as 50th Fighter Wing on 16 May 1949. Activated in the Reserve on 1 Jun 1949. Redesignated 50th Fighter-Interceptor Wing on 1 Mar 1950. Ordered to active service on 1 Jun 1951. Inactivated on 2 Jun 1951. Redesignated 50th Fighter-Bomber Wing on 15 Nov 1952. Activated on 1 Jan 1953. Redesignated 50th Tactical Fighter Wing on 8 Jul 1958.

Assignments. First Air Force, 1 Jun 1949 (attached to 33d Fighter [later, 33d Fighter-Interceptor] Wing, 1 Jun 1949–); Eastern Air Defense Force, 1 Sep 1950–2 Jun 1951 (remained attached to 33d Fighter-Interceptor Wing to 2 Jun 1951). Ninth Air Force, 1 Jan 1953; Twelfth Air Force, 9 Aug 1953; United States Air Forces in Europe, 1 Jan 1958; Seventeenth Air Force, 15 Nov 1959–.

Components. *Group.* 50th: 1 Jun 1949–2 Jun 1951; 1 Jan 1953–8 Dec 1957. *Squadrons.* 8th: attached 8 Mar–2 Apr 1973 and 6 Sep–6 Oct 1975. 9th: attached 11 Sep–7 Oct 1971 and 23 Sep–24 Oct 1976. 10th: 8 Dec 1957–. 68th: attached 10 May–7 Jun 1977. 69th Pilotless Bomber (later, 69th Tactical Missile): attached 14 Mar 1955–15 Apr 1956. 81st: 8 Dec 1957–15 Jul 1971 (detached 15 Jun–15 Jul 1971). 313th: 15 Nov 1976– (not operational, 15 Nov–26 Dec 1976). 355th: attached 5 Sep–16 Nov 1961. 417th: 8 Dec 1957–1 Jul 1968; attached 1–15 Jul 1968, 15 Jan–4 Apr 1969, 11 Sep–10 Oct 1970, 9 Sep–2 Oct 1971, 5 Feb–8 Mar 1973, 6 Mar–5 Apr 1974, 3 Oct–5 Nov 1975, and 24

Aug–26 Sep 1976. 421st: attached 5–25 Aug 1977. 428th: attached 1 Apr–c. 1 Oct 1957. 429th: attached 7 Oct 1956–1 Apr 1957. 430th: attached 20 Apr–7 Oct 1956. 435th: attached c. 24 Oct–11 Dec 1962. 457th: attached 20 Mar–c. 19 Aug 1958. 458th: attached c. 13 Aug 1958–c. 18 Feb 1959. 496th: attached 1–24 Nov 1968, assigned 25 Nov 1968–. 509th: attached 15 Jan–24 Mar 1958. 614th: attached 5 Sep–14 Nov 1961. *Detachment*. Det, 5th Fighter-Interceptor Squadron: attached 4–25 Sep 1975.

Stations. Otis AFB, Mass, 1 Jun 1949–2 Jun 1951. Clovis AFB, NM, 1 Jan–23 Jul 1953; Hahn AB, West Germany, 9 Aug 1953; Toul-Rosieres AB, France, 17 Jul 1956; Hahn AB, West Germany, 10 Dec 1959–.

Commanders. Brig Gen Bruce Johnson, 1 Jun 1949–1951. Col Wallace S. Ford, 1 Jan 1953; Col Melvin F. McNickle, 22 Jul 1954; Col Fred J. Ascani, 24 Jun 1955; Brig Gen Henry C. Newcomer, 26 Jul 1957; Col Frank L. Wood, Jr., Aug 1959; Col Jack S. Jenkins, 1 Sep 1959; Col William P. McBride, 16 Jul 1962; Col David T. McKnight, 12 Feb 1963; Col Louis J. Lamm, 9 Jun 1964; Col George W. McLaughlin, 20 Jul 1964; Col Richard C. Catledge, (by May) 1966; Col Robert L. Liles, 20 May 1966; Col Forrest L. Rauscher, 28 Jun 1968; Col John W. Smith, 14 Jun 1969; Col William B. Craig, 22 Apr 1970; Col Billy F. Rogers, 17 Nov 1970; Col William C. Norris, 1 Oct 1971; Brig Gen Michael E. DeArmond, 2 Jan 1973; Col Paul M. Ingram, 26 Aug 1974; Brig Gen James P. Albritton, 14 Mar 1975–.

Aircraft and Missiles. T–6, 1949–1951; T–33, 1949–1951; F–51, 1949–1950; F–84, 1949–1950; F–86, 1950–1951. F–51, 1953; F–86, 1953–1958; Matador, 1955–1956; ET–33, 1955–1956; F–100, 1957–1966; F–104, 1962; F–4, 1966–; F–102, 1968–1970; F–106, 1975.

Operations. Served as Reserve corollary of the 33d Fighter (later, Fighter-Interceptor) Wing, 1949–1951. Activated as a Tactical Air Command component in Jan 1953 and converted from F–51 to F–86F aircraft before moving to Europe as a component of USAFE. Provided tactical operations in support of USAFE, NATO, and U.S. Army forces beginning Aug 1953. Added air defense to its other tactical missions in Nov 1958. In Aug 1977, switched to a strike-attack role, with air defense as a secondary mission.

Service Streamers. None.

Campaign Streamers. None.

Decorations. Air Force Outstanding Unit Awards: 1 Nov 1970–15 Sep 1971; 1 Jan 1972–30 Jun 1973; 1 Jul 1973–30 Jun 1974.

Emblem. On a shield azure a griffin guardant effrontee, wings displayed argent, langued and breathing fire gules, his right talons surmounting an olive branch and his left talons surmounting a thunderbolt all or, all over an atomic cloud in pale, proper. *Motto:* MASTER OF THE SKY. (Approved on 23 Aug 1956.)

51st COMPOSITE WING (TACTICAL)

Lineage. Established as 51st Fighter Wing on 10 Aug 1948. Activated on 18 Aug 1948. Redesignated 51st Fighter-Interceptor Wing on 1 Feb 1950. Inactivated on 31 May 1971. Redesignated 51st Air Base Wing on 20 Oct 1971. Activated on 1 Nov 1971. redesignated 51st Composite Wing (Tactical) on 30 Sep 1974.

Assignments. 1st Air Division, 18 Aug 1948; Thirteenth Air Force, 1 Dec 1948; Twentieth Air Force, 16 May 1949 (attached to Fifth Air Force, 25 Sep 1950–1 Aug 1954 and further attached to 8th Fighter-Bomber Wing, 25 Sep–12 Oct 1950); 313th Air Division, 1 Mar 1955–31 May 1971. 314th Air Division, 1 Nov 1971–.

Components. *Group.* 51st: 18 Aug 1948–25 Oct 1957 (detached 26 Sep–12 Oct 1950, 16 Aug 1954–15 Mar 1955; not operational, 1 Jul–25 Oct 1957). *Squadrons.* 16th: attached 1 Jul–24 Oct 1957, assigned 25 Oct 1957–24 Dec 1964. 19th Tactical Air Control: 30 Sep 1974–. 25th: attached 1 Jul–24 Oct 1957, assigned 25 Oct 1957–8 Jun 1960 (not operational, 4 May–8 Jun 1960). 36th Tactical Fighter: 30 Sep 1974–. 82d: attached 17 Feb–24 Jun 1966, assigned 25 Jun 1966–31 May 1971 (detached 30 Jan–20 Feb 1968). 318th: attached 11–18 Feb 1968. 555th Tactical Fighter: attached 11 Dec 1964–15 Mar 1965 and 11 Nov 1965–25 Feb 1966. 558th Tactical Fighter: attached 12 Mar–15 Jun 1965. 559th Tactical Fighter: attached 12 Jun–15 Nov 1965.

Stations. Naha Afld (later, AB), Okinawa, 18 Aug 1948; Itazuke AB, Japan, 22 Sep 1950; Kimpo AB, South Korea, 10 Oct 1950; Itazuke AB, Japan, 10 Dec 1950; Tsuiki AB, Japan, 15 Jan 1951; Suwon AB, South Korea, 1 Oct 1951–26 Jul 1954; Naha AB, Okinawa, 1 Aug 1954–31 May 1971. Osan AB, South Korea, 1 Nov 1971–.

Commanders. Brig Gen Hugo P. Rush, 18 Aug 1948; Col John W. Egan, 25 Mar 1949; Col Richard M. Montgomery, 1 Apr 1949; Col John W. Weltman, 19 Sep 1949; Col Oliver G. Cellini, 24 Apr 1951; Col William P. Litton, c. 1 Nov 1951; Col George R. Stanley, 2 Nov 1951; Col Francis S. Gabreski, 6 Nov 1951; Col John W. Mitchell, 13 Jun 1952; Col William C. Clark, 31 May 1953; Col Ernest H. Beverly, 9 Aug 1953; Col William C. Clark, 11 Sep 1953; Col Benjamin O. Davis, Jr., Nov 1953; Col Barton M. Russell, 2 Jul 1954; Col Travis Hoover, 1 Aug 1954; Col Hilmer C. Nelson, 9 Aug 1954; Col Edwin C. Ambrosen, 16 Aug 1954; Col John H. Bell, 15 Nov 1955; Col Paul E. Hoeper, 2 Feb 1957; Col Robert L. Cardenas, 4 May 1957; Col Walter V. Gresham, Jr., 15 Jul 1957; Col Elliott H. Reed, 1 Aug 1957; Col Walter V. Gresham, Jr., 15 Aug 1957; Col Lester J. Johnson, 22 Nov 1957; Col William W. Ingenhutt, 25 Mar 1960; Col Lester C. Hess, 24 Jul 1962; Col Lloyd R. Larson, 11 Jun 1965; Col Frank E. Angier, 8 Apr 1967; Col John B. Weed, 13 Jun 1968; Col Roy D. Carlson, 30 Jun 1968–31 May 1971. Col Hewitt E. Lovelace, Jr., 1 Nov 1971; Col John H. Allison, 1 Aug 1972; Col Billie

J. Norwood, 7 Jun 1973; Col Alonzo L. Ferguson, 1 May 1974; Col Glenn L. Nordin, 30 Sep 1974; Brig Gen Vernon H. Sandrock, 12 Aug 1975; Col Frederick B. Hoenniger, 15 Jun 1977–.

Aircraft. F–61, 1948–1950; F–80, 1948–1951; F–82, 1949–1950; F–86, 1951–1960; F–94, 1954–1955; F–102, 1959–1964, 1966–1971; F–4, 1964–1965, 1965–1966; F–106, 1968. F–4, 1974–; OV–10, 1974–.

Operations. Replaced 301st Fighter Wing (which became non-operational) in Aug 1948, and absorbed the 301st's resources. Provided air defense of the Ryukyu Islands, Aug 1954–Sep 1950. Moved to Japan for combat in Korea, 22 Sep 1950–27 Jul 1953. Moved to Kimpo AB, South Korea, on 10 Oct 1950, and back to Japan 2 months later, while continuing combat in the war zone. Beginning May 1951, operated a detachment of wing elements at Suwon AB, South Korea, until the entire wing moved there in Oct 1951. Thereafter, operated maintenance and supply elements at Tsuiki AB, Japan, until Aug 1954, providing rear echelon support for the forward elements. The wing supported ground forces in Korea and flew patrol, escort, interdictory, and reconnaissance missions. Wing pilots frequently engaged the enemy's jet (MiG) fighters and reported numerous victories in aerial combat. Remained in Korea after the end of hostilities to provide air defense until late Jul 1954. Provided air defense of the Ryukyu Islands, Aug 1954–c. May 1971. From Aug 1954 through 1970, frequently deployed tactical aircraft, crews, and support personnel throughout the Far East, including Korea, Japan, Taiwan, and the Philippines. One squadron deployed at Tainan, Taiwan, 29 Aug 1958–26 Jan 1959, during the Taiwan Strait crisis. Wing F–86s flew numerous combat air patrol sorties to provide air cover for Nationalist Chinese Air Force flights resupplying besieged garrisons on Quemoy Island. In response to the *Pueblo* incident in 1968, the wing deployed one tactical squadron plus support personnel to Suwon AB, South Korea, 30 Jan–20 Feb 1968, and other personnel to support 314th Air Division at Osan AB, South Korea. A detachment of F–102s, crews, and support personnel deployed at Suwon AB from 28 Jun 1968 through 1970. The wing inactivated at Naha AB, Okinawa, on 31 May 1971, but was soon brought out of retirement to become an air base wing at Osan AB. From 1 Nov 1971 through 29 Sep 1974 the wing served primarily as a support wing, assuming tasks of the former 6314th Support Wing. It operated Osan AB and was responsible for remote site support and the Koon-Ni Range. On 15 Apr 1975 the wing also became responsible for Taegu AB, South Korea. During this "support" period the wing operated C–47 (1971), C–123 (1971–1973), CH–3 (1971–1974), VT–29 (1971–1974), and T–33 (1971–1976) aircraft, mostly in support of 314th Air Division. The wing assumed a tactical mission on 30 Sep 1974 when it gained an F–4E tactical fighter squadron and an OV–10 tactical air support squadron, but support responsibilities continued under a combat support group activated for this purpose. In Jan 1976 the wing gained a tactical control squadron, and in Apr 1976 a direct air support squadron and a tactical air control center squadron. These additions, with the tactical air support squadron already assigned, comprised the Korean tactical air control system. After 1974 the wing participated in numerous tactical exercises to maintain combat readiness.

Service Streamers. None.

Campaign Streamers. UN Offensive; CCF Intervention; First UN Counteroffensive; CCF Spring Offensive; UN Summer–Fall Offensive; Second Korean Winter; Korea Summer–Fall, 1952; Third Korean Winter; Korea Summer–Fall, 1953.

Decorations. Air Force Outstanding Unit Awards: 29 Aug 1958–19 Jan 1959; 26 Mar 1962–30 Sep 1963; 1 Jan 1965–31 Dec 1966; 1 Jan 1969–31 Dec 1970; 30 Sep 1974–31 Mar 1976. Republic of Korea Presidential Unit Citations: 20 Sep 1950–30 Jun 1951; 1 Jul 1951–31 Mar 1953; 19–20 Aug 1972.

Emblem. Per fess nebuly abased azure and or, issuing from partition line a demi–pegasus argent with a machine gun in each wing bendwise sable, gun fire proper. *Motto:* DEFTLY AND SWIFTLY. (Approved for 51st Group on 5 Feb 1942 and, in modified form, for 51st Wing on 2 May 1956.)

52d TACTICAL FIGHTER WING

Lineage. Established as 52d Fighter Wing, All Weather, on 10 May 1948. Activated on 9 Jun 1948. Redesignated: 52d Fighter-All Weather Wing on 20 Jan 1950; 52d Fighter-Interceptor Wing on 1 May 1951. Inactivated on 6 Feb 1952. Redesignated 52d Fighter Wing (Air Defense), and activated, on 11 Apr 1963. Organized on 1 Jul 1963. Inactivated on 30 Sep 1968. Redesignated 52d Tactical Fighter Wing on 12 Nov 1971. Activated on 31 Dec 1971.

Assignments. First Air Force, 9 Jun 1948 (attached to Eastern Air Defense Force, 10 Nov 1949–31 Aug 1950); Eastern Air Defense Force, 1 Sep 1950–6 Feb 1952. Air Defense Command, 11 Apr 1963; New York Air Defense Sector, 1 Jul 1963; 21st Air Division, 1 Apr 1966; 35th Air Division, 1 Dec 1967–30 Sep 1968. Seventeenth Air Force, 31 Dec 1971–.

Components. *Wing.* 84th: attached 1 Jun 1949–2 Jun 1951. *Group.* 52d: 9 Jun 1948–6 Feb 1952. *Squadrons.* 2d Fighter-Interceptor: 1 Jul 1963–30 Sep 1968. 23d: 31 Dec 1971–. 39th Tactical Electronic Warfare: 31 Dec 1971–1 Jan 1973 (not operational, 5 Dec 1972–1 Jan 1973). 58th: attached 8–22 Aug 1975. 81st: 15 Jan 1973–. 98th Fighter-Interceptor: 1 Jul 1963–30 Sep 1968. 105th: attached 1 Apr 1951–6 Feb 1952. 334th: attached 9–23 Sep 1975. 335th: attached 11–25 Jul 1975. 356th: attached 29 Aug–20 Sep 1976. 457th: attached 13–27 Aug 1977. 480th: 15 Nov 1976–. 562d: attached 12–30 Aug 1977. *Detachments.* Det, 17th Defense Systems Evaluation Squadron: attached 30 Aug–23 Oct 1974 and 29 Aug–25 Oct 1975. Det, 561st Tactical Fighter Squadron: attached 30 Aug–20 Sep 1976.

Stations. Mitchel Field (later, AFB), NY, 9 Jun 1948; McGuire AFB, NJ, 4 Oct 1949–6 Feb 1952. Suffolk County AFB, NY, 1 Jul 1963–30 Sep 1968. Spangdahlem AB, West Germany, 31 Dec 1971–.

Commanders. Col Roger V. Williams, 9 Jun 1948; Col Thomas C. Musgrave, Jr., 28 Jun 1948; Col Robert W. C. Wimmsatt, 1 Jul 1949; Col Edward C. Tates, 26 Sep 1949; Col Ernest H. Beverly, 16 Jul 1950; Col Edward W. Szaniawski, 4 Dec 1951; Lt Col LeRoy D. Hoerner, 1–6 Feb 1952. None (not manned), 11 Apr–30 Jun 1963; Col James H. Buckey, 1 Jul 1963; Col Ben H. Emmert, Jr., 1 Jul 1964; Col Francis S. Gabreski, 17 Aug 1964; Col Jack D. Gamble, 31 Oct 1967–30 Sep 1968. Col Thomas E. Clifford, 31 Dec 1971; Col James H. Ahmann, 16 Jul 1973; Col Robert F. C. Winger, 9 Nov 1973; Col Robert E. Buhrow, 7 Jul 1975; Col Richard E. Skelton, 10 Jun 1977–.

Aircraft. P (later, F)–61, 1947–1948; F–82, 1948–1952; F–94, 1950–1952; F–47, 1951–1952. F–101, 1963–1968. EB–66, 1971–1972; F–4, 1971–; EB–57, 1974, 1975; A–7, 1976; F–105, 1976, 1977.

Operations. Air defense in the northeastern United States, Jun 1948–Feb 1952, and Jul 1963–Sep 1968. In Dec 1971 became host wing at Spangdahlem AB, West Germany, and inherited tactical squadrons from 36th TFW at nearby Bitburg AB. Participated in numerous tactical exercises, operations, and tests of USAFE and NATO. Provided close air support, interdiction, and base defense operations. Cooperated with other NATO forces in frequent "squadron exchange" programs and hosted U.S.–based units on temporary duty in Europe.

Service Streamers. None.

Campaign Streamers. None.

Decorations. None.

Emblem. Quarterly per fess nebuly, first and fourth argent (white), each charged with a dagger in pale point downward gules (red), hilt and pommel of the same, grip or (gold); second quarter azure (blue); third quarter sable (black). *Motto:* SEEK, ATTACK, DESTROY. (Approved for 52d Group on 11 Jan 1951 and for 52d Wing on 10 May 1951.)

54th TACTICAL FIGHTER WING

Lineage. Established as 54th Troop Carrier Wing on 26 Feb 1943. Activated on 13 Mar 1943. Inactivated on 31 May 1946. Redesignated 54th Fighter Wing, and allotted to the Air National Guard, on 1 Jun 1946. Organized in the Georgia Air National Guard on 8 Jul 1946. Extended federal recognition on 2 Oct 1946. Ordered to active service on 10 Oct 1950. Inactivated, and returned to the control of the Department of the Air Force, on 11 Oct 1950. Redesignated 54th Tactical Fighter Wing on 5 Jun 1970. Activated on 15 Jun 1970. Inactivated on 31 Oct 1970.

Assignments. Fifth Air Force, 13 Mar 1943; Far East (later, Pacific) Air Service Command, 15 Jan–31 May 1946. Georgia Air National Guard, 8 Jul 1946; Fourteenth Air Force, 10–11 Oct 1950. Fifth Air Force, 15 Jun–31 Oct 1970 (attached to Detachment 1, Headquarters Fifth Air Force [5th ADVON], 15 Jul–30 Sep 1970).

Components. *Groups.* 2d Combat Cargo: 13 Dec 1944–5 Jan 1946. 116th: 10–11 Oct 1950. 317th: 1 Oct 1943–15 Jan 1946. 374th: 26 May–28 Sep 1943; attached 22 Sep 1944–c. 5 Jan 1945; assigned 26 Jan–15 May 1946. 375th: 12 Jul 1943–15 Jan 1946. 403d: 26 Jan–31 May 1946. 433d: 4 Oct 1943–5 Jan 1946. *Squadrons.* 1st Troop Carrier (Philippine Army): attached c. 26 Jan–31 May 1946. 9th: 15 Jan–c. Feb 1946; 15–31 May 1946. 16th: attached 15 Jun–7 Sep 1970. 65th: 13 Aug–9 Nov 1943. 66th: 13 Aug–9 Nov 1943. 311th: 15 Feb–15 May 1946. 316th: 15 Feb–25 Mar 1946. 478th: attached 15 Jun–2 Sep 1970.

Stations. Brisbane, Australia, 13 Mar 1943; Port Moresby, New Guinea, 3 May 1943; Nadzab, New Guinea, 18 Apr 1944; Biak, 5 Oct 1944; Dulag, Leyte, 14 Feb 1945; Clark Field, Luzon, 11 Jun 1945; Tachikawa, Japan, 25 Sep 1945; Manila, Luzon, c. 26 Jan–31 May 1946. Marietta AAB (later, Dobbins AFB), Ga, 8 Jul 1946–11 Oct 1950. Kunsan AB, South Korea, 15 Jun–31 Oct 1970.

Commanders. 1st Lt Edward A. Peters, 13 Mar 1943 (additional duty); none (not manned), 14–19 May 1943; Brig Gen Paul H. Prentiss, 20 May 1943; Brig Gen Warren R. Carter, 30 Mar 1944; Brig Gen Paul H. Prentiss, 19 Nov 1944; Brig Gen William D. Old, 30 Sep 1945; Col Audrin R. Walker, c. 13 Apr–31 May 1946. Unkn, 8 Jul 1946–11 Oct 1950. Col Henry L. Warren, 15 Jun 1970; Col James R. Davis, 4 Aug–30 Sep 1970; none (not manned), 1–31 Oct 1970.

Aircraft. C–47, 1943–1946; B–17, 1943–1944; C–46, 1944–1946; C–54, 1946. Unkn, 1946–1950. F–4, 1970.

Operations. Not operational from activation until 20 May 1943. Commenced air transport and medical air evacuation operations in support of Fifth Air Force on 26 May 1943, advancing as battle lines permitted. Employed C–47s almost exclusively, but during late 1943 and much of 1944 also used converted B–17s for armed transport missions in enemy-held territory. Supported every major advance made by the allies in the Southwest Pacific, operating from primitive airstrips carved from jungles and air-dropping cargo where airstrips unavailable. Took part in the airborne invasion of Nadzab, New Guinea, in Sep 1943 by dropping paratroopers of the 503d Parachute Infantry Regiment as well as Australian engineers and heavy equipment. In Jul 1944, dropped 1,418 paratroopers on Noemfoor Island to aid the allied invasion forces. Then assumed the task of handling all freight and personnel moving in troop carrier aircraft in the Southwest Pacific, in addition to scheduled and unscheduled air movement of cargo and troops, and air evacuation of wounded personnel. Some C–46s began operating within the wing in late 1944, and during 1945 large numbers of C–46s were used in addition to C–47s. By late 1944 and during the early months of 1945, most wing missions were flown to the Philippines. In Feb 1945, the wing flew three more airborne operations, all in the Philippines, to help encircle Japanese concentrations. Wing C–47s dropped napalm on Carabao Island, in Manila Bay, in Mar 1945. When hostilities ended, the wing moved the entire 11th Airborne Division (11,300 personnel) from the Philippines to Okinawa on short notice, and then began transporting occupation forces into Japan. During Sep 1945, the wing also evacuated over 17,000 former prisoners of war from Japan to the Philippines. The wing served as part of the occupation forces in Japan from 25 Sep 1945 to about 26 Jan 1946, while continuing routine air transport operations and a scheduled courier service. Beginning in Dec 1945 and continuing into mid–1946, most of the wing's components were reassigned to other units or inactivated, and on 15 Jan 1946 the wing became a component of the Far East (soon, Pacific) Air Service Command. Moving to the Philippines, the wing gained new components and flew scheduled routes between Japan, the Philippines, Australia, and the Hawaiian Islands. Replaced by the 403d Troop Carrier Group on 31 May 1946. As the 54th Fighter Wing, served the Georgia Air National Guard from Jul 1946 to Oct 1950. Ordered to active service on 10 Oct 1950 and inactivated the following day, with personnel used as fillers in other USAF units. In Jun 1970, as the 54th Tactical Fighter Wing, replaced the 354th TFW at Kunsan AB, South Korea. Used attached F–4 squadrons in the Republic of Korea.

Service Streamers. None.

Campaign Streamers. New Guinea; Leyte; Luzon.

Decorations. Philippines Presidential Unit Citation.

Emblem. None.

55th STRATEGIC RECONNAISSANCE WING

Lineage. Established as 55th Strategic Reconnaissance Wing on 29 Jun 1948. Activated on 19 Jul 1948. Inactivated on 14 Oct 1949. Redesignated 55th Strategic Reconnaissance Wing, Medium, on 27 Oct 1950. Activated on 1 Nov 1950. Redesignated 55th Strategic Reconnaissance Wing on 16 Aug 1966.

Assignments. 311th Air Division, Reconnaissance (later, 311th Air Division), 19 Jul 1948–14 Oct 1949. Second Air Force, 1 Nov 1950; 21st Air (later, 21st Strategic Aerospace) Division, 1 Oct 1952 (attached to 5th Air Division, 18 May–16 Aug 1955); 810th Strategic Aerospace Division, 1 Sep 1964; 12th Strategic Aerospace Division, 2 Jul 1966; 14th Strategic Aerospace (later, 14th Air) Division, 30 Jun 1971; 4th Air Division, 1 Oct 1976–.

Components. *Group.* 55th: 19 Jul 1948–14 Oct 1949 (not operational, 19 Jul–26 Oct 1948); 1 Nov 1950–16 Jun 1952 (not operational). *Squadrons.* 1st Airborne Command and Control: 1 Nov 1975–. 1st Strategic Reconnaissance (Provisional): attached 1 Sep–9 Oct 1948. 1st: attached 10–26 Oct 1948; attached 14 Jan–1 Jun 1949. 2d Airborne Command and Control: 1 Apr 1970–. 23d: attached 1–17 Jun 1949. 38th: attached 6 Jan 1951–15 Jun 1952, assigned

16 Jun 1952–1 Apr 1970. 323d: attached 19 Sep–10 Oct 1949. 338th: attached 25 Nov 1950–15 Jun 1952, assigned 16 Jun 1952–15 Jun 1963; assigned 25 Mar–25 Dec 1967. 343d: attached 19 Jul–26 Oct 1948; attached 4 Jan 1951–15 Jun 1952, assigned 16 Jun 1952–. 548th Strategic Missile: attached 1–31 Aug 1964, assigned 1 Sep 1964–25 Mar 1965.

Stations. Topeka (later, Forbes) AFB, Kans, 19 Jul 1948–14 Oct 1949. Ramey AFB, PR, 1 Nov 1950; Offutt AFB, Nebr, 16 Aug 1966–.

Commanders. Col Alfred F. Kalberer, 19 Jul 1948; Col William R. Yancey, 20 Oct 1948; Col John H. Davies, 17 Aug–14 Oct 1949. Col Richard T. King, 1 Nov 1950; Brig Gen Sydney D. Grubbs, Jr., 20 Dec 1950; Col Alfred F. Kalberer, 18 Feb 1952; Brig Gen Joseph D. C. Caldara, 1 Oct 1952; Col Clayton Stiles, 24 Dec 1952; Col Adam K. Breckenridge, 26 Jan 1953; Col Olbert F. Lassiter, 1 May 1955; Col James K. Johnson, 16 Feb 1957; Col Norton H. Van Sicklen, 1 Aug 1959; Col William D. Kyle, Jr., 2 Jul 1960; Col John G. Glover, 1 Jun 1961; Col Marion C. Mixon, 9 Jun 1963; Col William E. Riggs, 29 Aug 1966; Col Anthony Martinez, 17 Jul 1970; Col Marvin N. Morss, 30 Jun 1971; Col George D. Miller, 31 Aug 1972; Col Joe L. Church, 23 Jul 1974; Col Guy H. Winstead, Jr., 5 Mar 1976–.

Aircraft and Missiles. B/RB–17, 1948–1949; B/RB–29, 1948–1949; RC–54, 1948. B/RB–29, 1950–1951; RB–50, 1950–1954; EB/RB–47, 1954–1967; Atlas, 1964–1965; EC/KC–135, 1966–; RC–135, 1967–; E–4, 1975–; C–135, 1977–.

Operations. Provided precise Shoran and Hiran mapping and photographic reconnaissance, 1948–1949. Performed strategic reconnaissance, charting photography, precise electronic geodetic mapping, and electronic reconnaissance, 1950–1954. When mapping and charting functions transferred on 1 May 1954, wing assumed mission of global strategic reconnaissance, including electronic reconnaissance, weather reconnaissance (to Jun 1963), and photographic reconnaissance (to May 1964). Deployed at Ben Guerir AB, French Morocco, May–Aug 1955. Responsible for an Atlas missile complex, Aug 1964–Mar 1965. Became responsible for SAC's airborne command post and post attack command and control operations, Aug 1966. In addition, flew SAC logistic support missions after Sep 1971. Conducted K/E/RC–135 pilot receiver training as required. Gained an E–4 squadron in Nov 1975 and became responsible for the Advanced Airborne Command Post.

Service Streamers. None.

Campaign Streamers. None.

Decorations. Air Force Outstanding Unit Awards: Jul 1956–Nov 1957; 1 Jul 1963–30 Jun 1964; 1 Jul 1966–30 Jun 1967; 1 Jul 1972–30 Jun 1974; 1 Jul 1974–30 Jun 1976.

Emblem. On a light blue shield radiating saltirewise from a black aerial camera outlined in white, at the top of shield with aperture downward, four red lightning flashes with yellow upper edges; below and touching the flashes a green globe with white outlines to point of contact and white lines of latitude and longitude, the area between globe and flashes yellow; surmounting the globe a horizontal curved yellow flash inscribed with the code letters "SAC" in black. *Motto:* VIDEMUS OMNIA—We see all. (Approved on 4 Feb 1954.)

56th TACTICAL FIGHTER WING

Lineage. Established as 56th Fighter Wing on 28 Jul 1947. Organized on 15 Aug 1947. Discontinued on 1 Aug 1948. Activated on 1 Aug 1948. Redesignated 56th Fighter-Interceptor Wing on 20 Jan 1950. Inactivated on 6 Feb 1952. Redesignated 56th Fighter Wing (Air Defense), and activated, on 28 Dec 1960. Organized on 1 Feb 1961. Discontinued, and inactivated, on 1 Jan 1964. Redesignated 56th Air Commando Wing, and activated, on 16 Mar 1967. Organized on 8 Apr 1967. Redesignated: 56th Special Operations Wing on 1 Aug 1968; 56th Tactical Fighter Wing on 30 Jun 1975.

Assignments. Fifteenth Air Force, 15 Aug 1947; Strategic Air Command, 1 Oct 1947–1 Aug 1948. Strategic Air Command, 1 Aug 1948; Tenth Air Force, 1 Dec 1948 (attached to 26th Air Division [Defense], 10 Dec 1949–19 Feb 1950; 30th Air Division [Defense], 20 Feb 1950–); Eastern Air Defense Force, 1 Sep 1950–6 Feb 1952 (remained attached to 30th Air Division [Defense] to 6 Feb 1952). Air Defense Command, 28 Dec 1960; Sault Sainte Marie Air Defense Sector, 1 Feb 1961; Duluth Air Defense Sector, 1 Oct 1963; Strategic Air Command, 1 Jan 1964. Pacific Air Forces, 16 Mar 1967; Thirteenth Air Force, 8 Apr 1967 (attached to Seventh Air Force, 8 Apr 1967–26 Feb 1974; United States Support Activities Group/Seventh Air Force, 27 Feb 1974–30 Jun 1975); Tactical Air Command, 30 Jun 1975; Ninth Air Force, 30 Jun 1975–.

Components. *Group.* 56th: 15 Aug 1947–1 Aug 1948; 1 Aug 1948–6 Feb 1952. *Squadrons.* 1st: 20 Dec 1967–15 Dec 1972. 13th Tactical Fighter Training: 15 Jan 1976–. 18th: 25 Aug 1971–31 Dec 1972. 21st: 27 Nov 1967–30 Jun 1975. 22d: 25 Oct 1968–30 Sep 1970 (not operational, 18 Jul–30 Sep 1970). 23d Tactical Air Support: 15 Mar 1972–30 Jun 1975. 61st: 30 Jun 1975–. 62d: 1 Feb 1961–16 Dec 1963; 30 Jun 1975–. 63d: 30 Jun 1975–. 97th: attached 1 Dec 1950–20 May 1951. 361st Tactical Electronic Warfare: 1 Sep 1972–30 Jun 1974. 554th Reconnaissance: 15 Dec 1970–30 Sep 1972. 602d: 8 Apr 1967–31 Dec 1970 (not operational, 20–31 Dec 1970). 606th: 8 Apr 1967–15 Jun 1971. 609th: 15 Sep 1967–1 Dec 1969. 4501st Tactical Fighter Replacement: 30 Jun 1975–15 Jan 1976.

Stations. Selfridge Field (later, AFB), Mich, 15 Aug 1947–1 Aug 1948. Selfridge AFB, Mich, 1 Aug 1948–6 Feb 1952. K. I. Sawyer AFB, Mich, 1 Feb 1961–1 Jan 1964. Nakhon Phanom RTAFB, Thailand, 8 Apr 1967–30 Jun 1975; MacDill AFB, Fla, 30 Jun 1975–.

Commanders. Col William T. Hudnell, 15 Aug 1947–1 Aug 1948. Col William T. Hudnell, 1 Aug 1948; Lt Col

David T. McKnight, Jun 1949; Col James R. Gunn, Jr., 23 Aug 1949; Col George S. Brown, 15 Aug 1951–6 Feb 1952. None (not manned), 28 Dec 1960–31 Jan 1961; Col James F. Reed, 1 Feb 1961; Col John M. Konosky, 16 May 1963–1 Jan 1964. None (not manned), 16 Mar–7 Apr 1967; Col Harry C. Aderholt, 8 Apr 1967; Col Roland K. McCoskrie, 19 Nov 1967; Col Edwin J. White, Jr., 7 Nov 1968; Col Patrick M. Fallon, 31 May 1969; Col Edwin J. White, Jr., (by 18) Jun 1969; Col Samuel E. Crosby, Jr., 5 Oct 1969; Col Edward J. Walsh, Jr., 8 Aug 1970; Col Jack E. Robinson, 15 Jul 1971; Col Norbert L. Simon, 17 Jun 1972; Col Robert E. Wayne, 1 Dec 1972; Col William B. Owens, 30 Jun 1973; Col Ralph H. Bowersox, 15 Sep 1973; Col Charles E. Woods, 26 Sep 1973; Col Perry J. Dahl, 15 Jul 1974; Col Harry A. Goodall, 3 Feb 1975; Col Gerald J. Carey, Jr., 30 Jun 1975; Col Ernest A. Bedke, 11 Aug 1975–.

Aircraft. P (later, F)–80, 1947–1948. F–80, 1948–1950; F–86, 1950–1952; F–47, 1951–1952; F–51, 1951–1952; F–94, 1951–1952. F–101, 1961–1963. A–1, 1967–1972; A–26, 1967–1969; CH–3, 1967–1972; C–123, 1967–1971; T–28, 1967–1973; RT–28, 1967–1972; U–6, 1967; U–10, 1967–1969; UC–123, 1968–1971; C–47, 1969–1972; CH–53, 1970–1975; QU–22, 1970–1972; AC–119, 1971–1972; EC–47, 1972–1974; H–34, 1972; OV–10, 1972–1975; O–1, 1973; F–4, 1975–.

Operations. Supported exercises, operations, and training programs of Strategic Air Command, 1947–1948. Pioneered the first west-to-east jet fighter transatlantic crossing along the northern air route in Jul 1948. Provided air defense for a large portion of the northeastern United States, Dec 1948–Feb 1952. Provided air defense in the Mich area, 1961–1963. Combat in Southeast Asia, Apr 1967–Jan 1973, and combat support in the same general area until Jun 1975, employing a wide variety of aircraft to meet specialized needs. Moved to the United States on 30 Jun 1975 and absorbed resources of the 1st Tactical Fighter Wing. Operated MacDill AFB and nearby Avon Park Range, Fla, Jun 1975–. Conducted F–4E replacement training for pilots, weapon systems officers, and maintenance personnel, Jun 1975–. Conducted a service test of TAC's "production oriented maintenance organization" in 1976 and converted to the POMO concept in Mar 1977.

Service Streamers. None.

Campaign Streamers. Vietnam Air Offensive, Phase II; Vietnam Air Offensive, Phase III; Vietnam Air/Ground; Vietnam Air Offensive, Phase IV; TET 69/Counteroffensive; Vietnam Summer–Fall, 1969; Vietnam Winter–Spring, 1970; Sanctuary Counteroffensive; Southwest Monsoon; Commando Hunt V; Commando Hunt VI; Commando Hunt VII; Vietnam Ceasefire.

Decorations. Presidential Unit Citations (Southeast Asia): 1 Nov 1968–1 May 1969; 1 Oct 1969–30 Apr 1970; 1 Apr 1972–22 Feb 1973. Air Force Outstanding Unit Awards with Combat "V" Device: 1 Dec 1970–30 Nov 1971; 1 Dec 1971–29 Feb 1972; 23 Feb 1973–28 Feb 1974. Republic of Vietnam Gallantry Cross with Palm: 8 Apr 1967–28 Jan 1973.

Emblem. Tenne, on a chevron azure fimbriated or, two lightning flashes chevronwise of the last. *Motto:* CAVE TONITRUM—Beware of the thunderbolt. (Approved for 56th Group on 4 Apr 1942 and for 56th Wing on 19 Apr 1967.)

57th TACTICAL TRAINING WING

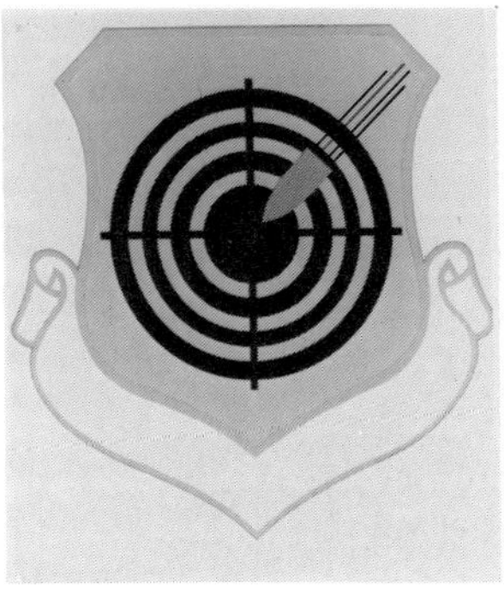

Lineage. Established as 57th Fighter Wing c. 15 Mar 1948. Organized on 20 Apr 1948. Discontinued on 20 Sep 1948. Activated on 20 Sep 1948. Redesignated 57th Fighter-Interceptor Wing on 20 Jan 1950. Inactivated on 1 Jan 1951. Redesignated 57th Fighter Weapons Wing on 22 Aug 1969. Activated on 15 Oct 1969. Redesignated 57th Tactical Training Wing on 1 Apr 1977.

Assignments. Alaskan Air Command, 20 Apr–20 Sep 1948. Alaskan Air Command, 20 Sep 1948–1 Jan 1951. USAF Tactical Fighter Weapons Center, 15 Oct 1969–.

Components. *Group.* 57th: 20 Apr–20 Sep 1948; 20 Sep 1948–1 Jan 1951 (detached 10 Dec 1950–1 Jan 1951). *Squadrons.* 4th Troop Carrier: attached 2 Dec 1948–28 Feb 1949; attached 14 Aug–14 Nov 1949. 7th Troop Carrier: attached 28 Feb–1 Jun 1949. 8th Troop Carrier: attached 1–20 Sep 1948; attached 20 Sep–2 Dec 1948; attached 1 Jun–15 Aug 1949. 37th Troop Carrier: attached 4 Jul–1 Sep 1948. 54th Troop Carrier: attached c. 20 Apr–c. 1 Jul 1948; attached 20 Sep 1949–31 Dec 1950 (not operational, 20 Sep–6 Nov 1949). 64th: 15 Oct 1972–. 65th: 15 Oct 1969– (not operational, c. 30 Dec 1969–c. 23 Jun 1972). 66th: 15 Oct 1969– (not operational, 26 Jul 1975–30 Sep 1977). 414th: 15 Oct 1969–. 422d: 15 Oct 1969–. 433d: 1 Oct 1976–. USAF Air Demonstration: 15 Feb 1974–.

Stations. Elmendorf AFB, Alaska, 20 Apr–20 Sep 1948. Elmendorf AFB, Alaska, 20 Sep 1948–1 Jan 1951. Nellis AFB, Nev, 15 Oct 1969–.

Commanders. Col Thomas L. Mosley, 20 Apr 1948; Col Harry W. Generous, 10–20 Sep 1948. Col Harry W. Generous, 20 Sep 1948; Brig Gen Donald R. Hutchinson, 24 May 1949; Col James T. Posey, 18 Sep 1950; Col James W. Andrew, 18 Dec 1950–1 Jan 1951. Col William B. Williamson, Sr., 15 Oct 1969; Col Brian J. Lincoln, 1 Feb 1970; Col Freddie L. Poston, 16 Feb 1971; Col David D. Young, 23 May 1972; Col Wilford E. Deming III, 5 Jul 1973; Col William L. Strand, 3 Mar 1975; Col Ronald M. Clements, 5 Aug 1977–.

Aircraft. F–51, 1948; F–80, 1948; C–47, 1948; C–54, 1948; C–82, 1948. F–80, 1948–1950; C–82, 1948–1949, 1950; C–54, 1949–1950. A–7, 1969–1975; F–4, 1969–; F–100, 1969; F–105, 1969–1975; F–111, 1969–; T–39, 1969–c. 1972; T–38, 1972–; F–5, 1975–; F–15, 1976–; A–10, 1977–.

Operations. Replaced 57th Fighter Wing (Provisional) in Apr 1948. Operated Elmendorf AFB, Alaska, and several satellite bases, and provided air defense of Alaska, Apr–Sep 1948 and Sep 1948–Dec 1950. Also provided intra-theater troop carrier and airlift support, 1948–1950, using several attached troop carrier squadrons. Replaced by 39th Air Depot Wing in Jan 1951. Replaced 4525th Fighter Weapons Wing at Nellis AFB, Nev, in Oct 1969. Trained tactical fighter aircrews, conducted tests, evaluations, and demonstrations of tactical fighter weapon systems, and developed fighter tactics, Oct 1969–. Assumed operation of Nellis AFB in Feb 1970.

Service Streamers. None.

Campaign Streamers. None.

Decorations. Air Force Outstanding Unit Award: 25 Oct 1969–25 Sep 1971.

Emblem. Argent (silver gray) a pellet within six annulets alternating or and sable, surmounted by a bomb bend sinisterwise gules, trailing speed lines of the fourth, all within a diminished bordure or. (Approved on 2 Sep 1970.)

58th TACTICAL TRAINING WING

Lineage. Established as 58th Fighter-Bomber Wing on 25 Jun 1952. Activated on 10 Jul 1952. Inactivated on 1 Jul 1958. Redesignated 58th Tactical Fighter Training Wing on 22 Aug 1969. Activated on 15 Oct 1969. Redesignated 58th Tactical Training Wing on 1 Apr 1977.

Assignments. Tactical Air Command, 10 Jul 1952 (attached to Fifth Air Force, 10 Jul 1952–28 Feb 1955; Korean Air Division, Provisional, 314th, 1–14 Mar 1955; 314th Air Division, 15 Mar 1955–31 Dec 1956); Far East Air Forces, 1 Jan 1957; 314th Air Division, 1 Jan 1957–1 Jul 1958. Twelfth Air Force, 15 Oct 1969; Tactical Training, Luke, 1 Apr 1977–.

Components. *Wings.* 49th: attached 16–31 Mar 1953. 474th: attached 1 Apr 1953–8 Nov 1954 (not operational). *Groups.* 49th: attached 16–31 Mar 1953. 58th: 10 Jul 1952–8 Nov 1957 (not operational, 1 Mar–8 Nov 1957). 474th: attached 1 Apr 1953–24 Nov 1954. *Squadrons.* 69th: attached 1 Mar–7 Nov 1957, assigned 8 Nov 1957–1 Jul 1958; assigned 15 Oct 1969–. 310th: attached 1 Mar–7 Nov 1957, assigned 8 Nov 1957–1 Jul 1958; assigned 15 Dec 1969–. 311th: attached 1 Mar–7 Nov 1957, assigned 8 Nov 1957–1 Jul 1958; assigned 18 Jan 1970– (not operational, 1 Apr–c. 31 Oct 1971). 333d: 22 Mar–31 Jul 1971 (not operational). 418th: 15 Oct 1969–1 Oct 1976 (not operational, 17 Aug–1 Oct 1976). 425th: 15 Oct 1969–. 426th: 18 Jan 1970– (not operational, 13 Sep–c. 2 Oct 1971). 461st: 1 Jul 1977–. 550th: 18 Jan 1970– (not operational, 1 Jul 1970–30 Jun 1971). 555th: 5 Jul 1974– (not operational, 5 Jul–13 Nov 1974). 4461st: 23 Jun 1976–1 Jul 1977. 4511th Combat Crew Training: 15 Oct

Thomas, 18 Jun 1970; Col Robert H. Campbell, 15 Jun 1971; Col Douglas L. Campbell, 15 Aug 1973; Col Paul E. Gardner, 23 May 1974; Col Franklin A. Ross, 2 Jun 1976–.

Aircraft. Primarily C–47, 1948; C–54, 1948, 1949–1950; and C–82, 1949–1951; but also flew (in single or small numbers) B–17, 1948–1949; L–5, 1948–1949, 1950; C–74, Sep 1948; YC–97, Jul 1949; C–47, 1949–1951; C–119, Aug 1950; and C–54, 1951. C–121, 1966; C–124, 1966–1969.

Operations. Participated in Berlin Airlift (Operation Vittles), 1 Jul–4 Nov 1948 and 10 Jul–17 Oct 1949. Operated Rhein-Main AB, West Germany, 1 Jul 1948–2 Jun 1951, and Templehof AB, West Germany, 1 Jul–5 Nov 1948. Also operated Tulln Airport in Austria, 1 Jul–10 Dec 1948. Flew theater airlift missions and participated in numerous exercises, Aug 1949–Jun 1951. The 61st TCG, the wing's primary group, deployed in South Korea for combat, Jul 1950–Jan 1951. Replaced by 60th Troop Carrier Wing on 2 Jun 1951. Replaced the 1502d Air Transport Wing in Hawaii in Jan 1966. Provided air transport and support functions for airlift operations in the entire Pacific Ocean area, Alaska to Antarctica, and the United States to Southeast Asia. Supported both scheduled and unscheduled airlift. Final combat squadron lost in Dec 1969; thereafter, wing concentrated entirely upon the support of airlift operations.

Service Streamers. None.

Campaign Streamers. None.

Decorations. Air Force Outstanding Unit Awards: 8–23 Jan 1966; 8 Jan–30 Jun 1966; 1 Jul 1966–30 Jun 1967; 1 Jul 1967–30 Jun 1968; 1 Jul 1968–30 Jun 1970; 1 Jul 1970–30 Jun 1972; 1 Jul 1972–30 Jun 1973.

Emblem. On a sky proper, issuant from chief two lightning flashes argent radiant to base saltirewise, surmounted in base by a roundel gules, winged or with details and outlines azure, the wings elevated and displayed to chief surrounding a sphere of the last bendwise with grid markings of the second and charged with three mullets and airlanes of the fourth, all within a diminished bordure silver. (Approved on 4 May 1966.)

62d MILITARY AIRLIFT WING

Lineage. Established as 62d Troop Carrier Wing on 28 Jul 1947. Organized on 15 Aug 1947. Discontinued on 24 Aug 1948. Redesignated 62d Troop Carrier Wing, Medium, and activated on 22 Aug 1948. Redesignated 62d Troop Carrier Wing, Heavy, on 12 Oct 1949. Inactivated on 1 Jun 1950. Activated on 17 Sep 1951. Redesignated: 62d Air Transport Wing, Heavy, on 1 Jan 1965; 62d Military Airlift Wing on 8 Jan 1966.

Assignments. Twelfth Air Force, 15 Aug 1947–24 Aug 1948. Twelfth Air Force, 22 Aug 1948; Fourth Air Force, 10 Dec 1948–1 Jun 1950. Eighteenth Air Force, 17 Sep 1951; Continental Division, Military Air Transport Service (later, Western Transport Air Force; Twenty-Second Air Force), 1 Jul 1957–.

Components. *Wings*. 302d: attached 27 Jun 1949–5 May 1950. 446th: attached 1 Jul 1973–. *Groups*. 61st: attached 21 Nov 1952–24 Aug 1954. 62d: 15 Aug 1947–24 Aug 1948; 22 Aug 1948–1 Jun 1950 (detached 2 May–1 Jun 1950); 1 Oct 1951–15 Jan 1960 (not operational, 8–15 Jan 1960). 939th: attached 25 Jul 1968–1 Jul 1973. *Squadrons*. 4th: attached 8–14 Jan 1960, assigned 15 Jan 1960–. 7th Logistic Support: 1 Jul 1963–1 Jul 1964. 7th: attached 8–14 Jan 1960, assigned 15 Jan 1960–22 Dec 1969. 8th: attached 8–14 Jan 1960, assigned 15 Jan 1960–. 19th Logistic Support (later, 19th Air Transport; 19th Military Airlift): 1 Jul 1963–22 Dec 1969. 28th: attached 1–7 Jul 1967, assigned 8 Jul 1967–8 Apr 1969. 36th Tactical Airlift: 1 Jul 1975–.

Stations. McChord Field (later, AFB), Wash, 15 Aug 1947–24 Aug 1948. McChord AFB, Wash, 22 Aug 1948–1 Jun 1950. McChord AFB, Wash, 17 Sep 1951; Larson AFB, Wash, 21 Apr 1952; McChord AFB, Wash, 13 Jun 1960–.

Commanders. Col Julius A. Kolb, 15 Aug 1947; Col Fred C. Nelson, 10 Apr–24 Aug 1948. Col Fred C. Nelson, 22 Aug 1948–1 May 1950; none (not manned), 2 May–1 Jun 1950. Brig Gen Harold W. Bowman, 17 Sep 1951; Col Edward T. Imparate, 19 Mar 1952; Brig Gen Harold W. Bowman, Apr 1952; Brig Gen George F. McGuire, 18 Sep 1954; Col John M. Hutchison, 26 May 1958; Col Harold M. Brecht, 13 Jun 1960; Col Allison C. Brooks, 15 Aug 1960; Col Tracy J. Petersen, (by 27) Feb 1963; Col Allison C. Brooks, May 1963; Col Tracy J. Petersen, 3 Jan 1964; Col Hugh E. Wild, 7 Aug 1964; Col Theodore P. Tatum, 16 Nov 1966; Brig Gen Clare T. Ireland, Jr., 9 Jun 1967; Col John H. Germeraad, 16 Feb 1969; Brig Gen Arthur W. Cruikshank, Jr., 19 May 1969; Brig Gen John H. Germeraad, 22 Aug 1969; Brig Gen Van N. Backman, 1 Mar 1970; Brig Gen Benjamin F. Starr, Jr., 31 May 1973; Col Donald W. Bennett, 12 Aug 1973; Brig Gen Edward J. Nash, 14 Aug 1973; Col Allan K. Andreason, 8 Aug 1975; Col Donald D. Brown, 1 Jul 1977–.

Aircraft. C–82, 1947–1948. C–82, 1948–1950; C–54, 1949–1950. C–124, 1951–1969; C–54, 1952; C–141, 1966–; C–130, 1975–.

Operations. Conducted troop carrier operations, tactical exercises, and humanitarian missions initially with C–82s and later with C–54s, 1947–1948 and 1948–1950. Provided training for 302d Troop Carrier Wing, a Reserve corollary, Jun 1949–May 1950. Not operational 2 May–1 Jun 1950. Trained in troop carrier operations with C–124s and C–54s at McChord AFB, Wash, in late 1951 and early 1952. Moved to Larson AFB, Wash, in Apr 1952. From Larson, routinely performed troop carrier, air transport, and humanitarian missions on a global scale. Participated in the airlift of French troops from France to Indo-China in Operation Bali-Hai, Apr–May 1954. Provided a major portion of the airlift needed to construct the distant early warning (DEW) line in northern Alaska and

Canada, 1955–1956, and thereafter periodically resupplied the DEW line stations. During the international geophysical year 1957–1958, and subsequently through 1962, supported scientific stations in the Arctic Ocean by airlanding and airdropping supplies on the drifting ice. Moved to McChord AFB in 1960. Helped transport UN troops and supplies to the Congo in 1960. Assumed responsibility in 1963 for worldwide airlift of nuclear weapons and associated equipment, continuing this mission through early 1971. Assumed airlift of Minuteman missiles from depots to operating sites in Apr 1971. From Oct 1975 to Oct 1977, maintained a detachment of C–130s in the Canal Zone to support USAF needs in Central and South America. In 1972, supported Presidential trips to China and the Soviet Union. From 12 Feb to 1 Apr 1973, transported former prisoners of war from North Vietnam to the Philippines and the United States. That same year, transported UN troops from Indonesia to Israel and Egypt as part of a peace-keeping effort.

Service Streamers. None.

Campaign Streamers. None.

Decorations. Air Force Outstanding Unit Awards: 1 Jan 1961–1 Nov 1962; 1 Jul 1965–15 Jul 1966; 1 Jul 1969–30 Jun 1970; 1 Jul 1973–30 Jun 1974.

Emblem. Gray, a globe with axis bendwise azure gridlined of the first above in base two arched olive branches, one to dexter and one to sinister vert, overall in pale a sword with blade argent, hilt or, the blade winged of the last, the point of the blade surmounting a sunburst of the like, all within a diminished bordure or. (Approved on 17 Nov 1969.)

63d MILITARY AIRLIFT WING

Lineage. Established as 63d Troop Carrier Wing, Medium, on 10 May 1949. Activated in the Reserve on 27 Jun 1949. Ordered to active service on 1 May 1951. Inactivated on 9 May 1951. Redesignated 63d Troop Carrier Wing, Heavy, on 18 Dec 1952. Activated on 8 Jan 1953. Redesignated 63d Military Airlift Wing on 8 Jan 1966.

Assignments. First Air Force, 27 Jun 1949–9 May 1951. Eighteenth Air Force, 8 Jan 1953; Continental Division, Military Air Transport Service (later, Western Transport Air Force), 1 Jul 1957; Eastern Transport Air Force (later, Twenty-First Air Force), 1 Oct 1958; Twenty-Second Air Force, 1 Apr 1967–.

Components. *Wings.* 64th: attached 15 Oct 1953–1 Mar 1954. 445th: attached 1 Jul 1973–. *Groups.* 61st: attached 25 Aug 1954–30 Jun 1957, assigned 1 Jul 1957–8 Oct 1959 (detached 23 Jul–c. 15 Sep 1958). 63d: 27 Jun 1949–9 May 1951; 20 Jun 1953–18 Jan 1963. 64th: attached 15 Oct 1953–15 Feb 1954. 465th: attached 15 Oct–30 Nov 1953. 944th: attached 25 Mar 1968–1 Jul 1973. *Squadrons.* 7th Air Transport: 1 Jul 1964–8 Jan 1966. 14th:

18 Jan 1963–. 15th: 18 Jan 1963– (not operational, c. Feb–14 Aug 1967). 21st Helicopter: attached 9 Jul 1956–30 Jun 1957. 52d: 18 Jan 1963–8 Jan 1967 (detached). 53d: 18 Jan 1963–8 Jul 1966; 8 Jan 1972–. 54th: 1 Jul 1957–8 Oct 1959; 18 Jan 1963–25 Jun 1965. 58th: 8 Jan–1 Jul 1966. 309th: attached 8 Oct 1954–9 Jul 1956.

Stations. Floyd Bennett NAS, NY, 27 Jun 1949–9 May 1951. Altus Muni Aprt (later, AFB), Okla, 8 Jan 1953; Donaldson AFB, SC, 15 Oct 1953; Hunter AFB, Ga, 1 Apr 1963; Norton AFB, Calif, 1 Apr 1967–.

Commanders. Brig Gen Robert L. Copsey, Jun 1949; Col Clayton Stiles, 9 Sep 1950–May 1951. Brig Gen Glynne M. Jones, 8 Jan 1953; Col Eston E. Selvey, Jan 1953; Brig Gen Glynne M. Jones, c. Mar 1953; Brig Gen Edgar W. Hampton, Feb 1955; Col Chester C. Moomaw, c. Sep 1958; Brig Gen Andrew B. Cannon, 15 Sep 1958; Col Roland J. Barnick, 29 Sep 1961; Col Leland W. Johnson, 24 Jun 1964; Col Gilbert L. Curtis, 8 Jul 1964; Col Lopez J. Mantoux, 7 Apr 1966; Col James A. Evans, Jr., 4 Nov 1966; Brig Gen Gilbert L. Curtis, 1 Apr 1967; Brig Gen Louis G. Griffin, 6 Jul 1968; Brig Gen John F. Gonge, 1 Feb 1970; Brig Gen Lester T. Kearney, Jr., 28 Feb 1971; Brig Gen Erskine Wigley, 12 Mar 1973; Brig Gen Benjamin F. Starr, Jr., 15 Aug 1974; Brig Gen William E. Carson, 15 Jul 1975; Brig Gen George B. Powers, Jr., 9 Jul 1976–.

Aircraft. T–6, 1949–1950; T–7, 1949–1951; T–11, 1949–1951; C–47, 1949–1951. C–119, 1953–1954; C–124, 1953–1967; H–19, 1954–1956; H–21, 1956–1957; C–141, 1967–.

Operations. Trained in the Reserve, 1949–1951, performed limited troop carrier operations from mid-1950 until ordered to active service and inactivated in 1951. While wing stationed at Altus AFB, Okla, tactical components underwent C–124 training, Jun–Oct 1953. Performed global airlift missions, including occasional humanitarian or mercy missions, using C–124s as primary carriers Oct 1953–Mar 1967, but also using C–119s, 1953–1954, and helicopters, 1954–1957. Switched to C–141s as primary aircraft in Apr 1967, upon moving to Norton AFB, Calif. Among the wing's notable operations were airlifts and airdrops in the North American arctic during construction and subsequent operation of the distant early warning (DEW) line, 1954–1956, and on floating ice islands in support of scientific stations in the Arctic Ocean, 1957–1966; airlift and airdrop support in the Antarctic in support of the Navy's Operation Deep Freeze, 1956–1966; maintenance of a complete tactical squadron on rotation in Europe, Aug 1956–Jan 1967; airlift missions to the Far East and Southeast Asia during the Southeast Asia conflict, 1967–1973; evacuation of former American prisoners of war from North Vietnam (Operation Homecoming) in early 1973; and support of airlift of Vietnam refugees from their homeland to the United States (Operation New Life) in 1975.

Service Streamers. None.

Campaign Streamers. None.

Decorations. Air Force Outstanding Unit Awards: 2 Mar–31 May 1955; 1 Jul 1957–10 Dec 1962; 1 Jul 1968–30 Jun 1969; 1 Jul 1970–30 Jun 1971.

Emblem. On a light blue shield with a green embattled base, a red lightning flash striking from upper right corner and crossing the corner of one embattlement and a white parachute with shroud lines touching the tip of the flash; above the parachute three white aircraft, on the green base a circle of six yellow stars at the left and a triangle of three yellow stars. *Motto:* OMNIA UBIQUE SEMPER—Anything, anywhere, anytime. (Approved on 2 Oct 1953.)

64th FLYING TRAINING WING

Lineage. Established as 64th Troop Carrier Wing, Medium, on 3 Jul 1952. Activated on 14 Jul 1952. Inactivated on 21 Jul 1954. Activated on 24 Oct 1960. Organized on 8 Feb 1961. Discontinued, and inactivated, on 1 Jan 1963. Redesignated 64th Troop Carrier Wing, and activated, on 7 Mar 1966. Organized on 1 Jul 1966. Redesignated 64th Tactical Airlift Wing on 1 May 1967. Inactivated on 31 May 1971. Redesignated 64th Flying Training Wing on 14 Apr 1972. Activated on 1 Oct 1972.

Assignments. Eighteenth Air Force, 14 Jul 1952–21 Jul 1954 (attached to 63d Troop Carrier Wing, Heavy, 15 Oct 1953–1 Mar 1954). Tactical Air Command, 24 Oct 1960; Ninth Air Force, 8 Feb 1961; Twelfth Air Force, 1 Jan 1962–1 Jan 1963. Tactical Air Command, 7 Mar 1966; 839th Air Division, 1 Jul 1966; Twelfth Air Force, 9 Mar 1970–31 May 1971. Air Training Command, 1 Oct 1972–.

Components. *Groups.* 64th: 14 Jul 1952–21 Jul 1954 (detached 15 Oct 1953–15 Feb 1954). 443d: attached 8 Jan–1 Feb 1953. 465th: attached 1 Feb–15 Oct 1953. *Squadrons.* 4th Liaison: attached 22 Jul 1952–23 Jan 1953. 7th Liaison: attached 20 Oct 1952–9 Jan 1953. 17th: 8 Feb 1961–1 Jan 1963. 18th: 8 Jan 1962–1 Jan 1963. 35th: 1 Oct 1972–. 54th: 1 Oct 1972–. 61st: 1 Jul 1966–31 May 1971 (detached 5 May–14 Aug 1967, 28 Mar–29 Jun 1968, 28 May–7 Jul 1970, 12 Oct–19 Dec 1970). 62d: 1 Jul 1966–31 May 1971 (detached 13 Dec 1967–c. 28 Mar 1968, 1 Jul–2 Oct 1968, 5 Nov 1969–17 Jan 1970, 2 Jul–31 Aug 1970, 2 Apr–31 May 1971).

Stations. Donaldson AFB, SC, 14 Jul 1952–21 Jul 1954. Dyess AFB, Texas, 8 Feb 1961–1 Jan 1963. Sewart AFB, Tenn, 1 Jul 1966; Little Rock AFB, Ark, 9 Mar 1970–31 May 1971. Reese AFB, Texas, 1 Oct 1972–.

Commanders. Brig Gen Franklin Rose, 14 Jul 1952; Brig Gen Glynne M. Jones, 1 Oct 1953 (additional duty); Col Bob Arnold, 28 Feb 1954; Col William C. Bentley, 1 May–21 Jul 1954. None (not manned), 24 Oct 1960–7 Feb 1961; Col Donald F. Blake, 8 Feb 1961; Lt Col Raymond J. Berger, 14 Jul 1962; Col Burl W. McLaughlin, 19 Jul 1962–1 Jan 1963. None (not manned), 7 Mar–30 Jun 1966; Col Jack W. Crawford, Jr., 1 Jul 1966; Col Robert D. Brown, 6 Jan

1967; Col Earle F. MacDonald, 20 Oct 1967; Col Leo A. Drake, Jr., 1 Aug 1968; Col Richard J. Gibney, 7 Jan 1970–31 May 1971. Col Walter H. Baxter III, 1 Oct 1972; Col Schuyler Bissell, 29 Jul 1974; Brig Gen Edward Mendel, 5 May 1975; Col Charles E. Bishop, 21 May 1977–.

Aircraft. C–82, 1952–1953; L–20, 1952–1953; C–119, 1953, 1954. C–130, 1961–1963. C–130, 1966–1971. T–41, 1972–1973; T–37, 1972–; T–38, 1972–.

Operations. Performed airlift and airdrop/airlanding of troops and cargo, routinely and during frequent maneuvers, 1952–1953. Began phasing down for inactivation in mid-Oct 1953, at which time tactical operations passed to 63d Troop Carrier Wing. In Feb 1954, however, began building up again in preparation for an overseas movement, but was inactivated instead. Activated at Dyess AFB, Texas, in Feb 1961 with a troop carrier/airlift mission, plus resupply of Distant Early Warning sites on the Greenland ice cap. Inactivated on 1 Jan 1963. Replaced Troop Carrier Wing Provisional, 4413th, in Jul 1966 at Sewart AFB, Tenn. Provided global airlift and aeromedical evacuation, Jul 1966–May 1971. Also provided C–130 combat crew training for other C–130 units, 1 Jul 1966–6 Mar 1970, with this activity being the wing's primary activity from 9 Aug 1968 to 6 Mar 1970. Replaced at Little Rock AFB, Ark, in May 1971 by 314th Tactical Airlift Wing. Replaced 3500th Pilot Training Wing in Oct 1972 and assumed mission of undergraduate pilot training and operation and maintenance of Reese AFB, Texas.

Service Streamers. None.

Campaign Streamers. None.

Decorations. Air Force Outstanding Unit Award with Combat "V" Device: [1 Jul 1966]–30 Jun 1967. Air Force Outstanding Unit Award: 1 Jun 1969–31 May 1971.

Emblem. Azure, a stylized eagle ascending bendwise with wings elevated, head, neck, wing tips, and tail feathers argent, body, beak, wings, legs, claws and talons are garnished brown and sable, grasping a lightning flash of the second, in dexter chief a mullet of five points of the like, all within a diminished bordure or. (Approved on 20 Feb 1973.)

65th STRATEGIC RECONNAISSANCE WING, MEDIUM

Lineage. Established as 65th Troop Carrier Wing, Medium, on 26 May 1952. Activated in the Reserve on 14 Jun 1952. Inactivated on 1 Apr 1953. Redesignated 65th Strategic Reconnaissance Wing, Medium, on 1 Apr 1953.

Assignments. First Air Force, 14 Jun 1952–1 Apr 1953.

Components. *Group.* 65th: 14 Jun 1952–1 Apr 1953.

Stations. Mitchel AFB, NY, 14 Jun 1952–1 Apr 1953.

Commanders. Col Charles K. Nelson, Jr., 14 Jun 1952; Col Howard C. Stelling, 31 Jul 1952–1 Apr 1953.

Aircraft. C–46, 1952–1953.

Operations. Reserve training toward proficiency with troop carrier aircraft. Never fully manned or equipped.

Service Streamers. None.

Campaign Streamers. None.

Decorations. None.

Emblem. None.

66th TACTICAL RECONNAISSANCE WING

Lineage. Established as 66th Tactical Reconnaissance Wing on 15 Nov 1952. Activated on 1 Jan 1953. Inactivated on 1 Apr 1970.

Assignments. Ninth Air Force, 1 Jan 1953; Twelfth Air Force, 7 Jul 1953; United States Air Forces in Europe, 1 Jan 1958; Seventeenth Air Force, 15 Nov 1959; Third Air Force, 1 Sep 1966–1 Apr 1970.

Components. *Group.* 66th: 1 Jan 1953–8 Dec 1957. *Squadrons.* 17th: 10 May 1959–12 Jan 1970. 18th: 1 Jun 1959–30 Jan 1970. 19th: 8 Dec 1957–8 Mar 1958 (detached 8 Jan–8 Mar 1958). 30th: 8 Dec 1957–8 Mar 1958 (detached 8 Jan–8 Mar 1958). 32d: attached 8 Jan–7 Mar 1958, assigned 8 Mar 1958–1 Oct 1965. 38th: attached 8 Jan–7 Mar 1958, assigned 8 Mar 1958–1 Jan 1966. 302d: 8 Dec 1957–20 Jun 1959. 303d: 8 Dec 1957–20 Jun 1959.

Stations. Shaw AFB, SC, 1 Jan–25 Jun 1953; Sembach AB, West Germany, 7 Jul 1953; Laon AB, France, 10 Jul 1958; RAF Upper Heyford, England, 1 Sep 1966–1 Apr 1970.

Commanders. Col Jacob W. Dixon, 1 Jan 1953; Col G. H. Fulcher, 27 Mar 1953; Col Hervey H. Whitfield, (by Sep) 1954; Col Earl H. Jacobson, 25 Apr 1957; Col Robert R. Gideon, Jr., 8 Jun 1957; Brig Gen Kyle L. Riddle, Aug 1959; Col Bernard R. Muldoon, 6 Jul 1961; Col Nathan J. Adams, 2 Jul 1963; Col Charlie Falletta, 24 May 1965; Col Frederick W. Dyer, 10 Jul 1965; Col Frank C. Malone, 13 Jul 1965; Col Robert J. Holbury, 6 Jul 1966; Col Kendell S. Young, 14 Aug 1967; Col Harry M. Chapman, 26 Jun 1968; Col Herman G. Tillman, Jr., 4 Jul 1968–1 Apr 1970.

Aircraft. RF–51, 1953; RB–26, 1953–1955; RF–80, 1953–1956; RB–57, 1954–1955, 1955–1958; B–57, 1955–1956; RF–84, 1955–1959; RB–66, 1957–1958; RB–45, 1957; RF–101, 1958–1970; RF–4, 1969–1970.

Operations. Replaced 118th Tactical Reconnaissance Wing in Jan 1953. Provided day and night tactical reconnaissance for TAC, and participated in several exercises, Jan–May 1953. Moved to Europe in May 1953. Provided day and night (primarily day, after Jan 1958) reconnaissance for USAFE and NATO, Jul 1953–Jan 1970. In addition, participated in a steady stream of tactical exercises and evaluations, readiness inspections, and training programs.

Service Streamers. None.

Campaign Streamers. None.

Decorations. Air Force Outstanding Unit Award: 1 Jan–31 Dec 1962.

Emblem. Per bend gules and azure, a bend nebule argent between a sprig of goldenrod or and a sprig of mountain laurel vert, fimbriated of the fourth. *Motto:* OMNIA CONSPICIMUS—We observe all. (Approved for 66th Group on 5 Jan 1943 and for 66th Wing on 26 May 1953.)

67th TACTICAL RECONNAISSANCE WING

Lineage. Established as 67th Reconnaissance Wing on 6 Nov 1947. Organized on 25 Nov 1947. Discontinued on 24 Aug 1948. Redesignated 67th Tactical Reconnaissance Wing, and activated on 22 Aug 1948. Inactivated on 28 Mar 1949. Activated on 25 Feb 1951. Discontinued, and inactivated, on 8 Dec 1960. Activated on 2 Aug 1965. Organized on 1 Jan 1966.

Assignments. Twelfth Air Force, 25 Nov 1947–24 Aug 1948 (attached to 1st Fighter Wing, 25 Nov 1947–24 Aug 1948). Twelfth Air Force, 22 Aug 1948 (attached to 1st Fighter Wing, 22 Aug 1948–); Fourth Air Force, 20 Dec 1948–28 Mar 1949 (remained attached to 1st Fighter Wing to 28 Mar 1949). Fifth Air Force, 25 Feb 1951; 41st Air Division, 10 Nov 1958–8 Dec 1960. Tactical Air Command, 2 Aug 1965; Twelfth Air Force, 1 Jan 1966; 831st Air Division, 15 Apr 1966; Twelfth Air Force, 20 Apr 1971–.

Components. *Group.* 67th: 25 Nov 1947–24 Aug 1948; 22 Aug 1948–28 Mar 1949; 25 Feb 1951–1 Oct 1957 (not operational, 1 Jun–24 Nov 1954; detached 1 Jul–1 Oct 1957). *Squadrons.* 4th: 15 Jul–15 Oct 1971. 7th: 15 Dec 1967–15 Oct 1971 (not operational, 15 Dec 1967–c. 19 Jan 1968). 9th: 15 Jul–31 Aug 1971. 10th: 1 Jan 1966–30 Jun 1971. 11th: attached 1 Jun–24 Nov 1954; attached 1 Jul–30 Sep 1957, assigned 1 Oct 1957–8 Mar 1960; assigned 1 Apr–25 Oct 1966. 12th: attached 1 Jun–24 Nov 1954; attached 1 Jul–30 Sep 1957, assigned 1 Oct 1957–8 Mar 1960; assigned 1 Jul–2 Sep 1966 (not operational, 1 Jul–28 Aug 1966); assigned 31 Aug 1971– (detached 5 May–4 Jun 1974 and 8–29 Sep 1977). 15th: attached 1 Jun–24 Nov 1954; attached 1 Jul–30 Sep 1957, assigned 1 Oct 1957–25 Apr 1960. 22d: 20 Sep 1966–15 Oct 1971 (detached 8–26 Oct 1968 and 15 Jul–15 Oct 1971). 45th: attached 1 Jun–24 Nov 1954; attached 1 Jul–30 Sep 1957, assigned 1 Oct 1957–25 Apr 1960; assigned 15 Oct 1971–31 Oct 1975 (detached 13 Jun–7 Jul 1973). 91st: 15 Jul 1971– (detached 26 Apr–25 May 1972 and 25 May–9 Jun 1977). 417th: 1 Jul 1968–15 Nov 1970 (detached 12 Jan–4 Apr 1969 and 11 Sep–10 Oct 1970). 421st Air Refueling: attached 17–30 Sep 1957, assigned 1 Oct 1957–8 Dec 1960 (detached 21 Nov–8 Dec 1960). 6021st: attached 1 Jul–8 Dec 1957 (not operational, c. 6 Sep–8 Dec 1960). 6091st: attached 1 Jul–30 Sep 1957, assigned 1 Oct 1957–8 Dec 1960 (detached 21 Nov–8 Dec 1960). *Flight.* 6166th Air Weather Reconnaissance: attached 25 Feb 1951–25 Nov 1953.

Stations. March Field (later, AFB), Calif, 25 Nov 1947–24 Aug 1948. March AFB, Calif, 22 Aug 1948–28 Mar 1949. Komaki AB, Japan, 25 Feb 1951; Taegu AB, South Korea, 21 Mar 1951; Kimpo AB, South Korea, 20 Aug 1951; Itami AB, Japan, 6 Dec 1954; Yokota AB, Japan, 1 Jul 1957–8 Dec 1960. Mountain Home AFB, Idaho, 1 Jan 1966; Bergstrom AFB, Texas, 15 Jul 1971–.

Commanders. Col Arthur R. DeBolt, 25 Nov 1947–24 Aug 1948. Col Arthur R. DeBolt, 22 Aug 1948; Lt Col Charles F. Scott, Jr., 4 Oct 1948; Lt Col Jack W. Hayes, Jr., 11 Oct 1948; Lt Col Horace A. Hanes, 1 Nov 1948; Lt Col Charles F. Scott, Jr., 12 Nov 1948; Col William H. Clark, 7 Jan 1949; Col Loren G. McCollom, 13 Jan 1949; Col Charles E. Marion, 16 Jan–28 Mar 1949. Col Karl L. Polifka, 25 Feb 1951; Col Bert N. Smiley, 1 Jul 1951; Col Vincent Howard, 4 Jul 1951; Col Edwin S. Chickering, 31 Oct 1951; Col Russell A. Berg, 13 Aug 1952; Col Charles F. Knierim, Jul 1953; Col Loren G. McCollom, 15 Aug 1953; Col Bernice S. Barr, c. Jul 1954; Col Prescott M. Spicer, 11 Aug 1954; Col Gwen G. Atkinson, 8 Nov 1956; Col Dalene E. Bailey, 22 Aug 1959; Col John G. Foster, 15 Jun–8 Dec 1960. None (not manned), 2 Aug–31 Dec 1965; Col Robert G. Williams, 1 Jan 1966; Col Wendell L. Bevan, Jr., 21 Nov 1966; Col Joseph Schreiber, 1 Jul 1968; Col Henry L. Warren, 1 Sep 1970; Col Walter F. Daniel, 15 Jul 1971; Col George A. Edwards, Jr., 28 Jul 1972; Col Thomas C. Pinckney, Jr., 8 Apr 1974; Col George M. Sauls, 2 Jul 1975; Col Davis C. Rohr, 19 May 1976; Col Robert L. Pearson, 3 Aug 1977–.

Aircraft. B/RB–26, 1947–1948; F–6, 1947; FA–26, 1947–1948; FP (later, RF)–80, 1947–1948. B/RB–26, 1948–1949; FA–26, 1948–1949; RF–80, 1948–1949. C–47, 1951–1952; RB–26, 1951–1957; WB–26, 1951–1957; RF–51, 1951–1953; RF–80, 1951–1955; RF–86, 1951–1956; T–6, 1951; F–80, 1952–1953; F–86, 1953; F–84, 1955; RF–84, 1955–1958; RB–66, 1956–1960; C–47, 1957–1958; SC–47, 1957–1960; C–54, 1957–1958; C–119, 1957–1958; RB/KB–50, 1957–1960; RB–57, 1957–1960; T–33, 1957–1959; WB–66, 1958–1960; RF–101, 1958–1960. RF–4, 1966–; F–4, 1968–1969, 1969–1970.

Operations. When the 67th Wing organized in Nov 1947, only its 67th Reconnaissance Group was fully operational. The entire 67th Wing was attached to the 1st Fighter Wing. The original (Table of Distribution) wing discontinued on 24 Aug 1948 and a new (Table of Organization) wing activated on 22 Aug 1948, the new wing absorbing resources of the original wing. Remained attached to 1st Fighter Wing until inactivated in 1949. The wing activated again in Feb 1951 for operations in Korea. It absorbed resources of the 543d Tactical Support Group and immediately commenced combat reconnaissance operations. Provided photographic coverage of enemy airfields and rail lines, with weather reconnaissance as a secondary task, during the Korean war. After the war, the wing remained in South Korea and later, in Japan, to provide reconnaissance as needed. On 1 Jul 1957, it became the sole reconnaissance wing in the Far

East, and in Sep 1957 added air refueling and military airlift to its mission, these new tasks continuing until the wing inactivated in Dec 1960. Six years later, the wing was organized at Mountain Home AFB, Idaho, charged with aerial, visual, optical, electronic, thermal, and radar reconnaissance. Added RF–4C replacement training to its mission in May 1966, and in Jun 1968, added tactical fighter operations with F–4Ds. This latter mission ceased in Nov 1970. The wing moved to Bergstrom AFB, Texas, in 1971, but from 15 May to 15 Jul 1971, the wing headquarters served in a dual role for the 67th TRW and the succeeding 347th TFW at Mountain Home AFB. At Bergstrom, the 67th absorbed the resources of the inactivated 75th TRW and continued the reconnaissance mission formerly handled by that wing.

Service Streamers. None.

Campaign Streamers. First UN Counteroffensive; CCF Spring Offensive; UN Summer–Fall Offensive; Second Korean Winter; Korea Summer–Fall, 1952; Third Korean Winter; Korea Summer–Fall, 1953.

Decorations. Air Force Outstanding Unit Awards: 1 Dec 1952–30 Apr 1953; 1 Aug 1966–31 May 1968; 15 Jul 1971–15 May 1973; 16 May 1974–15 May 1976. Republic of Korea Presidential Unit Citation: [25] Feb 1951–31 Mar 1953.

Emblem. On a shield per bend sinister, sky proper and azure between a lightning bolt gules, fimbriated sable, in bend sinister, the quarter section of a sun, issuing from the dexter chief, or, fimbriated sable, in sinister four stars argent, one, two and one, all the shield within a diminutive bordure sable. *Motto:* LUX EX TENEBRIS—Light from darkness. (Approved on 20 Mar 1952.)

68th BOMBARDMENT WING, HEAVY

Lineage. Established as 68th Strategic Reconnaissance Wing, Medium, on 4 Oct 1951. Activated on 10 Oct 1951. Redesignated: 68th Bombardment Wing, Medium, on 16 Jun 1952; 68th Bombardment Wing, Heavy, on 15 Apr 1963.

Assignments. 37th Air Division, 10 Oct 1951 (attached to 21st Air Division, 10 Oct 1951–c. 15 May 1952); Second Air Force, 28 May 1952; 806th Air Division, 16 Jun 1952 (attached to 7th Air Division, 14 Jun–7 Aug 1954 and 27 Sep 1957–8 Jan 1958); 825th Air (later, 825th Strategic Aerospace) Division, 15 Jun 1960; 822d Air Division, 15 Apr 1963; 57th Air Division, 1 Jul 1964; 822d Air Division, 1 Jul 1965; 57th Air Division, 2 Sep 1966; 823d Air Division, 2 Jul 1969; 42d Air Division, 30 Jun 1971–.

Components. *Group.* 68th: 10 Oct 1951–16 Jun 1952 (not operational). *Squadrons.* 24th: attached 10 Oct 1951–15 Jun 1952, assigned 16 Jun

1952–16 Jan 1953. 51st: attached 10 Oct 1951–15 Jun 1952, assigned 16 Jun 1952– (not operational, 20 Mar–14 Apr 1963 and 27 May 1972–Jul 1973). 52d: attached 10 Oct 1951–15 Jun 1952, assigned 16 Jun 1952–15 Apr 1963 (not operational, 20 Mar–15 Apr 1963). 68th Air Refueling: attached 8 Apr–28 May 1952 (not operational); assigned 25 Nov 1953–3 Sep 1957 (detached 14 Jun–7 Aug 1954). 656th: 16 Jan 1953–15 Apr 1963 (not operational, 20 Mar–15 Apr 1963). 657th: 1 Dec 1958–1 Jan 1962 (not operational, 1 Oct 1961–1 Jan 1962). 911th Air Refueling: 15 Apr 1963– (not operational, 27 May 1972–Jul 1973).

Stations. Lake Charles (later, Chennault) AFB, La, 10 Oct 1951; Seymour Johnson AFB, NC, 15 Apr 1963–.

Commanders. Capt William S. Glass, Jr., 10 Oct 1951; Col Lowell G. Sidwell, 26 Oct 1951; Brig Gen Joseph J. Nazzaro, 20 Aug 1952; Col Joel A. Carroll, Jr., 17 Jan 1953; Col Robert R. Gideon, Jr., 22 Jan 1953; Col Herbert O. Wangeman, Jun 1953; Col Robert R. Gideon, Jr., Sep 1953; Col Joel A. Carroll, Jr., 15 Oct 1954; Col Robert I. Barrowclough, 25 Oct 1954; Col Andrew J. Bratton, Jr., 11 Jun 1956; Col Robert I. Barrowclough, 7 Jul 1956; Col Andrew J. Bratton, Jr., 17 Jun 1957; Col Robert I. Barrowclough, 18 Jul 1957; Col Frank P. Bender, 27 Jul 1957; Col James T. Gribble, Jr., 1 Sep 1959; Col John W. Livingston, 3 Oct 1960; Col Edward D. Gaitley, Jr., c. 15 Feb 1963; Col Osce V. Jones, 15 Apr 1963; Col Walter A. Hardzog, Jr., 16 Jun 1963; Col Charles J. Beck, 1 Jul 1963; Col Raymond E. Buckwalter, 28 Sep 1965; Col Robert E. Brofft, 1 Sep 1966; Col Eugene L. Hudson, 28 Apr 1967; Col Harold E. Ottaway, 6 Jul 1968; Col Donald L. Stallsmith, 29 May 1969; Col Robert W. Daniels, 30 Apr 1970; Col LeRoy P. Hansen, 15 Oct 1970; Col Donald F. Ryan, 14 May 1971; Col Melvin G. Bowling, 7 Jun 1972; Col Jerome E. Wechter, 15 Feb 1973 (temporary), 10 May 1973 (permanent); Col George P. Tynan, 6 Jun 1974; Col James E. Myers, Sr., 28 Jul 1975; Col Caryl W. Calhoun, 22 Aug 1975; Col Henry L. Conn, 14 Jul 1977–.

Aircraft. B–29, 1951–1953; B–47, 1953–1963; KC–97, 1953–1957; B–52, 1963–1972, 1973–; KC–135, 1963–1972, 1973–.

Operations. Received initial cadre of 16 people from 44th Bombardment Wing in Oct 1951. Began operational training as a reconnaissance wing using borrowed B–29s in Oct 1951. Received own B–29s in May 1952 and trained as a bombardment wing. Converted to B–47s in late 1953. Added a refueling mission in Nov 1953. Conducted strategic bombardment training (May 1954–Jun 1963) and air refueling (May 1954–Sep 1957) to meet SAC's global commitments. Deployed at Fairford RAF Station, England, 14 Jun–7 Aug 1954 and at Brize Norton AB, England, 27 Sep 1957–8 Jan 1958. Moved without personnel or equipment to NC on 15 Apr 1963, replacing 4241st Strategic Wing at Seymour Johnson AFB. Conducted strategic bombardment training with B–52s and air refueling with KC–135s beginning Apr 1963. Deployed at Loring AFB, Maine, 28 Jul–28 Aug 1965. From 27 May 1972 to 15 Jul 1973, all wing aircraft, most aircrew and maintenance personnel, and about half of the wing's support people loaned to other SAC units for combat operations in Southeast Asia.

Service Streamers. None.

Campaign Streamers. None.

Decorations. None.

Emblem. On a shield, per chevron reversed, azure and gules; on a chevron reversed, indented and fracted argent, two lightning bolts gules; in chief six stars in fess argent, above a clenched mailed fist gules, fimbriated argent, holding an olive branch or; in base eight bombs argent. *Motto:* FOLLOW ME. (Approved on 3 Oct 1952.)

70th BOMBARDMENT WING, HEAVY

Lineage. Established as 70th Strategic Reconnaissance Wing, Medium, on 23 Mar 1953. Activated on 24 Jan 1955. Redesignated 70th Bombardment Wing, Medium, on 25 Oct 1961. Discontinued, and inactivated, on 25 Jun 1962. Redesignated 70th Bombardment Wing, Heavy, and activated, on 15 Nov 1962. Organized on 1 Feb 1963. Inactivated on 31 Dec 1969.

Assignments. Second Air Force, 24 Jan 1955 (attached to 801st Air Division, 24 Jan 1955–); 825th Air (later, 825th Strategic Aerospace) Division, 1 Aug 1955–25 Jun 1962 (remained attached to 801st Air Division to c. 19 Oct 1955; attached to 5th Air Division, 26 Oct–17 Dec 1956). Strategic Air Command, 15 Nov 1962; 816th Strategic Aerospace Division, 1 Feb 1963; 17th Strategic Aerospace Division, 1 Jul 1965–31 Dec 1969.

Components. *Squadrons.* 6th: 24 Jan 1955–25 Jun 1962 (not operational, 24 Jan–30 Apr 1955; detached 1 May–c. Oct 1955); 1 Feb 1963–31 Dec 1969 (not operational, 15 Apr–c. 1 Oct 1968 and Apr–Sep 1969). 26th (later, 681st): 24 Jan 1955–25 Jun 1962 (not operational, 24 Jan–2 Oct 1955). 61st: 24 Jan 1955–25 Jun 1962 (not operational, 24 Jan–10 Jul 1955; detached 15 Jul–c. Oct 1955). 70th Air Refueling: 1 Aug 1955–1 Aug 1961 (not operatinal, 1 Aug–14 Oct 1955; detached 27 Jan–16 Aug 1956, 24 Jun–c. 24 Sep 1957, 3 Sep 1958–12 Jan 1959, and 5 Oct 1960–11 Jan 1961). 902d Air Refueling: 1 Feb 1963–31 Dec 1969 (not operational, 15 Apr– c. 1 Oct 1968 and Apr–Sep 1969).

Stations. Little Rock AFB, Ark, 24 Jan 1955–25 Jun 1962. Clinton-Sherman AFB, Okla, 1 Feb 1963–31 Dec 1969.

Commanders. Col Lester C. Hess, 24 Jan 1955; Maj Lewis P. Gaby, 14 Feb 1955; Lt Col Albert S. Harwell, Jr., 14 Apr 1955; Col Lester C. Hess, 10 May 1955; Col William Burke, 26 Jun 1955; Col Donald O. Tower, 26 May 1958; Col John H. Kunkel, Jr., 6 Aug 1958; Col Irby V. Tedder, 1 Apr 1960; Col James O. Britt, 16 Apr 1960; Col George E. Glober, (by 4) May 1961–c. 25 Jun 1962. None (not manned), 15 Nov 1962–31 Jan 1963; Col Paul N. Bacalis,

1 Feb 1963; Col Orie O. Schurter, 12 Jun 1964; Col William R. Brown, 15 Nov 1965; Col Therwin S. Walters, 13 Apr 1968; Col William R. Brown, 5 Oct 1968; Col Raymond P. Lowman, 30 Nov 1968; Col Robert T. Calhoun, 26 Mar 1969; Col Raymond P. Lowman, 30 Sep–31 Dec 1969.

Aircraft. RB–47, 1955–1962; KC–97, 1955–1961; B–47, 1961–1962. B–52, 1963–1968, 1968–1969; KC–135, 1963–1968, 1968–1969.

Operations. Deployed at Lockbourne AFB, Ohio, 24 Jan–19 Oct 1955, while permanent base underwent construction. Few wing components manned until move to Little Rock AFB, Ark. Flew strategic reconnaissance to meet SAC's global commitments, Oct 1955–1962, but on a reduced scale after Feb 1958. Assumed an air refueling mission in 1955. Deployed at Sidi Slimane AB, Morocco, 26 Oct–17 Dec 1956. From Jun 1958 to Sep 1961, provided B/RB–47 combat crew training for other SAC units, while continuing RB–47 and KC–97 operations. The refueling squadron transferred in Aug 1961 and the final RB–47 class graduated in Oct 1961. Converted to B–47s in late 1961, but inactivated prior to becoming combat ready. Replaced the 4123d Strategic Wing at Clinton–Sherman AFB, Okla, in Feb 1963. Conducted strategic bombardment training and air refueling to meet SAC's global commitments, Feb 1963–Dec 1969. For several months each in 1968 and 1969, all wing aircraft, most of its aircrew and maintenance personnel, and some of its support people loaned to other SAC units engaged in combat operations in the Far East and Southeast Asia.

Service Streamers. None.

Campaign Streamers. None.

Decorations. Air Force Outstanding Unit Awards: 15 Feb–30 Dec 1957; 15 Apr–1 Oct 1968.

Emblem. On a medium blue shield within a narrow yellow border, near the top of the shield, two white cloud formations issuing from each side of the shield, on a horizontal plane originating in the center near the bottom of the shield two green olive branches, highlighted yellow encircling a light blue globe, rimmed and grid lines black with green land areas, the globe surmounting two red lightning bolts forming an X. Within the lightning bolts at the top of the shield a circle of seven yelloab01w stars. On the globe a black mated bomber and tanker flying horizontally. *Motto:* STRENGTH THROUGH UNITY. (Approved on 17 Feb 1964.)

71st FLYING TRAINING WING

Lineage. Established as 71st Tactical Reconnaissance Wing on 10 Aug 1948. Activated on 18 Aug 1948. Inactivated on 25 Oct 1948. Redesignated 71st Strategic Reconnaissance Wing, Fighter, on 4 Nov 1954. Activated on 24 Jan 1955.

Inactivated on 1 Jul 1957. Redesignated 71st Surveillance Wing (Ballistic Missile Early Warning System), and activated, on 6 Dec 1961. Organized on 1 Jan 1962. Redesignated 71st Missile Warning Wing on 1 Jan 1967. Inactivated on 30 Apr 1971. Redesignated 71st Flying Training Wing on 14 Apr 1972. Activated on 1 Nov 1972.

Assignments. 1st Air Division, 18 Aug–25 Oct 1948 (attached to 32d Composite Wing, 24 Aug–25 Oct 1948). Fifteenth Air Force, 24 Jan 1955–1 Jul 1957. Air Defense Command, 6 Dec 1961; 9th Aerospace Defense Division, 1 Jan 1962; Fourteenth Aerospace Force, 1 Jul 1968–30 Apr 1971. Air Training Command, 1 Nov 1972–.

Components. *Group.* 71st: 18 Aug–25 Oct 1948 (detached). *Squadrons.* 8th: 1 Nov 1972–. 23d: attached 18–24 Aug 1948. 25th: 24 Jan 1955–1 Jul 1957; 1 Nov 1972–. 82d: 24 Jan 1955–1 Jul 1957. 91st: 24 Jan 1955–1 Jul 1957.

Stations. Kadena, Okinawa, 18 Aug–25 Oct 1948. Larson AFB, Wash, 24 Jan 1955–1 Jul 1957. Ent AFB, Colo, 1 Jan 1962; McGuire AFB, NJ, 21 JUL 1969–30 Apr 1971. Vance AFB, Okla, 1 Nov 1972–.

Commanders. Col Edwin M. Day, 18–24 Aug 1948; none (not manned), 25 Aug–25 Oct 1948. None (not manned), 24 Jan–11 Feb 1955; Col Charles F. McKenna III, 12 Feb 1955; Col Charles A. Gayle, 26 Mar–1 Jul 1957. None (not manned), 6–31 Dec 1961; Col Robert L. Harriger, c. 1962; Col Edwin Bishop, Jr., c. 1965; Col Russell G. Ogan, 15 Jul 1968; Col William A. Larsen, 1 Jul 1969; Col Lincoln D. Faurer, 31 Dec 1970–30 Apr 1971. Col John P. Rollston, 1 Nov 1972; Col Schuyler Bissell, 24 Sep 1973; Col George T. Kertesz, 15 Jul 1974; Col James P. Smothermon, 10 Apr 1975; Col Thomas J. Magner, 17 Aug 1976–.

Aircraft. RB–17, 1948; RB–29, 1948. RF–84, 1955–1957; RBF–84, 1955–1956. T–41, 1972–1973; T–37, 1972–; T–38, 1972–.

Operations. Tactical group detached, but a single reconnaissance squadron was attached, 18–24 Aug 1948, to perform photographic reconnaissance. Wing not operational, 25 Aug–25 Oct 1948. Activated in Jan 1955 to perform strategic reconnaissance and test a technique for launching small RBF–84 aircraft from GRB–36 bombers, to extend the range of photographic reconnaissance and fighter escort. Tests ended in 1956, but wing continued strategic reconnaissance until inactivated in 1957. Activated in 1962 to operate and maintain the ballistic missile early warning system (BMEWS), including sites in Alaska, Greenland, and England. Also operated the sea launched ballistic missile detection and warning system, supported the USAF "Spacetrack" system, and monitored the "Over–the–horizon" radar system, 1969–1971. Replaced, and absorbed resources of, the 3575th Pilot Training Wing in Nov 1972 and assumed control of Vance AFB, Okla, and undergraduate pilot training for USAF, Air National Guard, Air Force Reserve, and selected foreign allies.

Service Streamers. None.

Campaign Streamers. None.

Decorations. Air Force Outstanding Unit Awards: 1 Jan 1962–15 Jul 1964; 1 Jun 1968–31 May 1970; 1 Jan–31 Dec 1975.

Emblem. Gules, in fess a stylized aircraft palewise argent between two piles issuant from base of the like, each bearing a stylized aircraft palewise azure, on a chief arched of the last a pair of wings displayed fesswise of the second, surmounted by an escutcheon blazoned azure, issuant from base a demi-sphere with axis bend sinisterwise, issuant from sinister base three rays pilewise in bend or, a chief arched argent grid lined sable, all within a diminished bordure or, the entire within a diminished bordure or. (Approved on 2 Jan 1973.)

72d BOMBARDMENT WING, HEAVY

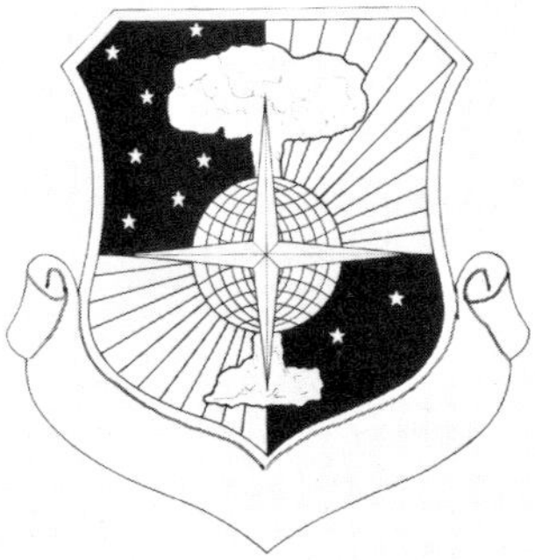

Lineage. Established as 72d Strategic Reconnaissance Wing, Heavy, on 4 Jun 1952. Activated on 16 Jun 1952. Redesignated 72d Bombardment Wing, Heavy, on 1 Oct 1955. Inactivated on 30 Jun 1971.

Assignments. Second Air Force, 16 Jun 1952; Eighth Air Force, 1 Jan 1959; 823d Air Division, 1 Oct 1962–30 Jun 1971.

Components. *Squadrons*. 60th: 16 Jun 1952–30 Jun 1971 (not operational, 16 Jun–4 Oct 1952 and 18 Nov 1958–13 Aug 1959). 73d: 16 Jun 1952–5 Jan 1959 (not operational, 16 Jun 1952–7 Jan 1953 and 1 Sep 1958–5 Jan 1959). 301st: 16 Jun 1952–17 Jun 1959 (not operational, 16 Jun 1952–c. 15 Mar 1953 and 11 Sep 1958–17 Jun 1959). 915th Air Refueling: 1 Sep 1958–30 Jun 1971.

Stations. Ramey AFB, PR, 16 Jun 1952–30 Jun 1971.

Commanders. Brig Gen Alfred F. Kalberer, 16 Jun 1952 (additional duty), 1 Oct 1952 (permanent); Col Virgil M. Cloyd, 29 Apr 1953; Col William E. Ruark, Jr., 22 May 1953; Brig Gen Alfred F. Kalberer, 24 May 1953; Col Virgil M. Cloyd, Jr., 10 Jun 1953; Col Frederick T. Prasse, 30 Jun 1953; Col Virgil M. Cloyd, 7 Jul 1953; Brig Gen Alfred F. Kalberer, 11 Jul 1953; Brig Gen Bertram C. Harrison, 2 Jul 1955; Brig Gen Henry R. Sullivan, Jr., 14 Sep 1957; Maj Gen William K. Martin, 28 Jun 1958; Brig Gen Joseph J. Preston, 13 Jul 1959; Col Samuel G. Porterfield, 20 Aug 1959; Maj Gen Joseph J. Preston, 12 Oct 1959; Brig Gen William E. Creer, 28 Sep 1960; Brig Gen Howard A. Davis, 6 Aug 1962; Col William H. Reddell, 27 Jul 1963; Brig Gen Roland A. Campbell, 1 May 1964; Col Madison M. McBrayer, 21 Jul 1965; Brig Gen Timothy J. Dacey, Jr., 1 Aug 1965; Col James M. Keck, 14 Jul 1966; Col George H. McKee, 6 Jul 1967; Col Clifford W. Hargrove, 1 Jul 1968; Col Frank L. Voigtmann, 6 May 1969; Col Kenneth E. Wehrman, 20 Mar 1970–30 Jun 1971.

Aircraft. RB–36, 1952–1958; KC–135, 1958–1971; B–52, 1959–1971.

Operations. Not operational, 16 Jun–30 Sep 1952. Absorbed residual resources of 55th Strategic Reconnaissance Wing in Oct 1952. Conducted global strategic reconnaissance, Mar

1953–1955, gradually shifting to a bombardment training mission beginning in 1954. Added air refueling to its global mission in 1958.

Service Streamers. None.

Campaign Streamers. None.

Decorations. Air Force Outstanding Unit Awards: 1 Oct 1957–1 Jun 1958; 1 Jul 1968–30 Jun 1969.

Emblem. A shield quarterly azure and or, the fess line debased; first and fourth quarters, semés of 9 stars, argent, 7 in the first and 2 in the fourth; second and third quarter lines radiant throughout of the first, 11 and 11, overall in pale a stylized atom burst proper, fimbriated azure, thereover, a globe proper, grid lines azure; debruising the atom burst and sphere a stylized compass star of the third, shaded proper and outlined of the first. (Approved on 29 Jun 1954.)

75th TACTICAL RECONNAISSANCE WING

Lineage. Established as 75th Tactical Reconnaissance Wing, and activated, on 17 May 1966. Organized on 1 Jul 1966. Inactivated on 15 Jul 1971.

Assignments. Tactical Air Command, 17 May 1966; 835th Air Division, 1 Jul 1966; Twelfth Air Force, 24 Dec 1969–15 Jul 1971.

Components. *Squadrons.* 4th: 18 Nov 1966–15 Jul 1971. 9th: 1 Sep 1969–15 Jul 1971. 14th: 3 Apr–6 Nov 1967 (detached 25 Oct–6 Nov 1957). 91st: 1 Jul 1967–15 Jul 1971 (not operational, 1 Jul–c. 15 Sep 1967).

Stations. Bergstrom AFB, Texas, 1 Jul 1966–15 Jul 1971.

Commanders. None (not manned), 17 May–30 Jun 1966; Col Frank C. Malone, 1 Jul 1966; Brig Gen James U. Cross, 1 Feb 1969; Col Walter F. Daniel, 28 Apr–15 Jul 1971.

Aircraft. RF–4, 1966–1971.

Operations. RF–4C replacement training, Feb 1967–Aug 1970, and tactical reconnaissance, Jul 1966–Jul 1971. Replaced by 67th Tactical Reconnaissance Wing.

Service Streamers. None.

Campaign Streamers. None.

Decorations. Air Force Outstanding Unit Awards: 1 Jan 1968–30 Apr 1969; 1 Nov 1969–31 May 1971.

Emblem. Per fess abased nebuly celeste and gules fimbriated argent throughout a pile azure between two rays in point argent bearing a sword in pale point to base of the like, grip gules, surmounted by wings erect in honour point or, both garnished celeste, charged with an eye quartered countercharged argent and celeste having a hurt bearing a mullet argent charged with a torteau; all within a diminished bordure or. *Motto:* APPERCEPTIVE. (Approved on 14 Apr 1967.)

76th MILITARY AIRLIFT WING

Lineage. Established as 76th Military Airlift Wing on 14 Sep 1977. Activated on 30 Sep 1977.

Assignments. Twenty-First Air Force, 30 Sep 1977–.

Components. *Group.* 89th: 30 Sep 1977–.

Stations. Andrews AFB, Md, 30 Sep 1977–.

Commanders. Maj Gen Benjamin F. Starr, Jr., 30 Sep 1977–.

Aircraft. C–12, 1977–; C–135, 1977–; CH–3, 1977–; CT–39, 1977–; UH–1, 1977–; VC–6, 1977–; VC–9, 1977–; VC–135, 1977–; VC–137, 1977–; VC–140, 1977–.

Operations. Replaced 76th Airlift Division, 89th Military Airlift Wing, and 1100th Air Base Wing at Andrews AFB, Md, and Bolling AFB, D.C., upon activation. Charged with special mission-type military airlift of the President, Cabinet members, Congressmen, and other VIPs; also performed many other support functions unique to this wing.

Service Streamers. None.

Campaign Streamers. None.

Decorations. None.

Emblem. Azure a drop bomb argent surmounted by a pair of binoculars bendwise gules winged or. *Motto:* OUR OBSERVATION, YOUR SECURITY. (Approved for 76th Reconnaissance Group on 5 Nov 1942, but never used by 76th Wing, which used emblem of the 76th Airlift Division in error.)

78th FLYING TRAINING WING

Lineage. Established as 78th Fighter Wing on 24 Sep 1948. Activated on 16 Nov 1948. Redesignated 78th Fighter-Interceptor Wing on 20 Jan 1950. Inactivated on 6 Feb 1952. Redesignated 78th Fighter Wing (Air Defense) on 14 Sep 1956. Activated on 18 Oct 1956. Inactivated on 31 Dec 1969. Redesignated 78th Flying Training Wing on 14 Apr 1972. Activated on 1 Dec 1972. Inactivated on 30 Sep 1977.

Assignments. Fourth Air Force, 16 Nov 1948 (attached to Western Air Defense Force, 10 Nov 1949–31 Jul 1950); Western Air Defense Force, 1 Aug 1950–6 Feb 1952. 28th Air Division, 18 Oct 1956; San Francisco Air Defense Sector, 1 Jul 1960; 28th Air Division, 1 Aug 1963; 26th Air Division, 1 Apr 1966; 27th Air Division, 15 Sep 1969; Tenth Air Force, 19 Nov–31 Dec 1969.

Air Training Command, 1 Dec 1972–30 Sep 1977.

Components. *Group.* 78th: 16 Nov 1948–6 Feb 1952 (not operational, 16 Nov–7 Dec 1948); 18 Oct 1956–1 Feb 1961. *Squadrons.* 82d: 1 Dec 1972–15 Jun 1976. 83d: 1 Feb 1961–1 Jul 1963 (not operational, 3 May–1 Jul 1963); 1 Dec 1972–30 Sep 1977. 84th: 1 Feb 1961–31 Dec 1969. 498th: 30 Sep 1968. 3389th: 1 Jan 1974–30 Sep 1977.

Stations. Hamilton AFB, Calif, 16 Nov 1948–6 Feb 1952. Hamilton AFB, Calif, 18 Oct 1956–31 Dec 1969. Webb AFB, Texas, 1 Dec 1972–30 Sep 1977.

Commanders. Col George L. Usher, 16 Nov 1948; Col George H. Steel, 1 Apr 1950; Col Brian O'Neill, 12 Mar 1951; Col James W. Andrew, 1 Jul 1951–6 Feb 1952. Col Wilton H. Earle, 18 Oct 1956; Col George F. Ceuleers, 27 Jul 1957; Col Benjamin B. Cassiday, Jr., 16 Jul 1960; Col Harvey E. Henderson, 28 Jul 1960; Col William F. Barns, 12 May 1962; Col William S. Harrell, 1 Jul 1962; Col William C. Miller, 15 Jul 1964; Col Charles D. Chitty, Jr., 30 Jul 1964; Col Harry W. Shoup, 23 Jun 1965; Col Donald H. Lynch, 17 Jun 1968–1969. Brig Gen Stanley M. Umstead, Jr., 1 Dec 1972; Col Robert G. Liotta, 21 Aug 1973; Col Robert A. Owens, 19 Jul 1974; Col Harry A. Spannaus, 8 Jun 1976–30 Sep 1977.

Aircraft. F–51, 1949–1952; F–84, 1949–1952; F–89, 1951–1952. F–86, 1956–1958; F–89, 1956–1959; F–102, 1957–1960; F–104, 1958–1960; F–101, 1959–1960, 1960–1968; F–106, 1959–1960, 1968–1969. T–37, 1972–1977; T–38, 1972–1977; T–41, 1972–1973.

Operations. Air defense of the U.S. Pacific coast area, 1949–1952, and again between 1956 and 1969. Replaced, and absorbed resources of, the 3560th Pilot Training Wing at Webb AFB, Texas, on 1 Dec 1972. Pilot training for both USAF and allied officers, 1972–1977.

Service Streamers. None.

Campaign Streamers. None.

Decorations. Air Force Outstanding Unit Award: 1 Jul 1968–30 Jun 1969.

Emblem. Per pale indented azure and gules, in chief five chain lengths conjoined fesswise or. *Motto:* ABOVE THE FOE. (Approved for 78th Group on 26 Sep 1942 and for 78th Wing on 19 Mar 1958.)

80th FLYING TRAINING WING

Lineage. Established as 80th Flying Training Wing on 25 May 1972. Activated on 1 Jan 1973.

Assignments. Air Training Command, 1 Jan 1973–.

Components. *Squadrons.* 88th: 1 Jan 1973–. 89th: 1 Jan 1973–. 90th: 1 Jan 1973–.

Stations. Sheppard AFB, Texas, 1 Jan 1973–.

Commanders. Col Robert G. Liotta, 1 Jan 1973; Col Kirk A. Brown, 28 Jun

1973; Col Spence M. Armstrong, 22 Jul 1974; Col Robert D. Caudry, 17 Jul 1976; Col William R. Deans, 1 Apr 1977–.

Aircraft. T–37, 1973–; T–38, 1973–.

Operations. Replaced, and absorbed resources of, the 3630th Flying Training Wing in Jan 1973. Provided undergraduate pilot training, initially for USAF, German Air Force, and South Vietnamese Air Force (VNAF) students. The last USAF students graduated in Jun 1975. VNAF student input ceased in Sep 1974. Began training under the security assistance program students from selected states, including Iran, El Salvador, Kuwait, Ecuador, and Saudi Arabia in Nov 1974.

Service Streamers. None.

Campaign Streamers. None.

Decorations. None.

Emblem. Per bend azure and sable a bend raguly or, all within a diminished bordure of the like. *Motto:* ANGELS ON OUR WINGS. (Approved for 80th Group on 14 Oct 1942 and for 80th Wing on 2 Jan 1973.)

81st TACTICAL FIGHTER WING

Lineage. Established as 81st Fighter Wing on 15 Apr 1948. Activated on 1 May 1948. Redesignated: 81st Fighter-Interceptor Wing on 20 Jan 1950; 81st Fighter-Bomber Wing on 1 Apr 1954; 81st Tactical Fighter Wing on 8 Jul 1958.

Assignments. 7th Air Division, 1 May 1948; Pacific Air Command, 3 Sep 1948; Twelfth Air Force, 21 May 1949 (attached to Western Air Defense Force, 10 Nov 1949–); Fourth Air Force, 1 Apr 1950 (remained attached to Western Air Defense Force to 1 Aug 1950); Western Air Defense Force, 1 Aug 1950 (attached to Third Air Force, 5–8 Sep 1951); Third Air Force, 9 Sep 1951 (attached to 49th Air Division, Operational [later, 49th Air Division (Operational)], 1 Mar 1954–1 Jul 1956); Seventeenth Air Force, 1 Jul 1961; Third Air Force, 1 Sep 1963–.

Components. *Group.* 81st: 1 May 1948–8 Feb 1955 (not operational, c. 22 Apr 1954–8 Feb 1955). *Squadrons.* 78th: attached c. 22 Apr 1954–7 Feb 1955, assigned 8 Feb 1955–. 91st: attached c. 22 Apr 1954–7 Feb 1955, assigned 8 Feb 1955–. 92d: attached c. 22 Apr 1954–7 Feb 1955, assigned 8 Feb 1955–. 116th: attached 10 Feb–9 Aug 1951 (further attached to 81st Fighter-Interceptor Group).

Stations. Wheeler AFB, TH, 1 May 1948–21 May 1949; Camp Stoneman, Calif, 27 May 1949; Kirtland AFB, NM, 5 Jun 1949; Moses Lake (later, Larson) AFB, Wash, 2 May 1950–16 Aug 1951; Bentwaters RAF Station (later, RAF Bentwaters), England, 6 Sep 1951–.

Commanders. Col Thomas W. Blackburn, 1 May 1948; Lt Col Francis R. Royal, 21 May 1949; Col Thomas W.

Blackburn, (by 28) Jun 1949; Col Gladwyn E. Pinkston, 28 Apr 1950; Col Robert F. Harris, 22 Aug 1951; Col Gladwyn E. Pinkston, 27 Sep 1951; Col Robert F. Harris, c. 3 Jan 1953; Col Gladwyn E. Pinkston, c. 20 Feb 1953; Col Robert J. Garrigan, 20 Jun 1953; Col Gladwyn E. Pinkston, c. 20 Aug 1953; Col Harold N. Holt, 2 Jun 1954; Col Ivan W. McElroy, 10 Jun 1955; Col Lester L. Krause, Jr., 18 Jun 1957; Col Henry L. Crouch, Jr., 8 Jul 1957; Col James R. DuBose, Jr., 6 May 1960; Col Eugene L. Strickland, 9 Jul 1960; Col William C. Clark, 9 Jul 1962; Col Robin Olds, 9 Aug 1963; Brig Gen DeWitt R. Searles, 26 Jul 1965; Col Ramon R. Melton, 28 Jul 1967; Col George S. Dorman, 5 Jul 1968; Col Devol Brett, 25 Sep 1968; Col David J. Schmerbeck, 29 Aug 1969; Col John C. Bartholf, 6 Mar 1970; Col James W. Enos, 4 Sep 1970; Col Dwaine L. Weatherwax, 22 Jun 1971; Brig Gen Charles E. Word, 16 Aug 1972; Col John R. Paulk, 19 Apr 1974; Brig Gen Clyde H. Garner, 14 Mar 1975; Col Gerald D. Larson, 11 Feb 1976; Col Rudolph F. Wacker, 6 May 1977–.

Aircraft. P (later, F)–47, 1948–1949; F–80, 1949; F–86, 1949–1955; F–51, 1951; F–84, 1954–1959; F–101, 1958–1966; F–4, 1965–; A–10, 1968–.

Operations. Conducted air defense of Hawaii, Dec 1948–May 1949. Moved to the United States and converted to F–80s and then F–86s. Became part of Western Air Defense Force's air defense structure in Nov 1949 and moved to the Pacific northwest in 1950 to provide air defense from Larson AFB, Geiger Field, and Whidbey Island, Wash. Moved to England in mid-1951. From 1951 to mid-1954, worked with Royal Air Force Fighter Command to provide air defense for a portion of England. Converted to F–84Fs in 1954 and changed from fighter-interceptor to fighter-bomber operations, using both conventional and nuclear weapons. Since 1954, charged with tactical operations in support of USAFE and NATO, with air defense as a secondary mission.

Service Streamers. None.

Campaign Streamers. None.

Decorations. Air Force Outstanding Unit Awards: 28 Mar 1959–30 Jun 1961; 1 Jul 1961–30 Jun 1963; 1 Jun 1966–31 May 1968; 1 Jul 1968–30 Jun 1970.

Emblem. Or, a dragon sailient wings displayed and addorsed azure, armed and langued gules, incensed proper, holding in its dexter claw a stylized boll weevil sable. *Motto:* LE NOM LES ARMES LA LOYAUTE—The name, the arms, and loyalty. (Approved for 81st Group on 2 Mar 1943 and for 81st Wing on 14 May 1958.)

82d FLYING TRAINING WING

Lineage. Established as 82d Fighter Wing on 28 Jul 1947. Organized on 15 Aug 1947. Discontinued on 1 Aug

1948. Activated on 1 Aug 1948. Inactivated on 2 Oct 1949. Redesignated 82d Flying Training Wing on 22 Jun 1972. Activated on 1 Feb 1973.

Assignments. Strategic Air Command, 15 Aug 1947–1 Aug 1948 (attached to 307th Bombardment Wing, Very Heavy, 15 Aug 1947–11 Jul 1948; 307th Bombardment Wing, Medium, 12 Jul–1 Aug 1948). Strategic Air Command, 1 Aug 1948 (attached to 307th Bombardment Wing, Medium, 1 Aug–15 Dec 1948); Fifteenth Air Force, 16 Dec 1948; First Air Force, 22 Aug–2 Oct 1949. Air Training Command, 1 Feb 1973–.

Components. *Group.* 82d: 15 Aug 1947–1 Aug 1948 (detached 4 Apr–29 Jun 1948); 1 Aug 1948–2 Oct 1949. *Squadrons.* 96th: 1 Feb 1973–. 97th: 1 Feb 1973–.

Stations. Grenier Field (later, AFB), NH, 15 Aug 1947–1 Aug 1948. Grenier AFB, NH, 1 Aug 1948–2 Oct 1949. Williams AFB, Ariz, 1 Feb 1973–.

Commanders. Col Edwin L. Tucker, 15 Aug 1947; Col Henry Viccellio, 19 Jan 1948; Col William B. Offutt, 16 Feb 1948; Col Henry Viccellio, 8 Jul–1 Aug 1948. Col Henry Viccellio, 1 Aug 1948; Col William P. Litton, 1–2 Oct 1949. Col Warren C. Moore, 1 Feb 1973; Brig Gen Norman C. Gaddis, 16 Feb 1974; Col William E. Brown, Jr., 17 Jun 1974; Col William S. Henderson, Jr., 1 Mar 1975; Col Carl G. Baily, 12 Jun 1976; Col Larry T. Cooper, 11 Jun 1977–.

Aircraft. P (later, F)–51, 1947–1948. F–51, 1948–1949. T–37, 1973–; T–38, 1973–.

Operations. Trained to maintain proficiency in fighter escort and tactical fighter operations, 1947–1948, and again in 1948–1949. Replaced, and absorbed resources of, the 3525th Pilot Training Wing in Feb 1973 and assumed undergraduate pilot training operations, plus operation and maintenance of Williams AFB, Ariz. Began undergraduate pilot training for females in Sep 1976 and graduated first class of ten women on 2 Sep 1977.

Service Streamers. None.

Campaign Streamers. None.

Decorations. None.

Emblem. On a shield per bend or and azure a lightning bolt in bend throughout point to base, with two beviles, per bend argent, gules and or, between three fleurs-de-lis, two and one, of the second, and eleven stars in bend, six and five, of the first; overall in dexter chief a roundle per fess, wavy of two, sable and vert. *Motto:* ADORIMINI—Up and at "em! (Approved on 4 Nov 1957 for 82d Fighter Group [Air Defense]; used since Feb 1973 by 82d FTW.)

83d FIGHTER-DAY WING

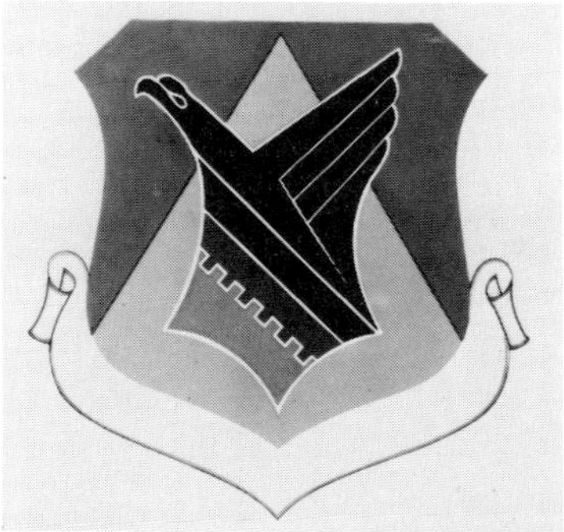

Lineage. Established as 83d Fighter-Day Wing on 24 Feb 1956. Activated on 8 Jul 1956. Inactivated on 8 Dec 1957.

Assignments. Ninth Air Force, 8 Jul 1956–8 Dec 1957.

Components. *Group.* 83d: 8 Jul 1956–11 Nov 1957 (not operational, 7–11 Nov 1957). *Squadrons.* 448th: 11 Nov–8 Dec 1957. 532d: attached 7–10 Nov 1957, assigned 11 Nov–8 Dec 1957. 533d: attached 7–10 Nov 1957, assigned 11 Nov–8 Dec 1957. 534th: attached 7–10 Nov 1957, assigned 11 Nov–8 Dec 1957.

Stations. Seymour Johnson AFB, NC, 8 Jul 1956–8 Dec 1957.

Commanders. Col Robert C. Richardson III, 8 Jul 1956; Col Ralph L. Merritt, Jr., 9 Jul 1956; Col Robert C. Richardson III, 1 Sep 1956–8 Dec 1957.

Aircraft. F–80, 1956; F–86, 1956–1957; F–100, 1957.

Operations. Replaced, and absorbed resources of, the 4435th Air Base Squadron in Jul 1956. Trained with C–45, C–47, C–119, B–25, T–33, and F–80 aircraft until F–86Hs began to arrive in Oct 1956. Fully operational and flying firepower demonstrations by Jun 1957. Converted to F–100Cs in late 1957. Replaced in Dec 1957 by 4th Fighter-Day Wing.

Service Streamers. None.

Campaign Streamers. None.

Decorations. None.

Emblem. On a shield per pile transposed azure and or; overall on an escutcheon per bend gules and medium blue, a bend embattled inverted, vert, fimbriated throughout argent; superimposed over the chief area of the escutcheon a stylized demi-falcon bendwise, in profile, sable, his head and wings raised upward above the escutcheon; his eyes gules, the falcon fimbriated throughout argent. (Approved on 29 Mar 1957.)

84th FIGHTER-ALL WEATHER WING

Lineage. Established as 84th Fighter Wing, All Weather, on 16 May 1949. Activated in the Reserve on 1 Jun 1949. Redesignated 84th Fighter-All Weather Wing on 1 Mar 1950. Ordered to active service on 1 Jun 1951. Discontinued, and inactivated, on 2 Jun 1951.

Assignments. First Air Force, 1 Jun 1949 (attached to 52d Fighter Wing, All Weather [later, 52d Fighter-All Weather Wing], 1 Jun 1949–); Eastern Air Defense Force, 1 Sep 1950–2 Jun 1951 (remained attached to 52d Fighter-All Weather Wing [later, 52d Fighter-Interceptor Wing] to 2 Jun 1951).

Components. *Group.* 84th: 1 Jun 1949–2 Jun 1951.

Stations. Mitchel AFB, NY, 1 Jun 1949; McGuire AFB, NJ, 10 Oct 1949–2 Jun 1951.

Commanders. Unkn, 1 Jun–9 Oct 1949; none (not manned), 10 Oct–13 Nov 1949; Lt Col Frederic N. Millen, 14 Nov 1949–unkn; unkn, c. Jul 1950–2 Jun 1951.

Aircraft. F–82 (of 52d Wing), 1950.

Operations. Activated in the Reserve in 1949 to train as a fighter corollary of the 52d Wing (Regular Air Force), but apparently undermanned and thus performed very little training. During its only 2-week summer encampment (12–26 Jun 1950), the wing had only four pilots capable of flying F–82s. Even nonflying units of the 84th Wing seem to have been poorly manned, and the 52d Wing made little use of its corollary units. The 84th Wing was ordered to active service on 1 Jun 1951, inactivated the next day, and its few people became "fillers" in other USAF units.

Service Streamers. None.

Campaign Streamers. None.

Decorations. None.

Emblem. Azure, a flash in pale between in dexter chief a gun sight and in sinister base a drop bomb palewise, all or. *Motto:* CURSUM PERFICIO—I accomplish my course. (Approved on 22 Jan 1943 for 84th Group.)

86th TACTICAL FIGHTER WING

Lineage. Established as 86th Fighter Wing, and activated, on 1 Jul 1948. Redesignated: 86th Fighter-Bomber Wing on 20 Jan 1950; 86th Fighter-Interceptor Wing on 9 Aug 1954; 86th Air Division (Defense) on 18 Nov. 1960. Inactivated on 14 Nov 1968. Redesignated: 86th Fighter-Interceptor Wing on 14 Nov 1968; 86th Tactical Fighter Wing on 13 Oct 1969. Activated on 1 Nov 1969.

Assignments. United States Air Forces in Europe, 1 Jul 1948; 2d Air Division, 10 Oct 1949; Twelfth Air Force, 7 May 1951; United States Air Forces in Europe, 1 Jan 1958; Seventeenth Air Force, 15 Nov 1959; United States Air Forces in Europe, 1 Jul 1963; Seventeenth Air Force, 1 Sep 1963; United States Air Forces in Europe, 20 May 1965; Seventeenth Air Force, 5 Oct–14 Nov 1968. Seventeenth Air Force, 1 Nov 1969–.

Components. *Group.* 86th: 1 Jul 1948–8 Mar 1958 (not operational, 22 May 1954–7 Oct 1955 and 10 Aug 1956–8 Mar 1958); 22 Sep 1975–. *Squadrons.* 7th Special Operations: 31 Jan–15 Mar 1973 (detached). 17th Tactical Reconnaissance: 12 Jan 1970–31 Jan 1973. 32d: 8 Apr 1960–1 Nov 1968. 38th Tactical Reconnaissance: attached 16–30 Jan 1973. 81st: attached 12 Jun–14 Jul 1971, assigned 15 Jul 1971–15 Jan 1973. 151st: 25 Nov 1961–11 Jul 1962. 197th: 25 Nov 1961–11 Jul 1962. 434th: attached 30 Sep–12 Dec 1961. 435th: attached 22 Sep 1961–14 Jan 1962 and 4 Nov–12 Dec 1962. 436th: attached 12 Jan–12 Apr 1962. 440th: attached 1 Jul 1954–7 Oct 1955; attached 10 Aug 1956–7 Mar 1958, assigned 8 Mar 1958–1 Jan 1960. 476th: attached 12 Apr–8 Aug 1962. 496th: attached 1 Jul 1954–7 Oct 1955; attached 10 Aug 1956–7 Mar 1958, assigned 8 Mar 1958–1 Nov 1968. 512th: 24 Mar 1958–1 Jul 1959. 513th: 25 Apr 1958–8 Jan 1961 (not operational, 22 Nov 1960–8 Jan 1961). 514th: 15 May 1958–8 Jan 1961 (not operational, 18 Nov 1960–8 Jan 1961). 525th: attached 22 May 1954–7 Oct 1955; attached 10 Aug 1956–7 Mar 1958, assigned 8 Mar 1958–1 Nov 1968. 526th: attached 22 May 1954–7 Oct 1955; attached 10 Aug 1956–7 Mar 1958, assigned 8 Mar 1958–1 Nov 1968; assigned 31 Jan 1973–22 Sep 1975. 527th: attached 22 May 1954–7 Oct 1955. *Detachments.* Det, 117th Tactical Reconnaissance Wing: attached 18 Mar–1 Apr 1976. Det, 127th Tactical Fighter Wing: attached 1–13 Nov 1975. Det, 178th Tactical Fighter Group: attached 9–25 Oct 1975. Det, 435th Tactical Fighter Squadron: attached 25 Oct–3 Nov 1962.

Stations. Neubiberg AB, West Germany, 1 Jul 1948; Landstuhl (later, Ramstein-Landstuhl; Ramstein) AB, West Germany, 21 Aug 1952–14 Nov 1968. Zweibrucken AB, West Germany, 1 Nov 1969; Ramstein AB, West Germany, 31 Jan 1973–.

Commanders. Col Clarence T. Edwinson, 1 Jul 1948; Col John S. Chennault, 31 May 1949; Col George R. Bickell, 16 Jun 1952; Col James O. Beckwith, 19 Jan 1955; Col Albert L. Evans, Jr., 8 Jun 1956; Col James W. Little, 9 Jun 1958; Col Charles M. Young, 30 Jun 1958; Col Robert J. Rogers, 4 Jul 1959; Col George W. Rogers, 15 Mar 1961; Brig Gen Frank W. Gillespie, 30 Jun 1961; Brig Gen Thomas L. Hayes, Jr., 10 Jul 1964; Brig Gen James M. Vande Hey, 12 Jan 1966; Brig Gen Richard N. Ellis, 28 Jun 1967–14 Nov 1968. Col Howard A. Jones, 1 Nov 1969; Col Wilbur L. Creech, 31 Dec 1969; Col Walter L. Doerty, Jr., 17 Nov 1970; Col John J. Knight, 1 Oct 1971; Col James E. McInerney, Jr., 19 Oct 1971; Brig Gen William F. Georgi, 31 Jan 1973; Col Edward J. Campbell, 13 Apr 1973; Col Lloyd C. Ulrich, 13 May 1974; Brig Gen Cornelius Nugteren, 22 Aug 1975; Brig Gen John H. Bennett, 15 Jul 1977–.

Aircraft. F–47, 1948–1950; F–84, 1950–1953; F–86, 1953–1960; F–102, 1959–1968; F–100, 1960; F–104, 1961–1962. RF–4, 1970–1973, 1976; F–4, 1971–; F–100, 1975.

Operations. Provided air defense, primarily in West Germany, Jul 1948–Nov 1968, initially as a wing but later as a division. During its 8 years as an air division, the organization supervised the improvement of a manual radar system to a semiautomatic air weapons control system. From Nov 1969 to Jun 1971, it was charged only with tactical reconnaissance, but added tactical fighter operations later in 1971. In Sep 1975, tactical responsibilities were placed in the 86th Tactical Fighter Group so other wing elements could concentrate on a multitude of "host wing" responsibilities connected with support of numerous military units located in the area of Ramstein AB, West Germany.

Service Streamers. None.

Campaign Streamers. None.

Decorations. Air Force Outstanding Unit Awards: 31 Oct 1955–31 Oct 1958; 1 Jul 1964–30 Jun 1965.

Emblem. Azure, a pile or, the shield edged of the last. *Motto:* VIRTUS PERDURAT—Courage will endure. (Approved for 86th Group on 17 Oct 1942 and, in modified form, for 86th Wing on 27 Jul 1956.)

87th TROOP CARRIER WING, MEDIUM

Lineage. Established as 87th Troop Carrier Wing, Medium, on 26 May 1952. Activated in the Reserve on 15 Jun 1952. Inactivated on 1 Feb 1953.

Assignments. 2d Air Reserve District, 15 Jun 1952–1 Feb 1953.

Components. *Group.* 87th: 15 Jun 1952–1 Feb 1953.

Stations. Atterbury AFB, Ind, 15 Jun 1952–1 Feb 1953.

Commanders. Col George C. Riley, 15 Jun 1952–1 Feb 1953.

Aircraft. T–7, 1952–1953; C–46, 1952–1953; C–47, 1953; B–25, 1952–1953; T–6, 1953.

Operations. Replaced, and absorbed resources of, the nonflying 923d Reserve Training Wing. Trained under supervision of 2d Air Reserve District and 2466th Air Force Reserve Training Center, using aircraft of the center. Experienced extreme difficulty recruiting and retaining qualified airmen. Replaced in Feb 1953 by 434th Troop Carrier Wing, Medium.

Service Streamers. None.

Campaign Streamers. None.

Decorations. None.

Emblem. None.

89th MILITARY AIRLIFT GROUP

Lineage. Established as 89th Troop Carrier Wing, Medium, on 10 May 1949. Activated in the Reserve on 27 Jun 1949. Ordered to active service on 1 May 1951. Inactivated on 10 May 1951. Redesignated 89th Fighter-Bomber Wing on 26 May 1952. Activated in the Reserve on 14 Jun 1952. Inactivated on 16 Nov 1957. Redesignated 89th Military Airlift Wing, Special Mission, and activated, on 27 Dec 1965. Organized on 8 Jan 1966. Redesignated 89th Military Airlift Group on 30 Sep 1977.

Assignments. First Air Force, 27 Jun 1949–10 May 1951. First Air Force, 14 Jun 1952–16 Nov 1957. Military Air Transport Service (later, Military Airlift Command), 27 Dec 1965; 76th Airlift Division, 1 Jul 1976; 76th Military Airlift Wing, 30 Sep 1977–.

Components. *Group.* 89th: 27 Jun 1949–10 May 1951; 14 Jun 1952–16 Nov 1957. *Squadrons.* 1st Helicopter: 1 Jul 1976–. 1st: 12 Sep 1977–. 98th: 8 Jan 1966–1 Sep 1977. 99th: 8 Jan 1966–12 Sep 1977. 1400th: 1 Apr 1975–. 1401st: 1 Apr 1975–. 1402d: 1 Apr 1975–. *Detachment.* Det 1, HQ 89th MAW, SM: 1 Jul–1 Oct 1975.

Stations. Hanscom Aprt (later, Laurence G. Hanscom Field), Mass, 27 Jun 1949–10 May 1951. Laurence G. Hanscom Field, Mass, 14 Jun 1952–16 Nov 1957. Andrews AFB, Md, 8 Jan 1966–.

Commanders. Brig Gen Ray J. Stecker, 27 Jun 1949; Lt Col William

Binder, Jan 1950; Col Howard C. Stelling, Feb 1950; Capt John F. Coughlin, 1–10 May 1951. Lt Col Thomas J. McGrath, 14 Jun 1952; Col Charles E. Flaherty, c. 28 Jun 1952; Col Arthur C. Carroll, 1 Apr 1955–16 Nov 1957. None (not manned), 27 Dec 1965–7 Jan 1966; Col Harlan C. Wilder, 8 Jan 1966; Col John G. Williams, 1 Mar 1967; Col Burgess Gradwell, 25 Nov 1969; Col Jay R. Wallace, 29 Dec 1972; Col Stewart Young, 28 Jul 1975; Brig Gen Paul E. Gardner, 23 Jun 1976–.

Aircraft. C–45, 1949–1950; C–46, 1949–1951; T–6, 1949–1950; T–7, 1949–1951; T–11, 1949–1951. T–6, 1952–1954; T–11, 1952; F–51, 1952–1954; C–46, 1952, 1956–1957; T–28, 1953–1956; T–33, 1953–1957; F–80, 1953–1957; C–45, 1955–1957; TC–47, 1955–1957; F–86, 1957; C–119, 1957. C–118, 1966–1972; VC–118, 1966–1974; C–121, 1966–1968; VC–121, 1966; C–131, 1966; VC–131, 1966–1977; C–135, 1966–1968, c. 1975–; VC–137, 1966–; C–140, 1966–1972; VC–140, 1966–; VC–6, 1966–; U–4, 1966–1969; VC–135, 1968–; VC–9, 1975–; T (later, TC)–39, 1975–; UH–1, 1976–; CH–3, 1976–; C–12, 1976–.

Operations. Trained 1949–1951 in the organized Reserve as a troop carrier wing. Ordered to active service in May 1951, the wing was soon inactivated and its people used to fill worldwide vacancies in regular units. Trained 1952–1957 in the organized Reserve as a fighter-bomber wing. From Jan 1966 (after replacing the 1254th Air Transport Wing), served Military Airlift Command as a special mission military airlift wing, charged with providing worldwide airlift for the Executive Department and high-ranking dignitaries of the U.S. Government and of foreign governments as directed. In mid-1975, assumed an additional mission of controlling all T–39 administrative airlift within the United States. Gained a helicopter squadron in Jul 1976 and added rescue and medical evacuation (in the D.C. area) to its mission. In Oct 1976, began training C–12 pilots for units in Alaska and West Germany, and for duty with defense attaché offices and military assistance units. Reduced in size in 1977 through transfer of many aircraft and inactivation of units, and became a group on 30 Sep 1977.

Service Streamers. None.

Campaign Streamers. None.

Decorations. Air Force Outstanding Unit Awards: 1 Jul 1966–30 Jun 1968; 1 Jul 1968–30 Jun 1970; 1 Jul 1970–30 Jun 1972; 1 Jul 1972–30 Jun 1974; 1 Jul 1974–31 Dec 1975; 1 Jan 1976–31 Jan 1977.

Emblem. A shield azure, issuing from base, clouds proper, supporting a sphere of the last, encircled with an orbit argent, lined vert, surmounted by an eagle volant or, wings, head, tail feathers and legs highlighted. *Motto:* EXPERTO CREDE—Trust one who has had experience. (Approved on 28 Apr 1966.)

90th STRATEGIC MISSILE WING (ICBM–MINUTEMAN)

Lineage. Established as 90th Bombardment Wing, Medium, on 20 Dec 1950. Activated on 2 Jan 1951. Redesignated 90th Strategic Reconnaissance Wing, Medium, on 16 Jun 1956. Discontinued on 20 Jun 1960. Redesignated 90th Strategic Missile Wing (ICBM–Minuteman) on 21 Feb 1963. Organized on 1 Jul 1963.

Assignments. Fifteenth Air Force, 2 Jan 1951 (attached to 92d Bombardment Wing, Heavy, 2–31 Jan 1951); 21st Air Division, 14 Mar 1951; Department of the Air Force, 20 Jun 1960; Strategic Air Command, 21 Feb 1963; 13th Strategic Missile Division, 1 Jul 1963; 821st Strategic Aerospace Division, 2 Jul 1966; 4th Strategic Missile (later, 4th Air) Division, 30 Jun 1971–.

Components. *Group.* 90th: 2 Jan 1951–16 Jun 1952 (not operational, 16 Feb 1951–16 Jun 1952). *Squadrons.* 90th Air Refueling: 5 Aug 1955–20 Jun 1960. 319th: attached 16 Feb 1951–15 Jun 1952, assigned 16 Jun 1952–20 Jun 1960; assigned 1 Oct 1963– (not operational, 1 Oct 1963–23 Jul 1964). 320th: attached 16 Feb 1951–15 Jun 1952, assigned 16 Jun 1952–20 Jun 1960; assigned 8 Jan 1964– (not operational, 8 Jan–c. Oct 1964). 321st: attached 16 Feb 1951–15 Jun 1952, assigned 16 Jun 1952–20 Jun 1960; assigned 9 Apr 1964– (not operational, 9 Apr–Dec 1964). 400th: 1 Jul 1964– (not operational, 1 Jul 1964–Feb 1965).

Stations. Fairchild AFB, Wash, 2 Jan 1951; Forbes AFB, Kans, 14 Mar 1951–20 Jun 1960. Francis E. Warren AFB, Wyo, 1 Jul 1963–.

Commanders. Col Conrad F. Necrason, 2 Jan 1951; Col Joseph S. Pirruccello, 14 Mar 1951; Col Gerald G. Robinson, 22 Mar 1951; Col Joseph S. Pirruccello, 4 Apr 1951; Col Conrad F. Necrason, 20 Apr 1951; Col Joseph S. Pirruccello, 21 Apr 1952; Col Conrad F. Necrason, 5 Jun 1952; Col Joseph S. Pirruccello, 19 Sep 1952; Col Albert J. Shower, 6 Dec 1952; Col Joseph S. Pirruccello, 27 Apr 1953; Col Albert J. Shower, 18 May 1955–unkn; Col Gordon F. Goyt, (by Mar) 1954; Col Jack E. Cunningham, (by 8 Apr) 1954; Col Albert J. Shower, 22 Apr 1954; Lt Col Vincent M. Crane, c. May 1954; Col Albert J. Shower, (by 7 May) 1954; Col Joseph S. Pirruccello, May 1954; Lt Col Vincent M. Crane, (by 7 Jun) 1954; Col Joseph S. Pirruccello, (by 25) Jun 1954; Col Olbert F. Lassiter, (by 30) Jun 1954; Col Albert J. Shower, Jul–3 Jul 1954; unkn, 4–5 Jul 1954; Col Gordon F. Goyt, (by 6) Jul 1954; Col George L. Robinson, (by 31) Jul 1954; Col Harold W. Ohlke, 23 Aug 1957; Col William W. Wilcox, (by 21) Apr 1958; Col Norman J. McGowan, 10–20 Jun 1960; none (not manned), 21 Jun 1960–30 Jun 1963; Col Floyd E. Wikstrom, 1 Jul 1963; Col Donald W. Johnson, 26 Aug 1965; Col Robert J. Hill, 16 Aug 1966; Col Robert R. Scott, 2 Aug 1968; Brig Gen Harold A. Strack, 18 Aug 1969; Col Paul E. Bell, 3 Jan 1972; Col Bobbie G. Guthrie, 2 Jul 1973; Col Christopher S. Adams, Jr., 13 Jun 1974; Col Ray E. Miller, 3 Dec 1975; Col James E. Cowan, 29 Sep 1976–.

Aircraft and Missiles. B–29, 1951–1954; RB–29, 1951, 1952–1954; TB–29, 1951–1952; KB–29, 1953–1954; RB–47, 1954–1960; KC–97, 1955–1960; Minuteman I, 1964–1974; Minuteman III, 1973–.

Operations. Served as operational training unit for B–29 aircrews and mechanics of the 376th, 308th, and 310th Bombardment Wings, in turn, May 1951–Sep 1952; as replacement training unit for B–29 aircrews (Jun 1951–Aug 1953) and RB–29 aircrews (Nov 1952–Aug 1953) for Far East Air Forces. Also trained Shoran personnel, SAC-wide, Nov 1952–Nov 1953. Flew strategic reconnaissance missions, Sep 1953–May 1958, and air refueling missions, Feb 1956–Jun 1960. Served as RB–47 combat crew training wing, May 1958–Jun 1960. Deployed at Eielson AFB, Alaska, 5 May–31 Aug 1955. Not operational, Jun 1960–Jun 1963. Supervised missile facility construction, Jul 1963–Jul 1964, and served as a strategic missile wing, using Minuteman I missiles from Jul 1964 to Oct 1974 and Minuteman III missiles from Jun 1973.

Service Streamers. None.

Campaign Streamers. None.

Decorations. Air Force Outstanding Unit Awards: 1 Jul 1968–30 Jun 1969; 1 Jul 1973–30 Jun 1975.

Emblem. Per chevron enhanced reversed azure and light blue a chevron reversed argent bearing six mullets of the first, issuant from base a demisphere of the last, rimmed and grid lined of the third surmounted by two olive branches one bendwise and one bend sinisterwise all of the like and overall in pale a missile ascending, terminating in fess or emitting a propulsion frail gules and two lightning flashes one to dexter fess enarriere and one to sinister fess of the like, in chief a pterodactyl in flight, wings elevated of the fourth, eye and tongue of the third, all within a diminished bordure of the fourth. *Motto:* IMPAVIDE—Undauntedly. (Approved on 29 Sep 1964.)

91st STRATEGIC MISSILE WING

Lineage. Established as 91st Strategic Reconnaissance Wing on 11 Oct 1948. Activated on 10 Nov 1948. Redesignated 91st Strategic Reconnaissance Wing, Medium, on 6 Jul 1950. Inactivated on 8 Nov 1957. Redesignated 91st Bombardment Wing, Heavy, and activated, on 15 Nov 1962. Organized on 1 Feb 1963. Redesignated 91st Strategic Missile Wing on 25 Jun 1968.

Assignments. 311th Air Division, Reconnaissance (later, 311th Air Division), 10 Nov 1948; Second Air Force, 1 Nov 1949; 4th Air Division, 10 Feb 1951; Second Air Force, 11 Sep 1951; 37th Air Division, 10 Oct 1951 (attached to Second Air Force, 10 Oct 1951–17 Mar 1952); 801st Air Division, 28 May 1952–8 Nov 1957. Strategic Air Command, 15 Nov 1962; 810th Strategic Aerospace Division, 1 Feb 1963; 18th Strategic Aerospace Division, 1 Jul 1963; 821st Strategic Aerospace Division, 1 Sep 1964; 810th Strategic Aerospace Division, 1 Jul 1966 (attached to Advanced Echelon, 3d Air Division, c. 5 Feb–15 Apr 1968); 4th Strategic Missile Division, 30 Jun 1971; Fifteenth Air Force, 30 Nov 1972 (attached to Air Division Provisional, 810th, 30 Nov 1972–14 Jan 1973); 47th Air Division, 15 Jan 1973; 57th Air Division, 22 Jan 1975–.

Components. *Groups*. 91st: 10 Nov 1948–28 May 1952 (not operational, 10 Feb 1951–28 May 1952). *Squadrons*. 16th: attached 10 Nov 1948–1 Jun 1949. 26th Air Refueling: attached 28 May 1952–1 Jun 1953. 38th: attached 1 Nov 1950–5 Jan 1951. 68th Air Refueling: attached 5–28 May 1952. 91st Air Refueling: attached 10 Feb 1951–27 May 1952, assigned 28 May 1952–8 Nov 1957 (detached 12 Jan–26 Feb 1954, 6 Oct–12 Nov 1954, 10 Jul–Oct 1955). 91st: attached 22 Jan–25 Mar 1949. 100th Air Refueling: attached 23 May–24 Nov 1953. 322d: attached 10 Feb 1951–27 May 1952, assigned 28 May 1952–8 Nov 1957; assigned 1 Feb 1963–25 Jun 1968 (detached c. 11 Sep 1966–c. 31 Mar 1967, c. 16 Feb–c. 30 Apr 1968; not operational, c. 1 May–25 Jun 1968). 323d: attached 10 Feb 1951–27 May 1952, assigned 28 May 1952–8 Nov 1957 (detached 12 Jan–26 Feb 1954). 324th: attached 10 Feb 1951–27 May 1952, assigned 28 May 1952–8 Nov 1957. 338th: attached 1–24 Nov 1950. 343d: attached 1 Nov 1950–3 Jan 1951. 740th: 25 Jun 1968–. 741st: 25 Jun 1968–. 742d: 25 Jun 1968–. 907th Air Refueling: 1 Jul 1963–25 Jun 1968 (detached c. 11 Sep 1966–c. 31 Mar 1967, c. 5 Feb–c. 16 Apr 1968; not operational, c. 1 May–25 Jun 1968).

Stations. McGuire AFB, NJ, 10 Nov 1948; Barksdale AFB, La, 1 Oct 1949; Lockbourne AFB, Ohio, 11 Sep 1951–8 Nov 1957. Glasgow AFB, Mont, 1 Feb 1963; Minot AFB, ND, 25 Jun 1968–.

Commanders. Col Frank L. Dunn, 10 Nov 1948; Col Audrin R. Walker, Mar 1949; Col Thomas W. Steed, 5 Aug 1949; Col Randolph L. Wood, 15 May 1950; Col Horace M. Wade, 24 May 1950; Col Thomas W. Steed, 19 Jun 1950; Col Randolph L. Wood, 19 Jul 1950; Col Henry K. Mooney, 21 Jul 1950; Col Horace M. Wade, 12 Aug 1950; Col Henry K. Mooney, 24 Aug 1950; Col Horace M. Wade, 13 Jan 1951; Col Landon E. McConnell, 10 Feb 1951; Col Lewis E. Lyle, 17 Feb 1951; Col Henry K. Mooney, 18 May 1951; Col Lewis E. Lyle, 22 May 1951; Col Joseph J. Preston, 22 Aug 1951; Col Everett W. Homstrom, 2 Jan 1953; Col Joseph J. Preston, 13 Mar 1953; Col John A. DesPortes, 14 Jan 1954; Col Joseph J. Preston, 23 Feb 1954; Col John A. DesPortes, 8 Apr 1954; Col Joseph J. Preston, 9 May 1954; Col Charles M. Eisenhart, 9 Jul 1954; Col Robert E. Kimmel, 24 Jan 1956; Col Elbert D. Reynolds, 9 Jul 1956; Maj Joseph D. Hales, 10 Aug 1956; Col Elbert D. Reynolds, c. 24 Oct 1956; Col Woodrow P. Swancutt, 12 Apr–8 Nov 1957. None (not manned), 15 Nov 1962–31 Jan 1963; Col Gerald G. Robinson, 1 Feb 1963; Col Rowland H. Worrell, Jr., 15 Jul 1963; Col William R. Grady, 3 Jun 1965; Col George Pfeiffer, Jr., 7 Jul 1965; Col Lawrence E. Stephens, 15 May 1968; Col Robert D. Gardner, 31 May 1968; Col B. H. Davidson, 25 Jun 1968; Col Robert E.

Mullin, 10 Jul 1969; Col Grover C. Graves, Jr., 4 Aug 1970; Col Charles E. McCartney, Jr., 19 Mar 1973; Col Pierce L. Smith, 1 May 1974; Col William R. Brooksher, 29 Jul 1976; Col Charles L. Lipscomb, 27 May 1977–.

Aircraft and Missiles. B/RB–17, 1948–1950; TRB–17, 1949; B–29, 1948–1949, 1950; RB–29, 1948–1951; TB–29, 1948–1949; TRB–29, 1949; RC–54, 1948–1949; B–50, 1949–1950; RB–50, 1950–1951; B/RB–45, 1950–1953; B–47, 1953; YRB–47, 1953–1954; RB–47, 1953–1957; KB–29, 1950–1953; KC–97, 1952–1953, 1953–1957. B–52, 1963–1966, 1967–1968; KC–135, 1963–1966, 1967–1968; Minuteman I, 1968–1971; Minuteman III, 1968–.

Operations. Performed global strategic reconnaissance, 1948–1957, with emphasis on aerial photography and mapping, 1948–1950, and aerial refueling, 1950–1957. Wing headquarters integrated with headquarters of 301st Bombardment Wing, 1 Apr 1950–9 Feb 1951, although each wing continued tactical operations independently. Tactical components occasionally detached for periods up to 3 months for duty with other USAF establishments. More frequently, wing maintained operational detachments comprised of aircraft and crews drawn from several components to provide reconnaissance support in overseas areas. Such detachments were maintained in England, 19 Jan 1951–20 Mar 1952, 18 Mar–11 May 1952, 21 Oct–12 Dec 1952 and 8 Apr–9 May 1954; in Japan, 23 Mar 1951–30 Nov 1953; in North Africa, 3 Aug–4 Nov 1956; in Newfoundland, 3 Aug–2 Nov 1956; and in Greenland, 1 Oct–8 Nov 1957. From Aug to Nov 1956 most of the wing deployed overseas in detachments not under operational control of the small establishment remaining in the United States. Inactivated in Nov 1957, but activated in Feb 1963 as a bombardment wing to train for global bombardment and aerial refueling. Except for a small rear echelon, the wing's headquarters staff, tactical aircraft and crews, and most support personnel were integrated in the Strategic Air Command Arc Light force for combat in Southeast Asia, c. 11 Sep 1966–c. 31 Mar 1967. Deployed in Okinawa in response to the *Pueblo* incident, 5 Feb–c. 15 Apr 1968. Not tactically operational c. 1 May–25 Jun 1968 while closing Glasgow AFB, Mont. Moved without personnel or equipment on 25 Jun 1968 to Minot AFB, ND, absorbing personnel and equipment of an inactivated missile wing. Thereafter operated and maintained strategic missiles in a state of operational readiness.

Service Streamers. None.

Campaign Streamers. None.

Decorations. Air Force Outstanding Unit Awards: 8 Sep 1953–8 Nov 1957; 1 Jul 1965–30 Jun 1966; 1 Jul 1966–30 Jun 1967; 1 Feb–1 Mar 1968; 2 Mar–15 Apr 1968; 1 Jul 1972–30 Jun 1973.

Emblem. Light blue, issuant from sinister base a mailed hand bendwise argent grasping three lightning flashes to chief and one to base or, in dexter base a sphere azure with land areas of the second and grid lines counterchanged of the last and the fourth, overall an entwining olive wreath vert, in dexter honor point a nuclear symbol of the second, all within a diminished bordure of the third. *Motto:* POISED FOR PEACE. (Approved c. 23 Aug 1963.)

92d BOMBARDMENT WING, HEAVY

Lineage. Established as 92d Bombardment Wing, Very Heavy, and organized, on 17 Nov 1947. Discontinued on 12 Jul 1948. Redesignated 92d Bombardment Wing, Medium, and activated on 12 Jul 1948. Redesignated: 92d Bombardment Wing, Heavy, on 16 Jun 1951; 92d Strategic Aerospace Wing on 15 Feb 1962; 92d Bombardment Wing, Heavy, on 31 Mar 1972.

Assignments. Fifteenth Air Force, 17 Nov 1947–12 Jul 1948. Fifteenth Air Force, 12 Jul 1948; 57th Air Division, 16 Apr 1951 (attached to 3d Air Division, 16 Oct 1954–12 Jan 1955 and 26 Apr–6 Jul 1956); Fifteenth Air Force, 4 Sep 1956; 18th Air (later, 18th Strategic Aerospace) Division, 1 Jul 1959 (attached to 14th Strategic Aerospace Division, 15 Jun–1 Jul 1968); 14th Strategic Aerospace Division, 2 Jul 1968; 4th Strategic Aerospace Division, 31 Mar 1970; 47th Air Division, 30 Jun 1971–.

Components. *Wings*. 90th: attached 2–31 Jan 1951. 98th: attached 17 Nov 1947–12 Jul 1948 (not operational); attached 12 Jul 1948–15 Apr 1950 (not operational); attached 16 May 1950–31 Mar 1951. *Groups*. 92d: 17 Nov 1947–12 Jul 1948; 12 Jul 1948–16 Jun 1952 (detached 7 Feb–19 May 1949 and 9 Jul–30 Oct 1950; not operational, 16 Feb 1951–16 Jun 1952). 98th: attached 17 Nov 1947–12 Jul 1948; attached 12 Jul–21 Aug 1948, 10 Dec 1948–16 May 1949, 18 Aug 1949–15 Apr 1950; rear echelon (no aircraft or crews) attached 2 Aug 1950–16 Apr 1951. 454th: attached 27 Jun 1949–16 Jun 1951. *Squadrons*. 22d Air Refueling: 15 Jun 1960–1 Jul 1962 (not operational, 14 Jun–1 Jul 1962). 43d Air Refueling: 2 Apr 1966– (detached c. 22 Mar–8 Jul 1968 and 9 Jun–14 Sep 1969). 92d Air Refueling: 1 Jul 1957 (detached 1 Jul–13 Sep 1957, 9 Jul–22 Sep 1968, and 15 Mar–9 Jun 1969). 325th: attached 16 Feb 1951–15 Jun 1952, assigned 16 Jun 1952– (detached c. 22 Mar–22 Sep 1968 and c. 15 Mar–14 Sep 1969; not operational, c. 1 Jun 1972–24 Oct 1973). 326th: attached 16 Feb 1951–15 Jun 1952, assigned 16 Jun 1952–1 Apr 1961 (detached 1 Mar–1 Apr 1961). 327th: attached 16 Feb 1951–15 Jun 1952, assigned 16 Jun 1952–1 Jun 1960 (not operational, 5 Feb–c. Jun 1957). 567th Strategic Missile: 1 Apr 1960–25 Jun 1965 (not operational, 6 Apr–25 Jun 1965).

Stations. Spokane AAFld (later, Spokane AFB), Wash, 17 Nov 1947–12 Jul 1948. Spokane (later, Fairchild) AFB, Wash, 12 Jul 1948–.

Commanders. Col Albert J. Shower, 17 Nov 1947; Col James E. Briggs, 12 Apr–12 Jul 1948. Col James E. Briggs, 12 Jul 1948; Lt Col James E. Johnson, 18 Aug 1948; Brig Gen James E. Briggs, c. 17 Sep 1948; Col Clifford H. Rees, 17 Mar 1949; Col Kermit D. Stevens, (by 26 Jul) 1950; Col Conrad F. Necrason, (by 29) Aug 1950; Col

Clifford H. Rees, (by 26) Sep 1950; Col Conrad F. Necrason, (by 30) Oct 1950; Col Clifford H. Rees, c. 1 Nov 1950; Col Conrad F. Necrason, 6 Jan 1951; Col Claude E. Putnam, Jr., 14 Apr 1951; Col McLyle G. Zumwalt, c. Jun 1951; Col Kenneth B. Hobson, (by 19) Jun 1951; Col Edgar S. Davis, 23 Jan 1952; Col David Wade, 9 Feb 1952; Col Jack J. Catton, 1 Nov 1952; Brig Gen James V. Edmundson, 18 Nov 1952; Col Jack J. Catton, 20 Mar 1954; Col Roland A. Campbell, 7 Jul 1955; Col Robert B. Hurley, Aug 1956; Col Clarence A. Neely, 8 Aug 1956; Col Robert B. Hurley, 22 Oct 1956; Col Clarence A. Neely, 25 Jan 1957; Col Edward A. Perry, 12 Dec 1957; Col Donald E. Hillman, 20 Jan 1958; Col Lester F. Miller, 30 May 1959; Col Reuben A. Baxter, 6 Jun 1962; Col Daniel V. MacDonald, 11 Jul 1962; Col Reuben A. Baxter, 26 Jul 1962; Col David I. Liebman, 6 Aug 1962; Col Edison F. Arnold, 15 May 1964; Col Alex W. Talmant, 15 Mar 1965; Col Woodrow A. Abbott, c. May 1967; Col Robert H. Gaughan, 17 Jan 1968; Col Robert L. Cooch, c. 22 Mar 1968; Col Robert H. Gaughan, 23 Sep 1968; Col Robert L. Cooch, 15 Mar 1969; Col Frank W. Elliott, Jr., 14 Sep 1969; Col Richard F. Heller, Jr., 23 Jan 1970; Col Clyde R. Denniston, Jr., 15 Jan 1971; Col Donald L. Keplinger, 18 Jun 1971; Col Martin C. Fulcher, 9 Apr 1973; Col Louis C. Buckman, 1 Feb 1974; Col John R. Stewart, Jr., 29 May 1975; Col Philip A. Brennan, 7 Apr 1976; Col Alan H. Lancaster, 13 Jun 1977–.

Aircraft and Missiles. B–29, 1947–1948. B–29, 1948–1950, 1950–1952; B–36, 1951–1957; KB–29, 1957; B–52, 1957–1968, 1968–1969, 1969–1972, 1973–; KC–135, 1958–; Atlas, 1961–1965.

Operations. Served as a double-sized B–29 bombardment wing, Nov 1947–Jul 1948, Jul 1948–Apr 1950, and May 1950–Apr 1951, although one bomb group was generally deployed overseas for training or combat. Supervised a Reserve corollary bomb group, Jun 1949–Feb 1951. Pioneered mass B–36 deployments to the Far East, Aug–Sep 1953. Deployed at Andersen AFB, Guam, 16 Oct 1954–12 Jan 1955 and 26 Apr–6 Jul 1956. Added air refueling operations to bombardment mission in Sep 1957. From Jul 1961 to Aug 1965, controlled an Atlas missile squadron. Supported SAC activities in Southeast Asia from early 1965 to Dec 1975 through deployment of bomber and tanker aircraft and crews. From Mar to Sep 1968 and Mar to Sep 1969, all wing B–52s and half its KC–135 resources, plus support personnel, were involved in Southeast Asia operations with other SAC units. From Jun 1972 to Oct 1973, all wing B–52s and most wing KC–135s, plus aircrew and support personnel, again supported SAC operations in Southeast Asia.

Service Streamers. None.

Campaign Streamers. None.

Decorations. Air Force Outstanding Unit Awards: 22 Aug–11 Sep 1953; 3 Mar–6 Oct 1959; 1 Jan 1961–31 Mar 1962; 1 Jul 1967–30 Jun 1968; 1 Jul–1 Oct 1968; 1 Jul 1969–30 Jun 1970; 1 Jul 1976–30 Jun 1977.

Emblem. Per bend of the sky proper and sable, in chief between two clouds argent an olive branch vert conjoined in base with a lightning flash gules fimbriated of the third bend sinisterwise throughout, over all issuant from base an armored hand fesswise grasping a two-edged broad sword bendwise throughout of the first, the hilt alternately or and azure. *Motto:* DUPLUM INCOLUMITATIS—Twofold security. (Approved on 21 Nov 1957.)

93d BOMBARDMENT WING, HEAVY

Lineage. Established as 93d Bombardment Wing, Very Heavy, on 28 Jul 1947. Organized on 15 Aug 1947. Discontinued on 12 Jul 1948. Redesignated 93d Bombardment Wing, Medium, and activated on 12 Jul 1948. Redesignated 93d Bombardment Wing, Heavy, on 1 Feb 1955.

Assignments. Fifteenth Air Force, 15 Aug 1947–12 Jul 1948. Fifteenth Air Force, 12 Jul 1948 (attached to 7th Air Division, 6 Dec 1951–6 Mar 1952); 47th Air (later, 47th Strategic Aerospace; 47th Air) Division, 1 Jul 1959; Second Air Force, 30 Jun 1971; Fifteenth Air Force, 15 Feb 1973; 14th Air Division, 1 Oct 1976–.

Components. *Groups*. 93d: 15 Aug 1947–12 Jul 1948 (detached 15 May–12 Jul 1948); 12 Jul 1948–16 Jun 1952 (detached 12 Jul–25 Aug 1948 and 15 Jul 1950–30 Jan 1951; not operational, 10 Feb 1951–16 Jun 1952). 447th: attached 10 Feb–16 Jun 1951. *Squadrons*. 90th Air Refueling: 18 Jan 1954–5 Aug 1955 (detached c. 3 Apr–18 May 1954 and 1 Apr–16 Jul 1955; not operational, c. 20 Jul–5 Aug 1955). 93d Air Refueling: attached 15 Jul 1950–30 Jan 1951; attached 10 Feb 1951–15 Jun 1952, assigned 16 Jun 1952– (detached c. 1 Apr–15 May 1954, 29 Jun–14 Aug 1954, 19 Jan–c. 15 Mar 1955, 18 Jun–c. 3 Jul 1955, 2 Nov 1955–5 Jan 1956, and 27 Sep–c. 24 Dec 1956). 328th: attached 10 Feb 1951–15 Jun 1952, assigned 16 Jun 1952–. 329th: attached 10 Feb 1951–15 Jun 1952, assigned 16 Jun 1952–30 Sep 1971 (not operational, 14–30 Sep 1971). 330th: attached 10 Feb 1951–15 Jun 1952, assigned 16 Jun 1952–15 Sep 1963. 340th Air Refueling: attached 20 Oct 1952–18 Jan 1954 (not operational, 20 Oct 1952–c. 15 Jan 1953). 341st Air Refueling: attached 11 Jun 1954–15 Aug 1955 (not operational, 11 Jun 1954–c. 20 Jul 1955). 924th Air Refueling: 1 Jul 1959–.

Stations. Castle Field (later, AFB), Calif, 15 Aug 1947–12 Jul 1948. Castle AFB, Calif, 12 Jul 1948–.

Commanders. Col Lee B. Coats, 15 Aug 1947; Lt Col William G. Gillespie, 5 May 1948; Lt Col Jack D. Whidden, 14 Jun 1948; Lt Col William G. Gillespie, 18 Jun 1948; Col Robert H. Terrill, 29 Jun–12 Jul 1948. Col Robert H. Terrill, 12 Jul 1948; Lt Col William G. Gillespie, 31 Jul 1948; Col Glendon P. Overing, 14 Aug 1948; Col Robert H. Terrill, 27 Aug 1948; Col David Wade, 13 Jul 1950; Col Charles W. Bicking, 15 Jul 1950; Col David Wade, 4 Oct 1950;

Brig Gen Robert H. Terrill, 1 Feb 1951; Col John E. Dougherty, 10 Apr 1951; Col Richard H. Carmichael, 16 Apr 1951; Col John E. Dougherty, 23 Apr 1951; Col Richard H. Carmichael, 3 May 1951; Col John E. Dougherty, 19 Oct 1951; Col Frank L. O'Brien, Jr., 10 Jun 1952; Col John E. Dougherty, c. Aug 1952; Col Frank L. O'Brien, Jr., 25 Nov 1952; Col John E. Dougherty, (by 31) Dec 1952; Col Frank L. O'Brien, Jr., 3 Feb 1953; Brig Gen William E. Eubank, Jr., 2 Jul 1953; Col Paul K. Carlton, 1 Jul 1958; Maj Gen William E. Eubank, Jr., 22 Jul 1958; Col George B. Thabault, Jul 1959; Col Lawrence S. Lightner, 11 Aug 1959; Col James V. Reardon, 21 Jul 1961; Col Roy C. Crompton, 17 Jan 1966; Col Charles Abbuhl, Jr., 9 Sep 1966; Col Woodrow A. Abbott, 26 Jan 1968; Brig Gen Bryan M. Shotts, 23 Jun 1969; Col Colin C. Hamilton, Jr., 16 Mar 1970; Brig Gen Charles I. Bennett, Jr., 23 Apr 1971 (additional duty), 30 Jun 1971 (permanent); Col James H. McGrath, 21 Jan 1972; Brig Gen John R. Kelly, Jr., 6 Mar 1972; Col Malcolm L. Landess, 13 Jan 1973; Brig Gen Richard N. Cody, 12 Mar 1973; Col Irving B. Reed, 1 Jul 1974; Col Jimmy R. Williams, 1 Apr 1975; Col Burr V. Miller, Jr., 14 May 1977–.

Aircraft. B–29, 1947–1948. B–29, 1948–1949; B–50, 1949–1950, 1950–1954; KB–29, 1950–1953; KC–97, 1953–1955, 1955, 1956, 1956–1957; B–47, 1954–1956; B–52, 1955–; KC–135, 1957–.

Operations. Maintained combat readiness for global strategic bombardment, Aug 1947–Jul 1948 and Jul 1948–Feb 1956, and aerial refueling, beginning Oct 1950. Was first SAC wing to convert to B–52 aircraft (in 1955–1956). Became SAC's primary B–52 aircrew training organization, adding KC–135 aircrew training in mid-1956. Served as the sole B–52/KC–135 aircrew training organization for SAC (sometimes extending training to other USAF commands and to friendly foreign nations) except for periods Sep 1959–Sep 1963 and Apr 1974–Mar 1977, when other SAC wings also performed such training. From Apr 1968 to Apr 1974, also operated a special B–52 replacement training unit to support SAC's B–52 operations in Southeast Asia. Although most of its components were used for aircrew training, after 1956 the 93d Wing sometimes maintained one or more of its units in a pure tactical role, with operational commitments. Notable operations include the deployment of the 93d Bombardment Group to Okinawa in 1948 (the first SAC bomb group to deploy in full strength to the Far East); deployment of its full tactical force, augmented by support personnel, to England, Jul 1950–Jan 1951; deployment of the entire 93d Wing to England, Dec 1951–Mar 1952; aerial refueling and navigational assistance for the Jul 1952 movement of the 31st Fighter-Escort Wing from the United States to Japan (the first jet fighter crossing of the Pacific Ocean); nonstop B–52 flights of some 16,000 miles around North America and to the North Pole in Nov 1956; the first jet aircraft nonstop flight around the world in Jan 1957 (with wing B–52s flying 23,574 miles in 45:19 hours); and a nonstop, unrefueled KC–135 flight from Yokota AB, Japan to Washington, D.C., in 13:58 hours in Apr 1958.

Service Streamers. None.

Campaign Streamers. None.

Decorations. Air Force Outstanding Unit Awards: 1 Jan 1956–1 Jul 1959; 1 Jun 1962–1 Apr 1963; 1 Apr 1973–30 Jun 1974.

Emblem. Azure, in front of a bend parti per bend sable and argent between two globes of the last with latitude and longitude lines of the second, the one in chief bearing a wreath vert and the one in base bearing a cross of four arrows, points out of the first, gules, or and of the fifth, a lightning flash bend sinisterwise or. (Approved on 4 Sep 1953.)

94th TACTICAL AIRLIFT WING

Lineage. Established as 94th Bombardment Wing, Light, on 10 May 1949. Activated in the Reserve on 26 Jun 1949. Ordered to active service on 10 Mar 1951. Inactivated on 1 Apr 1951. Redesignated 94th Tactical Reconnaissance Wing on 26 May 1952. Activated in the Reserve on 14 Jun 1952. Redesignated: 94th Bombardment Wing, Tactical, on 18 May 1955; 94th Troop Carrier Wing, Medium, on 1 Jul 1957. Ordered to active service on 28 Oct 1962. Relieved from active duty on 28 Nov 1962. Redesignated: 94th Military Airlift Wing on 1 Oct 1966; 94th Tactical Airlift Wing on 1 Jul 1972.

Assignments. Fourteenth Air Force, 26 Jun 1949–1 Apr 1951. Fourteenth Air Force, 14 Jun 1952; Tenth Air Force, 18 May 1955; First Air Force, 16 Nov 1957; Fourteenth Air Force, 25 Mar 1958; First Air Force Reserve Region, 15 Aug 1960; Ninth Air Force, 28 Oct 1962; First Air Force Reserve Region, 28 Nov 1962 (attached to Second Air Force Reserve Region, 1 May–23 Jun 1966); Eastern Air Force Reserve Region, 31 Dec 1969; Fourteenth Air Force (Reserve), 8 Oct 1976–.

Components. *Groups*. 94th: 26 Jun 1949–20 Mar 1951; 14 Jun 1952–14 Apr 1959. 901st: 11 Feb 1963–1 Jul 1972. 902d: 11 Feb 1963–25 Jan 1966. 905th: 1 Jul 1966–25 Feb 1972. 908th: 1 Jul 1972–. 911th: attached 1–20 Apr 1971, assigned 21 Apr 1971–25 Feb 1972. 914th: 1 Jan 1964–1 Jul 1966. 918th: 1 Jul 1972–1 Sep 1975. *Squadrons*. 700th: 1 Sep 1975–. 731st: 14 Apr 1959–11 Feb 1963. 732d: 14 Apr 1959–11 Feb 1963.

Stations. Marietta (later, Dobbins) AFB, Ga, 26 Jun 1949–1 Apr 1951. Dobbins AFB, Ga, 14 Jun 1952; Scott AFB, Ill, 18 May 1955; Laurence G. Hanscom Field, Mass, 16 Nov 1957; Dobbins AFB, Ga, 1 Jul 1972–.

Commanders. Brig Gen William L. Plummer, 26 Jun 1949; Col Harry Copeland, c. 10–19 Mar 1951; none (not manned), 20 Mar–1 Apr 1951. Col George H. Wilson, 14 Jun 1952; Col Edwin H. Lauth, 18 May 1955; Col Arthur C. Carroll, 16 Nov 1957; Brig Gen Charles D. Briggs, Jr., 29 Dec 1969; Col Dona J. LaCouture, Jr., 1 Jun 1971; Brig Gen Cecil T. Jenkins, 20 Jul

1971; Col Norman R. Mailloux, 23 Dec 1975 (temporary), 23 Jan 1976 (permanent); Brig Gen Sloan R. Gill, 21 Jul 1976–.

Aircraft. T–6, 1949–1950; T–7, 1949–1951; T–11, 1949–1951; B–26, 1949–1951. AT–6, 1952–1954; C–46, 1952–1955; TF–51, 1953–1955; F–51, 1953–1954; B–26, 1953–1955, 1955–1957; T–28, 1953–1954, 1955; C–45, 1953–1955; T–33, 1954–1955; F–80, 1954–1955; RB–26, 1954–1955; F–84, 1954–1955; C–47, 1955; C–119, 1957, 1957–1966; C–124, 1966–1972; C–7, 1972–.

Operations. Trained as a light bombardment wing in the Reserve, Jun 1949–Mar 1951. Upon being called to active duty during the Korean war, wing personnel augmented other active USAF units. Trained in the Reserve from Jun 1952, in turn as a tactical reconnaissance, bombardment, troop carrier, and airlift wing. Served briefly on active duty during the Cuban missile crisis of 1962. By mid-1958, wing personnel flew airlift missions with C–119s, and after Mar 1959 airlift operations and exercises were flown regularly both in the United States and overseas, including contingency operations in the Dominican Republic in 1965. After converting to C–124s in 1966, flew global airlift missions, including troop and cargo missions to Southeast Asia from 1966 to 1971, augmenting normal airlift resources of Military Airlift Command and Tactical Air Command. After switching to C–7s in mid-1972, the wing's primary operations involved support of U.S. Army airborne forces, tactical cargo airlift, and air evacuation missions. From Jul 1973 to May 1975, the wing also flew 685 C–7 "Coronet Round-up" missions in Puerto Rico, during which it airdropped 1.2 billion sterile screwworm flies as part of a U.S. Department of Agriculture project to eradicate the screwworm menance in Puerto Rico.

Service Streamers. None.

Campaign Streamers. None.

Decorations. Air Force Outstanding Unit Award: 1 Jul 1972–15 Mar 1974. Republic of Vietnam Gallantry Cross with Palm: 1 Apr 1966–24 Feb 1972.

Emblem. On a sky proper issuant from base in pale surmounting a cloud mass argent outlined azure and a sphere abased of the first with grid markings of the third, a Minute Man affrontee couped above the ankles silhouetted of the last, detailed of the second and winged or, the wings outlined and detailed of the third. *Motto:* MINUTEMAN WING. (Approved on 19 May 1959.)

95th STRATEGIC WING

Lineage. Established as 95th Bombardment Wing, Medium, on 4 Jun 1952. Activated on 16 Jun 1952. Redesignated 95th Bombardment Wing, Heavy, on 8 Nov 1952. Discontinued, and inactivated, on 25 Jun 1966. Redesignated 95th Strategic Wing, and activated, on 8 Aug 1966. Organized on 2 Oct 1966. Inactivated on 30 Sep 1976.

Assignments. 810th Air Division, 16 Jun 1952 (attached to 3d Air Division, 26 Jul–4 Nov 1955); 819th Strategic Aerospace Division, 1 Jul 1962; 12th Strategic Aerospace Division, 1 Jul 1964–25 Jun 1966. Strategic Air Command, 8 Aug 1966; 45th Air Division, 2 Oct 1966–30 Sep 1976.

Components. *Squadrons*. 334th: 16 Jun 1952–25 Jun 1966 (not operational, 16 Jun 1952–6 Sep 1953). 335th: 16 Jun 1952–15 Jan 1959 (not operational, 16 Jun 1952–6 Sep 1953). 336th: 16 Jun 1952–1 Jul 1959 (not operational, 16 Jun 1952–6 Sep 1953). 917th Air Refueling: 1 May 1959–15 Jan 1965.

Stations. Biggs AFB, Texas, 16 Jun 1952–25 Jun 1966. Goose AB (later, Goose Bay Aprt), Canada, 2 Oct 1966–30 Sep 1976.

Commanders. Brig Gen John D. Ryan, 16 Jun 1952 (additional duty); Col Bertram C. Harrison, Nov 1952–Mar 1953; unkn, Mar–23 Aug 1953; Col Edward W. Scott, Jr., 24 Aug 1953; Col Gerald G. Robinson, 3 Nov 1956; Col Thomas G. Netcher, 5 Nov 1960; Col Douglas M. Conlan, Nov 1963; Col Gerald W. Johnson, 1 Dec 1963; Col Douglas M. Conlan, 4 Jun 1965; Col George P. Cole, 26 Jul 1965–25 Jun 1966. None (not manned), 8 Aug–1 Oct 1966; Col Donald G. McPherson, 2 Oct 1966; Col James O. Britt, 28 Aug 1967; Col Lawrence F. McGuire, 14 Aug 1969; Col James B. Penrod, 27 Apr 1970; Col Duard Y. Jackson, 30 Mar 1971; Col John H. Moore, Jr., 28 Mar 1973; Col John R. Shipe, 14 Aug 1974; Col Caleb G. Pendley, 10 Jul 1975; Lt Col Milo L. Carlson, 14 Jul–30 Sep 1976.

Aircraft. B–36, 1953–1959; B–52, 1959–1966; KC–135, 1959–1965. KC–135 (attached), 1966–1975.

Operations. Manned as paper unit, Jun 1952–Jul 1953, and minimally manned, Jul–6 Sep 1953. Strategic bombardment training, Aug 1953–Feb 1966, and air refueling, Aug 1959–Jan 1965, to meet SAC's global commitments. Supported SAC's KC–135 alert tanker forces in eastern Canada and North Atlantic, Oct 1966–Dec 1975.

Service Streamers. None.

Campaign Streamers. None.

Decorations. Air Force Outstanding Unit Awards: 1 Jul 1970–30 Jun 1971; 27–30 Jun 1974.

Emblem. On a shield azure, a Justin cross throughout argent, over all a feather in bend gules, all within a narrow edge white. *Motto:* JUSTICE WITH VICTORY. (Approved for 95th Group on 26 Feb 1943 and, slightly modified, for 95th Wing on 3 Sep 1957.)

96th BOMBARDMENT WING, HEAVY

Lineage. Established as 96th Bombardment Wing, Heavy, on 23 Mar 1953. Redesignated 96th Bombardment Wing, Medium, on 6 Nov 1953. Activated on 18 Nov 1953. Redesignated: 96th Strategic Aerospace Wing on 1 Apr 1962; 96th Bombardment Wing, Heavy, on 31 Mar 1972.

Assignments. Eighth Air Force, 18 Nov 1953; Fifteenth Air Force, 1 Apr 1955 (attached to 3d Air Division, 10 Jan–7 Apr 1957); 819th Air (later, 819th Strategic Aerospace) Division, 3 Sep 1957; 19th Air Division, 2 Jul 1966; 12th Air Division, 1 Jul 1973–.

Components. *Squadrons.* 4th Strategic Support: 1 Sep 1959–15 Mar 1961. 11th Air Refueling: attached 16 Dec 1957–Mar 1958. 96th Air Refueling: 18 Nov 1953–3 Dec 1957 (not operational, 18 Nov 1953–Jan 1954; detached Jan–14 Mar 1954, 5 Oct–20 Nov 1954, 1 Aug–14 Sep 1955, 18–31 Jan 1956, 25 Jun–9 Oct 1956, 15 Nov–7 Dec 1956, and 10 Jan–7 Apr 1957). 321st Air Refueling: attached 3 Jul–8 Nov 1954 (not operational). 337th: 18 Nov 1953–15 Mar 1963 (not opertional, 18 Nov 1953–13 Mar 1955); 15 Sep 1963– (not operational, 15 Sep–c. 22 Dec 1963, c. 22 Jun–19 Sep 1970, and c. 8 Apr 1972–28 Oct 1973). 338th: 18 Nov 1953–15 Mar 1963 (not operational, 18 Nov 1953–13 Mar 1955). 339th: 18 Nov 1953–15 Mar 1963 (not operational, 18 Nov 1953–29 Apr 1955). 380th Air Refueling: attached 8 Nov 1954–1 Apr 1955. 413th: 1 Nov 1958–1 Jan 1962 (not operational, 1 Oct 1961–1 Jan 1962). 578th Strategic Missile: 1 Jul 1961–25 Mar 1965 (not operational, 1 Jul 1961–26 Apr 1962 and Feb–25 Mar 1965). 917th Air Refueling: attached 1–14 Jan 1965, assigned 15 Jan 1965– (not operational, c. 24 Jun–Dec 1970 and c. 8 Apr 1972–Mar 1973).

Stations. Altus AFB, Okla, 18 Nov 1953; Dyess AFB, Texas, 8 Sep 1957–.

Commanders. Col Dearl L. Beard, 18 Nov 1953 (additional duty), 15 Mar 1954 (permanent); Col Audrin R. Walker, 21 Apr 1954; Col Roger M. Crow, 11 Jan 1955; Col Robert B. Templeman, 26 Jan 1955; Col Roger M. Crow, 29 Jan 1955; Col Audrin R. Walker, 10 Mar 1955; Col Howard B. Walsh, c. 1 Oct 1957; Col Charles F. McKenna III, Oct 1957; Col Burton C. Andrus, Jr., 1 Nov 1958; Col William R. Yancey, 1 Dec 1958; Col Burton C. Andrus, Jr., 1 Mar 1959; Col William L. McDowell, Jr., 1 Jun 1961; Col Harold A. Radetsky, (by 27) Jun 1963; Col Eugene A. Stalzer, 2 Aug 1965; Col William H. Cooper, 16 Jun 1967; Col Edgar S. Harris, Jr., 16 Aug 1968; Col William P. Armstrong, 13 Feb 1970; Col Bertram G. Brunner, c. 5 Jun 1970; Col Evarice C. Mire, Jr., c. 22 Jun 1970–unkn; Col William P. Armstrong, (by 7 Oct) 1970; Col James D. Naler, 15 Mar 1971; Col Bill V. Brown, c. 8 Feb 1972; unkn, 4–9 Aug 1972; Col Eric W. Carlson, 10 Aug 1972; Col James D. Naler, 15 Nov 1972; Col Eric W. Carlson, 29 Jun 1973; Col Bill V. Brown, 23 Aug 1973; Col Eric W. Carlson, 1 May 1974; Col Frank J. Apel, Jr., 2 Jul 1975; Col Joseph S. Morison, 24 Aug 1977–.

Aircraft and Missiles. KC–97, 1954–1956, 1956–1958; B–47, 1955–1963; C–124, 1959–1961; Atlas, 1962–1965; B–52, 1963–1970, 1970–1972, 1973–; KC–135, 1965–1970, 1970–1972, 1973–.

Operations. Although activated in Nov 1953, wing headquarters and most wing components were not manned until Mar 1954; those components manned were controlled by the 96th Air Base Group, whose commander served additional duty as wing commander. Began air refueling operations in Mar 1954 and bombardment training in Apr 1955 in support of SAC's global commitments. Deployed at Andersen AFB, Guam, 10 Jan–7 Apr 1957. Controlled a strategic airlift squadron, Sep 1959–Mar 1961, and an Atlas missile squadron, Jul 1961–Mar 1965. The first Atlas missile went on alert in Apr 1962. During several months of 1970, and for a lengthy period in 1972–1973, all wing aircraft, crews, and most support personnel loaned to other SAC organizations based in the Far East or Southeast Asia for combat operations.

Service Streamers. None.

Campaign Streamers. None.

Decorations. Air Force Outstanding Unit Awards: 1 Jan 1959–31 Dec 1960; 1 Jul 1974–30 Jun 1975.

Emblem. Azure a falcon's head erased or, holding in its beak a drop bomb bendwise gules, that portion over the first fimbriated of the second. *Motto:* E SEMPRE L'ORA—It is always the hour. (Approved for 96th Group on 18 Feb 1943 and for 96th Wing on 22 Mar 1955.)

97th BOMBARDMENT WING, HEAVY

Lineage. Established as 97th Bombardment Wing, Very Heavy, on 11 Sep 1947. Organized on 1 Dec 1947. Discontinued on 12 Jul 1948. Redesignated 97th Bombardment Wing, Medium, and activated on 12 Jul 1948. Redesignated 97th Bombardment Wing, Heavy, on 1 Oct 1959.

Assignments. Fifteenth Air Force, 1 Dec 1947 (attached to Yukon Sector, Alaskan Air Command, 1 Dec 1947–12 Mar 1948; 301st Bombardment Wing, Very Heavy, 17 Mar–16 May 1948); Eighth Air Force, 16 May–12 Jul 1948. Eighth Air Force, 12 Jul 1948 (attached to 7th Air Division, 15 Mar–11 Jun 1952); 810th Air Division, 16 Jun 1952 (attached to 7th Air Division, 5 May–4 Jul 1956); 4th Air Division, 1 Jul 1959; 42d Air Division, 1 Jul 1963; 19th Air Division, 2 Jul 1969; 42d Air Division, 1 Jan 1970; 19th Air Division, 30 Jun 1971; 42d Air Division, 1 Jul 1973–.

Components. *Groups*. 97th: 1 Dec 1947–12 Jul 1948; 12 Jul 1948–16 Jun 1952 (detached 4 Nov 1948–15 Feb 1949 and c. 26 Jul 1950–9 Feb 1951; not operational, 10 Feb 1951–16 Jun 1952). 401st: attached 10 Feb–25 Jun 1951. *Squadrons*. 97th Air Refueling: attached 12 Jul 1950–15 Jun 1952, assigned 16 Jun 1952–1 Sep 1957 (detached c. 21 Nov–c. 20 Dec 1954, c. 31 May–10 Jul 1955, 1 May–9 Jul 1957, and 25 Aug–1 Sep 1957); assigned 23 Oct 1964–. 340th: attached 10 Feb 1951–15 Jun 1952, assigned 16 Jun

1952– (detached 16 Dec 1953–c. 15 Mar 1954 and 24 Sep–2 Nov 1957; not operational, 15 Jan–30 Sep 1959). 341st: attached 10 Feb 1951–15 Jun 1952, assigned 16 Jun 1952–15 Feb 1960 (detached c. 15 Mar– c. 12 Jul 1954 and 12 Aug–24 Sep 1957; not operational, 15 Jan 1959–15 Feb 1960). 342d: attached 10 Feb 1951–15 Jun 1952, assigned 16 Jun 1952–1 May 1960 (detached 10 Dec 1952– 19 Mar 1953 and 1 Jul–12 Aug 1957; not operational, 15 Jan 1959–1 May 1960). 914th Air Refueling: 1 Oct 1961–23 Oct 1964 (not operational, 1 Oct 1961–11 Jan 1962). 4024th: attached 1 Apr 1955–1 May 1956.

Stations. Mile 26 Air Field (later, Eielson AFB), Alaska, 1 Dec 1947–12 Mar 1948; Smoky Hill AFB, Kans, 16 Mar 1948; Biggs AFB, Texas, 22 May–12 Jul 1948. Biggs AFB, Texas, 12 Jul 1948; Blytheville AFB, Ark, 1 Jul 1959–.

Commanders. Col Jerome B. McCauley, 1 Dec 1947; Col George L. Robinson, c. 18 Mar–12 Jul 1948. Col George L. Robinson, 12 Jul 1948; Col Joel Q. Braddock, 6 Sep 1948; Col George L. Robinson, 25 Sep 1948; Brig Gen David W. Hutchison, 30 Dec 1948; Col Richard M. Montgomery, 13 Jul 1950; Brig Gen David W. Hutchison, 23 Jan 1951; Col Harvey C. Dorney, 20 Feb 1951; Brig Gen John D. Ryan, 16 Jul 1951–15 Jun 1952 (primary) and 16 Jun 1952 (additional duty); Col Clifford F. Macomber, c. 29 Nov 1952; Brig Gen John D. Ryan, (by 24) Jan 1953 (additional duty); Col Keith K. Compton, 10 Aug 1953; Col Charles F. McKenna III, 1 Dec 1953; Col Keith K. Compton, c. 4 Feb 1954; Col Harold D. Courtney, (by Apr) 1954; Col Keith K. Compton, (by Jun) 1954; Col Willard W. Smith, 2 Jul 1954; Col Lawrence M. Thomas, 2 Mar 1956; Col Anthony J. Perna, 30 Jul 1956; Col Salvatore E. Manzo, 18 Oct 1957; Col William C. Garland, 30 Jul 1958; Col Stephen P. Dillon, 24 Nov 1958–c. 15 Jan 1959 (primary) and c. 16–20 Jan 1959 (additional duty); Col Charles K. Nelson, Jr., 21 Jan 1959–unkn (additional duty); Col Eugene A. Stalzer, 1 Jul 1959 (additional duty); Col Ralph C. Jenkins, 13 Jul 1959; Col Eugene A. Stalzer, 21 Jul 1959 (additional duty); Col Van B. Haggard, 14 Aug 1959; Col Ralph C. Jenkins, Nov 1959; Col Richard G. Wilkinson, 5 Jun 1964; Col John W. Livingston, 1 Jul 1964; Col George H. McKee, 6 Jun 1966; Col Eugene D. Minietta, 5 Jun 1967; Col Kenneth E. Wehrman, 27 Jun 1969; Col Richard A. Bosworth, 9 Mar 1970; Col Bruce K. Brown, 1 Jul 1971; Col Thomas F. Rew, 19 Jun 1972; Col Thomas M. Mason, 6 Oct 1972; Col Thomas F. Rew, 17 Mar 1973; Col William L. Nicholson, III, 12 Apr 1973; Col Rodger L. Brooks, 5 Jun 1974; Col Thomas G. Darling, 23 Jul 1975; Col Melbourne Kimsey, 10 Feb 1977–.

Aircraft. B–29, 1947–1948. B–29, 1948–1950; B–50, 1950–1955; KB–29, 1950–1956; ERB–29, 1954–1956; RB–50, 1954–1956; KC–97, 1954–1957; B–47, 1955–1959; B–52, 1960–1972, 1973–; KC–135, 1962–1972, 1973–.

Operations. Organized in Dec 1947 in Alaska from components deployed there from Kansas. Flew training missions over the Arctic Ocean. Moved to Kansas in Mar 1948 and attached to another bomb wing for further training. Reorganized from very heavy to medium bomb wing in Jul 1948, after moving to Biggs AFB, Texas. Added a refueling mission in early 1950. Sent tactical units to England, Nov 1948–Feb 1949 and Jul 1950–Feb 1951. Entire wing deployed in England, 15 Mar–11 Jun 1952, and squadrons operated from Guam, Dec 1952–Mar 1953 and Dec 1953–Jul 1954. Added electronic reconnaissance to bombardment and refueling missions in Apr 1954, using ERB–29A and RB–50G/E aircraft, with reconnaissance missions operating from England and Japan. Transferred the reconnaissance mission in May 1956 but continued bombardment and air refueling training to meet SAC's global commitments. Deployed at RAF Upper Heyford, England, May–Jul 1956. This was last full-wing deployment, but wing components continued deploying overseas regularly, as needed. Phased down for inactivation at Biggs AFB in Dec 1958 and became non-operational 15 Jan 1959, but moved to Ark in Jul 1959 and was remanned and re-equipped later that year with B–52s. Gained KC–135s in Oct 1961. Earned an AFOUA for activities during the Cuban missile crisis of 1962. Supported SAC's combat operations in Southeast Asia in the mid-and late-1960s and early 1970s, furnishing aircraft and crews to other organizations. By mid-1972, all of the 97th's aircraft and over one-fourth of its people loaned to other SAC organizations in the Far East, Southeast Asia, and other overseas locations. A few KC–135s began returning to the wing in Apr 1973, but B–52s on loan until Oct 1973.

Service Streamers. None.

Campaign Streamers. None.

Decorations. Air Force Outstanding Unit Awards: 2 Jul–3 Nov 1957; 23 Oct–22 Nov 1962.

Emblem. On a shield azure, a spear in pale or, point to base, flammant and embrued; the shield is edged of the second. *Motto:* VENIT HORA—The hour has come. (Approved for 97th Group on 5 Mar 1943 and, in modified form, for 97th Wing on 2 May 1957.)

98th STRATEGIC WING

Lineage. Established as 98th Bombardment Wing, Very Heavy, on 24 Oct 1947. Organized on 10 Nov 1947. Discontinued on 12 Jul 1948. Redesignated 98th Bombardment Wing, Medium, and activated on 12 Jul 1948. Redesignated 98th Strategic Aerospace Wing on 1 Feb 1964. Discontinued, and inactivated, on 25 Jun 1966. Redesignated 98th Strategic Wing, activated, and organized, on 25 Jun 1966. Inactivated on 31 Dec 1976.

Assignments. Fifteenth Air Force, 10 Nov 1947–12 Jul 1948 (attached to 92d Bombardment Wing, Very Heavy, 17 Nov 1947–12 Jul 1948). Fifteenth Air Force, 12 Jul 1948 (attached to 92d Bombardment Wing, Medium, 12 Jul

1948–15 Apr 1950); Second Air Force, 16 May 1950 (attached to 92d Bombardment Wing, Medium, 16 May 1950–); Fifteenth Air Force, 28 Jul 1950 (remained attached to 92d Bombardment Wing, Medium, through 31 Mar 1951; attached to FEAF Bomber Command, Provisional, 1 Apr 1951–; rear echelon attached to 92d Air Base Group, 1 Apr 1951–); 57th Air Division, 16 Apr 1951 (remained attached to FEAF Bomber Command, Provisional, with rear echelon attached to 92d ABG to 25 Jul 1952); Fifteenth Air Force, 25 Nov 1953 (remained attached to FEAF Bomber Command, Provisional, through 17 Jun 1954; attached to Twentieth Air Force, 18 Jun–25 Jul 1954); 818th Air (later, 818th Strategic Aerospace) Division, 11 Oct 1954 (attached to 7th Air Division, 11 Nov 1955–29 Jan 1956); 810th Strategic Aerospace Division, 25 Mar 1965–25 Jun 1966. Strategic Air Command, 25 Jun 1966–31 Dec 1976.

Components. *Group.* 98th: 10 Nov 1947–12 Jul 1948 (detached); 12 Jul 1948–16 Jun 1952 (detached 12 Jul 1948–15 Apr 1950 and 2 Aug 1950–31 Mar 1951; not operational, 1 Apr 1951–16 Jun 1952). *Squadrons.* 98th Air Refueling: 16 Jun 1952–1 Jul 1953 (detached); 18 Feb 1954–15 Apr 1963 (detached 18 Feb–31 Jul 1954, 7 Jan–21 Feb 1955, 27 Dec 1956–14 Mar 1957, 28 Dec 1957–25 Mar 1958, 1 Apr–c. 8 Jul 1959, and 2 Oct 1962–7 Jan 1963; not operational, 2–15 Apr 1963). 307th Air Refueling: attached 8 Nov 1954–1 Feb 1955. 343d: attached 1 Apr 1951–15 Jun 1952, assigned 16 Jun 1952–25 Jun 1966 (not operational, 8 Dec 1965–25 Jun 1966). 344th: attached 1 Apr 1951–15 Jun 1952, assigned 16 Jun 1952–25 Jun 1966 (not operational, 8 Dec 1965–25 Jun 1966). 345th: attached 1 Apr 1951–15 Jun 1952, assigned 16 Jun 1952–25 Jun 1966 (not operational, 8 Dec 1965–25 Jun 1966). 380th Air Refueling: 1 Aug–8 Nov 1954. 415th: 1 Sep 1958–1 Jan 1962 (not operational, c. 1 Oct 1961–1 Jan 1962). 515th Strategic Missile: 1 Jan 1964–25 Jun 1965 (not operational, 12 Apr–25 Jun 1965).

Stations. Spokane AAFld (later, Spokane AFB), Wash, 10 Nov 1947–12 Jul 1948. Spokane (later, Fairchild) AFB, Wash, 12 Jul 1948–15 Aug 1953; Yokota AB, Japan, 15 Aug 1953–25 Jul 1954; Lincoln AFB, Nebr, 25 Jul 1954–25 Jun 1966. Torrejon AB, Spain, 25 Jun 1966–31 Dec 1976.

Commanders. Lt Col Joseph D. White, 10 Nov 1947 (additional duty [hereafter, addn dy]); Col Albert J. Shower, 17 Nov 1947 (addn dy); Col James E. Briggs, 12 Apr–12 Jul 1948 (addn dy). Col James E. Briggs, 12 Jul 1948 (addn dy); Lt Col James E. Johnson, 18 Aug 1948 (addn dy); Brig Gen James E. Briggs, c. 17 Sep 1948 (addn dy); Col Clifford H. Rees, 17 Mar 1949 (addn dy); Col Richard H. Carmichael, 16 May 1950 (addn dy); Col Kermit D. Stevens, c. 31 Jul 1950 (addn dy); Col Conrad F. Necrason, (by 29) Aug 1950 (addn dy); Col Clifford H. Rees, (by 26) Sep 1950 (addn dy); Col Conrad F. Necrason, (by 30) Oct 1950 (addn dy); Col Clifford H. Rees, c. 1 Nov 1950 (addn dy); Col Conrad F. Necrason, 6 Jan 1951 (addn dy); Col David Wade, 1 Apr 1951; Col Edwin F. Harding, Jr., c. 15 Sep 1951; Col Lewis A. Curtis, Nov 1951; Col Winton R. Close, May 1952; Col Charles B. Westover, 26 Oct 1952; Col Edgar S. Davis, 17 Jun 1953; Col George L. Robinson, 6 Jul 1953; Col

Joseph C. Reddoch, Jr., 3 Apr 1954; Lt Col Frank J. Puerta, 22 Jul 1954; Lt Col Harry C. Smith, 25 Jul 1954; Col Ervin Wursten, 1 Apr 1954; Col Don W. Bailey, 16 Aug 1954; Col Ervin Wursten, 4 Sep 1954; Col William F. Coleman, 10 Nov 1954; Col Wilson R. Wood, 14 Nov 1956; Col William C. Garland, c. 3 Dec 1958; Col James T. Gribble, Jr., 5 Jul 1961; Col Lee V. Wiseman, 30 Nov 1963; Col Edwin H. Garrison, 20 Aug 1964; Col Clifford J. Moore, Jr., 10 Aug 1965; Col Alvin R. Fortney, 14 Jan–25 Jun 1966. Col Louis M. Sowers, 25 Jun 1966; Col Bill H. Martin, 20 Jan 1968; Col Donald L. Stallsmith, 17 Aug 1970; Col Donald L. Keplinger, 23 Apr 1973; Col Gordon J. Krautkramer, 16 Jul 1976; Col Donald M. Griffin, 16 Aug–31 Dec 1976.

Aircraft and Missiles. B–29, 1950, 1951–1954; KC–97, 1954–1963; B–47, 1954–1965; Atlas, 1964–1965. KC–135 (attached), 1966–1976.

Operations. From Nov 1947 to Jul 1948 and Jul 1948 to Jul 1954, the 98th Wing headquarters often manned as a "paper" unit with most of its components attached to other establishments for long periods. The wing's tactical group was operational, but under control of other organizations from Nov 1947 to Apr 1950, and again from Aug 1950 to Apr 1951. On 1 Apr 1951 the tactical group became a paper unit and wing headquarters deployed to Japan to assume control over combat operations of the three tactical squadrons, while the remainder of the wing remained behind, attached to another wing. In Jun 1952, three maintenance squadrons joined the wing in Japan, as did the small rear echelon of wing headquarters that had remained at Fairchild AFB, Wash. Combat operations in Korea involved interdiction of enemy communications and support of United Nations ground forces, as well as propaganda leaflet drops. The wing's last combat mission, flown 25 Jul 1953, was followed 2 days later—on the day of truce—with a propaganda leaflet drop. Remained in Japan in combat-ready status for another year. Meanwhile, wing components not deployed in Japan moved to a reopened base in Nebr to supervise construction in preparation for movement there of deployed wing components. In Jul 1954, after disposing of B–29s in Ariz, the wing headquarters, flying units, and maintenance squadrons moved to Lincoln AFB, Nebr, and for the first time since 1947 all wing components were located at the same base, under wing control. Air refueling operations were already underway in Jul 1954, and the bombardment squadrons prepared to receive B–47s. Participated in SAC's worldwide bombardment training and air refueling commitments for the next decade. Deployed at Lakenheath RAF Station, England, 11 Nov 1955–29 Jan 1956. From Jan 1964 to Apr 1965, the wing also controlled an Atlas ICBM squadron. Inactivated on 25 Jun 1966 at Lincoln AFB but activated the same day at Torrejon AB, Spain, replacing the 3970th Strategic Wing. For the next decade, the wing had no tactical components assigned, but used attached KC–135 tankers and crews furnished by other SAC wings to provide air refueling support to meet operational, alert, and exercise commitments of SAC, TAC, USAFE, and NATO in an area including the eastern Atlantic, most of Europe, North Africa, and the Middle

East. In Oct 1976, the 306th Strategic Wing, based in West Germany, assumed this support task and the 98th phased down at Torrejon.

Service Streamers. None.

Campaign Streamers. First UN Counteroffensive; CCF Spring Offensive; UN Summer–Fall Offensive; Second Korean Winter; Korea Summer–Fall, 1952; Third Korean Winter; Korea Summer–Fall, 1953.

Decorations. Distinguished Unit Citation (Korea): 1 Dec 1952–30 Apr 1953. Air Force Outstanding Unit Awards: 1 Jul 1964–1 Jun 1965; 1 Jan 1970–31 Mar 1971; 1 Jul 1974–30 Jun 1976. Republic of Korea Presidential Unit Citation: [1 Apr 1951]–27 Jul 1953.

Emblem. Azure, a bend indented between a dexter mailed hand couped at the wrist, in bend, grasping a drop bomb and an olive wreath, all or. *Motto:* FORCE FOR FREEDOM. (Approved for 98th Group on 29 Jul 1942 and for 98th Wing on 29 Feb 1956.)

99th BOMBARDMENT WING, HEAVY

Lineage. Established as 99th Strategic Reconnaissance Wing, Heavy, and activated, on 1 Jan 1953. Redesignated 99th Bombardment Wing, Heavy, on 1 Oct 1955. Inactivated on 31 Mar 1974.

Assignments. 57th Air Division, 1 Jan 1953 (attached to 3d Air Division, 29 Jan–25 Apr 1956); 817th Air Division, 2 Jul 1969; 45th Air Division, 30 Jun 1971–31 Mar 1974.

Components. *Squadrons.* 99th Air Refueling: 1 Jan 1966–30 Sep 1973 (not operational, c. 1 Oct 1967–c. 1 Apr 1968, c. 22 Sep 1968–c. 21 Mar 1969, c. 15 Mar–c. 22 Jun 1970, Aug 1972–Feb 1973, and Jul–30 Sep 1973). 346th: 1 Jan 1953–31 Mar 1974 (not operational, 4 Sep–7 Dec 1956, c. 1 Oct 1967–c. 1 Apr 1968, c. 22 Sep 1968–c. 21 Mar 1969, c. 15 Mar–c. 22 Jun 1970, and c. 30 Apr 1972–31 Mar 1974). 347th: 1 Jan 1953–1 Sep 1961 (detached 1 Jan–12 Sep 1953; not operational, 20 Aug–13 Oct 1953 and 4 Sep–9 Dec 1956; detached 15–31 Aug 1961). 348th: 1 Jan 1953–30 Sep 1973 (not operational, 31 Jul–11 Dec 1956, c. 1 Oct 1967–c. 1 Apr 1968, c. 22 Sep 1968–c. 21 Mar 1969, c. 15 Mar–c. 22 Jun 1970, and c. 30 Apr 1972–30 Sep 1973).

Stations. Fairchild AFB, Wash, 1 Jan 1953; Westover AFB, Mass, 4 Sep 1956–31 Mar 1974.

Commanders. Col Salvatore E. Manzo, 1 Jan 1953; Col Edward D. Edwards, 2 Jul 1954; Col Bryson R. Bailey, 16 Apr 1955; Col John W. Gaff, Jr., 15 May 1956; Col Bryson R. Bailey, (by 10) Jul 1956; Col Selmon W. Wells, 4 Sep 1956; Col Gene F. Oholendt, 7 Oct 1956; Col Selmon W. Wells, 10 Nov 1956; Col Olbert F. Lassiter, 5 Jun 1958; Col Gordon F. Goyt, 3 Aug 1959; Col Olbert F. Lassiter, c. 9 Sep 1959; Col Delmore P. Wood, 19 Sep 1960; Col Gordon F. Goyt, 20 Sep 1960; Col Delmore P. Wood, c. 1 Nov 1960; Col Gordon F. Goyt, 8 Feb 1962; Col Edward M. Nichols, Jr., 1 Mar 1962; Col Charles V. Neil, 24 Feb 1964; Col Robert E. Brofft, 1 May 1967; Col Roy J. Sousley, Jr., c. 1 Oct 1967; Col Robert E. Brofft, c. 2 Apr 1968; Col Maxwell V. Judas, c. 22 Sep 1968; Col Robert E. Brofft, c. 21 Mar 1969; Col Harold E. Ottaway, 16 Jun 1969; Col William Wolfendon, c. 19 Mar 1970; Col Paul E. Clifford, 27 Apr 1970; Col Harold E. Ottaway, c. 23 Jun 1970; Col Alfred R. Grimm, 15 Jul 1970; Col LeRoy P. Hansen, 4 Jun 1971; Col Donald F. Ryan, 15 Jun 1972; Col Paul W. Maul, 13 Apr 1973; Col John W. Rosenbalm, 20 Aug 1973–31 Mar 1974.

Aircraft. RB-29, 1953; RB–36, 1953–1956; GRB–36, 1955–1956; B–52, 1956–1967, 1968, 1969–1970, 1970–1972; KC–135, 1966–1967, 1968, 1969–1970, 1970–1972, 1973; EC–135, 1966–1970.

Operations. Replaced the 111th Strategic Reconnaissance Wing in Jan 1953. Performed global reconnaissance, Jan 1953–Sep 1956. From Jan 1955 to Feb 1956, one tactical squadron additionally had a FICON (Fighter Interceptor Carrier, Reconnaissance) mission in which GRB–36s tested carrying of RF–84Fs under the fuselage of the bombers to extend the range of the interceptors. Gradually shifted to strategic bombardment training in late 1954. Gained a tanker squadron in Jan 1966 and added air refueling to its mission. The tanker squadron also operated EC–135s used in a PACCS (post attack command control system) role in support of Eighth Air Force until Mar 1970. All tactical and maintenance, and some support resources of the wing, loaned to SAC forces in the Pacific-Southeast Asia area for combat and combat support operations on several occasions beginning in 1967. During the periods c. 1 Oct 1967–c. 1 Apr 1968, c. 22 Sep 1968–c. 21 Mar 1969, c. 15 Mar–c. 22 Jun 1970, and c. 30 Apr 1972–31 Mar 1974, most of the wing's tactical forces and large portions of its support resources loaned to SAC units engaged in combat operations.

Service Streamers. None.

Campaign Streamers. None.

Decorations. Air Force Outstanding Unit Awards: 1 Oct 1967–1 Mar 1968; 2 Mar–1 Apr 1968; 1 Jul 1971–30 Jun 1972.

Emblem. Azure, in saltire, a bend rompu arraswise gules garnished argent and a lightning flash or striking from a cloud issuant from sinister chief of the third an atomic symbol in base of the like, all within a diminished bordure gray. *Motto:* CAVEANT AGGRESSORES—Let aggressors beware. (Approved on 7 Feb 1958.)

100th AIR REFUELING WING, HEAVY

Lineage. Established as 100th Bombardment Wing, Medium, on 23 Mar 1953. Activated on 1 Jan 1956. Redesignated: 100th Strategic Reconnaissance Wing on 25 Jun 1966; 100th Air Refueling Wing, Heavy, on 30 Sep 1976.

Assignments. Eighth Air Force, 1 Jan 1956; 817th Air Division, 1 Feb 1956 (attached to 7th Air Division, 29 Dec 1957–1 Apr 1958); 12th Strategic Aerospace Division, 25 Jun 1966; 14th Strategic Aerospace Division, 30 Jun 1971; 12th Strategic Missile (later, 12th Air) Division, 1 Aug 1972; 14th Air Division, 30 Sep 1976–.

Components. *Squadrons*. 9th: 30 Sep 1976–. 99th: 1 Nov 1972–30 Jun 1976 (not operational, 27 Mar–30 Jun 1976). 100th Air Refueling: 16 Aug 1956–25 Jun 1966 (not operational, 22 Dec 1965–25 Jun 1966). 349th: 1 Jan 1956– (not operational, 12 Feb–24 Jun 1966 and 11 Aug–30 Sep 1976). 350th: 1 Jan 1956–1 Jul 1976 (detached 4 Mar–c. 4 Apr 1958; not operational, 12 Feb–24 Jun 1966). 351st: 1 Jan 1956–25 Jun 1966 (not operational, 12 Feb–25 Jun 1966). 418th: 1 Mar 1959–1 Jan 1962 (not operational, c. 31 Oct 1961–1 Jan 1962). 509th Air Refueling: attached 8 Apr–8 Jul 1958.

Stations. Portsmouth (later, Pease) AFB, NH, 1 Jan 1956; Davis-Monthan AFB, Ariz, 25 Jun 1966; Beale AFB, Calif, 30 Sep 1976–.

Commanders. Col James W. Chapman, Jr., 1 Jan 1956; Brig Gen Walter E. Arnold, 25 Apr 1956; Col Ariel W. Nielsen, 4 Aug 1956; Col Gordon F. Goyt, 1 Sep 1957; Col Charles L. Wimberly, 23 Oct 1957; Col Winton R. Close, 15 Nov 1957; Col Charles L. Wimberly, 1 Apr 1958; Col Winton R. Close, 26 May 1958; Col Roland W. Bergamyer, 29 Jun 1959; Col Delmore P. Wood, 23 Jul 1959; Col Richard D. Reinbold, 16 Sep 1960; Col Wallace Wall, Jr., 2 Jul 1962; Col Raymond E. Buckwalter, 8 Jul 1965; Col James S. Howard, 21 Sep 1965; unkn, c. 1 Apr–24 Jun 1966; Col William D. Kyle, Jr., 25 Jun 1966; Col Marion C. Mixon, 15 Aug 1966; Col Raymond L. Haupt, 31 Jul 1970; Col Donald S. White, 29 Jun 1972; Col Charles B. Stratton, 7 May 1974; Col Lyman M. Kidder, 11 Jul 1976; Col John J. Tobin, 30 Sep 1976–.

Aircraft. B–47, 1956–1966; KC–97, 1956–1966; U–2, 1966–1976; WU–2, 1966–c. 1969; DC–130, 1966–1976; CH–3, 1966–1976; Q–147 (later, AQM–34) (drone), c. 1966–1976; KC–135, 1976–.

Operations. Performed global strategic bombardment training, Apr 1956–Feb 1966, and global air refueling, Aug 1956–Dec 1965. Deployed at Brize Norton RAF Station, England, Dec 1957–Apr 1958. Not operational, 1 Apr–24 Jun 1966. Moved without personnel or equipment to Davis-Monthan AFB, Ariz, in Jun 1966 and absorbed resources of the 4080th Strategic Wing. Performed global strategic reconnaissance with U–2 and drone aircraft, Jun 1956–1976, using one overseas-based squadron (99th SRS), and deployed operating locations as needed, 1972–1976. Transferred drone operations and associated DC–130 launchers and CH–3 recoverers to TAC in mid-1976, and transferred U–2 resources to 9th Strategic Reconnaissance Wing at Beale AFB, Calif, Jul–Sep 1976. Not operational, 11 Aug–29 Sep 1976, while phasing down at Davis-Monthan AFB. Moved without personnel or equipment to Beale AFB on 30 Sep 1976 and absorbed resources of the 17th Bombardment Wing, Heavy. Operated Beale AFB, and provided KC–135Q refueling support to 9th SRW, worldwide, Sep 1976–. Also provided air refueling as needed to other USAF strategic and tactical forces.

Service Streamers. None.

Campaign Streamers. None.

Decorations. Air Force Outstanding Unit Award with Combat "V" Device: 1 Jul 1972–30 Jun 1973. Air Force Outstanding Unit Award: 1 Jul 1968–30 Jun 1970.

Emblem. Gray, issuing from a base nebuly azure bearing in fess arched reversed six mullets argent, nine billets in chevron sable, surmounted by two lions respectant or langued gules, grasping in saltire a palm branch bend sinisterwise vert and a lightning flash of the sixth. *Motto:* PEACE THROUGH STRENGTH. (Approved on 22 Nov 1957.)

301st AIR REFUELING WING

Lineage. Established as 301st Bombardment Wing, Very Heavy, on 15 Oct 1947. Organized on 5 Nov 1947. Discontinued on 1 Aug 1948. Redesignated 301st Bombardment Wing, Medium, and activated on 1 Aug 1948. Redesignated 301st Air Refueling Wing on 15 Jun 1964.

Assignments. Fifteenth Air Force, 5 Nov 1947–1 Aug 1948. Fifteenth Air Force, 1 Aug 1948; Second Air Force, 1 Apr 1950; 4th Air Division, 10 Feb 1951 (attached to 7th Air Division, 3 Dec 1952–c. 4 Mar 1953; 5th Air Division, c. 10 Feb–c. 17 Apr 1954); 801st Air Division, 15 Apr 1958; 817th Air Division, 15 Mar 1965; 57th Air Division, 15 Nov 1965; 40th Air Division, 2 Jul 1966; 42d Air Division, 31 Mar 1970; 40th Air Division, 1 Jul 1973; 42d Air Division, 1 Jul 1975–.

Components. *Wings.* 22d Bombardment: attached 1 Aug 1948–9 May 1949 (not operational). 97th Bombardment: attached 17 Mar–16 May 1948. *Groups.* 22d Bombardment: attached 18 May–1 Aug 1948; attached 1 Aug–15 Nov 1948; attached Feb–9 May 1949. 301st: 5 Nov 1947–1 Aug 1948 (detached Jul 1948); 1 Aug 1948–16 Jun 1952 (detached 1 Aug 1948–Jan 1949, 15 May–30 Nov 1950; not operational, 10 Feb 1951–16 Jun 1952). *Squadrons.* 32d: attached 10 Feb 1951–15 Jun 1952, assigned 16 Jun 1952–8 Jun 1964; assigned 15 Mar 1965– (not operational, c. 9 Jun–8 Oct 1972). 91st: attached 4 May–14 Jun 1964, assigned 15 Jun 1964–1 Jul 1971. 301st: attached 10 Feb 1951–15 Jun 1952, assigned 16 Jun 1952–15 Apr 1958 (detached 20–26 Jun 1955, 10 Jul–18 Sep 1955, 27 Apr–27 Jun 1956, 15 Nov–6 Dec 1956, 27 Dec 1956–28 Feb 1957); assigned 30 Sep 1973–31 Dec 1975. 321st: 15 Apr 1958–15 Mar 1965 (detached 11 Apr–13 Jul 1960, 3

Oct 1961–Jan 1962). 352d: attached 10 Feb–20 Sep 1951; attached 20 Dec 1951–15 Jun 1952, assigned 16 Jun 1952–8 Jun 1964. 353d: attached 10 Feb 1951–15 Jun 1952, assigned 16 Jun 1952–8 Jun 1964. 376th: attached 1 Dec 1957–15 Apr 1958. 419th: 1 Dec 1958–1 Jan 1962. 4363d Post Attack Command and Control: attached 15–25 Mar 1965.

Stations. Smoky Hill Afld (later, AFB), Kans, 5 Nov 1947–1 Aug 1948. Smoky Hill AFB, Kans, 1 Aug 1948; Barksdale AFB, La, 7 Nov 1949; Lockbourne (later, Rickenbacker) AFB, Ohio, 15 Apr 1958–.

Commanders. Col Leslie G. Mulzer, 5 Nov 1947–1 Aug 1948. Col Leslie G. Mulzer, 1 Aug 1948; Col Joe W. Kelly, 3 Jan 1949; Col Thomas W. Steed, 1 Apr 1950; Col Randolph L. Wood, 15 May 1950; Col Horace M. Wade, 24 May 1950; Col Thomas W. Steed, 19 Jun 1950; Col Randolph L. Wood, 19 Jul 1950; Col Henry K. Mooney, 21 Jul 1950; Col Horace M. Wade, 12 Aug 1950; Col Vernon C. Smith, 24 Aug 1950; Col Thomas W. Steed, 8 Dec 1950; Col Horace M. Wade, 10 Feb 1951; Col George Y. Jumper, 11 Apr 1953; Col Horace M. Wade, 2 Jul 1953; Col John C. Jennison, Jr., 12 Jun 1954; Col Everett W. Holmstrom, 11 Jun 1955; Col Kenneth S. Steele, 13 Apr 1957; Col Osce V. Jones, 6 Mar 1958; Col William H. Reddell, 15 Apr 1958; Col Robert G. David, 16 Mar 1960; Col William H. Reddell, 14 Apr 1960; Col Robert G. David, 3 May 1960; Col Raymond F. Rudell, 23 Feb 1962; Col John W. Farrar, 15 Aug 1965; Col James O. Britt, 6 Jul 1966; Col George N. Payne, 18 Aug 1967; Col Raymond J. Bryan, 10 Apr 1968; Col Richard A. Bosworth, 16 Jul 1969; Col Irwin R. Stuhr, 5 Mar 1970; Col William L. Nicholson III, 21 Apr 1972; Col Jean M. Crane, 10 Jun 1972; Col Herman St. John, 15 Jul 1972; Col William E. Long, 8 Oct 1972; Col William L. Nicholson III, 8 Dec 1972; Col William E. Long, 19 Dec 1972; Col Roger K. Peterson, 5 Jan 1973; Col William L. Nicholson III, 18 Jan 1973; Col David A. Woods, Jr., 7 Apr 1973; Col Thomas W. Sherman, Jr., 10 May 1973; Col Edward F. Gehrke, 26 Nov 1973; Col David A. Woods, Jr., 24 Jul 1974; Col Caleb G. Pendley, 31 May 1975; Col Richard J. Smith, 21 Jun 1975; Col Caleb G. Pendley, 27 Jun 1975; Col Richard J. Kiefer, 3 Jul 1975; Col Regis F. A. Urschler, 11 Jul 1977–.

Aircraft. B–29, 1947–1948. B–29, 1948–1953; KB–29, 1949–1950, 1950–1953; B–47, 1953–1961, 1963–1964; KC–97, 1953–1960, 1960–1961, 1962–1963; RB–47, 1958; E–47, 1961–1964, 1965; EC–135, 1964–1966; KC–135, 1963–1972, 1972–.

Operations. Conducted strategic bombardment training, 1947–1948, and aerial gunnery training for other SAC organizations, Nov 1947–Jan 1948. Strategic bombardment training, 1948–1964, and aerial refueling 1949–. Deployed in England, Dec 1952–Mar 1953, and in French Morocco, Feb–Apr 1954. Added electronic countermeasures (ECM) activities to its other missions in Jul 1958, and soon devoted most of its activity to ECM work. Became an air refueling wing in Apr 1964, discontinuing all previous missions. In addition, participated in the post attack command and control system from 3 Mar 1965 to 30 Jun 1966. From c. 9 Jun to 8 Oct 1972, most of the wing headquarters staff, all tactical aircraft and crews, and most of the maintenance personnel, plus support personnel in various categories, deployed in Southeast Asia, attached to other SAC organizations. A reduced wing headquarters remained in the United States to administer activities of the combat support group and hospital at Lockbourne AFB, Ohio. From 19 Dec 1972 to 18 Jan 1973, the wing repeated previous deployed condition on a smaller scale, with deployed resources forming a provisional air refueling squadron in the Philippines.

Service Streamers. None.

Campaign Streamers. None.

Decorations. Air Force Outstanding Unit Awards: 1 Jan 1961–31 Dec 1962; 1 Oct 1966–1 Apr 1967.

Emblem. Light blue, on a chief nebuly azure, four mullets or, on a base nebuly of the second a lightning flash of the third, a spray of laurel bend sinisterwise argent, superimposed overall and throughout by a flight symbol gules fimbriated of the fourth, all within a diminished bordure of the like. *Motto:* WHO FEARS? (Approved on 22 Jul 1959.)

301st TACTICAL FIGHTER WING

Lineage. Established as 301st Fighter Wing on 5 Oct 1944. Activated on 15 Oct 1944. Inactivated on 20 Jan 1949. Redesignated 301st Tactical Fighter Wing on 19 May 1972. Activated in the Reserve on 1 Jul 1972.

Assignments. First Air Force, 15 Oct 1944 (attached to I Fighter Command); Twentieth Air Force, 21 May 1945 (attached to Army Air Forces, Pacific Ocean Area, 21 May 1945; Seventh Air Force, 1 Jun–14 Aug 1945); Eighth Air Force, 15 Aug 1945; 1st Air Division, 7 Jun 1946; Thirteenth Air Force, 1 Dec 1948–20 Jan 1949. Central Air Force Reserve Region, 1 Jul 1972; Tenth Air Force (Reserve), 8 Oct 1976–.

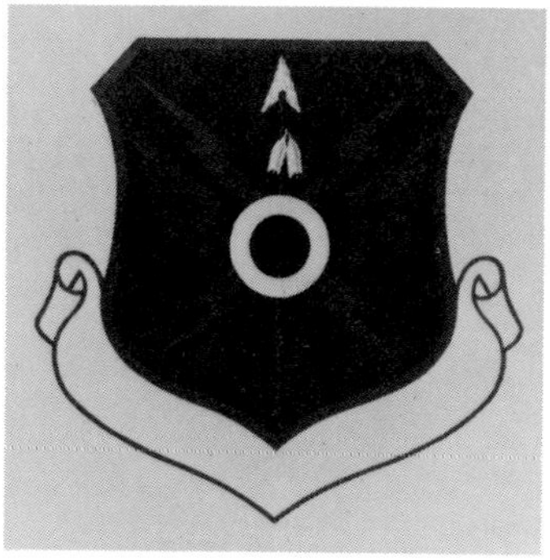

Components. *Groups*. 51st: 15 Oct 1946–18 Aug 1948. 318th: attached, 21 May–Nov 1945. 413th: 28 Oct 1944–15 Oct 1946. 414th: 28 Oct 1944–17 Apr 1945. 506th: 8 Jul 1972–25 Mar 1973. 507th: 26 Jun 1945–27 May 1946; 25 Jul 1972–25 Mar 1973; 17 Oct 1975–. 508th: 1 Jan–25 Mar 1973; 17 Oct 1975–. 945th Military Airlift: 1 Jul 1972–1 Jan 1973. *Squadrons*. 418th Night Fighter: 20 Mar 1946–20 Feb 1947. 457th: 25 Mar 1973–. 465th: 25 Mar 1973–17 Oct 1975. 466th: 25 Mar 1973–17 Oct 1975. 548th Night Fighter: attached 8 Jun–14 Jul 1945.

Stations. Seymour Johnson Field, NC, 15 Oct 1944; Mitchel Field, NY, 1 Nov 1944; Fort Lawton, Wash, 3–6 Jun 1945; Ie Shima, Ryukyus, 19 May 1945; Kadena, Okinawa, 29 Nov 1945; Yontan, Okinawa, c. 1 Apr 1946; Bisha Gawa, Okinawa, Nov 1946; Naha AAB (later, AB), Okinawa, 12 May 1947–20 Jan 1949. Carswell AFB, Texas, 1 Jul 1972–.

Commanders. Lt Col George H. Hollingsworth, 15 Oct 1944; Col Thayer S. Olds, 19 Oct 1944; Brig Gen Francis H. Griswold, 23 Aug 1945; Col Emmett F. Yost, 11 Sep 1945; Col Hanlon H. Van Auken, 1 Nov 1945; Col Mark E. Bradley, Jr., 4 Feb 1946; Col Loring F. Stetson, Jr., 30 Oct 1946; Brig Gen Robert C. Oliver, 1 Jan 1947; Col Loring F. Stetson, Jr., 24 Mar 1947; Col Joseph E. Barzynski, Jr., 21 Apr 1947; Brig Gen Hugo P. Rush, 1 May 1947–18 Aug 1948; none (not manned), 19 Aug 1948–20 Jan 1949. Unkn, 1 Jul–31 Dec 1972; Brig Gen John E. Taylor, Jr., 1 Jan 1973–.

Aircraft. P (later, F)–47, 1944–1948; P (later, F)–61, 1945–1948; P (later, F)–80, 1947–1948. F–105, 1972–.

Operations. Trained for B–29 escort operations, 1944–1945. Air echelon moved to Ie Shima, Ryukyus, in May, and commenced combat operations in early Jun 1945; ground echelon arrived on 31 Jul 1945. Operations included escort of B–29 and B–24 bombers, plus dive bombing and strafing attacks on Japanese shipping and lines of communication. Provided air defense of the Ryukyus in the post-war period. Not operational after 18 Aug 1948. Inactivated on 20 Jan 1949. Activated in the Reserve on 1 Jul 1972 replacing a military airlift group. On 8 Jul 1972 began converting from a MAC-gained C–124 unit to a TAC-gained F–105 organization. Trained Reservists for worldwide deployment, maintaining capability for deploying aircraft and personnel required for sustained combat operations, preparing as required to destroy enemy forces and facilities through conventional weapons delivery in support of counter-air, interdiction and close air support needs of the Tactical Air Command. Deployed 12–27 Aug 1977 at Norvenich AB, West Germany.

Service Streamers. None.

Campaign Streamers. Ryukyus.

Decorations. None.

Emblem. Azure two lightning bolts in saltire or behind in pale an Indian spear, head argent, shaft of the second and feathered proper, overall an annulet argent winged of the second and encircling a pomme. (Approved on 19 Dec 1978.)

302d TACTICAL AIRLIFT WING

Lineage. Established as 302d Troop Carrier Wing, Medium, on 16 May 1949. Activated in the Reserve on 27 Jun 1949. Redesignated 302d Troop Carrier Wing, Heavy, on 28 Jan 1950. Ordered to active service on 1 Jun 1951. Inactivated on 8 Jun 1951. Redesignated 302d Troop Carrier Wing, Medium, on 26 May 1952. Activated in the Reserve on 14 Jun 1952. Ordered to active service on 28 Oct 1962. Relieved from active duty on 28 Nov 1962. Redesignated: 302d Tactical Airlift Wing on 1 Jul 1967; 302d Special Operations Wing on 1 Jul 1970; 302d Tactical Airlift Wing on 2 Aug 1971.

Assignments. Fourth Air Force, 27 Jun 1949 (attached to 62d Troop Carrier Wing, Medium [later, 62d Troop Carrier Wing, Heavy], 27 Jun 1949–5 May 1950; 325th Fighter-All Weather Wing, 6 May 1950–); Western Air Defense Force, 1 Aug 1950–8 Jun 1951 (remained attached to 325th Fighter-All Weather [later, 325th Fighter-Interceptor] Wing to 8 Jun 1951). First Air Force, 14 Jun 1952; Fourteenth Air Force, 25 Mar 1958; Second Air Force Reserve Region, 15 Aug 1960; Ninth Air Force, 28 Oct 1962; Second Air Force Reserve Region, 28 Nov 1962; First Air Force Reserve Region, 24 Jan 1966; Eastern Air Force Reserve Region, 31 Dec 1969; Fourteenth Air Force (Reserve), 8 Oct 1976–.

Components. *Groups*. 302d: 27 Jun 1949–8 Jun 1951; 14 Jun 1952–14 Apr 1959. 901st: 1 Jul 1972–1 Apr 1974. 906th: 11 Feb 1963–1 Sep 1975. 907th: 11 Feb 1963–1 Sep 1975. 908th: 11 Feb–18 Mar 1963; attached 1–24 Oct 1971, assigned 25 Oct 1971–1 Jul 1972. 910th: 1 Jul 1966–15 Feb 1970. 911th: 25 Feb 1972–. 912th: 8 Jan 1965–1 Jul 1966. 913th: 8 Jan 1965–1 Jul 1966; attached 30 Jun–16 Sep 1970, assigned 17 Sep 1970–21 Apr 1971 (detached 1–21 Apr 1971). 914th: 1 Jul 1966–1 Sep 1969 (detached 31 Jul–1 Sep 1969). 930th: 31 Dec 1969–1 Jun 1970. *Squadrons*. 1st Combat Crew (later, 1st Tactical Airlift) Training: 1 Jul 1968–25 Mar 1973. Combat Crew Training Squadron Provisional, 302d: attached 1 Apr–1 Aug 1968 (not operational, 1 Jul–1 Aug 1968). 355th: 14 Apr 1959–11 Feb 1963; 1 Sep 1975–. 356th: 14 Apr 1959–11 Feb 1963; 1 Sep 1975–. 357th: 8 May 1961–11 Feb 1963.

Stations. McChord AFB, Wash, 27 Jun 1949–8 Jun 1951. Clinton County AFB, Ohio, 14 Jun 1952; Lockbourne (later, Rickenbacker) AFB, Ohio, 2 Aug 1971–.

Commanders. Col Gibbons, 27 Jun 1949–unkn. Brig Gen Donald J. Campbell, 14 Jun 1952; Brig Gen Ben J. Mangina, 15 Jun 1970; Col Clarence E. Horton, c. Nov 1973; Brig Gen Justin L. Townsley, 12 Dec 1973; Lt Col Billy R. Henderson, 10 Sep 1976; Brig Gen Donald M. Jenkins, 27 Sep 1976–.

Aircraft. C–82, 1949; C–54, 1949–1950. C–46, 1952–1957; C–119, 1956–1973; U–3, 1970, 1971–1972; C–130, 1970–1971; A–37, 1970; C–123, 1971–; UC–123, 1973–.

Operations. Reserve corollary of 62d Troop Carrier Wing, Jun 1949–May 1950, and of 325th Fighter-All Weather (later, 325th Fighter-Interceptor) Wing, May 1950–Jun 1951. After being ordered to active service, personnel absorbed by the 325th Wing and inactivated. Trained as a Reserve troop carrier wing from Jun 1952. Began flying airlift operations in the United States and overseas in mid-1950s. Converted to Air Reserve Technician (ART) program in Oct 1958 and became self-sufficient in Mar 1959. On active duty during Cuban missile crisis of 1962. From Apr 1968 to Mar 1973, provided C–119 gunship training for pilots, navigators, flight engineers, and mechanics of USAF active units and similar personnel from Jordan, Morocco, Ethiopia, and South Vietnam. By the mid-1960s, wing aircraft and crews performed worldwide airlift missions and participated in numerous tactical exercises. In Apr 1973, the wing assumed a rotational airlift task in support of USAF Southern Command, continuing this mission through Jan 1976. Also in Apr 1973, the wing assumed from an active squadron a UC-123 aerial spraying mission, which frequently took wing crews to Central America, the Caribbean, the Azores, North Africa, islands of the Pacific and to many U.S. points for insect-spraying missions.

Service Streamers. None.

Campaign Streamers. None.

Decorations. Air Force Outstanding Unit Award: 1 Jan–31 Dec 1970. Republic of Vietnam Gallantry Cross with Palm: 14 Feb 1968–28 Jan 1973.

Emblem. Azure, a thunderbolt in pale irradiated or, inflamed proper, winged, gules. *Motto:* JUSTEM ET TENACEM—Just and resolute. (Approved for 302d Group on 27 Feb 1943 and for 302d Wing on 23 Apr 1954.)

303d BOMBARDMENT WING, MEDIUM

Lineage. Established as 303d Bombardment Wing, Medium, on 27 Aug 1951. Activated on 4 Sep 1951. Discontinued, and inactivated, on 15 Jun 1964.

Assignments. 36th Air Division, 4 Sep 1951 (attached to 5th Air Division, 5 Oct–6 Nov 1952; 7th Air Division, 4 Mar–5 Jun 1954; 3d Air Division, 4 Jul–4 Oct 1956 and 5 Apr–4 Jul 1958); 12th Air (later, 12th Strategic Aerospace) Division, 15 Mar 1960–15 Jun 1964.

Components. *Group.* 303d: 4 Sep 1951–16 Jun 1952 (not operational). *Squadrons.* 9th Air Refueling: attached 15 Jan–5 Oct 1952 and 15 Nov 1952–25 Apr 1953. 43d Air Refueling: 15 Mar–15 Nov 1960. 303d Air Refueling: attached 4 Sep 1951–8 Apr 1952 (not operational); assigned 18 Feb 1953–1 Feb 1956 (detached 19 Apr–2 Jun 1955). 358th: attached 4 Sep 1951–15 Jun 1952, assigned 16 Jun 1952–15 Jun 1964. 359th: attached 4 Sep 1951–15 Jun 1952, assigned 16 Jun 1952–15 Jun 1964. 360th: attached 4 Sep 1951–15 Jun 1952, assigned 16 Jun 1952–15 Jun 1964. 427th: 1 Dec 1958–1 Jan 1962 (not operational, 1 Sep 1961–1 Jan 1962). *Detachment.* Det, 96th Air Refueling Squadron, Medium: attached c. 4 Jul–c. 4 Oct 1956.

Stations. Davis-Monthan AFB, Ariz, 4 Sep 1951–15 Jun 1964.

Commanders. Col Frederick J. Knorre, Jr., 4 Sep 1951; Col David Wade, 9 Oct 1951; Col John K. Hester, 14 Jan 1952; Col Manford J. Wetzel, 26 Jan 1953; Maj Henry G. Bussing, 2 Feb 1953; Col Manford J. Wetzel, 6 Feb 1953; Col John K. Hester, 30 Mar 1953; Col William J. Wrigglesworth, 12 Jun 1954; Col Donald W. Saunders, 19 Nov 1954; Col Lloyd H. Dalton, Jr., 25 Aug 1956; Col William W. Jones, 8 Dec 1956; Col Landon E. McConnell, 6 Oct

1958; Col William C. Bacon, 1 Nov 1958; Col Max W. Rogers, 1 Jan 1962–15 Jun 1964.

Aircraft. B–29, 1951–1953; KB–29, 1952, 1952–1953; B–47, 1953–1964; KC–97, 1953–1956, 1956, 1960.

Operations. Trained for strategic bombardment and air refueling operations to meet SAC's global commitments. Deployed at Sidi Slimane AB, French Morocco, 5 Oct–6 Nov 1952; Greenham Common RAF Station, England, 4 Mar–28 Apr 1954; Fairford RAF Station, England, 28 Apr–5 Jun 1954; and Andersen AFB, Guam, 4 Jul–4 Oct 1956 and 5 Apr–5 Jul 1958.

Service Streamers. None.

Campaign Streamers. None.

Decorations. Air Force Outstanding Unit Award: 1 Jan 1961–31 Mar 1962.

Emblem. Azure, a diminutive pile between four flashes of lightning, two issuant palewise from chief and one from dexter and sinister chief sides chevronwise inverted, issuant from base a burst of five rays, all or. *Motto:* MIGHT IN FLIGHT. (Approved for 303d Group on 9 Jan 1943 and for 303d Wing on 11 Dec 1951.)

305th AIR REFUELING WING

Lineage. Established as 305th Bombardment Wing, Medium, on 20 Dec 1950. Activated on 2 Jan 1951. Redesignated 305th Air Refueling Wing on 1 Jan 1970.

Assignments. Second Air Force, 2 Jan 1951; 6th Air Division, 10 Feb 1951 (attached to 7th Air Division, 4 Sep–5 Dec 1953; 5th Air Division, 3 Nov 1955–8 Jan 1956 and 7 Jan–8 Mar 1957); Second Air Force, 1 Jun 1959; 17th Air Division, 15 Jul 1959; 19th Air Division, 1 Jan 1961; 825th Strategic Aerospace Division, 1 Sep 1964; 42d Air Division, 1 Jan 1970; 40th Air Division, 1 Jul 1973–.

Components. *Group.* 305th: 2 Jan 1951–16 Jun 1952 (not operational, 10 Feb 1951–16 Jun 1952). *Squadrons.* 3d Airborne Command and Control: 1 Apr 1970–31 Dec 1975. 68th: 1 Jun 1959–25 Mar 1965. 70th: 1 Jan 1970–. 305th: attached 2 Jul 1951–15 Jun 1952, assigned 16 Jun 1952–1 May 1959 (detached 4 Jan–c. 16 Apr 1955); assigned 25 Mar 1965–. 364th: attached 10 Feb 1951–15 Jun 1952, assigned 16 Jun 1952–1 Jan 1970. 365th: attached 10 Feb 1951–15 Jun 1952, assigned 16 Jun 1952–1 Jan 1970. 366th: attached 10 Feb 1951–15 Jun 1952, assigned 16 Jun 1952–1 Jan 1970. 422d: 1 Jan–1 Oct 1959 (not operational, 1 Jun–1 Oct 1959); 8 Mar 1960–15 Feb 1961 (not operational).

Stations. MacDill AFB, Fla, 2 Jan 1951; Bunker Hill (later, Grissom) AFB, Ind, 1 Jun 1959–.

Commanders. Col Elliott Vandevanter, Jr., 2 Jan 1951; Col James F. Wilson, 17 Jul 1954; Col Frank A. Kurtz, 14 Feb 1956; Col Julian M. Bleyer, 27 Jun 1956; Col Frank L. O'Brien, Jr., 24 Feb 1958; Brig Gen Paul K. Carlton, 18 Nov

1963; Brig Gen Gerald W. Johnson, 1 Jul 1965; Col Howard J. Fry, 1 Jul 1966; Col Frank L. Voightmann, 24 Jul 1967; Col Hugh B. Robertson, Jr., 15 Jul 1968; Col William T. Gentry, 9 Feb 1970; Col George L. Miller, 5 Jun 1972; Col Robert L. Nicholl, 10 May 1973; Col Walter B. Ratliff, 20 Jun 1974; Col Jerome R. Barnes, Jr., 11 Feb 1975; Col Lyman E. Buzard, 14 May 1976; Col Donald K. Winston, 5 Aug 1977–.

Aircraft. B–29, 1951–1953; KC–97, 1951–1959; B–47, 1952–1961; RB–47, 1958; KC–135, 1959–; B/TB–58, 1961–1970; EC–135, 1966–.

Operations. Established at MacDill AFB, Fla, during the Korean war. Conducted strategic bombardment training, Feb 1951–Feb 1953. Added a refueling mission in Jul 1951. Converted to B–47s in late 1952. Deployed overseas three times, once to England (Sep–Dec 1953) and twice to North Africa (Nov 1955–Jan 1956 and Jan–Mar 1957), in keeping with its mission of global bombardment and air refueling operations. Two wing B–47s set speed records on 28 Jul 1953 when one flew from Goose Bay, Labrador, to Fairford RAF Station, England, in 4:14 hours and the other flew from Limestone AFB, Maine, to Fairford RAF Station in 4:45 hours. Moved to Ind in Jun 1959 and assumed responsibility for operating Bunker Hill (later, Grissom) AFB, Ind. Converted from KC–97 to KC–135 tankers in 1959 and from B–47 to B/TB–58 bombers in 1961, continuing its global bombardment and refueling mission. A wing B–58 set a new speed record on 16 Oct 1963 by flying from Tokyo, Japan, to London, England (via Alaska and Greenland), in 8:35 hours at an average speed of 938 mph. The wing operated a B–58 combat crew training school, Aug 1965–Dec 1969, and gained an EC–135 post attack command control system (PACCS) mission in mid-1966. The 305th lost all of its bombardment units in Jan 1970 and thereafter concentrated on air refueling and PACCS support.

Service Streamers. None.

Campaign Streamers. None.

Decorations. Air Force Outstanding Unit Awards: 1 Jan 1954–1 Mar 1957; 1 Jul 1972–30 Jun 1973; 1 Jul 1973–30 Jun 1974; 1 Jul 1975–30 Jun 1977.

Emblem. Celeste, issuing from base a demi-sphere argent, gridlined and rimmed azure, below an arched cloud formation of the second, overall issuing from chief in pale a refueling boom arraswise gray, all within a diminished bordure or. *Motto:* CAN DO. (Approved on 13 Apr 1978.)

306th STRATEGIC WING

Lineage. Established as 306th Bombardment Wing, Medium, on 11 Aug 1948. Activated on 1 Sep 1950. Redesignated 306th Bombardment Wing, Heavy, on 1 Apr 1963. Inactivated on 1 Jul 1974. Redesignated 306th Strategic

Wing on 14 Aug 1976. Activated on 15 Aug 1976.

Assignments. Second Air Force, 1 Sep 1950; 6th Air Division, 10 Feb 1951 (attached to 7th Air Division, 11 Jun–7 Sep 1953; 5th Air Division, 5 Jan–21 Feb 1955 and 23 Oct 1956–9 Jan 1957; Sidi Slimane Task Force, 9–15 Oct 1957); 823d Air Division, 6 Feb 1961; 42d Air Division, 30 Jun 1971–1 Jul 1974. Strategic Air Command, 15 Aug 1976–.

Components. *Group.* 306th: 1 Sep 1950–16 Jun 1952 (not operational, 10 Feb 1951–16 Jun 1952). *Squadrons.* 305th Air Refueling: attached 5 Jan 1954–21 Feb 1955; attached c. 20 Dec 1956–c. 9 Jan 1957; assigned 1 May 1959–15 Jan 1960. 306th Air Refueling: attached 10 Feb 1951–15 Jun 1952, assigned 16 Jun 1952–1 Jul 1962 (detached 8 Nov–22 Dec 1954, 5 Jan–21 Feb 1955, 20 Dec 1956–9 Jan 1957, c. 9–15 Oct 1957, 1 Jul–5 Oct 1958, 5 Apr–12 Jul 1961; not operational, 13 Jun–1 Jul 1962); assigned 1 Apr 1963–30 Sep 1973 (not operational, 1–30 Sep 1973). 367th: attached 10 Feb 1951–15 Jun 1952, assigned 16 Jun 1952–1 Jul 1974 (not operational, 3 Jan–1 Apr 1963 and c. 1 Nov 1973–1 Jul 1974). 368th: attached 10 Feb 1951–15 Jun 1952, assigned 16 Jun 1952–1 Apr 1963. 369th: attached 10 Feb 1951–15 Jun 1952, assigned 16 Jun 1952–1 Apr 1963 (not operational, 3 Jan–1 Apr 1963). 423d: 1 Jan 1959–1 Jan 1962 (not operational, 15 Oct 1961–1 Jan 1962). 919th Air Refueling: 25 Mar 1967–30 Jun 1971 (not operational, 15–30 Jun 1971). *Detachments.* Det 1, HQ 306th SW: 1 Oct 1976–. Det 2, HQ 306th SW: 15 Aug 1976– (not operational, 15 Aug–30 Sep 1976). Det 3, HQ 306th SW: 1 Oct 1976–.

Stations. MacDill AFB, Fla, 1 Sep 1950; McCoy AFB, Fla, 1 Apr 1963–1 Jul 1974. Ramstein AB, West Germany, 15 Aug 1976–.

Commanders. Col Thayer S. Olds, 1 Sep 1950; Col Michael N. W. McCoy, 10 Feb 1951; Brig Gen Hewitt T. Wheless, 10 Nov 1953; Col Richard N. Ellis, 12 Mar 1954; Col Kenneth O. Sanborn, 12 Apr 1954; Col Paul S. Emrick, 31 Jul 1954; Col Robert L. Snider, 17 Feb 1956; Col Robert J. Mason, 20 May 1956; Col Robert J. Nolan, 1 Mar 1958; Col Calvin W. Fite, Jr., 6 Apr 1959; Col Stanley I. Hand, 16 Jul 1960; Col William G. Walker, Jr., 1 Apr 1963; Col Sherman W. Wilkins, 8 Jun 1963; Col Stanley I. Hand, 19 Jul 1963; Col Earl L. Johnson, 27 Nov 1954–Sep 1966; unkn, Sep 1966–c. Mar 1967; Col Earl L. Johnson, c. Mar 1967; Col Gail D. Roberts, 1 Jul 1967; Col Salvador E. Felices, 1 Jun 1968; Col James S. Howard, (by 11 Oct) 1968; Col Jon E. White, c. Dec 1968; Col Salvador E. Felices, 4 Apr 1969; Col Howard P. McClain, 12 Apr 1969; Col Walter A. Carter, Jr., (by 10) Oct 1969; Col Howard P. McClain, c. Apr 1970; Col William A. Temple, 4 May 1970; Col Glen L. Pugmire, 16 Aug 1971; Col Robert N. Saye, Jr., 9 Feb 1972; Col Grady L. Friday, Jr., 17 Mar 1972; Col Glen L. Pugmire, 10 May 1972; Col Grady L. Friday, Jr., 19 Jun 1972; Col John J. Murphy, 10 Jul 1972; Col Grady L. Friday, Jr., 9 May 1973; Col Roy L. Harris, Jr., 29 Sep 1973; Col George A. Patterson, 31 Jan–1 Jul 1974. None (not manned), 15–22 Aug 1976; Col Doyle F. Reynolds, 23 Aug 1976–.

Aircraft. B–29, 1950–1951; B–50, 1951; B–47, 1951–1963; KC–97, 1951–1962; B–52, 1963–1973; KC–135, 1963–1973. KC–135 (attached), 1976–; RC–135 (attached), 1976–.

Operations. Provided B–29 transition training for SAC aircrews, Sep 1950–Feb 1951. Converted to B–47 bombers and KC–97 tankers during 1951. Developed combat procedures and techniques for B–47 jet bombers, 1952. From early 1953 until early 1963, maintained proficiency by constant training in strategic bombardment and aerial refueling operations. Deployed at Fairford RAF Station, England, Jun–Sep 1953, at Ben Guerir AB, French Morocco (later, Morocco), Jan–Feb 1955, Oct 1956–Jan 1957, and Oct 1957, and at Hunter AFB, Ga, Oct–Dec 1962. Phased down for inactivation in early 1963, but moved to a new base and reequipped with B–52s and KC–135s. From Apr 1963 to the autumn of 1973, maintained combat proficiency by constant training in strategic bombardment and air refueling operations. On several occasions, furnished aircraft and personnel to SAC combat forces in the Pacific and Southeast Asia to the point of depleting all home base resources. By the autumn of 1973, lost all tactical forces and began phasing down, at the same time closing McCoy AFB, Fla. Inactivated in Jul 1974. Activated in Aug 1976 to replace 98th Strategic Wing. Not operational, 15 Aug–30 Sep 1976, while becoming organized. Functioned as the focal point for all SAC operations in Europe, and as liaison between SAC and USAFE (and European Command), 1 Oct 1976–. Employed KC/RC–135 aircraft and crews on loan from U.S.-based SAC wings for air refueling and reconnaissance operations.

Service Streamers. None.

Campaign Streamers. None.

Decorations. Air Force Outstanding Unit Awards: 22 Jan 1953–8 Dec 1956; 1 Jul 1966–30 Jun 1967; 1 Oct 1968–1 Mar 1969.

Emblem. Light blue, issuant from sinister base an eagle ascending bendwise azure, head and neck argent, beak or, eyed of the second, grasping in its beak an olive branch of the like and emitting from its eye an electronic flash bend sinisterwise or, above the eagle's head a pattern of ten mullets of five points argent, issuing from sinister fess and surmounting the body of the eagle an air refueling ice shield arraswise gray garnished argent and azure, above a canton or fimbriated argent bearing the Indian symbol for rattlesnake's jaws gules and a chief dancette of the second between two triangular armor plates gray bolted argent, all within a diminished bordure gold. *Motto:* ABUNDANCE OF STRENGTH. (Approved on 10 Nov 1977.)

307th STRATEGIC WING

Lineage. Established as 307th Bombardment Wing, Very Heavy, on 28 Jul 1947. Organized on 15 Aug 1947. Discontinued on 12 Jul 1948. Redesignated 307th Bombardment Wing, Medium, and activated on 12 Jul 1948. Discontinued, and inactivated, on 25 Mar 1965. Redesignated 307th Strategic Wing on 21 Jan 1970. Activated on 1 Apr 1970. Inactivated on 30 Sep 1975.

Assignments. Strategic Air Command, 15 Aug 1947–12 Jul 1948. Strategic Air Command, 12 Jul 1948; Fifteenth Air Force, 16 Dec 1948; Second Air Force, 1 Apr 1950; 6th Air Division, 10 Feb 1951 (attached to Far East Air Forces Bomber Command, Provisional, 10 Feb–11 Aug 1951; Far East Air Forces Bomber Command, Provisional, ADVON, 12 Aug–11 Sep 1951; Far East Air Forces Bomber Command, Provisional, 12 Sep 1951–17 Jun 1954; Twentieth Air Force, 18 Jun 1954–); 818th Air (later, 818th Strategic Aerospace) Division, 11 Oct 1954–25 Mar 1965 (remained attached to Twentieth Air Force to 19 Nov 1954; attached to 7th Air Division, 7 Jul–5 Oct 1956). Eighth Air Force, 1 Apr 1970 (attached to Air Division Provisional, 17th, 1 Jun 1972–31 Dec 1974); 3d Air Division, 1 Jan–30 Sep 1975.

Components. *Wing*. 82d Fighter: attached 15 Aug 1947–12 Jul 1948; attached 12 Jul–15 Dec 1948. *Groups*. 306th: attached 1 Aug 1948–31 Aug 1950 (not operational, 1–12 Aug 1948). 307th: 15 Aug 1947–12 Jul 1948; 12 Jul 1948–16 Jun 1952 (detached 16 Jul–3 Nov 1948 and 8 Aug 1950–9 Feb 1951; not operational, 10 Feb 1951–16 Jun 1952.) *Squadrons*. 99th Strategic Reconnaissance: attached 1 Jan–30 Sep 1975. 307th Air Refueling: attached c. 1 Aug–15 Sep 1950 (not operational); assigned 16 Jun 1952–1 Jul 1953 (detached); assigned 8 Nov 1954–1 Jun 1960 (detached 8 Nov 1954–31 Jan 1955, 8 Apr–21 May 1955, 2 Jul–3 Oct 1957, c. 1 Oct 1958–9 Jan 1959, and c. 4 Jul–5 Oct 1969). Bombardment Squadron Provisional, 364th: attached 1 Jul 1972–30 Jun 1975 (not operational, 1 Jul 1972–c. 29 Jan 1973 and 9–30 Jun 1975). Bombardment Squadron Provisional, 365th: attached 1 Jul 1972–1 Jul 1974 (not operational, 1 Jul 1972–c. 29 Jan 1973). 370th: attached 10 Feb 1951–15 Jun 1952, assigned 16 Jun 1952–25 Mar 1965. 371st: attached 10 Feb 1951–15 Jun 1952, assigned 16 Jun 1952–25 Mar 1965. 372d: attached 10 Feb 1951–15 Jun 1952, assigned 16 Jun 1952–25 Mar 1965. 424th: 1 Sep 1958–1 Jan 1962. Air Refueling Squadron Provisional, 901st: attached 1 Jul 1974–30 Sep 1975. 4180th: 1 Oct 1970–31 Dec 1971 (not operational). 4181st: 1 Apr 1970–31 Mar 1972 (not operational). 4362d Support (later, 4362d Post Attack Command Control): attached 20 Jul 1962–24 Dec 1964 (not operational, 20–c. 31 Jul 1962).

Stations. MacDill Field (later, AFB), Fla, 15 Aug 1947–12 Jul 1948. MacDill AFB, Fla, 12 Jul 1948–14 Aug 1953; Kadena AB, Okinawa, 15 Aug 1953–19 Nov 1954; Lincoln AFB, Nebr, 20 Nov 1954–25 Mar 1965. U–Tapao AB, Thailand, 1 Apr 1970–30 Sep 1975.

Commanders. Col Bayard Johnson, 15 Aug 1947; Brig Gen Donald R. Hutchinson, c. 5 Sep 1947; Col Bayard Johnson, 28 Apr 1948; Brig Gen Donald R. Hutchinson, 17 May 1948–12 Jul 1948. Brig Gen Donald R. Hutchinson, 12 Jul 1948; Col Bayard Johnson, 16 Mar 1949; Brig Gen James E.

Briggs, 28 Mar 1949; Col Thayer S. Olds, c. 1 Aug 1950; Col John M. Reynolds, 23 Sep 1950; Col Thayer S. Olds, c. 8 Oct 1950; Col John A. Hilger, 10 Feb 1951; Col John M. Reynolds, 15 Mar 1951; Col William H. Hanson, 20 Aug 1951; Col John C. Jennison, Jr., 4 Feb 1952; Brig Gen Raymond L. Winn, 8 May 1952; Col Charles S. Overstreet, Jr., c. 1 Oct 1952; Col Austin J. Russell, 29 Dec 1952; Col James W. Wilson, 14 Sep 1953; Col Louis G. Thorup, 8 Jun 1954; Maj William T. Minor, 20 Nov 1954; Lt Col Douglas M. Conlan, 1 Dec 1954; Col Louis G. Thorup, 15 Dec 1954; Col Ernest C. Hardin, Jr., 11 Jan 1955; Col Ralph G. Vaughn, 23 Feb 1955; Col Ernest C. Hardin, Jr., 26 Feb 1955; Col Louis G. Thorup, 15 Mar 1955; Col Robert B. Nowell, 13 May 1957; Col Elkins Read, Jr., 18 May 1957; Col Walter W. Berg, 14 Oct 1960; Col William E. Bertram, 27 Nov 1961; Col William E. Riggs, 5 Apr 1963; Col Arthur W. Holderness, Jr., 18 Jan–c. 25 Mar 1965. Brig Gen Woodrow A. Abbott, 1 Apr 1970; Brig Gen John R. Hinton, Jr., 5 Jul 1970; Brig Gen Frank W. Elliott, Jr., 5 Jul 1971; Col Donald M. Davis, 1 Jun 1972; Col Bill V. Brown, 11 Feb 1973; Col Frank J. Apel, Jr., 21 Aug 1973; Col Ernest J. Stirman, 10 Apr 1974; Brig Gen George D. Miller, 1 Jan 1975; Col Ernest J. Stirman, 22 Jan 1975; Col Caryl W. Calhoun, 6 Mar 1975; Col George A. Dugard, 12 Aug–30 Sep 1975.

Aircraft. P (later, F)–51, 1947–1948; B–29, 1947–1948. F–51, 1948; B–29, 1948–1950, 1951–1954; B–50, 1950; B–47, 1955–1965; KC–97, 1955–1960; EB–47, 1962–1964. B–52, 1970–1975; KC–135, 1970–1972, 1974–1975; RC–135, 1975.

Operations. Replaced the 94th Combat Bombardment Wing, VHB (Provisional), and other organizations in Aug 1947. From Aug 1947 until 12 Jul 1948, and from 12 Jul to 15 Dec 1948, the 307th Wing controlled in addition to its own units the 82d Fighter Wing at Grenier Field, NH. From Sep 1947 to Jul 1948, and Jul 1948 to Aug 1950, trained other SAC combat units in antisubmarine warfare. From Feb 1949 through Aug 1950, operated a B–29 transition training school for SAC units, and provided combat crew standardization training for SAC units, Nov 1949–Aug 1950. The wing's 307th Bombardment Group deployed to Okinawa in Aug 1950 for combat operations under FEAF Bomber Command, Provisional. The attached 306th Bombardment Group transferred to its parent wing on 1 Sep 1950, and until 10 Feb 1951, the 307th Wing had no tactical mission. On that date, wing resources were used to man the 6th Air Division at MacDill, and the wing deployed without personnel to Kadena, where it absorbed resources of the 307th Bombardment Group and began flying combat missions. By the end of hostilities, the wing (including its tactical group) had flown 5,810 combat sorties during 573 combat missions. The wing remained in the Far East in combat ready status, and on 15 Aug 1953, Kadena AB, Okinawa, became its permanent base. Returned to the United States in Nov 1954, disposing of B–29s at Davis-Monthan AFB, Ariz, en route to a new base in Nebr. Gained B–47 and KC–97 aircraft in 1955, and, until Jan 1965 when the wing began phasing down for inactivation, conducted strategic bombardment training and air refueling operations to meet SAC's global commitments. Activated in Thailand in Apr 1970, replacing the 4258th Strategic Wing. Until inactivated in Sep 1975, the 307th was the only regular Air Force SAC wing in Southeast Asia. Using aircraft and crews loaned from other SAC wings, the 307th provided KC–135 aerial refueling of U.S. aircraft in Southeast Asia and conducted conventional bombardment operations as directed through the Military Assistance Command, Vietnam. Ended all combat operations on 14 Aug 1973. The final B–52 left the wing in Jun 1975, but the wing continued some KC–135 air refueling and RC–135 reconnaissance operations until inactivated in Sep 1975.

Service Streamers. None.

Campaign Streamers. First UN Counteroffensive; CCF Spring Offensive; UN Summer–Fall Offensive; Second Korean Winter; Korea Summer–Fall, 1952; Third Korean Winter; Korea Summer–Fall, 1953. Vietnam Winter–Spring, 1970; Sanctuary Counteroffensive; Southwest Monsoon; Commando Hunt V; Commando Hunt VI; Commando Hunt VII; Vietnam Ceasefire.

Decorations. Distinguished Unit Citation (Korea): 11–27 Jul 1953. Air Force Outstanding Unit Awards with Combat "V" Device: 1 Apr 1970–31 Mar 1971; 1 Apr 1971–31 Mar 1972; 1 Apr 1972–28 Jan 1973; 29 Jan–31 Dec 1973. Republic of Korea Presidential Unit Citation: 10 Feb 1951–27 Jul 1953. Republic of Vietnam Gallantry Crosses with Palm: [1 Apr 1970]–28 Jan 1973; 8 Feb–31 Mar 1971.

Emblem. Azure, a four-petalled dogwood bloom slipped or. (Approved for 307th Group on 21 Dec 1942 and for 307th Wing on 23 Dec 1952.)

308th STRATEGIC MISSILE WING (ICBM–TITAN)

Lineage. Established as 308th Bombardment Wing, Medium, on 4 Oct 1951. Activated on 10 Oct 1951. Discontinued, and inactivated, on 25 Jun 1961. Redesignated 308th Strategic Missile Wing (ICBM–Titan), and activated, on 29 Nov 1961. Organized on 1 Apr 1962.

Assignments. 38th Air Division, 10 Oct 1951 (attached to 21st Air Division, 10 Oct 1951–17 Apr 1952; 5th Air Division, 21 Aug–c. 26 Oct 1956); 820th Air Division, 15 Jul 1959–25 Jun 1961. Strategic Air Command, 29 Nov 1961; 825th Air (later, 825th Strategic Aerospace) Division, 1 Apr 1962; 42d Air Division, 1 Jan 1970; 17th Strategic Aerospace Division, 31 Mar 1970; 12th Strategic Missile (later, 12th Air) Division, 30 Jun 1971; 42d Air Division, 1 Apr 1973–.

Components. *Group.* 308th: 10 Oct 1951–16 Jun 1952 (not operational). *Squadrons.* 303d Air Refueling: attached 1 Feb 1956–15 Jul 1959. 308th Air Refueling: 8 Jul 1953–15 Jun 1959 (detached 1–21 Jun 1954, 5 Jan–4 Mar 1956, and 2 Apr–2 Jul 1958). 373d: attached 10 Oct 1951–15 Jun 1952 (not operational, 10 Oct–5 Nov 1951), assigned 16 Jun 1952–25 Jun 1961 (not operational, 15 Jul 1959–25 Jun 1961); assigned 1 Apr 1962–. 374th: attached 10 Oct 1951–15 Jun 1952 (not operational, 10 Oct–5 Nov 1951), assigned 16 Jun 1952–25 Jun 1961 (not operational, 15 Jul 1959–25 Jun 1961); assigned 1 Sep 1962–. 375th: attached 10 Oct 1951–15 Jun 1952 (not operational, 10 Oct–13 Nov 1951), assigned 16 Jun 1952–25 Jun 1961 (not operational, 15 Jul 1959–25 Jun 1961). 425th: 1 Oct 1958–25 Jun 1961 (not operational, 15 Jul 1959– 25 Jun 1961).

Stations. Forbes AFB, Kans, 10 Oct 1951; Hunter AFB, Ga, 17 Apr 1952; Plattsburgh AFB, NY, 15 Jul 1959–25 Jun 1961. Little Rock AFB, Ark, 1 Apr 1962–.

Commanders. None (not manned), 10 Oct–4 Nov 1951; Col George L. Newton, Jr., 5 Nov 1951; Col Charles B. Dougher, 5 Feb 1952; Col George L. Newton, Jr., 15 Mar 1952; Col Maurice A. Preston, 7 May 1952; Lt Col Perry P. Menzies, 20 Feb 1953; Col Maurice A. Preston, 28 Mar 1953; Col John F. Batjer, 5 Aug 1953; Col James H. Thompson, 15 Aug 1953; Col John F. Batjer, 24 Aug 1953; Col James H. Thompson, 27 Aug 1953; Col Ralph C. Jenkins, 29 Sep 1953; Col James H. Thompson, 1 Oct 1953; Brig Gen Maurice A. Preston, 23 Oct 1953; Col John F. Batjer, 12 Jan 1954; Lt Col John O. Vick, 21 Sep 1954; Col John F. Batjer, 12 Nov 1954; Col Paul W. Tibbetts, Jr., 9 Jun 1956; Col William L. Gray, 7 Jan 1958–14 Jul 1959; none (not manned), 15 Jul 1959–25 Jun 1961. None (not manned), 29 Nov 1961–31 Mar 1962; Col Charles P. Sullivan, 1 Apr 1962; Col Collier H. Davidson, 11 Jun 1962; Col Charles P. Sullivan, 1 Jul 1965; Col Edward A. Vivian, 28 Aug 1966; Col Don C. La Moine, 22 Aug 1969; Col William E. Bifford, 6 Jul 1971; Col Max M. Axelsen, 1 Sep 1972; Col Edward D. Bailey, 27 Apr 1973; Col William E. O'Neil, 15 Jul 1974; Col Joe P. Morgan, 17 Nov 1975–.

Aircraft and Missiles. B–29, 1951–1952, 1952–1953; B–47, 1953–1954, 1954–1959; KC–97, 1953–1959. Titan II, 1963–.

Operations. Strategic bombardment training, 1951–1959, and air refueling, 1953–1959, to meet SAC's global commitments. Deployed to bases in North Africa three times, twice in detachment form and once (Sidi Slimane AB, Morocco, 21 Aug–c. 26 Oct 1956) as a unit. From Nov 1956 to Mar 1957, tested SAC alert plan by maintaining one-third of its bomber and tanker force on continuous alert. Not operational, Jul 1959–Jun 1961. Organized in Apr 1962 as a Titan II strategic missile wing. Gained control over first missile complex in Aug 1962 and became fully operational with 18 sites in Dec 1963.

Service Streamers. None.

Campaign Streamers. None.

Decorations. Air Force Outstanding Unit Awards: 1 Nov 1956–1 Apr 1957; 1 Jul 1957–30 Jun 1968; 1 Jul 1972–30 Jun 1974; 1 Jul 1975–30 Jun 1977.

Emblem. Light blue, a pale gules fimbriated argent between in fess abased a mullet of 12 points of the last bearing a hurt voided of the third and a cloud formation of the last emitting three lightning flashes to base or, on a chief per chevron inverted of the fourth, fimbriated of the third, two bombs or between 18 mullets fesswise four, six, four, two and two of the third, overall in pale a futuramic missile of the last finned of the fifth emitting a vapor trail to base of the fourth, all within a diminished bordure of the fifth fimbriated of the fourth. *Motto:* NON SIBI SED ALIIS—Not for self, but for others. (Approved on 28 Feb 1963.)

310th STRATEGIC AEROSPACE WING

Lineage. Established as 310th Bombardment Wing, Medium, on 15 Mar 1952. Activated on 28 Mar 1952. Redesignated 310th Strategic Aerospace Wing on 1 Mar 1962. Discontinued, and inactivated, on 25 Jun 1965.

Assignments. Fifteenth Air Force, 28 Mar 1952 (attached to 21st Air Division, 28 Mar 1952–); 802d Air Division, 28 May 1952 (remained attached to 21st Air Division to 4 Sep 1952; attached to 7th Air Division, 10 Mar–8 Jun 1955 and 3 Oct 1956–9 Jan 1957); 819th Air (later, 819th Strategic Aerospace) Division, 20 Jun 1960; 22d Strategic Aerospace Division, 1 Jul 1962–25 Jun 1965.

Components. *Wing*. 40th: attached 6 Feb–1 May 1953. *Squadrons*. 40th Air Refueling: attached 9 Sep 1952–30 Apr 1953; assigned 1 Jun 1960–15 Mar 1963 (not operational, 1 Jan–15 Mar 1963). 310th Air Refueling: 8 Oct 1952–25 Jun 1965 (detached 1–28 Mar 1954, 28 Dec 1955–26 Feb 1956, 25 Nov–10 Dec 1957, 25 Mar–8 Jul 1958, and 15 Apr–25 Jun 1965). 379th: 28 Mar 1952–25 Mar 1965 (not operational, 28 Mar–4 Apr 1952 and 25 Feb–25 Mar 1965). 380th: 28 Mar 1952–25 Mar 1965 (not operational, 28 Mar–4 Apr 1952 and 25 Feb–25 Mar 1965). 381st: 28 Mar 1952–25 Mar 1965 (not operational, 28 Mar–4 Apr 1952 and 25 Feb–25 Mar 1965). 428th: 1 Feb 1959–1 Jan 1962 (not operational, 1 Oct 1961–1 Jan 1962). 550th Strategic Missile: 1 Apr 1961–25 Jun 1965 (not operational, 11 Mar–25 Jun 1965).

Stations. Forbes AFB, Kans, 28 Mar 1952; Smoky Hill (later, Schilling) AFB, Kans, 4 Sep 1952–25 Jun 1965.

Commanders. None (not manned), 28 Mar–4 Apr 1952; Col Robert J. Nolan, 5 Apr 1952; Col John H. de Russy, 28 Nov 1952; Col Robert J. Nolan, 12 Feb 1953; Col John H. de Russy, 10 Mar 1953; Col Willard W. Wilson, 16 Mar 1954; Col Robert E. Thacker, 27 Mar 1954; Col Willard W. Wilson, 6 May 1954; Col John H. de Russy, 28 May 1954; Col Murray A. Bywater, 9 Aug 1955; Col Delmore P. Wood, (by 16) Aug 1955; Col Robert E. Thacker, 17 Aug 1955; Col Selmon W. Wells, 20 Aug 1955; Col Delmore P. Wood, 20 Jun 1956; Col Bryson R. Bailey, 20 Sep 1956; Col Jean B. Miller, Jr., 13 Jan 1958; Col Walter Y. Lucas, 11 Apr 1959; Col James C. Robinson, Jr., Jun 1960; Col George Y. Jumper, 20 Jun 1960;

Col James C. Robinson, Jr., 25 Jan 1961; Col Jack W. Hayes, Jr., 3 Feb 1961; Col Edison F. Arnold, 15 Jul 1962; Col Roy C. Crompton, 22 May 1964; Col John F. Scanlon, 14–25 Jun 1965.

Aircraft and Missiles. B–29, 1952–1954; KC–97, 1952–1963; B–47, 1954–1965; Atlas F, 1962–1965; KC–135, 1964–1965.

Operations. Received B–29 bombardment training from 90th Bombardment Wing, Apr–Aug 1952. From Feb through May 1953, provided bombardment training to 40th Bombardment Wing. Converted to B–47s in 1954. Deployed at Upper Heyford RAF Station, England, 10 Mar–8 Jun 1955, and at RAF Greenham Common, England, 3 Oct 1956–9 Jan 1957. Gained a strategic missile squadron in Apr 1961. First Atlas missiles went on alert in Sep 1962. Began phasing down for inactivation in early 1965.

Service Streamers. None.

Campaign Streamers. None.

Decorations. Air Force Outstanding Unit Award: 1 Jan 1956–1 Jan 1959.

Emblem. On a blue shield between two 45° triangles with the long sides facing each other and placed diagonally from upper right to lower left, three white stars; in the upper triangle a white mailed right hand grasping a red lightning flash and in the lower triangle a white dove in flight to base carrying a green and black olive branch in its beak, hand and dove outlined in black; in a row across the bottom of shield 10 small white stars; the shield and triangles bordered with black, edged with white against the blue. (Approved on 7 Jan 1954.)

312th TACTICAL FIGHTER WING

Lineage. Established as 312th Fighter-Bomber Wing on 23 Mar 1953. Activated on 1 Oct 1954. Redesignated 312th Tactical Fighter Wing on 1 Jul 1958. Inactivated on 18 Feb 1959.

Assignments. Ninth Air Force, 1 Oct 1954; Eighteenth Air Force, 1 Oct 1957; 832d Air Division, 8 Oct 1957–18 Feb 1959.

Components. *Groups.* 312th: 1 Oct 1954–8 Oct 1957. 474th: attached 22 Dec 1954–8 Oct 1957. *Squadrons.* 386th: 8 Oct 1957–18 Feb 1959 (detached 12 Nov–6 Dec 1957). 387th: 8 Oct 1957–18 Feb 1959. 388th: 8 Oct 1957–18 Feb 1959 (detached 4 Sep–3 Dec 1958). 477th: 8 Oct 1957–18 Feb 1959 (detached 8 Sep–11 Dec 1958).

Stations. Clovis (later, Cannon) AFB, NM, 1 Oct 1954–18 Feb 1959.

Commanders. Col James B. Buck, 1 Oct 1954; Col Henry H. Norman, Jr., 17 Jul 1955; Col Donald J. M. Blakslee, 20 Aug 1955; Brig Gen William M. Momyer, c. 18 Sep 1955; Lt Col James M. Miller, 8 Oct 1957; Col Arlie J. Blood, 14 Oct 1957; Lt Col Richard L. Ryan, 15 Nov 1957; Col Arlie J. Blood,

6 Dec 1957; Col Gilbert L. Meyers, 2 Sep 1958–18 Feb 1959.

Aircraft. F–86, 1954–1957; F–100, 1956–1959.

Operations. Trained to maintain proficiency in fighter-bomber operations with conventional weapons until Sep 1955, then trained to maintain combat proficiency with atomic weapons. From Apr 1956 to Oct 1957, rotated tactical squadrons to France, 6 months at a time. Also furnished units for TAC composite air strike forces in the Far East, 1957–1958. Replaced by 27th TFW in Feb 1959.

Service Streamers. None.

Campaign Streamers. None.

Decorations. None.

Emblem. On a shield azure an eagle volant or, carrying with his talons a futuramic bomb argent, fire exhaust proper, and a branch of olive vert. (Approved on 30 Nov 1958.)

313th TACTICAL AIRLIFT WING

Lineage. Established as 313th Troop Carrier Wing on 28 Jul 1947. Organized on 15 Aug 1947. Discontinued on 26 Aug 1948. Redesignated 313th Troop Carrier Wing, Heavy, and activated on 23 Aug 1948. Inactivated on 20 Jan 1949. Redesignated 313th Troop Carrier Wing, Medium, on 26 Nov 1952. Activated on 1 Feb 1953. Inactivated on 25 Aug 1953. Activated on 15 Jun 1964. Organized on 1 Oct 1964. Redesignated 313th Tactical Airlift Wing on 1 May 1967. Inactivated on 30 Sep 1973.

Assignments. Ninth Air Force, 15 Aug 1947–26 Aug 1948. Ninth Air Force, 23 Aug 1948; Tactical Air Command, 25 Oct 1948; United States Air Forces in Europe, 5 Nov 1948 (attached to 1st Air Lift Task Force, 9–17 Nov 1948); 1st Air Lift Task Force, 18 Nov 1948–20 Jan 1949. Eighteenth Air Force, 1 Feb–25 Aug 1953. Tactical Air Command, 15 Jun 1964; 839th Air Division, 1 Oct 1964; 838th Air Division, 9 Nov 1964; Twelfth Air Force, 24 Dec 1969; 834th Air Division, 15 Mar 1972–30 Sep 1973.

Components. *Group.* 313th: 15 Aug 1947–26 Aug 1948; 23 Aug 1948–20 Jan 1949; 1 Feb–25 Aug 1953. *Squadrons.* 29th: 1 Oct 1964–1 Feb 1966. 38th: 1 Jul 1969–15 Nov 1971 (not operational, 1 Jul–31 Dec 1969; detached 4 Nov 1970–12 Jan 1971 and 9 Sep–15 Nov 1971). 47th: 1 Oct 1964–6 Jul 1973 (detached 26 Jul–19 Nov 1965, 25 Jan–c. 23 Jun 1966, 2 Sep– c. Nov 1966, c. Jan–25 Mar 1967, 27 Sep–4 Dec 1969, 16 Feb–19 Mar 1970, 5 Jun–11 Aug 1970, 3 May–12 Jul 1971, 6 Dec 1971–14 Feb 1972, 3 Aug–20 Oct 1972, 31 Dec 1972–11 Feb 1973). 48th: 1 Jan 1965–25 Jun 1967 (detached c. 17 Nov 1965–c. 28 Jan 1966, 23 Jun–Sep 1966, c. Nov 1966–c. Jan 1967); 15 Nov 1971–6 Aug 1973 (detached 3 Apr–28 Jun 1972 and 3 Oct–30 Dec 1972).

Stations. Bergstrom Field (later, AFB), Texas, 15 Aug 1947–26 Aug 1948. Bergstrom AFB, Texas, 23 Aug–22 Oct 1948; Fassberg RAF Station, West Germany, 9 Nov 1948–20 Jan 1949. Mitchel AFB, NY, 1 Feb–25 Aug 1953. Forbes AFB, Kans, 1 Oct 1964–30 Sep 1973.

Commanders. Col Raphael Baez, Jr., 15 Aug 1947–26 Aug 1948. Col Raphael Baez, Jr., 23 Aug 1948; Col Jesse C. Auton, 9 Nov 1948–20 Jan 1949. Brig Gen Arthur L. McCullough, 1 Feb–25 Aug 1953. None (not manned), 15 Jun–30 Sep 1964; Col George H. Kneen, Jr., 1 Oct 1964; Col Burl W. McLaughlin, Dec 1964; Col Joseph N. Donovan, 27 Jan 1965; Col Harold V. Sommers, Mar 1966; Col Marion F. Caruthers, 9 Jun 1966; Col William A. Dietrich, 30 Mar 1968; Col Robert C. Newman, Jr., 21 Feb 1970; Col Claude H. Turner, Jr., 16 Apr 1971; Col Warren Foss, 24 May 1972; Col Bruce D. Ferrier, 15 Aug–30 Sep 1973.

Aircraft. C–47, 1947–1948; C–54, 1947–1948; C–82, 1947–1948. C–47, 1948; C–54, 1948–1949; C–82, 1948. C–46, 1953; C–119, 1953. C–130, 1964–1973.

Operations. Trained in troop carrier operations, 1947–1948. Participated in Berlin Airlift, 1948–1949. Trained in troop carrier operations, 1953. Trained to become proficient and to maintain combat readiness in tactical airlift operations, 1964–1973. Frequently deployed tactical squadrons or segments thereof on a global basis to support airlift requirements of overseas commands. Participated in tactical exercises and disaster relief on a regular basis. Last C–130 transferred on 6 Aug 1973. Thereafter, until inactivation, the wing was involved in base closure operations.

Service Streamers. None.

Campaign Streamers. None.

Decorations. Air Force Outstanding Unit Award: 1 Jun 1968–1 Jun 1970.

Emblem. Per bend azure and gules the silhouette of a stylized winged aircraft or, charged with a mullet of the first between six mullets, three and three, of the third. (Approved for 313th Group on 3 Feb 1943 and for 313th Wing on 18 Jun 1953.)

314th TACTICAL AIRLIFT WING

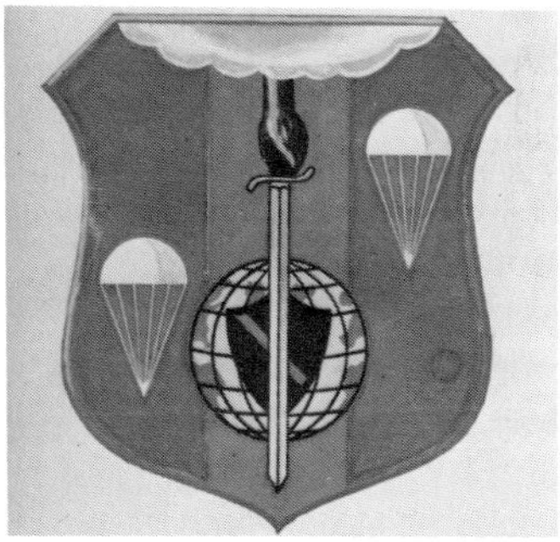

Lineage. Established as 314th Troop Carrier Wing, Medium, on 4 Oct 1948. Activated on 1 Nov 1948. Redesignated: 314th Troop Carrier Wing on 1 Jan 1967; 314th Tactical Airlift Wing on 1 Aug 1967.

Assignments. Ninth Air Force, 1 Nov 1948; Fourteenth Air Force, 1 Feb 1949; Tactical Air Command, 1 Aug 1950; Eighteenth Air Force (Troop Carrier) (later, Eighteenth Air Force), 1 Jun 1951; Ninth Air Force, 1 Sep 1957; 839th Air Division, 8 Oct 1957 (attached to 315th Air Division [Combat Cargo], 22–26 Jan 1966); 315th Air Division (Combat Cargo) (later, 315th Air Division), 27 Jan 1966; 327th Air Division, 1 Nov 1968; Twelfth Air Force, 31 May 1971; 834th Air Division, 15 Mar 1972; Twenty-Second Air Force, 31 Dec 1974– (attached to Operating Location A, Headquarters Twenty-Second Air Force, 1 Jan–30 Jun 1975).

Components. *Groups*. 309th: attached 26 Jun 1949–20 Feb 1951. 313th: attached 1 Oct 1953–8 Jun 1955. 314th: 1 Nov 1948–8 Oct 1957 (not operational, 1 Nov 1948–27 Jan 1949; detached 27 Aug 1950–14 Nov 1954). 316th: attached 4 Nov 1949–14 Nov 1954. 513th: attached 8 Nov 1955–8 Oct 1957. 516th: attached 8 Mar 1955–9 Jul 1956. *Squadrons*. 5th Liaison: attached 8 Sep 1952–22 Mar 1953. 16th Tactical Airlift Training: 1 Aug 1971–. 18th: 1 Jul 1963–1 Apr 1965 (detached Oct 1964–Jan 1965). 20th Helicopter: attached 9 Jul 1956–17 Jul 1959. 21st Helicopter: attached 30 Jun–c. 8 Oct 1957. 23d Helicopter: attached 9 Jul–c. 12 Oct 1956. 24th Helicopter: attached 9 Jul–c. 25 Sep 1956. 32d: 1 Sep 1973– (detached 5 Nov 1973–16 Jan 1974, 3 Feb–16 Apr 1975, 3 Sep–14 Nov 1975, 3 Jun–14 Aug 1976, 13 Feb–13 Apr 1977, 9 Sep 1977–). 48th: 6 Aug–1 Sep 1973. 50th: 8 Oct 1957–26 Dec 1965 (detached 29 Aug–c. 20 Dec 1958, 27 Mar–c. 15 Aug 1961, May–Jul 1965); 23 Feb 1966–31 May 1971; 15 Aug 1973– (not operational, 15 Aug–15 Sep 1973; detached 1 Jun–18 Aug 1974, 25 Apr–7 Jun 1975, 3 Dec 1975–18 Feb 1976, 4 Sep–13 Nov 1976, 4 Apr–14 Jun 1977). 61st: 8 Oct 1957–1 Dec 1965 (detached 19 Mar–5 Oct 1959, 7 Jan–20 Feb 1960, Jan–Mar 1965); 31 May 1971– (detached 13 May–8 Sep 1972, 3 Jan–17 Mar 1973, 12 Jun–16 Aug 1973, 3 Oct–16 Dec 1974, 4 Jun–17 Aug 1975, 5 Mar–17 May 1976, 3 Dec 1976–13 Feb 1977, 5 Jul–9 Sep 1977). 62d: 8 Oct 1957–1 Dec 1965 (detached 6 Jun–Aug 1961, 19 May–29 Jul 1962, 5 Aug–Oct 1964, Mar–May 1965); 31 May 1971– (detached 31 May–13 Jun 1971). 345th: attached 12 Nov 1958–1 Jun 1962; assigned 25 Mar 1966–31 May 1971. 346th: 15 Mar 1969–31 May 1971. 664th: attached 16 Dec 1952–8 Mar 1955. 776th: 25 Mar 1966–31 May 1971. 2601st Assault: attached 1 Oct–12 Dec 1949. Troop Carrier Squadron Provisional, 4418th: attached 15 May–1 Jul 1963.

Stations. Smyrna (later, Sewart) AFB, Tenn, 1 Nov 1948–c. 15 Jan 1966; Kung Kuan (later, Ching Chuan Kang) AB, Taiwan, 22 Jan 1966–31 May 1971; Little Rock AFB, Ark, 31 May 1971–.

Commanders. Col Hoyt L. Prindle, 1 Nov 1948; Col Norton H. Van Sicklen, 31 Aug 1950; Col Hoyt L. Prindle, 28 Dec 1950; Col Norton H. Van Sicklen, 1 Jun 1952; Col William H. DeLacey, 2 Jul 1952; Col Hoyt L. Prindle, 23 Aug 1952; Col Marvin L. McNickle, 6 Jul 1954; Col William Lewis, Jr., 1 Jul 1956; Col Adriel N. Williams, 21 Jul 1956; Col Charles W. Howe, 1 Aug 1957; Col John T. Hylton, Jr., 8 Oct 1957; Lt Col William F. Kelleher, 30 May 1958; Col Daniel F. Tatum, 16 Jul 1958; Col George M. Foster, 16 Jul 1960; Col William H. DeLacey, 17 Aug 1960; Col William G. Moore, Jr., 13 Aug 1962; Col Arthur C. Rush, 1 Sep 1963; Col Paul A. Jones, 14 Feb 1967; Col Lyle D. Lutton, 12 Mar 1968; Col Albert W. Jones, 12 Oct 1968; Col William T. Phillips, 15 Jul 1970; Col Ray C. Staley, 22 Jan 1971; Col Andrew P. Iosue, 15 May 1971; Col Richard J.

Gibney, 31 May 1971; Col Richard T. Drury, 31 Jul 1972; Col Frank W. Janssen, 14 May 1973; Brig Gen Eugene W. Gauch, Jr., 18 Oct 1973 (additional duty); Col Robert F. Coverdale, 3 Nov 1973; Col John E. Davis, 16 Jul 1974; Brig Gen Russell E. Mohney, 19 Jan 1976; Col Donald M. Nagel, 1 Aug 1977– .

Aircraft. C–82, 1948–1949, 1949–1951; C–47, 1948–1949, 1949–1953; CG–15 (glider), 1949–1951; YG–18 (glider), 1949–1951; C–119, 1949–1951; C–45, 1949–1951, 1954–1955; TC–46, 1950; YC–122, 1950–1954; YH–12, 1951; H–19, 1952–1955; C–46, 1952; L–5, 1952–1953; L–16, 1952–1953; L–20, 1952–1953, 1954; H–21, 1955–1959; C–123, 1956–1957, 1958–1961; C–130, 1956–.

Operations. From activation until Dec 1965, served as a primary troop carrier unit in the eastern United States, involved in joint airborne training with Army forces, developed assault airlift operations, and participated in aerial demonstrations, exercises, maneuvers, and joint operations. Wing operations extended worldwide. From Jan 1966 to May 1971, operated from Taiwan to provide passenger and cargo airlift throughout the Far East and combat airlift in Southeast Asia. Returned to the United States in May 1971 and again served as a principal airlift unit involved in worldwide airborne training, airlift, and special operations. Since Aug 1971, has served as the primary C–130 training organization for Department of Defense agencies and aircrews of selected foreign states.

Service Streamers. None.

Campaign Streamers. None.

Decorations. Air Force Outstanding Unit Award with Combat "V" Device: 1 Nov 1967–31 Dec 1969. Air Force Outstanding Unit Awards: 11 Jan–14 Feb 1955; 1 Jan 1960–31 Dec 1961; 1 Jan 1975–30 Jun 1976.

Emblem. Azure, in base on a pale or, between in bend sinister two open parachutes argent, a globe proper extending over the pale and surmounted by an escutcheon gules, a bendlet of the second, a bordure sable, overall in pale issuing from a bank of clouds proper in chief a left hand of the last grasping a sword of the third helted vert, all within a bordure gold. (Approved on 17 Jun 1954.)

315th MILITARY AIRLIFT WING (ASSOCIATE)

Lineage. Established as 315th Troop Carrier Wing, Medium, on 23 May 1952. Activated on 10 Jun 1952. Inactivated on 18 Jan 1955. Redesignated 315th Air Commando Wing, Troop Carrier, and activated, on 21 Feb 1966. Organized on 8 Mar 1966. Redesignated: 315th Air Commando Wing on 1 Aug 1967; 315th Special Operations Wing on 1 Aug 1968; 315th Tactical

Airlift Wing on 1 Jan 1970. Inactivated on 31 Mar 1972. Redesignated 315th Military Airlift Wing (Associate) on 29 Jan 1973. Activated in the Reserve on 1 Jul 1973.

Assignments. 315th Air Division (Combat Cargo), 10 Jun 1952–18 Jan 1955. Pacific Air Forces, 21 Feb 1966; 315th Air Division (Combat Cargo), 8 Mar 1966 (attached to 2d Air Division, 8–31 Mar 1966; Seventh Air Force, 1 Apr–15 Oct 1966); 834th Air Division, 15 Oct 1966; Seventh Air Force, 1 Dec 1971–31 Mar 1972. Eastern Air Force Reserve Region, 1 Jul 1973 (attached to 437th Military Airlift Wing, 1 Jul 1973–); Fourteenth Air Force (Reserve), 8 Oct 1976– (remained attached to 437th Military Airlift Wing).

Components. *Group.* 315th: 10 Jun 1952–18 Jan 1955. *Squadrons.* 8th: 31 Jul 1971–15 Jan 1972 (detached 5–15 Jan 1972). 9th: 30 Sep 1971–29 Feb 1972 (detached 9 Jan–29 Feb 1972). 12th: 15 Oct 1966–30 Sep 1970 (not operational, 20 Jul–30 Sep 1970). 19th: 8 Mar 1966–10 Jun 1971 (not operational, 1 May–10 Jun 1971). 300th: 1 Jul 1973–. 309th: 8 Mar 1966–31 Jul 1970 (not operational, 1–31 Jul 1970). 310th: 8 Mar 1966–15 Jan 1972, attached 16–26 Jan 1972. 311th: 8 Mar 1966–5 Oct 1971 (not operational, 15 Sep–5 Oct 1971). 701st: 1 Jul 1973–. 707th: 1 Jul 1973–. *Flight.* Royal Australian Air Force Air Transport Flight, Vietnam: attached 8 Mar–15 Oct 1966. *Detachments.* Det 5, HQ 315th Air Division (Combat Cargo): attached 8 Mar–15 Oct 1966. Det 6, HQ 315th Air Division (Combat Cargo): attached 8 Mar–15 Oct 1966. Det 1, HQ 315th Air Commando Wing, Troop Carrier: 1 Aug–15 Oct 1966.

Stations. Brady AB, Japan, 10 Jun 1952–18 Jan 1955. Tan Son Nhut AB, South Vietnam, 8 Mar 1966; Phan Rang AB, South Vietnam, 15 Jun 1967–31 Mar 1972. Charleston AFB, SC, 1 Jul 1973–.

Commanders. Col Kenneth W. Northamer, 10 Jun 1952; Col Robert O. Good, 26 Jul 1953; Col Adriel N. Williams, 29 Aug 1953; Col David B. Lancaster, 27 Feb 1954; Col Francis W. Williams, 10 Aug 1954–18 Jan 1955. None (not manned), 21 Feb–7 Mar 1966; Col George L. Hannah, Jr., 8 Mar 1966; Col Robert T. Simpson, 23 Jun 1966; Col Vernon W. Froehlich, 19 Nov 1966; Col Bill M. Richardson, 9 Aug 1967; Col Robert D. Brown, 20 Nov 1967; Col Noble F. Greenhill, Jr., 8 Jun 1968; Col John W. Pauly, 19 Jul 1968; Col Harry V. Bankard, 4 May 1969; Col John W. Pauly, 3 Jun 1969; Col Leslie J. Campbell, Jr., 10 Jun 1969; Col Charles S. Reed, 27 May 1970; Col Kenneth T. Blood, Jr., 31 Jan 1971; Col Ray C. Staley, 19 Nov 1971–31 Mar 1972. Col Richard P. McFarland, 1 Jul 1973; Col David Guminski, c. 31 Sep 1974; Lt Col David L. Webber, 1 Dec 1974; Lt Col Kenneth O. Mann, c. 25 Apr 1976; Col Marc M. McClelland, c. 20 Jun 1976–.

Aircraft. C–46, 1952–1955. CV–2, 1966; UC–123, 1966–1971; C–123, 1966–1972; C–130, 1966; A–37, 1971–1972; C–47, 1971–1972; O–2, 1971–1972. C–5, 1973; C–141, 1973–.

Operations. Flew troop and cargo airlift and airdrop, leaflet drop, spraying, air evacuation, search and rescue, and other allied missions between Japan and Korea during the Korean war. Continued airlift in Japan, Korea, French Indo-China, and other points in the Far East from Jul 1953 to 14 Dec 1954.

Inactivated in Jan 1955. Activated in South Vietnam in Mar 1966 and became responsible until 15 Oct 1966 for all in-country airlift in the Republic of Vietnam, including control over all USAF airlift assets, aerial port squadrons, an aeromedical evacuation squadron, and a special air transport flight of the Royal Australian Air Force. From 15 Oct 1966 to 15 Jan 1972, performed C–123 airlift operations in Vietnam. Operations included aerial movement of troops and cargo, flare drops, defoliation missions, aeromedical evacuation, and airdrops of critical supplies and paratroops. Conducted C–123 aircrew training for the South Vietnamese Air Force, 4 Jan–22 Sep 1971. Gained control over A–37 close air support and interdiction operations of the 8th Special Operations Squadron in Jul 1971, and over psychological warfare and visual reconnaissance operations of the 9th Special Operations Squadron in Sep 1971. Lost control over these special operations units early in 1972. Not tactically operational, 15 Jan–31 Mar 1972. Replaced 943d Military Airlift Group (Associate) on 1 Jul 1973 and became affiliated with the 437th Military Airlift Wing, with Reserve aircrews flying aircraft of the regular unit.

Service Streamers. Korean Theater.

Campaign Streamers. Vietnam Air; Vietnam Air Offensive; Vietnam Air Offensive, Phase II; Vietnam Air Offensive, Phase III; Vietnam Air/Ground; Vietnam Air Offensive, Phase IV; TET 69/Counteroffensive; Vietnam Summer–Fall, 1969; Vietnam Winter–Spring, 1970; Sanctuary Counteroffensive; Southwest Monsoon; Commando Hunt V; Commando Hunt VI; Commando Hunt VII.

Decorations. Presidential Unit Citations (Vietnam): 21 Jan–12 May 1968; 1 Apr–30 Jun 1970. Air Force Outstanding Unit Awards with Combat "V" Device: 15 Oct 1966–30 Apr 1967; 10 Jun–31 Dec 1967; 15 Jul 1968–30 Jun 1969; 1 Jan 1971–31 Mar 1972. Republic of Korea Presidential Unit Citation: [10 Jun 1952]–27 Jul 1953. Republic of Vietnam Gallantry Crosses with Palm: 1 Oct 1966–30 Oct 1971; 1 Jun 1969–1 Jun 1970; 1 Jul 1971–11 Mar 1972.

Emblem. Per fess nebuly light blue and argent fimbriated or on the first three mullets of five points fesswise of the third above an aircraft fesswise of the second in base a globe per pale argent and azure, grid lines counterchanged, all within a diminished bordure of the third. (Approved on 7 Nov 1973.)

316th TACTICAL AIRLIFT WING

Lineage. Established as 316th Troop Carrier Wing on 29 Jul 1947. Organized on 15 Aug 1947. Discontinued on 25 Aug 1948. Redesignated 316th Troop Carrier Wing, Medium, and activated on 23 Aug 1948. Inactivated on 20 Oct 1949. Redesignated

316th Troop Carrier Wing, Assault, and activated, on 15 Nov 1965. Organized on 25 Nov 1965. Redesignated: 316th Troop Carrier Wing on 1 Mar 1966; 316th Tactical Airlift Wing on 1 May 1967. Inactivated on 1 Oct 1975.

Assignments. Ninth Air Force, 15 Aug 1947–25 Aug 1948. Ninth Air Force, 23 Aug 1948; Fourteenth Air Force, 1 Feb–20 Oct 1949. Tactical Air Command, 15 Nov 1965; 840th Air Division, 25 Nov 1965; Ninth Air Force, 24 Dec 1969; 839th Air Division, 31 Mar 1970; Twenty-First Air Force, 31 Dec 1974–1 Oct 1975 (attached to Operating Location A, Headquarters Twenty-First Air Force, 31 Dec 1974–30 Jun 1975).

Components. *Group.* 316th: 15 Aug 1947–25 Aug 1948; 23 Aug 1948–20 Oct 1949. *Squadrons.* 29th: 1 Apr–15 Nov 1971. 36th: 1 Apr 1966–25 Mar 1968 (detached 28 Mar–29 Jun 1967); 5 Jul 1968–1 Jul 1975 (detached 25 Feb–15 Jun 1969, 24 Nov 1969–7 Feb 1970, 13 Aug–18 Oct 1970, 12 Jul–10 Sep 1971, 20 May–8 Sep 1972, 12 Mar–18 May 1973, 14 Jan–16 Mar 1974, and 13 Aug–16 Oct 1974). 37th: 1 Oct 1966–15 Sep 1975 (detached 24 Sep–21 Dec 1967, 27 Apr–13 May 1968, 24 Nov 1968–5 Mar 1969, 13 Jul–26 Sep 1969, 1 Mar–11 May 1970, 7 Feb–13 Apr 1971, 5 Jan–13 Mar 1972, 30 Nov 1972–15 Mar 1973, 31 Aug–16 Nov 1973, 12 Apr–29 Jun 1974, and 5 Apr–15 Jun 1975). 38th: 1 Jan 1967–1 Jul 1969 (detached 5 Feb–22 Jul 1968); 15 Nov 1971–31 Aug 1975 (detached 13 Mar–16 May 1972, 31 Aug–5 Dec 1972, 18 May–13 Jul 1973, 29 Aug–3 Oct 1973, 13 Dec 1974–15 Feb 1975; not operational, 1 Jul–31 Aug 1975).

Stations. Greenville AAB (later, AFB), SC, 15 Aug 1947–25 Aug 1948. Greenville AFB, SC, 23 Aug 1948–20 Oct 1949. Langley AFB, Va, 25 Nov 1965–1 Oct 1975.

Commanders. Col Paul H. Prentiss, 15 Aug 1947–25 Aug 1948. Col Paul H. Prentiss, 23 Aug 1948; Col Newton Longfellow, 11 Dec 1948; Col Louis M. Merrick, 26 Jun–20 Oct 1949. None (not manned), 15–24 Nov 1965; Col Raymond C. Bird, 25 Nov 1965; Col Clifford Nash, 25 Feb 1966; Col Raymond C. Bird, 10 Mar 1966; Col Thomas A. Twomey, 11 Apr 1966; Col Clifford Nash, 5 May 1966; Brig Gen Malcolm P. Hooker, 1 Aug 1968; Col Theodore P. Crichton, 23 Jul 1971; Col Patrick G. Long, 1 Mar 1973; Col Allan K. Andreason, 15 Feb 1974; Col Ivan D. Brown, 30 Jul–1 Oct 1975.

Aircraft. C–47, 1947–1948; C–82, 1947–1948; CG–15 (glider), 1947–1948. C–47, 1948–1949; C–82, 1948–1949; CG–15 (glider), 1948–1949. C–130, 1966–1975.

Operations. Participated in joint airborne training, glider training, exercises and maneuvers, and ferried freight in the United States and overseas, 1947–1948, and again in 1948–1949. Participated in worldwide tactical airlift operations, humanitarian missions, and special exercises and maneuvers, including joint airborne training, 1966–1975. Conducted C–130 replacement training, Jan 1966–Nov 1967, and C–130 maintenance training, Feb–Dec 1966. In 1973, participated in repatriation of South Vietnamese and American prisoners of war from North Vietnam.

Service Streamers. None.

Campaign Streamers. None.

Decorations. Air Force Outstanding Unit Awards: 1 May 1967–30 Apr 1969; 1 May 1970–30 Apr 1972; 1 May 1972–30 Apr 1974.

Emblem. Azure, nine parachutes argent, three, two, three, and one, all within a bordure per bend or and gules. *Motto:* VALOR WITHOUT ARMS. (Approved for 316th Group on 17 Aug 1951 and for 316th Wing on 14 Dec 1965.)

317TH TACTICAL AIRLIFT WING

Lineage. Established as 317th Troop Carrier Wing, Heavy, on 10 Aug 1948. Activated on 18 Aug 1948. Inactivated on 14 Sep 1949. Redesignated 317th Troop Carrier Wing, Medium, on 3 Jul 1952. Activated on 14 Jul 1952. Inactivated on 25 Sep 1958. Activated on 13 Mar 1963. Organized on 15 Apr 1963. Redesignated: 317th Troop Carrier Wing on 1 Mar 1966; 317th Tactical Airlift Wing on 1 May 1967.

Assignments. Fifth Air Force, 18 Aug 1948; 1st Air Lift Task Force, 8 Jan–14 Sep 1949. Twelfth Air Force, 14 Jul 1952 (attached to 322d Air Division [Combat Cargo], 1 Apr 1954–31 Jul 1955); 322d Air Division (Combat Cargo), 1 Aug 1955–25 Sep 1958. United States Air Forces in Europe, 13 Mar 1963; 322d Air Division (Combat Cargo), 15 Apr 1963; United States Air Forces in Europe, 1 Apr 1964 (attached to 322d Air Division [Combat Cargo], 1 Apr–20 Jun 1964); Ninth Air Force, 20 Jun 1964; 840th Air Division, 1 Oct 1964; Ninth Air Force, 24 Dec 1969; 839th Air Division, 31 Mar 1970; Twenty-First Air Force, 31 Dec 1974– (attached to Operating Location A, Headquarters Twenty-First Air Force, 31 Dec 1974–30 Jun 1975).

Components. *Group.* 317th: 18 Aug 1948–14 Sep 1949 (detached 21 Sep 1948–8 Jan 1949; not operational, c. 31 Aug–14 Sep 1949); 14 Jul 1952–12 Mar 1957 (not operational, 8 May 1955–12 Mar 1957). *Squadrons.* 18th: 1 Apr 1965–25 Jun 1967. 37th: 15 Sep 1975–1 Oct 1977. 39th: attached 8 May 1955–23 Jun 1956; assigned 8 Jul 1957–25 Sep 1958; assigned 15 Apr 1963–31 Jul 1971 (detached c. Feb–c. May 1965, 13 May–18 Jul 1968 and 15 Apr–22 Jul 1969; not operational, 1 Jun–31 Jul 1971); assigned 31 Aug 1971– (detached 12 Dec 1973–17 Feb 1974, 9 Jul–15 Sep 1974, 12 Jul–14 Sep 1975, 12 Apr–14 Jun 1976, 4 Jan–4 Mar 1977). 40th: attached 21 Sep–15 Nov 1948; attached 8 May 1955–11 Mar 1957, assigned 12 Mar 1957–25 Sep 1958 (detached 10 Apr–7 Jul 1957); assigned 15 Apr 1963– (detached 24 Nov 1964–19 Feb 1965, 16 Mar–26 May 1968; not operational, 12–30 Aug 1971; detached 31 Aug–17 Oct 1971, 7 Apr–16 Jun 1973, 4 Mar–7 May 1975, 12 Jan–15 Mar 1976, 4 Oct–15 Dec 1976, and 26 Apr–15 Jul 1977). 41st: attached 8 May 1955–11 Mar 1957, assigned 12 Mar

1957–25 Sep 1958 (detached 15 Mar–7 Jul 1957); assigned 15 Apr 1963–21 Nov 1965 (detached 6 Sep–21 Dec 1964); assigned 31 Aug 1971– (detached 6 Nov 1971–12 Jan 1972, 4 Jun–16 Aug 1972, 5 Feb–14 Apr 1973, 9 Aug–15 Oct 1973, 11 Mar–16 May 1974, 11 Nov 1974–15 Jan 1975, 4 Oct–15 Dec 1975, 13 Jul–10 Sep 1976, and 5 Mar–25 Apr 1977). 46th: attached 18 Aug–30 Sep 1948. 52d: attached 15 Apr 1963–31 Mar 1964. 780th: 8 Jul 1957–8 Mar 1958. 781st: 8 Jul 1957–8 Mar 1958. 782d: 8 Jul–20 Dec 1957. 4408th Combat Crew Training: 22 Sep 1969–15 Aug 1971.

Stations. Tachikawa AB, Japan, 18 Aug–2 Dec 1948; Celle RAF Station, West Germany, 9 Jan–14 Sep 1949. Rhein-Main AB, West Germany, 14 Jul 1952; Neubiberg AB, West Germany, 17 Mar 1953; Evreux-Fauville AB, France, 17 Apr 1957–25 Sep 1958. Evreux-Fauville AB, France, 15 Apr 1963-20 Jun 1964; Lockbourne AFB, Ohio, 20 Jun 1964; Pope AFB, NC, 31 Aug 1971–.

Commanders. Col Thomas K. Hampton, 18 Aug 1948; Col William A. Ross, c. 15 Aug–c. 14 Sep 1949. Col Donald J. French, 14 Jul 1952; Col Harry M. Pike, 23 Jul 1954; Col Clarence B. Hammerle, Jr., 29 Jul 1954; Col Joseph A. Cunningham, 9 Sep 1954 (additional duty only, 8–16 Apr 1957); none (not manned), 17 Apr–7 Jul 1957; Col Robert D. Forman, 8 Jul 1957; Col John B. Wallace, 11 Sep–25 Sep 1958. None (not manned), 13 Mar–14 Apr 1963; Col Arthur C. Rush, 15 Apr 1963; Col George W. Kinney, 20 Jun 1963; Col Harry S. Dennis, Jr., 27 Dec 1965; Col Robert M. Levy, 29 Jul 1966; Col Jack J. Schneider, 13 Sep 1967; Col James A. Giles, 28 Sep 1967; Col Bill M. Richardson, 18 Dec 1967; Col James A. Giles, 20 May 1968; Col Bill M. Richardson, 19 Jun 1968; Col Richard J. Downs, 2 Jan 1970; Col Thomas G. Cline, 14 Jul 1971; Col Billie J. Norwood, 31 Aug 1971; Col Edwin F. Rumsey, 13 Apr 1973; Col Stewart Young, 14 Sep 1973; Brig Gen Robert F. Coverdale, 6 Jun 1975; Col Benjamin Kraljev, Jr., 8 Aug 1977–.

Aircraft. C–46, 1948; C–54, 1948–1949. C–119, 1952–1957, 1957–1958; C–130, 1957–1958. C–130, 1963–1964, 1964–1971, 1971–; C–124, 1963–1964; C–123, 1969–1971.

Operations. Provided troop carrier and courier service in the Far East, 1948. Moved by ship from Japan to West Germany, Dec 1948–Jan 1949. Participated in Berlin Airlift, 9 Jan–31 Jul 1949. From Jul 1952 to Apr 1957 provided C–119 troop carrier and airlift service in support of USAFE, NATO, and UN, at same time participating in numerous exercises and humanitarian missions. Moved to France in Apr 1957, replacing 465th Troop Carrier Wing on 8 Jul. From Apr 1963 to Jun 1964, provided C–130 airlift in support of USAFE, NATO, and UN. Moved to Ohio in Jun 1964 and became involved in TAC's worldwide C–130 airlift operations, with airborne training a major responsibility. Provided C–130 replacement training support for PACAF, Oct 1965–Jul 1971 and Aug–Dec 1971. Also provided C–123 combat crew training for the U.S. and Republic of Vietnam crews, Sep 1969–Aug 1971. Pioneered in use of adverse weather aerial delivery system (AWADS) equipment in active combat operations in Southeast Asia, and from Sep 1977 to Jan 1978, trained aircrews in the AWADS for a C–130 squadron in Europe.

Service Streamers. None.

Campaign Streamers. None.

Decorations. Air Force Outstanding Unit Awards: 1 Apr 1964–30 Jun 1965; 1 May 1972–30 Apr 1973; 1 May 1973–30 Apr 1975; 1 May 1975–30 Apr 1977.

Emblem. Or issuant from chief a dexter arm, fist clenched inflamed proper, in base a fire of seven tongues of the last, on a chief nebuly azure, three piles of the first. Motto: I GAIN BY HAZARD. (Approved for 317th Group on 22 Dec 1942 and for 317th Wing on 15 May 1958.)

319th BOMBARDMENT WING, HEAVY

Lineage. Established as 319th Bombardment Wing, Light, on 10 May 1949. Activated in the Reserve on 27 Jun 1949. Inactivated on 2 Sep 1949. Activated in the Reserve on 10 Oct 1949. Ordered to active service on 10 Mar 1951. Inactivated on 28 Mar 1951. Redesignated 319th Fighter-Bomber Wing on 12 Apr 1955. Activated in the Reserve on 18 May 1955. Inactivated on 16 Nov 1957. Redesignated 319th Bombardment Wing, Heavy, and activated, on 15 Nov 1962. Organized on 1 Feb 1963.

Assignments. Ninth Air Force, 27 Jun–2 Sep 1949. Fourteenth Air Force, 10 Oct 1949–28 Mar 1951. Fourteenth Air Force, 18 May 1955–16 Nov 1957. Strategic Air Command, 15 Nov 1962; 810th Strategic Aerospace Division, 1 Feb 1963; 4th Strategic Aerospace Division, 1 Sep 1964; 47th Air Division, 30 Jun 1971; 4th Strategic Missile (later, 4th Air) Division, 15 Jan 1973; 57th Air Division, 22 Jan 1975–.

Components. *Group.* 319th: 27 Jun–2 Sep 1949 (not operational); 10 Oct 1949–22 Mar 1951 (not operational, c. 15–22 Mar 1951); 18 May 1955–16 Nov 1957. *Squadrons.* 46th: 1 Feb 1963–. 905th Air Refueling: 1 Feb 1963–.

Stations. Reading Muni Aprt, Pa, 27 Jun–2 Sep 1949. Birmingham Muni Aprt, Ala, 10 Oct 1949–28 Mar 1951. Memphis Muni Aprt, Tenn, 18 May 1955–16 Nov 1957. Grand Forks AFB, ND, 1 Feb 1963–.

Commanders. None (not manned), 27 Jun–2 Sep 1949. Brig Gen Henry L. Badham, Jr., 10 Oct 1949; Col Wilson R. Wood, c. 14–c. 28 Mar 1951. Brig Gen William F. Fry, c. 18 May 1955; Lt Col Van D. Dowda, 2 Apr 1956; Col William J. Johnson, Jr., 5 Jul 1956–1957. None (not manned), 15 Nov 1962–31 Jan 1963; Col Allen B. Rowlett, 1 Feb 1963; Col Pete C. Sianus, 23 Sep 1963; Col Robert J. Ray, 2 Mar 1965; Col George H. McKee, 14 Apr 1965; Col William H. Cooper, 18 May 1966; Col Keith A. Whitaker, 1 Jun 1967; Col Lawrence W. Steinkraus, 20 Jan 1968; Col Samuel G. Taylor, Jr., 4 Aug 1968; Col Robert C. Glenn, 4 Aug 1970; Col Lee R. Senter, 17 Jun 1971;

Col George D. Moore, Jr., 9 May 1973; Col Burr V. Miller, Jr., 24 May 1974; Col Donald D. Johnson, Jr., 6 May 1975; Col John A. Brashear, 4 Apr 1977–.

Aircraft. T–6, 1949–1951; T–7, 1949–1951; T–11, 1949–1951; B–26, 1949–1951. T–33, 1955–1957; F–84, 1955–1957; F–86, 1957. B–52, 1963–; KC–135, 1963–.

Operations. Replaced 514th Troop Carrier Wing in Oct 1949. Performed Reserve training until ordered to active service in Mar 1951, when wing personnel were used to fill other USAF units. Replaced 8710th Pilot Training Wing in May 1955. Performed Reserve training and, from Jul 1956 through Aug 1957, maintained two F–84s on "runway alert" at Memphis Municipal Airport under operational control of 20th Air Division, Air Defense Command. Replaced by 445th Troop Carrier Wing in Nov 1957. Replaced 4133d Strategic Wing in Feb 1963. Conducted global bombardment training and air refueling operations to meet SAC commitments.

Service Streamers. None.

Campaign Streamers. None.

Decorations. None.

Emblem. Azure, a mailed fist couped raguly gray, grasping a torch in pale of the like on which is a flight symbol edged sable, the torch enflamed proper, all within a diminished bordure or. *Motto:* DEFENSORES LIBERTATIS—Defenders of freedom. (Approved on 6 Jan 1964.)

320th BOMBARDMENT WING, HEAVY

Lineage. Established as 320th Bombardment Wing, Medium, and activated, on 1 Dec 1952. Discontinued on 15 Sep 1960. Redesignated 320th Bombardment Wing, Heavy, on 15 Nov 1962. Organized on 1 Feb 1963.

Assignments. 12th Air Division, 1 Dec 1952–15 Sep 1960 (attached to 7th Air Division, 3 Jun–4 Sep 1954; 3d Air Division, 5 Oct 1956–11 Jan 1957); Department of the Air Force, 16 Sep 1960–14 Nov 1962; Strategic Air Command, 15 Nov 1962; 14th Strategic Aerospace Division, 1 Feb 1963; 18th Strategic Aerospace Division, 1 Jul 1965; 47th Air Division, 2 Jul 1966; 14th Strategic Aerospace Division, 31 Mar 1970; 47th Air Division, 30 Jun 1971; 14th Air Division, 1 Oct 1972–.

Components. *Squadrons.* 320th Air Refueling: 1 Dec 1952–16 Jun 1960 (detached 2 May–15 Jun 1955, 1–c. 25 Oct 1955, 3 Mar–7 May 1956, 5 Oct 1956–11 Jan 1957, and 3 Jan–10 Apr 1958). 441st: 1 Dec 1952–15 Sep 1960 (not operational, 16 May–15 Sep 1960); 1 Feb 1963– (not operational, 11 Feb–c. 1 Jul 1965, 1 Dec 1965–c. 21 Mar 1966, and c. 3 Jun 1972–25 Oct 1973). 442d: 1 Dec 1952–15 Sep 1960 (not operational, 1–15 Sep 1960). 443d: 1 Dec 1952–15 Sep 1960 (not operational, 1–15 Sep 1960). 444th: 1 Jan 1959–15 Sep 1960 (not operational, 1 Jul–15 Sep 1960). 904th Air Refueling: 1 Feb 1963– (not operational, 11 Feb–c. 1 Jul 1965, 7 Dec 1965–31 Mar 1966, and c. 3 Jun 1972–25 Oct 1973).

Stations. March AFB, Calif, 1 Dec 1952–15 Sep 1960. Mather AFB, Calif, 1 Feb 1963–.

Commanders. Col Loran D. Briggs, 1 Dec 1952; Col Francis W. Nye, c. 28 Feb 1953; Col Olbert F. Lassiter, 11 May 1953; Lt Col Russell F. Ireland, 21 May 1953; Col Olbert F. Lassiter, 25 May 1953; Lt Col Russell F. Ireland, 26 May 1953; Col Loren D. Briggs, 4 Jun 1953; Col Ernest C. Eddy, 27 Apr 1954; Col William R. Large, Jr., 1 May 1954; Col Ernest C. Eddy, 25 Jun 1955; Col Robert B. Miller, 15 Jul 1955; Col Robert J. Hughey, 12 Jan 1957; Col William J. Crumm, 22 Apr 1957; Col Robert J. Hughey, 20 Oct 1958; Col David I. Liebman, 8 May 1959; Col Thomas G. Netcher, 10 Jul 1959; Col Frank W. Hansley, (by 20) Aug–15 Sep 1960; none (not manned), 16 Sep 1960–31 Jan 1963; Col Merrill N. Moore, 1 Feb 1963; Col Van R. Parker, 20 Jun 1963; Col Owen A. Weddle, c. 11 Feb 1965; Col Van R. Parker, (by 26) Jul 1965–c. 30 Nov 1965; unkn, c. 1 Dec 1965–c. 31 Mar 1966; Col Van R. Parker, c. 1 Apr 1966; Col Richard D. Butler, 31 Aug 1966; Col Clyde R. Denniston, Jr., 18 Jul 1969; Col Donald G. Prieve, 8 Jan 1971; Col Richard N. Cody, 28 Feb 1972; Col Lawton W. Magee, 8 Aug 1972; Col Richard N. Cody, 17 Feb 1973; Col Lawton W. Magee, 9 Mar 1973; Col William A. Eveland, 26 Mar 1973; Col Lawton W. Magee, 7 Nov 1973; Col Curtis R. Smith, 9 Sep 1974; Col William M. Charles, Jr., 31 Aug 1977–.

Aircraft. B–29, 1952–1953; KC–97, 1952–1960; YRB–47, 1953–1954; B–47, 1953–1960. B–52, 1963–; KC–135, 1963–; T–29, 1973.

Operations. Replaced 106th Bombardment Wing, Medium, in Dec 1952. Conducted global bombardment training and air refueling operations to meet SAC commitments, 1952–1960. Trained B–47 cadre for 96th Bombardment Wing, Medium, Dec 1953–Jan 1955. Deployed as a wing to Brize Norton RAF Station, England, 5 Jun–4 Sep 1954, and Andersen AFB, Guam, 5 Oct 1956–11 Jan 1957. Replaced 4134th Strategic Wing in Feb 1963. Performed global bombardment training and air refueling operations to meet SAC commitments, Feb 1963–1965 and later. Entire wing drastically reduced Feb–Jul 1965, Dec 1965–Mar 1966, and Jun 1972–Oct 1973, when all aircraft, crews, and most support personnel loaned to other SAC units for operations in Southeast Asia. During the latter period, trained T–29 pilots for Fifteenth Air Force.

Service Streamers. None.

Campaign Streamers. None.

Decorations. Air Force Outstanding Unit Awards: 18 Jun–31 Jul 1965 and 1 Dec 1965–1 Mar 1966; 2 Mar–1 Apr 1966; 1 Jun 1974–30 Jun 1976.

Emblem. Azure, three four-pointed stars or, trimmed argent, in fess enhanced, per fess debased dovetailed, dark azure, lower edge of dovetail fimbriated sable, in base, a bomb with a burst of four points, point downwards gules. Crest: A torch sable, trimmed argent, flamant or and gules, winged or; the base of the torch superimposed over the chief of the shield. *Motto:* STRENGTH THROUGH AWARE-

NESS. (Originally approved on 23 Nov 1951 for 106th Bombardment Wing, Medium; officially transferred to 320th Wing, by mutual consent of both units, on 5 Dec 1952.)

321st STRATEGIC MISSILE WING

Lineage. Established as 321st Bombardment Wing, Medium, on 23 Mar 1953. Activated on 15 Dec 1953. Discontinued, and inactivated, on 25 Oct 1961. Redesignated 321st Strategic Missile Wing, and activated, on 14 Aug 1964. Organized on 1 Nov 1964.

Assignments. Second Air Force, 15 Dec 1953 (attached to Air Division Provisional, 813th, 11 Jun–14 Jul 1954); 813th Air Division, 15 Jul 1954 (attached to 7th Air Division, 9 Dec 1954–5 Mar 1955; 5th Air Division, 9 Apr–3 Jul 1956); Second Air Force, 1 Jun 1956; 6th Air Division, 1 Jan 1959; Eighth Air Force, 1 Feb 1959; 6th Air Division, 1 Jul 1959; 823d Air Division, 6 Feb–25 Oct 1961. Strategic Air Command, 14 Aug 1964; 4th Strategic Aerospace (later, 4th Strategic Missile; 4th Air) Division, 1 Nov 1964; 57th Air Division, 22 Jan 1975–.

Components. *Squadrons.* 307th Air Refueling: attached 28 Sep–8 Nov 1954. 321st Air Refueling: 8 Nov 1954–16 Sep 1956 (detached 16 Aug–16 Sep 1956). 445th: 15 Dec 1953–25 Oct 1961 (not operational, 15 Dec 1953–31 May 1954 and c. 15 Sep–25 Oct 1961). 446th: 15 Dec 1953–25 Oct 1961 (not operational, 15 Dec 1953–31 May 1954 and c. 15 Sep–25 Oct 1961); 1 Jul 1965–. 447th: 15 Dec 1953–25 Oct 1961 (not operational, 15 Dec 1953–31 May 1954); 1 Feb 1965–. 448th: 1 Feb 1954–25 Oct 1961 (not operational, 23 May–25 Oct 1961); 15 Sep 1965–.

Stations. Pinecastle (later, McCoy) AFB, Fla, 15 Dec 1953–25 Oct 1961. Grand Forks AFB, ND, 1 Nov 1964–.

Commanders. Nonc (not manned), 15 Dec 1953–24 May 1954; Col Michael N. M. McCoy, 24 May 1954 (additional duty), 1 Jun 1954 (permanent); Col William L. Gray, 9 Oct 1957; Col Robert W. Strong, Jr., 18 Oct 1957; Col Clifford V. Warden, 1 Jul 1959; Col Winton R. Close, 16 Jul 1959; Lt Col Harry F. Baker, 15 Sep–25 Oct 1961. None (not manned), 14 Aug–31 Oct 1964; Col Gilbert F. Friederichs, 1 Nov 1964; Col Jack D. Lander, 31 May 1967; Col Gerald G. Fall, Jr., 21 Jun 1967; Brig Gen Paul Krause, 23 May 1970; Col Oliver C. Fought, 31 Jul 1972; Brig Gen Paul Krause, 15 Sep 1972; Col Stuart H. Sherman, Jr., 8 Nov 1972; Brig Gen William L. Shields, Jr., 16 Feb 1974; Col Joe L. Church, 10 Mar 1976–.

Aircraft and Missiles. B–47, 1954–1961; KC–97, 1954–1956; C–124, 1959–1961. Minuteman II, 1965–1973; Minuteman III, 1972–.

Operations. Absorbed resources of 4042d Flying Training Wing in late

May 1954. Conducted global bombardment training and air refueling operations to meet SAC commitments, 1954–1961. Wing deployed at RAF Station Lakenheath, England, 9 Dec 1954–5 Mar 1955, and at Sidi Slimane AB, Morocco, 9 Apr–3 Jul 1956. On 11–12 Aug 1957, a wing B–47 flew nonstop from Andersen AFB, Guam, to Sidi Slimane AB, Morocco—a distance of 11,450 miles—in 22:50 hours, establishing a new flight record. Replaced by 4047th Strategic Wing in Oct 1961. Monitored Minuteman II ICBM facility construction, Nov 1964–Nov 1966. First Minuteman II missile assigned in Aug 1965 and first squadron completely equipped in Apr 1966. Wing operational with 150 Minuteman missiles in Nov 1966.

Service Streamers. None.

Campaign Streamers. None.

Decorations. Air Force Outstanding Unit Award: 1 Jul 1968–30 Jun 1969.

Emblem. Light blue, on a pile fimbriated gold between in base a wreath of laurel in dexter and a wreath of olive in sinister, each of eight leaves gold garnished brown, six stars three, two, gold and one white with a red disc in center; all within a diminished bordure gold. *Motto:* SKILL–PROFESSIONALISM–DETERMINATION. (Approved on 27 Dec 1965.)

322d BOMBARDMENT WING, TACTICAL

Lineage. Established as 322d Bombardment Wing, Tactical, on 23 Mar 1953.

Assignments. None.

Components. None.

Stations. None.

Commanders. None.

Aircraft. None.

Operations. Never made active.

Service Streamers. None.

Campaign Streamers. None.

Decorations. None.

Emblem. None.

322d TACTICAL AIRLIFT WING

Lineage. Established as 322d Tactical Airlift Wing on 21 Nov 1969. Activated on 1 Jan 1970. Inactivated on 30 Jun 1975.

Assignments. Seventeenth Air Force, 1 Jan 1970–30 Jun 1975.

Components. *Squadrons.* 7th Special Operations: 15 Mar 1973–30 Jun 1975. 32d: attached 15 Feb–15 Apr 1975. 36th: attached 1 Jan–2 Feb 1970, 10 Aug–21 Oct 1970, 29 Sep–29 Oct 1971 and 16 Aug–16 Oct 1974. 37th: attached 4 Oct–1 Nov 1970, 8 Feb–10 Apr 1971, 1 Sep–5 Oct 1972, 16 Apr–25 Jun 1974, and 15 Apr–15 Jun 1975. 38th: attached 16 Dec 1974–15 Feb 1975. 39th: attached 15 Dec 1973–12 Feb 1974. 40th: attached 1 Sep–5 Oct 1971 and 11 Apr–5 Jun 1973. 41st: attached 12 Jun–11 Aug 1972, 11 Feb–13 Apr 1973, and 11

Aug–12 Oct 1973. 47th: attached 18 Feb–18 Mar 1970, 16 Jun–10 Aug 1970, 8 Dec 1971–14 Feb 1972, 11 Aug–20 Oct 1972, and 16 Dec 1972–11 Feb 1973. 48th: attached 12 Apr–11 Jun 1972 and 20 Oct–16 Dec 1972. 50th: attached 1 Jun–15 Aug 1974. 55th Aeromedical Airlift: 1 Jan 1970–31 Mar 1975. 61st: attached 21 Oct–19 Dec 1970, 5 Jun–11 Aug 1973, 16 Oct–16 Dec 1974, and 15–30 Jun 1975. 62d: attached 10 Apr–12 Jun 1971. 347th: attached 2 Feb–13 Apr 1970, 12 Jun–12 Aug 1971, and 14 Feb–17 Apr 1972. 348th: attached 5 Oct–8 Dec 1971. 772d: attached 12 Feb–16 Apr 1974. 774th: attached 12 Oct–15 Dec 1973. 778th: attached 12 Aug–1 Sep 1971. 779th: attached 13 Apr–16 Jun 1970 and 19 Dec 1970–7 Feb 1971. 7406th Support (later, 7406th Operations): 15 Nov 1971–30 Jun 1974. *Flight.* 7111th Support (later, 7111th Operations): 1 Feb 1972–1 Feb 1975.

Stations. Rhein-Main AB, West Germany, 1 Jan 1970–30 Jun 1975.

Commanders. Col Wilbert Turk, 1 Jan 1970; Brig Gen Thomas M. Sadler, 30 Aug 1971; Col Cornelius Nugteren, 12 Feb 1974–30 Jun 1975.

Aircraft. Primarily C–118, 1970–1972; C–130, 1970–1975; C–131, 1970–1972; VC–118, 1971–1972; and C–9, 1972–1975. Also flew, in fewer numbers, KC–135, 1970–1974; C–47, 1970–1972, 1973; VC–54, 1970; T/VT–29, 1970–1975; C–135, 1972, 1974; UH–1, 1973; C–131, 1973–1975; and VC–131, 1973–1974.

Operations. Replaced 7310th TAW on 1 Jan 1970. From Jan 1970 to Jun 1975, used rotational C–130 squadrons for tactical airlift in Europe, North Africa, and the Middle East. Used C–118s and C–131s for aeromedical airlift until late 1972, then shifted to C–9As for this work. Continued aeromedical airlift operations through Mar 1975. Used KC–135 (VIP equipped) to provide transportation for CINCUSAFE until early 1973, followed by KC–135B until early 1974 and by C–135C thereafter. Used VT–29 aircraft to support Air Force North (AFNORTH), a NATO component. In Mar 1973, the wing gained the 7th Special Operations Squadron, equipped with C–47, UH–1H, and C–130E aircraft, all but the C–130s transferred a few months later, to conduct unconventional warfare operations in Europe. Wing replaced by 435th TAW in Jun 1975.

Service Streamers. None.

Campaign Streamers. None.

Decorations. None.

Emblem. Tierce per fess azure and or, five piles, three conjoined between two transposed counterchanged. *Motto:* RECTO FACIENDO NEMINEM TIMEO—I fear none in doing right. (Approved for 322d Group on 9 Jan 1943.)

323d FLYING TRAINING WING

Lineage. Established as 323d Bombardment Wing, Light, on 10 May 1949. Activated in the Reserve on 27 Jun 1949. Ordered to active service on 10 Mar 1951. Inactivated on 28 Mar 1951. Redesignated 323d Fighter-Bomber Wing on 9 May 1955. Activated on 8 Aug 1955. Inactivated on 1 Sep 1957. Redesignated 323d Flying Training Wing on 28 Jul 1972. Activated on 1 Apr 1973.

Assignments. Twelfth Air Force, 27 Jun 1949; Fourteenth Air Force, 1 Jul 1950–28 Mar 1951. Ninth Air Force, 8 Aug 1955–1 Sep 1957. Air Training Command, 1 Apr 1973–.

Components. *Groups.* 323d: 27 Jun 1949–17 Mar 1951; 8 Aug 1955–1 Sep 1957. 386th: attached 8 Apr 1956–9 Apr 1957. *Squadrons.* 449th: 1 Apr 1973–. 450th: 1 Apr 1973–. 451st: 1 Apr 1973–. 452d: 1 Apr 1973–. 453d: 1 Apr 1973–. 454th: 1 Apr 1973–. 455th: 1 Apr 1973–.

Stations. Tinker AFB, Okla, 27 Jun 1949–28 Mar 1951. Bunker Hill AFB, Ind, 8 Aug 1955–1 Sep 1957. Mather AFB, Calif, 1 Apr 1973–.

Commanders. Brig Gen W. C. Lewis, 27 Jun 1949; Col Clint T. Johnson, c. Aug 1950–Mar 1951. Col Carter E. Duncan, 8 Aug 1955; Col Bernard R. Muldoon, 21 Dec 1955; Col Joseph H. Moore, 14 Jul 1956; Col Billy Cornett, 22 Jul 1957; Col Henry J. Chisholm, 15 Aug–1 Sep 1957. Col Norris M. Overly, 1 Apr 1973; Brig Gen Robert W. Bazley, 13 Oct 1973; Col Dennis B. Sullivan, 18 Jul 1975; Col Attilio Pedroli, 13 Sep 1976–.

Aircraft. T–6, 1949–1951; T–11, 1949–1951; B–26, 1949–1951; T–7, 1950–1951. F–86, 1955–1957; F–100, 1956–1957. T–29, 1973–1975; ET–29, 1973–1974; T–43, 1973–; T–37, 1974–.

Operations. Trained in the organized Reserve, 1949–1951. Ordered to active service on 10 Mar 1951; personnel used as "fillers" to meet USAF world-wide requirements for strategic and tactical forces. Trained to become proficient in tactical operations as part of TAC, Mar 1956–May 1957. Phased down and replaced on 1 Sep 1957 by 4041st Air Base Group. Replaced, and absorbed resources of, the 3535th Navigator Training Wing in Apr 1973. Operated Mather AFB, Calif, published *Navigator* magazine, and conducted training for navigators, navigator-bombardiers, and electronic warfare officers, Apr 1973–. Conducted operational test and evaluation of the T–43A aircraft, 1 Aug–31 Oct 1973. Began converting to T–43s in 1973. As the only USAF school teaching navigation, the wing served not only the USAF but also the Air National Guard, Air Force Reserve, and friendly foreign states. Began training U.S. Navy and U.S. Coast Guard flight officers in Jul 1976 and supporting Marine Aerial Navigation School (which moved from Texas to Mather AFB) in Jul 1976, although the USMC conducted its own navigation training. Began training female navigators in Mar 1977.

Service Streamers. None.

Campaign Streamers. None.

Decorations. Air Force Outstanding Unit Awards: 1 Apr–31 Dec 1973; 1 Jan 1976–28 Feb 1977.

Emblem. Per pale azure and gules a globe arraswise light blue, grid lined argent within the arced envelopment of a pair of stylized wings in base, conjoined or garnished of the third, in dexter chief a mullet of five points argent, issuing from chief in sinister and surmounting the globe, a lightning bolt bend sinisterwise or, all within a diminished bordure of the like. (Approved on 25 Sep 1973.)

325TH FIGHTER WING (AIR DEFENSE)

Lineage. Established as 325th Fighter Wing, All Weather, on 10 May 1948. Activated on 9 Jun 1948. Redesignated: 325th Fighter-All Weather Wing on 20 Jan 1950; 325th Fighter-Interceptor Wing on 1 May 1951. Inactivated on 6 Feb 1952. Redesignated 325th Fighter Wing (Air Defense) on 14 Sep 1956. Activated on 18 Oct 1956. Discontinued, and inactivated, on 1 Jul 1968.

Assignments. Fourth Air Force, 9 Jun 1948 (attached to Western Air Defense Force, 10 Nov 1949–31 Jul 1950); Western Air Defense Force, 1 Aug 1950–6 Feb 1952. 25th Air Division (Defense) (later, 25th Air Division [SAGE]), 18 Oct 1956; Seattle Air Defense Sector, 10 Feb 1960; 25th Air Division, 1 Apr 1966–1 Jul 1968.

Components. *Wing*. 302d Troop Carrier: attached 6 May 1950–8 Jun 1951. *Group.* 325th: 9 Jun 1948–6 Feb 1952; 18 Oct 1956–25 Mar 1960 (not operational, 18 Oct 1956–c. Jun 1957). *Squadrons*. 4th Troop Carrier: attached 1 May–17 Jul 1950. 123d: attached 1 Feb 1951–6 Feb 1952. 317th Fighter-Interceptor: attached 18 Oct 1956–c. Jun 1957. 318th Fighter-Interceptor: attached 18 Oct 1956–c. Jun 1957; assigned 25 Mar 1960–1 Jul 1968. 498th Fighter-Interceptor: attached 18 Oct 1956–c. Jun 1957. 318th Fighter-Interceptor: attached 18 Oct 1956–c. Jun 1957; assigned 25 Mar 1960–1 Jul 1968. 498th Fighter-Interceptor: 1 Jul 1963–25 Jun 1966.

Stations. Hamilton AFB, Calif, 9 Jun 1948; Moses Lake AFB, Wash, 23 Nov 1948; McChord AFB, Wash, 20 Apr 1950–6 Feb 1952. McChord AFB, Wash, 18 Oct 1956–1 Jul 1968.

Commanders. Col George L. Usher, 9 Jun 1948–unkn; Col Harold E. Kofahl, (by Nov) 1948; Col Thomas A. Bennett, 26 Jul 1949; Col Phillip E. Tukey, Jr., 14 Nov 1951; Col Thomas A. Bennett, 26 Nov 1951–6 Feb 1952. Col Henry L. Crouch, Jr., 18 Oct 1956–unkn; Col James C. Stewart, (by Jun) 1957; Col Vernone L. Stintzi, 10 Jul 1957; Col Henry S. Tyler, Jr., 6 Jun 1958; Col Charles W. King, 8 Jul 1958; Col James F. Reed, 15 Feb 1960; Col Donavon F. Smith, 5 Dec 1960; Col Jack E. McKee, Jul 1962; Col Dean Davenport, 28 Jul 1962; Col Louis W. Ford, 3 Aug 1965; Col Harry L. Downing, 21 Oct 1966–1 Jul 1968.

Aircraft. F–61, 1948; F–82, 1948–1951; F–94, 1950–1952; C–54, 1950; F–51, 1951–1952. F–86, 1956–1957; F–102, 1956–1960; F–106, 1960–1968.

Operations. Air defense of the U.S. west coast. During 1950, controlled a troop carrier squadron and from 6 May 1950 to 8 Jun 1951, provided training for elements of a troop carrier wing. From 9 Feb to 1 Jul 1968, had a large detachment at Osan AB, South Korea, to provide air defense.

Service Streamers. None.

Campaign Streamers. None.

Decorations. Air Force Outstanding Unit Award: 1 Jan 1967–1 Mar 1968.

Emblem. Per fess, sable and azure, a fess arched, argent, upper line nebuly, overall a lightning flash or, issuing from dexter chief. *Motto:* LOCARE ET LIQUIDARE—Locate and liquidate. (Approved for 325th Group on 1 Oct 1951 and for 325th Wing on 5 Mar 1957.)

328th FIGHTER WING (AIR DEFENSE)

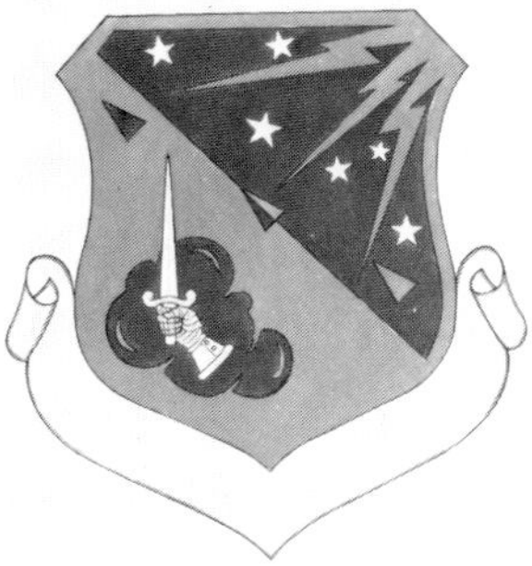

Lineage. Established as 328th Fighter Wing (Air Defense), and activated, on 28 Dec 1960. Organized on 1 Feb 1961. Discontinued, and inactivated, on 18 Jul 1968.

Assignments. Air Defense Command, 28 Dec 1960; Kansas City Air Defense Sector, 1 Feb 1961; Sioux City Air Defense Sector, 1 Jul 1961; 30th Air Division, 1 Apr 1966–18 Jul 1968.

Components. *Squadrons.* 71st Fighter-Interceptor: 16 Jan 1967–18 Jul 1968. 326th Fighter-Interceptor: 1 Feb 1961–2 Jan 1967.

Stations. Richards-Gebaur AFB, Mo, 1 Feb 1961–18 Jul 1968.

Commanders. None (not manned), 28 Dec 1960–31 Jan 1961; Col Jones E. Bolt, 1 Feb 1961; Col John W. Jacobs, Jr., 27 May 1961; Col Kenneth E. Rosebush, 25 Aug 1961; Col Joseph H. Belser, (by Jun) 1963; Col Donald H. Lynch, 19 Jul 1963; Col James T. Jarman, 15 Jul 1965; Col Ray A. Robinson, Jr., 1 Jul 1966; Col William F. Shaeffer, 19 Jul 1967–18 Jul 1968.

Aircraft. F–102, 1961–1966; F–106, 1967–1968.

Operations. Provided active air defense of a portion of the central United States. Maintained an air defense detachment at Homestead AFB, Fla, 19 Dec 1962–15 Feb 1963, and at Key West Naval Air Station, Fla, 1 Aug 1965–1 Jul 1966.

Service Streamers. None.

Campaign Streamers. None.

Decorations. None.

Emblem. Per bend azure and or, three delta-shaped projectiles bendwise respectively of the first, counterchanged and of the second between in chief a three-pronged lightning flash radiant from sinister chief of the last, the field stewn with stars argent, and in base a cloud of the first charged with a dexter gauntlet grasping a sword palewise over all proper, all within a diminished bordure gold. (Approved for 328th Group on 24 Nov 1958.)

330th TROOP CARRIER WING, MEDIUM

Lineage. Established as 330th Bombardment Wing, Medium, on 16 May 1949. Activated in the Reserve on 27 Jun 1949. Ordered to active service on 1 May 1951. Inactivated on 16 Jun 1951. Redesignated 330th Troop Carrier Wing, Medium, on 26 May 1952. Activated in the Reserve on 14 Jun 1952. Inactivated on 14 Jul 1952.

Assignments. Fourth Air Force, 27 Jun 1949; Strategic Air Command, 27 Jun 1949; Fifteenth Air Force, 27 Jun 1949–16 Jun 1951 (attached to 22d Bombardment Wing, Medium, 27 Jun 1949–30 Apr 1951; 12th Air Division, 1 May–16 Jun 1951). 1st Air Reserve District, 14 Jun–14 Jul 1952.

Components. *Group.* 330th: 27 Jun 1949–16 Jun 1951 (not operational, 1 May–16 Jun 1951); 14 Jun–14 Jul 1952.

Stations. March AFB, Calif, 27 Jun 1949–16 Jun 1951. Greater Pittsburgh Aprt, Pa, 14 Jun–14 Jul 1952.

Commanders. Col Duden, 27 Jun 1949–c. Mar 1950; unkn, c. Mar 1950–30 Apr 1951; none (not manned), 1 May–16 Jun 1951. Unkn, 14 Jun–14 Jul 1952.

Aircraft. B–29 (of 22d Bombardment Wing), 1950; T–6 and C–47 (of 22d Air Base Group), 1950–1951. Possibly C–46 (of 2253d Air Force Reserve Training Center), 1952.

Operations. Reserve training, 1949–1951.

Service Streamers. None.

Campaign Streamers. None.

Decorations. None.

Emblem. None.

332d FIGHTER WING

Lineage. Established as 332d Fighter Wing on 28 Jul 1947. Organized on 15 Aug 1947. Discontinued on 28 Aug 1948. Activated on 26 Aug 1948. Inactivated on 1 Jul 1949.

Assignments. Ninth Air Force, 15 Aug 1947–28 Aug 1948. Ninth Air Force, 26 Aug 1948–1 Jul 1949 (attached to First Air Force, 15 Jan–1 Feb 1949).

Components. *Group.* 332d: 15 Aug 1947–28 Aug 1948; 26 Aug 1948–1 Jul 1949.

Stations. Lockbourne AAB (later, AFB), Ohio, 15 Aug 1947–28 Aug 1948. Lockbourne AFB, Ohio, 26 Aug 1948–1 Jul 1949.

Commanders. Maj Edward C. Gleed, 15 Aug 1947; Col Benjamin O. Davis, Jr., 22 Aug 1947–28 Aug 1948. Col Benjamin O. Davis, Jr., 26 Aug 1948–1 Jul 1949.

Aircraft. P (later, F)–47, 1947–1948. F–47, 1948–1949.

Operations. Replaced 447th Composite Group and 580th Air Service Group in Jul 1947. Participated in firepower demonstrations, gunnery training, and operational missions to maintain combat proficiency, 1947–1948, and 1948–1949.

Service Streamers. None.

Campaign Streamers. None.

Decorations. None.

Emblem. Azure on a fess nebule or, a panther passant sable armed and incensed gules. Motto: SPIT FIRE. (Approved for 332d Group on 15 Jan 1943.)

340th BOMBARDMENT WING, HEAVY

Lineage. Established as 340th Bombardment Wing, Medium, on 3 Oct 1952. Activated on 20 Oct 1952. Redesignated 340th Bombardment Wing, Heavy, on 1 Sep 1963. Discontinued, and inactivated, on 2 Oct 1966.

Assignments. Second Air Force, 20 Oct 1952; Eighth Air Force, 1 Jul 1955 (attached to 7th Air Division, 13 Sep–3 Nov 1955); Second Air Force, 1 Jan 1959; 17th Air (later, 17th Strategic Aerospace) Division, 15 Jul 1959; 4th Air Division, 1 Sep 1963 (attached to 19th Air Division, c. 1–31 Aug 1964); 19th Air Division, 1 Sep 1964–2 Oct 1966.

Components. *Squadrons*. 34th Air Refueling: 1 Oct 1958–1 Oct 1959. 340th Air Refueling: 20 Oct 1952–1 Jul 1953 (detached); 18 Jan 1954–15 Oct 1962 (not operational, 18 Jan–Aug 1954; detached 29 Oct–31 Dec 1956, 25 Sep–28 Dec 1957, 5 Jan–9 Apr 1959, and 3 Jan–1 Apr 1961). 486th: 20 Oct 1952–2 Oct 1966 (not operational, 20 Oct 1952–Feb 1954). 487th: 20 Oct 1952–1 Sep 1963 (not operational, 20 Oct 1952–Feb 1954). 488th: 20 Oct 1952–1 Sep 1963 (not operational, 20 Oct 1952–Feb 1954). 489th: 1 Oct 1958–1 Jan 1962. 910th Air Refueling: 1 Sep 1963–2 Oct 1966.

Stations. Sedalia (later, Whiteman) AFB, Mo, 20 Oct 1952; Bergstrom AFB, Texas, 1 Sep 1963–2 Oct 1966.

Commanders. Lt Col Leonard S. Flo, 20 Oct 1952; Col Franklin K. Reyher, 18 Feb 1953; Col Chester C. Cox, 20 Nov 1953; Col Abe J. Beck, 2 Jul 1954; Col Robert T. Calhoun, 29 Jun 1957; Brig Gen Harold E. Humfeld, 23 Sep 1957; Col Robert T. Calhoun, c. 16 Jul 1959; Col George L. Newton, Jr., 1 Sep 1959; Col Willis F. Lewis, 1 May 1961; Col Carl G. Payne, 10 Jul 1963; Col Lowell B. Fisher, 13 Aug 1963; Col Frank P. Bender, 1 Sep 1963; Col Edwin H. Garrison, 16 Aug 1965; Col William Marchesi, 1 Jun–2 Oct 1966.

Aircraft. YRB–47, 1954–1956; B–47, 1954–1963; KC–97, 1954–1962; KC–135, 1959, 1963–1966; B–52, 1963–1966.

Operations. Replaced, and absorbed resources of, the 4224th Air Base Squadron in Oct 1952. Devoted to supervision of base rehabilitation and new construction until May 1954, through 340th Air Base Group. During this period, the wing headquarters, tactical and maintenance squadrons were minimum-manned "paper" units. Commenced initial tactical operations in Mar 1954. Phased down at Whiteman AFB, Mo, in mid-1963 and moved without personnel or equipment to Bergstrom AFB, Texas, absorbing resources and mission of former 4130th Strategic Wing. Continued global strategic bombardment training and air refueling operations until Oct 1966.

Service Streamers. None.

Campaign Streamers. None.

Decorations. None.

Emblem. A shield per fess nebuly, azure and argent, in chief two cloud formations proper, one issuing from the dexter and one issuing from the sinister, in base three stars of five points, of the first, two and one, all surmounted in fess, with an ear of wheat proper and a lightning flash, gules in saltire, an edge around the shield sable. *Motto:* ANYWHERE–ANYTIME. (Approved on 12 Sep 1955.)

341st STRATEGIC MISSILE WING (ICBM–MINUTEMAN)

Lineage. Established as 341st Bombardment Wing, Medium, on 23 Mar 1953. Activated on 1 Sep 1955. Discontinued, and inactivated, on 25 Jun 1961. Redesignated 341st Strategic Missile Wing (ICBM–Minuteman), and activated, on 1 Jul 1961. Organized on 15 Jul 1961.

Assignments. Fifteenth Air Force, 1 Sep 1955; 819th Air Division, 1 Feb 1956–25 Jun 1961 (attached to 3d Air Division, 9 Jan–c. 4 Apr 1958). Strategic Air Command, 1 Jul 1961; 22d Air Division, 15 Jul 1961; 821st Strategic Aerospace Division, 1 Jul 1962; 813th Strategic Aerospace Division, 1 Jul 1964; 18th Strategic Aerospace Division, 2 Jul 1966; 810th Strategic Aerospace Division, 2 Jul 1968; 4th Strategic Missile (later, 4th Air) Division, 30 Jun 1971; 47th Air Division, 15 Jan 1973–.

Components. *Squadrons.* 10th: 1 Sep 1955–25 Jun 1961; 1 Dec 1961–. 11th Air Refueling: 1 Dec 1955–1 Jun 1960 (detached 19 Dec 1956–10 Apr 1957, 9 Jan–c. 4 Apr 1958, and 10 Jul–26 Sep 1958). 12th: 1 Sep 1955–25 Jun 1961; 1 Mar 1962– (not operational, 1 Mar–c. 15 Jun 1962). 490th: 1 Sep 1955–25 Jun 1961; 1 May 1962– (not operational, 1 May–c. 15 Sep 1962). 491st: 1 Nov 1958–25 Jun 1961. 564th: 1 Apr 1966– (not operational, 1 Apr–c. Oct 1966).

Stations. Abilene (later, Dyess) AFB, Texas, 1 Sep 1955–25 Jun 1961. Malmstrom AFB, Mont, 15 Jul 1961–.

Commanders. Col Anthony J. Perna, 1 Sep 1955; Col Frank P. Sturdivant, c. 3 Dec 1955; Col Calvin E. Peeler, c. 31 Oct 1957; Col Anthony J. Perna, c. 1 Nov 1957; Col Jack W. Hayes, Jr., 9 Jun 1959; Col Ralph T. Holland, 3 Feb–25 Jun 1961. None (not manned), 1–14 Jul 1961; Col Burton C. Andrus, Jr., 15 Jul 1961; Brig Gen Lawrence S. Lightner, 20 Feb 1963; Col Rex Dowtin, 1 Jul 1964; Col Thomas F. Doyle, 3 Jun 1966;

Col John W. Carroll, 5 Jul 1966; Col Eugene J. Crahen, 13 Mar 1968; Brig Gen Gerald G. Fall, Jr., 27 May 1970; Brig Gen Kermit C. Kaericher, 7 Jun 1972; Col Ralph D. Scott, 7 Jun 1973; Col William R. Brooksher, 18 Jun 1975; Col Gerald E. McIlmoyle, 23 Jul 1976–.

Aircraft and Missiles. B–47, 1956–1961; KC–97, 1956–1960. Minuteman I, 1962–1969; Minuteman II, 1967–; Minuteman III, 1975–.

Operations. Performed strategic bombardment training operations on a global scale, Jan 1956–May 1961, and air refueling, Feb 1956–May 1960. Deployed at Andersen AFB, Guam, Jan –Apr 1958. Phased down for inactivation at Dyess AFB, Texas, Apr–Jun 1961. Replaced 4061st Air Refueling Wing in Jul 1961. Became USAF's first Minuteman ICBM wing. Supervised missile training and coordinated silo construction, Jul 1961–Jul 1963 and Oct 1964–May 1967. First missile squadron formed in Dec 1961. First Minuteman I missile arrived at Malmstrom on 23 Jul 1962; first missile emplaced in its silo on 17 Aug 1962. First missile on alert on 26 Oct 1962, and three squadrons became operational by early Jul 1963. A fourth squadron was added later, became combat ready in May 1967. Selected as SAC's "outstanding missile wing" for 1969.

Service Streamers. None.

Campaign Streamers. None.

Decorations. Air Force Outstanding Unit Awards: 22 Oct 1962–31 Dec 1963; 1 Jul 1975–30 Jun 1976; 1 Jul 1976 30 Jun 1977.

Emblem. On a shield per fess nebuly azure and argent, a semee of stars in chief of the last, overall in pale a sheathed sword proper, the rim of the sheath and winged hilt and pommel or; the blade entwined with a girdle of the last; the sword point downward between two bolts of lightning radiating upward gules; overall, in base a branch of olive vert, detail vein lines or. *Motto:* PAX ORBIS PER ARMA AERIA—World peace through air strength. (Approved on 5 Jun 1957.)

342d FIGHTER-DAY WING

Lineage. Established as 342d Fighter-Day Wing on 7 May 1956. Activated on 25 Jul 1956. Inactivated on 19 Nov 1956.

Assignments. Ninth Air Force, 25 Jul–19 Nov 1956.

Components. *Groups.* 342d: 25 Jul–19 Nov 1956. 455th: attached 25 Jul–19 Nov 1956.

Stations. Myrtle Beach AFB, SC, 25 Jul–19 Nov 1956.

Commanders. Col Robert G. Emmens, 25 Jul 1956; Col Francis S. Gabreski, 10 Sep–19 Nov 1956.

Aircraft. RF–80, 1956; T–33, 1956.

Operations. The wing activated in Jul 1956 when Myrtle Beach AFB, SC, was still in process of being reopened. During its short existence, the wing—which inherited a small cadre from the 4434th Air Base Squadron—endeavored to reach operational capability. Two tactical groups, each with three squadrons, were under wing control, but none of these squadrons achieved operational status before the wing inactivated.

Service Streamers. None.

Campaign Streamers. None.

Decorations. None.

Emblem. None.

345th BOMBARDMENT WING, TACTICAL

Lineage. Established as 345th Bombardment Wing, Tactical, on 23 Mar 1953. Activated on 8 Oct 1957. Inactivated on 25 Jun 1959.

Assignments. 836th Air Division, 8 Oct 1957–25 Jun 1959.

Components. *Squadrons.* 498th: 8 Oct 1957–25 Jun 1959 (detached 16 Jul–21 Oct 1958). 499th: 8 Oct 1957–25 Jun 1959 (detached 6 Sep–9 Dec 1958). 500th: 8 Oct 1957–25 Jun 1959 (not operational, 15–25 Jun 1959). 501st: 8 Oct 1957–25 Jun 1959 (not operational, 1–25 Jun 1959).

Stations. Langley AFB, Va, 8 Oct 1957–25 Jun 1959.

Commanders. Col Albert W. Satterwhite, 8 Oct 1957–25 Jun 1959.

Aircraft. B–57, 1957–1959.

Operations. Trained to maintain combat proficiency in locating, attacking, and destroying targets from all altitudes and under all conditions of weather and light.

Service Streamers. None.

Campaign Streamers. None.

Decorations. None.

Emblem. On a disc azure, an orle argent surmounting all the head, in profile, of an Apache, proper, wearing a feathered headdress of the second, with markings gules, and a string of animal's teeth of the second. *Motto:* AIR APACHES. (Approved for 345th Group on 21 May 1954 and for 345th Wing on 29 May 1958.)

347th TACTICAL FIGHTER WING

Lineage. Established as 347th Fighter Wing, All Weather, on 10 Aug 1948. Activated on 18 Aug 1948. Redesignated 347th Fighter-All Weather Wing on 20 Jan 1950. Inactivated on 24 Jun 1950. Redesignated 347th Tactical Fighter Wing, and activated, on 21 Dec 1967. Organized on 15 Jan 1968. Inactivated on 31 Oct 1972. Activated on 30 Jul 1973. Inactivated on 30 Jun 1975. Activated on 30 Sep 1975.

Assignments. 315th Air Division, 18 Aug 1948; Fifth Air Force, 1 Mar–24 Jun 1950. Pacific Air Forces, 21 Dec 1967; Fifth Air Force, 15 Jan 1968; Tactical Air Command, 15 May 1971; 832d Air Division, 15 May 1971–31 Oct

1972. Thirteenth Air Force, 30 Jul 1973–30 Jun 1975 (attached to Seventh Air Force, 30 Jul 1973–c. 14 Feb 1974; United States Support Activities Group/Seventh Air Force, c. 14 Feb 1974–30 Jun 1975). Ninth Air Force, 30 Sep 1975–.

Components. *Group.* 347th: 18 Aug 1948–24 Jun 1950. *Squadrons.* 34th: 15 Jan 1968–15 Mar 1971 (detached). 35th: 15 Jan 1968–15 Mar 1971 (detached 22 Mar–10 Jun 1968). 36th: 15 Jan 1968–15 May 1971. 68th: 30 Sep 1975–. 70th: 30 Sep 1975–. 80th: 15 Jan 1968–15 Mar 1971 (not operational, 15 Feb–15 Mar 1971). 339th: 30 Dec 1975– (not operational, 30 Dec 1975–4 May 1976). 389th: 15 Oct 1971–31 Oct 1972. 390th: 30 Jun–31 Oct 1972. 391st: 1 Jul 1971–31 Oct 1972. 428th: 30 Jul 1973–15 Jun 1975. 429th: 30 Jul 1973–21 Jun 1975. 556th Reconnaissance: 1 Jul 1968–15 May 1971. 4589th: 1 Sep–15 Oct 1971. 4590th: 1 Jan–30 Jun 1972. 6091st Reconnaissance: 15 Jan–1 Jul 1968.

Stations. Itazuke, Japan, 18 Aug 1948; Bofu Afld, Japan, 15 Oct 1948; Ashiya Afld (later, AB), Japan, 3 May 1949; Nagoya AB, Japan, 1 Apr–24 Jun 1950. Yokota AB, Japan, 15 Jan 1968–15 May 1971; Mountain Home AFB, Idaho, 15 May 1971–31 Oct 1972. Takhi RTAFB, Thailand, 30 Jul 1973; Korat RTAFB, Thailand, 12 Jul 1974–30 Jun 1975. Moody AFB, Ga, 30 Sep 1975–.

Commanders. Col Daniel A. Cooper, 18 Aug 1948; Col Robert D. McCarten, 21 Jan 1949; Col Daniel A. Cooper, 3 May 1949; Col Virgil L. Zoller, 23 Jun 1949; Col Walter C. White, 1 Apr–24 Jun 1950. None (not manned), 21 Dec 1967–14 Jan 1968; Col Paul P. Douglas, Jr., 15 Jan 1968; Col Allen K. McDonald, 23 Jan 1968; Col Thomas M. Carhart, 29 Jan 1968; Col Irby B. Jarvis, Jr., 3 Sep 1969; Col William L. Craig, 5 Jul 1970; Brig Gen Donald H. Ross, 15 Jul 1970; Brig Gen Henry L. Warren, 15 May 1971 (additional duty to 15 Jul 1971, in addition to commanding 67th TRW); Col Lynwood E. Clark, 10 Dec 1971–31 Oct 1972. Col Thomas E. Lacy, 30 Jul 1973; Col Cecil D. Crabb, 9 Mar 1974; Col Maurice E. Seaver, Jr., 21 Sep 1974; Col Russell E. Thoburn, 22 Mar 1975; Col James D. Covington, 21–30 Jun 1975. Col Robert L. Cass, 30 Sep 1975; Col Jack I. Gregory, 17 Aug 1976–.

Aircraft. F–51, 1948; F–61, 1948–1950; F–82, 1949–1950. F–105, 1968; F–4, 1968–1971; C–130, 1968–1971; EB–57, 1968–1971; RB–57, 1968; F–111, 1971–1972. F–111, 1973–1975. F–4, 1975–.

Operations. Air defense in Japan, Aug 1948–Mar 1950. Air defense in Japan and South Korea, plus aerial reconnaissance and contingency operations, Jan 1968–May 1971. Not operational, 15 May–14 Jul 1971. Proficiency training in F–111 aircraft, Jul 1971–Oct 1972. Combat operations in Cambodia, 30 Jul–15 Aug 1973, then maintained F–111As in Southeast Asia for possible contingency actions, Aug 1973–May 1975. Participated in numerous exercises, conducted firepower demonstrations, and, Jan–May 1975, flew sea surveillance missions. Participated in the recovery of the SS *Mayaguez*, an American merchant ship, from the Cambodians, 13–14 May 1975. Phased down and inactivated in Jun 1975. Replaced Det 1, 363d Combat Support Group (a holding organization) at Moody AFB,

Ga, in Sep 1973 and embarked on a training program to become combat ready in F–4E aircraft. Assumed responsibility for operating Moody AFB in Dec 1975. Became combat ready in Apr 1977 and deployed a force of 18 F–4s to Jever AB, West Germany, 17 May–7 Jun 1977.

Service Streamers. None.

Campaign Streamers. None.

Decorations. Air Force Outstanding Unit Award with Combat "V" Device: 30 Jul 1973–15 May 1975. Air Force Outstanding Unit Award: 15 Apr 1969–15 Apr 1971.

Emblem. Per bend argent and sable, on the first a silhouette of a knight in armor palewise, armed with a shield and lance all of the second, overall issuing from base in pale a demi-sphere checky of the first and of the second, supporting three knights (chess pieces) of the first mounted on a base of three arcs palewise or, gules and azure, all within a diminished bordure or. (Approved on 26 Mar 1967.)

349th MILITARY AIRLIFT WING (ASSOCIATE)

Lineage. Established as 349th Troop Carrier Wing, Medium, on 10 May 1949. Activated in the Reserve on 27 Jun 1949. Ordered to active service on 1 Apr 1951. Inactivated on 2 Apr 1951. Redesignated 349th Fighter-Bomber Wing on 26 May 1952. Activated in the Reserve on 13 Jun 1952. Redesignated 349th Troop Carrier Wing, Medium, on 1 Sep 1957. Ordered to active service on 28 Oct 1962. Relieved from active duty on 28 Nov 1962. Redesignated 349th Military Airlift Wing on 1 Jun 1966. Ordered to active service on 26 Jan 1968. Relieved from active duty on 1 Jun 1969. Redesignated 349th Military Airlift Wing (Associate) on 25 Jul 1969.

Assignments. Fourth Air Force, 27 Jun 1949–2 Apr 1951. 4th Air Reserve District, 13 Jun 1952; Fourth Air Force, 1 Dec 1952; Sixth Air Force Reserve Region, 1 Sep 1960; Twelfth Air Force, 28 Oct 1962; Sixth Air Force Reserve Region, 28 Nov 1962; Twenty-Second Air Force, 26 Jan 1968; Sixth Air Force Reserve Region, 2 Jun 1969 (attached to 60th Military Airlift Wing, 25 Jul 1969–); Western Air Force Reserve Region, 31 Dec 1969 (remained attached to 60th Military Airlift Wing); Fourth Air Force (Reserve), 8 Oct 1976– (remained attached to 60th Military Airlift Wing).

Components. *Groups*. 349th: 27 Jun 1949–2 Apr 1951; 13 Jun 1952–14 Apr 1959. 921st: 26 Jan 1968–2 Jun 1969 (not operational, 1 Aug 1968–1 Jun 1969). 938th: 11 Feb 1963–1 Jul 1973 (not operational, 29 Mar 1968–1 Jun 1969; detached 25 Jul–14 Dec 1969). 939th: 11 Feb 1963–26 Jan 1968; 15 Jun 1969–1 Jul 1973 (detached 25 Jul–14 Dec 1969). 940th: 11 Feb 1963–26 Jan

1968. 941st: 11 Feb 1963–25 Jul 1969 (not operational, 1 Aug 1968–21 May 1969). 944th: 25 Jul 1969–1 Jul 1973 (detached 25 Jul–14 Dec 1969). *Squadrons*. 67th: attached 1 Aug 1968–1 Jun 1969. 97th: 14 Apr 1959–11 Feb 1963; attached 1 Aug 1968–21 May 1969. 301st: 1 Jul 1973–. 312th: 14 Apr 1959–11 Feb 1963; attached 29 Mar 1968–1 Jun 1969; assigned 1 Jul 1973–. 313th: 14 Apr 1959–11 Feb 1963. 314th: 14 Apr 1959–11 Feb 1963. 708th: 1 Jul 1973–. 710th: 1 Jul 1973–. 733d: 28 Oct–28 Nov 1962. 8649th Replacement Training: attached 20 Aug 1954–6 Feb 1956.

Stations. Hamilton AFB, Calif, 27 Jun 1949–2 Apr 1951. Hamilton AFB, Calif, 13 Jun 1952; Travis AFB, Calif, 25 Jul 1969–.

Commanders. Brig Gen Franklin Rose, 27 Jun 1949–c. 2 Apr 1951. Brig Gen Harold P. Little, 13 Jun 1952; Brig Gen Rollin B. Moore, Jr., 10 Jan 1959; Col Jesse A. Irwin, 15 Jul 1968; Col Ray M. Foster, 25 Jul14 Dec 1969 (acting); Col Arthur C. Carroll, 15 Dec 1969; Col Billy C. Means, 8 Apr 1970; Brig Gen James L. Wade, 31 Dec 1973; Col Edward C. Black, Jr., 12 Jan 1976; Brig Gen Donald H. Balch, 1 Feb 1976–.

Aircraft. T–6, 1949–1950; T–7, 1949–1951; T–11, 1949–1951; C–46, 1949–1951. T–6, 1952–1954; C–46, 1952–1958; T–28, 1953–1956; F–51, 1953–1954; T–33, 1953–1957; F–80, 1953–1956; C–45, 1954–1956; C–47, 1955–1956; F–84, 1956–1957; C–119, 1958–1968; C–124, 1965–1969; C–141, 1969–; C–5, 1972–.

Operations. The 349th Wing has been ordered to active service three times. During the Korean war, the wing was called up and then inactivated, its personnel used as fillers in other wings. During the Cuban missile crisis of 1962, the wing served a month on active duty. The third mobilization followed the North Korean seizure of the USS *Pueblo* and lasted well over a year, during which time the wing airlifted vital cargo to the Far East, Southeast Asia, and points in Europe and the Middle East. The wing flew its own aircraft until becoming an associate wing in 1969; since then it has flown aircraft of the regular units with which it is associated. From 1969 to 1973, the wing and its components worked with Twenty-Second Air Force and the 60th, 62d, and 63d Military Airlift Wings. Since 1973 the wing has been associated only with the 60th MAW at Travis AFB, Calif.

Service Streamers. None.

Campaign Streamers. None.

Decorations. Air Force Outstanding Unit Awards: 23 Dec 1964–22 Jan 1965; 26 Jan 1968–1 Jun 1969; 1 Jul 1974–30 Jun 1975; 1 Jul 1975–30 Jun 1977. Republic of Vietnam Gallantry Cross with Palm: 1 Apr 1966–28 Jan 1973.

Emblem. Sable, abased a sphere light blue grid lined azure, surmounted by a wyvern with wings elevated and addorsed or, emitting three flames of the last, each within a puff of smoke argent, grasping in its dexter paw parachute straps of the last of a combat-ready paratrooper of the third and all within a diminished bordure of the fifth. *Motto:* IN OMNIA PARATUS—Prepared for all things. (Approved on 2 Sep 1960.)

351st STRATEGIC MISSILE WING (ICBM–MINUTEMAN)

Lineage. Established as 351st Strategic Missile Wing (ICBM–Minuteman), and activated, on 9 Aug 1962. Organized on 1 Feb 1963.

Assignments. Strategic Air Command, 9 Aug 1962; 17th Strategic Aerospace (later, 17th Strategic Missile; 17th Strategic Aerospace) Division, 1 Feb 1963; 4th Strategic Missile (later, 4th Air) Division, 30 Jun 1971; 40th Air Division, 1 Jul 1973–.

Components. *Squadrons.* 508th: 1 May 1963–. 509th: 1 Jun 1963–. 510th: 1 Jul 1963–.

Stations. Whiteman AFB, Mo, 1 Feb 1963–.

Commanders. None (not manned), 9 Aug 1962–31 Jan 1963; Col Harold D. Courtney, 1 Feb 1963; Col George T. Chadwell, 14 Dec 1963; Col James C. Adkins, 4 Oct 1966; Col George R. Brendle, 10 Oct 1966; Col William J. Grossmiller III, 30 Sep 1971; Col Charles W. Parker, 1 Jun 1973; Col William M. Kottas, 25 Jul 1974; Col Clifford D. Cork, 27 May 1976–.

Missiles. Minuteman I, 1964–1967; Minuteman II, 1966–.

Operations. Supervised missile training operations and coordinated construction of SM–80B (later, LGM–30B) Minuteman I missile facilities, 1 Feb 1963–29 Jun 1964. First missile arrived 14 Jan 1964 and was emplaced in its silo 2 days later. Last flight (of 15) accepted on 29 Jun 1964, giving the wing 150 fully operational missiles. The 508th SMS became combat-ready on 5 Jun, the 509th SMS on 10 Jun, and the 510th SMS on 29 Jun 1964. Meanwhile, as the 340th Bombardment Wing phased down for inactivation, the 351st SMW gradually assumed host-wing responsibility at Whiteman AFB, Mo, between 15 Jul and 1 Sep 1963. Won the Colonel Lee R. Williams Memorial Missile Trophy for Calendar Years 1965, 1967, and 1973. Converted to LGM–30F Minuteman II missiles between 7 May 1966 and 3 Oct 1967. Won the SAC missile combat competitions and Blanchard Trophy in 1967, 1971, and 1977. Named as SAC's "best Minuteman wing" in 1972.

Service Streamers. None.

Campaign Streamers. None.

Decorations. Air Force Outstanding Unit Awards: 1 Jul 1965–30 Jun 1966; 1 Jul 1967–30 Jun 1968; 1 Jul 1969–30 Jun 1971.

Emblem. Azure, issuant from sinister base a demisphere with axis bendwise or, rimmed and grid lined sable, surmounted by three spires bendwise gules and of the third, in chief a lightning bolt bend sinisterwise of the fourth, and in dexter flank an arched olive branch vert, all within a diminished bordure of the second. *Motto:* SENTINELS OF PEACE. (Approved on 7 Feb 1964.)

354th TACTICAL FIGHTER WING

Lineage. Established as 354th Fighter-Day Wing on 26 Sep 1956. Activated on 19 Nov 1956. Redesignated 354th Tactical Fighter Wing on 1 Jul 1958.

Assignments. Ninth Air Force, 19 Nov 1956; Twelfth Air Force, 1 Jul 1960; Ninth Air Force, 1 Jan 1962; 833d Air Division, 1 Oct 1964; Fifth Air Force, 5 Jul 1968 (attached to 4th Tactical Fighter Wing, 5–24 Jul 1968; Detachment 1, HQ Fifth Air Force [Fifth Air Force ADVON], 25 Jul 1968–14 Jun 1970); Ninth Air Force, 15 Jun 1970– (attached [as HQ 354th TFW (Advanced)] to Thirteenth Air Force, and further attached for control to Seventh Air Force, 14 Oct 1972–18 May 1974).

Components. *Groups*. 354th: 19 Nov 1956–25 Sep 1957. 455th: attached 19 Nov 1956–1 Jul 1957 (not operational, 1 Apr–1 Jul 1957). *Squadrons*. 16th: attached 29 May–14 Jun 1970. 20th Helicopter: 16 Jul 1959–8 Mar 1960. 68th: attached 20 Jun–9 Dec 1969. 74th: attached 5 Jul–28 Dec 1973. 127th: 5 Jul 1968–10 Jun 1969. 166th: 5 Jul 1968–10 Jun 1969. 334th: attached 16 Dec 1969–31 May 1970. 335th: attached 8 Dec 1969–23 May 1970. 352d: 25 Sep 1957–15 Aug 1966 (detached 16 Jul–26 Oct 1958, 14–23 Apr 1959, 12 Jan–14 May 1960, 30 Nov–5 Dec 1960, 15 Feb–4 Mar 1961, 14 Nov 1961–11 Mar 1962, 21 Oct–1 Dec 1962, 14 Jan–21 Apr 1963, 7–18 May 1963, 30 Jun–18 Sep 1963, 10 Dec 1963–12 Mar 1964, 20 Nov 1964–18 Mar 1965, and 14 Jul–13 Aug 1965). 353d: 25 Sep 1957–27 Apr 1966 (detached c. 9 Sep 1958–20 Feb 1959, 8–12 Jul 1959, 14 Sep 1959–19 Jan 1960, 15 Jul–16 Nov 1961, 8 Oct 1962–20 Jan 1963, 15 Sep–16 Dec 1963, 25 Aug–4 Dec 1964, 2–28 May 1965, 14 Jul–13 Aug 1965, and 25 Aug–6 Dec 1965); 15 Jul 1971–. 354th: attached 14 Jan–5 Jul 1973. 355th: 25 Sep 1957–22 Apr 1968 (detached 15 Jul–26 Oct 1958, 19 May–17 Sep 1959, 10 Sep 1960–16 Jan 1961, 5 Sep–19 Nov 1961, 7 Jul–14 Oct 1962, 21 Oct–1 Dec 1962, 6–20 Feb 1963, 3 Jul–17 Sep 1963, 8–15 Jun 1964, 15 Jun–28 Aug 1964, 2 Jul–25 Sep 1965, 4 Dec 1965–23 Apr 1966, and 3 Feb–22 Apr 1968); 1 Nov 1970–. 356th: 25 Sep 1957–29 Nov 1965 (detached 17 Jan–18 May 1959, 10 Oct–13 Nov 1959, 1 May–14 Sep 1960, 9–17 Jun 1961, 5 Mar–11 Jul 1962, 21 Oct–1 Dec 1962, 7 Apr–5 Jul 1963, 27 Oct–24 Nov 1963, 3 Mar–18 Jun 1964, 16 Mar–8 Jul 1965, and 14 Jul–13 Aug 1965); 15 May 1971– (detached 7 Sep–14 Nov 1974 and 30 Aug–22 Sep 1976). 358th: attached 28 Dec 1973–15 May 1974. 478th: attached 21 May–14 Jun 1970. 511th: 15 Jun 1970–15 Jul 1971 (not operational, 15 Jun–c. 8 Sep 1970). 560th: attached 23 Jun–17 Dec 1969. 4430th Combat Crew Training: 15 Jun 1970–31 Jul 1972. 4456th: 15 Jan–15 May 1971. 4554th Tactical

Fighter Replacement: 15 May 1972–15 Oct 1975 (not operational, 13 Sep–15 Oct 1975).

Stations. Myrtle Beach AFB, SC, 19 Nov 1956–2 Jul 1968; Kunsan AB, South Korea, 2 Jul 1968–14 Jun 1970; Myrtle Beach AFB, SC, 15 Jun 1970–.

Commanders. Col Francis S. Gabreski, 19 Nov 1956; Col Robert L. Petit, 13 Jul 1960; Brig Gen Gilbert L. Meyers, 3 Oct 1960; Col Joseph J. Kruzel, 1 Apr 1963; Col Franklin H. Scott, 12 Jan 1964; Col Herbert E. Ross, 15 May 1965; Col Harold L. Price, 27 Jul 1965; Col Warren R. Lewis, 29 Oct 1966; Col Edwin A. Schneider, 28 Nov 1966; Col William I. Williams, 1 May 1967; Col Wallace C. Bosworth, Jr., 19 Mar 1968; Col Waring W. Wilson, 22 Apr–2 Jul 1968 (additional duty); none (not manned), 3–4 Jul 1968; Col Donald W. Forney, 5 Jul 1968; Col Henry W. Ritter, 5 Jun 1969; Col Maurice G. Long, 14 Jun 1969; Col Albert R. Neville, Jr., 12 Jul 1969; Col Henry L. Warren, 25 Jan 1970; Col Evan W. Rosencrans, 15 Jun 1970; Col Thomas M. Knoles III, 21 Jun 1971; Col William D. Curry, Jr., 1 May 1973; Col Michael G. Filliman, 25 Oct 1974; Col Robert H. Reed, 5 Aug 1976–.

Aircraft. RF–80, 1956–1957; F–100, 1957–1969; H–21, 1959–1960; F–4, 1969–1970; T/AT–33, 1970–1972; A–7, 1970–1977; A–10, 1977–.

Operations. Replaced the 342d Fighter-Day Wing in Nov 1956. Switched from fighter-day to fighter-bomber training in Jul 1958. From Jul 1958 through Apr 1966, had one or more squadrons constantly deployed overseas. During the Cuban missile crisis of 1962, part of the wing manned a provisional air division at McCoy AFB, Fla. During the Dominican Republic crisis of 1965, the 354th deployed over 400 people and 18 F–100s to Ramey AFB, PR, and San Isidro AB, Dominican Republic. The conflict in Southeast Asia drained wing strength; one squadron moved to Japan in Nov 1965, another to Spain in Apr 1966, and another to South Vietnam in Aug 1966, leaving the wing with a single flying unit. This last squadron moved to South Vietnam in Apr 1968. The mobilized ANG 113th TFW moved to Myrtle Beach AFB, SC, in Apr 1968, absorbing resources of the 354th. The 354th had no units and existed primarily on paper until it moved to South Korea in early Jul 1968 to replace the 4th TFW. There, it was remanned primarily by ANG people on active duty under 4th TFW control. When the 4th TFW departed, the 354th assumed active F–100 operations. Its two ANG squadrons returned to the United States in Jun 1969, and for 10 days in South Korea the wing was again without tactical components. Several rotational squadrons provided needed tactical force after this brief lapse. On 14 Jun 1970, the 354th passed its resources to the 54th TFW and returned to the United States without personnel or equipment, absorbing resources of the 4554th TFW at Myrtle Beach AFB. Charged with T/AT–33 combat crew training and with becoming proficient with A–7 aircraft, on 10 Oct 1972 the wing split into Advance and Rear echelons, both under the wing commander, with each echelon having a designated commander. The Advance element moved to Thailand and commenced combat operations in Southeast Asia on 16 Oct 1972. The split-wing status continued until 23 May 1974;

during this period tactical units rotated between Thailand and the United States. Recombined at Myrtle Beach, the 354th continued routine A–7 operations until 1977, when it converted to A–10 aircraft.

Service Streamers. None.

Campaign Streamers. Vietnam Ceasefire.

Decorations. Presidential Unit Citation (Southeast Asia): 10 Oct 1972–30 Apr 1973. Air Force Outstanding Unit Awards: 1 Oct 1962–31 Dec 1963; 15 Jun 1970–31 May 1972; 1 May 1974–30 Apr 1976.

Emblem. Argent, four bendlets azure, or, vert, and gules between a demi-horse rampant of the last and two swords saltirewise proper grip and guard of the second fimbriated or. *Motto:* VALOR IN COMBAT. (Approved on 1 Jun 1971.)

355th TACTICAL FIGHTER WING

Lineage. Established as 355th Tactical Fighter Wing, and activated, on 13 Apr 1962. Organized on 8 Jul 1962. Inactivated on 10 Dec 1970. Activated on 1 Jul 1971.

Assignments. Tactical Air Command, 13 Apr 1962; 831st Air Division, 8 Jul 1962; 835th Air Division, 21 Jul 1964; Thirteenth Air Force, 8 Nov 1965–10 Dec 1970 (attached to 2d Air Division, 8 Nov 1965–31 Mar 1966; Seventh Air Force, 1 Apr 1966–10 Dec 1970). Twelfth Air Force, 1 Jul 1971; Ninth Air Force, 1 Jul 1976; Tactical Training, Davis-Monthan, 1 Apr 1977–.

Components. *Wing.* 4453d Combat Crew Training: attached 1 Jul–30 Sep 1971. *Squadrons.* 11th Tactical Drone: 1 Jul 1971–1 Jul 1976. 35th: attached 8–c. 9 Nov 1965. 40th: 1 Oct 1971–1 Jun 1972. 41st Tactical Reconnaissance (later, 41st Tactical Electronic Warfare): attached 8 Nov 1965–18 Sep 1966 and 8–14 Aug 1967, assigned 15 Aug 1967–31 Oct 1969. 42d Tactical Electronic Warfare: 1 Jan 1968–15 Oct 1970 (detached c. 23 Sep–15 Oct 1970). 44th: 15 Oct 1969–10 Dec 1970. 333d Tactical Fighter (later, 333d Tactical Fighter Training): 4 Dec 1965–10 Dec 1970; 31 Jul 1971–. 334th: attached 8 Nov 1965–5 Feb 1966. 335th: attached 8 Nov–6 Dec 1965. 354th: 8 Jul 1962–8 Nov 1965 (detached 24 Jan–21 Feb 1964, 2 May–c. 20 Sep 1964, 3 Mar–12 Jun 1965); 27 Nov 1965–10 Dec 1970; 1 Jul 1971– (detached 12 Jan–5 Jul 1973). 357th Tactical Fighter (later, 357th Tactical Fighter Training): 8 Jul 1962–8 Nov 1965 (detached 9 Aug–12 Dec 1964, 12 Jun–8 Nov 1965); 29 Jan 1966–10 Dec 1970; 1 Jul 1971–. 358th Tactical Fighter (later, 358th Tactical Fighter Training): 1 Jun 1972– (detached 28 Dec 1973–15 May 1974). 421st: 8 Jul 1962–8 Nov 1965 (not operational, 8 Jul 1962–c. Feb 1963; detached 15 Sep–23 Nov 1964, 7 Apr–20 Aug 1965). 469th: 8 Jul 1962–8 Nov

1965 (not operational, 8 Jul 1962–c. Oct 1963; detached 30 Nov 1964–13 Mar 1965). 562d: attached 8 Nov–c. 4 Dec 1965. 4455th Combat Crew Training: attached 1–8 Oct 1971. 6460th Tactical Reconnaissance (later, 6460th Tactical Electronic Warfare): attached 8 Jun–18 Sep 1966 and 8–14 Aug 1967, assigned 15 Aug 1967–1 Jan 1968.

Stations. George AFB, Calif, 8 Jul 1962; McConnell AFB, Kans, 21 Jul 1964–Oct 1965; Takhli RTAFB, Thailand, 8 Nov 1965–10 Dec 1970. Davis-Monthan AFB, Ariz, 1 Jul 1971–.

Commanders. None (not manned), 13 Apr–7 Jul 1962; Lt Col Adrian E. Drew, c. 8 Jul 1962; Col Olin E. Gilbert, 12 Jul 1962; Col Paul E. Adams, 20 Jul 1963; Col Edward A. McGough III, 3 Sep 1963; Col William H. Holt, 2 Aug 1965; Col Robert R. Scott, 4 Aug 1966; Col John C. Giraudo, 2 Aug 1967; Col Michael C. Horgan, 30 Jun 1968; Col Heath Bottomly, 27 Jun 1969; Col Clarence E. Anderson, Jr., 22 Jun–10 Dec 1970. Col John F. Barnes, 1 Jul 1971; Col Fred A. Haeffner, 23 Aug 1972; Col William J. Hosmer, 19 Jul 1974; Col Alonzo L. Ferguson, 30 Jan 1976; Brig Gen William D. Curry, Jr., 16 Aug 1976; Col Alonzo L. Ferguson, 1 Apr 1977; Col Ralph E. Adams, 11 Jul 1977–.

Aircraft. Primarily F–105, 1962–1970; and EB–66, 1967–1970; but also included RB–66, 1965–1966; EB–66, 1966; and F–111, 1968. F–4, 1971; A–7, 1971–; DC–130, 1971–1976; AQM–34 (drone), 1971–1976; CH–3, 1972–1976; BGM–34 (drone), c. 1974–1975; RC–130, c. 1975–1976; A–10, 1976–.

Operations. Trained in tactical fighter operations, Jul 1962–Nov 1965, and deployed tactical squadrons overseas as required, primarily to combat duty in Southeast Asia. Moved to Thailand in Nov 1965 and performed combat in Southeast Asia, 8 Nov 1965–6 Oct 1970, including air-to-air combat, strike missions, armed reconnaissance, close air support and electronic warfare. Had operational control of an F–111 detachment of the 428th Tactical Fighter Squadron, 17 Mar–19 Nov 1968. Began phasing down for inactivation on 7 Oct 1970. Final aircraft departed 10 Nov and wing inactivated in place on 10 Dec. Replaced the 4453d Combat Crew Training Wing at Davis-Monthan AFB, Ariz, in Jul 1971. That wing and the 355th shared commanders and staff through 30 Sep 1971, and built up the 355th as an A–7D unit while phasing down the 4453d as a F–4C unit. Ended F–4 training in mid-Oct 1971. Began training with A–7Ds in a close air support role in Jul 1971. Conducted tactical drone reconnaissance operations, Jul 1971–Jun 1976. Became combat ready with A–7s and 22 Aug 1972. Participated in numerous tactical exercises in the United States and overseas. Trained A–7 pilots for other USAF units. Maintained an A–7 detachment at Howard AFB, CZ, 15 Nov 1972–1 Feb 1974. Augmented an advanced echelon of the 354th TFW at Korat RTAFB, Thailand, Oct 1972–Jul 1973 and Dec 1973–May 1974. Began preparations early in 1975 for conversion to A–10s, and received first of these close air support aircraft in Mar 1976. Conducted A–10 pilot training and supported a follow-on test and evaluation of the aircraft system, beginning 25 Aug 1976. Served as host wing at home base, 30 Sep 1976–31 Mar 1977.

Service Streamers. None.

Campaign Streamers. Vietnam Defense; Vietnam Air; Vietnam Air Offensive; Vietnam Air Offensive, Phase II; Vietnam Air Offensive, Phase III; Vietnam Air/Ground; Vietnam Air Offensive, Phase IV; TET 69/Counteroffensive; Vietnam Summer–Fall, 1969; Vietnam Winter–Spring, 1970; Sanctuary Counteroffensive; Southwest Monsoon; Commando Hunt V.

Decorations. Presidential Unit Citations (Vietnam): 1 Jan–10 Oct 1966; 11–12 Aug and 24–28 Oct 1967; 12 Apr 1968–30 Apr 1969. Air Force Outstanding Unit Awards with Combat "V" Device: 12 Oct 1966–11 Apr 1967; 12 Apr 1967–11 Apr 1968; 1 Jul 1969–24 Nov 1970. Air Force Outstanding Unit Award: 1 Jul 1971–1 Jun 1973. Republic of Vietnam Gallantry Cross with Palm: 22 Apr 1966–10 Dec 1970.

Emblem: Azure on a pile issuant from sinister throughout or, flames of fire proper charged with a dagger fesswise point to dexter of the second. *Motto:* OUR MIGHT ALWAYS. (Approved on 16 Mar 1943 for 355th Fighter Group; used by wing, in slightly altered format since Jul 1962.)

360th STRATEGIC FIGHTER WING

Lineage. Established as 360th Strategic Fighter Wing on 23 Mar 1953.

Assignments. None.

Components. None.

Stations. None

Commanders. None

Aircraft. None.

Operations. Never made active.

Service Streamers. None

Campaign Streamers. None.

Decorations. None.

Emblem. None.

363d TACTICAL RECONNAISSANCE WING

Lineage. Established as 363d Reconnaissance Wing on 29 Jul 1947. Organized on 15 Aug 1947. Discontinued on 27 Aug 1948. Redesignated 363d Tactical Reconnaissance Wing, and activated on 27 Aug 1948. Inactivated on 26 Apr 1949. Activated on 1 Sep 1950.

Assignments. Ninth Air Force, 15 Aug 1947–27 Aug 1948. Ninth Air Force, 27 Aug 1948–26 Apr 1949 (attached to First Air Force, 15 Jan–1 Feb 1949). Tactical Air Command, 1 Sep 1950; Ninth Air Force, 2 Apr 1951; Tactical Air Division Provisional, 25 Apr 1951; Ninth Air Force, 11 Oct 1951 (attached to Twenty-Ninth Air Force [Tactical] [Provisional], 31 Oct–10 Dec 1955); 837th Air Division, 8 Feb 1958; USAF Tactical Air Reconnaissance Center, 1 Feb 1963; Ninth Air Force, 15

Jul 1963; 833d Air Division, 1 Oct 1964; Ninth Air Force, 24 Dec 1969–.

Components. *Groups*. 363d: 15 Aug 1947–27 Aug 1948; 27 Aug 1948–26 Apr 1949; 1 Sep 1950–8 Feb 1958 (detached 25 Apr–10 Oct 1951). 432d: attached 18 Mar 1954–30 Oct 1955; attached 10 Dec 1955–8 Feb 1958. 4402d Tactical Training: 1 Jul 1966–20 Jan 1968. 4403d Tactical Training: 1 Jul 1966–20 Jan 1968. *Squadrons*. 2d Liaison: attached 22 Jul 1952–18 Jun 1954. 9th: 8 Feb 1958–1 Jul 1966; 1 Feb 1967–1 Sep 1969 (not operational). 10th Fighter-Interceptor: attached 11 Sep–1 Dec 1950. 16th: 8 Feb 1958–27 Oct 1965; 15 Feb 1971–. 18th: 30 Jan 1970– (detached 12–29 Apr 1977). 19th: attached 20 Jul 1953–7 May 1954; assigned 1 Sep 1966–1 Feb 1967; assigned 20 Jan–31 Dec 1968. 20th: attached 8 Apr–17 May 1959, assigned 18 May 1959–12 Nov 1965. 22d: 15 Jul–15 Oct 1971. 29th: attached 8 Apr–17 May 1959, assigned 18 May 1959–1 Jul 1966; assigned 20 Jan 1968–24 Jan 1971. 31st Tactical Reconnaissance Training: 15 Oct 1969–18 Feb 1971. 33d Tactical Reconnaissance Training: 15 Oct 1969–. 39th Tactical Reconnaissance Training (later, 39th Tactical Electronic Warfare Training): 15 Oct 1969–15 Mar 1974. 41st: 8 Feb 1958–18 May 1959; 1 Oct–20 Nov 1965. 43d: 8 Feb 1958–18 May 1959 (detached c. 1 Feb–7 Apr 1959). 62d: 15 Oct 1971– (detached 5–24 Mar 1976). 72d Liaison: attached 9 Mar–1 Apr 1949. 84th Bombardment: attached 1 Sep 1950–12 Mar 1951. 85th Bombardment: attached 1 Sep 1950–12 Mar 1951. 165th: attached 25 Mar–3 May 1968. 2215th (later, 4400th) Combat Crew Training: attached 1 Sep 1950–12 Mar 1951. 4414th Combat Crew Training: 20 Jan 1968–15 Oct 1969. 4415th Combat Crew Training: 1 Feb 1967–15 Oct 1969. 4416th Test: 1 Jul 1966–1 Jul 1967. 4417th Combat Crew Training: 1 Jul 1966–1 Feb 1967; 20 Jan 1968–15 Oct 1969. 4426th Reconnaissance Crew Training: attached 9 Jan–1 Jun 1952. *Flights*. 2d Liaison: attached 1 Sep 1950–2 Feb 1951. 4415th Liaison: attached c. 16 Nov 1948–unkn 1949. *Detachments*. Det 1, 5th Helicopter Flight: attached 1 Sep 1950–12 Mar 1951. Det 001, HQ 363d Tactical Reconnaissance Wing: c. 26 Jan–31 Dec 1968 (detached).

Stations. Langley Field (later, AFB), Va, 15 Aug 1947–27 Aug 1948. Langley AFB, Va, 27 Aug 1948–26 Apr 1949. Langley AFB, Va, 1 Sep 1950–12 Mar 1951; Shaw AFB, SC, 2 Apr 1951–.

Commanders. Col Robert W. C. Wimsatt, 15 Aug 1947–27 Aug 1948. Col Robert W. C. Wimsatt, 27 Aug 1948–26 Apr 1949. Col Willis F. Chapman, 1 Sep 1950; Lt Col Harvey J. Watkins, 12 Mar 1951; Lt Col Victor N. Cabas, 13 Mar 1951; Col John R. Dyas, c. 2 Apr–24 Apr 1951; none (not manned), 25 Apr–10 Oct 1951; Col John R. Dyas, 11 Oct 1951; Col Richard A. Knobloch, 14 Jul 1954; Col Gene H. Tibbets, 17 Jul 1954; Brig Gen Stephen B. Mack, 4 Jun 1955; Col Derwood K. Smith, 8 Feb 1958; Col Thomas D. Brown, 25 Aug 1958; Brig Gen Thomas R. Ford, 5 Jun 1959; Col John D. Bridges, 21 Jul 1959; Col Franklin A. Nichols, 15 Jun 1961; Col Arthur A. McCartan, 1 Sep 1961; Col Arthur D. Thomas, 19 Aug 1963; Col Victor N. Cabas, 25 Jun 1965; Col Leslie J. Westburg, 5 Aug 1967; Col Allan T. Sampson, 23 Jun 1968; Brig Gen Kendell S. Young, 15 Jul 1968; Col Erwin A.

Hesse, 14 Jun 1969; Col Richard B. Collins, 16 May 1970; Col Philip V. Howell, Jr., 10 Jun 1971; Col Mark A. Welsh, Jr., 26 Jun 1972; Col William J. Bally, Jr., 25 Oct 1972; Col Rolland G. Hull, 2 Aug 1974; Col Albert G. Rogers, 28 Mar 1976; Col Paul A. Henkel, 12 Aug 1977–.

Aircraft. FP (later, RF)–80 and FA (later, RB)–26, 1947–1948. Primarily RF–80 and RB–26, 1948–1949; but also included F–6, 1948; H–5, 1949; and L–5, 1949. Primarily B–26, 1950–1951, 1951–1952; B–45, 1950–1951; RB–26, 1951, 1951–1957; RF–80, 1951, 1951–1955; B–25, 1952–1954; RB–45, 1954; RB–57, 1954–1956; RF–84, 1954–1958; RT–33, 1955–1956; WT–33, 1955–1956; RB–66, 1956–1969; WB–66, 1957–1964, 1968–1969; RF–101, 1957–1958, 1959–1971; RF–4, 1965–; and EB–66, 1966–1974; but also included, in fewer numbers: RB–26, 1950–1951; F–84, 1951; L–13, 1951–1954; L–20, 1951–1954; T–33, 1951–1955; TB–25, 1956–1958; TF–101, 1966–1969; and B–57, 1971–1976.

Operations. Provided day and night visual and photographic reconnaissance, 1947–1948 and again, 1948–1949. Besides performing tactical electronic and photographic reconnaissance, Sep 1950–Apr 1951, controlled light bombardment and provided B–26 crew replacement training. Wing headquarters was not operational, 25 Apr–10 Oct 1951. (During this period, all headquarters personnel were integrated into the Tactical Air Division Provisional, which directly controlled all wing components.) Regained wing integrity on 11 Oct 1951. Provided tactical reconnaissance from Oct 1951, also provided electronic reconnaissance, Nov 1953–Feb 1974, and weather reconnaissance, Nov 1953–Dec 1964. Provided combat crew training for reconnaissance crews, Oct 1951–Dec 1954 and Apr 1956–Apr 1959. Deployed aircraft and crews in small detachments, or as part of composite squadrons to support overseas reconnaissance needs. Deployed at Langley AFB, Va, 1 Jun–1 Oct 1959, and at MacDill AFB, Fla, 21 Oct–30 Nov 1962. From MacDill, played a major reconnaissance role during the Cuban missile crisis of 1962 and received an Air Force Outstanding Unit Award presented personally by President John F. Kennedy. Performed a major reconnaissance role during the Dominican Republic crisis of 1965–1966. Supported U.S. operations in Southeast Asia in the 1960s and early 1970s by deploying numerous detachments and transferring several highly trained squadrons to that area. Provided replacement training of tactical reconnaissance and tactical electronic warfare crews, and combat crew training, beginning Jan 1966. Flew many test projects for the Tactical Air Reconnaissance Center, 1966–1967 and 1970–1971. Deployed a detachment of EB–66s to the Far East during the *Pueblo* crisis of 1968. Also rotated EB–66 crews to Southeast Asia, 1972–1973. The wing, during all of these operations, also participated in numerous tactical exercises and operations, worldwide.

Campaign Streamers. None.

Decorations. Air Force Outstanding Unit Awards: 23 Oct–24 Nov 1962; 10–15 Feb 1973; 1 Jul 1974–1 Jul 1976.

Emblem. A shield quarterly, first quarter checky, argent and gules; second and third quarters, azure; fourth quarter gules, a lion rampant or, armed and langued azure, all within a diminutive of the bordure or. Wreath of the colors, argent and gules. *Motto:* VOIR C'EST SAVOIR—To see is to know. (Approved on 16 Jun 1952.)

366th TACTICAL FIGHTER WING

Lineage. Established as 366th Fighter-Bomber Wing on 15 Nov 1952. Activated on 1 Jan 1953. Redesignated 366th Tactical Fighter Wing on 1 Jul 1958. Inactivated on 1 Apr 1959. Activated on 30 Apr 1962. Organized on 8 May 1962.

Assignments. Ninth Air Force, 1 Jan 1953 (attached to Nineteenth Air Force, 15 Feb 1956–24 Sep 1957); 834th Air Division, 25 Sep 1957–1 Apr 1959. United States Air Forces in Europe, 30 Apr 1962; Seventeenth Air Force, 8 May 1962; Twelfth Air Force, 12 Jul 1963; 832d Air Division, 1 Oct 1964; 2d Air Division, 20 Mar 1966; Seventh Air Force, 1 Apr 1966; Thirteenth Air Force, 27 Jun 1972; 832d Air Division, 31 Oct 1972; Twelfth Air Force, 1 Jul 1975–.

Components. *Groups*. 366th: 1 Jan 1953–25 Sep 1957. 401st: attached 5 Feb 1954–25 Sep 1957. *Squadrons*. 4th: 12 Apr 1969–31 Oct 1972 (detached 29–31 Oct 1972). 20th Tactical Air Support: 15 Mar–27 Jun 1972. 35th: attached 3 Apr–12 Jun 1972. 352d: 15 Aug–10 Oct 1966. 362d Tactical Electronic Warfare: 1 Feb–27 Jun 1972. 388th Tactical Fighter Training: 1 Jul 1977–. 389th: 25 Sep 1957–1 Apr 1959 (detached 25 Sep–22 Dec 1957; not operational, 1 Jan–1 Apr 1959); 8 May 1962–15 Jun 1969 (detached 15 Sep–16 Dec 1965); attached 16–24 Jun 1969; assigned 31 Oct 1972– (detached 16 Sep–5 Oct 1976). 390th: 25 Sep 1957–1 Apr 1959 (not operational, 28 Jan–1 Apr 1959); 8 May 1962–29 Oct 1965; 10 Oct 1966–30 Jun 1972 (not operational, 15–30 Jun 1972); 31 Oct 1972– (detached 19 Aug–16 Sep 1976). 391st: 25 Sep 1957–1 Apr 1959 (not operational, 6 Feb–1 Apr 1959); 8 May 1962–26 Jan 1966; 31 Oct 1972–. 420th Air Refueling: attached 18 Mar 1954–22 Sep 1955 (not operational, 18–24 Mar 1954). 421st: 16 Apr 1969–31 May 1972 (not operational, 16–22 Apr 1969; detached 23 Apr–25 Jun 1969). 480th: 25 Sep 1957–1 Apr 1959 (not operational, 4 Mar–1 Apr 1959); 8 May 1962–1 Feb 1966; 10 Oct 1966–15 Apr 1959. 614th: 18 Sep–10 Oct 1966. 615th: 16 Jul–10 Oct 1966. 622d Air Refueling: attached 18 Jul 1955–1 Jul 1958. *Detachment*. Det 1, 612th Tactical Fighter Squadron: attached 15 May–10 Oct 1966.

Stations. Alexandria (later, England) AFB, La, 1 Jan 1953–1 Apr 1959. Chaumont AB, France, 8 May 1962–15 Jul 1963; Holloman AFB, NM, 15 Jul

1963–11 Mar 1966; Phan Rang AB, South Vietnam, 20 Mar 1966; Da Nang AB, South Vietnam, 10 Oct 1966; Takhli RTAFB, Thailand, 27 Jun–31 Oct 1972; Mountain Home AFB, Idaho, 31 Oct 1972–.

Commanders. Col Reginald F. C. Vance, 1 Jan 1953; Col William A. Daniel, 14 Jul 1953; Col Victor E. Warford, 29 Aug 1957; Col Clyde B. Slocumb, Jr., 25 Sep 1957; Lt Col David N. Harmon, 1 Jun 1958; Col Robert J. Rogers, 17 Jul 1958; Lt Col Frank L. McGuinness, 6 Mar 1959; Col Robert J. Rogers, 23 Mar–1 Apr 1959. None (not manned), 30 Apr–7 May 1962; Col James S. Coward, 8 May 1962; Col George S. Weart, 12 Mar 1964; Col Frank J. Collins, 16 Mar 1964; Col George S. Weart, 7 Jul 1965; Col Carlos M. Talbott, 15 Jul 1965; Col George S. Weart, May 1966; Col Allan P. Rankin, 10 Oct 1966; Col Jones E. Bolt, 20 Mar 1967; Col Robert W. Maloy, 27 May 1967; Col Clifford H. Meier, 19 Dec 1967; Col Paul C. Watson, 17 Jan 1968; Col John W. Roberts, 2 Jan 1969; Col Edward H. Risher, 19 Apr 1969 (temporary); Brig Gen John W. Roberts, 4 May 1969; Col Joseph C. Secino, 1 Oct 1969; Col Daniel C. Perry, 19 Sep 1970; Col John R. Spalding, Jr., 18 Feb 1971; Col Julian D. Sawyer, 7 Jul 1971; Col George W. Rutter, 22 Mar 1972; Col Lynwood E. Clark, 31 Oct 1972; Brig Gen Howard W. Leaf, 15 May 1973; Col Robert K. Parsons, 12 Jul 1974; Col Samuel Huser, 2 Jun 1976; Col John L. Pickitt, 8 Jan 1977–.

Aircraft. F–51, 1953; F–86, 1953–1955, 1956; F–84, 1954–1958; KB–29, 1954–1957; KB–50, 1957–1958; F–100, 1957–1959. F–84, 1962–1965; F–100, 1963, 1966; F–4, 1965–1972; EC–47, 1972; O–2, 1972; OV–10, 1972; F–111, 1972–.

Operations. Replaced the 132d Fighter-Bomber Wing when activated in Jan 1953. Trained to maintain combat proficiency. Conducted air refueling, Sep 1954–Jul 1958. Rotated tactical squadrons to France, 1954–1956, and to Italy, 1955–1957. Served as conventional strike force in Europe, 1962–1963. Moved to the United States in Jul 1963 and converted to F–4 aircraft in 1965. Moved to Southeast Asia in Mar 1966 for combat operations. In addition to its F–4 squadrons, also controlled several F–100 squadrons in 1966. On 10 Oct 1966, wing designation switched with that of 35th TFW at Da Nang AB, South Vietnam, giving the 366th new personnel, equipment, and facilities. By early 1967, many of the wing's combat missions involved flying cover for F–105 strike aircraft, offering numerous opportunities for aerial combat with North Vietnamese MiG aircraft. Wing pilots achieved 18 aerial victories in Southeast Asia. In 1972, gained the 362d TEWS, equipped with EC–47N/P/Q aircraft, and 20th TASS, flying O–2A and OV–10A aircraft. The former had an electronic countermeasures mission, while the latter had a forward air control mission. Moved to Thailand in Jun 1972 with little change in combat missions; aircraft now limited to F–4s. Continued combat operations until moved without personnel or equipment to the United States in Oct 1972. Replaced the 347th TFW at Mountain Home AFB, Idaho, becoming operational with F–111F aircraft. In 1977, in a three-way switch of aircraft, transferred F–111Fs to a wing in England and gained F–111A aircraft from a wing at Nellis AFB, Nev.

Service Streamers. None.

Campaign Streamers. Vietnam Air; Vietnam Air Offensive; Vietnam Air Offensive, Phase II; Vietnam Air Offensive, Phase III; Vietnam Air/Ground; Vietnam Air Offensive, Phase IV; TET 69/Counteroffensive; Vietnam Summer–Fall, 1969; Vietnam Winter–Spring, 1970; Sanctuary Counteroffensive; Southwest Monsoon; Commando Hunt V; Commando Hunt VI; Commando Hunt VII.

Decorations. Presidential Unit Citations (Southeast Asia): 23 Apr–1 Aug 1967; 1 Apr–31 Oct 1972. Air Force Outstanding Unit Awards with Combat "V" Device: 10 Oct 1966–31 Mar 1967; 1 Apr 1967–31 Mar 1968; 1 Apr 1968–31 Jul 1969; 1 Aug 1969–1 Aug 1970; 2 Aug 1970–31 Mar 1972. Air Force Outstanding Unit Awards: 17 Apr 1974–15 Apr 1976; 18 Aug–16 Sep 1976. Republic of Vietnam Gallantry Cross with Palm: 1 Apr 1966–31 Oct 1972.

Emblem. Gules, a pile azure fimbriated or between in base four flight symbols ascendant pilewise two in dexter and two in sinister, one over one, and bearing in honour point an escutcheon vert charged with a fleur-de-lis between six crosses, three in dexter and three in sinister, all or, within a bordure of the like; all within a diminished bordure of the last. *Motto:* AUDENTES FORTUNA JUVAT—Fortune favors the bold. (Approved on 8 Aug 1965.)

369th STRATEGIC FIGHTER WING

Lineage. Established as 369th Strategic Fighter Wing on 23 Mar 1953.

Assignments. None.
Components. None.
Stations. None.
Commanders. None.
Aircraft. None.
Operations. Never made active.
Service Streamers. None.
Campaign Streamers. None.
Decorations. None.
Emblem. None.

374th TACTICAL AIRLIFT WING

Lineage. Established as 374th Troop Carrier Wing, Heavy, on 10 Aug 1948. Activated on 17 Aug 1948. Inactivated on 1 Jul 1957. Redesignated 374th Troop Carrier Wing, and activated, on 27 Jun 1966. Organized on 8 Aug 1966. Redesignated 374th Tactical Airlift Wing on 1 Aug 1967.

Assignments. Marianas Air Materiel Area (Provisional), 17 Aug 1948 (attached to Twentieth Air Force, 17 Aug 1948–); Marianas Air Materiel Area, 1 Feb 1949 (remained attached to Twentieth Air Force to 5 Mar 1949); Fifth Air Force, 5 Mar 1949 (attached to 1st Troop Carrier Task Force [Provisional], 5–9 Sep 1950; Far East Air Forces Combat Cargo Command, Provisional, 10

Sep 1950–); 314th Air Division, 1 Dec 1950 (remained attached to Far East Air Forces Combat Cargo Command, Provisional, to 25 Jan 1951); 315th Air Division (Combat Cargo), 25 Jan 1951; Military Air Transport Service, 1 Jul 1957. Pacific Air Forces, 27 Jun 1966; 315th Air Division (Combat Cargo), 8 Aug 1966; 313th Air Division, 1 Nov 1968; 327th Air Division, 31 May 1971; Thirteenth Air Force, 15 Nov 1973; Twenty-Second Air Force, 31 Mar 1975–.

Components. *Groups*. 1st Troop Carrier Group, Medium (Provisional) (later, Troop Carrier Group [Medium], No. 1 Provisional): attached 26 Aug 1950–10 Jan 1951. 374th: 17 Aug 1948–1 Jul 1957 (not operational, 3 Feb 1956–1 Jul 1957). *Squadrons*. 6th: attached 3 Feb 1956–1 Jul 1957. 7th Air Command and Control: 22 May 1974–31 Mar 1975 (detached). 20th Operations (later, 20th Aeromedical Airlift): 31 Mar 1975–. 21st: attached 29 Jun 1951–28 Mar 1952; attached 3 Feb 1956–1 Jul 1957; assigned 8 Aug 1966– (not operational, c. 27 Apr–30 May 1971). 22d: attached 3 Feb 1956–1 Jul 1957 (not operational, 10 Jun–1 Jul 1957). 35th: 8 Aug 1966–31 Mar 1971 (not operational, 24–31 Mar 1971). 36th: attached 16 May–1 Sep 1972. 37th: attached 29 Nov 1972–28 Feb 1973. 38th: attached 1 Sep–29 Nov 1972. 41st: 8 Aug 1966–28 Feb 1971 (not operational, 21–28 Feb 1971). Troop Carrier Squadron (Medium) No. 47 Provisional: attached 10–26 Jan 1951. 50th: 31 May 1971–15 Aug 1973 (not operational, 8 Feb–15 Aug 1973); attached 29 Apr–c. 20 May 1975. 61st: attached 16 May–1 Sep 1972. 345th: 31 May 1971–. 772d: attached c. 10 May–6 Jun 1973. 773d: attached 28 Feb–c. 10 May 1973. 776th: 31 May 1971–31 Oct 1975. 815th: 1 Nov 1968–15 Dec 1969 (detached 1 Nov 1968–1 Apr 1969; not operational, 19 Oct–15 Dec 1969). 817th: 8 Aug 1966–15 Jun 1970 (not operational, 10 Apr–15 Jun 1970). 6475th (later, 6037th) Flying Training Squadron: attached 25 Nov 1954–18 May 1955. 6485th Operations: attached 17 Sep 1956–1 Jul 1957. *Units*. 6142d Air Transport: attached 1 Aug–1 Oct 1950. 6143d Air Transport: attached 26 Jul–1 Oct 1950. 6144th Air Transport: attached 26 Jul–1 Oct 1950. *Detachments*. Det 1, HQ 317th Troop Carrier Wing, Heavy: attached 3 Feb–17 Sep 1956. Royal Thailand Air Force Detachment: attached 1953–1 Jul 1957.

Stations. Harmon AFB, Guam, 17 Aug 1948; Tachikawa (later, Tachikawa AB), Japan, 5 Mar 1949–1 Jul 1957. Naha AB, Okinawa, 8 Aug 1966; Ching Chaun Kang AB, Taiwan, 31 May 1971; Clark AB, Philippines, 15 Nov 1973–.

Commanders. Col Charles K. Moore, 17 Aug 1948; Col James C. Jensen, Feb 1949; Col Troy W. Crawford, 19 Jun 1949; Col Charles W. Howe, Sep 1951; Col James W. Chapman, Jr., 9 Aug 1952; Col Adriel N. Williams, 1 Mar 1954; Col Francis W. Williams, 16 Jun 1956; Col James R. Haun, 22 Jun–1 Jul 1957. None (not manned), 27 Jun–7 Aug 1966; Col John R. Neal, 8 Aug 1966; Col Russell D. Crane, 16 Jun 1967; Brig Gen Kelton M. Farris, 25 Jan 1969; Col Noble F. Greenhill, Jr., 11 Jul 1970; Col Andrew P. Iosue, 31 May 1971; Col James I. Baginski, 18 May 1973; Col Albert M. Navas, 12 Feb 1975; Col James I. Baginski, 24 Apr 1975; Col Albert M. Navas, 1 Aug 1975; Col Gary G. Boettcher, 15 Aug 1977; Col Jimmy L. Maturo, 29 Aug 1977–.

Aircraft. C–54, 1948–1956, 1956–1957; C–46, 1949, 1950–1951, 1956–1957; C–47, 1951–1957; C–124, 1952–1957; C–119, 1951, 1956–1957; VB–17, 1951. C–130, 1966–1971, 1971–; C–9, 1975–.

Operations. Operated Harmon Field, Guam, Aug 1948–Mar 1949, and provided troop carrier operations in the Pacific and Far East. Moved to Japan in Mar 1949, assuming control over Tachikawa (later, Tachikawa AB), which it operated until 1 Jan 1956. Performed routine transport operations until the outbreak of war in Korea in Jun 1950. With assigned and attached components, performed combat airlift, airdrops, and aeromedical evacuation in Korea throughout the war. Also flew courier flights throughout the Pacific area. Transported the first of several groups of repatriated prisoners of war from Korea to Japan in Apr 1953 (Operation Little Switch), and subsequently transported United Nations prisoners of war (Operation Big Switch) from North Korea. Following hostilities, the wing resumed its normal troop carrier and airlift operations in the Far East and Pacific area, including participation in tactical exercises and humanitarian missions. Operated in Indo-China (now Vietnam) in 1954, flying in observers, maintenance personnel, and liaison officers and evacuating wounded French troops. Trained C–46 pilots of the Japanese Air Self Defense Force, Nov 1954–May 1955. On 1 Jul 1957, transferred to Military Air Transport Service and inactivated, replaced in part by 1503d Air Transport Wing. Nine years later, in Aug 1966, replaced the 6315th Operations Group at Naha AB, Okinawa, and assumed a mission heavily involved in airlift to Southeast Asia, as well as intra-theater airlift for elements of the Pacific Command. In addition, the wing supported Army Special Forces training, participated in tactical exercises, and flew search and rescue and humanitarian missions as needed. The wing phased down for inactivation in early 1971 and from 27 Apr to 31 May had no aircraft. On 31 May, the wing replaced the 314th Tactical Airlift Wing in Taiwan. Saved from inactivation and revived with new resources, the 374th remained heavily committed to support of operations in Southeast Asia, and also continued routine airlift in other areas. One of the wing's humanitarian missions—flood relief in the Philippines—earned it a Philippine Republic Presidential Unit Citation in 1972. The wing provided support in Mar 1973 for Operation Homecoming, the repatriation of American prisoners from Hanoi, North Vietnam. The wing maintained a forward operating location in Thailand until mid-1976, and was quite active in that area. It took part in Operation Baby Lift (evacuation of Vietnam orphans) and Operation New Life (evacuation of Vietnamese refugees) in Apr 1975. During the recovery of the SS *Mayaguez* from the Cambodians in May 1975, a wing aircraft dropped a 15,000-lb bomb on Koh Tang Island to create a helicopter landing area. The wing became part of the Military Airlift Command on 31 Mar 1975, at which time it gained an aeromedical airlift mission in the Far East.

Service Streamers. None.

Campaign Streamers. UN Defensive; UN Offensive; CCF Intervention; First

UN Counteroffensive; CCF Spring Offensive; UN Summer–Fall Offensive; Second Korean Winter; Korea Summer–Fall, 1952; Third Korean Winter; Korea Summer–Fall, 1953.

Decorations. Presidential Unit Citation (Vietnam): 8 Aug 1967–7 Aug 1968. Air Force Outstanding Unit Award with Combat "V" Device: 12 Feb–17 May 1975. Air Force Outstanding Unit Award: 8 Aug 1966–7 Aug 1967. Republic of Korea Presidential Unit Citation: 1 Jul 1951–27 Jul 1953. Republic of Vietnam Gallantry Cross with Palm: 1 Apr 1966–28 Jan 1973. Philippine Republic Presidential Unit Citation: 21 Jul–15 Aug 1972.

Emblem. Per bend azure and or, in chief a hand couped in armour, holding a dagger, point upward, issuing from its handle an arrow and a wheat stalk or, in base a winged foot azure. *Motto:* CELERITER PUGNARE—Swiftly to fight. (Approved for 374th Group on 3 Jul 1951 and for 374th Wing on 20 Dec 1951.)

375th AEROMEDICAL AIRLIFT WING

Lineage. Established as 375th Troop Carrier Wing, Medium, on 10 May 1949. Activated in the Reserve on 27 Jun 1949. Ordered to active service on 15 Oct 1950. Inactivated on 14 Jul 1952. Activated in the Reserve on 14 Jul 1952. Inactivated on 16 Nov 1957. Redesignated 375th Aeromedical Airlift Wing, and activated, on 27 Dec 1965. Organized on 12 Jan 1966.

Assignments. Ninth Air Force, 27 Jun 1949; First Air Force, 1 Aug 1950; Tactical Air Command, 16 Oct 1950; Eighteenth Air Force, 1 Jun 1951–14 Jul 1952. 1st Air Reserve District, 14 Jul 1952; First Air Force, 14 Jan 1954–16 Nov 1957. Military Air Transport Service (later, Military Airlift Command), 27 Dec 1965–.

Components. *Groups.* 171st: 13 May–12 Dec 1968. 375th: 27 Jun 1949–14 Jul 1952; 14 Jul 1952–16 Nov 1957. 932d: attached 25 Jul 1969–. *Squadrons.* 10th: 12 Jan 1966–8 Mar 1969. 11th: 12 Jan 1966–. 12th: 12 Jan 1966–8 Jun 1969. 13th: 12 Jan 1966–8 Dec 1968.

Stations. Greater Pittsburgh Aprt, Pa, 27 Jun 1949; Greenville (later, Donaldson) AFB, SC, 16 Oct 1950–14 Jul 1952. Pittsburgh, Pa, 14 Jul 1952–16 Nov 1957. Scott AFB, Ill, 12 Jan 1966–.

Commanders. Brig Gen Emil H. Molthan, 27 Jun 1949–unkn; Col William S. Johnston, 14 Sep 1949; Lt Col Stanley V. Fowler, c. Aug 1950; Col Lance Call, Sep 1950; Col Glynne M. Jones, 3 Mar 1952; Brig Gen Franklin Rose, 22 May–14 Jul 1952. Col Arthur R. Anderson, 14 Jul 1952; Col Jack R. Adams, Mar 1953; Col Albert B. Starr, 1 Sep 1955–16 Nov 1957. None (not manned), 27 Dec 1965–11 Jan 1966; Col William E. Nix, 12 Jan 1966;

Col Felix G. Brenner, 3 Aug 1966; Col Harry L. Waesche, 6 Sep 1966; Col Robert L. Moeller, 1 Oct 1968; Col John W. Self, 1 Nov 1969; Col Muller L. Jones, 13 May 1971; Col Frank W. Contestable, 24 May 1971; Col Charles C. Irions, 31 May 1974; Col Paul A. Bergerot, 30 Jun 1975; Col Hubert S. Diamond, 29 Jan 1976–.

Aircraft. T–6, 1949–1950; T–7, 1949–1951; T–11, 1949–1951; C–46, 1949–1950; C–82, 1950–1952; C–45, 1951. C–46, 1952–1955; C–119, 1954–1957. C–118, 1966–1969; C–131, 1966–1969; C–121, 1968; C–9, 1968–.

Operations. Reserve flying training, Jun 1949–Oct 1950. On active duty, wing participated in troop carrier/airlift operations and paratroop drops and other exercises, Oct 1950–Jul 1952. Reserve training, Jul 1952–Nov 1957. Conducted domestic aeromedical airlift/evacuation operations in the United States, Alaska, and off-shore areas of the North Atlantic and the Caribbean from Jan 1966 for MAC, other Department of Defense agencies, the U.S. Public Health Service, and the Veterans Administration (VA), with the C–9 Nightingale as principal mission aircraft beginning in 1969, and augmented by aircraft of ANG (1968) and other MAC units. Used missions to train personnel of ANG and Reserve in aeromedical evacuation. Between Jan 1966 and Apr 1975 wing maintained and scheduled support aircraft at Scott AFB, Ill, and from Aug 1966 to Apr 1975 wing used mostly aircrews of other Scott-based units to provide scheduled air shuttle/courier service to the east and west coasts. From Jan 1966 to Sep 1968 and since Jun 1973 wing operated and maintained Scott AFB. Airlifted over 700 VA hospital patients from Biloxi and Gulfport, Miss, to safety during Hurricane Camille in Aug 1969; during Project Homecoming in early 1973 the wing flew 119 sorties to airlift some 350 U.S. POWs to 26 hospitals in the United States. In Oct 1973 an aeromedical evacuation center, established under wing control at Scott AFB, assumed the functions previously handled by smaller centers at Scott, McGuire AFB, NJ, and Travis AFB, Calif. In Apr 1975, when the aeromedical evacuation support units in West Germany and the Philippines came under wing control, the wing became the single-point manager for worldwide DOD aeromedical evacuation services.

Service Streamers. None.

Campaign Streamers. None.

Decorations. Air Force Outstanding Unit Awards: [12]–31 Jan 1966; 19–20 Aug 1969; 20 Aug 1969–30 Jun 1971; 24 Jul 1975–23 Jul 1977.

Emblem. Gules, a pile reversed throughout azure, overall an eagle displayed with wings inverted or, grasping in both talons a sphere of the second grid markings bendwise argent. *Motto:* DESUPER ADUIMENTUM—Help from above. (Approved on 31 Jan 1966.)

376th STRATEGIC WING

1947–1977

Lineage. Established as 376th Bombardment Wing, Medium, on 25 May 1951. Activated on 1 Jun 1951. Discontinued, and inactivated, on 15 Mar 1965. Redesignated 376th Strategic Wing on 23 Jan 1970. Activated on 1 Apr 1970.

Assignments. 4th Air Division, 1 Jun 1951 (attached to 21st Air Division, 1 Jun–10 Oct 1951); 801st Air Division, 3 Dec 1957–15 Mar 1965. Eighth Air Force, 1 Apr 1970; 3d Air Division, 1 Jan 1975–.

Components. *Group.* 376th: 1 Jun 1951–16 Jun 1952 (not operational). *Squadrons.* 82d Strategic Reconnaissance: 1 Apr 1970–30 Sep 1976 (not operational, 11–30 Sep 1976). 91st Air Refueling: 1 Dec 1957–15 Jun 1964 (not operational, 8 Jan–4 Apr 1963). 376th Air Refueling: 18 Aug 1953–1 Dec 1957. 512th: attached 1 Jun 1951–15 Jun 1952, assigned 16 Jun 1952–15 Mar 1965. 513th: attached 1 Jun 1951–15 Jun 1952, assigned 16 Jun 1952–15 Mar 1965. 514th: attached 1 Jun 1951–15 Jun 1952, assigned 16 Jun 1952–15 Mar 1965. 515th: 1 Dec 1958–1 Jan 1962 (not operational, c. 15 Oct 1961–1 Jan 1962). 909th Air Refueling: 1 Jul 1971–. Air Refueling, Provisional, 4102d: attached 6 Jun–8 Nov 1972. Air Refueling, Provisional, 4102d: attached 18 Dec 1972–22 Jan 1973. 4180th Bombardment: 1 Apr–1 Jul 1970 (not operational). 4220th Air Refueling: 1 Apr 1970–31 Jan 1971 (not operational, 15 Nov 1970–31 Jan 1971). 4363d Support (later, 4363d Post Attack Command and Control): attached 20 Jul 1962–15 Feb 1965 (not operational, Jul–Nov 1962).

Stations. Forbes AFB, Kans, 1 Jun 1951; Barksdale AFB, La, 10 Oct 1951; Lockbourne AFB, Ohio, 1 Dec 1957–15 Mar 1965. Kadena AB, Okinawa (later, Japan), 1 Apr 1970–.

Commanders. Col Cecil E. Combs, 1 Jun 1951; Col Frederick J. Sutterlin, c. 15 Apr 1952; Col Clifton Pyle, 23 Apr 1952; Col Frederick J. Sutterlin, May 1952; Col John P. Proctor, c. 1 Aug 1953; Col John C. Jennison, Jr., 4 Jan 1954; Col Robert T. Calhoun, 8 Jan 1954; Col John W. Carroll, 1 Feb 1954; Col John C. Jennison, Jr., 4 Feb 1954; Lt Col Elmon R. Cobb, 15 Feb 1954; Col John P. Proctor, 4 Mar 1954; Col Stephen D. McElroy, 1 Jul 1955; Col Robert W. Strong, Jr., 1 May 1957; Col Ralph J. White, c. Nov 1957; Col Woodrow P. Swancutt, 1 Dec 1957; Col Charles L. Wimberly, 1 Apr 1959; Col Alan F. Adams, 22 Jul 1961–15 Mar 1965. Brig Gen Alan C. Edmunds, 1 Apr 1970; Col Jack A. Weyant, 2 Sep 1970; Col Dudley G. Kavanaugh, 30 Aug 1972; Col Raymond L. Horvath, 10 Sep 1974; Col Lyman E. Buzard, 30 Sep 1977–.

Aircraft. B–29, 1951–1954; B/E/EB–47, 1954–1965; E–47, 1958–1961; KC–97, 1953–1963; KC–135, 1963–1964. B–52, 1970; KC–135, 1970–; RC–135, 1970–.

Operations. Trained in strategic bombardment, Aug 1951–Feb 1965, with bombardment operations sometimes overshadowed by electronic countermeasures operations, which became the wing's primary mission in Sep 1953. Included EB–47 post attack command and control operations, Dec 1962–Feb 1965, and air refueling, Sep 1953–Jun 1964. Conducted B–52 combat operations in Southeast Asia, Apr–Sep 1970, air refueling and electronic reconnaissance in the Western Pacific,

Apr 1970–, and airborne radio relay operations, Apr–Nov 1970, Feb–Jun 1971, and Mar 1972–c. Aug 1973.

Service Streamers. None.

Campaign Streamers. Vietnam Winter–Spring, 1970; Sanctuary Counteroffensive; Southwest Monsoon.

Decorations. Air Force Outstanding Unit Awards with Combat "V" Device: 1 Apr 1970–31 Mar 1972; 1 Apr 1972–28 Jan 1973. Air Force Outstanding Unit Awards: 29 Jan 1973–31 Mar 1974; 1 Jul 1974–30 Jun 1976; 1 Jul 1976–30 Jun 1977. Republic of Vietnam Gallantry Cross with Palm: 1 Apr 1970–28 Jan 1973.

Emblem. Azure, in base, a stylized winged sphinx or, shaded tenne, and fimbriated azure, on a terra cotta. mound sanguine, in dexter chief a bomb or, point downward, charged with a roundle and a lozenge, sanguine, a triangle azure and a square sanguine, all within a diminutive of a border or. *Motto:* LIBERANDOS. (Approved on 8 Nov 1951.)

377th AIR BASE WING

Lineage. Established as 377th Combat Support Group, activated, and organized on 8 Apr 1966. Redesignated 377th Air Base Wing on 17 Jan 1972. Inactivated on 28 Mar 1973.

Assignments. Seventh Air Force, 8 Apr 1966–28 Mar 1973.

Components. *Squadrons.* 8th Special Operations: 15 Jan–1 Oct 1972; attached 12–25 Oct 1972. 9th Special Operations: attached 12 Jan–29 Feb 1972. 21st Tactical Air Support: 15 Mar 1972–23 Feb 1973 (not operational, 21–23 Feb 1973). 310th Tactical Airlift: 15 Jan–15 Nov 1972 (not operational, 1–15 Nov 1972). 360th Tactical Electronic Warfare: 1 Feb–24 Nov 1972 (not operational, 15–24 Nov 1972). 6252d Operations: 10 Jun 1966–1 Jan 1967.

Stations. Tan Son Nhut AB, South Vietnam, 8 Apr 1966–28 Mar 1973.

Commanders. Col George Budway, 8 Apr 1966; Col Grover K. Coe, 8 Oct 1966; Col Farley E. Peebles, 4 Oct 1967; Col Benjamin B. Shields, 26 Jul 1968; Col Frank E. Marek, (by Sep) 1969; Col Harold E. Hobbs, 31 Jul 1970; Col Charles D. Gunn, Jr., 10 Jul 1971; Col David A. Odell, 27 Jun 1972–28 Mar 1973.

Aircraft. C/VC–47, 1966, 1972–1973; VC–54, 1966; VC–123, 1966, 1972; C/VC–118, 1972–1973; T–39, 1972–1973; A–37, 1972; C–123, 1972; C–7, 1972; EC–47, 1972; O–2, 1972–1973.

Operations. Replaced 6250th Combat Support Group in Apr 1966. Responsible for operation and maintenance of USAF portion of Tan Son Nhut AB, South Vietnam, Apr 1966–Mar 1973. Responsibilities included housing numerous tenant organizations including Seventh Air Force, base defense, and liaison with South Vietnamese Air Force. Underwent numerous enemy attacks. Further responsible for Binh Thuy AB, South Vietnam, 12 May–1 Jul 1970. Provided support for Seventh Air Force flying operations with C–47, C–123 and C–54 aircraft, Jun–Dec 1966. In Sep 1971 again became responsible for supporting base flight T–39, C–54, C–47 and C–118, as well as C–130 aircraft of 834th Air Division. Elevated to Air Base Wing in Jan 1972 and gained a tactical mission and combat units. Operated the Southeast Asia Central Instructor Pilots School, in which the 360th TEWS used C/EC–47s, 15 Feb–c. Nov 1972. Operated a Combat Crew Training School at Phu Cat, South Vietnam, with C–7 aircraft, 15 Mar–Oct 1972. Resumed base flight operations at Tan Son Nhut in Jan 1972, operating and maintaining C–47, C–118, and T–39 aircraft. With the 8th Special Operations Squadron (A–37s), performed strike missions, Jan–Oct 1972. With the 9th Special Operations Squadron (O–2 and C–47), conducted psychological warfare operations, Jan–Feb 1972. With the 21st Tactical Air Support Squadron (Light), conducted air liaison officer and forward air controller operations, Mar 1972–28 Jan 1973. With the 310th Tactical Airlift Squadron (C/UC–123s, Jan–Jun 1972 and C–7s, Mar–Oct 1972), performed airlift and airdrop missions, Jan–Oct 1972. With the 360th Tactical Electronic Warfare Squadron (C/EC–47s), conducted airborne radio direction finding operations Feb–Nov 1972 and psychological warfare operations, Feb–Aug 1972. An operating location of the wing headquarters was established at Bien Hoa AB, South Vietnam, on 14 Apr 1972 to provide turn-around service for F–4s of other organizations. It was replaced on 20 Jun 1972 by Detachment 1 of the wing headquarters, which continued the F–4 turn-around service and added A–7 turn-around service on 30 Oct 1972. The detachment continued operations through 11 Feb 1973. Wing phased down for inactivation, Feb–Mar 1973, transferring many assets to South Vietnamese Air Force.

Service Streamers. None.

Campaign Streamers. Vietnam Air; Vietnam Air Offensive; Vietnam Air Offensive, Phase II; Vietnam Air Offensive, Phase III; Vietnam Air Offensive, Phase IV; TET 69/Counteroffensive; Vietnam Summer–Fall, 1969; Vietnam Winter–Spring, 1970; Sanctuary Counteroffensive; Southwest Monsoon; Commando Hunt V; Commando Hunt VI; Commando Hunt VII; Vietnam Ceasefire.

Decorations. Air Force Outstanding Unit Awards with Combat "V" Device: 8 Apr 1966–31 May 1967; 31 Jan–31 Mar 1968; 1 Apr 1969–31 Mar 1971; 17 Jan 1972–28 Mar 1973. Republic of Vietnam Gallantry Cross with Palm: [8] Apr 1966–28 Jan 1973.

Emblem. Light blue, a bend triparted gules, argent, and azure, between in chief a flight symbol of the last fimbriated argent, emitting a vapor trail fesswise to sinister chief and bend sinisterwise to base passing under the triparted bend all azure, and in base a plate rimmed and gridlined azure surmounted by a tiger's head affronte couped or garnished brown and argent with mouth gules, all within a diminished bordure or. *Motto:* SERVING FREEDOM'S FINEST. (Emblem approved on 17 Jul 1967; motto approved on 31 Jul 1969.)

379th BOMBARDMENT WING, HEAVY

Lineage. Established as 379th Bombardment Wing, Medium, on 23 Mar 1953. Activated on 1 Nov 1955. Redesignated 379th Bombardment Wing, Heavy, on 9 Jan 1961.

Assignments. Second Air Force, 1 Nov 1955 (attached to 813th Air Division, 1 Nov 1955–31 May 1956); 823d Air Division, 1 Jun 1956 (attached to 5th Air Division, 6 Mar–12 May 1957); 40th Air Division, 9 Jan 1961–.

Components. *Squadrons.* 19th Air Refueling: attached 1 Feb–30 Jun 1956. 524th: 1 Nov 1955–. 525th: 1 Nov 1955–9 Jan 1961. 526th: 1 Nov 1955–9 Jan 1961. 527th: 1 Nov 1958–9 Jan 1961. 920th Air Refueling: 9 Jan 1961–.

Stations. Homestead AFB, Fla, 1 Nov 1955; Wurtsmith AFB, Mich, 9 Jan 1961–.

Commanders. Maj James C. Harrington, 1 Nov 1955; Lt Col William L. Hosler, Jr., 2 Nov 1955; Col Travis M. Hetherington, 10 Nov 1955; Col William H. Cleveland, 1 Jun 1957; Col John B. McPherson, 3 Mar 1958; Col Joseph A. Kelly, 18 Sep 1959; Col Roland W. Bergamyer, 15 Oct 1959; Col Richard R. Stewart, 1 Aug 1960; Col John H. Kunkel, Jr., 9 Jan 1961; Col Gerard G. Wolke, 13 Jun 1962; Col Paul K. Carlton, 25 Jun 1962; Col Boyd B. White, 18 Nov 1963; Col Andrew J. Bratton, Jr., 9 Jan 1964; Col Boyd B. White, 19 May 1965; Col William R. Calhoun, Jr., 15 Jun 1965; Col Pat H. Earhart, 15 Jun 1966; Col Lawrence W. Steinkraus, 9 Aug 1968; Col Colin C. Hamilton, Jr., 21 Apr 1969; Col John W. Burkhart, 23 Feb 1970; Col Thomas M. Ryan, Jr., 14 Jul 1972; Col Perrin W. Gower, Jr., 25 Oct 1972; Col Kelly H. Burke, 3 Jan 1973; Col Donald N. Webster, 13 Jun 1974; Col Edwin L. Smith, 15 Apr 1975; Col Henry W. Boardman, 8 Jul 1975; Col John J. Doran, Jr., 11 Jul 1977–.

Aircraft. KC–97, 1956; B–47, 1956–1960; B–52, 1961–; KC–135, 1961–.

Operations. Replaced 4276th Air Base Squadron at Homestead AFB, Fla, in Nov 1955 and spent next few months becoming organized and manned. Received tactical aircraft in Apr 1956 and commenced training for air refueling and strategic bombardment operations. Deployed at Sidi Slimane AB, Morocco, Mar–May 1957. Transferred B–47s beginning Oct 1960 and moved to Wurtsmith AFB, Mich, without equipment in Jan 1961. Reequipped with KC–135 and B–52 aircraft, conducted air refueling operations since Jan 1961 and strategic bombardment training since May 1961. Supported combat operations in Southeast Asia with KC–135 aircraft and crews and B–52 crews, 1965–1975.

Service Streamers. None.

Campaign Streamers. None.

Decorations. Air Force Outstanding Unit Awards: 1 Jul 1963–30 Jun 1964; 1 Jul 1970–30 Jun 1971.

Emblem. On a shield per bend azure and gules, on a lightning bolt per bend throughout, or, seven stars per bend argent; all between a dart, with three stars arched and an atomic symbol encircled by nine stars, all of the last. *Motto:* DILIGENTIA ET ACCURATIO—Precision and accuracy. (Approved on 23 Aug 1956.)

380th BOMBARDMENT WING, MEDIUM

Lineage. Established as 380th Bombardment Wing, Medium, on 23 Mar 1953. Activated on 11 Jul 1955. Redesignated: 380th Strategic Aerospace Wing on 15 Sep 1964; 380th Bombardment Wing, Medium, on 1 Jul 1972.

Assignments. Eighth Air Force, 11 Jul 1955; 820th Air (later, 820th Strategic Aerospace) Division, 1 Feb 1956 (attached to 7th Air Division, 3 Apr–3 Jul 1957); 817th Air Division, 25 Jun 1965; 45th Air Division, 1 Jul 1968; 817th Air Division, 2 Jul 1969; 45th Air Division, 30 Jun 1971–.

Components. *Squadrons.* 26th Air Refueling: attached 7 Aug 1957–31 Jul 1959, assigned 1 Aug 1959–1 Apr 1961. 310th Air Refueling: 25 Jan 1967–. 380th Air Refueling: 16 Aug 1956–1 Apr 1961; 15 Sep 1964–. 528th: 11 Jul 1955– (not operational, 11–31 Jul 1955, 14 Dec 1965–18 Jun 1966, and 6 Jan–c. 16 Jul 1971). 529th: 11 Jul 1955–25 Jun 1966 (not operational, 11–31 Jul 1955 and 11–25 Jun 1966); 1 Jan 1971– (not operational, 1 Jan–30 Sep 1971). 530th: 11 Jul 1955–25 Jun 1966 (not operational, 11–31 Jul 1955 and 11–25 Jun 1966). 531st: 1 May 1959–1 Jan 1962. 556th Strategic Missile: 15 Sep 1964–25 Jun 1965 (not operational, 1 May–25 Jun 1965). 4007th Combat Crew Training: 31 Dec 1971–. 4365th Support (later, 4365th Post Attack Command Control): attached 20 Jul 1962–24 Dec 1964 (not operational, 12 Sep–24 Dec 1964).

Stations. Plattsburgh AFB, NY, 11 Jul 1955–.

Commanders. Col Alvan N. Moore, 11 Jul 1955; Col Alvan C. Gillem II, 20 Dec 1957; Col Harold J. Whiteman, 1 Apr 1961; Col Robert G. Moll, 25 Jun 1965; Col Wallace Wall, Jr., 10 Jul 1965; Col Warren D. Johnson, 1 Jul 1966; Col Howard P. McClain, 1 Jul 1967; Col Wesley L. Pendergraft, 7 Apr 1969; Col Gerhard R. Abendhoff, 20 Feb 1970; Col John M. Parker, 14 Jun 1972; Col Donald R. Nicholas, 19 Apr 1973; Col Robert E. Chapman, 8 Mar 1974; Col Earl T. O'Loughlin, 12 Apr 1974; Col John R. Shipe, 18 Jul 1975; Col Harold J. M. Williams, 26 Jul 1977–.

Aircraft and Missiles. B–47, 1955–1965; KC–97, 1956–1961; EB–47, 1962–1964; KC–135, 1964–; Atlas, 1964–1965; B–52, 1966–1971; FB–111, 1971–.

Operations. Trained in strategic bombardment, Aug 1955–Dec 1965. Flew worldwide air refueling missions, Sep 1956–Apr 1961 and again since Sep 1964; also flew EB–47 post attack command control missions, Jul 1962–Nov 1964. Conducted combat training through a wing detachment at Pinecastle AFB, Fla, 10 Jan–25 Jun 1956, while Plattsburgh AFB, NY, facilities were completed. Deployed at Brize Norton RAF Station, England, 3 Apr–3 Jul 1957. Service tested a "super" wing concept (70 B–47s and 40 KC–97s), Jul 1959–Jun 1960. Briefly controlled Atlas ICBM operations, Sep 1964–Apr 1965. Commenced global strategic bombardment training with B–52s in Jun 1966 and continued through Jan 1971. Converted to FB–111 medium bombers in 1971. Commenced FB–111 strategic bombardment mission in Jul 1971 and FB–111 combat crew training in Aug 1971. Won the SAC bombing and navigation competition, and Fairchild Trophy, in 1974, 1976, and 1977.

Service Streamers. None.

Campaign Streamers. None.

Decorations. Air Force Outstanding Unit Award: 1 Jul 1974–30 Jun 1975.

Emblem. Azure, two cloud formations argent, fesswise, one issuing from dexter enhanced, one from sinister abased, surmounted by a sword in pale, point to base, or, hilt, grip and pommell gules, entwined with an olive branch vert. *Motto:* STRENGTH AND CONFIDENCE. (Approved on 26 Nov 1956.)

381st STRATEGIC MISSILE WING (ICBM–TITAN)

Lineage. Established as 381st Strategic Missile Wing (ICBM–Titan), and activated, on 29 Nov 1961. Organized on 1 Mar 1962.

Assignments. Strategic Air Command, 29 Nov 1961; 42d Air (later, 42d Strategic Aerospace) Division, 1 Mar 1962; 17th Strategic Aerospace Division, 1 Jul 1963; 12th Strategic Missile (later, 12th Air) Division, 30 Jun 1971; 19th Air Division, 1 Jul 1973–.

Components. *Squadrons*. 532d: 1 Mar 1962–. 533d: 1 Aug 1962–.

Stations. McConnell AFB, Kans, 1 Mar 1962–.

Commanders. None (not manned), 29 Nov 1961–28 Feb 1962; Col George W. Von Arb, 1 Mar 1962; Col Julius Pickoff, 11 Jan 1965; Col Theodore J. Michel, 18 Aug 1967; Col James A. Bryant, 30 Sep 1970; Col Bobbie G. Guthrie, 27 Mar 1962; Col Eugene J. Shattuck, Jr., 18 Jun 1973; Col Jimmy F. Scott, 19 Jul 1974; Col Donald F. Gaylor, 7 May 1976–.

Missiles. Titan II, 1963–.

Operations. Trained personnel and prepared to receive intercontinental ballistic missiles, Mar 1962–Jun 1963. Placed first Titan II missiles on alert in Jul 1963. Became the host organization at McConnell AFB, Kans, on 1 Jul 1972.

Service Streamers. None.

Campaign Streamers. None.

Decorations. Air Force Outstanding Unit Awards: 1 Jan 1966–30 Jun 1967; 1 Jul 1971–30 Jun 1972; 1 Jul 1974–30 Jun 1975.

Emblem. Per pale gules and azure, a pale argent surmounted by two olive branches, one in dexter flank and one in sinister flank, conjoined in middle base and extending to chief vert, overall in honor point a globe of the field with land masses and rim sable surmounted by a missile palewise of the like trailing a vapor stream to base of the first, all within a diminished bordure of the third. *Motto:* PEACE, POWER, AND PROTECTION. (Approved on 19 Sep 1962.)

384th AIR REFUELING WING, HEAVY

Lineage. Established as 384th Bombardment Wing, Medium, on 23 Mar 1953. Activated on 1 Aug 1955. Discontinued, and inactivated, on 1 Sep 1964. Redesignated 384th Air Refueling Wing, Heavy, on 15 Nov 1972. Activated on 1 Dec 1972.

Assignments. 825th Air (later, 825th Strategic Aerospace) Division, 1 Aug 1955–1 Sep 1964 (attached to 7th Air Division, 3 Jan–5 Apr 1957). 12th Strategic Missile (later, 12th Air) Division, 1 Dec 1972; 19th Air Division, 1 Jul 1973–.

Components. *Squadrons.* 70th: 1 Aug 1961–1 Sep 1964 (detached 31 Jul–28 Sep 1962 and c. 19 Aug–1 Sep 1964). 91st: 1 Dec 1972–. 384th: 30 Sep 1973–. 544th: 1 Aug 1955–1 Sep 1964. 545th: 1 Aug 1955–1 Sep 1964. 546th: 1 Aug 1955–1 Sep 1964. 547th: 1 Sep 1958–1 Jan 1962.

Stations. Little Rock AFB, Ark, 1 Aug 1955–1 Sep 1964. McConnell AFB, Kans, 1 Dec 1972–.

Commanders. Col Malcolm A. Bailey, 1 Aug 1955; Lt Col Edward D. Gaitley, Jr., Oct 1955; Col George D. Hughes, 1 Nov 1955; Col Delmar E. Wilson, 18 Nov 1955; Col Robert H. Strauss, 14 Jan 1957; Col Davison Dalziel, 3 Dec 1958; Col Willis F. Lewis, 3 Feb 1960; Col James O. Britt, 1 May 1961; Col Henry L. Hogan III, 13 Jun 1962; Col Sherman F. Martin, 13 Jun 1963; Col Stanley Lucich, 25 Jun–1 Sep 1964. Col Harold R. Austin, 1 Dec 1972; Col Ray C. O'Neal, 11 May 1973; Col John A. Bradford, 31 Aug 1974; Col Marion S. Hardin, 24 Feb 1977–.

Aircraft. B–47, 1956–1964; KC–97, 1961–1962, 1962–1963; KC–135, 1964. KC–135, 1972–.

Operations. Poorly manned and without aircraft in 1955. Trained to maintain proficiency in strategic bombing, Feb 1956–Jul 1964, and in aerial refueling, Aug 1961–Oct 1963 and Apr–Aug 1964. Deployed at RAF Station Brize

Norton, England, 3 Jan–5 Apr 1957. Operated out of McConnell AFB, Kans, from Dec 1972. Deployed KC–135 aircraft and crews on a worldwide basis, engaging in actual and simulated tactical and strategic operations, including air refueling support for the evacuation of South Vietnamese and Americans from Vietnam in 1975. Maintained proficiency in air refueling in support of SAC units and other units as directed.

Service Streamers. None.

Campaign Streamers. None.

Decorations. Air Force Outstanding Unit Awards: 15 Feb–30 Dec 1957; 1 Jul 1974–30 Jun 1976.

Emblem. On a shield of the sky, between two cloud formations in chief and one in base throughout proper, five stars, one, two, and two or, the one in chief emitting a ray to each star of the like voided azure, and a lightning flash palewise to base point gules fimbriated argent, all within a diminutive border of the last. *Motto:* KEEP THE SHOW ON THE ROAD. (Approved on 9 Apr 1958.)

385th STRATEGIC AEROSPACE WING

Lineage. Established as 385th Strategic Aerospace Wing, and activated, on 15 Nov 1962. Organized on 1 Jan 1963. Discontinued, and inactivated, on 15 Dec 1964.

Assignments. Strategic Air Command, 15 Nov 1962; 818th Strategic Aerospace Division, 1 Jan 1963–15 Dec 1964.

Components. *Squadrons.* 34th Air Refueling: 1 Jan–15 Dec 1964 (detached 10–15 Dec 1964). 549th Strategic Missile: 1 Jan 1963–15 Dec 1964 (not operational, 1–15 Dec 1964).

Stations. Offutt AFB, Nebr, 1 Jan 1963–15 Dec 1964.

Commanders. None (not manned), 15 Nov–31 Dec 1962; Col Edwin H. Garrison, 1 Jan 1963; Col Allen A. Lathan, 20 Aug–15 Dec 1964.

Aircraft and Missiles. KC–135, 1963–1964; Atlas D, 1963–1964.

Operations. Controlled a mixture of strategic missiles and air refueling aircraft in the 1960s; the former served as a deterrent force and the latter provided airborne command post services and supported SAC's global air refueling mission.

Service Streamers. None.

Campaign Streamers. None.

Decorations. None.

Emblem. None.

386th TROOP CARRIER WING, MEDIUM

Lineage. Established as 386th Troop Carrier Wing, Medium, on 23 Mar 1953.

Assignments. None.

Components. None.

Stations. None.

Commanders. None.

Aircraft. None.

Operations. Never made active.

Service Streamers. None.

Campaign Streamers. None.

Decorations. None.

Emblem. None.

388th TACTICAL FIGHTER WING

Lineage. Established as 388th Fighter–Day Wing on 23 Mar 1953. Redesignated 388th Fighter-Bomber Wing on 5 Nov 1953. Activated on 23 Nov 1953. Inactivated on 10 Dec 1957. Redesignated 388th Tactical Fighter Wing, and activated, on 1 May 1962. Organized on 1 Oct 1962. Discontinued, and inactivated, on 8 Feb 1964. Activated on 14 Mar 1966. Organized on 8 Apr 1966.

Assignments. Ninth Air Force, 23 Nov 1953; Twelfth Air Force, 12 Dec 1954–10 Dec 1957. Tactical Air Command, 1 May 1962; Twelfth Air Force, 1 Oct 1962–8 Feb 1964. Pacific Air Forces, 14 Mar 1966; Thirteenth Air Force, 8 Apr 1966 (attached to Seventh Air Force, 8 Apr 1966–14 Feb 1973; U.S. Support Activities Group/Seventh Air Force, 15 Feb 1973–c. 30 Jun 1975); 17th Air Division, 1 Jul 1975; Twelfth Air Force, 23 Dec 1975–.

Components. *Group.* 388th: 23 Nov 1953–10 Dec 1957 (not operational, 1 Jul–10 Dec 1957). *Squadrons.* 3d: 15 Mar 1973–15 Dec 1975. 4th: 23 Dec 1975– (not operational, 23 Dec 1975–9 Mar 1976). 7th Airborne Command Control: 30 Apr 1972–22 May 1974. 13th: attached 15 May 1966–20 Oct 1967 (not operational, 18–20 Oct 1967). 16th Special Operations: attached 19 Jul 1974–8 Dec 1975. 17th Wild Weasel: 1 Dec 1971–15 Nov 1974 (not operational, 29 Oct–15 Nov 1974). 34th: attached 15 May 1966–14 Mar 1971, assigned 15 Mar 1971– (not operational, 29 Jun–1 Jul 1974 and 23 Dec 1975–31 Mar 1976). 35th: attached c. 12 Jun–c. 10 Oct 1972. 42d Tactical Electronic Warfare: attached c. 21 Sep–14 Oct 1970, assigned 15 Oct 1970–15 Mar 1974 (not operational, 17 Jan–15 Mar 1974). 44th: 25 Apr 1967–15 Oct 1969 (detached 10–15 Oct 1969). 421st: 8 Apr 1966–25 Apr 1967; 23 Dec 1975– (not operational, 23 Dec 1975–2 Aug 1976; detached 9–23 Aug 1977). 469th: 8 Apr 1966–31 Oct 1972. 553d Reconnaissance: 15 Dec 1970–31 Dec 1971 (not operational, 6–31 Dec 1971). 560th: 1 Oct 1962–8 Feb 1964. 561st: attached 1 Jul–10 Dec 1957; assigned 1 Oct 1962–8 Feb 1964 (not operational, 1 Oct 1962–30 Jun 1963). 562d: attached 1 Jul–10 Dec 1957; assigned 1 Oct 1962–8 Feb 1964 (not operational, 1 Oct 1962–30 Jun 1963). 563d: attached 1 Jul–10 Dec 1957; assigned 1 Oct 1962–8 Feb 1964 (not operational, 1 Oct 1962–30 Jun 1963). 6010th Wild Weasel: 1 Nov 1970–1 Dec 1971.

Stations. Clovis AFB, NM, 23 Nov 1953–28 Nov 1954; Etain–Rouvres AB, France, 12 Dec 1954–10 Dec 1957. McConnell AFB, Kans, 1 Oct 1962–8 Feb 1964. Korat RTAFB, Thailand, 8 Apr 1966–23 Dec 1975; Hill AFB, Utah, 23 Dec 1975–.

Commanders. Lt Col Thomas O. Crandall, 23 Nov 1953; Col Clayton L. Peterson, 15 Dec 1953; Col Harold J.

Whiteman, 11 Jan 1954; Brig Gen James F. Whisenand, 23 Feb 1954; Col Harold J. Whiteman, 22 Feb 1955; Col Joseph L. Dickman, 1 Jul 1956–10 Dec 1957. None (not manned), 1 May–30 Sep 1962; Col Richard C. Banbury, 1 Oct 1962; Col Olin E. Gilbert, 1 Oct 1963–8 Feb 1964. None (not manned), 14 Mar–7 Apr 1966; Col Monroe S. Sams, 8 Apr 1966; Brig Gen William S. Chairsell, c. 17 Aug 1966; Col Edward B. Burdett, 1 Aug 1967; Col Jack C. Berger, 18 Nov 1967; Col Neil J. Graham, 22 Nov 1967; Col Norman P. Phillips, 19 Jan 1968; Col Paul P. Douglas, Jr., 24 Jan 1968; Col Allen K. McDonald, 23 Jul 1968; Col Paul P. Douglas, Jr., 19 Aug 1968; Col Allen K. McDonald, 15 Dec 1968; Col John A. Nelson, 11 Jun 1969; Col James M. Breedlove, 5 Dec 1969; Col Ivan H. Dethman, 30 Jun 1970; Col Irby B. Jarvis, Jr., 1 Aug 1970; Col Webb Thompson, 26 Jul 1971; Col Stanley M. Umstead, Jr., 15 Dec 1971; Col Richard E. Markling, 5 Aug 1972; Col Mele Vojvodich, Jr., 25 Jan 1973; Col Robert K. Crouch, 1 Jul 1973; Col Thomas H. Normile, 3 Jan 1974; Col John P. Russell, 3 Jul 1974; Col Neil L. Eddins, 11 Jul 1975; Col Robert L. Rodee, 19 Apr 1977; Col Davis C. Rohr, 3 Aug 1977–.

Aircraft. F–86, 1954–1957; F–100, 1957. F–100, 1962–1964; F–105, 1963–1964. F–105, 1966–1969, 1970–1974; F–4, 1969–1975, 1976–; EB–66, 1970–1974; EC–121, 1970–1971; C–130, 1972–1974; A–7, 1973–1975; AC–130, 1974–1975.

Operations. Trained as a fighter-bomber wing in NM, Feb–Oct 1954. Moved to four European bases in Nov–Dec 1954. Participated in NATO operations and exercises, Dec 1954–Dec 1957. Replaced by 49th Fighter-Bomber Wing in Dec 1957. Trained with F–100s and F–105s at McConnell AFB, Kans, and Nellis AFB, Nev, Oct 1962–Jan 1964. Replaced by 23d Tactical Fighter Wing in Feb 1964. Replaced 6234th Tactical Fighter Wing in Thailand in Apr 1966. Flew combat missions in Southeast Asia, 8 Apr 1966–15 Aug 1973, initially with F–105s and later with F–4s. Added a variety of other special-purpose aircraft and related missions as the war progressed. Following the final ceasefire in Aug 1973, entered into intensive training program to maintain combat readiness. Provided air cover and escort during the evacuation of Americans from Phnom Penh, Cambodia, and of Americans and selected Vietnamese from Saigon, South Vietnam, in Apr 1975. Participated in the rescue of the crew and recovery of the SS *Mayaguez* from the Cambodians in May 1975. Ceased all aircraft operations on 28 Nov 1975 and moved in name only to Hill AFB, Utah, on 23 Dec 1975, replacing a holding unit—Det 1, HQ 67th Combat Support Group. Received F–4Ds in Jan 1976 and commenced F–4D flying operations on 15 Mar 1976. Began initial preparations in Apr 1977 to convert to F–16 aircraft in 1979.

Service Streamers. None.

Campaign Streamers. Vietnam Air; Vietnam Air Offensive; Vietnam Air Offensive, Phase II; Vietnam Air Offensive, Phase III; Vietnam Air/Ground; Vietnam Air Offensive, Phase IV; TET 69/Counteroffensive; Vietnam Summer–Fall, 1969; Vietnam Winter–Spring, 1970; Sanctuary Counteroffensive; Southwest Monsoon; Commando Hunt V; Commando Hunt

VI; Commando Hunt VII; Vietnam Ceasefire.

Decorations. Presidential Unit Citation (Southeast Asia): 10 Mar–1 May 1967. Air Force Outstanding Unit Awards with Combat "V" Device: 29–30 Jun 1966; 1 Jul 1966–30 Jun 1967; 1 Jul 1967–30 Jun 1968; 1 Jul 1968–15 Sep 1969; 10 Oct 1970–20 May 1971; 18 Dec 1972–15 Aug 1973; 15 Oct 1974–12 May 1975; 13–15 May 1975. Republic of Vietnam Gallantry Cross with Palm: 8 Apr 1966–28 Jan 1973.

Emblem. Per bend azure and gules, on a bend or, a lightning flash sable. The shield is supported by two wings light blue, feathered and detail black, below the shield on a scroll the motto. Motto: LIBERTAS VEL MORS—Liberty or death. (Approved on 11 Mar 1955.)

389th STRATEGIC MISSILE WING (ICBM–ATLAS)

Lineage. Established as 389th Strategic Missile Wing (ICBM–Atlas), and activated, on 26 Apr 1961. Organized on 1 Jul 1961. Discontinued, and inactivated, on 25 Mar 1965.

Assignments. Strategic Air Command, 26 Apr 1961; 13th Air (later, 13th Strategic Missile) Division, 1 Jul 1961–25 Mar 1965.

Components. *Squadrons*. 564th: 1 Jul 1961–1 Sep 1964 (not operational, 3 Aug–1 Sep 1964). 565th: 1 Jul 1961–1 Dec 1964 (not operational, Oct–1 Dec 1964). 566th: 1 Jul 1961–25 Mar 1965 (not operational, c. 15 Feb–25 Mar 1965).

Stations. Francis E. Warren AFB, Wyo, 1 Jul 1961–25 Mar 1965.

Commanders. None (not manned), 26 Apr–30 Jun 1961; Col George T. Chadwell, 1 Jul 1961; Col Julius B. Summers, Jr., 12 Dec 1963–25 Mar 1965.

Missiles. Atlas, 1961–1965.

Operations. Replaced 706th SMW (ICBM–Atlas) in Jul 1961. Conducted strategic missile training operations as directed by higher headquarters.

Service Streamers. None.

Campaign Streamers. None.

Decorations. None.

Emblem. Azure, issuant from dexter base a demi-globe dark blue in front of a cloud in fess throughout dark gray and bendwise in pale overall a missile ascendant argent tipped gules and finned or emitting to base three flashes of the fifth; all within a diminished bordure dimidiated of the sixth and of the second. (Approved on 15 May 1962.)

390th STRATEGIC MISSILE WING (ICBM–TITAN)

Lineage. Established as 390th Bombardment Wing, Medium, on 23 Mar 1953. Redesignated 390th Strategic Missile Wing (ICBM–Titan), and activated, on 28 Nov 1961. Organized on 1 Jan 1962.

Assignments. Strategic Air Command, 28 Nov 1961; 12th Air (later, 12th Strategic Aerospace; 12th Strategic Missile; 12th Air) Division, 1 Jan 1962–.

Components. *Squadrons*. 570th: 1 Jan 1962–. 571st: 1 May 1962–.

Stations. Davis-Monthan AFB, Ariz, 1 Jan 1962–.

Commanders. None (not manned), 28 Nov–31 Dec 1961; Col Raymond D. Sampson, 1 Jan 1962; Col John C. Fahringer, (by 5) Jun 1962; Col Clyde J. Johnson, c. 26 Jul 1962; Col Raymond D. Sampson, Aug 1962; Col Robert J. Hill, 15 Dec 1965; Col Robert R. Scott, 1 Aug 1966; Col Charles R. Hammack, 25 Jul 1968; Col Edward P. Denton, 6 Jan 1969; Col Edgar A. Northrup, Jr., 7 Dec 1971; Col Eugene D. Scott, 29 Jan 1973; Col Joseph P. Cerny, 10 Feb 1975; Col George Holt, Jr., 15 Jul 1976; Col Charles H. Greenley, 30 Sep 1977–.

Missiles. Titan II, 1963–.

Operations. Formed from "scratch" in Jan 1962, although some cadre came from the 303d Bombardment Wing at Davis-Monthan AFB, Ariz. Supervised and coordinated SM–68B Titan II intercontinental ballistic missile personnel training and facility construction, Jan 1962–Nov 1963. First Titan II missile arrived on 27 Nov 1962 and was installed in its silo on 8 Dec 1962. The wing accepted its first Titan II missile complex on 31 Mar 1963. The 570th Squadron became fully operational on 13 Jun 1963 and the 571st Squadron on 30 Nov 1963. Wing was declared fully operational on 1 Dec 1963. Named as "Best Titan Wing in SAC" following missile combat competitions in 1969, 1970, 1974 and 1977.

Service Streamers. None.

Campaign Streamers. None.

Decorations. Air Force Outstanding Unit Awards: 1 Jul 1969–30 Jun 1970; 1 Jul 1976–30 Jun 1977.

Emblem. Per pale argent and azure, originating in dexter flank and arched to chief an olive branch vert, in sinister three mullets chevronwise to dexter of the first, over all in base a cloud gules enfiled by an open mailed hand with fingers outstretched, the finger tips surmounted by a missile both palewise of the first, all within a diminished bordure or. *Motto:* NON NOBIS SOLUM—Not for ourselves alone. (Approved on 2 Mar 1964.)

392d STRATEGIC MISSILE WING

Lineage. Established as 392d Bombardment Wing, Light, on 16 May 1949. Activated in the Reserve on 27 Jun 1949. Inactivated on 10 Nov 1949. Redesignated 392d Fighter-Day Wing on 23 Mar 1953. Redesignated 392d Strategic Missile Wing, and activated, on 6 Oct 1961. Organized on 18 Oct 1961. Discontinued, and inactivated, on 20 Dec 1961.

Assignments. Twelfth Air Force, 27 Jun–10 Nov 1949 (attached to 47th Bombardment Wing, Light, 27 Jun–2 Oct 1949). Strategic Air Command, 6 Oct 1961; 1st Strategic Aerospace Division, 18 Oct–20 Dec 1961.

Components. *Group.* 392d: 27 Jun–10 Nov 1949. *Squadron.* 576th: 18 Oct–20 Dec 1961 (detached 18–19 Oct and 15–20 Dec 1961).

Stations. Barksdale AFB, La, 27 Jun–10 Nov 1949. Vandenberg AFB, Calif, 18 Oct–20 Dec 1961.

Commanders. Brig Gen T. B. Herndon, 27 Jun–10 Nov 1949. None (not manned), 6–19 Oct 1961; Brig Gen Roger M. Crow, 20 Oct–14 Dec 1961; none (not manned), 15–20 Dec 1961.

Aircraft and Missiles. B–26, 1949. Atlas, Minuteman, and Titan, 1961.

Operations. Reserve corollary of 47th Bombardment Wing, Light, 1949. Formed in 1961 to control missile training operations, but eliminated by reorganization of 1st Strategic Aerospace Division.

Service Streamers. None.

Campaign Streamers. None.

Decorations. None.

Emblem. None.

397th BOMBARDMENT WING, HEAVY

Lineage. Established as 397th Bombardment Wing, Heavy, and activated, on 15 Nov 1962. Organized on 1 Feb 1963. Discontinued, and inactivated, on 25 Apr 1968.

Assignments. Strategic Air Command, 15 Nov 1962; 6th Air Division, 1 Feb 1963; 45th Air Division, 2 Jul 1966–25 Apr 1968.

Components. *Squadrons.* 19th Air Refueling: 1 Feb–15 Jun 1963. 71st Air Refueling: 1 Feb 1963–25 Apr 1968 (detached 1–25 Apr 1968). 341st Air Refueling: 1 Feb–1 Sep 1963 (not operational, c. 15 Jul–1 Sep 1963). 596th: 1 Feb 1963–25 Apr 1968 (detached 1–25 Apr 1968).

Stations. Dow AFB, Maine, 1 Feb 1963–25 Apr 1968.

Commanders. None (not manned), 15 Nov 1962–31 Jan 1963; Col Harry R. Burrell, 1 Feb 1963; Col John W. Kline, 10 Jul 1963; Col James L. Flanagan, 1 May 1964–25 Apr 1968.

Aircraft. B–52, 1963–1968; KC–97, 1963–1964; KC–135, 1964–1968.

Operations. Replaced the 4038th Strategic Wing in Feb 1963. Conducted bombardment training and air refueling operations to meet SAC commitments.

Service Streamers. None.

Campaign Streamers. None.

Decorations. None.

Emblem. Sable, a bend azure, in dexter base a demi-sphere or, grid lines of the first, issuant from the sphere and arched to dexter chief a trail argent terminating behind an aircraft bend sinisterwise between two three-pointed stars all of the like, all within a diminished bordure of the last. *Motto:* CUSTODES LIBERTATIS—Guardian of freedom. (Approved on 30 Oct 1963.)

401st TACTICAL FIGHTER WING

Lineage. Established as 401st Fighter-Bomber Wing on 23 Mar 1953. Activated on 25 Sep 1957. Redesignated 401st Tactical Fighter Wing on 1 Jul 1958.

Assignments. 834th Air Division, 25 Sep 1957; Twelfth Air Force, 1 Apr 1959 (attached to Air Division Provisional, 4481st, 1 Jan–30 Jun 1964); 834th Air Division, 1 Jul 1964; Sixteenth Air Force, 27 Apr 1966–.

Components. *Squadrons.* 90th: attached c. 5 Dec 1965–c. 7 Feb 1966. 307th: 27 Apr 1966–15 Jul 1971. 353d: 27 Apr 1966–15 Jul 1971. 531st: attached 19 Nov–c. 10 Dec 1965. 612th: 25 Sep 1957–3 Nov 1965; 15 Jul 1971–. 613th: 25 Sep 1957–. 614th: 25 Sep 1957–27 Apr 1966; 15 Jul 1971–. 615th: 25 Sep 1957–27 Apr 1966.

Stations. England AFB, La, 25 Sep 1957–22 Apr 1966; Torrejon AB, Spain, 27 Apr 1966–.

Commanders. Col Chester L. Van Etten, 25 Sep 1957; Brig Gen Ivan W. McElroy, 1 Apr 1959; Col Albert W. Schinz, 10 Jun 1960; Col Niven K. Cranfill, 11 Mar 1962; Col Richard V. Travis, 15 Mar 1962 (additional duty, 1 Jan–22 Sep 1964); Col William P. McBride, 23 Sep 1964; Col Harold G. Shook, 14 Jun 1965; Col Clayton M. Isaacson, 7 May 1966; Brig Gen Sanford K. Moats, 20 Apr 1967; Col Herndon F. Williams, 2 Nov 1968; Col James M. Hoag, Jr., 8 Jan 1970; Col Wilbur L. Creech, 17 Nov 1970; Col Tony M. Greget, 19 Jul 1971; Col Richard G. Collins, 6 Sep 1972; Col Charles L. Donnelly, Jr., 1 Nov 1973; Col Benjamin R. Battle, 17 Jul 1975; Col Anthony T. Sheehan, 14 Jul 1977–.

Aircraft. F–84, 1957; F–100, 1957–1970; F–4, 1970–.

Operations. From Sep 1957 to Apr 1966, the wing participated in numerous firepower demonstrations, tactical exercises and maneuvers in the United States and overseas, and deployed its tactical squadrons to bases in Europe and the Middle East in support of NATO. From 19 Oct to 5 Dec 1962, during the Cuban missile crisis, all wing tactical and support elements not deployed overseas operated from Homestead AFB, Fla. From Feb 1964 to Nov 1965, squadron deployments shifted to the Far East and Southeast Asia in support of operations in that area, then returned to support operations in Europe-Middle East. The wing moved to Spain in Apr 1966, and from Torrejon AB continued NATO support by keeping deployed tactical squadrons on alert status. The only break in this status came during conversion from F–100 to F–4 aircraft in 1970.

Service Streamers. None.

Campaign Streamers. None.

Decorations. Air Force Outstanding Unit Award: 1 Jan–31 Dec 1963.

Emblem. Azure, within a diminutive border argent a sheaf of four lances bend sinisterwise of the last, surmounted by a fess chequy sable and of the second overall a bend wavy vert, gules, or and of the first each fimbriated silver. *Motto:* CAELUM ARENA NOSTRA—The sky is our arena. (Approved on 9 Sep 1958.)

402d FIGHTER-DAY WING

Lineage. Established as 402d Fighter-Day Wing on 23 Mar 1953.
Assignments. None.
Components. None.
Stations. None.
Commanders. None.
Aircraft. None.
Operations. Never made active.
Service Streamers. None.
Campaign Streamers. None.
Decorations. None.
Emblem. None.

403d RESCUE AND WEATHER RECONNAISSANCE WING

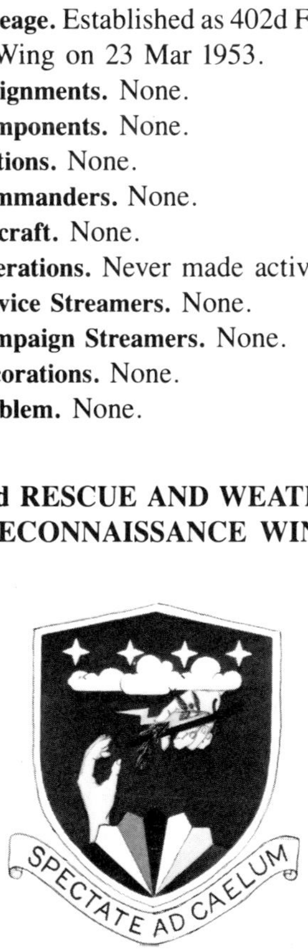

Lineage. Established as 403d Troop Carrier Wing, Medium, on 10 May 1949. Activated in the Reserve on 27 Jun 1949. Ordered to active service on 1 Apr 1951. Inactivated on 1 Jan 1953. Activated in the Reserve on 1 Jan 1953. Ordered to active service on 28 Oct 1962. Relieved from active duty on 28 Nov 1962. Redesignated: 403d Tactical Airlift Wing on 1 Jul 1967; 403d Composite Wing on 31 Dec 1969; 403d Tactical Airlift Wing on 29 Jul 1971; 403d Aerospace Rescue and Recovery Wing on 15 Mar 1976; 403d Rescue and Weather Reconnaissance Wing on 1 Jan 1977.

Assignments. Fourth Air Force, 27 Jun 1949; Tactical Air Command, 2 Apr 1951; Eighteenth Air Force, 1 Jun 1951–1 Jan 1953 (attached to 315th Air Division [Combat Cargo], 14 Apr 1952–1 Jan 1953). Fourth Air Force, 1 Jan 1953; Tenth Air Force, 16 Nov 1957; Fifth Air Force Reserve Region, 1 Sep 1960; Twelfth Air Force, 28 Oct 1962; Fifth Air Force Reserve Region, 28 Nov 1962; Central Air Force Reserve Region, 31 Dec 1969; Eastern Air Force Reserve Region, 1 Apr 1971; Western Air Force Reserve Region, 15 Mar 1976; Fourth Air Force (Reserve), 8 Oct 1976–.

Components. *Groups*. 314th: attached 14 Apr–31 Dec 1952. 403d: 27 Jun 1949–1 Jan 1953; 1 Jan 1953–14 Apr 1959. 913th: 21 Apr 1971–8 Jan 1976. 914th: 21 Apr 1971–8 Jan 1976. 920th: 1 Jan 1977–. 927th: 11 Feb 1963–31 Dec 1969; 1 Jun 1970–15 Mar 1976. 928th: 11 Feb 1963–1 Dec 1969. 929th: 11 Feb 1963–1 Jan 1964. 930th: 1 Jun 1970–15 Jan 1971. 931st: 1 Jun 1970–15 Jan 1971. *Squadrons*. 21st: attached 14 Apr–1 Dec 1952. 53d: attached 14 Apr–c. 12 Sep 1952. 63d: 14 Apr 1959–11 Feb 1963. 64th: 14 Apr 1959–11 Feb 1963. 65th: 14 Apr 1959–11 Feb 1963. 301st: 15 Mar

1976–. 303d: 15 Mar 1976–. 304th: 15 Mar 1976–. 305th: 15 Mar 1976–. 6461st: attached 1–31 Dec 1952.

Stations. Portland Aprt (later, Intl Aprt), Ore, 27 Jun 1949–25 Mar 1952; Ashiya AB, Japan, 14 Apr 1952–1 Jan 1953. Portland Intl Aprt, Ore, 1 Jan 1953; Selfridge AFB (later, ANG Base), Mich, 16 Nov 1957–.

Commanders. Brig Gen Chester E. McCarty, 27 Jun 1949; Col Sidney S. Murphy, c. Jul 1951; Brig Gen Chester E. McCarty, Aug 1951; Lt Col Robert E. Harrington, 6 Dec 1951; Brig Gen Chester E. McCarty, 8 Feb 1952; Col Philip H. Best, 14 Apr 1952; Col Maurice F. Casey, 15 May 1952–1 Jan 1953. Unkn, 1 Jan 1953–unkn; Col Robert W. Sheets, (by Jan 1954); Col James H. McPartlin, 16 Nov 1957; Col Carl F. King, 1 Aug 1961; Col George L. Kittle, 1 Dec 1970; Brig Gen George H. Wilson, 22 Mar 1971; Brig Gen Roy M. Marshall, 25 Jun 1973; Col James S. Brown, 22 Jul 1976; Lt Col Elmer C. Apel, 27 Aug 1976; Col James C. Wahleithner, 18 Jan 1977–.

Aircraft. T–7, 1949–1951; T–11, 1949–1951; C/TC–46, 1949–1952; C/VC–47, 1952; C–54, 1952; C–119, 1952. C–46, 1953–1957; TC–47, 1957–unkn; C–119, 1957–1969, 1970; U–3, 1969, 1970–1971; O–2, 1970–1971; A–37, 1970–1971; C–130, 1971–1976, 1977–; HH–1, 1976–; HH–3, 1976–; CH–3, 1976–; HC–130, 1976–; WC–130, 1977–.

Operations. Trained as a Reserve troop carrier wing until called to active service in Apr 1951, then trained to gain combat proficiency. Moved to Japan in Apr 1952 and for remainder of that year supported troop carrier and tactical airlift requirements of the Far East Command and United Nations. Inactivated in Japan and activated at Portland Intl Aprt on 1 Jan 1953, again as a Reserve wing. Until Nov 1957, trained as a Reserve troop carrier wing. Moved without personnel or equipment to Selfridge AFB, Mich, in Nov 1957, absorbing resources of another Reserve wing. Continued training as a Reserve troop carrier wing, beginning the Air Reserve Technician (ART) program in Apr 1958. Participated in many tactical exercises and humanitarian missions. Had a 1-month tour of active duty during the Cuban missile crisis of 1962. Assumed an additional mission of tactical air support and trained with U–3As for a short period in 1969. Had no components (except its headquarters) from 31 Dec 1969 to 1 Jun 1970. Assumed a tactical air support and special operations mission in Jun 1970, using O–2, U–3, and A–37 aircraft. Lost O–2, U–3, and A–37 aircraft in 1971 and gained C–130s for tactical airlift missions. For the next 5 years, the wing performed tactical airlift operations, participating in many exercises and humanitarian missions. Flights were made on a global basis, many to Southeast Asia. Shifted to a rescue and recovery mission in 1976, controlling all four Air Force Reserve rescue squadrons. In Jan 1977, added weather reconnaissance to its mission.

Service Streamers. Korean Theater.

Campaign Streamers. None.

Decorations. Republic of Korea Presidential Unit Citation: [14 Apr 1952]–[31 Dec 1952]. Republic of Vietnam Gallantry Cross with Palm: 14 Feb–11 Mar 1968.

Emblem. Azure, two hands in bend sinister proper, the upper a dexter hand issuing from a cloud argent and holding an olive branch of the second, a lightning flash or and a sword sable, the lower sinister hand in profile issuing from a fan indented of seven sections, which in turn issue from base, above the cloud four mullets of four points of the third, all within a diminished bordure of the last. *Motto:* SPECTATE AD CAELUM—Look to the skies. (Approved on 9 Jan 1953.)

405th FIGHTER WING

Lineage. Established as 405th Fighter-Bomber Wing on 15 Oct 1952. Activated on 1 Dec 1952. Inactivated on 1 Jul 1958. Redesignated 405th Fighter Wing on 11 Mar 1959. Activated on 9 Apr 1959. Inactivated on 16 Sep 1974.

Assignments. Ninth Air Force, 1 Dec 1952; Tactical Air Command, 16 Apr 1953; Ninth Air Force, 1 Jul 1956; 836th Air Division, 8 Oct 1957–1 Jul 1958. Thirteenth Air Force, 9 Apr 1959; 6th Air Division, 1 Aug 1968; Thirteenth Air Force, 15 Dec 1969–16 Sep 1974.

Components. *Groups*. 305th Bombardment: attached 19 Jul 1954–8 Oct 1957. 405th: 1 Dec 1952–8 Oct 1957. 4400th Combat Crew Training: attached 1 May 1953–19 Jul 1954. *Squadrons*. 1st Test: 30 Apr 1970–16 Sep 1974 (detached). 8th Bombardment (later, 8th Special Operations; 8th Fighter): attached 9 Apr–4 Aug 1964 and 4–17 Nov 1964, assigned 18 Nov 1964–15 Jan 1968 (detached 18 Jun–15 Aug 1965, 16 Oct–16 Dec 1965, 15 Feb–18 Apr 1966, 15 Jun–15 Aug 1966, 12 Oct–12 Dec 1966, 11 Feb–12 Apr 1967, 7 Jun–2 Aug 1967, 26 Sep–21 Nov 1957); attached 15–17 Jan 1968; assigned 1 Oct 1972–1 Mar 1974 (not operational). 13th Bombardment (later, 13th Fighter): attached 10 Apr–17 Nov 1964, assigned 18 Nov 1964–15 Jan 1968 (detached 5 Aug–3 Nov 1964, 17 Feb–21 Jun 1965, 16 Aug–16 Oct 1965, 16 Dec 1965–17 Feb 1966, 17 Apr–17 Jun 1966, 14 Aug–13 Oct 1966, 12 Dec 1966–11 Feb 1967, 11 Apr–8 Jun 1967, 1 Aug–26 Sep 1967, 21 Nov 1967–15 Jan 1968); assigned 24 Dec 1972–30 Sep 1973 (not operational). 20th Operations: 31 Dec 1971–16 Sep 1974. 26th Tactical Fighter: 30 Sep 1973–16 Sep 1974 (not operational). 43d Tactical Fighter: attached 17 Aug–20 Oct 1965. 46th Tactical Fighter: attached 15 May–2 Aug 1965. 64th Tactical Fighter: 10 Jun 1966–15 Dec 1969 (detached 3 Feb–28 Jun 1968; not operational, 1–15 Dec 1969). 68th Tactical Fighter: 30 Sep 1973–16 Sep 1974 (not operational). 90th Tactical Fighter (later, 90th Special Operations; 90th Tactical Fighter): attached 7 Feb–c. 8 May 1965; assigned 15 Dec 1972–16 Sep 1974 (not operational, 15 Dec 1972–31 Aug 1973). 390th Tactical Fighter: attached c. 4–18 Nov 1965. 422d Bombardment: attached 1 May–c. 11 Dec 1953. 429th Air Refueling: attached 19 Jul 1954–1 Jul 1958. 478th Tactical Fighter: attached

23 May–8 Jun 1962. 508th: 8 Oct 1957–1 Apr 1958 (not operational, 20 Mar–1 Apr 1958). 509th: 8 Oct 1957–1 Jul 1958 (detached 8 Oct 1957–24 Mar 1958; not operational, c. 28 Mar–1 Jul 1958); 9 Apr 1959–24 Jul 1970 (detached Aug 1964–Nov 1965; not operational, 17–24 Jul 1970). 510th: 8 Oct 1957–1 Jul 1958 (not operational, 15 Apr–1 Jul 1958); 9 Apr 1959–16 Mar 1964 (detached 16 May–8 Jun 1962); attached c. 8 May–17 Aug 1965. 511th: 8 Oct 1957–1 Jul 1958 (not operational, 15 May–1 Jul 1958). 522d Tactical Fighter: attached 15 Aug–c. 23 Nov 1965. 523d Tactical Fighter: 20 Nov 1965–31 Aug 1973 (detached 9 Apr–24 Oct 1972). 531st Tactical Fighter: attached 6 Nov 1964–7 Feb 1965. 612th Tactical Fighter: attached 28 Feb–c. 4 Jun 1964. 615th Tactical Fighter: attached c. 4 Jun–6 Jun 1964. 774th Tactical Airlift: 31 Dec 1971–15 Sep 1972 (not operational, 2–15 Sep 1972). *Flights.* 4424th Helicopter: attached 1 May 1953–c. 23 Aug 1954. Flight A, 2d Liaison Squadron: attached 1 May 1953–18 Jun 1954.

Stations. Godman AFB, Ky, 1 Dec 1952; Langley AFB, Va, 16 Apr 1953–1 Jul 1958. Clark AB, Philippines, 9 Apr 1959–16 Sep 1974.

Commanders. Col Robert L. Delashaw, 1 Dec 1952; Brig Gen Charles D. Jones, 18 Apr 1953; Col Donald A. Baccus, 17 Jun 1953; Col Burton K. Sams, 6 Jul 1953; Brig Gen Charles D. Jones, 13 Jul 1953; Col Donald A. Baccus, 30 Sep 1953; Brig Gen Charles D. Jones, 26 Oct 1953; Brig Gen Edwin S. Chickering, 23 Aug 1954; Col William I. Williams, 8 Oct 1957–1 Jul 1958. Col James K. Dowling, 9 Apr 1959; Col Edward W. Szaniawski, 6 Jul 1959; Col Roscoe C. Crawford, Jr., c. 23 Jun 1962; Col George Laven, Jr., 10 Aug 1963; Col James E. Hill, 30 Sep 1964; Col Vermont Garrison, 5 Jan 1966; Col Charles E. Yeager, 4 Aug 1966; Col Duncan C. Myers, 4 Jan 1968; Col Edward P. McNeff, 5 Feb 1968; Col Walter J. Brown, 10 Jan 1970; Col James E. Tilton, 1 Jun 1971; Col John R. Geyer, 1 Jan 1972; Col Henry C. Gordon, 6 Jun 1972; Col Lacy W. Breckenridge, 8 Jun 1974; Col George L. Schulstad, 15 Jun–16 Sep 1974.

Aircraft. Primarily F–47, 1952; F–84, 1953–1956; B–45, 1953; B–26, 1953–1956; B/RB–57, 1954–1957; RB–29, 1954; KB–29, 1954–1956; F–100, 1956–1958; and KB–50, 1956–1958; but also flew, in fewer numbers, H–19, 1953–1956; L–20, 1953–1956; C–45, 1954–1956; C/VC–47, 1954–1956; C–119, 1954–1956; VC–54, 1955; and VC–131, 1955. F–86, 1959–1960; F–100, 1959–1964, 1964–1967; F–102, 1960–1970; F–4, 1965, 1967–1974; B–57, 1964–1968; C–130, 1972; C–118, 1972; and C–9, 1972–1974.

Operations. Replaced 108th Fighter-Bomber Wing in Dec 1952. Operated Godman AFB, Ky, Dec 1952–Apr 1953, and Langley AFB, Va, May 1953–Oct 1957. At the latter base, replaced 4430th Air Base Wing and operationally controlled numerous tactical and support components until Oct 1957. Operations included gunnery and bombardment training, firepower demonstrations, weapons delivery training, and numerous tactical exercises, 1952–1958, plus air refueling, 1954–1958. Replaced 6200th Air Base Wing at Clark AB, Philippines, in Apr 1959. Provided air defense and offensive fighter operations in the Philippines, Taiwan, and other Far Eastern points, Apr 1959–Jun 1962. Operated Clark AB and its satellite facilities, Apr 1959–Mar 1965 and Dec 1971–Sep 1974. Provided air defense training for Royal Thai Air Force personnel, from a base in Thailand, Nov 1961–Feb 1966. From mid–1962 until the end of the conflict in Southeast Asia, frequently deployed assigned and attached components to bases in Southeast Asia for air defense and combat operations under operational control of other organizations. When not so involved, components trained in air defense and other tactical exercises in Taiwan and the Philippines. During Jul–Aug 1972, provided extensive flood relief to Philippine areas inundated by monsoon rains. During Feb–Mar 1973, provided medical, logistical, and administrative support for former prisoners of war, on their way to the United States from North Vietnam. Replaced by 3d Tactical Fighter Wing in Sep 1974.

Service Streamers. None.

Campaign Streamers. None.

Decorations. Air Force Outstanding Unit Awards: 1 Nov 1960–30 Jun 1961; 5 Aug 1964–31 Mar 1965. Philippine Republic Presidential Unit Citation: 21 Jul–15 Aug 1972.

Emblem. On a shield azure, a sphere argent, land marking and grid lines sable, surmounted by a bend gules, charged with a lightning flash or, between a fleur-de-lis of the last and two olive branches in saltire, proper, all within a diminutive bordure of the second. *Motto:* MOVERE ET AGGREDI—Deploy and attack. (Approved on 10 Nov 1955.)

406th TACTICAL FIGHTER TRAINING WING

Lineage. Established as 406th Fighter-Bomber Wing on 25 Jun 1952. Activated on 10 Jul 1952. Redesignated 406th Fighter-Interceptor Wing on 1 Apr 1954. Inactivated on 15 May 1958. Redesignated 406th Tactical Fighter Training Wing on 20 Jun 1972. Activated on 15 Jul 1972.

Assignments. Third Air Force, 10 Jul 1952–15 May 1958 (attached to Twelfth Air Force, 10 Jul 1952–31 Mar 1954; RAF Fighter Command, 1 Apr 1954–15 Feb 1958). Sixteenth Air Force, 15 Jul 1972–.

Components. *Group.* 406th: 10 Jul 1952–1 May 1956. *Squadrons.* 87th: attached 21 Dec 1954–8 Sep 1955. 512th: 1 May 1956–24 Mar 1958. 513th: 1 May 1956–25 Apr 1958. 514th: 1 May 1956–15 May 1958.

Stations. RAF Station Manston (later, RAF Manston), England, 10 Jul 1952–15 May 1958. Zaragoza AB, Spain, 15 Jul 1972–.

Commanders. Col Philip P. Ardery, 10 Jul 1952; Col George F. Ceuleers, 13 Oct 1952; Col Conrad J. Herlick, 26 Oct 1952; Col William S. Harrell, 15 Jun

1955; Col Hugh B. Manson, Jr., 8 Jul 1955–15 May 1958. Col Richard G. Collins, 15 Jul 1972; Col Carl H. Cathey, Jr., 30 Aug 1972; Col Richard E. Skelton, 20 Apr 1974; Col Benjamin R. Battle, 25 Apr 1975; Col David W. Forgan, 14 Jul 1975; Col Harley N. Wills, 14 Jul 1977–.

Aircraft. F–84, 1952–1953; F–86, 1953–1958.

Operations. Replaced 123d Fighter-Bomber Wing in Jul 1952. Trained in fighter-bomber and air defense operations, 1952–1953. Provided air defense in the United Kingdom, 1954–1958, and in the Netherlands, 1954–1955. Phased down for inactivation, 15 Feb–15 May 1958. Replaced 406th Tactical Fighter Training Group in Jul 1972. Assumed responsibility for operating and maintaining Zaragoza AB, Spain, and associated gunnery ranges and air combat tactics training area. Combat units of the United States Air Forces in Europe (USAFE) sent weapons training detachments to Zaragoza for training. These detachments were fully supported, and temporarily controlled, by the 406th TFTW, although the wing had no tactical squadrons or aircraft permanently assigned. In addition to range training, attached detachments often participated in tactical exercises. Beginning in Sep 1972 the wing also operated the USAFE Tactical Forces Employment School, and in May 1976 began operating the USAFE Instructor Pilot School. Weapons training detachments were principally F–4 aircraft, although F–111s used the wing's ranges for a short period in 1974 and U.S. Navy A–7s also used range facilities in Jun 1974, operating temporarily from Zaragoza. From 1 Nov to 17 Dec 1976, and 5 Jan to 2 Mar 1977, OV–10 detachments used the ranges, and from 15 Nov to 17 Dec 1976, and 5 Jan to 29 Apr 1977, F–5s also used the ranges. The 406th TFTW began full maintenance support of a SAC KC–135 detachment on a permanent basis in Nov 1976.

Service Streamers. None.

Campaign Streamers. None.

Decorations. Air Force Outstanding Unit Awards: [15 Jul 1972]–30 Jun 1973; 1 Jul 1974–30 Jun 1976.

Emblem. Azure, a bend gules fimbriated argent, overall a dexter hand in spiked mail gauntlet palewise proper, grasping a three-pronged lightning flash or and surmounted at the cuff by a chain of four links of the last. *Motto:* ASCENDE ET DEFENDE—Rise and defend. (Approved on 14 May 1953.)

407th STRATEGIC FIGHTER WING

Lineage. Established as 407th Strategic Fighter Wing on 23 Mar 1953. Activated on 18 Dec 1953. Inactivated on 1 Jul 1957.

Assignments. Fifteenth Air Force, 18 Dec 1953–1 Jul 1957 (attached to 39th Air Division [Defense], 8 Aug–10 Nov 1954).

Components. *Squadrons.* 91st Strategic Reconnaissance: attached 20 Dec 1954–15 Jul 1955. 407th Air Refueling: 18 Dec 1953–1 Jul 1957. 515th: 18 Dec 1953–1 Jul 1957. 516th: 18 Dec 1953–1 Jul 1957 (detached 5 Feb–9 May 1957). 517th: 18 Dec 1953–1 Jul 1957 (detached 6 Feb–8 May 1956).

Stations. Great Falls (later, Malmstrom) AFB, Mont, 18 Dec 1953–1 Jul 1957.

Commanders. Col Lester S. Harris, 18 Dec 1953; Col Charles A. Gayle, 25 Jun 1955; Col Murray A. Bywater, 21 Jul 1955; Lt Col George T. Walker, c. Nov 1955; Col Charles A. Gayle, c. Dec 1955; Col Murray A. Bywater, c. Feb 1956; Col Salvador P. LaBarbera, c. Apr 1956; Col Murray A. Bywater, c. 8 May 1956; Col John C. Edwards, c. Jun 1956; Col Murray A. Bywater, c. Jul 1956–1 Jul 1957.

Aircraft. F–84, 1954–1957; KB–29, 1954–1957; RBF–84, 1955; KC–97, 1957.

Operations. At first undermanned, operational training delayed until Jun 1954. Provided air defense of northern Japan, while in deployed status, 8 Aug–10 Nov 1954. Provided long-range fighter support and air refueling in support of SAC bombers, Nov 1954–Jun 1957.

Service Streamers. None.

Campaign Streamers. None.

Decorations. None.

Emblem. On a shield azure, over an Indian bow and arrow proper, in saltire, an Indian shield argent, edged black, charged with a war bird gules, markings sable, 12 feathers pendented from the base of the shield, proper. (Approved on 1 Jun 1955.)

408th STRATEGIC FIGHTER WING

Lineage. Established as 408th Strategic Fighter Wing on 23 Mar 1953.

Assignments. None.

Components. None.

Stations. None.

Commanders. None.

Aircraft. None.

Operations. Never made active.

Service Streamers. None.

Campaign Streamers. None.

Decorations. None.

Emblem. Azure, a lightning bolt, bendwise, or, between two jet-like eagles volant proper with trailing speed vapor proper. *Motto:* DEFEND WITH VIGILANCE. (Approved for 408th Fighter Group on 22 May 1957.)

410th BOMBARDMENT WING, HEAVY

Lineage. Established as 410th Bombardment Wing, Heavy, and activated, on 15 Nov 1962. Organized on 1 Feb 1963.

Assignments. Strategic Air Command, 15 Nov 1962; 40th Air Division, 1 Feb 1963; 4th Strategic Aerospace Division, 1 Sep 1964; 40th Air Division, 31 Mar 1970–.

Components. *Squadrons.* 46th Air Refueling: 1 Feb 1963–. 644th: 1 Feb 1963–.

Stations. K. I. Sawyer AFB, Mich, 1 Feb 1963–.

Commanders. None (not manned), 15 Nov 1962–31 Jan 1963; Col William B. Kyes, 1 Feb 1963; Col Madison M. McBrayer, 27 Feb 1963; Col Frederick R. Ramputi, 1 May 1963; Col Pete C. Sianis, 1 Mar 1965; Col Robert J. Ray, 8 Jul 1966; Col Richard M. Hoban, 26 Jun 1967; Brig Gen John R. Hinton, Jr., 15 Jul 1968; Col Jules M. Blomberg, 11 May 1970; Col Andrew B. Anderson, Jr., 15 Oct 1970; Col Robert J. Thompson, 23 Mar 1971; Col Morris E. Shiver, 6 Oct 1972; Col Jack L. Watkins, 14 May 1973; Col Morris E. Shiver, 24 Aug 1973; Col Nathaniel A. Gallagher, 26 Feb 1974; Col Judson H. Ruth, 21 May 1975; Col George A. Dugard, 29 Jun 1977–.

Aircraft. B–52, 1963–; KC–135, 1963–.

Operations. Replaced 4042d Strategic Wing on 1 Feb 1963. Conducted strategic bombardment training and air refueling operations on a global scale to meet SAC commitments, Feb 1963–. Supported combat operations in Southeast Asia with KC–135 aircraft and crews, 1964–1975, and with B–52 crews, 1968–1975.

Service Streamers. None.

Campaign Streamers. None.

Decorations. Air Force Outstanding Unit Awards: 1 Feb–31 Mar 1963; 1 Jul 1975–30 Jun 1976.

Emblem. Per quarter light blue and azure, within a pattern of five mullets, one in dexter chief and one in sinister base of the last, one in sinister chief, one in dexter base and one in middle base argent, a circular pattern of 12 mullets, 10 of the last, one at 10 o'clock and one at 4 o'clock of the second, the mullets encircling a globe of the first, rimmed and gridlined of the second (rim argent on second and third quarters), on the globe a winged bomb gules surmounted by a lightning bolt bendwise or bearing three mullets of the second, all within a diminished bordure of the fifth. (Approved on 17 Jul 1964.)

413th TACTICAL FIGHTER WING

Lineage. Established as 413th Strategic Fighter Wing on 23 Mar 1953. Redesignated 413th Fighter-Day Wing on 26 Sep 1957. Activated on 8 Oct 1957. Redesignated 413th Tactical Fighter Wing on 1 Jul 1958. Inactivated on 15 Mar 1959.

Assignments. 831st Air Division, 8 Oct 1957–15 Mar 1959.

Components. *Squadrons.* 1st: 8 Oct 1957–15 Mar 1959 (detached 27 Jun–c. 12 Nov 1958). 21st: 8 Oct 1957–15 Mar 1959 (detached 14–15 Mar 1959). 34th: 8 Oct 1957–15 Mar 1959. 474th: 8 Oct 1957–15 Mar 1959 (detached 11 Nov 1958–c. 14 Mar 1959).

Stations. George AFB, Calif, 8 Oct 1957–15 Mar 1959.

Commanders. Lt Col Samuel V. Blair, 8 Oct 1957; Col Gordon F. Blood, 10 Oct 1957; Col Robert W. Stephens, 13 Jul 1958–15 Mar 1959.

Aircraft. F–100, 1957–1959.

Operations. Trained to maintain combat readiness by participation in tactical exercises, firepower demonstrations, joint training with U.S. Army and U.S. Marine Corps units, and tactical evaluations. Provided augmentation of Sixteenth Air Force, in Spain, through deployment of assigned squadrons on a rotational basis.

Service Streamers. None.

Campaign Streamers. None.

Decorations. None.

Emblem. Argent, within a diminutive border per border of the like and azure a sheaf of broad swords points upward gules of the second, vert and or, all with hilts of the first. *Motto:* SIVA (Hindu god of destruction). (Approved for 413th Group on 26 Apr 1955 and for 413th Wing on 29 Jan 1958.)

416th BOMBARDMENT WING, HEAVY

Lineage. Established as 416th Bombardment Wing, Heavy, and activated, on 15 Nov 1962. Organized on 1 Feb 1963.

Assignments. Strategic Air Command, 15 Nov 1962; 6th Air Division, 1 Feb 1963; 57th Air Division, 2 Jul 1966; 817th Air Division, 2 Sep 1966; 45th Air Division, 2 Jul 1969; 40th Air Division, 30 Jun 1971; 45th Air Division, 1 Jul 1973–.

Components. *Squadrons.* 41st Air Refueling: 1 Feb 1963–. 668th: 1 Feb 1963–.

Stations. Griffiss AFB, NY, 1 Feb 1963–.

Commanders. None (not manned), 15 Nov 1962–31 Jan 1963; Col Robert G. David, 1 Feb 1963; Col William M. Shy, 31 Jul 1964; Col Clifford W. Hargrove, 8 Jul 1966; Col Eugene Q. Steffes, Jr., 12 Jul 1966; Col Salvador E. Felices, 28 Jun 1967; Col Hilding L. Jacobson, Jr., 24 May 1968; Col William A. Temple, 10 Apr 1969; Col Charles L. Britton, 21 Apr 1970; Col Bruce K. Brown, 23 Jun 1972; Col Richard Y. Newton, Jr., 30 Apr 1973; Col William B. Maxson, 11 Jun 1973;

Col Caryl W. Calhoun, 30 May 1974; Col Jack L. Watkins, 3 Jul 1974; Col George P. Tynan, 1 Aug 1975; Col Richard J. Kiefer, 15 Jul 1977–.

Aircraft. B–52, 1963–; KC–135, 1963–.

Operations. Replaced and absorbed resources of 4039th Strategic Wing on 1 Feb 1963. Conducted strategic bombardment training and air refueling operations on a global scale to meet SAC commitments, Feb 1963–. Supported SAC operations in the Far East and Southeast Asia with tankers and crews, Dec 1964–Dec 1975, and with B–52 crews, Jun 1968–1975. Assumed host wing responsibility at Griffiss AFB, NY, on 1 Jul 1970.

Service Streamers. None.

Campaign Streamers. None.

Decorations. None.

Emblem. On a shield divided diagonally from the viewer's lower right to upper left, light blue on the viewer's left, a bend convergent to sinister base blue, black on the viewer's right, in the lower right an Air Force blue demisphere with diagonal axis, grid lined and rimmed white below two stylized yellow aircraft outlined Air Force blue ascending to the viewer's upper left. In the top of the shield, arched to the viewer's right, three white stars, one on the blue portion and two on the black. Around the shield a narrow yellow border. (Approved on 2 Mar 1964.)

419th TROOP CARRIER WING, MEDIUM

Lineage. Established as 419th Troop Carrier Wing, Medium, on 10 May 1949. Activated in the Reserve on 27 Jun 1949. Ordered to active service on 1 May 1951. Inactivated on 2 May 1951.

Assignments. Tenth Air Force, 27 Jun 1949–2 May 1951.

Components. *Group.* 419th: 27 Jun 1949–2 May 1951.

Stations. Scott AFB, Ill, 27 Jun 1949–2 May 1951.

Commanders. Brig Gen James H. Howard, 27 Jun 1949; Col Billy G. Dilworth, Jr., 12 Jan 1950; Col Enoch O. Paulson, (by 19) Jan–2 May 1951.

Aircraft. T–6, 1949–1951; T–7, 1949–1951; T–11, 1949–1951; C/TC–46, 1949–1951.

Operations. Trained under administration of 2469th Air Force Reserve Training Center. Held annual summer encampments at Atterbury AFB, Ind, 16–30 Sep 1949, and at Memphis Muni Aprt, Tenn, 12–27 Jul 1950.

Service Streamers. None.

Campaign Streamers. None.

Decorations. None.

Emblem. Per pale azure and vert, on a pile argent a point in point reversed gules between the wings of an eagle volant, sable, his head and detail of the third, grasping with his talons the left hand of a Roman warrior and lowering him to base; the warrior holding a sword in his right hand; all between three stars, argent, one in chief, one in dexter base, one in sinister base. (Approved for 419th Group on 25 Jun 1957.)

432d TACTICAL DRONE GROUP

Lineage. Established as 432d Tactical Reconnaissance Wing on 23 Mar 1953. Activated on 8 Feb 1958. Inactivated on 18 Jun 1959. Activated on 19 Aug 1966. Organized on 18 Sep 1966. Redesignated 432d Tactical Fighter Wing on 15 Nov 1974. Inactivated on 23 Dec 1975. Redesignated 432d Tactical Drone Group on 24 May 1976. Activated on 1 Jul 1976.

Assignments. 837th Air Division, 8 Feb 1958–18 Jun 1959. Pacific Air Forces, 19 Aug 1966; Thirteenth Air Force, 18 Sep 1966 (attached to Seventh Air Force, 18 Sep 1966–c. 15 Aug 1973; United States Support Activities Group/Seventh Air Force, c. 15 Aug 1973–30 Jun 1975); 17th Air Division, 1 Jul 1975–23 Dec 1975. Twelfth Air Force, 1 Jul 1976–.

Components. *Group.* 4411th Combat Crew Training: attached 8 Apr–17 May 1959. *Squadrons.* 4th: attached 29–30 Oct 1972, assigned 31 Oct 1972–23 Dec 1975 (not operational, 7–23 Dec 1975). 7th Airborne Command and Control: 31 Oct 1968–30 Apr 1972 (detached 31 Oct 1968–30 Apr 1972). 11th: 25 Oct 1966–10 Nov 1970; 1 Jul 1976–. 13th: attached 21 Oct–14 Nov 1967, assigned 15 Nov 1967–30 Jun 1975. 14th: attached 28 Oct–5 Nov 1967, assigned 6 Nov 1967–30 Jun 1975. 17th: 8 Feb 1958–10 May 1959 (detached 6 Sep–9 Dec 1958). 18th: 8 Feb 1958–1 Jun 1959. 20th: 8 Feb 1958–18 May 1959 (detached 8 Apr–17 May 1959); 18 Sep 1966–1 Nov 1967. 22d: 1 Jul 1976–. 25th: 5 Jul 1974–18 Dec 1975. 29th: 8 Feb 1958–18 May 1959 (detached 8 Apr–17 May 1959). 41st: 18 Sep 1966–15 Aug 1967 (detached 8–15 Aug 1967). 43d: attached c. 1 Feb–7 Apr 1959. 58th: attached 9 May–14 Oct 1972. 307th: attached c. 29 Jul–28 Oct 1972. 308th: attached 9 May–c. 29 Jul 1972. 421st: 31 Oct 1972–23 Dec 1975 (detached 14–23 Dec 1975). 523d: attached 9 Apr–25 Oct 1972. 555th: attached 28–31 May 1968, assigned 1 Jun 1968–5 Jul 1974. 6460th: 18 Sep 1966–15 Aug 1967 (detached 8–15 Aug 1967). 6461st: 18 Sep–8 Nov 1966 (not operational, 25 Oct–8 Nov 1966).

Stations. Shaw AFB, SC, 8 Feb 1958–18 Jun 1959. Udorn RTAFB, Thailand, 18 Sep 1966–23 Dec 1975. Davis-Monthan AFB, Ariz, 1 Jul 1976–.

Commanders. Col John G. Foster, 8 Feb 1958; Col Robert C. Rawl, 25 Aug 1958–18 Jun 1959. None (not manned), 19 Aug–17 Sep 1966; Col Robert W. Schick, 18 Sep 1966; Col Victor N. Cabas, 16 Sep 1967; Col Wendell L. Bevan, Jr., 3 Sep 1968; Brig Gen Darrell S. Cramer, 7 Jun 1969; Col David S.

Mellish, 25 Feb 1970; Col Lloyd R. Leavitt, Jr., 26 Nov 1970; Col Lyle E. Mann, 3 Apr 1971; Col Charles A. Gabriel, 29 Oct 1971; Col Scott G. Smith, 14 Jun 1972; Col Robert W. Clement, 18 Mar 1973; Col William P. Acker, 15 Mar 1974; Col William D. Mol, 12 Mar–23 Dec 1975. Col Bennie E. Higgins, Jr., 1 Jul 1976; Col James E. Witzel, 10 Mar 1977–.

Aircraft. RF–84, 1958; RF–101, 1958–1959; RB–66, 1959. In addition to EB–66, 1966–1967; RF–101, 1966–1967; RF–4, 1966–1975; and F–4, 1967–1975; also flew a few RC–47, 1966–1969; and a few AC–47, 1969–1970. AQM–34 (drone), 1976–; DC–130, 1976–; RC–130, 1976–; CH–3, 1976–.

Operations. Replaced the 432d Tactical Reconnaissance Group in Feb 1958, assuming tactical reconnaissance mission. Operated USAF Advanced Flying Training School, Tactical Reconnaissance, Mar 1958–Jun 1959. Inactivated in Jun 1959. Organized in Southeast Asia in Sep 1966 to perform combat tactical reconnaissance. Added tactical fighter operations in Oct 1967, initially using fighters to provide combat air patrol and cover for unarmed reconnaissance planes, but later to fly strike missions. Wing fighter units destroyed many enemy aircraft: 36 confirmed aerial victories between 17 Dec 1967 and 8 Jan 1973. Also used AC–47D gunships to provide air defense of friendly Laotian outposts, Jun 1969–Jun 1970. Ceased combat in Vietnam in Jan, in Laos in Feb, and in Cambodia in Aug 1973. The wing remained in Southeast Asia to perform reconnaissance and routine training to remain combat proficiency, changing designations from reconnaissance to fighter in Nov 1974. The wing supported the evacuation of U.S. personnel from Phnom Penh, Cambodia, on 12 Apr 1975, and the evacuation of American and certain South Vietnamese personnel from Saigon on 29 Apr 1975. From 13 to 15 May 1975, the wing played a major role in locating the SS *Mayaguez* and in the military operations associated with the recovery of that American commercial vessel and its crew from the Cambodians. The wing was relieved of all operational commitments on 30 Nov and inactivated at Udorn RTAFB, Thailand, on 23 Dec 1975.

Organized as 432d Tactical Drone Group in Jul 1976 to perform photographic reconnaissance and to support tactical air and surface forces with tactical drones. Used AQM–34L/M/V drones, DC–130 launch vehicles, and CH–3 recovery helicopters. Conducted follow-on testing and evaluation of the AQM–34V model drone and initial operational testingand evaluation and developmental testing and evaluation of the DC–130H "mother ship." Supported testing and evaluation of the BQM–34C drone at Hill AFB, Utah.

Service Streamers. None.

Campaign Streamers. Vietnam Air Offensive; Vietnam Air Offensive, Phase II; Vietnam Air Offensive, Phase III; Vietnam Air/Ground; Vietnam Air Offensive, Phase IV; TET 69/Counteroffensive; Vietnam Summer–Fall, 1969; Vietnam Winter–Spring, 1970; Sanctuary Counteroffensive; Southwest Monsoon; Commando Hunt V; Commando Hunt VI; Commando Hunt VII; Vietnam Ceasefire.

Decorations. Presidential Unit Citations (Southeast Asia): 19 Sep 1967–1 Nov 1968; 1 Nov 1968–31 Oct 1969. Air Force Outstanding Unit Awards with Combat "V" Device: 18 Sep 1966–18 Sep 1967; 21 Nov 1969–20 Nov 1970; 21 Nov 1970–6 Apr 1971; 18 Dec 1972–27 Jan 1973. Republic of Vietnam Gallantry Cross with Palm: 18 Sep 1966–28 Jan 1973.

Emblem. On a shield gules, a stylized owl, holding in his dexter claws two lightning bolts in saltire, all sable, detail of the field. *Motto:* On a red scroll lettered black: VICTORIA PER SCIENTIAM—Victory through knowledge. (Approved for 432d Group on 2 Jun 1955 and for 432d Wing on 4 Aug 1958.)

433d TACTICAL AIRLIFT WING

Lineage. Established as 433d Troop Carrier Wing, Medium, on 10 May 1949. Activated in the Reserve on 27 Jun 1949. Ordered to active service on 15 Oct 1950. Inactivated on 14 Jul 1952. Activated in the Reserve on 18 May 1955. Redesignated: 433d Tactical Airlift Wing on 1 Jul 1967; 433d Military Airlift Wing on 25 Jul 1969; 433d Tactical Airlift Wing on 29 Jun 1971.

Assignments. Ninth Air Force, 27 Jun 1949; First Air Force, 1 Aug 1950; Tactical Air Command, 16 Oct 1950; Eighteenth Air Force, 1 Jun 1951 (attached to Twelfth Air Force, 5–7 Aug 1951); Twelfth Air Force, 8 Aug 1951–14 Jul 1952. Fourteenth Air Force, 18 May 1955; Tenth Air Force, 25 Mar 1958; Fourth Air Force Reserve Region, 1 Sep 1960; Central Air Force Reserve Region, 31 Dec 1969; Fourth Air Force (Reserve), 8 Oct 1976–.

Components. *Groups.* 433d: 27 Jun 1949–14 Jul 1952; 18 May 1955–14 Apr 1959. 908th: 1 Mar 1968–25 Apr 1969. 916th: 18 Mar–1 Jul 1963; 21 Apr 1971–8 Jul 1972. 921st: 17 Jan 1963–26 Jan 1968; 2 Jun 1969–1 Nov 1974. 922d: 17 Jan 1963–30 Jun 1974. 923d: 17 Jan 1963–25 Nov 1965. 924th: 1 Jul 1972–. 926th: 1 Mar 1968–1 Oct 1969. 929th: 1 Jan 1964–1 Jul 1966. *Squadrons.* 67th: 14 Apr 1959–17 Jan 1963. 68th: 14 Apr 1959–17 Jan 1963; 1 Nov 1974–. 69th: 14 Apr 1959–17 Jan 1963. 705th Tactical Airlift Training: 1 Jul–1 Sep 1972.

Stations. Cleveland Muni Aprt, Ohio, 27 Jun 1949; Greenville (later, Donaldson) AFB, SC, 16 Oct 1950–20 Jul 1951; Rhein-Main AB, West Germany, 5 Aug 1951–14 Jul 1952. Brooks AFB, Texas, 18 May 1955; Kelly AFB, Texas, 1 Nov 1960–.

Commanders. Brig Gen Robert A. Nagle, 27 Jun 1949; unkn, c. 7–c. 14 Oct 1950; Col Harry W. Hopp, c. 15 Oct 1950; Col Louis M. Merrick, 15 Jan 1951; Col Harry W. Hopp, 20 Jul 1951, Col Donald J. French, 14 Jan–14 Jul 1952. Brig Gen John H. Foster, 18 May 1955; Lt Col Tom E. Marchbanks, Jr., 7 Nov 1960; Brig Gen Roger L. Zeller, 21

Nov 1961; Brig Gen Tom E. Marchbanks, Jr., 26 Jun 1962; Brig Gen Ralph M. Lain, 8 Jan 1968; Col William A. Willis, 15 Jun 1970–12 Jun 1972; unkn, 13 Jun–c. 31 Jul 1972; Brig Gen Harry J. Huff II, c. 1 Aug 1972; Maj Gen John W. Huff, Jan 1976; Brig Gen Cecil T. Jenkins, 7 Jun 1976–.

Aircraft. T–6, 1949–1950; T–7, 1949–1950; T–11, 1949–1950; C–46, 1949–1950; C–119, 1950–1952. T–28, 1955; C–45, 1955–c. 1956; C–46, 1955–1958; C–119, 1957–1971; C–124, 1963, 1966–1972; C–130, 1971–.

Operations. Trained in the Reserve, Jun 1949–Oct 1950. Ordered to active service and served TAC for several months before moving to Europe to serve USAFE, primarily participating in tactical exercises and special missions. Inactivated in mid-1952. When activated in the Reserve in 1955, replaced a pilot training wing. Until 1958, depended upon an active Air Reserve Flying Center for assistance, then became self-supporting under the Air Reserve Technician (ART) program. By 1958, participating in numerous tactical exercises and flying airlift missions as well as training with Army special forces. By the mid-1960s, the wing was operating on a global basis to perform airlift and exercise missions. One wing component had a special mission of delivering sterile screwworms to Puerto Rico, while another component conducted USAF's C–130A pilot and flight engineer school, used not only by reservists but by all Department of Defense C–130 operators.

Service Streamers. None.

Campaign Streamers. None.

Decorations. Air Force Outstanding Unit Award: 1 Jul–31 Dec 1964. Republic of Vietnam Gallantry Cross with Palm: 1 Apr 1966–28 Jun 1971.

Emblem. Or, on and over a demiglobe issuant from base azure with land areas light blue three lightning flashes gules chained of the first and suspended from a parachute of the second; in chief above a constellation of 10 mullets bendwise 4, 3 and 3 of the second a front view of the Alamo of the like winged argent, all within a diminished bordure of the last fimbriated. (Approved on 7 Jul 1961.)

434th TACTICAL FIGHTER WING

Lineage. Established as 434th Troop Carrier Wing, Medium, and activated in the Reserve, on 1 Jul 1949. Ordered to active service on 1 May 1951. Inactivated on 1 Feb 1953. Activated in the Reserve on 1 Feb 1953. Ordered to active service on 28 Oct 1962. Relieved from active duty on 28 Nov 1962. Redesignated 434th Tactical Airlift Wing on 1 Jul 1967. Inactivated on 31 Dec 1969. Redesignated 434th Special Operations Wing on 12 Jan 1971. Activated in the Reserve on 15 Jan 1971. Redesignated 434th Tactical Fighter Wing on 1 Oct 1973.

Assignments. Tenth Air Force, 1 Jul 1949; Tactical Air Command, 2 May 1951; Eighteenth Air Force, 1 Jun 1951–1 Feb 1953. 2d Air Reserve District, 1 Feb 1953; Tenth Air Force, 15 Apr 1953; Fifth Air Force Reserve Region, 1 Sep 1960; Twelfth Air Force, 28 Oct 1962; Fifth Air Force Reserve Region, 28 Nov 1962–31 Dec 1969. Central Air Force Reserve Region, 15 Jan 1971; Tenth Air Force (Reserve), 8 Oct 1976–.

Components. *Groups*. 434th: 1 Jul 1949–1 Feb 1953; 1 Feb 1953–14 Apr 1959. 908th Tactical Air Support: 1 Jul–25 Oct 1971 (detached 1–25 Oct 1971). 910th: 21 Apr 1971–. 917th: 25 Feb 1972–. 930th: 11 Feb 1963–13 May 1968; 18 Jun–31 Dec 1969; 15 Jan 1971–1 Jul 1975. 931st: 11 Feb 1963–31 Dec 1969; 15 Jan 1971–1 Jul 1975. 932d: 11 Feb 1963–1 Oct 1966. *Squadrons*. 45th: 1 Jul 1975–. 46th: 1 Jul 1975–. 71st: 14 Apr 1959–11 Feb 1963. 72d: 14 Apr 1959–11 Feb 1963. 73d: 14 Apr 1959–11 Feb 1963.

Stations. Atterbury AFB, Ind, 1 Jul 1949; Lawson AFB, Ga, 23 Jan 1952–1 Feb 1953. Atterbury (later, Bakalar) AFB, Ind, 1 Feb 1953–31 Dec 1969. Grissom AFB, Ind, 15 Jan 1971–.

Commanders. Brig Gen Lacey V. Murrow, 1 Jul 1949; Col Troy W. Crawford, 5 Jan 1952; Col Wallace L. Linn, 23 Jan 1952; Brig Gen Lacey V. Murrow, 5 Feb 1952; Col Troy W. Crawford, 20 Feb 1952; Brig Gen Lacey V. Murrow, 18 Apr 1952; Col Troy W. Crawford, 12 Jan–1 Feb 1953. Col George C. Riley, 1 Feb 1953; Brig Gen John O. Bradshaw, 22 Apr 1953; Brig Gen John W. Hoff, 13 Oct 1962; Brig Gen Alfred Verhulst, 16 Jul 1967; Col William J. Johnson, Jr., c. 1 Oct–31 Dec 1969. Unkn, 15 Jan 1971; Col John C. Riley, (by Apr) 1971; Brig Gen Sidney S. Novaresi, Oct 1971; Col Joseph A. Thomas, 13 Nov 1973; Col Charles E. Jones III, c. 1 Mar 1974; Brig Gen Sidney S. Novaresi, c. 16 Jun 1974; Col Charles E. Jones III, 28 Sep 1975; Col Billy R. Henderson, 8 Aug 1977–.

Aircraft. T–7, 1949–1952; T–11, 1949–1952; C–47, 1949; C–46, 1949–1953. T–6, 1953; T–11, 1953; C–45, 1953–1957; C–46, 1953–1957; C–119, 1957–1969; U–3, 1969. O–2, 1971; U–3, 1971; A–37, 1971–; C–124, 1972.

Operations. Trained as a Reserve troop carrier wing under supervision of the 2466th Air Force Reserve Training Center, Jul 1949–Feb 1951. Ordered to active service and flew airlift missions and participated in tactical exercises, May 1951–Jan 1953. Also provided C–46 combat crew training in support of Far East requirements, Sep 1952–Jan 1953. Trained as a Reserve troop carrier wing under supervision of the 2466th Air Force Reserve Combat Training Center (later, 2466th Air Reserve Flying Center), Feb 1953–Oct 1958, using C–46s as primary training aircraft to Jan 1957 and C–119s thereafter. Began Air Reserve Technician program in Oct 1958 and soon became capable of flying overseas missions; participated in numerous tactical exercises on a regular basis. Went on 1-month active duty in 1962 during the Cuban missile crisis. Converted to tactical groups in Feb 1963; one transferred in 1966 and another went on active duty from May 1968 to Jun 1969. One group converted from C–119s to U–3As in Jun 1969, with a forward air controller training mission. Wing inactivated in Dec 1969 but was activated in Jan 1971 and charged with becoming proficient in A–37 fighter-bomber aircraft. Provided combat crew training in A–37s for all USAF and selected foreign aircrews. Trained as fighter-bomber unit to provide close air support for ground forces.

Service Streamers. None.

Campaign Streamers. None.

Decorations. Republic of Vietnam Gallantry Cross with Palm: 14 Feb–11 Mar 1968.

Emblem. Azure, a base embattled fesswise throughout or masoned of the first below a demi-sun issuing from sinister chief of the second and a pattern of four mullets of five points in dexter chief argent, issuing from base a demisphere of the last, gridlined of the first supporting a hurt charged with a mullet of five points argent, on which is centered a torteau enveloping the hurt and arced to dexter chief, four jet streams vert, gules, azure and maroon, all fimbriated argent, all within a diminished bordure of the last. (Approved on 30 Jun 1975.)

435th TACTICAL AIRLIFT WING

Lineage. Established as 435th Troop Carrier Wing, Medium, on 10 May 1949. Activated in the Reserve on 26 Jun 1949. Ordered to active service on 1 Mar 1951. Inactivated on 1 Dec 1952. Activated in the Reserve on 1 Dec 1952. Redesignated 435th Troop Carrier Wing, Heavy, on 18 Sep 1961. Ordered to active service on 1 Oct 1961. Relieved from active duty on 27 Aug 1962. Redesignated 435th Troop Carrier Wing, Medium, on 1 Jul 1963. Discontinued, and inactivated, on 1 Dec 1965. Redesignated 435th Military Airlift Support Wing on 25 Nov 1968. Activated on 24 Dec 1968. Redesignated 435th Tactical Airlift Wing on 1 Jul 1975.

Assignments. Fourteenth Air Force, 26 Jul 1949; Tactical Air Command, 2 Mar 1951; Eighteenth Air Force, 1 Jun 1951–1 Dec 1952. Fourteenth Air Force, 1 Dec 1952; Third Air Force Reserve Region, 15 Jul 1970; Ninth Air Force, 1 Oct 1961; Third Air Force Reserve Region, 27 Aug 1962–1 Dec 1965. Twenty-First Air Force, 24 Dec 1968–.

Components. *Groups.* 435th: 26 Jun 1949–1 Dec 1952; 1 Dec 1952–14 Apr 1959; 1 Jul 1975–. 908th: 18 Mar 1963–1 Dec 1965. 915th: 17 Jan 1963–1 Dec 1965. 916th: 17 Jan–18 Mar 1963. 917th: 17 Jan–1 Jul 1963. *Squadrons.* 55th Aeromedical Airlift: 31 Mar 1975–. 58th: 1 Sep 1977–. 76th: 14 Apr 1959–1 Oct 1961; 27 Aug 1962–17 Jan 1963. 77th: 14 Apr 1959–17 Jan 1963. 78th: 8 May 1959–17 Jan 1963.

Stations. Miami Intl Aprt, Fla, 26 Jun 1949–1 Dec 1952. Miami Intl Aprt, Fla, 1 Dec 1952; Homestead AFB, Fla, 25 Jul 1960–1 Dec 1965. High Wycombe AS, England, 24 Dec 1968; Rhein-Main AB, West Germany, 1 Jul 1969–.

Commanders. Col Laurence B. Hickam, 1949–unkn; Col Maurice F. Casey, (by May 1950); Col James L. Daniel, Jr., 19 Dec 1951; Maj William J. Frazier, Jr., 24 Oct–1 Dec 1952. Unkn, 1 Dec 1952–unkn; Lt Col William Niedernhofer, (by Apr 1953); Lt Col John R. Pountnay, 1953; Lt Col William C. Wilson, 1 Dec 1953–unkn; Col John R. Pountnay, (by Aug 1955); Lt Col Robert C. Hutton, (by Dec) 1957; Col Forrest R. Harsh, Feb 1959; Lt Col Clifford C. Root, 11 Dec 1963; Col Ben J. Mangina, 1 Apr 1964; Col Clifford C. Root, Jul–1 Dec 1965. Brig Gen Hugh E. Wild, 24 Dec 1968; Col Michael F. Robinson, 7 Jan 1970; Col Alden G. Glauch, 1 Apr 1970; Col E. Scott Minnich, 20 Mar 1971; Col John D. Hollowell, 20 Jan 1973; Brig Gen Theodore P. Crichton, 1 Jul 1975–.

Aircraft. T–6, 1949–1951; T–7, 1949–1951; T–11, 1949–1951; C–46, 1949–1951; C–119, 1951–1952. C–46, 1952–1957; C–119, 1957–1965; C–124, 1961–1963. C–130, 1975–; C–9, 1975–; VC–135, 1977–; VC–140, 1977–.

Operations. Trained as a Reserve troop carrier wing from Jul 1949 to Feb 1951, and again from Dec 1952 to Dec 1958 under supervision and guidance of the 2585th Air Force Reserve Training Center (later, 2585th Air Reserve Flying Center). From Mar 1951 to Dec 1952, the wing served on active duty with Tactical Air Command and trained C–46 aircrews for assignment to the Far East. The 435th was replaced by the 456th Troop Carrier Wing in Dec 1952 and itself replaced the 482d TCW as the Miami-based Reserve wing. By 1956, the wing was capable of flying overseas missions, particularly in the Caribbean area to Central America. Began the Air Reserve Technician (ART) program in Apr 1958 and became able to operate independently by Dec 1958. Two squadrons converted to C–124s in 1961 just before being ordered to active service. After training to become combat ready, participated in worldwide airlift and tactical exercises. Returned to Reserve status in Aug 1962 and regained C–119 squadron that had not been on active duty. Switched completely to C–119s in 1963. Inactivated in 1965. From Dec 1968 to Jul 1975, served as a support wing of Military Airlift Command, operating air terminals and providing aircraft maintenance at aerial ports in Europe, the Middle East, and Africa. Combined with a tactical wing in Jul 1975 and, while continuing to function as a tactical and support wing, gained the mission of aeromedical evacuation in Europe and the Middle East.

Service Streamers. None.

Campaign Streamers. None.

Decorations. Air Force Outstanding Unit Award: 1 Jul 1972–30 Jul 1974.

Emblem. Per bend sinister argent and azure, four flight symbols fesswise in bend sinister of the first garnished of the second between in dexter flank a stylized figure of the last supported by an open parachute celeste below in chief a cross couped gules winged fesswise of the field garnished silver, and issuing from base in para a demiglobe celeste gridlined argent below in sinister flank a crate on a platform all or, roped and garnished celeste, all within a diminished bordure gold. (Approved on 4 Oct 1976.)

436th MILITARY AIRLIFT WING

Lineage. Established as 436th Troop Carrier Wing, Medium, on 10 May 1949. Activated in the Reserve on 27 Jun 1949. Ordered to active service on 1 Apr 1951. Inactivated on 16 Apr 1951. Activated in the Reserve on 18 May 1955. Inactivated on 15 May 1958. Redesignated 436th Military Airlift Wing, and activated, on 27 Dec 1965. Organized on 8 Jan 1966.

Assignments. Ninth Air Force, 27 Jun 1949; First Air Force, 1 Aug 1950–16 Apr 1951. First Air Force, 18 May 1955; Fourteenth Air Force, 25 Mar–15 May 1958. Military Air Transport Service (later, Military Airlift Command), 27 Dec 1965; Twenty-First Air Force, 8 Jan 1966–.

Components. *Wing*. 512th: attached 1 Jul 1973–. *Groups*. 436th: 27 Jun 1949–16 Apr 1951; 18 May 1955–15 May 1958. 912th: attached 25 Sep 1968–30 Jun 1973. *Squadrons*. 1st: 8 Jan 1966–30 Jun 1971. 3d: 1 Aug 1973–. 9th: 8 Jan 1966–8 Sep 1968; 1 Apr 1971–. 20th: 8 Jan 1966–1 Aug 1973. 31st: 8 Jan 1966–8 Apr 1969. 39th: 8 Jan 1966–31 Mar 1971. 52d: 8 Jan 1967–8 Feb 1969 (detached). 58th: 1 Jul 1966–15 Aug 1971.

Stations. Godman AFB, Ky, 27 Jun 1949; Standiford Muni Aprt (later, Standiford Field), Ky, 20 Oct 1950–16 Apr 1951. New York NAS (later, USNAS, New York), NY, 18 May 1955–15 May 1958. Dover AFB, Del, 8 Jan 1966–.

Commanders. Brig Gen Albert M. Woody, 27 Jun 1949–16 Apr 1951. Col Peyton Gibson, 18 May 1955; Col Michael P. Yannell, 1 Feb–c. 14 Nov 1957; none (not manned), 15 Nov 1957–15 May 1958. None (not manned), 27 Dec 1965–7 Jan 1966; Brig Gen John B. Wallace, 8 Jan 1966; Brig Gen Fred W. Vetter, Jr., 29 Jan 1969; Col Horace W. Patch, c. 10 Feb 1969; Brig Gen Fred W. Vetter, Jr., 6 Mar 1969; Brig Gen Kelton M. Farris, 1 Aug 1970; Col Willum H. Spillers, Jr., 24 Aug 1972; Brig Gen Charles F. G. Kuyk, Jr., 11 Jun 1973; Col Click D. Smith, Jr., 3 Apr 1975–.

Aircraft. C–45, 1949; T–7, 1949–1951; T–11, 1949–1951; C–47, 1949–1951. T–28, 1955; T–33, 1955; C–45, 1955–1957; C–46, 1955–1957; C–119, 1957. C–124, 1966–1969; C–133, 1966–1971; C–141, 1966–1973; C–5, 1971–.

Operations. Trained as a Reserve troop carrier wing Jun 1949–Apr 1951 under supervision of the 2236th Air Force Reserve Training Center, and again during May 1955–Nov 1957 under supervision of the 2230th Air Reserve Flying Center. In between, ordered to active service and inactivated almost immediately, personnel serving as fillers for other USAF units. Replaced the 1607th Air Transport Wing in Jan 1966 as the MAC host wing at Dover AFB, Del. Initially flew C–124, C–133, and C–141 aircraft, but gradually replaced C–124 and C–133 types with C–5s. By mid-1973, flew only the C–5. Participated in joint training with Army forces, including troop and cargo drops and landings; took part in numerous tactical exercises in the United States and overseas, particularly in support of NATO; flew aeromedical evacuation, humanitarian, and mercy missions, special weapons airlift, and worldwide airlift of personnel, cargo, and mail. During the late 1960s and early 1970s, flew numerous missions to Southeast Asia, although primary wing routes served Europe, the Middle East, and Africa.

Service Streamers. None.

Campaign Streamers. None.

Decorations. Air Force Outstanding Unit Awards: 13 Nov–18 Dec 1967; 1 Jan 1968–31 Dec 1969; 1 Sep 1971–30 Jun 1972; 13 Oct–14 Nov 1973; 1 Jan 1974–30 Apr 1975; and 1 May 1975–31 May 1976.

Emblem. On a shield or, bordered argent, an American bald eagle volant, azure, highlighted bluebird, his wings superimposed over the border, airlifting with his talons a sphere of the second, fimbriated, longitude, latitude lines, grappling iron attached to upper area of sphere, all of the fourth. *Motto:* ROBUSTUM AUXILIUM—Powerful support. (Approved on 14 Jul 1966.)

437th MILITARY AIRLIFT WING

Lineage. Established as 437th Troop Carrier Wing, Medium, on 10 May 1949. Activated in the Reserve on 27 Jun 1949. Ordered to active service on 10 Aug 1950. Inactivated on 10 Jun 1952. Activated in the Reserve on 15 Jun 1952. Inactivated on 16 Nov 1957. Redesignated 437th Military Airlift Wing, and activated, on 27 Dec 1965. Organized on 8 Jan 1966.

Assignments. Tenth Air Force, 26 Jun 1949; Tactical Air Command, 14 Aug 1950; Fifth Air Force, 8 Nov 1950 (attached to FEAF Combat Cargo Command, Provisional, 8 Nov 1950–); 314th Air Division, 1 Dec 1950 (remained attached to FEAF Combat Cargo Command, Provisional, through 24 Jan 1951); 315th Air Division (Combat Cargo), 25 Jan 1951–10 Jun 1952. Tenth Air Force, 15 Jun 1952–16 Nov 1957. Military Air Transport Service (later, Military Airlift Command), 27 Dec 1965; Twenty-First Air Force, 8 Jan 1966–.

Components. *Wing.* 315th: attached 1 Jul 1973–. *Groups.* 437th: 27 Jun 1949–10 Jun 1952; 15 Jun 1952–16 Nov 1957. 943d: attached 25 Sep 1969–1 Jul 1973. *Squadrons.* 3d: 8 Jan 1966–1 Aug 1973. 17th: 8 Jan 1966–8 Apr 1969. 20th: 1 Aug 1973–. 41st: 8 Jan 1966–. 76th: 8 Jan 1966–.

Stations. Chicago–Orchard Aprt (later, O'Hare Field–Chicago Intl Aprt), Ill, 27 Jun 1949; Shaw AFB, SC, 14 Aug–16 Oct 1950; Brady Field, Japan, 8 Nov 1950–10 Jun 1952. O'Hare Intl Aprt, Ill, 15 Jun 1952–16 Nov 1957. Charleston AFB, SC, 8 Jan 1966–.

Commanders. Brig Gen John P. Henebry, 27 Jun 1949; Col John W. Lacey, 26 Jan 1951; Col John R. Roche, 26 Feb 1951; Col Kenneth W. Northamer, May–10 Jun 1952. Col Reed G. Landis, 15 Jun 1952; Lt Col Edwin L. Preston, 1 Sep 1954; Col John W. Lacey, 19 Jan 1955; Lt Col Joseph E. Whitwell, 2 May–16 Nov 1957. None (not manned), 27 Dec 1965–7 Jan 1966; Brig Gen Howard W. Kreidler, 8 Jan 1966; Brig Gen William V. McBride, 26 Jul 1966; Brig Gen Clare T. Ireland, Jr., 1 Mar 1969; Brig Gen Thomas B. Kennedy, 1 Aug 1970; Brig Gen Robert L. Moeller, 1 Apr 1972; Brig Gen Thomas M. Sadler, 1 Feb 1974; Brig Gen Tedd L. Bishop, 14 Mar 1975–.

Aircraft. T–7, 1949–1950; T–11, 1949–1950; C–46, 1949–1952. C–46, 1952–1957; C–47, 1955–1957; C–119, 1957. C–124, 1966–1969; C–130, 1966–1967; C–141, 1966–; C–5, 1970–1973.

Operations. Trained as a Reserve troop carrier wing under supervision of the 2471st Air Force Reserve Training Center, Jun 1949–Aug 1950 and Jun 1952–Nov 1957. Served between Aug 1950 and Jun 1952 on active duty. After concentrated training in the United States, moved to Japan and flew combat airlift missions, 10 Nov 1950–10 Jun 1952. Helped evacuate threatened airfields, hauled gasoline, napalm, and other explosives, dropped cargo and paratroops, flew spraying missions to rid areas of insects, and also flew routine courier missions until replaced by another wing in Jun 1952. Replaced the 1608th Air Transport Wing in 1966 as the MAC host wing at Charleston AFB, SC. Flew joint training missions with Army forces, aeromedical evacuation missions, mercy and humanitarian missions as needed, and airlifted personnel, cargo, and mail worldwide, primarily to Europe, the Middle East and Africa, but also to South America. Participated in numerous tactical operations and exercises, particularly those of NATO. From 1966 to the early 1970s, flew numerous missions to the Far East and Southeast Asia. Wing aircrews were augmented by attached Reserve aircrews.

Service Streamers. None.

Campaign Streamers. CCF Intervention; First UN Counteroffensive; CCF Spring Offensive; UN Summer–Fall Offensive; Second Korean Winter; Korea Summer–Fall, 1952.

Decorations. Air Force Outstanding Unit Awards: 11 Jul 1966–10 Jul 1967; 11 Jul 1967–10 Jul 1968; 11 Jul 1968–12 Jun 1969; 13 Jun 1969–12 Jun 1970; 1 Jul 1972–30 Jun 1973. Republic of Korea Presidential Unit Citation: 1 Jul 1951–[10 Jun 1952].

Emblem. On a yellow shield, within a narrow blue border and a narrow white border, a running "Minute Man" with rifle at high port, all in blue silhouette, in front of a pair of wings elevated and conjoined. (Approved on 24 Nov 1953.)

438th MILITARY AIRLIFT WING

Lineage. Established as 438th Troop Carrier Wing, Medium, on 10 May 1949. Activated in the Reserve on 27 Jun 1949. Ordered to active service on 10 Mar 1951. Inactivated on 14 Mar

1951. Redesignated 438th Fighter-Bomber Wing on 26 May 1952. Activated in the Reserve on 15 Jun 1952. Inactivated on 16 Nov 1957. Redesignated 438th Military Airlift Wing, and activated, on 27 Dec 1965. Organized on 8 Jan 1966.

Assignments. Tenth Air Force, 27 Jun 1949–14 Mar 1951. Tenth Air Force, 15 Jun 1952–16 Nov 1957. Military Air Transport Service (later, Military Airlift Command), 27 Dec 1965; Twenty-First Air Force, 8 Jan 1966–.

Components. *Wing*. 514th: attached 1 Jul 1973–. *Group*. 438th: 27 Jun 1949–14 Mar 1951; 15 Jun 1952–16 Nov 1957. 903d: attached 25 Sep 1968–30 Jun 1973. *Squadrons*. 6th: 8 Apr 1970–. 18th: 8 Jan–15 Jun 1966 (not operational, 1 Feb–15 Jun 1966); 1 Aug 1968–. 29th: 8 Jan 1966–31 Aug 1968 (not operational, 12–31 Aug 1968). 30th: 8 Apr 1967–. 40th: 8 Jan 1966–4 Mar 1968 (not operational, 1 Dec 1967–4 Mar 1968). 45th: 3 Jul 1967–31 Aug 1968 (not operational, 12–31 Aug 1968). Military Airlift Squadron Provisional, 1645th: attached 15 Mar–3 Jul 1967. Naval Air Transport Squadron VR–3: attached 1 Feb 1966–1 Jul 1967.

Stations. Offutt AFB, Nebr, 27 Jun 1949–14 Mar 1951. General Billy Mitchell Field, Wisc, 15 Jun 1952; Milwaukee, Wisc, 5 Jan 1953–16 Nov 1967. McGuire AFB, NJ, 8 Jan 1966–.

Commanders. Col Robert E. Flesher, 27 Jun 1949–14 Mar 1951. Col Robert E. Haynes, 15 Jun 1952; Lt Col Joseph J. Lingle, 19 Sep 1956–c. Nov 1957. None (not manned), 27 Dec 1965–7 Jan 1966; Brig Gen Roland J. Barnick, 8 Jan 1966; Col Gilbert G. Smith, Jr., 25 Jul 1967 (acting), 1 Aug 1967 (permanent); Brig Gen John H. Herring, Jr., 1 Aug 1968; Col Gilbert G. Smith, Jr., 14 Jun 1969; Brig Gen John W. Harrell, Jr., 11 Aug 1969; Brig Gen Keith L. Christensen, 30 Sep 1970; Brig Gen George M. Wentsch, 15 Jun 1972; Brig Gen Emil N. Block, Jr., 28 Jan 1974; Col James L. Gardner, Jr., 1 May 1976–.

Aircraft. T–6, 1949–1951; C–46, 1949–1951. T–6, 1952–1954; C–46, 1953; F–51, 1953–1954; T–33, 1954–1957; F–80, 1954–1957; F–86, 1957. C–130, 1966–1968; C–135, 1966–1967; C–141, 1967–.

Operations. Replaced the 1611th Air Transport Wing, Heavy, in Jan 1966. Transported military cargo, mail, and passengers worldwide, particularly in the eastern United States, Atlantic, European, and Mediterranean areas, with frequent special missions to the Arctic, the Antarctic, South America, the Far East, and to the Southeast Asia combat area during the conflict there.

Service Streamers. None.

Campaign Streamers. None.

Decorations. Air Force Outstanding Unit Award: 1 Jun 1966–30 Apr 1968. Republic of Vietnam Gallantry Cross with Palm: 1 Apr–31 Oct 1968.

Emblem. A shield per fess nebuly abaisse, azure and argent, two flanches representing hemispheres proper, latitude and longitude lines of the first, superimposed with three stylized aircraft, of the second, flying in pale, detail of the third. *Motto:* FIDELITAS PROELIIS DOMIQUE—Dependability in war and peace. (Approved on 16 May 1966.)

439th TACTICAL AIRLIFT WING

Lineage. Established as 439th Troop Carrier Wing, Medium, on 19 May 1949. Activated in the Reserve on 27 Jun 1949. Ordered to active service on 1 Apr 1951. Inactivated on 3 Apr 1951. Redesignated 439th Fighter-Bomber Wing on 26 May 1952. Activated in the Reserve on 15 Jun 1952. Inactivated on 16 Nov 1957. Redesignated 439th Tactical Airlift Wing on 14 Mar 1974. Activated in the Reserve on 1 Apr 1974.

Assignments. Tenth Air Force, 27 Jun 1949–3 Apr 1951. Tenth Air Force, 15 Jun 1952–16 Nov 1957. Eastern Air Force Reserve Region, 1 Apr 1974; Fourteenth Air Force (Reserve), 8 Oct 1976–.

Components. *Groups*. 439th: 27 Jun 1949–3 Apr 1951; 15 Jun 1952–16 Nov 1957. 914th: 25 Jan 1976–. *Squadrons*. 337th: 1 Apr 1974–. 731st: 1 Apr 1974–.

Stations. Selfridge AFB, Mich, 27 Jun 1949–3 Apr 1951. Selfridge AFB, Mich, 15 Jun 1952–16 Nov 1957. Westover AFB, Mass, 1 Apr 1974–.

Commanders. Col Lloyd E. Arnold, 27 Jun 1949; Col George R. Weinbrenner, c. Dec 1950; Col Kenneth R. Strauss, c. 20 Jan 1951; Col George R. Weinbrenner, 12 Mar–3 Apr 1951. Brig Gen Felix L. Vidal, 15 Jun 1952; Lt Col Richard M. Thornburn, 1 Mar 1955; Col James M. McPartlin, c. 25 Dec 1956–16 Nov 1957. Col James W. Kehoe, 1 Apr 1974; Col Ronald C. Dunn, 30 Jun 1974; Brig Gen Billy M. Knowles, 5 Sep 1974–.

Aircraft. T–6, 1949–1950; T–7, 1949–1951; T–11, 1949–1951; TC–46, 1949–1951. T–6, 1952–1954; C–46, 1952–1955; T–28, 1953–1955; F–51, 1953–1954; T–33, 1953–1957; F–80, 1953–1956; F–84, 1956–1957; F–86, 1957; TC–47, 1957; C–119, 1957. C–130, 1974–; C–123, 1974–.

Operations. Trained as a Reserve troop carrier organization under supervision of 2242d Air Force Reserve Training Center, 1949–1951. Ordered to active service on 1 Apr 1951 and inactivated 2 days later, personnel being used as USAF fillers, worldwide. Trained as a Reserve fighter-bomber organization under supervision of 2242d Air Force Reserve Combat Training Center, 1952–1957. Replaced 901st and 905th Tactical Airlift Groups at Westover AFB, Mass, in Apr 1974 and assumed mission of Reserve tactical airlift, special operations, SAC satellite support, and aeromedical evacuation. Replaced SAC's 4040th Air Base Squadron as host organization at Westover AFB on 1 May 1974. Participated in tactical exercises, global airlift, and humanitarian missions. Gained a separate tactical group, plus responsibility for operating the military portion of Niagara Falls Intl Aprt, NY, on 25 Jan 1976.

Service Streamers. None.

Campaign Streamers. None.

Decorations. Air Force Outstanding Unit Award: 1 Jan 1975–31 Dec 1976.

Emblem. Azure, between in chief a pair of wings conjoined in leure and in base three billets or, a chevron gules fimbriated argent, all within a diminished bordure of the second. (Approved on 13 May 1974.)

440th TACTICAL AIRLIFT WING

Lineage. Established as 440th Troop Carrier Wing, Medium, on 10 May 1949. Activated in the Reserve on 27 Jun 1949. Ordered to active service on 1 May 1951. Inactivated on 4 May 1951. Redesignated 440th Fighter-Bomber Wing on 26 May 1952. Activated in the Reserve on 15 Jun 1952. Redesignated 440th Troop Carrier Wing, Medium, on 8 Sep 1957. Ordered to active service on 28 Oct 1962. Relieved from active duty on 28 Nov 1962. Redesignated 440th Tactical Airlift Wing on 1 Jul 1967.

Assignments. Tenth Air Force, 27 Jun 1949–4 May 1951. Tenth Air Force, 15 Jun 1952; Fifth Air Force Reserve Region, 1 Sep 1960; Twelfth Air Force, 28 Oct 1962; Fifth Air Force Reserve Region, 28 Nov 1962; Central Air Force Reserve Region, 31 Dec 1969; Fourth Air Force (Reserve), 8 Oct 1976–.

Components. *Groups*. 440th: 27 Jun 1949–4 May 1951; 15 Jun 1952–14 Apr 1959. 914th: 1 Sep 1969–21 Apr 1971. 928th: 17 Sep 1970–. 933d: 11 Feb 1963–1 Sep 1975. 934th: 11 Feb 1963–. *Squadrons*. 95th: attached 16 Nov 1957–13 Apr 1959, assigned 14 Apr 1959–11 Feb 1963; assigned 1 Sep 1975–. 96th: 14 Apr 1959–11 Feb 1963.

Stations. Wold-Chamberlain Muni Aprt (later, Minneapolis-St. Paul Intl Aprt), Minn, 27 Jun 1949–4 May 1951. Ft Snelling, Minn, 15 Jun 1952; Minneapolis-St. Paul Intl Aprt, Minn, 15 Aug 1952; General Mitchell Field, Wisc, 16 Nov 1957–.

Commanders. Col Carl A. Hustad, 27 Jun 1949–4 May 1951. Unkn, 15 Jun 1952–unkn; Col C. Esco Obermann, (by Aug) 1952; Col Russell F. Gustke, c. 23 Jan 1953; Brig Gen Joseph J. Lingle, 16 Nov 1957; Col Earl W. Steinke, 13 Aug 1972; Brig Gen Charles E. Corcilius, 7 Jan 1973–.

Aircraft. T–6, 1949; C–46, 1949–1951; T–7, 1950–1951; T–11, 1950–1951. T–6, 1952–1955; C–46, 1952–1957; F–51, 1953–1954; T–33, 1954–1957; F–80, 1954–1957; C–119, 1957–1971; C–130, 1970–.

Operations. Trained as a Reserve troop carrier wing, Jun 1949–May 1951, as a Reserve fighter-bomber wing, Jun 1952–Jun 1957, and as a Reserve troop carrier wing, Jun 1957–Dec 1958, all under supervision of the 2465th Air Force Reserve Training (later, Air Reserve Flying) Center until Nov 1957 and the 2473d Air Reserve Flying Center, Nov 1957–Dec 1958. Converted to the Air Reserve Technician program in 1958. Performed Reserve troop carrier/tactical airlift functions, Dec 1958–, serving 1 month on active duty during the Cuban missile crisis of 1962. Routinely flew airlift missions by 1958 and soon participated in tactical exercises and operations in the United States and overseas. Wing was awarded the Air Force Association's trophy as the outstanding Air Force Reserve flying unit for 1963, 1964, 1966, and 1968.

Service Streamers. None.

Campaign Streamers. None.

Decorations. Republic of Vietnam Gallantry Cross with Palm: 14 Feb–11 Mar 1968.

Emblem. Argent, on and over the upper edge of a targe azure bearing Polaris and Ursa Major of the field within an orle or, a winged viking helmet of the like, behind the targe a sword and spear in saltire of the last all detailed and fimbriated of the second; all within an orle of the last and a diminished border gold. *Motto:* NUNQUAN NON PARATUS—Never unprepared. (Approved on 14 Nov 1958.)

441st TROOP CARRIER WING, MEDIUM

Lineage. Established as 441st Troop Carrier Wing, Medium, on 10 May 1949. Activated in the Reserve on 27 Jun 1949. Ordered to active service on 10 Mar 1951. Inactivated on 14 Mar 1951.

Assignments. Tenth Air Force, 27 Jun 1949–14 Mar 1951.

Components. *Group.* 441st: 27 Jun 1949–14 Mar 1951.

Stations. Chicago-Orchard Aprt (later, O'Hare Field-Chicago Intl Aprt), Ill, 27 Jun 1949–14 Mar 1951.

Commanders. Col Byron Jacobs, c. 27 Jun 1949; Col John S. Gulledge, (by Oct) 1949–14 Mar 1951.

Aircraft. T–6, 1949; T–7, 1949–1951; T–11, 1949–1951; C/TC–46, 1949–1951.

Operations. Trained as a Reserve troop carrier wing under supervision of the 2471st Air Force Reserve Training Center.

Service Streamers. None.

Campaign Streamers. None.

Decorations. None.

Emblem. None.

442d TACTICAL AIRLIFT WING

Lineage. Established as 442d Troop Carrier Wing, Medium, on 10 May 1949. Activated in the Reserve on 27 Jun 1949. Ordered to active service on

10 Mar 1951. Inactivated on 12 Mar 1951. Activated in the Reserve on 15 Jun 1952. Redesignated 442d Troop Carrier Wing, Heavy, on 8 May 1961. Ordered to active service on 1 Oct 1961. Relieved from active duty on 27 Aug 1962. Redesignated: 442d Air Transport Wing, Heavy, on 1 Dec 1965; 442d Military Airlift Wing on 1 Jan 1966; 442d Tactical Airlift Wing on 29 Jun 1971.

Assignments. Tenth Air Force, 27 Jun 1949–12 Mar 1951. Tenth Air Force, 15 Jun 1952; Fifth Air Force Reserve Region, 1 Sep 1960; Ninth Air Force, 1 Oct 1961; Twelfth Air Force, 1 Feb 1962; Fifth Air Force Reserve Region, 27 Aug 1962; Central Air Force Reserve Region, 31 Dec 1969; Fourth Air Force (Reserve), 8 Oct 1976–.

Components. *Groups.* 442d: 27 Jun 1949–12 Mar 1951; 15 Jun 1952–14 Apr 1959. 507th Tactical Fighter: 20 May–25 Jul 1972 (detached). 916th: 1 Jul 1963–8 Jan 1965. 917th: 1 Jul 1963–5 Feb 1965. 926th: 1 Jul 1972–. 932d: 1 Oct 1966–1 Apr 1969. 935th: 17 Jan 1963–1 Nov 1974. 936th: 17 Jan 1963–30 Jun 1974. 937th: 17 Jan 1963–5 Feb 1965; 21 Apr 1971–20 May 1972. *Squadrons.* 303d: 14 Apr 1959–17 Jan 1963; 1 Nov 1974–. 304th: 14 Apr 1959–17 Jan 1963. 305th: 14 Apr 1959–17 Jan 1963.

Stations. Fairfax Field, Kans, 27 Jun 1949; Olathe NAS, Kans, 27 May 1950–12 Mar 1951. Olathe NAS, Kans, 15 Jun 1952; Grandview (later, Richards-Gebaur) AFB, Mo, 3 Apr 1955–.

Commanders. Col Russell W. DeLany, 27 Jun 1949; Col Archie W. League, c. Aug 1950; Col Loyd C. Waldorf, (by 30) Sep 1950; Col Lyman H. Goff, Jr., 1 Oct 1950–12 Mar 1951. Col Frank E. Vrooman, 15 Jun 1952; Col Charles D. Daily, 11 Jul 1953; Col James H. McPartlin, 8 Aug 1961; Maj Edward J. Struewing, Jr., 28 Aug 1962; Brig Gen James H. McPartlin, 12 Sep 1962; Col George L. Cooper, 3 Jun 1965; Brig Gen Ben J. Mangina, 8 Jul 1965; Brig Gen Ralph M. Lain, 28 Jun 1970; Col George L. Cooper, (by Jun) 1971; Brig Gen Alvin J. Moser, 20 Jul 1971–.

Aircraft. T–6, 1949–1950; T–7, 1949–1951; T–11, 1949–1951; C/TC–46, 1949, 1950–1951; C–47, 1949–1950. C–46, 1952–1957; C–119, 1957–1961, 1966–1967; C–124, 1961–1972; C–130, 1971–.

Operations. Trained as a Reserve troop carrier wing under supervision of the 2472d Air Force Reserve Training (later, Air Reserve Flying) Center, Jun 1949–Feb 1951 and Jun 1952–Mar 1959. Ordered to active service during Korean war, but personnel used as fillers. By the mid-1950s, participated regularly in troop/cargo drops, airlift operations and exercises. Converted to the Air Reserve Technician program in 1958–1959. On active duty, Oct 1961–Aug 1962, when tactical squadrons completed conversion to C–124s. Flew numerous overseas missions, particularly to the Far East and Southeast Asia, by the mid-1960s and thereafter until the early 1970s. Flew humanitarian and mercy missions on numerous occasions in addition to worldwide airlift operations.

Service Streamers. None.

Campaign Streamers. None.

Decorations. Republic of Vietnam Gallantry Cross with Palm: 1 Apr 1966–28 Jun 1971.

Emblem. Per bend light blue and gules, a bendlet argent, overall an ellipsoid azure gridlined with the latitude lines terminating into arrows on each end of the third, in chief three mullets fesswise of the last, all within a diminished bordure or. *Motto:* SI JEUNESSE SAVAIT, SI VIELLESSE POUVAIT—If youth knew, if age were able. (Approved on 23 Jan 1963.)

443d MILITARY AIRLIFT WING, TRAINING

Lineage. Established as 443d Troop Carrier Wing, Medium, on 10 May 1949. Activated in the Reserve on 27 Jun 1949. Ordered to active service on 1 May 1951. Inactivated on 8 Jan 1953. Redesignated 443d Military Airlift Wing, Training, and activated, on 27 Dec 1965. Organized on 8 Jan 1966.

Assignments. Twelfth Air Force, 27 Jun 1949; Fourteenth Air Force, 1 Jul 1950; Tactical Air Command, 2 May 1951; Eighteenth Air Force, 1 Jun 1951–8 Jan 1953. Military Air Transport Service (later, Military Airlift Command), 27 Dec 1965; Twenty-Second Air Force, 1 Apr 1973–.

Components. *Group.* 443d: 27 Jun 1949–8 Jan 1953. *Squadrons.* 56th: 8 Jan 1966– (not operational, 5 Nov 1958–unkn 1969). 57th: 8 Jan 1966–.

Stations. Hensley Field, Texas, 27 Jun 1949; Donaldson AFB, SC, 9 Aug 1951–8 Jan 1953. Tinker AFB, Okla, 8 Jan 1966; Altus AFB, Okla, 5 May 1969–.

Commanders. Brig Gen Robert J. Smith, 27 Jun 1949; Col William E. Shuttles, 11 Aug 1950–8 Jan 1953. None (not manned), 27 Dec 1965–7 Jan 1966; Col Mahlon B. Hammond, 8 Jan 1966; Col Jerome M. Triolo, 30 Jun 1966; Col Weldon D. Newquist, 14 Aug 1968; Col George M. Wentsch, 18 Sep 1970; Brig Gen Eugene B. Sterling, 9 Jun 1972; Brig Gen Tedd L. Bishop, 14 May 1973; Col Harry F. Smith, Jr., 7 Mar 1975–.

Aircraft. T–6, 1949–1950; T–7, 1949–1951; T–11, 1949–1952; C–46, 1949–1952; C–119, 1952–1953. C–124, 1966–1968; C–141, 1966–; C–5, 1969–.

Operations. Trained as a Reserve troop carrier wing under supervision of the 2596th Air Force Reserve Training Center, Jun 1949–Apr 1951. On active duty, May 1951–Jan 1953; participated in tactical exercises and operations, trained C–46 aircrews for assignment to the Far East, and worked closely with other troop carrier wings to test and evaluate new troop carrier doctrine and procedures. Replaced the 1707th Air Transport Wing, Heavy, in Jan 1966. Became the primary USAF wing charged with training air and ground crews of C–124 and C–141 transports, while simultaneously maintaining a capability to perform airlift operations worldwide. C–124 training diminished in 1967 and ceased in 1968, but C–5 air and ground crew training began in late 1969.

Service Streamers. None.

Campaign Streamers. None.

Decorations. Air Force Outstanding Unit Awards: 1 Apr 1967–31 Mar 1969; 1 Apr 1970–31 Mar 1972.

Emblem. Light blue in fess point two wings conjoined elevated and displayed to chief or enveloping an arc of six mullets argent, the wings surmounted by a mullet of the last bearing a torteau, overall issuing from base a cover azure rolled and unfurled pilewise displaying a light blue reverse, surmounted by a lamp gray enflamed gules and or, all within a diminished bordure of the last. (Approved on 3 Jul 1967.)

445th MILITARY AIRLIFT WING (ASSOCIATE)

Lineage. Established as 445th Fighter-Bomber Wing on 24 Jun 1952. Activated in the Reserve on 8 Jul 1952. Redesignated: 445th Troop Carrier Wing, Medium, on 6 Sep 1957; 445th Troop Carrier Wing, Assault, on 25 Sep 1958. Ordered to active service on 28 Oct 1962. Relieved from active duty on 28 Nov 1962. Redesignated: 445th Troop Carrier Wing, Heavy, on 1 Oct 1965; 445th Air Transport Wing, Heavy, on 1 Dec 1965; 445th Military Airlift Wing on 1 Jan 1966. Ordered to active service on 26 Jan 1968. Relieved from active duty on 1 Jun 1969. Inactivated on 29 Jun 1971. Redesignated 445th Military Airlift Wing (Associate) on 29 Jan 1973. Activated in the Reserve on 1 Jul 1973.

Assignments. First Air Force, 8 Jul 1952; Fourteenth Air Force, 16 Nov 1957; Third Air Force Reserve Region, 15 Jul 1960; Ninth Air Force, 28 Oct 1962; Third Air Force Reserve Region, 28 Nov 1962; Twenty-First Air Force, 26 Jan 1968; Third Air Force Reserve Region, 2 Jun 1969; Eastern Air Force Reserve Region, 31 Dec 1969–29 Jun 1971. Western Air Force Reserve Region, 1 Jul 1973 (attached to 63d Military Airlift Wing, 1 Jul 1973–); Fourth Air Force (Reserve), 8 Oct 1976 (remained attached to 63d Military Airlift Wing).

Components. *Groups*. 445th: 8 Jul 1952–25 Sep 1958. 904th: 26 Jan 1968–1 Jun 1969 (not operational, 15 Aug 1968–1 Jun 1969). 915th: 1 Dec 1965–26 Jan 1968; 1 Sep 1969–21 Apr 1971 (detached 1–21 Apr 1971). 918th: 11 Feb 1963–21 Apr 1971 (not operational, 15 Aug 1968–1 Jun 1969; detached 1–21 Apr 1971). 919th: 11 Feb 1963–15 Dec 1965 (not operational, c. 25 Oct–15 Dec 1965). 920th: 11 Feb 1963–15 Dec 1965 (not operational, c. 25 Oct–15 Dec 1965). *Squadrons*. 76th: 1 Oct 1961–27 Aug 1962. 336th: attached 15 Aug 1968–1 Jun 1969. 700th: attached 16 Nov 1957–24 Sep 1958, assigned 25 Sep 1958–11 Feb 1963; attached 15 Aug 1968–1 Jun 1969. 701st: 25 Sep 1958–11 Feb 1963 (detached). 702d: 25 Sep

1968–11 Feb 1963 (detached). 728th: 1 Jul 1973–. 729th: 1 Jul 1973–. 730th: 1 Jul 1973–. *Detachment.* Det 1, HQ 445th Troop Carrier Wing, Assault: 25 Oct 1958–11 Feb 1963.

Stations. Buffalo, NY, 8 Jul 1952; Niagara Falls Muni Aprt, NY, 15 Jun 1955; Dobbins AFB, Ga, 16 Nov 1957–29 Jun 1971. Norton AFB, Calif, 1 Jul 1973–.

Commanders. Col Carlton C. Proctor, 8 Jul 1952; Lt Col Talmon R. Mager, 11 Aug 1952–unkn; Col William G. Blum, c. 1955; Col Harry A. Staley, 1955; Brig Gen George H. Wilson, 16 Nov 1957; Col Carl F. Rudder, 1 Jan 1970–29 Jun 1971. Col Ronald R. Blalack, 1 Jul 1973; Col Leonard F. Deist, 14 Oct 1973; Lt Col Rollin L. Ratchen, 30 Apr 1976; Col Alan G. Sharp, 1 Jul 1976; Col William M. Conley, 15 Jul 1977; Col Robert E. Dotson, 15 Sep 1977–.

Aircraft. Primarily T–6, 1952–1955; F–51, 1953–1954; F–80, 1953–1956; F–84, 1955–1957; C–119, 1957, 1957–1959, 1961–1962, 1965–1966; C–123, 1958–1965; and C–124, 1965–1971; but also included C–46, 1952–1956, 1957–1958; TF–51, 1953–1954; TF–80, 1953–1956; T–33, 1953–1957; T–28, 1954–1956; C–45, 1955–1957, 1957–1960; TC–47, 1956–1957, 1957–1958; F–86, 1957–1958; C–47, 1959–1968, 1969–1971; U–3, 1961–1965, 1970–1971; VC–117, 1966–1968; C–117, 1969–1970; VC–47, 1969–1970; HU–16, 1969–1971; and T/VT–29, c. 1970–1971. C–141, 1973–.

Operations. Trained as an Air Force Reserve organization to maintain operational proficiency as a fighter-bomber unit, 1952–1956, and as a troop carrier (later, military airlift) unit, 1956–1971. On active duty during the Cuban missile crisis in 1962 and during the period of international tension following the *Pueblo* incident, 1968-1969. Supported Tactical Air Command during the former period and the Military Airlift Command during the latter period. Components of the wing were collocated in NY until Nov 1957. From Nov 1957 to Jun 1971 operated primarily from a base in northern Ga, but with many of its tactical and support components based in other states. Not operational, 1 Apr–29 Jun 1971. Replaced 944th Military Airlift Group (Associate) in Jul 1971. Associated with the 63d Military Airlift Wing of the regular establishment, whose C–141s were flown and maintained in part by Reserve personnel.

Service Streamers. None.

Campaign Streamers. None.

Decorations. Air Force Outstanding Unit Award: 26 Jan 1968–31 Mar 1969. Republic of Vietnam Gallantry Cross with Palm: 1 Apr 1966–29 Jun 1971.

Emblem. Per chevron gules and or, in pale a gauntlet argent grasping a lightning bolt palewise and two arrows saltirewise sable, on a chief azure a fillet of the third thirteen mullets six and seven of the like, all within a diminished bordure of the last. *Motto:* READINESS IN RESERVE. (Approved on 10 Jan 1964.)

446th MILITARY AIRLIFT WING (ASSOCIATE)

Lineage. Established as 446th Troop Carrier Wing, Medium, on 11 Apr 1955. Activated in the Reserve on 25

May 1955. Redesignated 446th Tactical Airlift Wing on 1 Jul 1967. Inactivated on 1 Jul 1972. Redesignated 446th Military Airlift Wing (Associate) on 29 Jan 1973. Activated in the Reserve on 1 Jul 1973.

Assignments. Fourteenth Air Force, 25 May 1955; Tenth Air Force, 25 Mar 1958; Fourth Air Force Reserve Region, 1 Sep 1960; Central Air Force Reserve Region, 31 Dec 1969–1 Jul 1972. Western Air Force Reserve Region, 1 Jul 1973 (attached to 62d Military Airlift Wing, 1 Jul 1973–); Fourth Air Force (Reserve), 8 Oct 1976– (remained attached to 62d Military Airlift Wing).

Components. *Groups*. 446th: 25 May 1955–14 Apr 1959. 908th: 1 Dec 1965–1 Mar 1968. 917th: 21 Apr 1971–25 Feb 1972. 924th: 17 Jan 1963–1 Jul 1972. 925th: 17 Jan 1963–25 Mar 1968. 926th: 17 Jan 1963–1 Mar 1968; 1 Oct 1969–1 Jul 1972. *Squadrons*. 97th: 1 Jul 1973–. 313th: 1 Jul 1973–. 357th: 14 Apr 1959–8 May 1961. 704th: 14 Apr 1959–17 Jan 1963. 705th: 14 Apr 1959–17 Jan 1963; 25 Mar 1968–1 Jul 1972. 706th: 14 Apr 1959–17 Jan 1963.

Stations. Ellington AFB, Texas, 25 May 1955–1 Jul 1972. McChord AFB, Wash, 1 Jul 1973–.

Commanders. Col John W. Williams, 25 May 1955; Col Forrest R. Harsh, c. Jul 1955; Brig Gen Russell F. Gustke, 1 Nov 1958; Col Richard E. George, 1 Jan 1970; Brig Gen William G. Hathaway, 15 Jun 1970–1 Jul 1972. Col Donald F. Beyl, 1 Jul 1973; Col Paul A. Wriggle, 28 Aug 1975; Col Edward C. Black, Jr., 10 May 1976–.

Aircraft. C–45, 1955–1958; C–46, 1955–1958; C–119, 1957–1968, 1969–1970; C–130, 1968–1972; RC–130, 1970–1972; C–124, 1971–1972. C–141, 1973–.

Operations. Replaced 8706th Pilot Training Wing in May 1955. Performed Reserve troop carrier (later, tactical airlift) operations, 1955–1972, including aeromedical evacuation, 1970–1972, and military airlift, 1971–1972. Flew numerous disaster relief missions. Transported cargo and troops during exercises and maneuvers, some overseas. Supported National Aeronautics and Space Administration, airdropping experimental spacecraft, 1962–1967. Became the first Reserve organization to start the Air Reserve Technician (ART) program, in 1958. Operated the USAF Combat Crew Training School (Tactical Airlift—C–130), 1968–1972, to train aircrews of the USAF, other services, the Air National Guard, and other AF Reserve units. Manned primarily by ART personnel, the school became the first Reserve facility to train members of the active establishment. Ferried many C–130s to Taiwan in 1966 and to Southeast Asia, 1968–1970. Replaced 939th Military Airlift Group (Associate) in Jul 1973 and became associated with the 62d Military Airlift Wing, whose C–141s were flown and maintained in part by Reserve personnel.

Service Streamers. None.

Campaign Streamers. None.

Decorations. Air Force Outstanding Unit Awards: 1 Dec 1967–10 Jan 1972; 1 Jul 1973–30 Jun 1974. Republic of Vietnam Gallantry Cross with Palm: 1 Apr 1966–29 Jun 1971.

Emblem. Azure, between in base a pair of wings displayed argent and dark blue, charged in the center with a bezant, and in chief a skystreak proper, surmounted in the center by a mullet or with three rays to fess point of the second, a constellation consisting of twelve mullets in the form of a diamond of the third, and in fess bendwise overall a sword of the fourth, all within a diminished bordure of the second. (Approved on 3 Aug 1960.)

448th FIGHTER-BOMBER WING

Lineage. Established as 448th Bombardment Wing, Light, on 10 May 1949. Activated in the Reserve on 27 Jun 1949. Ordered to active service on 17 Mar 1951. Inactivated on 21 Mar 1951. Redesignated 448th Fighter-Bomber Wing on 12 Apr 1955. Activated in the Reserve on 18 May 1955. Inactivated on 16 Nov 1957.

Assignments. Fourth Air Force, 27 Jun 1949–21 Mar 1951. Fourteenth Air Force, 18 May 1955–16 Nov 1957.

Components. *Group.* 448th: 27 Jun 1949–21 Mar 1951; 18 May 1955–16 Nov 1957.

Stations. Long Beach Muni Aprt, Calif, 27 Jun 1949–21 Mar 1951. Dallas NAS, Texas, 18 May 1955–16 Nov 1957.

Commanders. Brig Gen Douglas Keeney, 27 Jun 1949; Col Robert E. Dake, (by Sep) 1950–21 Mar 1951. Brig Gen Jerry W. Davidson, 18 May 1955–c. Nov 1957.

Aircraft. T–6, 1949–1950; T–7, 1949–1951; T–11, 1949–1951; B–26, 1949–1951. T–28, 1955, 1955–1957; T–33, 1955–1957; F–80, 1955–1957; F–86, 1957.

Operations. Trained as a Reserve bombardment wing under supervision of the 2347th Air Force Reserve Training Center, 1949–1951. Lost more than half of its personnel in the call-up of another wing in Aug 1950. Ordered to active service in Mar 1951, but personnel used as fillers in other units. Replaced the 8708th Pilot Training Wing in May 1955 and trained as a Reserve fighter-bomber wing until inactivated in 1957.

Service Streamers. None.

Campaign Streamers. None.

Decorations. None.

Emblem. None.

449th BOMBARDMENT WING, HEAVY

Lineage. Established as 449th Fighter-Bomber Wing on 23 Mar 1953. Redesignated 449th Bombardment Wing, Heavy, and activated, on 15 Nov 1962. Organized on 1 Feb 1963. Inactivated on 30 Sep 1977.

Assignments. Strategic Air Command, 15 Nov 1962; 40th Air Division, 1 Feb 1963–30 Sep 1977.

Components. *Squadrons.* 716th: 1 Feb 1963–30 Sep 1977. 908th Air Refueling: 1 Jul 1963–30 Sep 1977.

Stations. Kincheloe AFB, Mich, 1 Feb 1963–30 Sep 1977.

Commanders. None (not manned), 15 Nov 1962–31 Jan 1963; Col Louis M. Sowers, 1 Feb 1963; Col Charles W. Johnson, Jr., 9 May 1964; Col Joseph D. White, 16 May 1964; Col Arthur W. Holderness, Jr., 8 Jul 1965; Col Robert E. Huyser, 29 Dec 1966; Col George N. Payne, 9 Apr 1968; Col Ernest L. Benton, 1 May 1970; Col Kenneth M. Holloway, 1 Jun 1971; Col Robert T. Herres, 12 Apr 1972; Col Kenneth M. Holloway, c. 10 Oct 1972; Col Robert T. Herres, 27 Nov 1972; Col John E. Wolter, 16 Mar 1973; Col Otto L. Kovar, Jr., 3 Aug 1973; Col Robert T. Herres, 14 Sep 1973; Col Otto L. Kovar, Jr., 8 Feb 1974; Col Donald L. Jolly, 7–30 Sep 1977.

Aircraft. B–52, 1963–1977; KC–135, 1963–1977.

Operations. Replaced the 4239th Strategic Wing and assumed a mission of training for strategic bombardment on 1 Feb 1963. Added air refueling to the mission in Jul 1963. Supported SAC combat operations in Southeast Asia by furnishing KC–135 aircraft and crews, Nov 1965–Dec 1975, and B–52 crews, May 1968–Jun 1975. Responsible for phasing down Kincheloe AFB, Mich, for closure, Jul–Sep 1977.

Service Streamers. None.

Campaign Streamers. None.

Decorations. Air Force Outstanding Unit Award: 1 Jul 1974–30 Jun 1976.

Emblem: A shield divided into a horizontal gray embattlement in base just below the horizontal center and diagonally from the viewer's upper right to lower left above the embattlement, the top portion medium blue and the bottom portion black, the upper portion bearing a yellow lightning bolt originating along top of the shield to the viewer's right and extending along the division line between the blue and black areas. Around the shield a narrow white border. *Motto:* NUMQUAM NON PARATUS—Never unprepared. (Approved on 7 Feb 1964.)

450th BOMBARDMENT WING, HEAVY

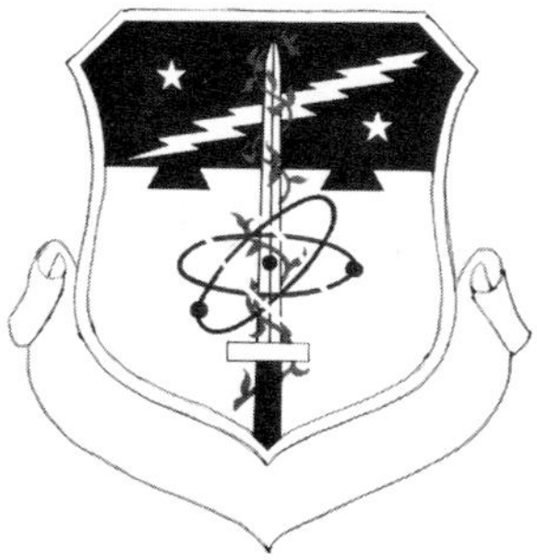

Lineage. Established as 450th Fighter-Bomber Wing on 23 Mar 1953. Activated on 1 Jul 1954. Redesignated 450th Fighter-Day Wing on 8 Mar 1955; 450th Tactical Fighter Wing on 1 Jul 1958. Inactivated on 18 Dec 1958.

Redesignated 450th Bombardment Wing, Heavy, and activated, on 15 Nov 1962. Organized on 1 Feb 1963. Discontinued, and inactivated, on 25 Jul 1968.

Assignments. Ninth Air Force, 1 Jul 1954; Eighteenth Air Force, 1 Oct 1957; Twelfth Air Force, 1 Jan–18 Dec 1958. Strategic Air Command, 15 Nov 1962; 810th Strategic Aerospace Division, 1 Feb 1963–25 Jul 1968.

Components. *Groups*. 322d: attached 1 Jul 1954–18 Nov 1957 (not operational, 24 Oct–18 Nov 1957). 450th: 1 Jul 1954–11 Dec 1957. *Squadrons*. 720th: 11 Dec 1957–18 Dec 1958 (not operational, Jul–18 Dec 1958); 1 Feb 1963–25 Jul 1968. 721st: 11 Dec 1957–18 Dec 1958 (not operational, Jul–18 Dec 1958). 722d: 11 Dec 1957–18 Dec 1958 (not operational, Jul–18 Dec 1958). 723d: 11 Dec 1957–18 Dec 1958 (not operational, 16 Aug–18 Dec 1958). 906th Air Refueling: 1 Feb 1963–25 Jul 1968.

Stations. Foster AFB, Texas, 1 Jul 1954–18 Dec 1958. Minot AFB, ND, 1 Feb 1963–25 Jul 1968.

Commanders. Col Frank L. Dunn, 1 Jul 1954; Col Joe L. Mason, 20 Jun 1955; Col Wallace E. Hopkins, 1 Jul 1957; Col Edmund F. Freeman, 12 Jul 1957; Brig Gen Avelin P. Tacon, Jr., 25 Jul 1957; Col Wallace E. Hopkins, 12 Nov 1957; Brig Gen Avelin P. Tacon, Jr., 11 Dec 1957; Col Edmund F. Freeman, 11 Aug–18 Dec 1958. None (not manned), 15 Nov 1962–31 Jan 1963; Col Howard J. Fry, 1 Feb 1963; Col Jerrold M. Vivian, 9 Jul 1964; Col Joel A. Carroll, Jr., 10 Aug 1964; Col John R. Hinton, Jr., 8 Jun 1967; Col William W. Culbertson, 10–25 Jul 1968.

Aircraft. F–86, 1954–1955; F–100, 1955–1958. B–52, 1963–1968; KC–135, 1963–1968; EC–135, 1967–1968.

Operations. Replaced 3580th Pilot Training Wing in Jul 1954. Trained with F–86 and later F–100 aircraft to maintain tactical proficiency for combat operations. Phased down for inactivation in Jul 1958. During final months, active in closing Foster AFB, Texas. Replaced 4136th Strategic Wing in Feb 1963. Trained in global bombardment and air refueling operations. Added post attack command and control system (PACCS)/airborne launch control system (ALCS) missions in 1967 and began active PACCS/ALCS missions in Feb 1968. Supported SAC combat operations in Southeast Asia by furnishing KC–135 aircraft and crews, Dec 1964–Jul 1968, and B–52 crews, Jun–Jul 1968. Replaced by 5th Bombardment Wing, Heavy, in Jul 1968.

Service Streamers. None.

Campaign Streamers. None.

Decorations. None.

Emblem. Argent, on a chief dovetailed azure between two mullets of the first, a lightning flash bend sinisterwise or, overall issuant from base in pale a sword of the first, guard of the third and handle striped bendwise gules and dark blue, the sword entwined by an olive branch vert and surmounted in fess by two orbital rings of the fourth and one of the third, all within a diminished bordure of the last. (Approved on 7 Feb 1964.)

451st STRATEGIC MISSILE WING (ICBM–TITAN)

Lineage. Established as 451st Strategic Missile Wing (ICBM–Titan), and activated, on 26 Apr 1961. Organized on 1 Jul 1961. Discontinued, and inactivated, on 25 Jun 1965.

Assignments. Strategic Air Command, 26 Apr 1961; 13th Air (later, 13th Strategic Missile) Division, 1 Jul 1961–25 Jun 1965.

Components. *Squadrons*. 724th: 1 Jul 1961–25 Jun 1965. 725th: 1 Jul 1961–25 Jun 1965.

Stations. Lowry AFB, Colo, 1 Jul 1961–25 Jun 1965.

Commanders. None (not manned), 26 Apr–30 Jun 1961; Col John P. Proctor, 1 Jul 1961; Col Julius Pickoff, 13 Mar 1962; Col Donald W. Johnson, 9 Jan–c. 25 Jun 1965.

Missiles. Titan I, 1962–1965.

Operations. Replaced 703d SMW (ICBM–Titan) in Jul 1961. First wing missile complex accepted 18 Apr 1962. All wing missiles off alert status on 26 Mar 1965, and wing phased down for inactivation.

Service Streamers. None.

Campaign Streamers. None.

Decorations. Air Force Outstanding Unit Award: 1 Jul 1963–30 Jun 1964.

Emblem. Azure, above a portion of a sphere in sinister base with axis bendwise light blue, grid lines argent, an orbiting missile arras-wise in bend of the third enflamed proper, emitting to chief and to base a lightning flash gules and trailing from its point four shock waves two and two of the third, sprinkled with nine mullets of the like above in base a wreath vert, all within a diminished bordure of the third. *Motto:* EXEMPLUM PROFERIMUS—We serve as an example. (Approved on 29 Jun 1962.)

452d AIR REFUELING WING

Lineage. Established as 452d Bombardment Wing, Light, on 10 May 1949. Activated in the Reserve on 27 Jun 1949. Ordered to active service on 10 Aug 1950. Inactivated on 10 May 1952. Redesignated 452d Tactical Reconnaissance Wing on 6 Jun 1952. Activated in the Reserve on 13 Jun 1952. Redesignated: 452d Bombardment Wing, Tactical, on 22 May 1955; 452d Troop Carrier Wing, Medium, on 1 Jul

1957; 452d Military Airlift Wing on 1 Apr 1972; 452d Air Refueling Wing on 1 Oct 1976.

Assignments. Fourth Air Force, 27 Jun 1949; Tactical Air Command, 10 Aug 1950; Fifth Air Force, 15 Nov 1950–10 May 1952 (attached to 8th Fighter-Bomber Wing, 15–30 Nov 1950; 314th Air Division, 1 Dec 1950–25 May 1951). 4th Air Reserve District, 13 Jun 1952; Fourth Air Force, 1 Dec 1952; Sixth Air Force Reserve Region, 1 Sep 1960; Western Air Force Reserve Region, 31 Dec 1969; Tenth Air Force (Reserve), 8 Oct 1976–.

Components. *Groups*. 452d: 27 Jun 1949–10 May 1952; 13 Jun 1952–14 Apr 1959. 904th: 31 Dec 1969–1 Sep 1975. 939th: 26 Jan 1968–15 Jun 1969 (detached 25 Jul 1968–15 Jun 1969). 940th: 26 Jan 1968–. 942d: 17 Jan 1963–1 Jan 1972. 943d: 17 Jan 1973–25 Apr 1969. 944th: 17 Jan 1963–25 Jul 1969 (detached 25 Mar 1968–25 Jul 1969). 945th: 17 Jan 1963–1 Jul 1972 (detached 15 Feb–1 Jul 1972). *Squadrons*. 336th: 1 Sep 1975–. 728th: 14 Apr 1959–17 Jan 1963. 729th: 14 Apr 1959–17 Jan 1963. 730th: 14 Apr 1959–17 Jan 1963. 733d: 14 Apr 1959–28 Oct 1962; 28 Nov 1962–17 Jan 1963.

Stations. Long Beach Muni Aprt, Calif, 27 Jun 1949; George AFB, Calif, 10 Aug–c. 22 Oct 1950; Itazuke AB, Japan, 25 Oct 1950; Miho AB, Japan, 12 Dec 1950; Pusan East AB, South Korea, 23 May 1951–10 May 1952. Long Beach Muni Aprt, Calif, 13 Jun 1952; March AFB, Calif, 14 Oct 1960; Hamilton AFB, Calif, 1 Jan 1972; March AFB, Calif, 12 Jan 1976–.

Commanders. Brig Gen Luther W. Sweetser, Jr., 27 Jun 1949; Col Brooks A. Lawhon, 12 May 1951; Col Reginald J. Clizbe, (by 20) Aug 1951; Col Albert W. Fletcher, 10 Feb–10 May 1952. Col George M. Miller, Jr., 13 Jun 1952; Brig Gen Joseph S. Marriott, c. Oct 1952; Maj Gen John R. Alison, 15 May 1955; Lt Col George F. Schlagel, 1 Oct 1959; Brig Gen Earl O. Anderson, 16 Jun 1960; Col Merle E. Larson, 1 May 1969; Col Harry J. Huff II, 13 Sep 1969; Brig Gen William G. Hathaway, Jul 1972; Brig Gen James L. Wade, 12 Jan 1976–.

Aircraft. T–11, 1949–1950; B–26, 1949–1952. Primarily flew F/TF–51, 1953–1954; B–26, 1953–1957; F/TF–80, 1954–1955; TB–26, 1954–1957; C–46, 1957–1958; C–119, 1958–1969; C–124, 1965–1972; C–130, 1972–1976; and KC–135, 1976–; also flew, in fewer numbers, T–6, 1952–1954; C–46, 1952–1954; T–28, 1953–1955; T–33, 1953–1955; FB–26, 1953–1954; C–45, 1953–1955, 1957–1958; TB–25, 1954–1955; and C–47, 1957–1958.

Operations. Trained in Reserve as a light bombardment wing, 1949–1950. Ordered to active service during the Korean war. From 27 Oct 1950 to 10 May 1952, flew reconnaissance, medium-level bombardment, and close air support for ground forces in Korea, accumulating nearly 14,000 combat sorties. Trained in Reserve as a tactical reconnaissance wing, 1952–1955, as a tactical bombardment wing, 1955–1957, as a troop carrier wing, 1957–1966, as a military airlift wing, 1966–1972, as a tactical airlift wing, 1972–1976, and as an air refueling wing since 1976.

Service Streamers. None.

Campaign Streamers. UN Defensive; UN Offensive; CCF Intervention; First

UN Counteroffensive; CCF Spring Offensive; UN Summer–Fall Offensive; Second Korean Winter; Korea Summer–Fall, 1952.

Decorations. Republic of Korea Presidential Unit Citation: 27 Oct 1950–27 Oct 1951. Republic of Vietnam Gallantry Cross with Palm: 1 Jan 1967–31 Dec 1971.

Emblem. Or, on a hurt spattered with mullets argent and having a border rayonne gules, a horse rampant bearing a knight in armor of the first and detailed brown, grasping a lance point to chief flying a pennant fesswise also of the first outlined azure. *Motto:* LABOR AD FUTURUM—Work for the future. (Approved on 10 Feb 1960.)

454th BOMBARDMENT WING, HEAVY

Lineage. Established as 454th Troop Carrier Wing, Medium, on 26 May 1952. Activated in the Reserve on 13 Jun 1952. Inactivated on 1 Jan 1953. Redesignated 454th Bombardment Wing, Heavy, and activated, on 15 Nov 1962. Organized on 1 Feb 1963. Inactivated on 2 Jul 1969.

Assignments. Fourth Air Force, 13 Jun 1952–1 Jan 1953. Strategic Air Command, 15 Nov 1962; 4th Air Division, 1 Feb 1963; 42d Air Division, 1 Jul 1963–2 Jul 1969.

Components. *Group.* 454th: 13 Jun 1952–1 Jan 1953. *Squadrons.* 736th: 1 Feb 1963–2 Jul 1969. 901st Air Refueling: 1 Feb 1963–2 Jul 1969.

Stations. Portland Intl Aprt, Ore, 13 Jun 1952–1 Jan 1953. Columbus AFB, Miss, 1 Feb 1963–2 Jul 1969.

Commanders. Col Robert W. Sheets, 13 Jun 1952–1 Jan 1953. None (not manned), 15 Nov 1962–31 Jan 1963; Col Orie O. Schurter, 1 Feb 1963; Col Flavel P. Sabin, 28 May 1964; Col William T. Cumiskey, 10 Jun 1964; Col Samuel P. Jordan, c. 16 Nov 1965; Col William T. Cumiskey, c. 1 Apr 1966; Col William F. Seith, 10 Jun 1966; Col Edward O. Martin, 1 May 1967; Col William A. Adams, Jr., c. 27 Jun 1967; Col Edward O. Martin, c. 10 Dec 1967; Col John H. Archer, Jr., c. 28 Jun 1968; Col Frank L. Scurlock, c. 21 Dec 1968–2 Jul 1969.

Aircraft. C–46, 1952. B–52, 1963–1965, 1966–1967, 1967–1968, 1968–1969; KC–135, 1963–1965, 1966–1967, 1967–1968, 1968–1969.

Operations. Replaced 922d Reserve Training Wing in Jun 1952. Trained as a Reserve troop carrier wing. Replaced by 403d Troop Carrier Wing on 1 Jan 1953. Replaced 4228th Strategic Wing in Feb 1963. Conducted air refueling operations and trained in bombardment operations. The wing's headquarters staff, tactical aircraft and crews, and maintenance personnel integrated into SAC combat forces in the Pacific and Southeast Asia, 16 Nov 1965–31 Mar 1966, 27 Jun– c. 23 Dec 1967, and c. 28 Jun–c. 20 Dec 1968. During these periods, the 454th Combat Support Group continued to operate Columbus AFB, Miss. Began phasing down for inactivation in May 1969 and ceased flying operations 2 days before inactivation.

Service Streamers. None.

Campaign Streamers. None.

Decorations. Air Force Outstanding Unit Awards: 1 Dec 1965–1 Mar 1966; 2 Mar–1 Apr 1966 and 1 Jul–31 Dec 1967; 1 Jul–1 Dec 1968.

Emblem. Quarterly, first and fourth quarters azure, on a bend sable, between two mullets or, a lightning flash point inward of the last, second quarter argent, issuant from sinister a mail gauntlet bendwise of the third, third quarter of the fourth, a pennant bendwise gules flying from a pole of the second with a spearhead of the third, all within a diminished bordure of the last. *Motto:* DETER OR DESTROY. (Approved on 19 Aug 1963.)

455th STRATEGIC MISSILE WING (ICBM–MINUTEMAN)

Lineage. Established as 455th Fighter-Bomber Wing on 23 Mar 1953. Redesignated 455th Strategic Missile Wing (ICBM–Minuteman), and activated, on 28 Jun 1962. Organized on 1 Nov 1962. Discontinued, and inactivated, on 25 Jun 1968.

Assignments. Strategic Air Command, 28 Jun 1962; 810th Strategic Aerospace Division, 1 Nov 1962–25 Jun 1968.

Components. *Squadrons.* 740th: 1 Nov 1962–25 Jun 1968. 741st: 1 Dec 1962–25 Jun 1968. 742d: 1 Jan 1963–25 Jun 1968.

Stations. Minot AFB, ND, 1 Nov 1962–25 Jun 1968.

Commanders. None (not manned), 28 Jun–31 Oct 1962; Col Gilbert F. Friederichs, 1 Nov 1962; Col John P. Couch, c. 1 Aug 1964; Col B. H. Davidson, 23 Jun 1967–25 Jun 1968.

Missiles. Minuteman I, 1963–1968.

Operations. Prepared for operational capability with intercontinental ballistic missiles, Nov 1962–Mar 1964. First missile arrived on 6 Sep 1963 and was emplaced 3 days later. The 150th missile was emplaced in its silo on 26 Feb 1964 and, by late Mar 1964, the wing became combat ready. Maintained combat readiness until replaced by 91st Strategic Missile Wing in Jun 1968.

Service Streamers. None.

Campaign Streamers. None.

Decorations. None.

Emblem. Argent on a chief nebuly light blue semee of mullets of the first a laurel branch arched fesswise or, overall between in base two lightning flashes parewise gules, in fess a sphere of the first and of the second with grid lines counterchanged surmounted by a missile palewise azure emitting a vapor trail to base of the third, all within a diminished bordure of the last. (Approved c. Oct 1963.)

456th BOMBARDMENT WING, HEAVY

Lineage. Established as 456th Troop Carrier Wing, Medium, on 15 Oct 1952. Activated on 1 Dec 1952. Inactivated on 9 Jul 1956. Redesignated 456th Strategic Aerospace Wing, and activated, on 15 Nov 1962. Organized on 1 Feb 1963. Redesignated 456th Bombardment Wing, Heavy, on 1 Jul 1972. Inactivated on 30 Sep 1975.

Assignments. Eighteenth Air Force, 1 Dec 1952–9 Jul 1956 (attached to 1st Air Division [Meteorological Survey], c. 22 Apr 1955–26 Mar 1956; 463d Troop Carrier Wing, 10 May–9 Jul 1956). Strategic Air Command, 15 Nov 1962; 14th Strategic Aerospace Division, 1 Feb 1963; 47th Air Division, 30 Jun 1971; 14th Air Division, 1 Oct 1972–30 Sep 1975.

Components. *Group.* 456th: 1 Dec 1952–1 Mar 1955. *Squadrons.* 9th Air Refueling: 1 Jan 1970–30 Sep 1975. 744th: 1 Mar 1955–9 Jul 1956; 1 Feb 1963–30 Sep 1975. 745th: 1 Mar 1955–9 Jul 1956. 746th: 1 Mar 1955–9 Jul 1956. 851st Strategic Missile: 1 Feb 1963–25 Mar 1965. 903d Air Refueling: 1 Feb 1963–30 Sep 1975. *Detachments.* Det 1, 744th Troop Carrier Squadron: attached 14 Feb 1955–9 Jul 1956. Det 1, 745th Troop Carrier Squadron: attached 14 Feb 1955–9 Jul 1956. Det 1, 746th Troop Carrier Squadron: attached 14 Feb 1955–9 Jul 1956.

Stations. Miami Intl Aprt, Fla, 1 Dec 1952; Charleston AFB, SC, 25 Jul 1953–16 Oct 1955; Shiroi AB, Japan, 10 Nov 1955–10 May 1956; Ardmore AFB, Okla, 25 May–9 Jul 1956. Beale AFB, Calif, 1 Feb 1963–30 Sep 1975.

Commanders. Maj William J. Frazier, Jr., 1 Dec 1952; Col James L. Daniel, Jr., c. 10 Dec 1952–9 Jul 1956. None (not manned), 15 Nov 1962–31 Jan 1963; Col Sam J. Byerley, 1 Feb 1963; Col William L. Reynolds, 20 Feb 1963; Col Rowland H. Worrell, Jr., 19 Jun 1965; Col Jack D. Templin, 26 Aug 1966; Col Richard G. Wilkinson, 22 Sep 1966; Col Wendell W. Sanders, (by 26) Jul 1968; Col George E. Burch, 23 Sep 1968; Col Carlton J. Koncz, 1 Jun 1970; Col Charles D. Youree, Jr., 17 Mar 1972; Col Vernon R. Huber, 23 Apr 1973; Col Philip A. Brennan, 11 Sep 1973; Col Vernon R. Huber, 22 Nov 1973; Col Philip A. Brennan, 30 Jun–30 Sep 1975.

Aircraft and Missiles. C–119, 1952–1956. B–52, 1963–1975; Titan I, 1963–1965; KC–135, 1963–1975.

Operations. Replaced 435th Troop Carrier Wing, a Reserve unit released from active duty, in Dec 1952. From then until early 1955, participated in numerous tactical exercises in the United States and overseas, mostly in conjunction with Army airborne forces. Reorganized on 1 Mar 1955. The tactical group and all support components inactivated and the wing assumed control over three tactical squadrons plus three squadron-size detachments, each squadron/detachment having eight specially modified C–119s and manned for self-sufficient operations. Participated in Project Drag Net, part of Project C–119L. The wing's task was to perform air recovery of balloon-borne instrument packages. From c. 22 Apr 1955 to 26 Mar 1956 the wing was controlled by the 1st Air Division (Meteorological Survey) in support of the high-altitude research program. Wing headquarters moved to Shiroi AB, Japan, and components were located at other points in Japan, the Aleutian Islands, Alaska, and Okinawa. On 26 Mar 1956 the wing was released from its attachment to the 1st Air Division and on 10 May began its return to the United States. At Ardmore AFB, Okla, the 456th Wing was attached to the 463d Troop Carrier Wing until the 456th inactivated in Jul 1956. Eight years later the 456th, redesignated as a strategic aerospace wing, replaced the 4126th Strategic Wing at Beale AFB, Calif, and assumed a mission of strategic bombardment training and air refueling. It also controlled a Titan I strategic missile squadron until early 1965. The wing's bombardment and air refueling squadrons frequently deployed aircraft and crews to meet USAF requirements, often having nearly all of their resources scattered around the world at various operating locations. Inactivated in Sep 1975 and replaced by the 17th Bombardment Wing.

Service Streamers. None.

Campaign Streamers. None.

Decorations. Air Force Outstanding Unit Award: 1 Apr 1955–20 Mar 1956.

Emblem. Azure, within a diminished bordure argent, in bend a flight symbol throughout arched to chief dark blue fimbriated of the second, between in chief an atom symbol of the third garnished gules and in base superimposed upon a lightning flash bendwise of the last highlighted or, a laurel branch bend sinisterwise of the like. (Approved on 23 Aug 1972.)

459th TACTICAL AIRLIFT WING

Lineage. Established as 459th Troop Carrier Wing, Medium, on 30 Dec 1954. Activated in the Reserve on 26 Jan 1955. Redesignated: 455th Military Airlift Wing on 1 Jul 1966; 459th Tactical Airlift Wing on 29 Jun 1971.

Assignments. First Air Force, 26 Jan 1955; Fourteenth Air Force, 25 Mar 1958; Second Air Force Reserve Region, 15 Aug 1960; First Air Force Reserve Region, 24 Jun 1966; Eastern Air Force Reserve Region, 31 Dec 1969; Fourteenth Air Force (Reserve), 8 Oct 1976–.

Components. *Groups*. 459th: 26 Jan 1955–14 Apr 1959. 904th: 1 Jul 1966–26 Jan 1968; 2 Jun–31 Dec 1969. 905th: 25 Feb 1972–1 Apr 1974. 909th: 17 Jan 1963–1 Sep 1975. 910th: 17 Jan 1963–1 Jul 1966. 911th: 17 Jan 1963–21 Apr

1971 (detached 1–21 Apr 1971). 913th: 8 Jan 1976–. 915th: 26 Jan 1968–1 Sep 1969. 918th: attached 1–20 Apr 1971, assigned 21 Apr 1971–1 Jul 1972. 919th: 30 Jul 1971–1 Dec 1974. 920th: 25 Apr 1973–1 Jan 1976. 927th: 15 Mar 1976–. *Squadrons*. 756th: 14 Apr 1959–17 Jan 1963; 1 Sep 1975–. 757th: 14 Apr 1959–17 Jan 1963. 758th: 14 Apr 1959–17 Jan 1963.

Stations. Andrews AFB, Md, 26 Jan 1955–.

Commanders. Unkn, 26 Jan–13 Apr 1955; Brig Gen Ramsey D. Potts, Jr., 14 Apr 1955; Brig Gen Charles D. Briggs, Jr., 19 Jun 1960; Col George A. Amsler, c. 1 Jan 1970; Brig Gen William J. Crandall, 1 Jun 1970; Brig Gen Edward Dillon, 14 Jun 1973; Col Joseph W. Bourassa, 1 Jul 1975; Brig Gen Donald E. Haughen, 16 Jul 1975–.

Aircraft. C–45, 1955–1958; C–46, 1955–1957; C–119, 1957–1967; C–124, 1966–1972; RC–130, 1971–1973; C–130, 1971–; C–7, 1972.

Operations. Trained in the Reserve to maintain proficiency in troop carrier and airlift operations. Converted to the Air Reserve Technician program in Apr 1958. Supported airlift requirements of Tactical Air Command from activation until Jul 1966 and from Jun 1971 to Dec 1974, and of Military Airlift Command from Jul 1966 to Jun 1971, and again from Dec 1974 onward. Participated in numerous exercises during short summer encampments and at other times, and gradually assumed a greater share in airlift support of the Air Force within the United States and overseas.

Service Streamers. None.

Campaign Streamers. None.

Decorations. Air Force Outstanding Unit Award: 1 Apr 1971–31 Mar 1973. Republic of Vietnam Gallantry Cross with Palm: 1 Apr 1966–29 Jun 1971.

Emblem. On a shield an American eagle proper flying over clouds in the base argent between two parachutes, one in chief transporting an airman, one in base transporting supplies all of the last; in chief a canton argent charged with the Capitol dome of the second. *Motto:* IN HONOR OF CONGRESS. (Approved on 17 Jan 1958.)

460th TACTICAL RECONNAISSANCE WING

Lineage. Established as 460th Tactical Reconnaissance Wing, and activated, on 2 Feb 1966. Organized on 18 Feb 1966. Inactivated on 31 Aug 1971.

Assignments. Pacific Air Forces, 2 Feb 1966; 2d Air Division, 18 Feb 1966; Seventh Air Force, 1 Apr 1966–31 Aug 1971.

Components. *Squadrons*. 12th: 2 Sep 1966–31 Aug 1971. 16th: 18 Feb 1966–15 Mar 1970. 20th: 18 Feb–18 Sep 1966. 41st: 18 Feb–18 Sep 1966. 45th: attached 30 Mar–7 Jul 1966. 360th Tactical Electronic Warfare: 8 Apr 1966–31 Aug 1971. 361st Tactical Electronic Warfare: 8 Apr 1966–31 Aug 1971.

362d Tactical Electronic Warfare: 1 Feb 1967–31 Aug 1971. 6460th: 8 Jun–18 Sep 1966. 6461st: 29 Jul–18 Sep 1966. *Detachments*. Det 1, 45th TRS: attached 8 Jul 1966–31 Dec 1970. Det 1, 360th TEWS: attached 1 Jun 1970–31 Aug 1971. Det 1, 361st RS: attached 8 Sep 1966–1 Feb 1967. Det 1, Headquarters 460th TRW: 18 Feb 1966–31 Aug 1971. Det 2, Headquarters 460th TRW: 8 Apr 1969–1 Jun 1970.

Stations. Tan Son Nhut AB, South Vietnam, 18 Feb 1966–31 Aug 1971.

Commanders. None (not manned), 2–17 Feb 1966; unkn, 18 Feb–13 Mar 1966; Col Edward H. Taylor, 14 Mar 1966; Col Robert G. Williams, (by Mar) 1967; Brig Gen Robert J. Holbury, 21 Dec 1967; Col Leslie J. Westberg, 8 Jul 1968; Col Hal L. Fitzpatrick, 28 May 1969; Col Harry M. Chapman, 21 Jun 1969; Col James E. Tilton, 1 May 1970; Col Dale L. Flowers, 15 Apr 1971; Col Jerome F. O'Malley, 1–31 Aug 1971.

Aircraft. RB–57, 1966–1971; EB/RB–66, 1966; RF–4, 1966–1971; RF–101, 1966–1970; RC–47, 1966–1967; EC–47, 1967–1971.

Operations. Organized in Feb 1966 to control and administer tactical reconnaissance resources in Southeast Asia. Assigned and attached tactical reconnaissance and tactical electronic warfare squadrons, and squadron-size detachments flew day and night visual, photographic, radar, thermographic, and electronic reconnaissance to meet the combat needs of 2d Air Division until Apr 1966 and for the Seventh Air Force thereafter. Divided reconnaissance in Southeast Asia with another wing in Sep 1966. In Oct 1966, assumed aircraft maintenance responsibility for all USAF organizations using Tan Son Nhut AB, South Vietnam. Continued reconnaissance operations through Aug 1971.

Service Streamers. None.

Campaign Streamers. Vietnam Air; Vietnam Air Offensive; Vietnam Air Offensive, Phase II; Vietnam Air Offensive, Phase III; Vietnam Air/Ground; Vietnam Air Offensive, Phase IV; TET 69/Counteroffensive; Vietnam Summer–Fall, 1969; Vietnam Winter–Spring, 1970; Sanctuary Counteroffensive; Southwest Monsoon; Commando Hunt V; Commando Hunt VI.

Decorations. Presidential Unit Citations (Southeast Asia): 18 Feb 1966–30 Jun 1967; 1 Sep 1967–10 Jul 1968; 11 Jul 1968–31 Aug 1969; 1 Feb–31 Mar 1971. Air Force Outstanding Unit Awards with Combat "V" Device: 1 Jul 1969–30 Jun 1970; 1 Jul 1970–30 Jun 1971. Republic of Vietnam Gallantry Cross with Palm: 1 Aug 1966–31 Aug 1971.

Emblem. Per fess gules and azure a fess rampu bambu rayonee to chief in flank or, in chief on and over a bar argent two swords in saltire, argent hilted or surmounted by a crown of the last lined azure, in base a winged orb argent centered by a hurt emitting to chief and base three rays or all within a diminished bordure of the like. (Approved on 30 Aug 1966.)

461st BOMBARDMENT WING, HEAVY

Lineage. Established as 461st Bombardment Wing, Light, on 11 Dec 1953. Activated on 23 Dec 1953. Redesignated 461st Bombardment Wing, Tactical, on 1 Oct 1955. Inactivated on 1 Apr 1958. Redesignated 461st Bombardment Wing, Heavy, and activated, on 15 Nov 1962. Organized on 1 Feb 1963. Discontinued, and inactivated, on 25 Mar 1968.

Assignments. Ninth Air Force, 23 Dec 1953–1 Apr 1958 (attached to Nineteenth Air Force, 15 Apr 1956–1 Apr 1958). Strategic Air Command, 15 Nov 1962; 22d Strategic Aerospace Division, 1 Feb 1963; 819th Strategic Aerospace Division, 1 Jul 1964; Second Air Force, 1 Jul 1965; 19th Air Division, 2 Jul 1966–25 Mar 1968.

Components. *Group.* 461st: 23 Dec 1953–8 Jan 1958. *Squadrons.* 764th: 1 Feb 1963–25 Mar 1968. 909th Air Refueling: 1 Apr 1963–25 Jun 1966.

Stations. Hill AFB, Utah, 23 Dec 1953; Blytheville AFB, Ark, 8 Apr 1956–1 Apr 1958. Amarillo AFB, Texas, 1 Feb 1963–25 Mar 1968.

Commanders. Lt Col Gus Weiser, 23 Dec 1953; Lt Col Thomas R. Ford, 29 Jan 1954–1 Apr 1958. None (not manned), 15 Nov 1962–31 Jan 1963; Col William R. Calhoun, Jr., 1 Feb 1963; Col John B. Paine, 11 Jun 1965; Col Charles D. Lewis, 2 Jul 1965; Col John B. Paine, 21 Jul 1967; Col William H. Hill, 19 Jan–25 Mar 1968.

Aircraft. B–26, 1953–1956; C–47, 1954–1956; B–57, 1955–1958. B–52, 1963–1968; KC–135, 1963–1966.

Operations. Organized to increase air support of ground forces and air interdiction during the Korean war. Although the Air Force envisioned equipping the 461st with B–57s, these were unavailable at the time of activation. The 461st therefore received the B–26. The wing trained assigned units and personnel for light bombardment and tactical bombardment proficiency. Participated in actual and simulated exercises involving the deployment of aircraft and crews. Wing also operated Blytheville AFB, Ark, from 8 Apr 1956 to inactivation in 1958. Activated at Amarillo AFB, Texas, in 1963, the 461st absorbed the personnel and equipment of the inactivating 4128th Strategic Wing. Trained with B–52s to maintain heavy bombardment proficiency, and participated in numerous operational readiness inspections and actual and simulated exercises as directed by the Strategic Air Command. Deployed B–52 aircraft and crews to Anderson AFB, Guam, 18 Jan–4 Jul 1967, for combat operations in Southeast Asia. Maintained combat proficiency until 21 Jan 1968 when last B–52 transferred. Inactivated on 25 Mar.

Service Streamers. None.

Campaign Streamers. None.

Decorations. Air Force Outstanding Unit Award: 1 Jul 1966–30 Jun 1967.

Emblem. A shield per bend azure and light blue, superimposed over the bend a thunderbolt, bendwise, or, piercing through a cloud formation proper, over an increscent moon to the sinister chief, and a sun to the dexter base of the third; on a chief argent, over a bar to base of chief, embattled gules, an olive branch and seven arrows in saltire, between two spheres all proper. (Approved on 4 Aug 1955.)

462d STRATEGIC AEROSPACE WING

Lineage. Established as 462d Strategic Aerospace Wing, and activated, on 15 Nov 1962. Organized on 1 Feb 1963. Discontinued, and inactivated, on 25 Jun 1966.

Assignments. Strategic Air Command, 15 Nov 1962; 18th Strategic Aerospace Division, 1 Feb 1963–25 Jun 1966.

Components. *Squadrons*. 43d Air Refueling: 1 Feb 1963–2 Apr 1966. 568th Strategic Missile: 1 Feb 1963–25 Mar 1965 (not operational, 9 Feb–25 Mar 1965). 768th Bombardment: 1 Feb 1963–2 Apr 1966.

Stations. Larson AFB, Wash, 1 Feb 1963–25 Jun 1966.

Commanders. None (not manned), 15 Nov 1962–31 Jan 1963; Col David A. Tate, 1 Feb 1963; Col Alex W. Talmant, 19 Jul 1965; Col Clyde W. Owen, c. 15 Mar–25 Jun 1966.

Aircraft and Missiles. Titan I, 1963–1965; B–52, 1963–1966; KC–135, 1963–1966.

Operations. Conducted strategic bombardment, air refueling, and missile training operations, 1963–1965, and bombardment training and air refueling thereafter until Apr 1966.

Service Streamers. None.

Campaign Streamers. None.

Decorations. None.

Emblem. Light blue, in dexter chief a lightning bolt gules and an olive branch argent saltirewise, overall an air foil bendwise of the third and or, in dexter base a sphere azure with land masses of the third, in sinister chief seven mullets of the fifth highlighted of the third and all within a diminished bordure of the last. (Approved on 7 Feb 1963.)

463d TACTICAL AIRLIFT WING

Lineage. Established as 463d Troop Carrier Wing, Medium, on 1 Dec 1952. Activated on 16 Jan 1953. Redesignated: 463d Troop Carrier Wing, Assault, on 1 Oct 1962; 463d Troop Carrier Wing, Medium, on 15 May 1965; 463d

Troop Carrier Wing on 8 Dec 1965; 463d Tactical Airlift Wing on 1 Aug 1967. Inactivated on 31 Dec 1971. Activated on 1 Jun 1972.

Assignments. Eighteenth Air Force, 16 Jan 1953; Ninth Air Force, 1 Sep 1957; 838th Air Division, 25 Sep 1957; Ninth Air Force, 11 Dec 1957; 839th Air Division, 15 Jan 1959; Ninth Air Force, 1 Jul 1963; 838th Air Division, 1 Oct 1963; 840th Air Division, 9 Nov 1964; 315th Air Division (Combat Cargo), 23 Nov 1965; 6th Air Division, 1 Nov 1968; Thirteenth Air Force, 15 Dec 1969–31 Dec 1971. 834th Air Division, 1 Jun 1972; Twenty-Second Air Force, 31 Dec 1974–.

Components. *Wing*. 456th: attached 10 May–9 Jul 1956 (not operational). *Groups*. 309th: attached 8 Jul 1955–c. 21 May 1956. 419th: attached 9 Jul 1956–25 Sep 1957. 463d: 16 Jan 1953–25 Sep 1957. *Squadrons*. 16th: attached 14 Nov 1954–8 Jul 1955. 18th Tactical Airlift Training: 1 Jun–31 Aug 1972 (not operational, 25–31 Aug 1972). 20th Operations: 17 Feb 1970–31 Dec 1971. 29th: attached 30 Jan–24 Mar 1966, assigned 25 Mar 1966–31 Oct 1970 (not operational, 1 Jul–31 Oct 1970). 47th: 6 Jul–1 Aug 1973. 360th Tactical Electronic Warfare: 24 Nov 1972–1 Jul 1973 (not operational). 772d: 25 Sep 1957–23 Nov 1965; 7 Feb 1966–15 Jun 1971 (not operational, 1–15 Jun 1971); 1 Jun 1972– (detached 9 Jul–15 Sep 1972, 10 Nov 1972–10 Jan 1973, 6 May–4 Jun 1973, 5 Feb–8 Apr 1974, 5 Jan–15 Mar 1975, 28 May–9 Aug 1975, 3 Nov 1975–16 Jan 1976, 3 Aug–15 Oct 1976). 773d: 25 Sep 1957–31 Oct 1971 (detached 15 Nov 1954–19 May 1955; 3 Jan–6 Mar 1961; not operational, 15–31 Oct 1971); 1 Jun 1972– (detached 1 Jun–8 Jul 1972, 16 Sep–16 Nov 1972, 23 Feb–12 May 1973, 3 Jul–10 Sep 1973, 5 May–15 Jul 1974, 3 May–16 Jul 1975, 9 Aug–12 Oct 1975, 3 Feb–9 Apr 1976, 7 Nov 1976–15 Jan 1977, 5 Aug–5 Oct 1977). 774th: 25 Sep 1957–31 Dec 1971 (detached 21 Mar–19 Jun 1961; not operational, 26 Dec 1962–1 Apr 1963); 1 Aug 1973– (detached 3 Oct–16 Dec 1973, 3 Sep–Dec 1974, 7 Apr–28 May 1975, 4 Aug–15 Oct 1975, 3 May–7 Jul 1976, 3 Jan–5 Aug 1977). Troop Carrier Squadron Provisional, 4480th: attached 3 Jan–1 Apr 1963. 6485th Operations: 1 Sep–1 Dec 1968.

Stations. Memphis Muni Aprt, Tenn, 16 Jan 1953; Ardmore AFB, Okla, 1 Sep 1953; Sewart AFB, Tenn, 15 Jan 1959; Langley AFB, Va, 1 Jul 1963–22 Nov 1965; Mactan Isle Afld, Philippines, 23 Nov 1965; Clark AB, Philippines, 15 Jul 1968–31 Dec 1971. Dyess AFB, Texas, 1 Jun 1972–.

Commanders. Col George L. Holcomb, 16 Jan 1953; Brig Gen Cecil H. Childre, 20 Aug 1954; Col James L. Daniel, Jr., 4 Jun 1957; Col Luther O'Hern, 25 Sep 1957; Col James L. Daniel, Jr., 11 Dec 1957; Col George G. Norman, 25 Jun 1958; Col George G. Byrnes, Jr., 18 Jun 1960; Col Earl W. Worley, 22 Sep 1960; Col George G. Byrnes, Jr., 9 Jul 1962; Col Ralph A. Reeve, 22 Aug 1962; Col Arthur Aenchbacher, 17 Oct 1964; Col Lopez J. Mantoux, 7 Nov 1966; Col Thomas A. Twomey, 7 Dec 1967; Col Marion F. Caruthers, 12 Apr 1968; Col Charles S. Wolfe, 9 May 1969; Col John R. Geyer, 2 Jul 1970; Col Stewart Young, 2 Sep–31 Dec 1971. Col Richard T. Drury, 1 Jun 1972; Col Robert F. Coverdale, 20 Jun 1972; Col Bruce D. Ferrier,

2 Nov 1973; Col Russell E. Mohney, 11 Feb 1975; Col Sam B. Barrett, 13 Jan 1976; Col Ivan D. Brown, 7 Mar 1977–.

Aircraft. C–46, 1953; C–119, 1953–1957; YC–122, 1954–1955; C–122, 1955; C–123, 1955–1956, 1956–1957; C–130, 1956–1971; C–118, 1968, 1970–1971; C–124, 1970–1971. C–7, 1972; C–130, 1972–.

Operations. Airlifted, airdropped, and landed troops and cargo to support tactical operations, special missions, and U.S. Army and joint airborne exercises, worldwide, 1953–1965. Supported forces deployed during crises in Lebanon (Jul 1958), Taiwan (Aug 1958), Berlin (Sep 1961), Cuba (Oct–Nov 1962), the Gulf of Tonkin (Aug–Dec 1964), Southeast Asia (Feb and Apr–Nov 1965), and the Dominican Republic (Apr–Sep 1965). Moved to the Far East in Nov 1965 and assumed responsibility for operating a C–130 combat airlift support unit (later, Det 5, 315th Air Division) at Tan Son Nhut AB, South Vietnam, and Det 2 (later, Det 9), 315th Air Division, at Clark AB, Philippines, through Nov 1968. Began furnishing aircraft and crews on 3 Dec 1965 to fly missions in Southeast Asia under operational control of the 315th Air Division (to Oct 1966) and 834th Air Division (Oct 1966–Oct 1971). Also flew aeromedical evacuation missions, Feb 1970–Dec 1971. Ceased all aircraft operations in Southeast Asia on 25 Oct 1971 and began phasing down for inactivation. Replaced 516th Tactical Airlift Wing at Dyess AFB, Texas, in Jun 1972, charged with worldwide tactical airlift, humanitarian missions, exercise participation, and special missions as required. Tactical components deployed frequently to support requirements in Europe, the Pacific, and the Canal Zone.

Service Streamers. None.

Campaign Streamers. None.

Decorations. Air Force Outstanding Unit Awards with Combat "V" Device: 1 Jan 1967–31 May 1968; 1 Jun 1968–30 Jun 1969; 1 Jul 1970–31 May 1971. Air Force Outstanding Unit Awards: 15 Dec 1960–1 Apr 1961; 1 Jul 1964–15 Jun 1966. Republic of Vietnam Gallantry Cross with Palm: 1 Jan 1967–31 Dec 1971.

Emblem. A shield azure (light sky blue), on a representation of a cloud argent a silhouette of mythical Pegasus drawing a chariot driven by Mars, the mythical Roman god of war, all sable. (Approved on 30 Aug 1954.)

464th TACTICAL AIRLIFT WING

Lineage. Established as 464th Troop Carrier Wing, Medium, on 15 Dec 1952. Activated on 1 Feb 1953. Redesignated 464th Troop Carrier Wing, Assault, on 1 Dec 1958; 464th Troop Carrier Wing, Medium, on 8 Jan 1964; 464th Troop Carrier Wing on 1 Mar

1966; 464th Tactical Airlift Wing on 1 May 1967. Inactivated on 31 Aug 1971.

Assignments. Eighteenth Air Force, 1 Feb 1953; Ninth Air Force, 1 Sep 1957; 838th Air Division, 1 Jul 1963; 839th Air Division, 9 Nov 1964–31 Aug 1971.

Components. *Group.* 464th: 1 Feb 1953–11 Nov 1957. *Squadrons.* 310th: attached 8 Feb 1955–7 Sep 1956. 346th: attached 1 Jul 1958–1 Apr 1963. 347th: attached 8 Oct 1955–1 Jul 1963. 775th: 1 Apr–1 Jul 1964 (detached 15 Apr–1 Jul 1964). 776th: 11 Nov 1957–1 Jul 1963; 8 Jul 1963–26 Dec 1965. 777th: 11 Nov 1957–1 Jul 1963 (detached 6 Jun–unkn 1962 and 5 Apr–1 Jul 1963); 8 Jul 1963–31 Aug 1971 (not operational, 8 Jul–30 Sep 1963; detached 10 Apr–1 Aug 1968, 10 May–10 Aug 1969, 5 Jan–19 Mar 1970, 30 Sep–8 Nov 1970, and 3 Mar–17 May 1971). 778th: 11 Nov 1957–31 Aug 1971 (detached 1–23 Aug 1968, 13 Jan–15 Apr 1969, 13 Oct–31 Dec 1969, and 5 Jul–16 Sep 1970). 779th: 1 Jul 1963–31 Aug 1971 (detached 4 Feb–c. 10 Apr 1968, 25 Sep–22 Nov 1968, 3 Aug–22 Oct 1969, 5 Apr–19 Jun 1970, and 15 Dec 1970–17 Feb 1971). 4419th Flying Training: attached 1 May–1 Aug 1953 (not operational).

Stations. Lawson AFB, Ga, 1 Feb 1953; Pope AFB, NC, 21 Sep 1954–31 Aug 1971.

Commanders. Col Troy W. Crawford, 1 Feb 1953; Col Charles D. Birdsall, 20 Apr 1953; Col Troy W. Crawford, 18 May 1953; Brig Gen Theodore G. Kershaw, 15 Aug 1955; Col James I. Cox, 11 Jun 1959; Brig Gen Clyde Box, 7 Jul 1959; Col James I. Cox, 31 May 1960; Brig Gen Clyde Box, 27 Jun 1960; Col Arthur P. Hurr, 12 Jun 1961; Brig Gen Clyde Box, 14 Aug 1961; Col Arthur P. Hurr, 9 Oct 1961; Col William T. Daly, 17 Oct 1961; Col William L. Welch, 23 Jul 1963; Col James G. Silliman, 31 May 1966; Col William H. Mason, 31 May 1967; Col Clarence B. Slaughter, Jr., 1 Sep 1967; Col Norman T. Lawrence, 25 Apr 1969; Col Billie J. Norwood, 15 Jan–31 Aug 1971.

Aircraft. C–46, 1953–1954; C–119, 1953–1958; H–19, 1955–1956; C–123, 1955–1964; C–130, 1963–1971.

Operations. Replaced the 434th Troop Carrier Wing in 1953. Provided tactical airlift of troops and cargo, participated in joint airborne training with Army forces, and took part in tactical exercises in the United States and overseas, 1953–1971. Provided aeromedical airlift and flew humanitarian missions as required. From late 1954 until inactivated, usually had two or more tactical squadrons deployed overseas at any one time, supporting airlift operations in Central America, Europe, the Middle East, the Far East, and Southeast Asia. Conducted C–123 combat crew training, Jun 1962–Apr 1964, and C–130 replacement training, Nov 1969–Aug 1971. Received the Mackay Trophy for humanitarian operations in the Congo in 1964. Participated in contingency airlift operations in the Dominican Republic, Apr 1965–Sep 1966. Replaced by the 317th Tactical Airlift Wing in Aug 1971.

Service Streamers. None.

Campaign Streamers. None.

Decorations. Air Force Outstanding Unit Awards: 28 Nov 1961–1 May 1963; 20–28 Nov 1964; 1 Jul 1967–30 Jun 1968.

Emblem. Azure, surmounting a cloud argent, an American eagle descendant, wings endorsed proper, between his beak four lightning streaks, two and two gules, speed lines of the first all inclosed by two bendlets sinister vert, edged or. *Motto:* CERTISSIMUS IN INCERTIS—Most certain in uncertainties. (Approved on 15 Apr 1954.)

465th BOMBARDMENT WING, HEAVY

Lineage. Established as 465th Troop Carrier Wing, Medium, on 21 Aug 1953. Activated on 25 Aug 1953. Inactivated on 8 Jul 1957. Redesignated 465th Bombardment Wing, Heavy, and activated, on 15 Nov 1962. Organized on 1 Feb 1963. Discontinued, and inactivated, on 25 Jul 1968.

Assignments. Eighteenth Air Force, 25 Aug 1953; Twelfth Air Force, 1 Apr 1954 (attached to 322d Air Division [Combat Cargo], 1 Apr 1954–31 Jul 1955); 322d Air Division (Combat Cargo), 1 Aug 1955–8 Jul 1957. Strategic Air Command, 15 Nov 1962; 822d Air Division, 1 Feb 1963 (attached to 57th Air Division, 10 Aug–1 Sep 1966); 57th Air Division, 2 Sep 1966–25 Jul 1968.

Components. *Groups*. 313th: attached 25 Aug–30 Sep 1953. 465th: 25 Aug–26 Dec 1953 (detached 25 Aug–30 Nov 1953); 1 Apr 1954–12 Mar 1957 (not operational, 1 Dec 1956–12 Mar 1957). *Squadrons*. 39th: attached 1 Dec 1956–11 Mar 1957, assigned 12 Mar–8 Jul 1957. 40th: attached 10 Apr–7 Jul 1957. 41st: attached 15 Mar–7 Jul 1957. 780th: attached 1 Dec 1956–11 Mar 1957, assigned 12 Mar–8 Jul 1957. 781st: attached 1 Dec 1956–11 Mar 1957, assigned 12 Mar–8 Jul 1957; assigned 1 Feb 1963–25 Jul 1968. 782d: attached 1 Dec 1956–11 Mar 1957, assigned 12 Mar–8 Jul 1957. 912th Air Refueling: 1 Feb 1963–25 Jul 1968.

Stations. Mitchel AFB, NY, 25 Aug 1953–23 Mar 1954; Toul-Rosieres AB, France, 2 Apr 1954; Evreux (later, Evreux-Fauville) AB, France, 23 May 1955–8 Jul 1957. Robins AFB, Ga, 1 Feb 1963–25 Jul 1968.

Commanders. Brig Gen Franklin Rose, 25 Aug 1953; Col Earl W. Worley, 12 May 1954; Col James A. Evans, Jr., 31 Jul 1956; Col Robert D. Forman, 15 Aug 1956–8 Jul 1957. None (not manned), 15 Nov 1962–31 Jan 1963; Col James M. Keck, 1 Feb 1963; Col Gordon F. Goyt, 20 Jan 1965; Col Madison M. McBrayer, 1 Jun 1966; Col Ralph D. Gahl, 14 Jan 1967; Col Wesley L. Pendergraft, 31 Jan–25 Jul 1968.

Aircraft. C–119, 1953, 1954–1957. B–52, 1963–1968; KC–135, 1963–1968.

Operations. Replaced 313th Troop Carrier Wing, Medium, in Aug 1953 at Mitchel AFB, NY. The 465th Troop Carrier Group operated under control of other wings from Aug through 30 Nov 1953, when it commenced an overseas movement. Meanwhile, the 465th Wing controlled the 313th Troop Carrier Group from 25 Aug to 30 Sep 1953 in normal troop carrier operations and training. From 1 Oct 1953 until the wing itself was relocated in Europe in early Apr 1954, no tactical operations were performed. The wing participated in numerous troop carrier and airlift operations, tests, and exercises in the European area in support of USAFE and NATO, Apr 1954–Jul 1957. In Jul 1957 the wing was replaced by the 317th Troop Carrier Wing, Medium. Activated as a bombardment wing in Feb 1963, the 465th replaced the 4137th Strategic Wing at Robins AFB, Ga. Conducted strategic bombardment training and air refueling operations, Feb 1963–Jul 1968. Replaced by 19th Bombardment Wing, Heavy, in Jul 1968.

Service Streamers. None.

Campaign Streamers. None.

Decorations. None.

Emblem. Light blue, on a bend azure fimbriated gules fifteen mullets one point upward, four, six, and five argent, issuant to chief a wing of the last, and in base a chess knight sable garnished of the fourth. *Motto:* CHECKMATE TO AGGRESSION. (Approved on 24 Mar 1964.)

473d FIGHTER-DAY WING

Lineage. Established as 473d Fighter-Day Wing on 23 Mar 1953.

Assignments. None.

Components. None.

Stations. None.

Commanders. None.

Aircraft. None.

Operations. Never made active.

Service Streamers. None.

Campaign Streamers. None.

Decorations. None.

Emblem. None.

474th TACTICAL FIGHTER WING

Lineage. Established as 474th Fighter-Bomber Wing on 25 Jun 1952. Activated on 10 Jul 1952. Inactivated on 8 Nov 1954. Activated on 8 Oct 1957. Redesignated 474th Tactical Fighter Wing on 1 Jul 1958.

Assignments. Tactical Air Command, 10 Jul 1952–8 Nov 1954 (attached to Fifth Air Force, 10 Jul 1952–1 Apr 1953; 58th Fighter-Bomber Wing, 1 Apr 1953–8 Nov 1954). 832d Air Division, 8 Oct 1957; USAF Tactical Fighter Weapons Center, 20 Jan 1968; 832d Air Division, 20 Mar 1968 (attached to Seventh Air Force, ADVON, c. 27 Sep 1972–c. 23 Mar 1973); Twelfth Air Force, 1 Jul 1975–.

Components. *Group.* 474th: 10 Jul 1952–8 Nov 1954 (detached 1 Apr 1953–8 Nov 1954). *Squadrons.* 428th: 8 Oct 1957–30 Jul 1973 (detached Feb–Jun 1959, 31 May–23 Jun 1960, 2 Oct 1961–15 Feb 1962, 18 Oct–30 Nov 1962, 9 Jan–14 Apr 1963, 12 Feb–8 May 1964, 24 Nov 1964–13 Mar 1965; not operational, 15 Sep 1965–30 Jan 1967, c. 30 Jun 1967–20 Jan 1968; detached c. 23 Mar–30 Jul 1973); 15 Jun 1975–. 429th: 8 Oct 1957–30 Jul 1973 (detached Jun–Nov 1959, 1 Sep–Nov 1961, 11 Jun–22 Oct 1962, 22 Oct–28 Nov 1962, 3 Jul–13 Nov 1963, 7 Apr–c. May 1964, 16 Nov 1964–12 Feb 1965, 13 Jul–16 Dec 1965; not operational, c. 16 Dec 1965–15 May 1967; detached 15 May 1967–15 May 1968, c. 23 Mar–30 Jul 1973); 21 Jun 1975–. 430th: 8 Oct 1957–15 Nov 1966 (detached Nov 1959, 7 Jun–Oct 1960, 5 Sep–28 Nov 1961, 2–18 Apr 1962, 1 Sep–16 Dec 1962, 30 Apr–18 May 1963, 20 Oct 1963–Feb 1964, 25 Aug–Nov 1964, 13 May–unkn 1965; not operational, 15 Sep 1965–15 Nov 1966); 15 Sep 1968–. 442d Tactical Fighter Training: 15 Oct 1969–31 Jul 1977. 478th: 8 Oct 1957–1 Nov 1966 (detached 7 Oct 1960–21 Feb 1961, 5–24 Feb 1962, 20 May–3 Sep 1962, 17 Oct–30 Nov 1962, 19 Apr–5 Jul 1963, 1 Jun–Aug 1964, 11 Feb–15 May 1965; not operational, 15 Sep 1965–1 Nov 1966). 4474th Tactical Training: 1 Dec 1968–15 Jun 1970 (not operational). 4527th Combat Crew Training: 20 Jan 1968–15 Oct 1969.

Stations. Misawa AB, Japan, 10 Jul 1952; Kunsan AB, South Korea, 10 Jul 1952; Taegu AB, South Korea, 1 Apr 1953–8 Nov 1954. Cannon AFB, NM, 8 Oct 1957; Nellis AFB, Nev, 20 Jan 1968–.

Commanders. Col William W. Ingenhutt, 10 Jul 1952; none (not manned), 1 Apr 1953–8 Nov 1954. Col Franklin H. Scott, 8 Oct 1957; Lt Col Jake L. Wilk, Jr., 15 Jul 1958; Col Thomas D. Robertson, 19 Jul 1958; Col William L. Curry, 8 Aug 1958; Col Gust Askounis, 30 Jul 1960; Col William L. Mitchell, Jr., 18 Aug 1960; Col Niven K. Cranfill, 6 Jun 1962; Col Francis E. Binnell, 21 Aug 1964; Col Paul P. Douglas, Jr., 3 Sep 1964; Lt Col Benjamin H. Clayton, 14 Jul 1965; Col Oscar L. Watson, 28 Aug 1965; 1st Lt Robert R. De Cocco, 15 Sep 1965 (additional duty); Col Ivan H. Dethman, 1 Oct 1966; Lt Col Maurice A. Spenny, 9 Aug 1967–unkn (additional duty); Col Chester L. Van Etten, 20 Jan 1968; Col Gelvin S. Nicely, 11 Jun 1968; Col Carmel M. Shook, 20 Jun 1968; Col Frederick C. Blesse, 5 Jun 1969; Col Herbert J. Gavin, 26 Jun 1970; Col Kenneth P. Miles, 22 Jun 1971; Col William R. Nelson, 1 Aug 1972; Col James N. McClelland, 25 Jul 1973; Col Thomas E. Wolters, 28 Feb 1975; Col Maurice E. Seaver, Jr., 24 May 1976; Col Reginald R. Davis, 5 Aug 1977–.

Aircraft. F–84, 1952–1953. F–100, 1957–1965; F–111, 1968–1977; F–4, 1977–.

Operations. Activated in Japan and moved the same day to South Korea with tactical components to begin combat operations. Tactical components were detached on 1 Apr 1953, while the rest of the wing reduced to "paper" status, a condition which prevailed until the wing inactivated in 1954. Activated in the United States in Oct 1957 and until mid-Sep 1964 maintained proficiency in tactical fighter operations, deploying components, aircraft, and crews on a global basis in support of NATO, PACAF, AAC, and other organizations. Deployed three squadrons to southeastern United States during the Cuban missile crisis of 1962. Entire wing, except for a deployed squadron in Southeast Asia, reverted to "paper" status on 15 Sep 1965, the single detached squadron being reduced to "paper" status upon its return to the United States. Wing gained sparse manning on 1 Oct 1966 in anticipation of conversion to F–111 aircraft, and c. 30 Jun 1967 again reverted to "paper" status. On 20 Jan 1968 the 474th TFW, 474th FMS, and the 428th TFS moved without personnel or equipment to Nellis AFB, Nev, and the 474th AEMS and 474th MMS inactivated. The units that moved to Nellis absorbed the resources of an inactivating wing. Gaining the 474th CSG, 474th Tactical Hospital, and 474th Supply Squadron, the 474th Wing became host unit for Nellis. There it acquired the F–111 equipped 4527th CCTS. On 20 Jan 1968 the 428th TFS organized Detachment 1, which also received F–111 aircraft. This detachment deployed c. 18 Mar to 22 Nov 1968 to Southeast Asia. On 15 May 1968 the 429th TFS discontinued attachment to another wing and rejoined the 474th Wing without personnel or equipment. A former component, the 430th TFS, became part of the wing on 15 Sep 1968. Tactical components of the wing received their initial F–111s between Nov 1968 and Mar 1969 and began training for proficiency in the new weapon system. The 4527th CCTS trained F–111 aircrews for the wing and for other USAF units until replaced in Oct 1969 by the 442d TFTS, which assumed the mission. The 4474th TTS, assigned 1 Dec to 15 Jun 1970, was sparsely manned and never equipped with F–111s. Upon inactivation of the 474th CSG, 474th Tactical Hospital, and 474th Supply Squadron in Feb 1970, the 474th Wing became a tenant at Nellis AFB. Wing assumed an operationally ready status between 31 Jan and 8 Sep 1971, and from Sep 1971 initiated tactical exercises for the maintenance of tactical operational proficiency. Over 1,600 tactical and support personnel of the wing deployed on 27 Sep 1972 to Takhli RTAFB, Thailand, to participate in combat operations in Southeast Asia. A rear echelon of wing headquarters remained at Nellis to control units not deployed. The 430th TFS returned to Nellis on 23 Mar 1973, assuming a replacement training unit mission; on 30 Jul 1973, the 428th and 429th Squadrons became subordinate units of the 347th TFW in Southeast Asia. In 1975 both of these overseas squadrons were again assigned to the 474th Wing. On 6 Aug the last F–111 aircraft and crews were transferred to Mountain Home AFB, Idaho, and the 474th Wing absorbed the F–4D aircraft, crews, and resources of the inactivating Tactical Fighter Wing Provisional, 4474th. Trained combat-ready force of aircrews and maintained a rapid-reaction capability to execute fighter attacks against enemy forces and facilities in time of crisis, 1975–.

Service Streamers. None.

Campaign Streamers. Korea Summer–Fall, 1952; Third Korean Winter; Korea Summer–Fall, 1953; Vietnam Ceasefire.

Decorations. Air Force Outstanding Unit Award with Combat "V" Device: 28 Sep 1972–22 Feb 1973. Air Force Outstanding Unit Award: 9 Mar 1961–9 Mar 1962. Republic of Korea Presidential Unit Citation: 10 Jul 1952–30 Mar 1953. Republic of Vietnam Gallantry Cross with Palm: 28 Sep 1972–22 Feb 1973.

Emblem. A shield per bend azure and or, in bend a lightning bolt throughout bendwise gules, fimbriated or, between a sphere argent, grid lines sable, and a stylized jet tail pipe vert emitting eight fire blasts gules, the pipe charged with an annulet of the first, fimbriated or, a semee of stars of the fourth on the azure field. (Approved for 474th Group on 22 Jun 1955 and for 474th Wing on 14 Nov 1958.)

475th AIR BASE WING

Lineage. Established as 475th Fighter Wing on 10 Aug 1948. Activated on 18 Aug 1948. Inactivated on 1 Apr 1949. Redesignated 475th Tactical Fighter Wing, and activated, on 21 Dec 1967. Organized on 15 Jan 1968. Inactivated on 15 Mar 1971. Redesignated 475th Air Base Wing on 20 Oct 1971. Activated on 1 Nov 1971.

Assignments. 315th Air Division, 18 Aug 1948–1 Apr 1949. Pacific Air Forces, 21 Dec 1967; Fifth Air Force, 15 Jan 1968–15 Mar 1971. Fifth Air Force, 1 Nov 1971–.

Components. *Group.* 475th: 18 Aug 1948–1 Apr 1949. *Squadrons.* 16th Tactical Reconnaissance: 16 Mar 1970–15 Feb 1971, attached 16–22 Feb 1971. 45th Tactical Reconnaissance: 15 Jan 1968–15 Mar 1971 (not operational). 67th: 15 Jan 1968–15 Mar 1971. 356th: 15 Jan 1968–15 Mar 1971. 391st: 22 Jul 1968–28 Feb 1971. 421st: attached 23 Apr–25 Jun 1969. 556th Reconnaissance: 1 Nov 1971–30 Jun 1972. 612th: 15 Jan 1968–15 Mar 1971 (not operational).

Stations. Itazuke Afld, Japan, 18 Aug 1948; Ashiya Afld, Japan, 25 Mar–1 Apr 1949. Misawa AB, Japan, 15 Jan 1968–15 Mar 1971. Yokota AB, Japan, 1 Nov 1971–.

Commanders. Col John M. Price, 18 Aug 1948; unkn, 25 Mar–1 Apr 1949. None (not manned), 21 Dec 1967–14 Jan 1968; Col Oliver B. Bucher, Jr., 15 Jan 1968; Col Vernon J. Henderson, 15 Jun 1968; Col William R. Eichelberger, 27 Jul 1970; Col Abner M. Aust, Jr., 8–15 Mar 1971. Col Harry H. Elmendorf, 1 Nov 1971; Col Nicholas Arabinko, 5 Nov 1971; Col John W. Grow, Jr., 25 Jan 1972; Col Robert H. Lee, 14 Jun 1972; Col John W. Grow, Jr., 28 Jun 1972; Col Robert H. Lee, 8 Sep 1972; Col John W. Grow, Jr., 30 Sep 1972; Col John C. Reed, 1 Dec 1972; Col Mathias J. Martin, 24 Oct 1975; Col Sharman R. Stevenson, 11 Nov 1975–.

Aircraft. F–51, 1948–1949. F–100, 1968; F–4, 1968–1971; RF–4, 1970–1971. C–130, 1971–1972; C–123, 1971–1976.

Operations. Provided air defense in Japan, 1948–1949. Replaced the 39th Air Division at Misawa AB, Japan, in Jan 1968 and trained for offensive and reconnaissance operations, 1968–1971. Two assigned squadrons (45th Tactical Reconnaissance and 612th Tactical Fighter) were "paper" units during their entire assignment, since each unit had all of its resources in a detachment in Southeast Asia. The wing maintained forward operating locations at Kunsan, South Korea (Jan 1968–Mar 1971) and Taegu, South Korea (Jul 1968–Apr 1970), and maintained squadrons or segments thereof at each location, with periodic rotation back to Misawa. A major earthquake on 16 May 1968 caused over $1 million damage to Misawa facilities. Phased down at Misawa in early 1971 and inactivated on 15 Mar, all resources moving to Kunsan AB, South Korea, for the 3d Tactical Fighter Wing. Replaced the 6100th Air Base Wing at Yokota AB, Japan, on 1 Nov 1971 and inherited a huge support complex, with some 47 installations in all parts of Japan, including Yokota and Tachikawa Air Bases, Fuchu and Chitose Air Stations, and numerous family housing complexes in the Tokyo area. Briefly controlled a C–130 airborne communications reconnaissance squadron (Nov 1971–Jun 1972) and a Royal Thailand Air Force C–123 detachment (Nov 1971–Jul 1976). The Thai detachment provided airlift support to the United Nations Command (Rear). In support of Fifth Air Force, the wing also controlled: C–54 (1971–1972), VC–118 (1971–1975), T–29 (1971–c. 1972), T–33 (1971–1972), T–39 (1971–) and UH–1P (1971–). The wing gradually closed down many of its installations, sites, and facilities, inactivating operating units thereof, and was preparing to close Tachikawa AB, Japan, in Sep 1977.

Service Streamers. None.

Campaign Streamers. None.

Decorations. Air Force Outstanding Unit Award: 1 Apr 1973–31 Mar 1975.

Emblem. Per fess dancette of four azure and light blue, in chief a double end wrench fesswise or, surmounted overall by a pair of dividers expanded argent between a mullet of the like and in base two wings conjoined in lure elevated of the third between a sphere of the first with longitude and latitude lines of the second and all within a diminished bordure or. (Approved on 29 Jul 1974.)

478th FIGHTER WING (AIR DEFENSE)

Lineage. Established as 478th Fighter-Day Wing on 23 Mar 1953. Redesignated 478th Fighter Wing (Air Defense), and activated, on 28 Dec 1960. Organized on 1 Feb 1961. Discontinued, and inactivated, on 1 Jul 1963.

Assignments. Air Defense Command, 28 Dec 1960; Grand Forks Air Defense Sector, 1 Feb 1961–1 Jul 1963.

Components. *Squadron.* 18th Fighter-Interceptor: 1 Feb 1961–1 Jul 1963.

Stations. Grand Forks AFB, ND, 1 Feb 1961–1 Jul 1963.

Commanders. None (not manned), 28 Dec 1960–31 Jan 1961; Col Leon G. Lewis, 1 Feb 1961; Col Robert J. Ahern, (by Jul) 1961–unkn; Col Raymond S. Brown, (by Jul) 1962–unkn; Col George O. Commenator, (by Sep) 1962–c. Jul 1963.

Aircraft. F–101, 1961–1963.

Operations. Replaced 478th Fighter Group (Air Defense) in Feb 1961. Provided air defense for a segment of north-central United States.

Service Streamers. None.

Campaign Streamers. None.

Decorations. None.
Emblem. None.

479th TACTICAL TRAINING WING

Lineage. Established as 479th Fighter-Bomber Wing on 15 Oct 1952. Activated on 1 Dec 1952. Redesignated: 479th Fighter-Day Wing on 15 Feb 1954; 479th Tactical Fighter Wing on 1 Jul 1958. Inactivated on 1 Oct 1971. Redesignated 479th Tactical Training Wing on 22 Oct 1976. Activated on 1 Jan 1977.

Assignments. Ninth Air Force, 1 Dec 1952 (attached to Nineteenth Air Force, 15 Mar–19 Apr 1956); Eighteenth Air Force, 1 Oct 1957; 831st Air Division, 8 Oct 1957; Twelfth Air Force, 20 Apr–1 Oct 1971. Twelfth Air Force, 1 Jan 1977; Tactical Training, Holloman, 1 Aug 1977–.

Components. *Groups*. 413th: attached 11 Nov 1954–8 Oct 1957. 479th: 1 Dec 1952–8 Oct 1957 (not operational, 1 Dec 1952–11 Jan 1953). *Squadrons*. 1st Liaison: attached 8 Apr 1953–c. 18 Jan 1954. Combat Crew Training Squadron Provisional, 1st: attached 3 Jan–30 Jun 1962. 68th: attached 6 Dec 1965–14 May 1968, assigned 15 May–1 Oct 1968. 431st: attached 6 Dec 1965–14 Jun 1968, assigned 15 Jun 1968–30 Oct 1970 (not operational, 1 Jan–1 Mar 1969 and 1 Jun–30 Oct 1970). 434th: attached 1 Dec 1952–11 Jan 1953; assigned 8 Oct 1957–1 Oct 1971 (detached 15 Mar–c. 15 Aug 1960, 11 Aug–17 Dec 1961; not operational, 3 Jan 1962–c. 1 Nov 1966); assigned 1 Jan 1977–. 435th: 8 Oct 1957–c. 20 Jul 1966 (detached 7 Dec 1960–c. 15 Apr 1961, 19 Sep 1961–22 Jan 1962, 3 Aug–19 Dec 1962, 30 Mar–23 Jun 1964, 12 Oct–20 Dec 1965; 1 Jan 1977–. 436th: attached 3 Dec 1952–11 Jan 1953, assigned 8 Oct 1957–15 Jul 1968 (detached c. 11 Aug–c. 11 Dec 1960, c. 18 Jan–c. 12 Apr 1962, 15 Dec 1962–3 Apr 1963, 15–30 Nov 1963, 25 Jan–17 Feb 1965, 1 Jul–14 Oct 1965; not operational, 1 Jul 1967–15 Jul 1968); assigned 30 Oct 1970–8 Mar 1971 (not operational); assigned 1 Jan 1977– (not operational, 1 Jan–24 Apr 1977). 476th: 8 Oct 1957–25 Sep 1968 (detached 12 Nov 1959–28 Mar 1960, 8 Apr–17 Aug 1961, 8 Apr–10 Aug 1962, 6 Jan–1 Apr 1964, 7 Apr–11 Jul 1968; not operational, 25 May–28 Jul 1966). 497th: attached 6–8 Dec 1965 (not operational). 4452d Combat Crew Training: 16 Jan 1967–1 Oct 1971 (not operational, 16 Jan 1967–24 Sep 1968). 4535th Combat Crew Training: 25 Sep 1968–1 Oct 1971.

Stations. George AFB, Calif, 1 Dec 1952–1 Oct 1971. Holloman AFB, NM, 1 Jan 1977–.

Commanders. Col Virgil L. Zoller, 1 Dec 1952; Col William C. Clark, 9 Feb 1953; Col Virgil L. Zoller, c. 9 Mar 1953; Col Robert L. Delashaw, 20 Jun 1953; Col Irwin H. Dregne, 27 Jun 1955; Col George Laven, Jr., 1 Jul 1957;

Col William B. Harris, 8 Oct 1957; Lt Col James R. Wilson, 18 Jun 1958; Col Darrell S. Cramer, 3 Sep 1958; Col George Laven, Jr., 18 Dec 1958; Col Paul E. Adams, 6 Jul 1959; Col George I. Ruddell, 1 Aug 1959; Col Paul E. Adams, 19 Jun 1961; Col William D. Dunham, 23 Aug 1961; Col Billy Cornett, 6 Jul 1962; Col Darrell S. Cramer, (by 6) Jan 1964; Col Donald H. Ross, 28 Feb 1966; Col Robert V. Spencer, 8 Feb 1967; Col Harry B. Trimble, 5 Sep 1967; Col John S. Clarke, Jr., 5 Apr 1969; Col Earl J. Archer, Jr., 24 Jun 1970; Col Fred A. Treyz, 9 Jul–1 Oct 1971. Col William P. Crum, 1 Jan 1977–.

Aircraft. F–51, 1952–1953; F–86, 1953–1956; F–100, 1954–1959; F–104, 1958–1967; F–4, 1965–1971. T/AT–38, 1977–.

Operations. Replaced the 131st Fighter-Bomber Wing at George AFB, Calif, in Dec 1952. Operated George AFB, 1 Dec 1952–7 Oct 1957 and 1 Jul 1967–1 Oct 1971. Maintained tactical proficiency with F–51s, later with F–86s. Tactical components participated in numerous exercises, augmented air defenses of the West Coast, and deployed overseas to support other commands. Converted to F–100s beginning Sep 1954 and to F–104s beginning Oct 1958. Trained F–104 pilots of foreign states, Jan 1962–Aug 1963. Had one squadron deployed at Key West NAS, Fla, during the Cuban missile crisis of 1962. During 1965, deployed three squadrons to Taiwan and South Vietnam to provide air defenses of northern area of the Republic of Vietnam. Gained two F–4 squadrons in Dec 1965, and began F–4 replacement training in Feb 1966. Transferred one F–104 squadron to Southeast Asia in mid-1966 and conducted F–104 replacement training until early 1967. Transferred all F–104s in Jul 1967. Began training foreign personnel in F–4 operations and maintenance in Mar 1969, including pilots from Israel, Iran, Japan, and West Germany. Inactivated, and replaced by the 35th TFW, in Oct 1971. Activated, and replaced the Tactical Training Wing Provisional, 4479th, in Jan 1977. Assumed a mission of T/AT–38 pilot training.

Service Streamers. None.

Campaign Streamers. None.

Decorations. Air Force Outstanding Unit Award: 19 Nov 1965–31 Mar 1967.

Emblem. Or, a broad sword gules in bend piercing a cloud proper, between a point sinister pointed gules, charged with six stars argent, three, two, and one, and a point in base vert, all within a diminished bordure azure. Motto: PROTECTORS LIBERATIS—Defenders of liberty. (Approved on 10 Sep 1954.)

482d FIGHTER-BOMBER WING

Lineage. Established as 482d Troop Carrier Wing, Medium, on 26 May 1952. Activated in the Reserve on 14 Jun 1952. Inactivated on 1 Dec 1952. Redesignated 482d Fighter-Bomber Wing on 12 Apr 1955. Activated in the Reserve on 18 May 1955. Inactivated on 16 Nov 1957.

Assignments. Fourteenth Air Force, 14 Jun–1 Dec 1952. Fourteenth Air Force, 18 May 1955–16 Nov 1957.

Components. *Group.* 482d: 14 Jun–1 Dec 1952; 18 May 1955–16 Nov 1957.

Stations. Miami Intl Aprt, Fla, 14 Jun–1 Dec 1952. Dobbins AFB, Ga, 18 May 1955–16 Nov 1957.

Commanders. Lt Col Frederick W. Baggott, 14 Jun 1952; Lt Col William Niedernhofer, (by 30) Jun–1 Dec 1952. Col George H. Wilson, 18 May 1955–16 Nov 1957.

Aircraft. C–46, 1952. F–80, 1955; F–84, 1955–1957; T–28, 1955–1957; T–33, 1955–1957; F–86, 1957; C–119, 1957.

Operations. Reserve training as a troop carrier wing under supervision of the 2585th Air Force Reserve Training Center, 1952. Replaced by 435th Troop Carrier Wing in Dec 1952. Replaced the 94th Tactical Reconnaissance Wing in May 1955. Trained as a Reserve fighter-bomber wing under supervision of the 2589th Air Reserve Flying Center, May 1955–Nov 1957. Replaced by 445th Troop Carrier Wing in Nov 1957.

Service Streamers. None.

Campaign Streamers. None.

Decorations. None.

Emblem. None.

483d TACTICAL AIRLIFT WING

Lineage. Established as 483d Troop Carrier Wing, Medium, on 15 Nov 1952. Activated on 1 Jan 1953. Discontinued, and inactivated, on 25 Jun 1960. Redesignated 483d Troop Carrier Wing, and activated, on 12 Oct 1966. Organized on 15 Oct 1966. Redesignated 483d Tactical Airlift Wing on 1 Aug 1967. Inactivated on 31 May 1972.

Assignments. Tactical Air Command, 1 Jan 1953 (attached to 315th Air Division [Combat Cargo], 1 Jan 1953–30 Jun 1954); 315th Air Division (Combat Cargo), 1 Jul 1954–25 Jun 1960. Pacific Air Forces, 12 Oct 1966; 834th Air Division, 15 Oct 1966; Seventh Air Force, 1 Dec 1971–31 May 1972.

Components. *Groups*. 314th: attached 1 Jan 1953–15 Nov 1954. 316th: attached 15 Nov 1954–18 Jun 1957 (not operational, 15 Mar 1956–18 Jun 1957). 483d: 1 Jan 1953–8 Dec 1958 (not operational, 15 Mar 1956–8 Dec 1958). Tactical Group Provisional, 6483d: attached 15 Mar 1969–30 Jun 1970. *Squadrons*. 20th Special Operations: 1 Sep 1971–1 Apr 1972. 21st: attached 1 Jul 1957–7 Dec 1958, assigned 8 Dec 1958–25 Jun 1960. 36th: attached 15 Mar 1956–18 Jun 1957. 37th: attached 15 Mar 1956–18 Jun 1957. 75th: attached 15 Mar 1956–18 Jun 1957. 90th Special Operations: 1 Sep 1971–15 Apr 1972. 360th Tactical Electronic Warfare: 31 Aug 1971–1 Feb 1972. 361st Tactical Electronic Warfare: 31 Aug–1 Dec 1971 (not operational, 15 Oct–1 Dec 1971). 362d Tactical Electronic Warfare: 31 Aug 1971–1 Feb 1972. 457th: 1 Jan 1967–30 Apr 1972 (not operational, 1–30 Apr 1972). 458th: 1 Jan 1967–1 Mar 1972. 459th: 1 Jan 1967–1 Jun 1970 (not operational, 15 May–1 Jun 1970). 535th: 1 Jan 1967–24

Jan 1972 (detached 15 Mar 1969–25 Jun 1970). 536th: 1 Jan 1967–15 Oct 1971 (detached 15 Mar 1969–30 Jun 1970). 537th: 1 Jan 1967–31 Aug 1971. 773d: attached c. 30 Aug–c. 10 Dec 1958. 815th: attached 15 Mar 1956–7 Dec 1958, assigned 8 Dec 1958–25 Jun 1960. 816th: attached 15 Mar–18 Sep 1956 (not operational, 9–18 Sep 1956). 817th: attached 15 Mar 1956–7 Dec 1958, assigned 8 Dec 1958–25 Jun 1960. 6461st Troop Carrier (later, 6461st Air Transport): attached 1 Jan 1953–24 Jun 1955. *Detachments*. Det C–119: 5 Dec 1953–27 Jul 1954. Det, 772d Troop Carrier Squadron: attached 8 Mar–16 Aug 1958.

Stations. Ashiya AB, Japan, 1 Jan 1953–25 Jun 1960. Cam Ranh Bay AB, South Vietnam, 15 Oct 1966–31 May 1972.

Commanders. Col Maurice F. Casey, 1 Jan 1953; Col Jamie Gough, 13 May 1954; Col William C. Lindley, 6 Aug 1955; Col LeRoy M. Stanton, 13 Aug 1955; Col John H. Herring, Jr., 30 May 1959–25 Jun 1960. None (not manned), 12 Oct–3 Nov 1966; Col Paul J. Mascot, 4 Nov 1966; Col William H. Mason, 8 Oct 1967; Col Wilbert Turk, 30 Sep 1968; Col Keith L. Christensen, 4 Sep 1969; Col Abbott C. Greenleaf, 23 Mar 1970; Col Rodney H. Newbold, 11 Apr 1971; Col William G. Christensen, 2 Sep 1971 (temporary); Col Rodney H. Newbold, 17 Sep 1971; Col Duane H. Erickson, 25 Feb–15 May 1972; none (not manned), 16–31 May 1972.

Aircraft. C–119, 1951–1959; C–47, 1953–c. 1959; C–130, 1958–1960. C–7, 1967–1972; C–47, 1970–1971; EC–47, 1971–1972; C–130, 1971–1972; UH–1, 1971–1972.

Operations. Replaced 403d Troop Carrier Wing, Medium, in Jan 1953. Performed troop carrier and air transport operations in the Far East, including landing of troops and cargo in forward areas of the combat zone, air transportation of airborne troops and equipment, and air evacuation of casualties. In Jun 1953, as the Korean war neared an armistice, all wing C–119s airlifted the entire 187th Regimental Combat Team (Airborne) from Japan to Seoul and Chunch'on, South Korea, to preclude enemy breakthroughs. This was the largest mass movement of personnel in the history of combat cargo to that time. Between Apr 1953 and Sep 1954, the wing aided the French Air Force in Indo-China by training aircrews, evacuating wounded, and maintaining aircraft. Provided intra-theater airlift of cargo and personnel to specified organizations in Southeast Asia beginning Jan 1967, initially with C–7A aircraft transferred from the U.S. Army. Gained a tactical electronic warfare mission in mid-1971 and a special operations mission in the autumn of 1971. Phased down for inactivation beginning early 1972.

Service Streamers. None.

Campaign Streamers. Third Korean Winter; Korea Summer–Fall, 1953; Vietnam Air Offensive; Vietnam Air Offensive, Phase II; Vietnam Air Offensive, Phase III; Vietnam Air/Ground; Vietnam Air Offensive, Phase IV; TET 69/Counteroffensive; Vietnam Summer–Fall, 1969; Vietnam Winter–Spring, 1970; Sanctuary Counteroffensive; Southwest Monsoon; Commando Hunt V; Commando Hunt VI; Commando Hunt VII; Vietnam Ceasefire.

Decorations. Presidential Unit Citations (Southeast Asia): 21 Jan–12 May 1968; 1 Apr–30 Jun 1970. Air Force Outstanding Unit Awards with Combat "V" Device: 1 Jan–30 Apr 1967; 1 May 1967–30 Apr 1968; 1 Jul 1970–31 Dec 1971. Air Force Outstanding Unit Award: 6 May 1953–10 Sep 1954. Republic of Korea Presidential Unit Citation: [1 Jan]–27 Jul 1953. Republic of Vietnam Gallantry Crosses with Palm: 12 Oct 1966–31 Oct 1971; 15 Oct 1966–31 May 1972.

Emblem. On a shield of the sky, a sphere encircled with an orbit all or, latitude and longitude lines azure, over the sphere a hand proper supporting a parachute proper, an aircraft proper, and artillery proper; encircling the upper section of the sphere, three clouds proper and an increscent moon and four stars of the second color; on a chief of the third, 13 stars argent, the chief fimbriated or. *Motto:* EFFECTIVE AIRLIFT SUPPORT. (Approved on 2 Feb 1956.)

484th BOMBARDMENT WING, HEAVY

Lineage. Established as 484th Bombardment Wing, Heavy, and activated, on 15 Nov 1962. Organized on 1 Feb 1963. Discontinued, and inactivated, on 25 Mar 1967.

Assignments. Strategic Air Command, 15 Nov 1962; 822d Air Division, 1 Feb 1963; 823d Air Division, 2 Sep 1966–25 Mar 1967.

Components. *Squadrons.* 824th: 1 Feb 1963–25 Jan 1967 (not operational, 1 Apr–c. 29 Sep 1966). 919th Air Refueling: 1 Feb 1963–25 Mar 1967 (not operational, 1 Apr–c. 29 Sep 1966).

Stations. Turner AFB, Ga, 1 Feb 1963–25 Mar 1967.

Commanders. None (not manned), 15 Nov 1962–31 Jan 1963; Col Donald G. McPherson, 1 Feb 1963; Col Harold J. Whiteman, 28 Jun 1965–c. 1 Apr 1966; none (not manned), 1 Apr–c. 29 Sep 1966; Col Willard A. Beauchamp, c. 29 Sep 1966–25 Mar 1967.

Aircraft. B–52, 1963–1966, 1966–1967; KC–135, 1963–1966, 1966–1967.

Operations. Strategic bombardment training and air refueling operations to meet operational commitments of SAC. From 1 Apr to c. 29 Sep 1966, all wing aircraft and crews, all wing headquarters personnel, and most wing support personnel in deployed status as part of 3d Air Division for combat operations in Southeast Asia.

Service Streamers. None.

Campaign Streamers. None.

Decorations. Air Force Outstanding Unit Award: 1 Apr–30 Sep 1966.

Emblem. Azure, on and over a bendlet dark blue a stylized aircraft bendwise gules, between two mullets or, issuant from dexter chief and middle chief two lightning flashes bendwise throughout of the fourth, and in base a section of a globe argent gridlined of the second and in dexter flank a nuclear symbol with three orbits and six electrons of the last, all within a diminished bordure of the fourth. (Approved on 19 Mar 1964.)

494th BOMBARDMENT WING, HEAVY

Lineage. Established as 494th Bombardment Wing, Heavy, and activated, on 15 Nov 1962. Organized on 1 Feb 1963. Discontinued, and activated, on 2 Apr 1966.

Assignments. Strategic Air Command, 15 Nov 1962; 816th Strategic Aerospace Division, 1 Feb 1963; 4th Air Division, 1 Jul 1963; 816th Strategic Aerospace Division, 1 Jul 1964; 819th Strategic Aerospace Division, 1 Jul 1965; 19th Air Division, 1 Oct 1965–2 Apr 1966.

Components. *Squadrons*. 864th: 1 Feb 1963–2 Apr 1966. 900th Air Refueling: 1 Feb 1963–2 Apr 1966.

Stations. Sheppard AFB, Texas, 1 Feb 1963–2 Apr 1966.

Commanders. None (not manned), 15 Nov 1962–31 Jan 1963; Col Frederick D. Berry, Jr., 1 Feb 1963; Col Roger L. Hicks, Jr., 7 Jul 1964; Col Merrill N. Moore, 17 Aug 1964; Col Roger L. Hicks, Jr., 11 Jan 1965–2 Apr 1966.

Aircraft. B–52, 1963–1966; KC–135, 1963–1966.

Operations. Strategic bombardment training and air refueling operations to meet operational commitments of SAC.

Service Streamers. None.

Campaign Streamers. None.

Decorations. None.

Emblem. Azure, issuant from sinister chief a cloud formation fesswise argent emitting a lightning flash or, terminating in pale above a demi-sphere issuant from base of the second, outlined and gridlined vert, in dexter chief a circle of six mullets of the second, all within a diminished bordure of the third. (Approved on 11 Feb 1964.)

497th AIR REFUELING WING

Lineage. Established as 497th Air Refueling Wing, and activated, on 15 Nov 1962. Organized on 1 Jan 1963. Discontinued, and inactivated, on 15 Sep 1964.

Assignments. Strategic Air Command, 15 Nov 1962; 820th Strategic

Aerospace Division, 1 Jan 1963–15 Sep 1964.

Components. *Squadrons.* 26th: 1 Jan 1963–15 Sep 1964 (not operational, 8–15 Sep 1964). 380th: 1 Jan 1963–15 Sep 1964 (not operational, 7 Jun–15 Sep 1964).

Stations. Plattsburgh AFB, NY, 1 Jan 1963–15 Sep 1964.

Commanders. None (not manned), 15 Nov–31 Dec 1962; Col Fred W. Miller, 1 Jan 1963; Col James O. Frankosky, 12 Mar 1963; Col Vernon K. Cammack, 1 Nov 1963; Col John H. M. Linebaugh, 1 Jul 1964; Col Robert G. Moll, 15 Jul–15 Sep 1964.

Aircraft. KC–97, 1963–1964.

Operations. Replaced 4108th Air Refueling Wing in Jan 1963. Supported global air refueling mission of SAC and other USAF needs as required.

Service Streamers. None.

Campaign Streamers. None.

Decorations. Air Force Outstanding Unit Award: 1 Jan–30 Jun 1963.

Emblem. Per bend light blue and argent, a bend vert garnished or between two cotises azure fimbriated of the second, in chief a mullet above a cloud formation issuant from sinister fesswise all of the last, in base 19 stripes palewise of the fifth, on the bend five mullets of the fourth, all within a diminished bordure of the last. *motto:* PARATI STAMUS—We stand ready. (Approved on 7 Feb 1963.)

499th AIR REFUELING WING

Lineage. Established as 499th Air Refueling Wing, and activated, on 15 Nov 1962. Organized on 1 Jan 1963. Discontinued, and inactivated, on 25 Jun 1966.

Assignments. Strategic Air Command, 15 Nov 1962; 57th Air Division, 1 Jan 1963–25 Jun 1966.

Components. *Squadrons.* 11th: 1 Jan 1963–1 Jul 1964. 19th: 15 Jun 1963–1 Jul 1964. 99th: 1 Jan 1963–1 Jan 1966. 303d: 1 Jan–15 Jun 1963. 305th: 1 Jan 1963–1 Jul 1964. 384th: 1 Jan 1963–25 Jun 1966 (not operational, c. 21 Dec 1965–25 Jun 1966).

Stations. Westover AFB, Mass, 1 Jan 1963–25 Jun 1966.

Commanders. None (not manned), 15 Nov–31 Dec 1962; Col William R. Brown, 1 Jan 1963; Col Therwin S. Walters, 1 Jul 1965; Col Edward D. Wooten, 30 Nov 1965–25 Jun 1966 (additional duty).

Aircraft. KC–97, 1963–1965; KC–135, 1963–1965; EC–135, 1965.

Operations. Replaced 4050th Air Refueling Wing in Jan 1963. Supported SAC bombardment and TAC fighter aircraft with air-to-air refueling and occasionally deployed segments of its tanker force overseas to support unit movements and special operations. Also flew EC–135s on a post attack command control system (PACCS) airborne command post mission in support of Eighth Air Force. From Nov 1965 until inactivated, wing components operated under a bomb wing at Westover AFB, Mass.

Service Streamers. None.

Campaign Streamers. None.

Decorations. None.

Emblem. None.

500th AIR REFUELING WING

Lineage. Established as 500th Air Refueling Wing, and activated, on 15 Nov

1962. Organized on 1 Jan 1963. Discontinued, and inactivated, on 15 Dec 1964.

Assignments. Strategic Air Command, 15 Nov 1962; 17th Strategic Aerospace Division, 1 Jan 1963; 40th Air Division, 1 Jul 1963–15 Dec 1964.

Components. *Squadrons.* 44th: 1 Jan 1963–15 Dec 1964 (detached 10 Jul–10 Oct 1963). 307th: 1 Jan 1963–15 Dec 1964 (detached 31 Jul–5 Oct 1963).

Stations. Selfridge AFB, Mich, 1 Jan 1963–15 Dec 1964.

Commanders. None (not manned), 15 Nov–31 Dec 1962; Col Ervin Wursten, 1 Jan 1963; Col James H. Coats, 7 Jun 1963; Col Joseph J. Young, 16 Sep–15 Dec 1964.

Aircraft. KC–97, 1963–1964.

Operations. Replaced 4045th Air Refueling Wing in Jan 1963. Supported SAC bombardment and TAC fighter aircraft with air-to-air refueling and occasionally deployed segments of its tanker force overseas to support unit movements and special operations.

Service Streamers. None.

Campaign Streamers. None.

Decorations. None.

Emblem. Per bend azure and vert, issuant from base a demi-sphere argent grid lined and outlined sable, in fess two stylized aircraft refueling detailed and fimbriated of the third between in sinister chief a moon increscent with a mullet between its points silver gray, and in dexter flank a sun radiant or, detailed of the fourth, all within a diminished bordure of the sixth. *Motto:* SEMPER PARATUS—Always prepared. (Approved on 19 Feb 1964.)

506th TACTICAL FIGHTER WING

Lineage. Established as 506th Strategic Fighter Wing on 20 Nov 1952. Activated on 20 Jan 1953. Redesignated 506th Fighter-Day Wing on 1 Jul 1957; 506th Fighter-Bomber Wing on 1 Jan 1958; 506th Tactical Fighter Wing on 1 Jul 1958. Inactivated on 1 Apr 1959.

Assignments. Eighth Air Force, 20 Jan 1953 (attached to 39th Air Division [Defense], 13 Aug–7 Nov 1953); Second Air Force, 1 Apr 1955; Ninth Air Force, 1 Jul 1957; Eighteenth Air Force, 1 Oct 1957; Twelfth Air Force, 1 Jan 1958–1 Apr 1959.

Components. *Squadrons.* 457th: 20 Jan 1953–1 Apr 1959 (detached 20 Mar–c. 19 Aug 1958). 458th: 20 Jan 1953–1 Apr 1959 (detached c. 13 Aug

1958–c. 18 Feb 1959). 462d: 20 Jan 1953–1 Apr 1959. 470th: 25 Sep 1957–1 Apr 1959. 506th Air Refueling: 25 Sep 1953–1 Mar 1955.

Stations. Dow AFB, Maine, 20 Jan 1953; Tinker AFB, Okla, 20 Mar 1955–1 Apr 1959.

Commanders. Col William B. David, 20 Jan 1953; Col William E. Bertram, 13 Feb 1953; Col Richard O. Hunziker, 20 May 1954; Col James S. Coward, 1 Oct 1956; Lt Col Walter A. Smith, 18 Oct 1956; Col James S. Coward, 22 Oct 1956; Col Richard O. Hunziker, 23 Oct 1956; Col Joseph L. Laughlin, 8 Aug 1957; Col Albert S. Kelly, 29 Nov 1958–1 Apr 1959.

Aircraft. F–84, 1953–1957; KB–29, 1954–1955; F–100, 1957–1958.

Operations. Replaced the 4009th Air Base Squadron at Dow AFB, Maine, in Jan 1953. Trained as a strategic fighter wing, charged with providing air defense and escort, Apr 1953–Jun 1957. Provided air defense of northern Japan while deployed at Misawa AB, 13 Aug–7 Nov 1953. Transferred from SAC to TAC on 1 Jul 1957 and converted from F–84 to F–100 aircraft. Participated in tactical exercises and rotated squadrons to Europe, 1957–1958. Phased down for inactivation, Dec 1958–Apr 1959.

Service Streamers. None.

Campaign Streamers. None.

Decorations. None.

Emblem. On a barry wavy of four argent and azure, second bar semee of stars of the first, overall an escutcheon, per pale argent and or, a crest of a stylized wing of the first, fimbriated of the second, the escutcheon surmounting a sword bendwise, hilt and pommel or, blade of the last, shaded gules; on a chief of the second, a sphere argent, land areas vert, over two lightning flashes in saltire gules, fimbriated of the first. (Approved on 21 Jul 1955.)

507th FIGHTER WING (AIR DEFENSE)

Lineage. Established as 507th Fighter Wing (Air Defense), and activated, on 28 Dec 1960. Organized on 1 Feb 1961. Discontinued, and inactivated, on 30 Sep 1968.

Assignments. Air Defense Command, 28 Dec 1960; Saulte Sainte Marie Air Defense Sector, 1 Feb 1961; Duluth Air Defense Sector, 1 Oct 1963; 29th Air Division, 1 Apr 1966–30 Sep 1968.

Components. *Squadron.* 438th Fighter-Interceptor: 1 Feb 1961–30 Sep 1968 (not operational, 13–30 Sep 1968).

Stations. Kincheloe AFB, Mich, 1 Feb 1961–30 Sep 1968.

Commanders. None (not manned), 28 Dec 1960–31 Jan 1961; Col Thomas W. Hornsby, 1 Feb 1961; Col Ward W. Martindale, 5 Aug 1963; Col Robert L. Hinchee, 1 Jul 1967; Col William P. Brierty, 31 Aug 1967; Col Howard C. Johnson, 10 Jun 1968; Col Robert L.

Hinchee, 1 Jul 1968; Col Howard C. Johnson, 12 Aug 1968; Col Robert L. Hinchee, 19 Aug–30 Sep 1968.

Aircraft. F–106, 1961–1968.

Operations. Air defense for an assigned segment of the north central United States.

Service Streamers. None.

Campaign Streamers. None.

Decorations. Air Force Outstanding Unit Award: 1 Jun 1966–1 Jun 1968.

Emblem. On a shield azure, edged argent, over a point pointed in point bendwise and arched gules, fimbriated of the second, a falcon flying downward per bend argent between two planets and a star in sinister chief, and the Great Dipper in dexter base, all proper. *Motto:* DEFENDIMUS USQUE AD ASTRA—We defend even to the stars. (Approved for 507th Group on 17 Aug 1950; used by 507th Wing, 1961–1968.)

508th STRATEGIC FIGHTER WING

Lineage. Established as 508th Fighter-Escort Wing on 19 Jun 1952. Activated on 1 Jul 1952. Redesignated 508th Strategic Fighter Wing on 20 Jan 1953. Inactivated on 11 May 1956.

Assignments. 40th Air Division, 1 Jul 1952–11 May 1956 (attached to 39th Air Division [Defense], c. 8 Feb–c. 13 May 1953 and 12 Feb–c. 7 May 1954).

Components. *Squadrons.* 466th: 1 Jul 1952–11 May 1956 (not operational, 1 Jul–Sep 1952). 467th: 1 Jul 1952–11 May 1956. 468th: 1 Jul 1952–11 May 1956 (not operational, 1 Jul–Sep 1952). 508th Air Refueling: 25 Nov 1953–11 May 1956 (detached 10 Feb–1 Jun 1954 and 4 Jul–15 Oct 1954).

Stations. Turner AFB, Ga, 1 Jul 1952–11 May 1956.

Commanders. Col Robert P. Montgomery, 1 Jul 1952; Col Gerald W. Johnson, 29 Jul 1952; Col Cy Wilson, 2 Aug 1952; Lt Col Howard E. Cody, 29 Dec 1954; Col Gerald W. Johnson, 4 Jan 1955; Col Nathan J. Adams, 2–11 May 1956.

Aircraft. F–84, 1952–1956; KB–29, 1953–1956.

Operations. Strategic fighter operations training and aerial refueling, 1953–1956. Deployed at Misawa AB, Japan, to provide air defense, Feb–May 1953 and Feb–May 1954.

Service Streamers. None.

Campaign Streamers. None.

Decorations. None.

Emblem. Per bend engrailed azure and gules, in bend a chain or and in chief an atomic cloud argent issuing from a base gray, overall three figures representing the "Spirit of '76" sable fimbriated of the fourth. *Motto:* KNOWLEDGE AND COURAGE. (Approved on 14 Sep 1953.)

509th BOMBARDMENT WING, MEDIUM

Lineage. Established as 509th Bombardment Wing, Very Heavy, on 3 Nov

1947. Organized on 17 Nov 1947. Discontinued on 1 Aug 1948. Redesignated 509th Bombardment Wing, Medium, and activated on 1 Aug 1948. Redesignated: 509th Bombardment Wing, Heavy, on 2 Apr 1966; 509th Bombardment Wing, Medium, on 1 Dec 1969.

Assignments. Eighth Air Force, 17 Nov 1947–1 Aug 1948. Eighth Air Force, 1 Aug 1948 (attached to 3d Air Division, 1 Feb 1951–); 47th Air Division, 10 Feb 1951 (remained attached to 3d Air Division to 4 May 1951; attached to 7th Air Division, 4 Jun–2 Sep 1952; 3d Air Division, 10 Jul–8 Oct 1954; 7th Air Division, 26 Jan–30 Apr 1956); 817th Air Division, 1 Jul 1958; 45th Air Division, 30 Jun 1971–.

Components. *Wing*. 33d Fighter: attached 17 Nov 1947–1 Aug 1948 (not operational); attached 1 Aug–15 Nov 1948 (not operational). *Groups*. 33d Fighter: attached 17 Nov 1947–1 Aug 1948; attached 1 Aug–15 Nov 1948. 509th: 17 Nov 1947–1 Aug 1948 (not operational); 1 Aug 1948–16 Jun 1952 (not operational, 1 Aug–14 Sep 1948 and 10 Feb 1951–16 Jun 1952). *Squadrons*. 34th Air Refueling: 25 Jun 1966–31 Mar 1976. 393d: attached 17 Nov 1947–1 Aug 1948; attached 1 Aug–14 Sep 1948; attached 1 Feb 1951–15 Jun 1952, assigned 16 Jun 1952– (detached 18 Jun–c. 18 Sep 1953; not operational, 23 Nov 1965–22 Mar 1966, 1 Apr–1 Oct 1968, 18 Mar–9 Sep 1969, and 19 Nov 1969–Jan 1971). 509th Air Refueling: attached 19 Jul–1 Aug 1948 (not operational); attached 1 Aug–14 Sep 1948 (not operational, 1–c. 31 Aug 1948); attached 1 Feb 1951–15 Jun 1952, assigned 16 Jun 1952–5 Jan 1958 (detached 10 Jul–5 Nov 1954, 14 Jun–5 Aug 1955, and 27 Feb–1 May 1957); assigned 8 Jul 1958–25 Jun 1965 (not operational, 11–25 Jun 1965); assigned 2 Oct 1966–. 661st: 1 Mar 1959–1 Jan 1962 (not operational, 15 Oct 1961–1 Jan 1962). 715th: attached 17 Nov 1947–1 Aug 1948; attached 1 Aug–14 Sep 1948; attached 1 Feb 1951–15 Jun 1952, assigned 16 Jun 1952–25 Jun 1966 (not operational, 23 Nov 1965–25 Jun 1966); assigned 1 Jan 1970– (not operational, 1 Jan 1970–Jan 1971). 830th: attached 17 Nov 1947–1 Aug 1948; attached 1 Aug–14 Sep 1948; attached 1 Feb 1951–15 Jun 1952, assigned 16 Jun 1952–25 Jun 1966 (detached 15 Mar–19 Jun 1953; not operational, 23 Nov 1965–25 Jun 1966). 900th Air Refueling: 2 Apr–25 Jun 1966.

Stations. Roswell AAFld (later, Walker AFB), NM, 17 Nov 1947–1 Aug 1948. Walker AFB, NM, 1 Aug 1948; Pease AFB, NH, 1 Jul 1958–.

Commanders. Col William H. Blanchard, 17 Nov 1947–1 Aug 1948. Col John D. Ryan, 1 Aug 1948; Brig Gen Clarence S. Irvine, 15 Sep 1948; Col James A. DeMarco, 3 Jan 1950; Brig Gen Hunter Harris, Jr., 15 Jan 1950; Col Thomas S. Jeffrey, Jr., 10 Jan 1951; Col John D. Ryan, 1 Feb 1951; Col

Berton H. Burns, (by 19) Jul 1951; Col William H. Blanchard, 21 Jul 1951; Col Berton H. Burns, c. 15 Jan 1952; Brig Gen William H. Blanchard, c. 7 Apr 1952; Col Wilson R. Wood, 11 Feb 1953; Col Howard E. Jackson, 22 Apr 1953; Col Harold E. Humfeld, (by 12) May 1953; Col Wilson R. Wood, c. 15 May 1953; Col Harold E. Humfeld, 30 Jul 1953; Col Wilson R. Wood, 23 Nov 1953; Col Clifford F. Macomber, 16 May 1955; Col Neil W. Wemple, (by 8) Jan 1957; Col Clifford F. Macomber, (by 29) Jan 1957; Col Brooks A. Lawhon, 11 Feb 1959; Col Donald G. McPherson, 1 Jun 1960; Col Edward D. Edwards, 10 Mar 1962; Col James O. Frankosky, 21 Oct 1963; Col Joseph V. Adams, Jr., 27 Jan 1966; Col James O. Frankosky, c. 2 Mar 1966; Col Madison M. McBrayer, 23 Jan 1967; Col Joseph V. Adams, Jr., 28 Mar 1968; Col Robert E. Blauw, c. 1 Oct 1968; Col William R. Thorstenson, 19 Mar 1969; Col Robert E. Blauw, 20 Sep 1969; Col William R. Thorstenson, 18 Nov 1969; Col Winston E. Moore, 11 Dec 1969; Col John M. Parker, 22 Feb 1972; Col Alan L. Hichew, 14 Jun 1972; Col Isaac M. Glass, 26 Mar 1973; Col Paul W. Maul, 21 Aug 1973; Col Richard A. Burpee, 26 Feb 1974; Col Fredric E. Roth, 1 Apr 1975; Col Guy L. Hecker, Jr., 3 May 1976–.

Aircraft. F–51, 1947–1948; F–84, 1948; B–29, 1947–1948. F–51, 1948; F–84, 1948; B–29, 1948–1952; B–50, 1949–1951; KB–29, 1951–1954; KC–97, 1954–1958, 1958–1965; B–47, 1955–1965; B–52, 1966–1969; KC–135, 1966–; FB–111, 1970–.

Operations. Maintained combat proficiency with B–29 bombers and F–51 and F–84 fighters, 1947–1948. Added air refueling in Sep 1948, initially with B–29M hose-type tankers and later with B/KB–29P boom-type tankers. Charged with strategic bombardment training and air refueling, 1949–1958. Deployed as a wing several times in the early 1950s, three times to England and once to Guam, and also deployed individual squadrons at other times. Temporarily had no refueling unit during 1958. Phased down for inactivation in late 1965, but was converted to a B–52/KC–135 wing in 1966. Supported SAC combat and contingency operations in Southeast Asia with KC–135 aircraft and crews, Nov 1966–Dec 1975, with B–52 aircraft and crews, Nov 1966–Sep 1969, and with B–52 crews, 1970. From 1 Apr to 1 Oct 1968 and 26 Mar to c. 20 Sep 1969, over one-half of the wing was involved in SAC operations in Southeast Asia. From Nov 1969 to Dec 1970, the wing had no bombardment aircraft, but continued refueling operations and performed FB–111 ground training. Resumed bombardment flying training in Dec 1970 and FB–111 alert commitments on 1 Jul 1971.

Service Streamers. None.

Campaign Streamers. None.

Decorations. Air Force Outstanding Unit Award: 1 Apr–1 Oct 1968.

Emblem. On a shield or, in base a label of three points gules, surmounted by an atomic cloud proper, between a pair of wings conjoined in base azure. *Crest:* On a wreath of the colors, or and azure, an atomic cloud or, with broken pattern gules, between two lightning bolts gules. *Motto:* DEFENSOR VINDEX—Defender avenger. (Approved on 10 Jul 1952.)

512th MILITARY AIRLIFT WING (ASSOCIATE)

Lineage. Established as 512th Troop Carrier Wing, Medium, on 4 Aug 1949. Activated in the Reserve on 2 Sep 1949. Ordered to active service on 15 Mar 1951. Inactivated on 1 Apr 1951. Activated in the Reserve on 14 Jun 1952. Ordered to active service on 28 Oct 1962. Relieved from active duty on 28 Nov 1962. Redesignated: 512th Troop Carrier Wing, Heavy, on 8 Jan 1965; 512th Air Transport Wing, Heavy, on 1 Dec 1965; 512th Military Airlift Wing on 1 Jan 1966. Inactivated on 29 Jun 1971. Redesignated 512th Military Airlift Wing (Associate) on 29 Jan 1973. Activated in the Reserve on 1 Jul 1973.

Assignments. Ninth Air Force, 2 Sep 1949; First Air Force, 1 Aug 1950–1 Apr 1951. 1st Air Reserve District, 14 Jun 1952; First Air Force, 14 Jan 1954; Fourteenth Air Force, 25 Mar 1958; Second Air Force Reserve Region, 15 Aug 1960; Ninth Air Force, 28 Oct 1962; Second Air Force Reserve Region, 28 Nov 1962; Fourth Air Force Reserve Region, 8 Jan 1965; Central Air Force Reserve Region, 31 Dec 1969–29 Jun 1971. Eastern Air Force Reserve Region, 1 Jul 1973 (attached to 436th Military Airlift Wing, 1 Jul 1973–); Fourteenth Air Force (Reserve), 8 Oct 1976– (remained attached to 436th Military Airlift Wing).

Components. *Groups*. 512th: 2 Sep 1949–1 Apr 1951; 14 Jun 1952–14 Apr 1959. 912th: 11 Feb 1963–8 Jan 1965. 913th: 11 Feb 1963–8 Jan 1965. 914th: 11 Feb 1963–1 Jan 1964. 916th: 8 Jan 1965–21 Apr 1971 (detached 1–21 Apr 1971). 917th: 5 Feb 1965–21 Apr 1971 (detached 1–21 Apr 1971). 937th: 5 Feb 1965–21 Apr 1971 (detached 1–21 Apr 1971). *Squadrons*. 326th: 14 Apr 1959–11 Feb 1963; 1 Jul 1973–. 327th: 14 Apr 1959–11 Feb 1963. 328th: 14 Apr 1959–11 Feb 1963. 709th: 1 Oct 1973–.

Stations. Reading Muni Aprt, Pa, 2 Sep 1949; New Castle County Aprt, Del, 12 Apr 1950–1 Apr 1951. New Castle County Aprt, Del, 14 Jun 1952; U.S. Naval Air Station Willow Grove, Pa, 20 Jul 1958; Carswell AFB, Texas, 8 Jan 1965–29 Jun 1971. Dover AFB, Del, 1 Jul 1973–.

Commanders. Brig Gen Emil H. Molthan, 2 Sep 1949–1 Apr 1951. Col Frank W. Davis, 14 Jun 1952; Brig Gen John S. Bagby, 5 Aug 1952; Col Stanley V. Rush, c. 8 Jan 1965; Brig Gen John W. Hoff, 16 Jul 1967; Brig Gen George H. Wilson, 1 Jun 1970; Col George H. Bergmark, Jr., c. Apr–29 Jun 1971. Maj William J. Cox, 1 Jul 1973; Lt Col David L. Webber, 2 Aug 1973; Col Donald H. Balch, 30 Nov 1974; Lt Col William J. Cox, 1 Feb 1976; Lt Col David L. Webber, 1 May 1976–.

Aircraft. AT–7, AT–11, and C–46, 1949–1951. C–46, 1952–1957; C–119, 1957–1965; C–124, 1965–1971. C–141, 1973; C–5, 1973–.

Operations. Reserve training in troop carrier operations, 1949–1951. Upon call to active service in 1951, personnel used to meet USAF worldwide requirements. Reserve training in troop carrier operations, 1952–1965, and in military airlift operations, 1965–1971. Called to active service for 1 month during Cuban missile crisis. Assumed active role in providing military airlift support for Vietnam conflict. Reserve training in military airlift operations, 1973 to present, in association with 436th Military Airlift Wing.

Service Streamers. None.

Campaign Streamers. None.

Decorations. Air Force Outstanding Unit Awards: 1 Aug 1967–25 Oct 1968; 13 Oct–14 Nov 1973; 1 Jan 1974–30 Apr 1975. Republic of Vietnam Gallantry Cross with Palm: 1 Apr 1966–[29 Jun 1971].

Emblem. Per bend celeste and azure, a sphere with axis bendwise argent gridlined sable surmounted by a beveled flight symbol quartered gules and or trailing an orbital ring enveloping the sphere of the like all between three mullets of five points, one in dexter flank, one in sinister chief and one in base of the last, all within a diminished bordure gold. *Motto:* MASTERS OF THE GLOBE. (Emblem approved on 23 Jul 1973. Motto approved on 26 May 1967, along with previous emblem.)

513th TACTICAL AIRLIFT WING

Lineage. Established as 513th Troop Carrier Wing, Assault, Fixed Wing, on 26 Sep 1957. Activated on 8 Oct 1957. Redesignated 513th Troop Carrier Wing, Assault, on 1 Jul 1958. Inactivated on 1 Dec 1958. Redesignated 513th Troop Carrier Wing, and activated, on 6 Apr 1966. Organized on 15 Apr 1966. Redesignated 513th Tactical Airlift Wing on 1 Jul 1967.

Assignments. 839th Air Division, 8 Oct 1957–1 Dec 1958. United States Air Forces in Europe, 6 Apr 1966 (attached to 322d Air Division for tactical operations, 15 Apr 1966–); Third Air Force, 1 Jul 1966 (remained attached to 322d Air Division); United States Air Forces in Europe, 1 Jul 1967 (remained attached to 322d Air Division); Third Air Force, 1 Nov 1968– (remained attached to 322d Air Division to 24 Dec 1968).

Components. *Squadrons.* 10th Airborne Command Control: 1 Jan 1970–. 32d: attached 5 Nov 1973–15 Jan 1974 and 5 Sep–14 Nov 1975. 36th: attached 21 Mar–22 Jun 1967, 26 Feb–19 Jun 1969, 13 Jul–14 Sep 1971, 5 Mar–16 May 1973, and 3 Jan–15 Mar 1974. 37th: attached 21 Sep–21 Dec 1967, 2 Dec 1958–26 Feb 1969, 2 Mar–13 May 1970, 13 Jan–14 Mar 1972, and c. 5 Sep–15 Nov 1973. 38th: attached 5 Nov 1970–7 Jan 1971, 13 Sep–16 Nov 1971, 11 Mar–6 May 1972, and 7 May–15 Jul 1973. 39th: attached 27 May–8 Jul 1968, 7 Jul–15 Sep 1974, and 4 Jul–14

Sep 1975. 40th: attached 11 Mar–27 May 1968 and 5 Mar–15 May 1975. 41st: attached 12 Nov 1971–17 Jan 1972, 3 Mar–15 May 1974, and 5 Nov 1974 16–Jan 1975. 47th: attached 12 May–16 Jul 1971. 48th: attached 10 Jun–c. Jul 1972. 61st: attached 6 May–11 Aug 1967, 8 Apr–c. 29 Jun 1968, 27 May–6 Jul 1970, and 5 Jan–16 Mar 1973. 62d: attached 15 Dec 1967–8 Apr 1968, 29 Jun–2 Oct 1968, 16 Nov 1969–11 Jan 1970, and 3 Jul–30 Aug 1970. 330th: 8 Oct 1957–1 Dec 1958 (not operational, 15 Sep–1 Dec 1958). 331st: 8 Oct 1957–1 Dec 1958 (not operational, 15 Oct–1 Dec 1958). 332d: 8 Oct 1957–1 Dec 1958 (not operational, 15 Nov–1 Dec 1958). 345th: attached 8 Oct 1957–12 Nov 1958. 346th: attached 8 Oct 1957–30 Jun 1958 and 13 Feb–11 Mar 1968. 347th: attached 22 Jun–23 Sep 1967, 15 Jun–6 Sep 1969, and 5 Sep–15 Nov 1970. 348th: attached 6 Sep–16 Nov 1969, 17 Feb–4 Mar 1970, 7 May–13 Jul 1970, 5 Jan–15 Mar 1971, and 6 May–1 Jun 1972. 772d: attached 5 Jul–21 Sep 1972, 3 Nov 1972–16 Jan 1973, 5 Jan–16 Mar 1975, and 5 Nov 1975–15 Jan 1976. 773d: attached 1 Jun–14 Jul 1972, 28 Aug–16 Nov 1972, 5 Jul–5 Sep 1973, 5 May–15 Jul 1974, and 5 May–14 Jul 1975. 774th: attached 5 Sep–15 Nov 1974. 777th: attached 6 Aug–13 Nov 1967, 10 May–7 Aug 1969, 11 Jan–19 Mar 1970, 1–31 Oct 1970, and 13 Mar–12 May 1971. 778th: attached 7 Nov 1967–13 Feb 1968, 18 Oct–21 Dec 1969, and 7 Jul–16 Sep 1970. 779th: attached 26 Sep–2 Dec 1968 and 7 Aug–18 Oct 1969. Military Airlift Squadron Provisional, 1648th: attached 8 Jul 1968–10 May 1969. 7120th Airborne Command Control: 1 Jul 1966–1 Jan 1970. Troop Carrier Squadron Provisional, 7441st: attached 20 Jul 1966–1 Mar 1967. Troop Carrier Squadron Provisional, 7442d: attached 20 Jul 1966–1 Jun 1967. *Detachments.* Det, 313th TAS: attached 18 Sep–c. 7 Nov 1970. Det, 464th TAS: attached 19 Sep–c. 7 Nov 1970. Det (composite), 313th TAW, 464th TAW, and 516th TAW: attached 14–30 Jun 1971. Det (composite), 47th TAS and 61st TAS: attached 6–27 Oct 1971. Det (composite), 41st TAS, 86th TAS, and 756th TAS: attached c. 6 Sep–7 Oct 1972. Det (composite from several AF Reserve and Air National Guard units): attached 10 Sep–11 Oct 1973.

Stations. Sewart AFB, Tenn, 8 Oct 1957–1 Dec 1958. Evreux-Fauville AB, France, 15 Apr 1966; RAF Mildenhall, England, 1 Jul 1966–.

Commanders. Col John R. Roche, 8 Oct 1957; Lt Col Raymond J. Berger, 16 Sep 1958; Lt Col Earl V. Riley, 7 Nov–1 Dec 1958. None (not manned), 6–14 Apr 1966; Col Harold G. Fulmer, 15 Apr 1966; Col William W. Kingery, 28 Jun 1968; Col Thomas J. Sims, 11 Jul 1969; Col Eugene H. Dyke, 17 Sep 1969; Col Robert W. Koernig, 2 Sep 1971; Col Webb Thompson, 10 Nov 1972; Col James E. Poore, 1 Mar 1974; Col Clarence W. Thomas, 9 May 1975; Col Walter J. Ford, 8 Jun 1977–.

Aircraft. C–123, 1957–1958. C–130, 1966–1976; EC–135, 1966–; C–124, 1968–1969.

Operations. Replaced and absorbed resources of the 513th Troop Carrier Group in Oct 1957. Participated in numerous tactical exercises and operations of TAC to maintain assault airlift proficiency, Oct 1957–Nov 1958, controlling three assigned and two attached flying squadrons. Organized at Evreux-

Fauville AB, France, in Apr 1966. Operated that base until 1 Jul 1966, then moved to England and assumed responsibility for operation and maintenance of RAF Mildenhall. The wing provided after Apr 1966 EC–135 aircraft and crews to support the European Command's airborne command post. From Apr 1966 to Jan 1976, the wing also provided intra-theater airlift in support of U.S. Air Forces in Europe, European Command, and North Atlantic Treaty Organization operations and exercises. C–130s and crews for this airlift mission were provided by U.S.-based wings of Tactical Air Command and Military Airlift Command. From Jul 1968 to May 1969 the wing also briefly controlled C–124 airlift operations in Europe, using planes and crews furnished by the 904th, 918th, 921st, 938th, and 941st Military Airlift Groups of the Air Force Reserve. Since Jan 1976, when another wing assumed control over rotational C–130 units and the intra–theater airlift mission, the 513th has continued its base operation and its airborne command post support with a drastic decrease in exercise par–ticipation, but with more emphasis on support of tenant organizations at RAF Mildenhall.

Service Streamers. None.

Campaign Streamers. None.

Decorations. Air Force Outstanding Unit Awards: 1 Jul 1966–30 Jun 1967; 1 Jul 1969–30 Jun 1970; 1 Jul 1972–30 Jun 1973; 1 Jul 1974–30 Jun 1975.

Emblem. On a shield per fesse dancette azure and vert, an American bald eagle volant, marked with three stars, red, blue, and green, wings spread upward, carrying with his talons an aircraft wing section loaded with a gun, supply box, and a combat soldier, all or; in chief a lightning bolt of the last. *Motto:* SUBSIDIA FERIMUS—We fly men and materiel. (Approved on 8 Apr 1958.)

514th MILITARY AIRLIFT WING (ASSOCIATE)

Lineage. Established as 514th Troop Carrier Wing, Medium, on 10 May 1949. Activated in the Reserve on 26 Jun 1949. Ordered to active service on 1 May 1951. Inactivated on 1 Feb 1953. Activated in the Reserve on 1 Apr 1953. Redesignated: 514th Tactical Airlift Wing on 1 Jul 1967; 514th Military Airlift Wing (Associate) on 25 Sep 1968.

Assignments. Fourteenth Air Force, 26 Jun 1949; First Air Force, 10 Oct 1949; Tactical Air Command, 2 May 1951; Eighteenth Air Force, 1 Jun 1951–1 Feb 1953. First Air Force, 1 Apr 1953; Fourteenth Air Force, 25 Mar 1958; First Air Force Reserve Region, 15 Aug 1960; Eastern Air Force Reserve Region, 31 Dec 1969 (attached to 438th Military Airlift Wing, 1 Jul 1973–); Fourteenth Air Force (Reserve), 8 Oct 1976– (remained attached to 438th Military Airlift Wing).

Components. *Groups*. 514th: 26 Jun 1949–1 Feb 1953; 1 Apr 1953–14 Apr 1959. 903d: 17 Jan 1963–1 Jul 1973. 904th: 17 Jan 1963–1 Jul 1966. 905th: 17 Jan 1963–1 Jul 1966. 912th: 1 Jul 1966–1 Jul 1973. 913th: 1 Jul 1966–17 Sep 1970 (detached 1 Jul–17 Sep 1970). 932d Military (later, 932d Aeromedical) Airlift: 1 Apr 1969–1 Jan 1972. 943d: 25 Sep 1969–1 Jul 1973. *Squadrons*. 335th: 14 Apr 1959–17 Jan 1963; 1 Jul 1973–. 336th: 14 Apr 1959–17 Jan 1963. 337th: 14 Apr 1959–17 Jan 1963. 702d: 1 Jul 1973–. 732d: 1 Jul 1973–.

Stations. Birmingham Muni Aprt, Ala, 26 Jun 1949; Mitchel AFB, NY, 10 Oct 1949–1 Feb 1953. Mitchel AFB, NY, 1 Apr 1953; McGuire AFB, NJ, 15 Mar 1961–.

Commanders. Brig Gen Henry L. Badham, Jr., 26 Jun 1949; Brig Gen Arthur L. McCullough, 10 Oct 1949–1 Feb 1953. Lt Col Arthur E. Tappan, 1 Apr 1953; Maj Gen Clayton Stiles, 6 Jun 1953; Brig Gen Campbell Y. Jackson, 1 Oct 1959; Col Clair S. Hazell, 16 Oct 1972; Brig Gen Campbell Y. Jackson, c. Jan 1973; Col Clair S. Hazell, 16 Feb 1973; Brig Gen James E. McAdoo, 15 May 1974; Lt Col Robert Q. Head, 1 Dec 1976; Col Alan G. Sharp, 15 Jul 1977–.

Aircraft. C/TC–46, 1949, 1949–1953; T–6, 1949, 1949–1951; T–7, 1949–1951; T–11, 1949, 1949–1951; C–119, 1952–1953. C–45, 1953; C–46, 1953–1954; C–119, 1954–1970; C–124, 1966, 1969; C–141, 1968–; C–9, 1969–1971; C–5, 1973.

Operations. Formed in Jun 1949 at Birmingham, Ala, from resources of 19th Air Division and 99th Bombardment Group. Trained as a Reserve troop carrier organization under supervision of the 2587th Air Force Reserve Training Center. Moved without personnel or equipment to Mitchel AFB, NY, in Oct 1949, leaving resources for the 319th Bombardment Wing, Light, at Birmingham, and taking over resources of the 84th Fighter Wing at Mitchel AFB. Trained as a Reserve troop carrier wing under supervision of the 2233d AFRTC until ordered to active service in May 1951. From then until inactivated in Feb 1953, performed troop carrier operations and took part in numerous tactical exercises and joint training operations. Operated a C–46 combat crew training school, 15 Sep 1952–20 Jan 1953. Began converting to C–119 aircraft on 31 Dec 1952. Replaced by 313th Troop Carrier Wing, Medium, on 1 Feb 1953. Activated in the Reserve at Mitchel AFB on 1 Apr 1953, replacing 65th Troop Carrier Wing, Medium. Trained under supervision of 2233d Air Force Reserve Combat Training Center (later, 2233d Air Reserve Flying Center) to 1958, initially with C–46s but with C–119s by Aug 1954. Summer camps conducted at Mitchel (and later, McGuire AFB, NJ) and at many other bases. Began participating in the Air Reserve Technician (ART) program on 1 Apr 1958 and from 14 Jul to 1 Oct 1958 absorbed functions and some personnel of the 2233d ARFC, which then inactivated. After 1958, the wing increasingly participated in airlift missions, tactical exercises, humanitarian missions, and mercy flights. By the mid-1960s the wing was augmenting Military Air Transport Service (later, Military Airlift Command) airlift operations on a regular basis. The wing trained South Vietnamese aircrews and maintenance personnel, and Royal

Hellenic Air Force maintenance personnel, in C–119 aircraft, 10 Aug to 18 Dec 1967, and ferried many C–119s to South Vietnam in 1968. Shortly after two of its groups began converting to C–124s in 1966 the wing lost these groups, but gained two C–119 groups. In 1968 two of the wing's groups shifted from Tactical Airlift to Military Airlift (Associate) status, transferring their C–119s and thereafter flying C–141s of the regular wings with which they were associated—the 436th MAW at Dover AFB, Del, and the 438th MAW at McGuire AFB. A third C–119 group was retained until mid-1970. Gained a C–124 group in Apr 1969, but it soon converted to an Aeromedical Airlift Group (Associate), flying C–9s of the 375th Aeromedical Airlift Wing. This group remained with the wing through 1971. A third C–141 associate group joined the wing in Sep 1969, associated with the 437th MAW at Charleston AFB, SC. In Jul 1973, however, the wing's groups at Dover and Charleston were replaced by new Reserve wings, and the 514th Wing itself absorbed all of the squadrons of what had been its 903d Group at McGuire AFB. Named as Air Force Association's "outstanding Reserve flying wing" for 1976.

Service Streamers. None.

Campaign Streamers. None.

Decorations. Air Force Outstanding Unit Award: 1 Jul 1973–31 Jan 1975. Republic of Vietnam Gallantry Crosses with Palm: 10 Aug–18 Dec 1967; 25 Aug 1968–28 Jan 1973.

Emblem. Per pairle abased argent, gules and azure, in chief the outline of an open parachute of the second surmounted by the silhouette of a stylized aircraft of the third, in dexter base a dexter hand in armor of the first holding a partially drawn sword in bend of the last the handle and hilt of the third the sheath of the like garnished of the first, in sinister base two lightning flashes in bend sinister of the first issuing from a storm cloud of the second fimbriated of the first. (Approved on 9 Sep 1954.)

516th TACTICAL AIRLIFT WING

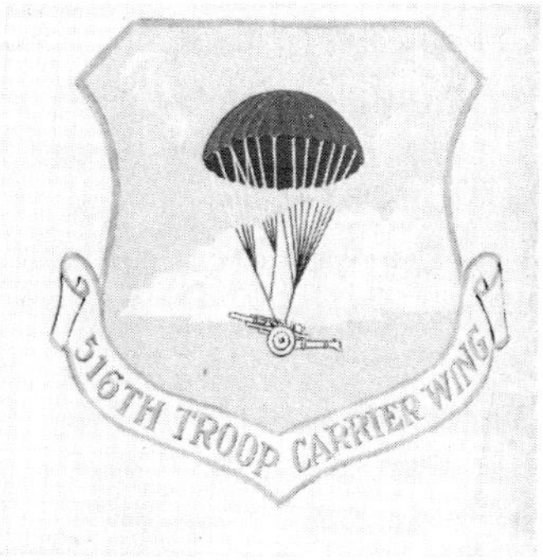

Lineage. Established as 516th Troop Carrier Wing, Medium, on 10 May 1949. Activated in the Reserve on 26 Jun 1949. Ordered to active service on 16 Apr 1951. Inactivated on 16 Jan 1953. Activated on 19 Jul 1962. Organized on 1 Jan 1963. Redesignated: 516th Troop Carrier Wing on 1 Mar 1966; 516th Tactical Airlift Wing on 1 May 1967. Inactivated on 1 Jun 1972.

Assignments. Fourteenth Air Force, 26 Jun 1947; Tactical Air Command, 17 Apr 1951; Eighteenth Air Force, 1 Jun 1951–16 Jan 1953. Tactical Air Command, 19 Jul 1962; Twelfth Air Force, 1 Jan 1963; 839th Air Division, 1 Jul 1963; 838th Air Division, 9 Nov 1964; Twelfth Air Force, 24 Dec 1969; 834th Air Division, 15 Mar–1 Jun 1972.

Components. *Group.* 516th: 26 Jun 1949–16 Jan 1953. *Squadrons.* 17th: 1 Jan 1963–15 Jun 1964. 18th: 1 Jan–1 Jun 1963; 15 Oct 1969–1 Jun 1972. 345th: 8 Jan 1963–27 Nov 1965. 346th: 1 Apr 1963–15 Mar 1969 (detached 1 Jul–c. 1 Sep 1964, 5 Feb–30 May 1968). 347th: 1 Jul 1963–1 Jun 1972 (detached 18 May–c. 20 Jul 1964, 22 Jun–27 Sep 1967, 27 Jan–11 Mar 1968, 18 Jun–15 Oct 1968, 25 Feb–28 May 1969, 13 Jun–3 Sep 1969, 3 Feb–10 Apr 1970, 7 Sep–11 Nov 1970, 4 Jun–10 Aug 1971, 4 Feb–17 Apr 1972). 348th: 5 Jul 1968–1 Jun 1972 (detached 15 Oct 1968–10 Jan 1969, 1 Sep–13 Nov 1969, 5 May–7 Jul 1970, 5 Jan–10 Mar 1971, 5 Oct–17 Dec 1971, 8 May–1 Jun 1972). 4449th Combat Crew Training: 27 Aug–15 Oct 1969.

Stations. Memphis Muni Aprt, Tenn, 26 Jun 1949–16 Jan 1953. Dyess AFB, Texas, 1 Jan 1963–1 Jun 1972.

Commanders. Brig Gen Everett H. Cook, 26 Jun 1949–unkn; Col Willis W. Mitchell, (by May 1950)–16 Jan 1953. None (not manned), 19 Jul–31 Dec 1962; Col Burl W. McLaughlin, 1 Jan 1963; Col William G. Duncan, 18 Jan 1965; Col Vernon W. Froehlich, 7 Oct 1965; Col William G. Duncan, 3 Dec 1965; Col Albert W. Jones, 10 Jun 1967; Col Charles W. Borders, 25 Jan 1968; Col Joel C. Stevenson, 13 Jan 1970; Col Robert F. Coverdale, 31 May 1971; Col Richard T. Drury, 15 Jun 1971–1 Jun 1972.

Aircraft. T–7, 1949–1951; T–11, 1949–1951; C–46, 1949–1953; C–119, 1952–1953. C–130, 1963–1972; C–7, 1969–1972.

Operations. Performed Reserve troop carrier training under supervision of 2584th Air Force Reserve Training Center, Jun 1949–Apr 1951. Upon entering active duty in Apr 1951, assumed responsibility for operating and maintaining Memphis Muni Aprt and participated in tactical exercises and worldwide airlift. Converted from C–46 to C–119 aircraft in 1952. Replaced by 463d Troop Carrier Wing in Jan 1953. Replaced 64th Troop Carrier Wing in Jan 1963. Until replaced by 463d Tactical Airlift Wing in Jun 1972, performed worldwide tactical airlift and participated in a constant stream of tactical exercises and operations. Frequently deployed squadrons overseas in Europe, the Far East, and the Canal Zone. Conducted C–7 combat crew training in addition to other missions, Aug 1969–May 1972 (for USAF personnel) and Aug–Oct 1971 (for South Vietnamese crews).

Service Streamers. None.

Campaign Streamers. None.

Decorations. Air Force Outstanding Unit Award: 1 Jan 1964–31 Dec 1965.

Emblem. On a shield azure, issuing from sinister in fess, a cloud formation proper, thereover a parachute gules, lines and ropes argent and shaded, carrying a howitzer proper; in dexter chief a small parachute bendwise argent carrying a box of supplies; in sinister chief a small parachute sinister bendwise, carrying an airman argent; all within a diminutive bordure or. (Approved on 5 Jun 1952.)

550th GUIDED MISSILES WING

Lineage. Established as 550th Guided Missiles Wing on 27 Jun 1949. Activated on 20 Jul 1949. Inactivated on 30 Dec 1950.

Assignments. Air Proving Ground, 20 Jul 1949; Long Range Proving Ground Division, 1–30 Dec 1950.

Components. *Squadrons.* 1st Guided Missiles Squadron, Air-to-Surface Missile: attached 20 Jul 1949–31 Jul 1950, assigned 1 Aug–30 Dec 1950 (not operational, 11–30 Dec 1950). 2d Guided Missiles Squadron, Surface-to-Surface Missile: attached 20 Jul 1949–31 Jul 1950, assigned 1 Aug–30 Dec 1950 (not operational, 1 Jun–24 Oct 1950). 3d Guided Missiles Squadron, Interceptor: 1 Aug–30 Dec 1950. 3200th Drone: attached 26 Apr–30 Jun 1950, assigned 1 Jul–1 Dec 1950 (not operational, 20 Sep–1 Dec 1950).

Stations. Eglin AFB, Fla, 20 Jul 1949; Patrick AFB, Fla, 11–30 Dec 1950.

Commanders. Col Thomas J. Gent, Jr., 20 Jul 1949; Col George M. McNeese, 23 Oct–30 Dec 1950.

Aircraft. B–17, 1949–1950; B–29, 1949–1950; T–33, 1950; F–80, 1950; F–86, 1950.

Operations. Replaced 1st Experimental Guided Missiles Group in Jul 1949. Developed tactics and techniques for employment of USAF guided missiles and drone aircraft. Service tested radio-controlled B–17, B–29, and T–33 aircraft. Monitored research and development of several air-to-surface and surface-to-surface guided missiles, including Lark, Matador, GAPA, Falcon, Shrike, Rascal, Snark, and Boojum types. Replaced by 4800th Guided Missile Wing in Dec 1950.

Service Streamers. None.

Campaign Streamers. None.

Decorations. None.

Emblem. None.

551st AIRBORNE EARLY WARNING AND CONTROL WING

Lineage. Established as 551st Airborne Early Warning and Control Wing on 11 Oct 1954. Activated on 18 Dec 1954. Inactivated on 31 Dec 1969.

Assignments. 8th Air Division (Airborne Early Warning and Control), 18 Dec 1954; Eastern Air Defense Force, 1 Jul 1957; 26th Air Division (SAGE), 1 Jul 1959; First Air Force, 1 Apr 1966; 21st Air Division, 4–31 Dec 1969.

Components. *Squadrons.* 960th: 8 Mar 1955–31 Jul 1969. 961st: 18 Dec 1954–31 Dec 1969. 962d: 8 Jul 1955–31 Dec 1969. 966th: 1 Feb 1962–1 May 1963.

Stations. Otis AFB, Mass, 18 Dec 1954–31 Dec 1969.

Commanders. Col Oliver G. Cellini, 18 Dec 1954; Col Arthur A. McCartan, 20 Feb 1956; Col Richard W. DaVania, 17 Jul 1957; Col Ernest J. White, Jr., (by 28) Aug 1959; Col James A. Harwell, (by 30 Jun) 1962; Col Rudolph B. Walters, 31 Jul 1962; Col Raymond K. Gallagher, 10 Aug 1964; Col Wright J. Sherrard, 14 Feb 1966; Col James P. Lyle, 1 Aug 1966; Col John M. Konosky, (by 31) Mar 1967; Col Max W. Rogers, 10

Jun 1967; Lt Col Jesse M. Doyle, (by 30 Jun) 1968; Col Max W. Rogers, (by 31 Dec) 1968–31 Dec 1969.

Aircraft. C–121, 1955–1969; RC–121, 1955–1962; EC–121, 1963–1969.

Operations. Performed airborne early warning and control operations for air defense purposes.

Service Streamers. None.

Campaign Streamers. None.

Decorations. Air Force Outstanding Unit Award: 1 Jul 1957–31 Oct 1958.

Emblem. On a shield argent, two bends sable, on a chief wavy azure a symbol of three radar pulses of the first, the shield bordered with an edge or. *Motto:* VIDERE EST PARAI—To see is to be prepared. (Approved on 22 Dec 1955.)

552d AIRBORNE WARNING AND CONTROL WING

Lineage. Established as 552d Airborne Early Warning and Control Wing on 30 Mar 1955. Activated on 8 Jul 1955. Redesignated 552d Airborne Early Warning and Control Group on 1 Jul 1974. Inactivated on 30 Apr 1976. Redesignated 552d Airborne Warning and Control Wing on 5 May 1976. Activated on 1 Jul 1976.

Assignments. 8th Air Division (Airborne Early Warning and Control), 8 Jul 1955; Western Air Defense Force, 1 Jul 1957; 28th Air Division (SAGE), 1 Jul 1960; Fourth Air Force, 1 Apr 1966; Tenth Air Force, 15 Sep 1969; Aerospace Defense Command, 15 Nov 1969–30 Apr 1976. Tactical Air Command, 1 Jul 1976–.

Components. *Squadrons.* 7th Airborne Command and Control: 1 Oct 1976–. 963d: 8 Jul 1955–30 Apr 1976; 1 Jul 1976–. 964th: 8 Jul 1955–30 Jun 1974; 1 Jul 1977–. 965th: 8 Aug 1955–30 Jun 1971. 966th: 1 May 1963–1 Jul 1969; 15 Nov–31 Dec 1969; 1 Jul 1976–.

Stations. McClellan AFB, Calif, 8 Jul 1955–30 Apr 1976. Tinker AFB, Okla, 1 Jul 1976–.

Commanders. Col Leeman J. Hipson, 8 Jul 1955; Col Richard W. DaVania, (by Dec) 1955; Col Septime S. Richard, Jr., (by Dec) 1956; Col Charles R. Heffner, 18 Oct 1957; Col Charles F. Knierim, 28 May 1959; Col Robert J. Loughry, 17 Oct 1960; Col James P. Lyle, 18 Oct 1963; Col Wright J. Sherrard, 28 Aug 1964; Col William R. Nevitt, 2 Feb 1966; Col Olin E. Gilbert, 31 May 1968; Col Henry L. Timmermans, 1 Nov 1969; Col Robert P. Halpenny, 28 Apr 1972; Col Harold P. Knutty, 26 Jul 1974; Col Francis B. Henkel, 27 Jun 1975–30 Apr 1976. Brig Gen John L. Piotrowski, 1 Jul 1976–.

Aircraft. RC–121, 1955–c. 1959, c. 1961–1963; TC–121, 1959–c. 1961, 1967–1969; EC–121, 1963–1976; C–121, 1967–1976. EC–130, 1976–; WC–135, 1977–; E–3A, 1977–.

Operations. The 552d operated from McClellan AFB, Calif, 1955 until inactivated in 1976. Through its squadrons, detachments and operating locations, it extended air defense radar coverage and fighter control seaward beyond the range of shore-based stations. Late in 1958, the 552d assumed the additional mission of performing gap-filler duty for temporarily inoperative ground radar stations. Tracked ballistic missiles in the Pacific after 1957 and provided support for *Discoverer* and *Mercury* space flight projects. On 11 Aug 1960 wing aircraft vectored and controlled the aircraft that recovered the *Discoverer XIII* capsule. Deployed aircraft and crews to McCoy AFB, Fla, (19 Oct–5 Dec 1962) during the Cuban missile crisis. Operated extensively in Southeast Asia, 1965–1974, as part of the Big (later, College) Eye Task Force. During this time the 552d expanded operations to the eastern coast of the United States and to Iceland. Redesignated as a group on 1 Jul 1974 because of a reduction in components and a reduced mission; remained in this status until inactivated on 30 Apr 1976. Redesignated 552d Airborne Warning and Control Wing, and activated on 1 Jul 1976 at Tinker AFB, Okla, the wing provided worldwide operation of Airborne Warning and Control E–3A aircraft as directed by the Tactical Air Command.

Service Streamers. None.

Campaign Streamers. None.

Decorations. Air Force Outstanding Unit Awards with Combat "V" Device: 1 Jul 1969–30 Jun 1970; 1 Jul 1971–31 Dec 1972. Air Force Outstanding Unit Awards: 1 Jul 1961–30 Jun 1963; 15 Apr 1965–1 Jul 1966; 2 Jul 1966–1 Jul 1968; 1 Jul 1970–30 Jun 1971; 1 Jul 1974–30 Jun 1975. Republic of Vietnam Gallantry Cross with Palm: 1 Apr 1966–28 Jan 1973.

Emblem. Per bend the sky proper and the base field per bend sinister of azure and of argent, a bendlet or between a compass of the third and sable and two lightning flashes issuing from the dexter, points to fess argent, and a silhouetted winged tower sable. *Motto:* ROBUR EX VIGILANTIA—In vigilance is strength. (Approved on 6 Feb 1956.)

553d RECONNAISSANCE WING

Lineage. Established as 553d Reconnaissance Wing, and activated, on 9 Feb 1967. Organized on 25 Feb 1967. Inactivated on 15 Dec 1970.

Assignments. Air Defense Command, 9 Feb 1967; First Air Force, 25 Feb 1967 (attached to Thirteenth Air Force, 19–30 Oct 1967); Thirteenth Air Force (attached to Seventh Air Force), 31 Oct 1967–15 Dec 1970.

Components. *Squadrons.* 553d: 25 Feb 1967–15 Dec 1970 (not operational, 25–28 Feb 1967). 554th: 25 Feb

1967–15 Dec 1970 (not operational, 25–28 Feb 1967).

Stations. Otis AFB, Mass, 25 Feb–Oct 1967; Korat RTAFB, Thailand, 31 Oct 1967–15 Dec 1970.

Commanders. None (not manned), 9–28 Feb 1967; Col Gus Weiser, 1 Mar 1967; Col Henry L. Timmermans, 8 Jul 1968; Col Ted H. Ostendorf, 1 Jul 1969; Col John W. Mitchell, 7 Dec 1969; Col Robert M. Slans, 11–15 Dec 1970.

Aircraft. EC–121, 1967–1970; YQU–22 (drone), 1968–1969; QU–22 (drone), 1970.

Operations. Electronic reconnaissance in Southeast Asia, 25 Nov 1967–15 Dec 1970. A wing detachment provided combat evaluation of YQU–22A drone aircraft and associated equipment from Nakhon Phanom, Thailand, Dec 1968–Aug 1969. Wing operated from U-Tapao, Thailand, 30 Jan–28 Feb 1969. Provided combat evaluation of QU–22B drone aircraft and associated equipment, Jul–Sep 1970.

Service Streamers. None.

Campaign Streamers. Vietnam Air Offensive, Phase II; Vietnam Air Offensive, Phase III; Vietnam Air/Ground; Vietnam Air Offensive, Phase IV; TET 69/Counteroffensive; Vietnam Summer–Fall, 1969; Vietnam Winter–Spring, 1970; Sanctuary Counteroffensive; Southwest Monsoon; Commando Hunt V.

Decorations. Air Force Outstanding Unit Awards with Combat "V" Device: 1 Apr 1967–31 May 1968; 1 Jul 1968–15 Apr 1969. Republic of Vietnam Gallantry Cross with Palm: 1 Apr 1967–15 Dec 1970.

Emblem. Or, in dexter chief a plate over three lightning bolts one in bend and two in saltire celeste charged with the ancient sign for sulpher gules, issuant from base a demi-sphere argent rimmed and gridded sable and overall in pale a batcat proper (azure shaded sable, eyes, teeth, lower lip and claws argent, tongue gules), all within a diminished bordure or. (Approved on 19 Jun 1967.)

580th AIR RESUPPLY AND COMMUNICATIONS WING

Lineage. Established as 580th Air Resupply and Communications Wing on 15 Mar 1951. Activated on 16 Apr 1951. Inactivated on 8 Sep 1953.

Assignments. Air Resupply and Communications Service, 16 Apr 1951; United States Air Forces in Europe, 1 Oct 1952–8 Sep 1953.

Components. *Group.* 580th: 16 Apr 1951–8 Sep 1953 (not operational, 8 Apr 1952–8 Sep 1953). *Squadron.* 580th: attached 8 Apr 1952–8 Sep 1953.

Stations. Mountain Home AFB, Idaho, 16 Apr 1951–17 Sep 1952; Wheelus Field, Libya, 22 Sep 1952–8 Sep 1953.

Commanders. Col William O. Eareckson, 16 Apr 1951; Col John R. Kane, 12 Nov 1951; Col Frederick J. Knorre,

Jr., 8 May 1952; Col John R. Kane, 2 Jun 1952; Col Frederick J. Knorre, Jr., 18 May 1953; Col Vincent M. Miles, 27 May–8 Sep 1953.

Aircraft. C–119, 1951–1953; B–29, 1951–1953; SA–16, 1951–1953; C–47, 1953.

Operations. Performed psychological warfare and unconventional operations.

Service Streamers. None.

Campaign Streamers. None.

Decorations. None.

Emblem. Quarterly, first and fourth, or, a stylized aircraft sable, nose to dexter; second and third, azure, a horse's head couped or; on a chief, gules over a wreath of two branches of olive, a sword in fess, all or. *Motto:* LIBERTAS PER VERITATEM—Freedom through truth. (Approved on 8 Nov 1951.)

581st AIR RESUPPLY AND COMMUNICATIONS WING

Lineage. Established as 581st Air Resupply and Communications Wing on 9 Jul 1951. Activated on 23 Jul 1951. Inactivated on 8 Sep 1953.

Assignments. Air Resupply and Communications Service, 23 Jul 1951; Thirteenth Air Force, 18 Jul 1952–8 Sep 1953.

Components. *Group.* 581st: 23 Jul 1951–8 Sep 1953 (not operational, 17 Apr 1952–8 Sep 1953). *Squadron.* 581st: attached 17 Apr 1952–8 Sep 1953.

Stations. Mountain Home AFB, Idaho, 23 Jul 1951–26 Jun 1952; Clark AB, Philippines, 18 Jul 1952–8 Sep 1953.

Commanders. Lt Col Rupert E. Herr, 23 Jul 1951; Col John K. Arnold, Jr., 1 Aug 1951; Maj John F. Zinn, 10 Aug 1951; Lt Col George H. Pittman, Jr., 31 Aug 1951; Col John K. Arnold, Jr., 1 Oct 1951; Col Lawrence C. Gilbert, 16 Jan 1952; Col John K. Arnold, Jr., c. 18 Feb 1952; Col Lawrence C. Gilbert, 12 Jan–8 Sep 1953.

Aircraft. C–119, 1951–1953; B–29, 1951–1953; SA–16, 1951–1953; H–19, 1952–1953; C–54, 1952; C–118, 1952–1953.

Operations. Performed psychological warfare and unconventional operations. Conducted limited operations in French Indo-China in 1953.

Service Streamers. None.

Campaign Streamers. None.

Decorations. None.

Emblem. On a shield azure, a torch, base argent, flame or, flame moving toward the dexter, over the flame a quill argent bend sinister, all between three links of a chain sable, the center link couped, with one and one-half links on each side of the torch; on a chief gules two branches, of olive, surmounted by a sword in fess, hilt and pommel to the dexter, all or. *Motto:* LIBERTAS PER VERITATEM—Freedom through truth. (Approved on 12 Jun 1952.)

582d AIR RESUPPLY AND COMMUNICATIONS WING

Lineage. Established as 582d Air Resupply and Communications Wing on 3 Sep 1952. Activated on 24 Sep 1952. Inactivated on 14 Aug 1953.

Assignments. Air Resupply and Communications Service, 24 Sep 1952–14 Aug 1953.

Components. *Group.* 582d: 24 Sep 1952–14 Aug 1953 (not operational). *Squadron.* 582d: attached 20 May–14 Aug 1953.

Stations. Mountain Home AFB, Idaho, 24 Sep 1952; Great Falls AFB, Mont, 1 May–14 Aug 1953.

Commanders. Col Robert W. Fish, 24 Sep 1952; Col Earl J. Livesay, 8 Jul–14 Aug 1953.

Aircraft. C–119, 1953; B–29, 1953; SA–16, 1953.

Operations. Performed psychological warfare and unconventional operations.

Service Streamers. None.

Campaign Streamers. None.

Decorations. None.

Emblem. Per fess indented or and azure, the silhouette of a transport plane sable and in base a broken chain of three links proper below two lightning bolts points conjoined argent, on a chief gules a wreath surmounted by a sword fesswise, hilt to dexter both of the first. *Motto:* LIBERTAS PER VERITATEM—Freedom through truth. (Approved on 14 Apr 1953.)

633d SPECIAL OPERATIONS WING

Lineage. Established as 633d Special Operations Wing, and activated, on 9 Jul 1968. Organized on 15 Jul 1968. Inactivated on 15 Mar 1970.

Assignments. Pacific Air Forces, 9 Jul 1968; Seventh Air Force, 15 Jul 1968–15 Mar 1970.

Components. *Squadron.* 6th: 15 Jul 1968–15 Nov 1969.

Stations. Pleiku AB, South Vietnam, 15 Jul 1968–15 Mar 1970.

Commanders. None (not manned), 9–14 Jul 1968; Col George P. Birdsong, Jr., 15 Jul 1968; Col Samuel D. Berman, 25 Apr 1969–15 Mar 1970.

Aircraft. A–1, 1968–1969.

Operations. Engaged in combat in Southeast Asia, including close air support, air escort, day and night interdiction, and visual and photographic reconnaissance, Jul 1968–Nov 1969.

Service Streamers. None.

Campaign Streamers. Vietnam Air Offensive, Phase III; Vietnam Air/Ground; Vietnam Air Offensive, Phase IV; TET 69/Counteroffensive; Vietnam Summer-Fall, 1969; Vietnam Winter-Spring, 1970.

Decorations. Air Force Outstanding Unit Award with Combat "V" Device: 15 Jul 1968–31 May 1969. Republic of Vietnam Gallantry Cross with Palm: 15 Jul 1968–15 Mar 1970.

Emblem. Per fess nebuly gules and azure fimbriated or in base six lightning flashes radiating fesswise three to dexter and three to sinister argent surmounted by a tiger's paw affronte couped proper, overall a crossbow purpure fitted with an arrow in pale point to base of the first, all within a diminished bordure or. *Motto:* ATTACK. (Approved on 29 May 1969.)

656th SPECIAL OPERATIONS WING

Lineage. Established as 656th Special Operations Wing on 14 May 1975. Activated on 30 Jun 1975. Inactivated on 22 Sep 1975.

Assignments. Thirteenth Air Force, 30 Jun 1975; 17th Air Division, 1 Jul–22 Sep 1975.

Components. *Squadrons.* 21st: attached 30 Jun–22 Sep 1975. 23d Tactical Air Support: attached 30 Jun–22 Sep 1975.

Stations. Nakhon Phanom Aprt, Thailand, 30 Jun–22 Sep 1975.

Commanders. Col Robert D. Janca, 30 Jun–22 Sep 1975.

Aircraft. CH–53, 1975; OV–10, 1975.

Operations. Formed to absorb resources left following movement of 56th Special Operations Wing. Charged with closing U.S. portion of Nakhon Phanom and, with attached squadrons, certain contingency operations.

Service Streamers. None.

Campaign Streamers. None.

Decorations. None.

Emblem. None.

701st TACTICAL MISSILE WING

Lineage. Established as 701st Tactical Missile Wing on 3 Aug 1956. Activated on 15 Sep 1956. Inactivated on 18 Jun 1958.

Assignments. Twelfth Air Force, 15 Sep 1956; United States Air Forces in Europe, 1 Jan–18 Jun 1958.

Components. *Groups.* 585th: 15 Sep 1956–18 Jun 1958. 586th: 15 Sep 1956–18 Jun 1958. 587th: 15 Sep 1956–18 Jun 1958.

Stations. Hahn AB, West Germany, 15 Sep 1956–18 Jun 1958.

Commanders. Lt Col Robert F. Zachman, 15 Sep 1956; Col Theodore H. Runyon, 7 Jan 1957–18 Jun 1958.

Missiles. Matador, 1956–1958.

Operations. First tactical missile wing of the U.S. Air Force, comprised of three groups, each with three squadrons.

Service Streamers. None.

Campaign Streamers. None.

Decorations. Air Force Outstanding Unit Award: 15 Sep 1956–30 Apr 1958.

Emblem. A shield quartered: first and fourth quarters, or, on a bend azure an arrow of the first in bend; second quarter, azure a griffin segreant or, langued gules; third quarter, azure a torch in pale, flamed, between two branches of olive or; on an escutcheon of pretence gules an astral crown or. *Motto:* VALOR WITH PROGRESS. (Approved on 20 Jun 1957.)

702d STRATEGIC MISSILE WING (ICM–SNARK)

Lineage. Established as 702d Strategic Missile Wing (ICM–Snark) on 17 Jun 1958. Activated on 1 Jan 1959. Discontinued, and inactivated, on 25 Jun 1961.

Assignments. 45th Air Division, 1 Jan 1959–25 Jun 1961.

Components. *Squadron.* 556th: 1 Apr–16 Jul 1959.

Stations. Presque Isle AFB, Maine, 1 Jan 1959–25 Jun 1961.

Commanders. Lt Col Harry W. Robb, 1 Jan 1959; Col Richard W. Beck, 15 Apr 1959; Col Roger A. Stevenson, 22 May–25 Jun 1961.

Missiles. Snark, 1959–1961.

Operations. Performed Snark intercontinental missile test operations from Patrick AFB, Fla, Apr–Jul 1959, and from Atlantic Missile Range, Cape Canaveral, Fla, c. Dec 1959–Jun 1961. Was only Snark missile wing in USAF. Briefly controlled a missile squadron at Patrick AFB in 1959, and later a detachment at the same base.

Service Streamers. None.

Campaign Streamers. None.

Decorations. None.

Emblem. Azure, in base a demi-sphere light blue segmented by six arcs throughout argent, saltirewise overall issuant from sinister base a missile of the last with jet trail gules and from dexter base arras-wise a cubit arm proper grasping a sword of the third; in center chief a mullet of the like, all within a diminished bordure or. *Motto:* READY, ABLE. (Approved on 15 Feb 1961.)

703d STRATEGIC MISSILE WING (ICBM-TITAN)

Lineage. Established as 703d Strategic Missile Wing (ICBM-Titan) on 5 Sep 1958. Activated on 25 Sep 1958. Discontinued, and inactivated, on 1 Jul 1961.

Assignments. 1st Missile Division, 25 Sep 1958; Fifteenth Air Force, 15 Jan

1959; 13th Air Division, 1 Jul 1959–1 Jul 1961.

Components. *Squadrons.* 848th: 1 Feb 1960–1 Jul 1961. 849th: 1 Aug 1960–1 Jul 1961.

Stations. Lowry AFB, Colo, 25 Sep 1958–1 Jul 1961.

Commanders. 1st Lt William M. McCormick, Jr., 25 Sep 1958 (acting); Lt Col John B. Howard, 11 Dec 1958; Maj Norman W. Bashant, 20 Dec 1958; Col John C. Fahringer, 3 Jan 1959; Col John P. Proctor, 10 Aug 1959–1 Jul 1961.

Missiles. None.

Operations. Not operational to c. 10 Dec 1958 and only partially operational from then to Mar 1960. Replaced by 451st SMW (ICBM-Titan) in Jul 1961 before becoming fully operational.

Service Streamers. None.

Campaign Streamers. None.

Decorations. None.

Emblem. None.

704th STRATEGIC MISSILE WING (ICBM)

Lineage. Established as 704th Strategic Missile Wing on 20 May 1957. Activated on 1 Jul 1957. Redesignated 704th Strategic Missile Wing (ICBM) on 1 Apr 1958. Inactivated on 1 Jul 1959.

Assignments. Air Research and Development Command, 1 Jul 1957 (attached to Air Force Ballistic Missile Division, 1–31 Jul 1957); 1st Missile Division, 1 Aug 1957–1 Jul 1959.

Components. *Squadrons.* 576th: 1 Apr 1958–1 Jul 1959 (detached 6 Apr–1 Jul 1959). 644th: 15 Jan–1 Jul 1959 (detached 6 Apr–1 Jul 1959). 672d: 1 Jan–20 May 1958. 864th: 23 Feb 1958–1 Jul 1959 (detached 1 Nov 1958–1 Jul 1959). 865th: 1 Jul 1958–1 Jul 1959 (detached 1 Nov 1958–1 Jul 1959). 866th: 1 Sep 1958–1 Jul 1959 (detached 1 Nov 1958–1 Jul 1959).

Stations. Cooke (later, Vandenberg) AFB, Calif, 1 Jul 1957–1 Jul 1959.

Commanders. Col Francis B. Howes, Jr., 1 Jul 1957 (acting); Col David K. Lyster, Jr., 16 Jul 1957 (additional duty); Col William S. Rader, 26 Aug 1957 (additional duty); Col David K. Lyster, Jr., 27 Aug 1957 (additional duty); Col William S. Rader, 20 Sep 1957 (additional duty), 13 Nov 1957–5 Apr 1959 (permanent), and 6 Apr 1959–unkn (additional duty); unkn, c. 10 Jun–1 Jul 1959.

Missiles. Atlas, 1958–1959; Jupiter, 1958; Thor, 1958–1959; Titan, 1959.

Operations. Not operational, 1 Jul–12 Nov 1957. Training of ICBM and IRBM units, Nov 1957–Apr 1959. Not operational, 6 Apr–1 Jul 1959.

Service Streamers. None.

Campaign Streamers. None.

Decorations. None.

Emblem. Per fess enhanced azure and light blue, the chief strewn with stars argent, between two clouds issuant one from sinister chief the other from dexter base of the last and issuant bendwise from sinister base a demi-sphere with grid lines of the first, land masses brown and seas of the third with overall a torch or enflamed proper between two lightning flashes radiant from its base gules, in bend a missile with enflamed trail of the fifth and surmounted in chief by a segment of a star overall of the third, all within a diminished bordure of the last. *Motto:* LEADERSHIP–KNOWLEDGE–DYNAMIC APPLICATION. (Approved on 26 Jun 1958.)

705th STRATEGIC MISSILE WING (IRBM-THOR)

Lineage. Established as 705th Strategic Missile Wing on 6 Feb 1958. Activated on 20 Feb 1958. Redesignated 705th Strategic Missile Wing (IRBM-Thor) on 1 Apr 1958. Discontinued on 1 Apr 1960.

Assignments. 7th Air Division, 20 Feb 1958–1 Apr 1960; Department of the Air Force, 1 Apr 1960–.

Components. None.

Stations. RAF Lakenheath, England, 20 Feb 1958; USAB South Ruislip (later, South Ruislip Air Station), England, 15 Mar 1958–1 Apr 1960.

Commanders. None, 20 Feb 1958; Col William R. Yancey, 18 Mar–10 Nov 1958 (additional duty); unkn, 11 Nov 1958–1 Apr 1960.

Missiles. None.

Operations. Wing never became operational and was manned only by additional-duty personnel of 7th Air Division.

Service Streamers. None.

Campaign Streamers. None.

Decorations. None.

Emblem. None.

706th STRATEGIC MISSILE WING (ICBM-ATLAS)

Lineage. Established as 706th Strategic Missile Wing on 13 Feb 1958. Activated on 23 Feb 1958. Redesignated 706th Strategic Missile Wing (ICBM-Atlas) on 1 Apr 1958. Discontinued, and inactivated, on 1 Jul 1961.

Assignments. 1st Missile Division, 23 Feb 1958; Fifteenth Air Force, 15 Jan 1959; 13th Air Division, 1 Jul 1959–1 Jul 1961.

Components. *Squadrons.* 549th: 1 Oct 1960–1 Jul 1961. 564th: 1 Jul 1958–1 Jul 1961 (not operational, 1 Jul 1958–30 Jan 1959). 565th: 1 Dec 1958–1 Jul 1961 (not operational, 1 Dec 1958–30 Jan 1959).

Stations. Francis E. Warren AFB, Wyo, 23 Feb 1958–1 Jul 1961.

Commanders. Col Hilbert F. Muenter, 23 Feb 1958; Brig Gen William R. Large, Jr., 15 Jan 1959; Col William S. Rader, 10 Jun 1959 (permanent) and 1 Jul 1959 (additional duty); Col George T. Chadwell, 24 Aug 1959–1 Jul 1961.

Missiles. Atlas, 1960–1961.

Operations. Replaced 4320th Strategic Wing (Missile) in Feb 1958. Accepted first two missile complexes in Aug 1960, gaining initial operational capability. Replaced by 389th SMW (ICBM–Atlas) in Jul 1961.

Service Streamers. None.

Campaign Streamers. None.

Decorations. None.

Emblem. Azure, issuing from base to dexter chief throughout a cloud argent bearing in bend a ribbon of the first semee of mullets of the second surmounted by a globe or bearing lines of longitude and latitude dark blue, overall in pale a missile of the like front fins gules emitting to base three flashes of the last both globe and missile spiralled from dexter base to sinister chief by an olive branch proper. (Approved on 14 Oct 1958.)

APPENDICES

Appendix I

Lineage Terms

Each unit and establishment of the Air Force possesses a separate identity, its own lineage and history. The War Department and, later, the Department of the Air Force have sought to preserve these separate organizational identities. In recent years, however, the Department of the Air Force introduced two changes in this basic policy. In a major adjustment, the service temporarily bestowed, under certain conditions, the history and honors of combat groups on similarly numbered combat wings. This practice began in 1954 and continues today. A second, minor adjustment substituted the Table of Organization (T/O) units and establishments created in 1948 for the Table of Distribution (T/D) organizations used in the 1947–1948 service test of the wing-base plan.* This volume treats these initial T/D and subsequent T/O organizations as single entities instead of separate establishments and units.

Between 1947 and 1977 the Air Force was composed of primary elements called units and establishments. The units divide among three primary categories: *squadrons* (later, the numbered flight was added as a "small" squadron), *miscellaneous* (a category including such organizations as bands, infirmaries, hospitals, etc.), and *headquarters*. The headquarters units served as headquarters for establishments. Establishments are Air Force organizations at group echelon or higher, having a headquarters unit as their primary component.

Headquarters units were "designated and organized" for the wings included in the 1947–1948 service test of the wing-base plan, and discontinued when the service test concluded in 1948. Headquarters units for the wings subsequently were "constituted and activated" (1948–1959 and 1968–current), or were "constituted, activated, and organized" (1959–1968). The units were "inactivated" (1948–1959 and 1968–current), or "discontinued and inactivated" (1959–1968),

*Details of this service test appear in the introduction to this volume.

when no longer needed. The establishments to which the headquarters units belonged, however, were "established" concurrently with the designation or constitution of their headquarters unit. If the Air Force disbanded a wing's headquarters unit (example: see 24th Composite Wing), the wing was "disestablished," and, when the headquarters unit was reconstituted, the wing was "reestablished." Otherwise, the lineage terms for establishments parallel those of the units.

The lineage of each wing establishment contained in this book is ultimately determined by the language employed in the War Department and Department of the Air Force letters and command orders relating to organizational actions. The following glossary defines the more important terms that appear in the lineage and honors histories.

Glossary of Terms

Activate. To bring into physical existence by assignment of personnel to the headquarters unit (from 1922 to 1959, and again after 1968). An establishment is activated when its headquarters unit is activated. During the period 1959–1968, however, activate meant to place on the active list, available to be organized.

Assign. To place in a military organization, as a permanent element or component of that organization.

Attach. To place one military organization temporarily with another for operational control and other purposes, including administration and logistical support.

Consolidate. To combine or merge one establishment with another, so that the lineage and history of both become one. Establishments are consolidated effective with the consolidation of their headquarters units. Consolidation can only occur when the establishments involved were active at different times. (Example: see 26th Tactical Reconnaissance Wing.)

Designation. The name of a unit or establishment. The designation includes all parts of the name: numerical, functional, and generic. A designation also applies to named activities and certain functions. To further identify a unit, descriptive words are sometimes added parenthetically. Such words are not a part of the official designation, but are used to clarify the official designation.

Discontinue. To withdraw all personnel from the headquarters unit (1959–1968). This action placed the establishment and its headquarters unit on the inactive list for those wings involved in the 1947–1948 service test of the wing-base plan.

Disestablish. To terminate an establishment concurrent with disbandment of its headquarters unit, until reestablished.

Establish. To assign a designation concurrent with the designation (1947–1948) or the constitution (1922–1947 and 1948–current) of the headquarters unit.

Establishment. A military organization at group or higher echelon, composed of a headquarters unit and any other elements that might be assigned. Personnel are not assigned to an establishment, but to its components.

Inactivate. To withdraw all personnel from the headquarters unit and place the establishment and its headquarters unit on the inactive list (from 1922 to 1959 and from 1968 to date). During the period 1959–1968, however, to be inactivated meant to be transferred from the active to the inactive list, after being discontinued.

Order to Active Service. Reserve establishments are ordered to active service from Reserve status for a period of extended active duty with the regular Air Force.

Organization. As used in this volume, the term organization applies to units and establishments.

Organize. To assign personnel to the headquarters unit (1947–1948 service test organizations). During the period 1959–1968, being organized also involved the assignment of personnel to the headquarters unit, after the headquarters unit and the establishment were activated.

Redesignate. To change the designation (number or number and name) of both the establishment and its headquarters unit.

Reestablish. To return a previously existing establishment from disestablished status to the active list, so it can be activated.

Relieve from Active Duty. Reserve units are relieved from active duty with the regular Air Force upon completion of a period of extended active duty.

Appendix II

Streamers

SERVICE STREAMERS

World War II

American Theater: 7 Dec 1941–2 Mar 1946.

European-African-Middle Eastern (EAME) Theater: 7 Dec 1941–8 Nov 1945.

Asiatic-Pacific Theater: 7 Dec 1941–2 Mar 1946.

Korean War

Korean Theater: 27 Jun 1950–27 Jul 1953.

Vietnam

Vietnam Theater: 1 Jul 1958–14 Nov 1961.

CAMPAIGN STREAMERS

World War II

American Theater:

Antisubmarine: 7 Dec 1941–2 Sep 1945.

EAME Theater:

Air Combat: 7 Dec 1941–11 May 1945.

Antisubmarine: 7 Dec 1941–2 Sep 1945.

Egypt-Libya: 11 Jun 1942–12 Feb 1943.

Air Offensive, Europe: 4 Jul 1942–5 Jun 1944.

Algeria-French Morocco: 8–11 Nov 1942.

Tunisia: 12 Nov 1942–13 May 1943.

Sicily: 14 May–17 Aug 1943.
Naples-Foggia: 18 Aug 1943–21 Jan 1944.
Anzio: 22 Jan–24 May 1944.
Rome-Arno: 22 Jan–9 Sep 1944.
Normandy: 6 Jun–24 Jul 1944.
Northern France: 25 Jul–14 Sep 1944.
Southern France: 15 Aug–14 Sep 1944.
North Apennines: 10 Sep 1944–4 Apr 1945.
Rhineland: 15 Sep 1944–21 Mar 1945.
Ardennes-Alsace: 16 Dec 1944–25 Jan 1945.
Central Europe: 22 Mar–11 May 1945.
Po Valley: 5 Apr–8 May 1945.

Asiatic-Pacific Theater:

Air Combat: 7 Dec 1941–2 Sep 1945.
Antisubmarine: 7 Dec 1941–2 Sep 1945.
Central Pacific: 7 Dec 1941–6 Dec 1943.
Philippine Islands: 7 Dec 1941–10 May 1942.
Burma: 7 Dec 1941–26 May 1942.
East Indies: 1 Jan–22 Jul 1942.
India-Burma: 2 Apr 1942–28 Jan 1945.
Air Offensive, Japan: 17 Apr 1942–2 Sep 1945.
Aleutian Islands: 3 Jun 1942–24 Aug 1943.
China Defensive: 4 Jul 1942–4 May 1945.
Papua: 23 Jul 1942–23 Jan 1943.
Guadalcanal: 7 Aug 1942–21 Feb 1943.
New Guinea: 24 Jan 1943–31 Dec 1944.
Northern Solomons: 23 Feb 1943–21 Nov 1944.
Eastern Mandates: 7 Dec 1943–16 Apr 1944.
Bismarck Archipelago: 15 Dec 1943–27 Nov 1944.
Western Pacific: 17 Apr 1944–2 Sep 1945.
Leyte: 17 Oct 1944–1 Jul 1945.
Luzon: 15 Dec 1944–4 Jul 1945.
Central Burma: 29 Jan–15 Jul 1945.
Southern Philippines: 27 Feb–4 Jul 1945.
Ryukyus: 26 Mar–2 Jul 1945.
China Offensive: 5 May–2 Sep 1945.

APPENDIX II

Korean War

United Nations Defensive: 27 Jun–15 Sep 1950.

United Nations Offensive: 16 Sep–2 Nov 1950.

Chinese Communist Forces Intervention: 3 Nov 1950–24 Jan 1951.

First United Nations Counteroffensive: 25 Jan–21 Apr 1951.

Chinese Communist Forces Spring Offensive: 22 Apr–8 Jul 1951.

United Nations Summer–Fall Offensive: 9 Jul–27 Nov 1951.

Second Korean Winter: 28 Nov 1951–30 Apr 1952.

Korea Summer–Fall, 1952: 1 May–30 Nov 1952.

Third Korean Winter: 1 Dec 1952–30 Apr 1953.

Korea Summer–Fall, 1953: 1 May–27 Jul 1953.

Vietnam War

Vietnam Advisory: 15 Nov 1961–1 Mar 1965.

Vietnam Defense: 2 Mar 1965–30 Jan 1966.

Vietnam Air: 31 Jan–28 Jun 1966.

Vietnam Air Offensive: 29 Jun 1966–8 Mar 1967.

Vietnam Air Offensive, Phase II: 9 Mar 1967–31 Mar 1968.

Vietnam Air/Ground: 22 Jan–7 Jul 1968.

Vietnam Air Offensive, Phase III: 1 Apr–31 Oct 1968.

Vietnam Air Offensive, Phase IV: 1 Nov 1968–22 Feb 1969.

TET 69/Counteroffensive: 23 Feb–8 Jun 1969.

Vietnam Summer–Fall, 1969: 9 Jun–31 Oct 1969.

Vietnam Winter–Spring, 1970: 1 Nov 1969–30 Apr 1970.

Sanctuary Counteroffensive: 1 May–30 Jun 1970.

Southwest Monsoon: 1 Jul–30 Nov 1970.

Commando Hunt V: 1 Dec 1970–14 May 1971.

Commando Hunt VI: 15 May–31 Oct 1971.

Commando Hunt VII: 1 Nov 1971–29 Mar 1972.

Vietnam Ceasefire: 30 Mar 1972–28 Jan 1973.

Appendix III

Unit Decorations

AMERICAN

Distinguished Unit Citation (DUC).

Used by the U.S. Army and Army Air Forces. First established by Executive Order 9075 on 26 Feb 1942, awarded for extraordinary valor in action on or after 7 Dec 1941.

Presidential Unit Citation (PUC).

Equivalent to the Distinguished Unit Citation. The PUC is used by the U.S. Navy and was awarded to a number of AAF units that operated under Navy control or in close support of the Navy. After 1965, the U.S. Air Force adopted the Presidential Unit Citation instead of the Distinguished Unit Citation to recognize outstanding combat performance of its tactical units.

Air Force Outstanding Unit Award with Combat "V" Device (AFOUA/V).

The AFOUA/V is awarded in lieu of the AFOUA (below) to recognize achievement in combat by USAF units and establishments. The Combat "V" Device was first used during the conflict in Southeast Asia.

Air Force Outstanding Unit Award (AFOUA).

A relatively new USAF decoration used to recognize outstanding efforts and meritorious actions of USAF units and establishments in peace and war, the AFOUA was announced in Department of the Air Force General Orders No. 1 on 6 Jan 1954. (Several units and establishments received this award retroactively, for meritorious actions during the Korean war.)

Meritorious Unit Commendation (MUC).

The U.S. Army's Meritorious Unit Commendation, roughly equivalent to the AFOUA (above), has been earned by a number of AAF and USAF units. This decoration recognizes outstanding and meritorious actions in both peace and war, but these actions are considered to be of a lesser consequence than those recognized by a Distinguished Unit Citation (above).

Navy Unit Commendation (NUC).

The U.S. Navy Unit Commendation, also roughly equivalent to the AFOUA (above), has been awarded to a few AAF and USAF units which worked closely with the Navy. The award recognizes outstanding and meritorious actions in both peace and war, but these actions are considered to be of a lesser consequence than those recognized by a Presidential Unit Citation (above).

FOREIGN

Belgium.

Citation in the Order of the Day, Belgian Army.

A citation by decree of the Belgian Government. Numerous AAF units and establishments which operated in or over Belgium during World War II received this award.

Belgian Fourragere.

A decoration awarded, by decree of the Belgian Government, to units cited twice in the Order of the Day, Belgian Army.

France.

Croix de Guerre.

A citation by decree of the French Government, awarded to Army Air Forces units and establishments. Generally identified as French Croix de Guerre with Palm.

French Fourragere.

A decoration, awarded by decree of the French Government, to units and establishments cited twice for the Croix de Guerre.

Korea.

Republic of Korea Presidential Unit Citation.

A citation for achievement during the Korean war. Most commonly presented to units based in Korea and carrying out combat operations there, but also awarded to some units, both combat and support types, based in adjacent areas. Since the cessation of hostilities in Korea in July 1953, this decoration has been awarded rarely to USAF units and establishments, usually in recognition of outstanding support in the defense of Korea.

Philippines.

Philippine Presidential Unit Citation.

A citation for achievement while serving in the Philippines during the periods 7 Dec 1941–10 May 1942 or 17 Oct 1944–4 Jul 1945. No date is connected with the citation. Only one award is authorized for every eligible unit, including units which served in the Philippines during both periods.

Philippine Republic Presidential Unit Citation.

A number of USAF units stationed in the Republic of the Philippines in July and August 1972 earned this citation in recognition of their participation in disaster relief operations.

Vietnam.

Republic of Vietnam Gallantry Cross with Palm.

This unit decoration was usually awarded to units and establishments actually engaged in combat in defense of the Republic of Vietnam, but in numerous instances it was also awarded to combat support organizations and tactical units that were based outside the Vietnam Theater yet flew missions to the theater or provided essential services to organizations flying to or operating within the theater.

Appendix IV

Abbreviations

The following glossary of abbreviations used in the volume does not include many standard abbreviations, such as those for the months of the year or names of the states.

AAA	antiaircraft artillery
AAB	Army Air Base
AAC	Alaskan Air Command
AAF	Army Air Forces
AAFld	Army Air Field
AB	Air Base
ABG	Air Base Group
ABW	Air Base Wing
AC&CS	Airborne Command and Control Squadron
ADC	Air Defense Command (see also, ADCOM)
ADCOM	Air (later, Aerospace) Defense Command (see also, ADC)
addn	additional
ADVON	advanced echelon
AEMS	Armament and Electronics Maintenance Squadron
AF	Air Force
AFB	Air Force Base
AFCON	Air Force-controlled
afld	airfield
AFNORTH	Air Force North (a NATO component)
AFOMO	Air Force Office of Manpower and Organization
AFOUA	Air Force Outstanding Unit Award
AFRTC	Air Force Reserve Training Center
AFS	Air Force Station
AFSC	Air Force Systems Command
ALCS	Airborne Launch Control System
ANG	Air National Guard
Aprt	Airport
ARADCOM	Army Air Defense Command
ARFC	Air Reserve Flying Center
ART	Air Reserve Technician
AS	Air Station
AWADS	Adverse Weather Aerial Delivery System

BMEWS	Ballistic Missile Early Warning System
Brig Gen	Brigadier General
c.	*circa* (about, or approximately)
Capt	Captain
CCF	Chinese Communist Forces (Korean war)
CCTS	Combat Crew Training Squadron
CCTW	Combat Crew Training Wing
CINCPAC	Commander in Chief, Pacific Command
CINCPACAF	Commander in Chief, Pacific Air Forces
CINCSAC	Commander in Chief, Strategic Air Command
CINCUSAFE	Commander in Chief, United States Air Forces in Europe
Col	Colonel
CONAD	Continental Air Defense Command
CSG	Combat Support Group
CZ	Canal Zone (in Panama)
DAF	Department of the Air Force
Det	detachment
DEW	Distant Early Warning
DOD	Department of Defense
DUC	Distinguished Unit Citation
dy	duty
EAME	European-African-Middle Eastern
ECM	Electronic Countermeasures
ETO	European Theater of Operations
FAC	Forward Air Control(ler)
FBG	Fighter Bomber Group
FEAF	Far East Air Forces (later named PACAF)
FICON	Fighter-Interceptor Carrier, Reconnaissance
1st Lt	First Lieutenant
FMS	Field Maintenance Squadron
Ft	Fort
FTW	Flying Training Wing
HQ	Headquarters
IBC	Iceland Base Command
ICBM	intercontinental ballistic missile
ICM	intercontinental missile (i.e., the Snark)
Intl	International
IRBM	intermediate range ballistic missile
Lt Col	Lieutenant Colonel
MAC	Military Airlift Command (earlier called MATS)
Maj	Major
Maj Gen	Major General
MAJCON	major command-controlled
MATS	Military Air Transport Service (later called MAC)
MAW	Military Airlift Wing
MiG	Soviet fighter aircraft named for its designers, Arten Mikovan and Mikhail Gurevich
MMS	Munitions Maintenance Squadron

mph	miles per hour
MTO	Mediterranean Theater of Operations
MUC	Meritorious Unit Commendation
Muni	Municipal
NAS	Naval Air Station
NATO	North Atlantic Treaty Organization
NEACP	National Emergency Airborne Command Post
NORAD	North American Air Defense Command
NUC	Navy Unit Commendation
OMS	Organizational Maintenance Squadron
PACAF	Pacific Air Forces (earlier called FEAF)
PACCS	Post Attack Command and Control System
POMO	Production Oriented Maintenance Organization
POW	Prisoner(s) of War
PR	Puerto Rico
PUC	Presidential Unit Citation
RAAF	Royal Australian Air Force
RAF	Royal Air Force (of Great Britain)
RS	Reconnaissance Squadron
RTAFB	Royal Thai(land) Air Force Base
SAC	Strategic Air Command
SAGE	semi-automatic ground environment
2d Lt	Second Lieutenant
SMS	Strategic Missile Squadron
SMW	Strategic Missile Wing
SOS	Special Operations Squadron
SRS	Strategic Reconnaissance Squadron
SRW	Strategic Reconnaissance Wing
SW	Strategic Wing
TAC	Tactical Air Command
TAS	Tactical Airlift Squadron
TASS	Tactical Air Support Squadron
TAW	Tactical Airlift Wing
TCG	Troop Carrier Group
TCW	Troop Carrier Wing
T/D	Table of Distribution
TEWS	Tactical Electronic Warfare Squadron
TFS	Tactical Fighter Squadron
TFTS	Tactical Fighter Training Squadron
TFTW	Tactical Fighter Training Wing
TFW	Tactical Fighter Wing
TH	Territory of Hawaii (state of Hawaii after 1959)
T/O	Table of Organization
TRS	Tactical Reconnaissance Squadron
TRW	Tactical Reconnaissance Wing
TTS	Tactical Training Squadron

UN	United Nations
unkn	unknown
U.S.	United States (of America)
USAB	United States Air Base
USAF	United States Air Force
USAFE	United States Air Forces in Europe
USARPAC	United States Army, Pacific
USMC	United States Marine Corps
USN	United States Navy
USNAS	United States Naval Air Station
VA	Veterans Administration
VHB	Very Heavy Bombardment
VIP	very important person(s)
VNAF	Vietnamese Air Force

Appendix V

USAF Bestowed History*

During World War II, combat squadrons were normally organized into combat groups, with three or four squadrons in each group, the group serving as the basic combat element of the Air Force. In many commands, although the practice was not uniform throughout the Air Force, two or more combat groups formed a wing for administrative or operational control (see *Air Force Combat Units of World War II, passim.*).

This organization changed in 1947 when the Air Force adopted the wing-base plan. Each combat wing was given one combat group (with three or four combat squadrons) and three support groups (air base, supply and maintenance, and medical). The wings required by this plan were new organizations, the old World War II wings being redesignated divisions (see wing histories in *Air Force Combat Units of World War II*). The combat wing and its integral combat group carried the same numerical and functional designations; for example, the 9th Bombardment Group was an integral part of the 9th Bombardment Wing.

In February 1951 the Strategic Air Command (SAC) began to eliminate its combat groups by reducing group headquarters to token strength (one officer and one enlisted man) and attaching the combat squadrons directly to the wings. Thus, the wing replaced the group as the basic combat element of SAC. On 16 June 1952, with the approval of Headquarters USAF, Headquarters SAC inactivated the headquarters of all combat groups (that had remained active under token manning) and assigned the remaining combat squadrons to the wings. The SAC reorganization also retired the World War II histories and honors of SAC's combat groups, while the SAC wings, having been created during or after 1947, possessed no World War II histories or honors.

---

*This appendix is based on Attachment 1 (Wing-Group Relations, Inheritance of History and Honors) to Air Force Pamphlet 210–2, Guide to Lineage and Unit History, 2 Jun 1975.

Deviations from the wing-base plan by other commands, particularly Air Defense Command (ADC), also affected the perpetuation of histories and honors of World War II groups. In 1954 SAC and ADC leaders asked Headquarters USAF to perpetuate the histories and honors of the World War II combat groups. The *ad hoc* committee which reviewed these requests rejected the idea of redesignating combat groups as wings. Instead, the committee recommended that combat groups and wings be maintained as separate and distinct organizations, and that the histories and honors of combat groups be bestowed upon the similarly designated combat wings.

Although the *ad hoc* committee's proposed bestowals ran counter to a long-standing policy of the Air Force against transferring history and honors from one unit to another, Headquarters USAF accepted the committee's recommendations. In November 1954 the Department of the Air Force issued a series of AFOMO letters which bestowed upon each active combat wing the history and honors of its similarly designated combat group; for example, SAC's 9th Bombardment Wing received by bestowal the history and honors of the 9th Bombardment Group. This bestowal of honors fell into two classes:

a. Those where the combat groups were now inactive (as in SAC).

b. Those where the combat groups remained active components of their related wings (as in TAC). In the second instance, however, Headquarters USAF went beyond the original intention of SAC, to perpetuate in the new wings the histories and honors of *inactive* World War II groups.

Since the initial bestowals in November 1954, the Department of the Air Force has continued to bestow the histories and honors of inactive groups on active wings of a similar designation. But, in some cases the letters have bestowed group histories a second time on wings that had been covered already by the bestowals made in November 1954, then subsequently inactivated. In other cases, the bestowals were newly made to wings not active in November 1954.

Other commands followed SAC's lead, eliminating combat groups and assigning squadrons directly to the wings. The Air Force, however, has continued to regard each combat group, albeit inactive, as an integral part of the similarly designated combat wing. Despite the trend to do away with combat groups, some survived as active organizations, and from time to time inactive groups have been activated. Beginning about 1957, active combat groups have usually been assigned to divisions or higher organizations, rather than to wings. The major exceptions appear in the reserve forces, where, since 1963, tactical wings usually have had two or more tactical groups (with numerical designations different from their wings), with one tactical squadron assigned to each group.

In bestowing group histories and honors on wings, Department of the Air Force directives have not specified any conditions or limitations except to note, in AFOMO letters issued after the initial bestowals of November 1954, that such bestowals are temporary. For a variety of reasons, particularly organizational developments after the initial bestowals, the Air Force found it necessary to formulate rules to govern temporary bestowals of histories and honors. In 1963 the interested USAF agencies agreed that the exceptional bestowal of history and honors:

1. Will be made only from AFCON combat groups to AFCON combat wings, with the bestowal in each case being from the group that has the same numerical designation as the recipient wing, and which is regarded by the Air Force as the primary-mission group, and thus an integral part of the wing, even though the group is inactive.

2. May be made if the group is:
   a. Inactive.
   b. Active and assigned to the similarly designated wing.

3. Will not be made if:
   a. The group is active and assigned to any organization other than the similarly designated wing.
   b. Any combat group other than the one related by similarity of designation is assigned to the wing.

4. Will apply only to that portion of the group's history which the group accrued, and to those honors which the group earned, during a period when the wing was not active.

5. Is temporary and:
   a. Becomes effective upon activation of the wing's headquarters.
   b. Terminates under any of the following circumstances:
      (1) The group is assigned to any organization other than its similarly designated wing.
      (2) The wing is assigned another combat group in place of, or in addition to, the similarly designated group from which it received the bestowal.
      (3) The wing's headquarters is inactivated.

Index of Aircraft and Missiles

Aircraft

Missiles

Index of Wing Commanders

Cabas, Victor N.: 192, 225
Caldara, Joseph D. C.: 89
Calhoun, Caryl W.: 108, 155, 224
Calhoun, Frederick E.: 37

☆ GPO : 1984 0 - 449-562